Inside the Bataan Death March

Inside the Bataan Death March

Defeat, Travail and Memory

KEVIN C. MURPHY

McFarland & Company, Inc., Publishers
Jefferson, North Carolina

ISBN 978-0-7864-9681-5 (softcover : acid free paper) ∞
ISBN 978-1-4766-1854-8 (ebook)

LIBRARY OF CONGRESS CATALOGUING DATA ARE AVAILABLE

BRITISH LIBRARY CATALOGUING DATA ARE AVAILABLE

© 2014 Kevin C. Murphy. All rights reserved

No part of this book may be reproduced or transmitted in any form or by any means, electronic or mechanical, including photocopying or recording, or by any information storage and retrieval system, without permission in writing from the publisher.

Cover photograph: Filipino and American prisoners of war at the start of the Bataan Death March, 1942 (Library of Congress)

Printed in the United States of America

McFarland & Company, Inc., Publishers
Box 611, Jefferson, North Carolina 28640
www.mcfarlandpub.com

For my daughter Maggie,
whose dreams will
surely come true

Table of Contents

Preface — 1
Introduction — 5

1. Virtue and Vice — 19
2. An Army's Ethos — 32
3. An Army Apart — 64
4. Chaos Meets *Kata* — 95
5. The Lens of Memory — 126
6. Remembering and Forgetting — 151
7. The Wages of Defeat — 190
8. Facing Filipinos — 215
9. Kinds of Kindness — 239

Conclusion — 267
Chapter Notes — 279
Bibliography — 303
Index — 317

*Der Blick des Forschers fand nicht selten mehr,
als er zu finden wünschte.*—Ephram Gotthold Lessing

Preface

Id ego longe aliter iudico esse.—Livy, *History*

During the spring of 1942, a compelling drama occurred that has come to be known as the Bataan Death March. Its *dramatis personae* were Americans, Japanese and Filipinos and, like all well-populated human events, it was complex, involving thousands of individual biographies and the cultural dispositions of the three civilizations they represented. A strange plant called the *tac-a-mona* grows on Bataan. Its name means "wait a minute" because its reverse spines allow one in but not out. So it has been with me—Bataan would not let me go once I began to sense its new contours and, most of all, its ironies.

I have found that the ironies reside in three aspects of this historical episode. The first is that of *defeat*. The defeat of the Fil-American army was complete, overwhelming and humiliating. The American contingent, some 10,000 men, was anything but a coherent force before the Japanese attacked; at the moment of defeat it dissolved into little more than a chaotic mob. Unprepared for what rigors the march required, poorly led, lacking unit cohesion and even basic discipline, American soldiers encountered Japanese guards who valued order and form above all, and it was at this intersection of culture that many, if not most, Americans died at the hands of their captors.

Another aspect is the different dimensions of *travail* these men experienced. There was, of course, the suffering of some men on the march itself, though how many suffered and to what degree remains an open question. Another form of travail was the men's experience in Japanese prisons for forty months after the march concluded. Here the strong often preyed on the weak in a raw, exploitative camp economy that rewarded physical power and connections rather than kindness and cooperation. The travail was psychological as well—these veterans firmly believed that they had been abandoned by their government and their commander, and came to realize that, even during the war, Americans at home soon forgot their ordeal. Survivors were embittered as they encountered an unsympathetic peacetime society, many falling victim to high rates of alcoholism, divorce, joblessness and even suicide.

It is this travail, I suggest, that defines the crucial aspect of *memory*. The available records, with the exception of some Japanese testimony at the post-war trial of the Japanese commander, are virtually all on the American side. The problem of this imbalance is greatly amplified when one considers the nature of these sources—the recollections of men who sat down to write of the experience years, usually decades, after their

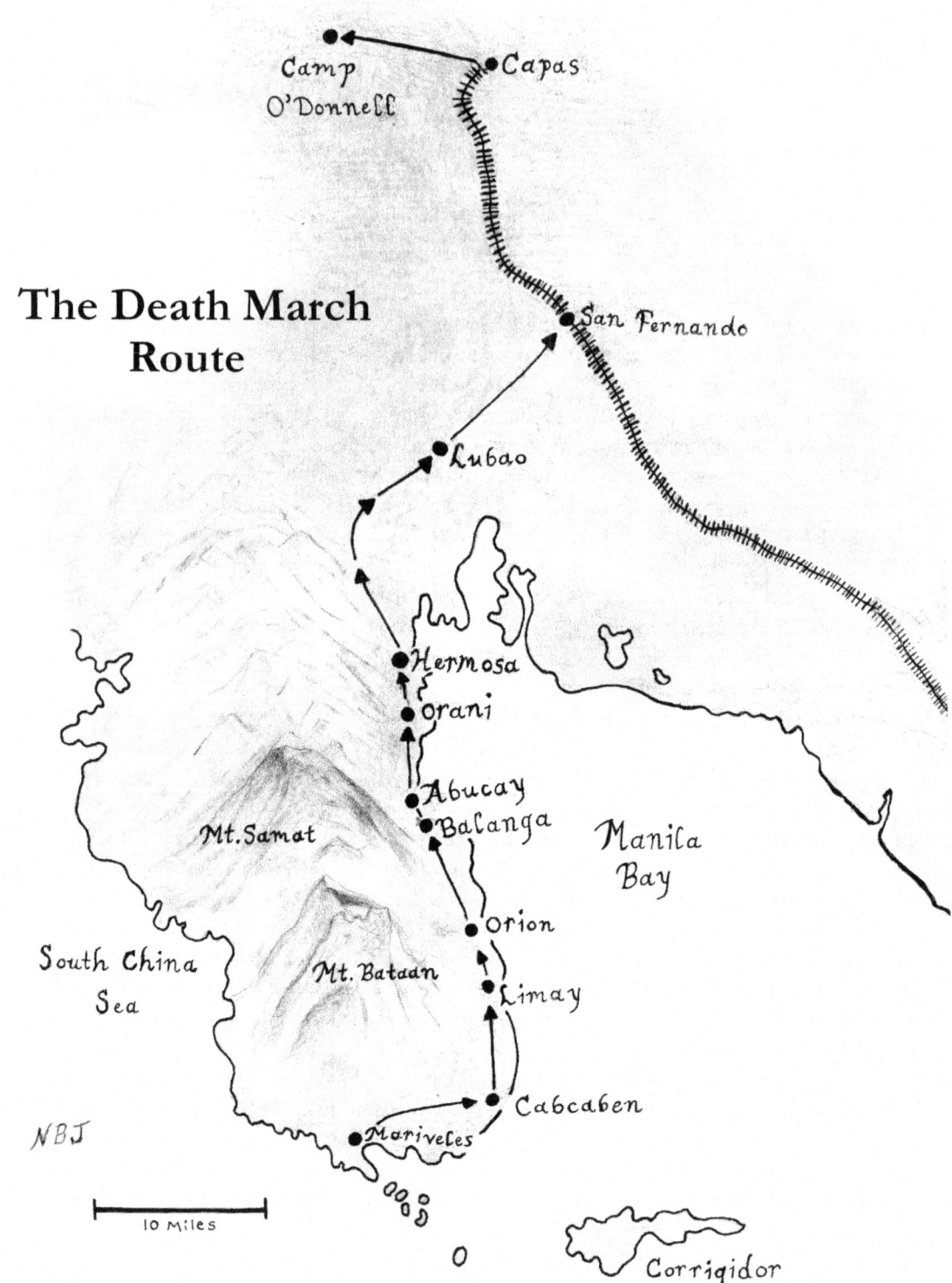

liberation at war's end. Here I was confronted with a choice. One way of proceeding was to follow the path of previous work, and essentially take the survivors of the Death March at their word—to assume that their version of the past could, or should, be the final one, something approximating objective truth, even though these men often emphasized or exaggerated their suffering at the hands of the Japanese to replace any narrative of their own less-than-heroic behavior while waiting for liberation. This approach reduces the dimensions of the story significantly and ignores the variety of issues that distort memory.

Such lenses have filtered out much light, focusing our attention in ways that force the past into a simple pattern—in this case Japanese cruelty, Filipino sympathy, American innocence and suffering. This book engages not just the past but the way the past is made, the universal problem of human memory's fallibility, and the uncertainty that inevitably results. The venture here is into another realm, where the lines between virtue and vice, innocence and guilt, cruelty and comity, blame and forgiveness all become blurred. I have striven here to avoid the historian's cardinal sin—limiting my search to find only that which confirms some pre-determined notion of truth. I have listened carefully and with some respect to what these men have said, and their words inform the narrative I relate here. I have not, however, allowed them to define its contours. The inevitable result is discomfort—we are left with a kind of distilled ambiguity. So it should be. The past is pregnant with meaning, but is not the place for polemic expression.

As this book gestated over six years, the words of the fourteenth century poet Yoshida Kenko frequently came to mind: "To sit alone in the lamplight with a book spread out before you, and hold intimate converse with men of unseen generations—such is a pleasure beyond compare." My conversation with those men, while producing the pleasure of discovery will, I suspect, also produce abrasions. All people tell themselves stories, comforting myths of noble quests, of frontiers tamed, of ideals sustained, of good wars fought, enemies vanquished. Even so, any good historian believes that the task of mastering the past is a serious one, a way to keep self-delusion at bay.

After surviving the Death March and imprisonment, Abie Abraham stayed on Bataan after the war, looking for graves of men who died during the ordeal. As he walked the route he had taken four years before, he spoke to local people, many of whom claimed to hear the soft voices of men rising in the night, breaking off suddenly as if ordered by a Japanese guard. Others claimed to see the outlines of men under a spreading mango tree where prisoners rested and the "night marchers" who kicked up dust during their trek.

As I personally walked the route of the march many years later, I heard the same ghostly stories, listened carefully in the night, and wondered about the line separating the living from the dead. I wondered about the gray areas between what we wish to believe and something closer to truth. I came home and wrote, thinking about the things I learned, or learned again—that bitterness defines a perspective as much as hope, that our pretentions blind us, that generalizations are dangerous, that memory is

Opposite: **The route of the march—sixty-five miles to San Fernando, thirty miles by train to Capas, then five miles to Camp O'Donnell (courtesy Nichole Murphy).**

the most malleable of substances, and that kindness can appear in the most unlikely of places.

I extend my gratitude to Robert Boughner, Andrew E. Mathis, Paul Moreno, Jeff Hearn, Wayne McWilliams and Margie Reinhart, each of whom improved this book. Thanks also to Christopher Leet, whose illustrations enhance meaning in ways my words could not. Throughout the text, Japanese names appear with the last name first.

Introduction

There is more to understand. Hold fast to that. —T.S. Eliot
With knowledge comes more doubt. —Goethe

This book was born at the intersection of geography, culture and memory. In the spring of 2008 I found myself at an international school in Thailand for a semester. I had brought a group of American students to a town south of Bangkok and worked for four months teaching them and a mixed bag of other Asian students when, near the end of the term, two free weeks appeared in the schedule, begging to be filled with travel. I had been eying that block of freedom from duties *in loco parentis* for some time, and as May approached, I walked with considerable purpose to my street-corner travel agent in Hua Hin to explore possibilities. Over Singha beers we looked over the map—the defining logic, as always, to go someplace new. Kathmandu was close enough, but connections from Bangkok too complicated; Kuala Lumpur close but maybe not quite different enough from southern Thailand. Brunei was too far and I was not in the mood for Singapore's discipline. Manila ... direct flights from Bangkok, not too far, interesting. A snap decision, the Philippines would do nicely.

Over shimmering rice fields I pondered an itinerary before touching down in Manila. For me, interest in the intersection of Japan and the world is never far beneath the surface, so a cab ride to the docks, then a short ferry ride over to Corregidor—and the purpose of my trip suddenly took precise form. I would tour the island battlefield of 1942, hire a *banca* and make my way over to the southern tip of the Bataan peninsula, the gathering point for the defeated Fil-American army after its exhausting struggle with the Japanese. Then I could head north along the route of the infamous "Death March" that began with General Edward King's surrender on April 9, the largest capitulation of American forces since Robert E. Lee had surrendered on the same day in 1865.

* * * * *

A short boat ride from Corregidor lies the town of Mariveles, where I find a small park containing memorials to the Death March. It is a place of quiet repose when I arrive; three young Filipinos talk in murmurs on a stone bench behind a large sign:

World War II DEATH MARCH MEMORIAL SHRINE
STARTING POINT OF
DEATH MARCH

APRIL 09–17, 1942
KM 00
MARIVELES, BATAAN

To the left of the sign stands a twice life-sized sculpture of an Allied rifle with fixed bayonet, upside down with a solder's helmet balanced on the butt as if marking a grave. The effect is sobering—there is no text, only a dignified suggestion of the suffering it represents. Behind and to the right is a stone wall with two plaques, one in Tagalog and the other in English, dating from 1967, sponsored by the National Historical Commission:

THE DEATH MARCH
OF FILIPINO AND AMERICAN PRISONERS OF
WAR FROM MARIVELES AND BAGAC TO
CAMP O'DONNELL, CAPAS, TARLAC
APRIL 1942

Already suffering from battle fatigue, the Filipino and American troops were strained to utter exhaustion by this long march on foot. Many were ill, most were feverish, but none might rest, for the enemy was brutal with those who lagged behind. Thousands fell along the way. Townspeople on the roadside risked their lives by slipping food and drink to the Death Marchers as they stumbled by.

Nearby stands the first of more than 100 obelisks that mark each kilometer of the route. They are more than six feet high and made of heavy stone—the earlier, smaller signs pilfered over time by souvenir-hungry tourists. The route out of Mariveles north is well marked, the obelisk at each kilometer bearing a silhouette of an American soldier helping a stumbling Filipino. There before me was the past explained—the meaning of the Death March memorialized with elegant simplicity.

As I started along the route of what survivors called "The Hike," I wondered about that simplicity and, once again, about the degree of tolerance we might have for the often messy complexity that a closer examination of the past so often reveals. Those who took the earlier signs found memory packaged neatly in a single image—a past that does little but confirm a simple understanding. That past has clear, even stark outlines: Brutal Japanese captors mistreated defeated and helpless American (and Filipino) victims, in front of equally helpless, yet sympathetic Filipino civilian onlookers. Each group's assigned part fits neatly in comfortable, interlocking symmetry. Here only the Japanese had agency; the Americans marched and suffered and the Filipinos, in despair over the defeat of their defenders, wept and watched. The pattern reinforces pleasing notions of the "good war" against a barbarous enemy and loyal allies enlisted in a righteous cause.

* * * * *

The U.S. had acquired the Philippines after its successful war against Spain in 1898. Always ambivalent about Asians' ability to govern themselves, U.S. policy finally concluded that granting independence was the best course of action, promised in 1934, with a delay in implementation until 1946. Rising tensions with Japan soon suggested the islands' strategic importance, and their defense was to have been according to "War Plan Orange 3." Completed just eight months before the war, this plan assumed that the Allied army comprising 65,000 Filipinos and 13,000 Americans could not defend the entire archipelago; rather it focused on holding central Luzon and then falling back to the Bataan peninsula, where it was expected to hold until reinforcements arrived, courtesy of the U.S. Navy.

Japan's invasion of Manchuria in 1931 and greater China in 1937 brought conflict with the U.S. nearer, and the American decision to cut off oil and scrap iron exports to Japan produced a crisis. Unwilling to withdraw from China, Japan's militarist leaders realized that without American oil, the Japanese navy would be starved for fuel. This left the conquest of the Dutch East Indies with its rich oil reserves as the only solution to the immediate problem. The decision to eliminate the only instrument that could interfere with this agenda followed naturally, and Japanese bombs rained on Pearl Harbor on December 7, 1941.

At the outbreak of hostilities with the U.S., Japan deployed its Southern army under the command of Terauchi Hisaichi. This force comprised four armies, the 14th, 15th, 16th, and 25th. Its goal was to capture the Philippines, Hong Kong, British Malaya, Burma, Java, Sumatra, the Celebes, Borneo, the Bismarck Islands, and Dutch Timor. Homma Masaharu's 14th army, comprising the 16th and 48th Infantry divisions and the 65th Independent mixed brigade, a force of some 43,000 men, battle-hardened by experience in China, was responsible for the conquest of the Philippines.[1] Japanese plans anticipated that the decisive battle would take place near Manila, and the campaign was expected to last fifty days, after which half of the 14th army would be dispatched for further operations in the south.[2]

General Douglas MacArthur assumed command of the Allied army in July 1941 and decided to reject "Plan Orange," designed to delay the invader by retreating to the Bataan peninsula. This he considered defeatist, and he introduced an alternative designed to defend the beaches. This in turn necessitated re-locating huge amounts of supplies from their storage areas on the Bataan peninsula to locations near the anticipated site of action. MacArthur had miscalculated badly, since the beaches proved indefensible, and large quantities of valuable supplies were lost.[3] Caught by surprise in the aftermath of Pearl Harbor, MacArthur also saw the bulk of his air force destroyed on the ground and he withdrew his forces to the Bataan peninsula, their destination according to the original plan.

The Imperial Japanese Army splashed ashore on the Philippine archipelago on December 10, 1941. In order to complete the campaign within the allotted fifty days, Homma lunged for the capital of Manila rather than the Fil-American army.[4] By January 2 he occupied the open city of Manila and set about completing the conquest of the island of Luzon, then reduce and capture the island fortress of Corregidor just offshore, commanding Manila Bay. The easy conquest of Manila convinced Japanese Imperial Headquarters that the Philippine campaign could be concluded without the 48th division, and it was transferred to the south in early January, replaced by a brigade of soldiers intended only for occupation duties. In the meantime, MacArthur recovered his senses and conducted a retreat to Bataan, the only course of action left to him after the capital fell. As it happened, the campaign lasted far longer than the Japanese anticipated, and Homma's inability, without the 48th division, to bring it to a successful conclusion left him in increasingly severe disfavor with Imperial Headquarters. Only reorganization and the arrival of 15,000 soldiers of the 4th division—bringing his total force to 50,000—assured final victory.

Such American and Japanese miscalculations set the stage for the following three months of bitter combat. Between January and final surrender on April 9, the Allied and Japanese armies were locked in intermittent, sanguinary battle that left both forces exhausted, disease-riddled and decimated. Only the Japanese, however, had the advantage of re-supply, since the Fil-American forces were cut off and gradually strangled. By spring, the Allied army occupied only the narrow area at the southern tip of the peninsula and MacArthur had abandoned his command, leaving subordinates to endure the inevitable defeat. With no hope of relief or re-supply, the campaign's outcome was a foregone conclusion, but not before each army was reduced to a shadow of its original self. After three months, General King, commanding the forces on Bataan, finally succumbed to exhaustion, disease and hopelessness, and surrendered on April 9.

What followed has entered historical consciousness as one of the four great Japanese atrocities during World War II. Along with the Rape of Nanjing, The Burma-Siam Death Railway and the Rape of Manila, it stands as one of the ultimate measures of Japanese wartime barbarity. "The Bataan Death March" is a phrase that still evokes strong emotion. After more than three months of resistance, the combined Fil-American army of some 75,000 men (about 10,000 of whom were American) was compelled to march some sixty-five miles from Mariveles, on the southern tip of the Bataan peninsula, to the railhead of Capas, where they were loaded onto trains for another thirty miles, then walked the remaining five to their destination of Camp O'Donnell, a facility that had been used for training Filipino soldiers before the war. This sad drama was played out before the eyes of thousands of Filipinos who watched as the procession made its way north.

Japanese miscalculation extended beyond the battle's conclusion. The Fil-American army had put up stiff resistance since January, and Homma estimated that it would take until the end of April to force surrender, leaving considerably less time for planning the evacuation of his prisoners than had been originally anticipated. The central implementation problem Homma faced stemmed from misinformation concerning the number of men he had captured; his staff had assured him that between 25,000 and 35,000 soldiers defended Bataan. However, when surrender came the Japanese were, quite simply, overwhelmed by the transportation problem that confronted them—65,000 Filipino and 10,000 American soldiers awaited their fate in captivity. Marching distances of twenty-five miles a day was routine in the Japanese army, and the assumption that their prisoners could do the same defined much of the Japanese plan for evacuation. Furthermore, Homma's staff failed to take into account the physical condition of the Allied force, its near starvation, and especially the extent to which malaria and other diseases, more prevalent in southern Bataan, had weakened its soldiers.

So, on April 9, three weeks ahead of schedule, he was faced with the huge task of removing severely weakened prisoners with inadequate transport in numbers far beyond his imagining—while still conducting a campaign to reduce the island fortress of Corregidor in Manila Bay, which would not surrender for another month.[5] These compounding difficulties rendered an already formidable logistical problem utterly insurmountable. Under intense pressure to reduce Corregidor, and lacking adequate transport for the huge number of prisoners they had captured, the Japanese began the movement of prisoners from southern Bataan to a holding camp far to the north, a haphazard and chaotic affair that came to be known as the Death March. Depending on an individual soldier's luck and circumstances, what survivors called "The Hike" lasted between forty-eight hours and ten days. For virtually the entire group of American and Filipino prisoners, it was over in two weeks. By April 23 the last of the stragglers arrived at Camp O'Donnell.

* * * * *

Such is the bare outline of the events. Yet such a description conceals as much as it reveals. What happened on the Death March? What is the existing consensus on its meaning? The prevailing agreement about this meaning is suffused with nostalgia about what Studs Terkel, though with considerable intended irony, called "the Good War." In a post 9–11 world, beset with uncertainties born of new economic and global tensions, we are inclined to revisit World War II with nostalgic yearning. David M. Kennedy speaks to the comfort that era offers us: "It was one of the rare wars in which history judges the victors to have fought for a just cause, and to have achieved an outcome of unarguable moral clarity."[6] Dwight D. Eisenhower, ruminating on the meaning of the war while in North Africa, wrote, "It seems to me that in no other war in history has the issue been so distinctly drawn between the forces of arbitrary oppression on one side and, on the other, those conceptions of individual liberty, freedom and dignity, under which we have been raised in our great Democracy."[7] Tom Brokaw called the generation that emerged from the depression and fought it "the greatest," arguing that these men and women persevered not for fame and recognition, but because of their righteous cause.[8]

A key moment in the recent HBO miniseries *The Pacific* echoes the familiar theme when one of the main characters says, "History is full of wars, fought for a hundred reasons, but this war, our war.... I have to believe ... every man who's wounded, every man I lose, that it's all worthwhile because our cause is just." In Steven Spielberg's highly successful *Saving Private Ryan,* the title character, years after the guns fell silent, tearfully asks his wife to tell him he's "a good man," making clear the connection between wartime sacrifice and constructive peacetime citizenship and domestic, family life. And in *Band of Brothers,* Captain Nixon serves as an interesting foil to the phlegmatic hero, Major Winters. Just before Easy Company discovers a German concentration camp, Nixon asks if Winters still believes that men killed in war "died as heroes." Without hesitation, Winters responds, "Yeah, I do."

At the heart of this vision is a belief in progress and redemption. We visit World War II over and over in novels, film and in popular history because of its power and clarity—a slumbering, isolationist, peaceful America awakened from dark depression by the perfidy of the sneak attack at Pearl Harbor, the aid given to our loyal British ally, the arsenal of democracy marshaled to smite the forces of tyranny and fascism, the great crusade of D-Day, the twin sweeps across Europe and the Pacific to liberate oppressed peoples, all punctuated with the unimaginable technological achievement detonated over Hiroshima. The United States redeemed the world, saving it from the forces of darkness, and in 1945 the country stood at the apex of military and economic power.

Every such crusade requires a suitably evil object to expiate. Thirty years ago Americans fretted over Japanese real estate purchases, trade deficits and import restrictions. Those concerns produced a variety of books and a brief infatuation with Japanese production techniques. Now Japan has once again faded into the background of American consciousness, replaced by the challenges of the Muslim world and rising Chinese power. Even still, that nation remains a mystery. During the war, Americans remained ambivalent about their German enemy, sharing as they did so much ethnic and cultural heritage with their Teutonic cousins. War with the Japanese, however, was another matter entirely. On the other side of the world, racial difference and almost total unfamiliarity defined an enemy far more dangerous and alien.

The cultural yield was what John Dower has called a "war without mercy," a war to exterminate an enemy whose behavior justified the most extreme measures, terminating with two atomic blasts.[9] Before Pearl Harbor, Americans had been mostly ignorant about Japan, but that event and the reality of fighting an alien people clarified the nature of the enemy as was never possible in Europe—and the Japanese seemed to give full cooperation to Americans seeking to demonize them as alien, even sub-human. How, it seems fair to wonder, did such an apparently savage enemy become such a stalwart ally so quickly after 1945? If understanding the shift from hated foe to reliable friend is so challenging, what must have produced the savagery to begin with?

As for Americans, it may seem foolhardy, if not unpatriotic, to put any kind of finer point on the suffering that some U.S. soldiers undoubtedly endured on the Death March. The place of the veteran in the national consciousness is sacrosanct—even those who survived the debacle of Vietnam have been rehabilitated to respectability. To be sure, the existing understanding dictates that Japanese cruelty and American suffering exist in proportion to each other. Re-casting the degree of a veteran POW's suffering—especially one at the mercy of such a barbaric foe—is tricky business indeed, but business that needs transacting.

Again with Japanese cruelty as the essential reference point, Filipino civilians who watched the Death March, to the extent they are mentioned at all, are almost uniformly described as sympathetic to the U.S. and her soldiers who ascended their Calvary. After all, the U.S. had liberated the Philippines from Spain in the "splendid little war" of 1898, and was in the process of granting the islands their promised independence when the Japanese interrupted the process so violently. There would seem little need to question Filipino loyalty or sympathy for the U.S. soldiers who, along with their countrymen, defended the archipelago against a hated invader.

Perhaps now is as good a time as any to re-visit these aspects of World War II. My focus is entirely on the two weeks of the march, but it soon became clear that if I wished to go beyond such simple characterizations, I needed to address related questions: Who were the American soldiers who experienced the Death March, who were their Japanese captors and who were the Filipinos who watched? How did each group's circumstances define its behavior? On the American side, this involved examining the many accounts survivors left behind. American ex–POWs, however gradually and painfully, wrote about their ordeal of the Death March, many with the explicit purpose of seeking some public recognition of their suffering. The accounts these men left were informed by years in POW camps, often intense hatred of the Japanese, and they expressed their bitterness freely and copiously. Throughout, I have assumed that memory is a valuable but imprecise and imperfect instrument and that these men, most of whom sat down to write years, even decades after 1942, told their stories in specific ways for specific reasons.

Yet if we leave the past, that past, in the hands of veterans, it is frozen in time—incomplete, biased, unrevised. Many might assume that the recollections of these veterans occupy a special place, any challenge to which is subject to the inevitable charges: lack of patriotism, bomb's relationship to the end of the war, but on its effects on the Japanese who suffered from radiation and the nuclear arms race that continues to plague our species. Clearly, the United States was unwilling to challenge any "heroic narrative" that placed the bomb at conclusion of the truly good war. In its Resolution 257, the U.S. Senate expressed the resentment felt by much of the country at any redefinition of the bomb's delivery, condemning the exhibition as "revisionist and offensive to many World War II veterans." Federal law, it continued, required that "the valor and sacrificial service of the men and women of the Armed Forces shall be portrayed as an inspiration to the present and future generations of America." Federal law, if understood to contain the First Amendment, requires no such thing. The tension between such pronouncements and the responsible practice of the historian's craft is nearly unbearable.[13]

The lesson I took from that evening and that debate: a veteran's perspective, even when contrived, and dreadfully under-informed by factual knowledge or actual combat experience, was assigned special validity. One Bataan veteran offered the familiar chant: "Reunion is a time to recall memories—good and bad—but only those who were there can relate to the days of horror and the ... sacrifice the Battling Bastards of Bataan made to stonewall the Japanese advance across Asia."[14] That many others had absorbed this lesson seemed even clearer when I noted that Brokaw's *The Greatest Generation* had made the bestseller lists. I understand and appreciate the impulse to honor veterans and to build a public memory that legitimates sacrifice, even though relatively few actually made it. However, no historical event involving thousands of characters can be bent to the comfort of simplicity my host, or the U.S. Senate, or popular memory, often demands.

I was not entirely without sympathy for my host's position, though surely from a distance. Long ago, as an undergraduate majoring diligently if not with great inspiration in history at a large state university, I wrote a quite unmemorable paper on a topic that meant something to me—the battle of Gettysburg. Like many a similar undergraduate effort, it was neither inspired nor original, and in it I had parroted some of the more obvious apologies for Robert E. Lee's generalship. The paper came back with a grade of "B+," but with something far more valuable—a comment that began to lead to an understanding of what I was doing, or of what I had failed to do. At the end of the paper, the professor had written, "Why do you believe what these people have said about Lee—because their explanation is what you want to hear, or because you've looked at the relevant documents and decided that for yourself?"

I had organized my paper around someone else's truth, surely a venial sin for an undergraduate, but I did begin to understand how to look at the past—with some strange yet empowering balance of wonder and distrust. It was dawning on me that no story is complete, and that the quest for a bigger truth, a better truth, one that encompasses more source material assembled in new and responsible ways, is eternal. Without revision, understanding remains static. If I lacked then a coherent historical vision, I was beginning to understand the problems involved in telling a responsible story, and I began to apprehend some reasons why the search for truth is so often truncated.

Sloth, bias, inflexibility and insecurity all combine to tell us something is true. Someone else (usually in authority) has said it is true; because it serves a selfish interest to be true; because it has always been true; because saying so eliminates the need to expend effort to investigate further. I came to believe that the past does not exist to confirm old prejudices, nor is its purpose to salve old wounds, least of all to serve the interests of any self-appointed custodians, even ones who have suffered.

Years interceded before I returned to the serious study of history, and many of those years were, and continue to be, bound up with Japan. In the American consciousness, Japan has gone from exotic fairyland to dreaded enemy, to Cold War ally, to feared economic competitor, to ally in China's shadow. Four years residence and a dozen return trips across the Pacific have connected me to that place on the map and in my mind in some ways easy to describe, in others almost impossible to apprehend; the idea of the place bored into my thinking and studies with determination and persistence. Having lived in Japan and wrestled with its language and culture, I wondered about the human intersection, and as an apprentice I wrote about Americans living in Japan in the nineteenth century.

I had dutifully completed all the required examinations, and sent draft after draft of my tome to my advisor. One day no more drafts seemed necessary and the time came for me to be anointed with the degree. I entered the room master of the material, sure of my emerging, if modest place in the literature of U.S.-Japan relations. My 400 pages argued, somewhat too strenuously, that Americans' cultural attitudes had unnecessarily limited their business profits over a forty-year period. I was prepared to do battle over the themes and details, but the first question I faced rocked me into silence. Most of the committee knew that I had lived in Japan for several years, and one of them, seated immediately to my right at the seminar table, wasted no time getting to the crux of the matter. "How," he intoned, "do we know that you, frustrated by your inability to penetrate Japanese culture and society to your satisfaction, have not simply projected this frustration onto these men you studied?"

I suppose many students on the brink of their degrees are cowed into humble silence. I certainly was. This question left me at the edge of a precipice both unexpected and unwelcome. I felt the five incline toward me and heard the earth turn on its axis for ten endless seconds before I said, slowly and evenly, "Professor, I know that I have done that to some degree. But I also know that without my experience in Japan, I would have written a lesser study." He looked at me squarely, smiled warmly, pivoted smartly toward the rest of the assembled intellect, and said lightly, "If he had said anything different, I would have voted against awarding him the degree." I sighed exquisite relief. Now, twenty-five years later, that is the only question I remember from my dissertation defense, and it remains the one whose essence keeps me connected to the study of the past, and the ironic, often uncomfortable intersections one finds there.

I have wondered about the nature of memory and of truth for some time. The past always emerges through the lens of the present, and I confess at the outset that my perspective on life, history, and the Bataan Death March is deeply informed by my long experience and residence in Japan. For this I do not apologize, as I do not apologize for Japanese wartime behavior. Instead, I hope my perspective has situated me more responsibly at this fascinating cultural intersection. My own substantial ambivalence regarding Japan is no doubt reflected here, perhaps in ways that illuminate the Japanese side of the story with appropriate nuance. As Clifford Geertz, reminds us, "where are we when we can no longer claim some unique form of psychological closeness, a sort of transcultural identification, with our subjects? What happens to *verstehen* when *einfühlen* disappears?"

* * * * *

In May 1992, at a reunion on the fiftieth anniversary of the fall of Bataan and Corregidor, Ben Llamzon was taping interviews of many in attendance. As he approached Richard

Gordon, mike in hand, the veteran said, "All those tapes—how will you sort out the truth?"[15] The sorting process is challenging indeed; the need to revise toward a better, deeper understanding is a permanent requirement. I have found that existing material on the Death March has done little to challenge an essentially simple understanding of a very complex episode. The temptation toward complacency is often strong, but no version of the past should ever be left alone, no memory should be left undisturbed. The author of a review of a recent book dealing with the Bataan Death March wondered, after all of the writing done on the subject, if the wall of this story needed "another brick."[16] It does, mostly because the bricks are all part of an edifice permanently under construction. Charles Beard, a historian I greatly admire, wrestled with the issue of "one more brick" in his essay "That Noble Dream":

> The effort to grasp at the totality of history must and will be continued, even though the dream of bringing it to earth must be abandoned. This means a widening of the range of ... interests hitherto neglected.... Certainly by this broadening process the scholar will come nearer to the actuality of history as it has been.

And so I have grasped at "the totality" of the Death March even as I recognize that bringing it fully to earth is a receding dream.

Robert Cowley, in the introduction to his *No End Save Victory: Perspectives on World War II*, suggests that "the particulars of those 2194 days from September 1, 1939, to September 2, 1945, remain as appalling and fascinating as ever, and as open to fresh examination, dispute and reinterpretation."[17] Kermit Lay, 2nd Lieutenant, I Philippine Corps, survivor of the march and of subsequent years in Japanese prisons, hinted at the complexity of this past, his past: "Now some people think there was one Death March. There were many Death Marches."[18] Cowley and Lay are right—behind the simplicity of that façade lurks a complexity and an ambiguity that is the stuff of genuine fascination. Further and different inquiry into what has come to be called the Death March yields a different product—one more nuanced, complicated, discomfiting and, I believe, ultimately more interesting than the relatively flat characterizations that have defined our understanding until now.

Tillman Routledge, custodian of the Battling Bastards of Bataan website, writes, "History should not be what you want it to be." His assertion was meant to discourage men from pretending to be Death March survivors, but I understand it to suggest the imperative of finding another, a different, a better truth as a permanent obligation, one that imposes a difficult task on even the most refined sensibilities. How does one proceed with the sure knowledge that truth behaves like quicksilver, sliding away just when it seems most firmly in our grasp, while remaining steadfastly committed to the quest for a better, more complete version of the past? To regard the past with reverence is a high ideal, and I have written this book with the sure knowledge that the "whole" truth of any event, especially one as many-sided as the Bataan Death March, can never be recovered. Even so, this is my effort to tell *more* of the story and in so doing, come closer to a more complete, and therefore more compelling truth.

William Evans' 1986 book, *Kora!*, stated the chronologically inevitable: "In a few short years we'll all be gone."[19] Indeed, we are now entering the period when memory, whether the veterans would approve or not, is replaced by post-memory. The few American and Japanese alive and soldiering in Bataan in 1942 are now at least in their mid-eighties, and soon their voices, except for the writings they left behind, will be stilled. I have read their many accounts. The passing of these men should not be the occasion to enshrine their version of the past on stone obelisks with fixed inscriptions. Instead, it is an opportunity to build on the foundation they have left. This book is really about memory—how it is made and by whom. Men who experienced the Death March chose to render a particular version of that experience. In turn, historians writing secondary works have largely accepted the main themes the survivors expressed.

* * * * *

In his lovely essay "Just This Side of Byzantium," Ray Bradbury speaks of the joy of exploration: "And, after all, isn't that what life is all about, the ability to go around back and come up inside other people's heads to look out at the damned fool miracle and say: oh, so that's how you see it!? Well, now, I must remember that."[20] I wondered if Americans and Japanese and Filipinos experienced the Death March in far greater variety and ambiguity than their monuments—public and private—wanted us to understand. My story started to have meaning; I wanted to know if there were any miracles—or at least surprises—as I went "around back" and came up inside these other people's heads.

Because I am attracted to irony in the human experience, I have asked different questions of this material and found different answers. My point of departure is the widely accepted triangulation of Japanese cruelty, American victimhood and Filipino sympathy. As I write this, the U.S. is at war in the Middle East and perhaps it is not quite politic to challenge the memory of soldiers, especially those who fought "The Good War" and suffered in captivity. Yet the questions persist: How faithfully does another, closer reading of this past show the actors to have played the desired parts of cruel captor, helpless victim and sympathetic onlooker? What if the captors were not as uniformly cruel as we have heretofore believed? What if the Filipinos who watched were not entirely sympathetic? And, what if the prisoners themselves demonstrated behavior during captivity that revealed unwelcome variation, and afterward distorted their experience?

Addressing these questions liberates all three groups from one-dimensional understanding and explains each of their roles in ways heretofore well concealed. It does these men no honor to fold them up neatly and put them away as helpless victims and cruel savages, flat characters without nuance, to force them into neat, facile categories that serve the interests of comfort more than of truth. No stage across which so many thousands of actors walked could ever be so simple and ultimately insulting to their memory.

William Faulkner once observed, "The past is never dead. It's not even past." It still is not, either for me, or for those who may read this interpretation. I have often found history to be a compelling and cruel mistress. The subject calls on us to seek the truth in ways that are as often uncomfortable as they are thrilling, a reality that calls to mind the words of Albert Einstein—"If you are out to describe the truth, leave elegance to the tailor." The past these survivors constructed remains alive, but like every set of memories, it sometimes conceals as much as it illuminates. My goal in this book is to render porous whatever barriers these men erected—not to inflict dishonor by tearing them down. Here I hope to avoid the distortion against which Ralph Ellison once warned: "That which we remember is, more often than not, that which we would like to have been; or that which we hope to be ... our history ever a tall tale told by inattentive idealists." Of a certain kind idealism I may be guilty but not, I hope, of inattention; if my tale is tall, may it stand among responsible histories with some integrity.

My interpretation is seasoned with many italicized vignettes and anecdotes, drawn from my long experience in Japan and from my walk along the route of the march that I hope will shed light on the main themes I have undertaken to explain. In this will be obvious my belief that fundamental cultural characteristics only change imperceptibly over time; in Japan, as elsewhere, they have been formed over a long process to which change is often an unwelcome intruder. Japanese behavior on the Death March at all the levels I can understand was a function of those characteristics, and the yield of a closer look at that relationship has been fascinating.

* * * * *

And so I set out from Mariveles from the obelisk marked "00 km," up a long and winding hill, and began to tick off the kilometers one by one, touching each obelisk, once again ruminating on the meaning of the past and on the difficult process of re-making it. Laboring up the same hill that Americans climbed as they began their march, I remembered other sites. I recalled admonitions of the custodians at the Arizona memorial at Pearl Harbor to keep voices lowered as I looked down at the sunken hulk, and the hush that hung over S-21, the high school that was the place of Khmer Rouge horror in Phnom Penh. And I remembered Auschwitz and the oppressive weight of the past at the death camp of Birkenau, the caught-at-the-throat sense of penetrating evil.

There I walked softly through the opening at the gate where the trains arrived, past the platform where SS men and their barking dogs greeted the victims, down to the ruins of the crematoria, destroyed as the Russian army approached, but still breathing memory of the organized might of a bureaucracy's will, focused on destruction, intent with gruesome efficiency. I could almost smell the Zyklon B. I remembered walking the battlefield of Sekigahara, where locals believe the spirits of those defeated by Tokugawa Ieyasu still roam. The places were worlds apart, yet in each I felt I had to part the air, it was so heavy with history.

But as I walked out of town, up toward the mountains, and as I passed a factory and a gas station and local bus stop, it dawned on me that this trek would be different, that somehow the point of contact with history would lead elsewhere, and what would follow would be worth the telling. Once upon a time Imelda Marcos, eager to stimulate Filipino national pride, planned to turn the route of the Death March into "a tree-lined memorial," but nothing came of it.[21] After leaving Mariveles with its modest remembrances, the route of the Death March bears no obvious signs beyond the markers at each kilometer, nothing to guide understanding of that past. The workers at the factory stood and smoked, the bus discharged its passengers, the clerk at the gas station sold me water for my trek, and I began to apprehend that the work-a-day world of Bataan's present did not bear down with the weight of Auschwitz. All at once it seemed that in the enormous space between those obelisks lay a thousand stories yet unwritten.

In his poem "The Wound Dresser," Walt Whitman offered the timeless challenge:

The author near Cabcaben.

> Now be witness again, paint the mightiest armies on earth,
> Of those armies so rapid so wondrous what saw you to tell us?
> What stays with you latest and deepest? Of curious panics,
> Of hard-fought engagements or sieges tremendous what deepest remains?

What parts of the past would I find that these men, American, Japanese and Filipino, had denied? As the sweat began, I hoped to find greater depth, embrace the complexity of their experience and meet it on its own ground.

My steps grew lighter as I began my ascent.

1
Virtue and Vice

The world is horror within magnificence, absurdity within intelligibility, suffering within joy.—Albert Schweitzer

All civilizations have their notions of justice and balance, of ideals by which to live, and of punishing those who diverge from those ideals. For the Japanese, this idea is expressed in the aphorism *Kanzen chōaku* (rewarding good, punishing evil). Such ideas often reside in folklore, and every Japanese school child knows the story of *Momotarō*, the peach boy. Since the seventeenth century, mothers have told their children one version or another of the old couple who found a giant peach floating in a river and discovered inside the boy who came to earth from heaven to be their son. The couple raised the boy, who later departed to fight marauding, terrible *oni*, or demons, on a faraway island. On his way the young warrior enlisted the aid of a dog, monkey and pheasant and triumphed in the ensuing battle. He then returned home with the captured *oni* chief and the stolen treasure. The *oni* conquered and the treasure restored, Momotarō and his family lived on in peace and comfort. Evil punished, good protected and rewarded.

Such is one expression of an ideal. Experience, however, is often full of bitter irony, and study of the Death March offers one of the most unsettling of the war and its aftermath. The careers of General Homma Masaharu and Colonel Tsuji Masanobu intersected for ten days on Bataan, and in many ways they represent the extremities of virtue and vice in the context of war. These extremities resided in different aspects of the code of *bushido*, and in the careers and sensibilities of these two men. Homma, the commander of sthe Japanese Fourteenth Army during the Bataan campaign, was a man of cosmopolitan and fundamentally humanistic sensibilities who advocated humane treatment of prisoners. Tsuji, a staff officer who appeared on Bataan after participating in the massacre of some 5,000 Chinese after the fall of Singapore, saw the conflict as a race war, and openly advocated brutality and death for those captured. In a grotesque turn of events, Homma, who was steadfastly opposed to war's darker expressions, was executed as a war criminal, while Tsuji, a xenophobic killer, escaped to enjoy decades of postwar freedom under American protection.

* * * * *

While imprisoned after the Death March, John Ball recorded his notion of *bushido* in iambic tetrameter:

> And a prayer that was quite common
> I have often heard them tell,
> was that these barbarian heathens will forever burn in hell.
> They were men and mostly good men, driven to the Promised Land,
> by starvation, thirst and beating by Bushido and his land.

Yet when he and others arrived at Camp O'Donnell after the Death March, they were greeted by a speech by the commandant, Captain Tsuneyoshi Yoshio, who told the POWs that he "could destroy them all but the spirit of Bushido forbade such action."[1] Here is reflected fundamental confusion about the nature of *bushido*, sometimes translated as "the way of the warrior." During wartime and afterward, survivors equated the term with cruelty, a monolithic warrior ethic that justified, even encouraged mistreatment of American prisoners.

In spite of the certainty with which many of the more than 9,000 Americans who survived the Death March defined it, few Japanese terms are more misunderstood in the West. Karl Friday's nicely titled essay "Bushido or Bull" makes clear the elasticity of the concept, and that "any connection between Japan's modern and pre-modern military traditions is thin ... which is to say that [those] who condemn the *samurai* tradition, who blame the legacy of Japan's warrior past for the atrocities and other wartime misbehavior committed by the Imperial Japanese Army, are distorting history."[2] Reasonably enough, neither John Ball nor many of the other survivors would ask, "What *form* of *bushido*?" nor would most inquire more deeply into the broader historical context from which it arose.

Before 1600, Japan was riven with internal wars, a time when scores of independent feudal domains competed and fought to ensure their survival and, if possible, expansion. It was a confused and dangerous period when any feudal lord, or *daimyo*, each commanding a force of *samurai*, could ill afford to ignore any means at hand to advance his political and military aims. In the struggles of the period, deception, betrayal and subterfuge were at least as common as loyalty and zealous self-sacrifice. Peace came after Tokugawa Ieyasu's decisive victory in 1600, and such arts were not much needed for the next two and a half centuries, a time when *samurai*, now with no wars to occupy them, became administrators and bureaucrats in service to their lords.

It was more than one hundred years into this period without war that we find a genuine definition of the term *bushido*. Alone in a small hermitage, a set of conversations with the *samurai* Yamamoto Tsunetomo yielded a work called *Hagakure*, usually translated as "Hidden Leaves." The ideas in the book essentially expressed "a search for the proper role of a warrior class in a world without war" and his ideas had little to do with the dark and stormy warring states period.[3] Even a cursory reading of this rambling work reveals that it is anything but a coherent philosophy. Among the many subjects on which Yamamoto ruminated was that of death—and the opening line of the work, "The Way of the Samurai is found in death," provided the basis upon which later generations, with agendas far different from legitimating the existence of a parasitical warrior class, would build.[4]

Another century and a half passed, and the ideas embedded in Yamamoto's rather disjointed conversations waited, fertile ideological ground from which a more precise definition of *bushido* would grow. The West intruded upon Japan in 1853 when Commodore Matthew Perry's "Black Ships" arrived and, after a brief civil war, a cadre of oligarchs took control of the nation. These men, eager to transform Japan into a power capable of resisting Western imperialism and avoiding the fate of China, found some of Yamamoto's ideas quite useful.

Under the slogan *fukoku kyohei* (Rich Country, Strong army) a generation of visionary leaders revived the imperial institution as a highly effective device to ensure popular submission to their goals. To this end, the government produced a series of texts specifically geared to the socialization of soldiers who would form the backbone of a modern army.

As early as 1879 the Japanese philosopher Nishi Amane's book *Heika Tokugyo* (*The Moral Virtue of the Soldier*) "emphasized the need to maintain the traditional Japanese values of benevolence and right conduct—values that are the essence of *bushido*." This version held military officers to the high standard of its essential elements. Included among these were "commitment to justice and duty and despising of cowardice" (righteousness), "love, tolerance, and sympathy for others.... Humanity toward the weak or the defeated is seen as the most honorable way for a warrior to conduct himself; therefore the ill-treatment of POWs is completely opposed to this element" (humanity), "the realization of humanity in acts of kindness" (propriety). The honorable warrior, he wrote, was obedient but never blindly so, and could not violate the code "without feeling great shame." These ideas had considerable traction, as Nishi participated in drafting the Imperial Code of Military Conduct in 1882.[5]

The *Gunjin Chokuyu* (Imperial Rescript to Soldiers and Sailors), promulgated the same year, contained unmistakably humanistic features, warning, "If you affect valor and act with violence, the world will in the end detest you and look upon you as wild beasts."[6] In 1899 the author and educator Nitobe Inazo added similar meaning to the term's definition in his book *Bushido: The Soul of Japan*. He noted the ideas of the Chinese thinkers Mencius and Confucius as they influenced *bushido*:

> The bravest are the tenderest, the loving are the daring. *Bushi no nasake*—the tenderness of a warrior—had a sound which appealed at once to whatever was noble in us ... because it implied mercy where mercy was not a blind impulse, but where it recognized due regard to justice, and where mercy did not remain merely a certain state of mind, but where it was backed by power to save or kill.

Nitobe reached into an imagined past, and suggested that "benevolence to the weak, the down-trodden or the vanquished, was ever extolled as peculiarly becoming to a samurai."[7] Nitobe was thoroughly cosmopolitan, an educator, women's rights advocate, diplomat and author, fluent in English, with years of experience abroad, and influenced by the Quaker community of Philadelphia where he lived with his American wife. He wrote the book in English, to explain Japan as he imagined it to the West.[8]

Echoes of Nishi's definition reverberate. This was the idealized version of Japan so appealing to an American audience in the throes of adapting to the jolting *fin de siècle* changes accompanying immigration, urbanization and industrialization. Americans could still regard Japan to some degree as exotic and quaint, a harmless land of cherry blossoms and *geishas*. Seeking comfort in stories of a pristine past unsullied by the complications of modern life, early twentieth century Americans saw sales of Edgar Rice Burroughs' *Tarzan of the Apes* (1912) and Owen Wister's *The Virginian* (1902) skyrocket. Nitobe's descriptions of a premodern, ethically pure Japan fit the same category.[9]

Even so, Nitobe's version emphasized humanistic dimensions of the code, and vestiges of this sensibility persisted beyond Pearl Harbor. In early 1942, Japan agreed to observe the Geneva Red Cross Convention *mutatis mutandis* (when it did not "conflict with its existing laws, policies and regulations") regarding the treatment of prisoners. And only one month before the Death March began, Japanese foreign minister Togo wrote the Swiss government:

"I desire to inform your Excellency that the Imperial Government intends to take into consideration, with regard to provisions and clothing to be distributed, the national and racial customs of American war prisoners and civilian internees placed under Japanese power."[10]

* * * * *

Toward the end of the sanguinary Bataan campaign, Homma asked for honorable surrender "in accordance with the humanitarian principles of *bushido*."[11] For him, this was not an empty gesture, nor was the code he cited unrelated to a certain standard of military behavior, even as Japan set upon the road to conquest. Homma had far more exposure to the world than did any of his contemporaries, and was far more cosmopolitan. He spent several years abroad as a military attaché, in 1918 serving with the British army in France. In all he spent six years in India and the United Kingdom, and because of his long association with the British, his fellow officers called him "the linguist with the red nose." He returned to field command later in the 1930s.[12] In all, he spent eight years outside Japan, became fluent in English, and developed both an understanding of and respect for the West.

He earned the second highest marks in his class at Staff College, and contemporaries rightly regarded Homma as brilliant, but the general's personal life raised eyebrows. For an officer in the Imperial Japanese Army, many thought him unconventional because of his interest in art and decoration, his poetry and talent for Western languages. He spent his time writing plays and chose to marry for love. While posted to England in 1919, he came to suspect his first wife of infidelity, and "was only saved with difficulty from throwing himself out the window" of his hotel. At his post-war trial, Homma's wife spoke of the response to his liberal attitudes:

> Because he studied about the United States and England, because he was always interested in world trends and kept his eyes open on it, and also because he understood Japan thoroughly, he realized that the spread of war was not only a misfortune for Japan but to all mankind.... People used to call him pro–American.

Homma corroborated this, stating that he belonged to a minority of liberal, pro–British officers, those who had learned English, opposed to Tojo Hideki, whose "dogmatic ideas were objectionable" to him. A British general, Francis S.G. Piggott, intimate with Homma during his time in London, offered an affidavit at his trial, stating that Homma's "views were independent, moderate, humanitarian and definitely pro–British."[13]

Japan's war of conquest in China began in earnest in 1937 and, when Nanking fell that year, he declared publicly, "unless peace is achieved immediately it will be disastrous" and then privately that he considered Tojo a poor choice for minister of war. "War against the USA would be a disaster, I knew, but I could not show any feeling in it, as ... I would have been called a traitor," Homma wrote. "Tojo [did] not understand Anglo-Saxon temperament and its potential strength.... Japan was already exhausted from its prolonged war in China and was not in a position to wage another against the U.S. and Great Britain. It was sheer madness."[14]

His attitude toward the conquered was generous. He examined orders "in light of common sense and humanity" and some considered him "indulgent to the point of negligence" with the Filipino population. Indeed, Homma had "pleaded for an enlightened and humane administration" of the Philippines ordering, for example, Western missionaries released from internment, in direct contradiction of orders from Tokyo.[15] The historian Murakami Hyoe called Homma "a man of common sense, whose long service in England helped him realize that lenient rule of the Philippines was the best policy to ensure cooperation, indeed he wanted to "govern still more liberally than the Americans had." In one instance, on his approach to Manila, Homma stopped his columns and ordered the men to clean up and tighten formations, knowing that unkempt soldiers are more likely to loot and rape. Aware of the shame a rapist would face in his home village, Homma ordered that copies of such court-martial reports be sent to the miscreants' parents.[16]

Some American survivors reasoned that Homma was so humiliated by the effective resistance on Bataan that he decided to take revenge on the Allied survivors. Though understandable from a POW perspective, this was hardly the case. In truth, Homma was far more concerned with the reduction of the island fortress of Corregidor than with any such action against his defeated enemy. Busy with such plans, he only met one American after Bataan's surrender on April 9. Colonel Collier, an officer on General King's staff, chatted easily with him in English while sitting in folding metal chairs in a mango grove. At the end of what Collier described as "relaxed" conversation, Homma smiled and said, "Your worries are over. Japan treats her prisoners well. You may even see my country in cherry-blossom time and that is a beautiful sight."[17] Under intense pressure from Tokyo and completely absorbed in preparations for the siege of Corregidor, Homma had already approved the evacuation plan and assumed that it was being carried out.

From the Japanese point of view, especially that of the Imperial Staff in Tokyo, the campaign had not gone well. The conquest of the Philippines had been allotted just fifty days in order to secure the flank of the more important thrust—toward the Dutch East Indies and its oil, a supply to replace what the U.S. embargo had choked off. After the easy conquest of Manila, Homma lost his best fighting division to the southern advance, and encountered stiff resistance on the Bataan peninsula and the disease its unforgiving jungle offered to his army and that of his enemies alike. Though he had lost the confidence of the Imperial Staff by March, he was left in command until the surrender of Corregidor on May 6. In June, in some disgrace, he was relieved and reassigned to Japan, where he lived quietly with his wife until the surrender.[18]

At the war's conclusion, Americans were eager to mete out justice to those believed responsible for wartime atrocities. In September 1945 he was summoned to Tokyo, where reporters were waiting and demanding an interview. He was nonplussed when the men kept "asking [him] about the march of Death."[19] At this point Douglas MacArthur, whom Homma had defeated and forced to flee to Australia, ordered his old enemy tried by an American military tribunal, an organ under his direct supervision, rather than the International Allied War Crimes Commission that held its proceedings in Tokyo.[20] The commission was directed to "apply the rules of evidence and pleading ... with the greatest liberality" and, whatever the commission's sentence, the final authority to approve or modify it was MacArthur.

In December 1945, proceedings began in the High Commissioner's Residence in Manila, putatively "confined strictly to a fair, expeditious hearing," but sentiment favoring revenge ran high. During the war, naturally Homma was routinely portrayed in uniformly negative terms. The February 2, 1942, edition of *Newsweek* called him "choleric," and a glory-seeker, his major bid for fame his management of the blockade of the British Concession in

Tientsin, where foreign women were "stripped, searched and manhandled by the Japanese soldiery." In the 1945 film *Back to Bataan*, Leonard Strong portrayed him in the most stereotypical tones—devious and unctuous, informing Filipinos that Japan "has been waiting to embrace you, to welcome you back into the fold, providing you behave yourselves. Remember, we are kindly, but not indulgent. We shall not hesitate to spank the unruly ones." He had acquired the alliterative sobriquet "Beast of Bataan."

From April 9, the date of the surrender, until April 28, his headquarters was in Balanga, about 500 meters from the coastal road along which the prisoners were marching. During his trial on January 10, a Death March survivor named Sergeant Jimmy Baldassarre took the stand. Like many who testified, Baldassarre spared no detail as he described the horrors of the Hike, and claimed that he saw "hundreds and hundreds" of bodies along the route. Unique among the witnesses, however, was his claim to have seen and recognized Homma on the coastal road, in an "official car with some kind of yellow sticker on the front." Baldassare added some detail, stating that Homma "dressed differently, and he was more stout then," but that his memory was clear and precise—Homma was in the courtroom with him. Homma acknowledged his occasional presence on the road, but denied seeing any bodies.[21]

It is highly unlikely that a sergeant in the U.S. army would have recognized Homma, but few were interested in any account that conflicted with Baldassarre's. Another scenario is more likely:

> The view of their routes was blocked by other buildings and trees. If General Homma saw any of the parties plodding by, he was observing men who were in the preliminary stages of the long march.... What General Homma may have seen could easily have lead [sic] him to conclude that his instructions were being carried out in the fashion he desired. From April 9th until April 19th he neither asked for nor received any progress reports ... in the Japanese army that was an indication that matters were going well.[22]

To be sure, Homma saw prisoners walking by his headquarters, but from his vantage point he did not see "anything extraordinary" and he was satisfied that the plan conformed to Geneva Convention guidelines for the treatment of prisoners. Orders to his staff specifically instructed that the prisoners be treated "in a friendly spirit." Indeed, his transportation officer, General Kawane Yoshikata, submitted a plan that would have provided "transportation, food and medical supplies for the prisoners in a model of humane treatment. Homma approved it, but everything went wrong."[23]

In his work *The War with Catiline*, the Roman historian Sallust once wrote that in "the highest position there is the least freedom of action." A millennium later, the Allied commander-in-chief Dwight Eisenhower wrote to his brother Edgar: "I suffer from the usual difficulty that besets the higher commander—things can be ordered and started, but actual execution at the front has to be turned over to someone else."[24] Both speak to the fundamental issue on which Homma was convicted, that of "command responsibility."[25] Lead defense counsel John H. Skeen's defense was based on several facts—Homma never ordered the commission of any atrocities, never consented to their commission, and took all reasonable precautions to prevent them, all of which were true.

During the trial, no evidence surfaced that indicated Homma ordered or condoned the brutality of Japanese guards. In his even-handed biography of MacArthur, the historian William Manchester stated flatly that no "hard evidence linked Homma with the Death March of 1942. At most he was an ineffectual commander, unable to control the brutality of his men." Other sources suggest something of his response upon learning of some of his soldiers' behavior—when he "heard the truth of the Bataan Death March, he erupted in anger," and he went to his death claiming that he knew nothing of whatever atrocities his soldiers committed on the Death March. At one point in the hearings, he wrote a note to his lawyers that said, "I am horrified to learn these things happened under my command.... I am ashamed of our troops."[26]

His defense lawyers relied on the argument that no orders had been issued for the Death March, and that it "had developed as an unpremeditated act of passion on the part of vengeful Japanese soldiers." Unconvinced, the court sentenced Homma to death. Essentially, he was condemned for the actions of his soldiers, for which he was held responsible, by which logic hardly any commander whose soldiers misbehaved would be innocent. Beyond even this, the foundation of societies governed by laws and courts is third-party punishment, clearly not the case since MacArthur defined the jurisdiction and claimed final authority on the verdict.[27]

Skeen stated that the proceedings were a "highly irregular trial, conducted in an atmosphere that left no doubt as to what the ultimate outcome would be." Supreme Court Associate Justice Frank Murphy protested the verdict, stating: "Either we conduct such a trial as this in the noble spirit and atmosphere of our Constitution or we abandon all pretense to justice, let the ages slip away and descend to the level of revengeful blood purges." Murphy wanted no part in such activity, and in his dissenting opinion made clear that Homma's life was "taken without regard to due process of law."[28]

After rejecting Homma's wife's plea for her husband's life, MacArthur allowed the man who had defeated him on the battlefield to be shot rather than ignominiously hanged. Yet he could not resist justifying his decision—Homma had "violated a fundamental code of chivalry, which has ruled all honorable military men throughout the ages in treatment of defeated opponents."[29] Defending the fairness of the trial, he offered what many wished to hear in the immediate postwar:

> If the defendant does not deserve his judicial fate, none in jurisdictional history ever did. There can be no greater, more heinous or more dangerous crime than the mass destruction, under guise of military authority or military necessity, of helpless men, incapable of further contribution to the war effort. A failure of law process to punish such acts of criminal enormity would threaten the very fabric of world society.[30]

Though MacArthur was in Tokyo, his presence was felt throughout the entire trial; Homma and another general, Yamashita Tomoyuki, were "tried and convicted by kangaroo courts which flouted justice with the Supreme Commander's approval and probably at his urging."[31]

Even so, during his trial, Homma stated, "I am morally responsible for whatever happened in anything under my command." Shortly before he was executed, he gave his wife a small box containing a lock of his hair and some fingernail clippings. After Fujiko left, he wrote the following verse:

> Laid down on the altar I am
> Offered as a victim to God
> For the sake of
> My newly born country.

As a final insult, to prevent the appearance of a pilgrimage site, MacArthur had his body burned, "and the ashes disposed of in great secrecy."[32]

Clearly, Homma did not know of the deeds of some of his men on the Death March. In perhaps the saddest of many ironies, perhaps he also did not know that the behavior of others of his soldiers reflected his optimism and generosity of spirit. Reflecting on his fate just before his execution, he quoted an aphorism from the Meiji period, *kateba kangun, makereba, zokugun* (Win and you are the official army, lose and you are the rebels).[33] Had he known the fate of another player in Bataan's post-war drama, he might have chosen a different maxim.

* * * * *

That player was Tsuji Masanobu, whose actions were consistent with quite a different form of *bushido*, one eventually associated with the most virulent nationalism. Like its inverse, this form took decades to gestate, helped along by the racist, imperial agenda of some Japanese. Late nineteenth century oligarchs, building a new Japanese state with a trowel in one hand and a sword in the other, used their nation's *samurai* tradition, but drew only selectively on its content. Lacking the luxury of time, operating during an era when a quarter of the earth's land was being divided among European powers, Japanese leaders found the concept of *bushido* to be useful mortar as they constructed their new state edifice. The *Gunjin Kunkai* (Admonition to Soldiers and Sailors), issued in 1878, demanded that the "ethos of the modern army must be founded on the traditional way of warriors," with loyalty, courage, and respect among the virtues; commoners were told that serving the emperor in the armed forces was a great privilege:

> During the past feudal period, *bushi* occupied a status superior to … commoners. Only *bushi* were expected to be loyal and courageous, to serve their lords, to respect their honour, and in failure to admit their shame. The virtues of the *bushi* were widely known among commoners…. Today's soldiers are undoubtedly *bushi*, even if their status is not hereditary. It is therefore beyond question that they should exhibit loyalty and courage as their prime virtues, according to the best tradition of the *bushi* of bygone days.[34]

The document makes clear a new ideal after which to be striven, with heavy emphasis on loyalty and obedience. Soldiers were not to question superiors or government policy.

Ten years later, *Gunjin Chokuyu* (Imperial Rescript to Soldiers and Sailors), though containing earlier strains of thought, pounded home the theme of obedience, making clear extent of expected loyalty—"Duty is weightier than a mountain, death is lighter than a feather." Such enunciations, useful for the purpose of state building, omitted the "spiritual underpinning" and "compassion and sensitivity" of *bushido*'s other forms. Like Yamamoto's earlier ideas, this new version of *bushido* waited, fertile ground for still another ideological crop.

The economic crash of 1929 called Japan's decade-long experiment with democracy and political parties into question, and the military was able to paint itself as representing *kokutai* (the national essence), willing and able to rescue the nation from the corrupt, Western-influenced political parties and ideas of liberalism. Just as the oligarchs refashioned the inchoate ideas of Yamamoto into a tool of national self-defense, the militarists who took control of Japan in the 1930s found it useful for their own jingoistic and xenophobic purposes—and took *bushido* even further away from its earlier, more humanistic roots. Here was the opportunity for yet another inscription on this most useful ideological palimpsest—the militarists virtually silenced what earlier had only been muted. As the historian Gavin

1. Virtue and Vice 27

Tsuji and Homma: Vice and virtue, dark and light (courtesy Christopher Leet).

Daws pointed out, by this time "Bushido, the way of the warrior, meant whatever officers wanted it to mean."³⁵

By the 1930s, the earlier emphasis on the need for loyalty to the emperor now took a more chauvinistic turn, toward virulent nationalism, what U.S. propaganda frequently referred to as the "modern cult" of *bushido*. Under pressure from the military, the Thought Bureau of the Ministry of Education pulled together several strands of thought in 1937 with the publication of *Kokutai no Hongi* (*Cardinal Principles of the National Polity*). Here the connection to previous versions of *bushido* primarily hinged on the emperor. This text asserted that Japanese were "intrinsically quite different from the so-called citizens of Occidental countries" due to an "original condition" that was peculiarly Japanese. The influence on the educational system was profound, with all exposed continuously to the excruciatingly arcane justification for the key chapter's opening sentence: "The Land of Japan stands high above the other nations of the world, and her people excel the peoples of the world."³⁶

For soldiers, such ideas found clear expression in the pamphlet all Japanese soldiers were given to read as they sailed to the Philippines. *Kore dake Yomeba Ware wa Kateru* (Read This and the War Is Won) stated flatly that "the present war is a struggle between races, and we must achieve the satisfaction of our just demands with no thought of leniency to Europeans":

> When you encounter the enemy after landing, regard yourself as an avenger come at last face to face with his father's murderer.... Here before you is the man whose death will lighten your heart of its burden of brooding anger. If you fail to destroy him utterly, you can never rest at peace.

In essence, the pamphlet described whites as interlopers in Asia, imperialists who exploited the human and natural resources of a richly abundant and productive region. "The aim of the present war is the realization, first in the Far East, of His Majesty's august will and ideal that the peoples of the world should each be granted possession of their rightful homelands."[37]

According to the new, corrupted form of *bushido*, surrendered prisoners were "objects of contempt," to Japanese soldiers, since their own manual had told them explicitly not to surrender. The April 24 issue of the *Japan Times and Advertiser*, speaking specifically of the horde of Americans caught on Bataan, stated: "they cannot be treated as ordinary prisoners of war.... To show them mercy is to prolong the war.... Hesitation is uncalled for, and the wrong doers must be wiped out."[38]

* * * * *

If Homma suggested something of the cosmopolitan and humane, Colonel Tsuji Masanobu is as clear an example of the racist, xenophobic strain in Japanese culture as one can locate in any era. Tsuji graduated at the top of his class from Nagoya Army Elementary School, where he had shown a strong interest in *kendo*. Only 5'2", but very strong physically, he was known "for beating his opponents into submission with smashing blows." He graduated from the War College in 1931 and served as operations staff officer in the Kwantung army in China as a major.[39]

He was known to shun those he disliked, but also for favoring the small coterie of kindred spirits to the exclusion of others. Tsuji boasted often of having been wounded in five countries, but his frequent transfers were due to his habit of offending superiors. In China, he criticized them for "spending secret funds on women and drink; at a key battle his reckless advance had led to failure, he was forced from headquarters at Hankow for attempting a coup."[40] Tsuji was quick to apply the principle of *gekokujo*, a form of insubordination, or, taking individual initiative when an officer determined that his superiors were misguided.

In early 1942 the Japanese advance rolled southward, into Malaya and Singapore, and Tsuji's star rose as one of its chief architects, the "god of operations." During the campaign some Japanese soldiers raped women on the island capital of Georgetown. The commanding general, Yamashita Tomoyuki, ordered the men responsible executed and an officer named Kobayashi, the commander of the men's unit, punished. Concerned with restraint, Yamashita wrote, "I want my troops to behave with dignity.... This is very important now that Japan is taking her place in the world. These men must be educated up to their new role in foreign countries."[41] Tsuji, however, objected vehemently to the punishment of Kobayashi. His attitude presaged extraordinarily brutal plans.

Singapore fell in February and Tsuji, along with the garrison commander Kawamura Saburo, the chief of staff Lt. Gen. Suzuki Sosaku and *Kempeitai* (secret police) commander Lt. Col. Oishi Masayuki, planned and orchestrated the purge of the Chinese community.

Chinese elite, especially the wealthy, including lawyers, doctors, school teachers, merchants and laborers, were gathered together, then placed in trucks and taken away to be shot.

> Under this scheme, Chinese males between the ages of 18 and 50 were ordered to report to mass screening centers. Those deemed anti–Japanese were detained, loaded onto lorries, and taken away to the coast or to other isolated places where they were machine-gunned and bayoneted to death.

The massacres of Chinese had been part of Tsuji's vision of a race war from his appointment as chief planning officer for the campaign more than a year earlier.

The massacres of February 21 to 23, during which some 5,000 were murdered, were not violations of the law. To deal with resistance to the conquest of Manchuria, the puppet government there was forced to legalize the execution of any anti–Japanese activists "on the spot without trial." Such procedures were called *Genju Shobun* (Harsh Disposal). A decade later, Kawamura published his memoirs, in which "he expressed condolences to the victims of Singapore and prayed for the repose of their souls." Tsuji wrote the foreword to the book, but he "showed no regrets and offered no apology to the victims."[42]

By April, Homma's star was waning with imperial headquarters in Tokyo, and the commander of the southern theater, Field Marshal Terauchi, was becoming more and more critical of the stalled conquest of Bataan and Corregidor. Tsuji was sent for the purpose of liaison and governing, and to stiffen the performance of Homma's army, bogged down and behind schedule. Tsuji was only on the Bataan peninsula for less than two weeks, but he came to the Philippines on April 1 preceded by a reputation comprising equal parts of brilliance and cruelty. He was riding the crest of his considerable influence after the conquest of Malaya and Singapore.

Though it demanded complete obedience from its lowest echelons, the Imperial Japanese Army was a confusing welter of cliques and conflicting interests. One historian of the institution states, "one cannot say that the whole army was either under strict control or evinced a clear singleness of purpose. Areas of responsibility were exceedingly ill-defined." Tsuji had cultivated a personal relationship with Tojo Hideki, and with his close friend Hattori Takushiro, with whom he had served in Manchuria, now Tojo's secretary and Adjutant of the War Ministry.[43] Like *Ryogenokan*, officials during the Heian period (794 to 1185 CE), whose posts did not exist as part of the official government structure, Tsuji appeared on Bataan with the prestige and influence of the imperial staff.

Tsuji immediately set about undermining Homma's authority by issuing oral orders about which the commander knew nothing. His goal was "establishing his personal coterie of militarist-minded officers" whose purpose was to kill all prisoners—Americans because they were white colonialists, Filipinos because they had betrayed the Asian cause. Clearly he saw the conflict in racial terms.[44] When surrender came on April 9, Tsuji was on hand, and "through his supporting staff officers, he issued such orders to unit commanders. Wachi Takeji, testifying at Homma's trial, stated that Tsuji advocated "severe treatment should be meted out" to Filipinos. One source claims that after arriving in Mariveles, Tsuji pulled out a pistol and shot a prisoner dead, claiming "This is the way to treat bastards like this."[45]

Some officers responded. Others, whose sensibilities more nearly resembled Homma's, did not. A colonel commanding Japanese troops at Mount Limay was ordered to "kill all prisoners and those offering to surrender." Objecting, Colonel Imai was told that the order came from imperial headquarters, whereupon he ordered all prisoners in his command released. Colonel Watanabe Saburo, a senior staff officer, met Tsuji near Mariveles on April 9, just as the Death March was beginning. Seeing a column of U.S. prisoners on the road, Tsuji turned to Watanabe and suggested, "How about we kill them?" When Watanabe refused, Tsuji accused him of having "no guts." Tsuji then found the commander of the 16th division, General Morioko, who also refused, stating, "Don't be stupid, we can't do that kind of thing." Another refusal came from General Torao Ikuta, who declined to kill prisoners without a written order.[46] The historian Ian Ward concludes,

> It is difficult to be precise about the percentage of Death March casualties directly attributable to the activities of Tsuji. But unquestionably his influence was highly significant, if not the dominant motivating force. Large numbers of prisoners were undoubtedly executed on verbal [sic] instructions originating from this newly-arrived celebrity troubleshooter.... Tsuji's manipulations ... ensured that, at the staff level echelon, a level of appalling brutality would be accepted during the Death March phase and pass unchallenged.

John Toland agrees, suggesting that "additional murders resulted directly from the unauthorized, oral order emanating from Colonel Tsuji." And in his magisterial *Embracing Defeat*, John Dower states that Tsuji "bore heavy responsibility for massacres in both Singapore and the Philippines, and was also implicated in isolated atrocities extending to an act of cannibalism following his execution of an American prisoner."[47]

When Japan surrendered in August 1945, Tsuji was in Thailand. Aware that the British wanted him for the Chinese massacres, he made his way to China.[48] He took on the alias "Aoki Norinobu," printed a phony death-note indicating he was going to commit suicide, and soon made contact in Bangkok with Chinese anti–Communist forces. He left Bangkok disguised as a Chinese businessman (or a priest in another account) and arrived in China and remained until 1948, "where his knowledge of military intelligence and his virulent anticommunism made him useful to the Nationalist forces under Chiang Kai-shek."[49]

Tsuji flourished in a post-war world where, after 1949, China had succumbed to Mao Zedong's vision of Communism, where the Soviet Union possessed the atomic bomb and Japan was the only reliable U.S. ally in the Far East. The U.S. feared what it considered a monolithic Communist menace above all, and it sometimes mattered little where useful information was found. One of the very darkest locations was in China, where at war's conclusion the U.S. granted full immunity to the Japanese physicians of what was euphemistically called the "Epidemic Prevention and Water Purification Department," otherwise known as Unit 731. There thousands of Chinese were subject to a wide range of barbaric experimentation, including vivisection and other, unspeakably cruel procedures. What interested the U.S. most was these doctors' research on biological warfare, including the means by which various diseases could be spread—and preventing the Soviet Union from acquiring it.[50]

In 1948 he returned to Japan under a different alias, "Aoki Kenshin," bearing identification papers from the Classical History Department of the University of Beijing. He arrived back home at just the right time. U.S. policy was in the midst of the pivot, called the reverse course, whereby the earlier emphasis on the disarmament of Japan was replaced by attention to restoring Japanese industrial strength under the protective wing of American nuclear umbrella. The new reality meant Japan, just a few years previously the dreaded enemy, was now recast as the stable, democratic ally, an essential part of the bulwark against rising Chinese Communist power. Global containment of Communism was now the central national priority. MacArthur's chief of intelligence was General Charles Willoughby, a virulent anti–

Communist. Aware of the continuing interest of the British in bringing Tsuji to justice, he arranged to keep Tsuji out of sight until the crisis subsided, to "keep the British misinformed."[51] By January 1950, Tsuji was free to move about in the open as the occupation authorities lifted his war criminal designation.

There soon followed two bestsellers, one on his escape after the war's end, the other dealing with the battle of Guadalcanal. In 1952 he published a third work, this time on the conquest of Singapore and, as the occupation was ending, he was elected to the Japanese Diet.[52] He wrote copiously about his storied career, selling the serial rights to *Mainichi* magazine under the title "Underground Escape." There and in his books he represented himself "as the architect of every successful strategem, the hero of death-defying encounters ... prescient, dynamic and misunderstood." Tsuji was now a public figure, speaking out strongly against Communism as he stood as independent candidate for the Japanese Diet from his district in Ishikawa prefecture, where won with a plurality of 20,000 votes. In 1957, he was appointed as emissary to Egypt, then to Yugoslavia. He finally died 1968 in Laos under mysterious circumstances.[53]

Directly responsible for the brutalization of native populations, Tsuji seemed "like a Japanese Rasputin, bobbing up in every theater of war with his taste for violence and his capacity for escalating it unimpaired." Toward the end of the war, General Suzuki Sosaku reflected on what had gone wrong. "It was the Ishiwara-Tsuji clique," he wrote, "that brought the Japanese army to this deplorable situation." He called Tsuji insubordinate and insolent, and he advised his superior in Malaya, General Yamashita, to punish and dismiss him. "I tell you," he complained, "as long as they exert influence on the army, it can only lead to ruin. Extermination of these poisonous insects should take precedence over all other problems."[54]

Tsuji survived Homma by twenty-two years.

* * * * *

Reflecting on his military experience, Glen Gray suggested that "war compresses the greatest opposites into the smallest space in the shortest time." He continued:

> Inhuman cruelty can give way to superhuman kindness. Inhibitions vanish, and people are reduced to their essence ... in moments of this kind I was as much inspired by the nobility of some of my fellows as appalled by the animosity of others, or, more exactly, by both qualities in the same person. The average degree, which we commonly know in peacetime, conceals as much as it reveals about the human creature.[55]

The simultaneous presence of such opposite qualities in the same person is hardly surprising, perhaps only in warfare does it seem more obvious and anomalous. There in the thickness of victory or defeat lay limitless opportunities for extracting the best and worst from a single individual; in war's nasty environs, the two are sometimes indistinguishable.

Yet in some, one of the qualities—humanistic or its opposite—preponderates. Homma was *Eros* to Tsuji's *Thanatos*. If men are driven by these urges—one to preserve, toward connection to others, the other toward death and destruction, in many ways these two represent the extremes of human behavior in the context of war. In between are all the shades of gray this study seeks to explore.

2

An Army's Ethos

Nothing is easier than denouncing the evil doer; nothing is more difficult than understanding him.—Doestoyevsky

The Imperial Japanese Army began its life in the late nineteenth century as part of the country's remarkable emergence from isolation to international power. As the nation underwent the upheavals that inevitably accompanied industrialization, integration into the world market, and entry into competition for colonial possessions, the army's definition of itself and of its role changed in fundamental ways. Once the agent of modernization as it defeated a band of reactionary samurai in 1877, by 1942 it had become intensely reactionary itself, an inward-looking entity, focused on what it perceived were threats to its definition of the "pure" essence of Japan. Intolerant of impurity in the form of Japanese infected with foreign ideas, rioting citizens, ethnic Koreans, Communists, or enemies on foreign battlefields, it never hesitated to act, wielding its rifles and bayonets against foes internal as well as external.

Closely related was another defining reality. Facing a lack of resources that prevented modernization and mechanization, the army leadership chose instead to believe it could develop in its soldiers an especially powerful *seishin* (fighting spirit) that could overcome better-supplied, more numerous enemies. The crude tactics employed on Bataan—overreliance on unsupported infantry frontal assaults—allowed the fractured Allied forces to hold out for more than three months while Homma's army suffered enormous casualties.

* * * * *

Japan goes to great lengths to represent itself as the ultimate example of consensus, a place somehow free of the divisiveness and conflicts that plague other societies. At different times and for different reasons, the West has enthusiastically embraced such a definition. Recent images have been clear and compelling—a smoothly running economy managed brilliantly by government and industry's cooperation, churning out high-quality products, manned by a highly competent work force, committed to the success of Japan, Inc. Its workers seemed uniform in their appearance and in their attitudes, "economic animals" willing to endure long commutes and long work hours in pursuit of the holy grail of what the Greater East Asia Co-Prosperity Sphere failed to achieve in the 1940s—security for an island nation, poor in most natural resources, except its population's astonishing ability to pull together as one behind its government's stated goals.

The *Nihonjin-ron*, loosely translated as "the debate over what it means to be Japanese," is a fine example of the Japanese obsession with their putative "uniqueness" and "collective self." Bookstores have whole sections devoted to the related cluster of topics, and the fringes of the discussion contain ludicrous assertions about the unique physical characteristics of Japanese—including the shape of their hips and the side of the brain on which thought occurs. When a Japanese, speaking to a foreigner, utters the phrase, "*Ware ware Nihonjin*" (We Japanese), it is meant to convey serious *gravitas*—a man speaking with the full authority of his tribe. During the war, the term *ichioku* (one hundred million) suggested this kind of powerful cultural unity. The battlefield no-surrender ferocity and *kamikaze* tactics near the war's end stemmed from the imperative of self-sacrifice, embodied in phrases such as *ichioku gyokusai*, "The hundred million as shattered jewel."[1]

Such is the image Japan projects, and such is the image that Westerners, relieved of the obligation to look deeper, have largely embraced. Works such as Ezra Vogel's *Japan as Number One* and James Fallows' *Looking into the Sun* all genuflected deeply at the altar of Japan, a nation that seemed to have solved many of the problems of the modern age. During the war, it was even easier to accept the Japanese self-assessment, and turn it to excellent use for propaganda. Frank Capra's 1945 production for the U.S. government, *Know Your Enemy: Japan*, offered a vision of the Japanese that, quite understandably, reduced a complex culture and society to a crude stereotype. There the narration defined the enemy soldier as little more than a mindless cog in a totalitarian machine—"He and his brother soldiers are as much alike as photographic prints off the same negative." The stereotype gives the lie to the reality.

On the battlefields of World War II, Japanese imperial soldiers were famous for their refusal to surrender. Few Americans facing their fanatic resistance on any Pacific battlefield failed to comment on this salient feature of their enemy's behavior. Less well known is that, when captured, individual Japanese often turned into active collaborators, freely cooperating and offering their erstwhile enemies information. One explanation for this seeming contradiction is that the Imperial Japanese Army offered no instruction to its soldiers regarding such security, since the possibility of capture was never contemplated. One Japanese officer put the matter succinctly, stating that his "army maintains the position that Japanese prisoners of war do not exist."[2]

But deeply rooted in Japanese culture lay another reality. Upon capture, the Japanese soldier crossed a crucially important boundary. On one side was all he knew, all of the ordered, hierarchical connections of his life. On the other was the outside world where nothing he knew or understood any longer obtained. He surrendered, quite literally, his Japaneseness, and ceased to be, at some fundamental level, a human being. He became the ultimate outsider.

All peoples, to some extent, define themselves in relationship to outsiders, those whose physical appearance is different, or do not assign similar meaning to the material or spiritual realms of existence. For Japanese, the difference between what is inside, safe and familiar (*uchi*) and that which is outside, threatening and unknown (*soto*) is of particular cultural significance. The term *uchi* is laden with meaning, and connotes a place wherein the individual exists in fixed, known association with others. In conversation, depending on the context, the term can denote the individual self, a person's family, school, hometown, company or, when speaking to a foreigner, all of Japan—"To a Japanese, being Japanese is the primary fact of life.... It means to be forever an inside man—inside a family, inside a village, inside a company, inside the Japanese islands surrounded by sea."³

The term conveys the concentric circles of meaning for Japanese, and defines an individual's identity with great precision. Beyond this, however, there is another dimension. The difference between *uchi* and *soto* is also intimately bound up with ideas of purity and impurity, but

> not the relatively simple idea of purity-impurity that most westerners have. Purity in Japan does not just mean undiluted or clean, it can include such concepts as perfection and normalcy. Impurity can include not just the mixed and the dirty, but also the sick and impaired, the spiritually or ritually tainted, the primitive, the selfish, the failure and others who fall from the grace of perfection.⁴

This way of dividing the world into the known and the threatening, the pure and the impure—so basic to Japanese sensibilities—is extremely useful in understanding the behavior of the modern Imperial Japanese Army from its birth in the nineteenth century through its actions on the Bataan peninsula in 1942. The American prisoners it captured were merely the most visible of the threats that the army perceived as it drew in upon itself, a well-defined *uchi*, firmly convinced of its role as the defender of what it labeled the pure Japanese essence.

Where I lived in the town of Ashiya, I frequented an izakaya *in the evenings after class, and came to know the master, a nice guy named Takahashi, rather well. Sometimes he would run a tab for me and allow my bar bill to extend to payday. On the walls of the bar were* omiyage—*souvenirs that regular customers had brought back from various placed they'd been— islands on the inland sea, temples in Kyoto, the emperor's palace in Tokyo. I had, I believed, become part of the* uchi *of "my" neighborhood bar. As such, when I made a trip to Hokkaido, I returned with a small, bearded, wooden doll of a "hairy Ainu" (what the Japanese call the indigenous people of the far north) on which Takahashi happily wrote my name in* katakana *before hanging it up. Two years later, during a return trip, I visited the bar again and saw, to my embarrassment, that my present was a silly caricature, much like a "Sambo" doll would be offensive to an African American. While living there, I had been seeking, even on the periphery allowed a foreigner, to define the other and maintain my connection to the* uchi.

Though the Japanese share a common language, history and cultural heritage, genuine homogeneity is a myth. Japanese history is as full of conflict, intrigue, betrayal, murder and war as that of any nation. As John Dower correctly observes, "Japanese society was honeycombed with groups suspicious of one another, and the blue-eyed barbarians from across the seas became absorbed into patterns of thinking that had emerged centuries earlier as a response to ... tense and threatening insider/outsider relationships."⁵ In fact, Japan, like any other large and complex society, is riven with contradictions and conflicts, with groups that strive assiduously to maintain their integrity, while remaining profoundly suspicious of others. If it were otherwise, the prodigious effort expended before the Pacific War to ensure a highly integrated and loyal population would surely have been unnecessary.

The Japanese claim of homogeneity is indeed spurious. Such a flat reality would be tedious, and Japan has never been that. Anyone spending an hour in front of a Japanese television or seeing one of Kurosawa's historical epics will note the numerous dramas based on the endless civil wars during which *samurai* slaughtered each other with great abandon. In modern times, there was the bloody conflict in 1960 over the ratification of the U.S.-Japan Security Treaty, the ten-year conflict between radical students, allied with farmers, over the construction of Tokyo's Narita airport that did not end until the early 1990s, and the horror of the sarin gas subway attacks carried out by the Aum Shinrikyo cult in 1995. Other examples include the frequency of labor unions' "spring offensives" that often result in violence, and *taishu danko*, the practice of confronting, sometimes violently, officials against whom groups have specific grievances. In the 1930s, young officers employed the notion of *gekokujō* (principled disobedience of superiors), and counted assassination among their tools.

There persists in Japan an essential "village mentality." Any threat to the harmony of one's immediate group produces strong reaction, and factions abound—"Group affiliations in Japan are very important, but the Japanese tend to emphasize these even beyond reality, attempting to interpret everything in terms of such things as personal factional alignments (*habatsu*) in politics, family interrelationships, university provenance (the "academic clique" or *gakubatsu*), and personal patronage and recommendations." Japanese society is arranged vertically, and doubtless part of its genius is the competition this structure breeds. But in such a society, "every co-worker is a rival. All those related to you horizontally—that is, all your peers—are a threat.... The Japanese expression *yokoyari* (an interruption, literally 'side-spearing') describes the nature of the threat posed by colleagues."[6]

If we consider for a moment Japanese society from the point of view of the "mainstream," there are numerous groups that qualify as outsiders—the hereditary caste of the *eta* (full of filth), the "primitive" Ainu of northern Japan, Koreans, organized crime in the form of the *yakuza*, Okinawans who are not "truly" culturally Japanese, day laborers and vagrants, those with obvious diseases, the physically disabled, the mentally impaired, and foreigners. Taken as a whole, these groups constitute a hefty portion of Japan's population, and denote the reality of considerable tension within Japanese society. Each group represents a threat to the purity of the whole.[7]

* * * * *

The arrival of Commodore Perry's Black Ships in 1853 generated a severe national crisis. After more than two centuries of near-complete isolation, the Japanese engaged in an immediate and ultimately fruitful debate about how to respond. Broadly put, one side of the debate was summed up in the reactionary slogan *sonno joi* (revere the emperor and expel the barbarian). The other was defined by the slogans *fukkoku kyohei* (rich country, strong army) and, later, *bunmei kaika* (civilization and enlightenment). A brief civil war settled the issue in favor of the latter approach to dealing with the Western challenge. It was a great challenge indeed, since Japan entered its modern age when Western powers were carving up the "Chinese melon" and dividing nearly a quarter of the earth's land among themselves as colonial masters. In this context, an obvious and necessary component of the Japanese response was the creation of a modern military force. Though any Death March survivor would claim the opposite, the weight of Japanese history suggests that, instead of harboring a desire to conquer, Japanese leaders have been motivated by a powerful urge to keep others from conquering them. It was out of this fear that the modern Imperial Japanese Army was born.

That army's first order of business was putting down a sizeable internal rebellion of discontented *samurai* who rejected the vision of a modernizing Japan, with the Western influence that vision implied. This, the subject of Edward Zwick's U.S. film *The Last Samurai* in

2003, the new conscript army handily accomplished in 1877. In the late nineteenth century, the army saw itself as a crucially important force for modernization, a key to the maintenance of Japanese sovereignty, essential protection against the dangers of *soto*—defined as those who, within or outside Japan, might challenge the consolidation of national power.

The role of infantry changed little over the years leading up to World War II. Before then, battlefields were invariably crowded places, with men frequently fighting shoulder-to-shoulder. Greek hoplites, Roman legionnaires, soldiers of Napoleon and infantry going over the top in World War I all shared the common experience of fighting in close company with their fellows.[8] The Japanese army's tactics at the turn of the century were no different, so demonstrated during its second task. During the Sino-Japanese war of 1894–95, when encountering the enemy,

> columns maneuvered into a skirmish line supported by densely packed ranks of infantrymen who rushed forward en masse for a short distance, threw themselves on the ground, and then repeated the maneuver. Junior officers led frontal assaults in short rushes ... the tightly packed formations preserved unit integrity and fire discipline, ensured tactical command and control.

Such tactics, combined with Chinese weakness, produced a Japanese victory. The application of pre-determined tactics was the key, with the infantry manual of 1898 validating "mass formations relying on bayonet attacks because that was the only way for a company commander to control his unit."[9]

The military then turned its attention to thwarting Russian imperial ambitions in Asia. During the resulting Russo-Japanese War of 1904–05, *seishin* seemed once again triumphant. During the siege of Port Arthur and later, on the plains of Manchuria at Mukden, Japanese soldiers hurled themselves as "human bullets" against Russian machine-gun fire, leaving some 90,000 corpses on those fields. The country mourned its dead, but battlefield success resulted in the acquisition of Port Arthur, Russian withdrawal from Manchuria and the eventual annexation of Korea. This was a dramatic and successful further incursion into the world of colonial competition, and the Japanese army was, understandably enough, reluctant to change the tactics that had yielded such gains. The historian Hayashi Saburo has suggested that such conservatism "was nothing less than a smug delusion born of incomplete comprehension of modern war's nature."[10] Yet Hayashi's indictment applied equally to Western armies, as battlefield tactics everywhere lagged behind technological innovations such as the machine gun. Reliance on the "spirit of the attack" in massed infantry assaults of World War I would demonstrate the results in the most shocking and gruesome way imaginable.

French military doctrine held that the courage of the French soldier in attack was unmatched. "Like strong wine, their *élan* made them insensible to their own weaknesses.... It was truly believed that, in combat, moral superiority would outweigh advantage in firepower." At the outset of World War I the French version of *seishin* would, the general staff believed, fully compensate for the lack of artillery and automatic weapons compared to the Germans.[11] The French were not alone in the commitment to offensive battlefield tactics. The Austrian army's 1911 regulations made clear that infantry, even without the support of other arms, could be victorious if they were "tough and brave." The Russian, British and German armies operated according to similar doctrines, with the result that the battles of World War I, especially the early ones, "closely resembled those fought by Napoleon a hundred years earlier."[12]

During the British offensive at Loos in 1915 — "the German defenders were astounded" by the sight of the entire field before them covered with advancing infantry in ten columns of a thousand men each. German machines guns scythed the British with devastating effect, one gun having fired more than 12,000 rounds; hundreds fell before the raking fire. A year later, assault tactics had not changed, nor, apparently, had the fatalism of the soldiers been much affected, some battalions kicking footballs ahead of their ranks as they advanced into withering fire.[13] Recalling his experience in the squalid trenches, Adolf Hitler criticized those mired in a stultifying past: "Who says I'm going to start a war like those fools in 1914? Are not all our efforts bent toward preventing this? Most people have no imagination.... The creative genius stands always outside the circle of the experts."[14] The generals who crafted the slaughter of the Russo-Japanese and Great Wars did not share the advantage of such hindsight. Yet by the outbreak of World War II, Western tactics, driven by an awareness of technology, had responded to the new battlefield reality.[15] Japanese tactics did not.

For the Japanese army, the emphasis on *seishin* legitimated an approach to military power that avoided the problems inevitably associated with technological innovation and resource management that were fundamental to modern, total war. Japan lacked the financial, industrial and technical backing that would have allowed it to modernize according to the demands of changing military technology. Simply put, the nation faced an uphill battle to continue the process of modernization it had so brilliantly begun in the nineteenth century. One observer put the problem succinctly, calling Japan an "overpopulated, have-not country" that "possessed a pygmy economy by the standards of advanced industrial powers and little appreciation of the totality of modern war in coping with the huge civil and military requirements it set for itself."[16]

Once after an afternoon of cherry blossom viewing in Osaka I boarded a Hankyu train and rode to Koshien stadium where the Hanshin Tigers played their home games. Their guests that evening were the Tokyo Giants, and the game the Tigers played was as sloppy a nine inning stretch as I had ever seen. Their two shortstops managed four errors between them, the outfielders missed the cut-off man twice, and the starting pitcher threw two wild pitches and three homerun balls. That the Tigers' drubbing only occurred to the tune of an 8 to 1 score struck me as remarkable. I had begun to chat with the fan next to me, who was willing to trade ideas with a foreigner. Over shared beer and bentō *we lamented the team's performance, and after the third booted grounder he muttered that the manager, Goto Tsuguo, needed to be replaced because he could not repair the lousy morale on the team. I replied that the players just did not have the skill to perform at their opponents' level, but he was insistent: "Ano hito kantosho katteinai desho" (He'd never win the "fighting spirit award") — the prize given at every tourney to the sumo wrestler who demonstrated it best. The fan's comment clearly reflected his belief in morale — spirit over matter could fix his team. Goto, without sufficient fighting spirit, led his team to last place that year.*

What seemed an unchallengeable lesson, drawn from a recent war against a formidable Western opponent, was intensely appealing to elements of a nation and military that had always been ambivalent about their nation's relationship to the outside world (*soto*), and to the West in particular. Now modern *samurai*, having bestrode the battlefields of Manchuria, settled into a mindset that tended to ignore the coming challenges of technology, organization and training. In order to build up a "wealthy nation and a strong army" within a short period of time, industry and technology from the West were essential ingredients. Yet, "from the beginning there was a conflict ... rationalism prevailed in the sphere of technology, traditionalism or non-rationalism in the sphere of morality."[17]

Reliance on *seishin* served another purpose. Anachronistic celebration of fighting spirit was, to men at the uncomfortable intersection of tradition and modernity, East and West, a simple way to build on an imagined, mythic cultural tradition that confirmed Japanese uniqueness. Japan had always been ambivalent about the West. Already facing a deficit of resources, army planners "generated tactics that drew upon values, attitudes and behavior unique to Japanese society.... Reaffirmation of faith in moral attributes and psychological drives amounted to a callous evasion (but not total ignorance) of the realities of modern firepower, mechanization, and aviation." Resistance due to financial and structural constraints was rooted even more deeply in culture:

> The deeper cultural resistance to change manifested itself as the cluster of uniquely Japanese values found in expressions such as bushido or *yamato damashii*. In short, powerful natural and historical forces worked against sweeping military renovation in Japan during World War II.[18] Lacking raw materials to sustain a long, protracted war, the Japanese general staff turned to offensive plans designed to take maximum advantage of soldiers' putative "spiritual superiority" to quickly defeat enemies. The Japanese officer corps came to believe that "all of their men had to be imbued with what they call Nippon *seishin*.... Troops with Japanese spirit, it was argued, could triumph where all others would fail. It is extraordinary how this view dominated the popular thinking of a whole nation for almost a quarter century."[19]

Indeed, Japanese commanders, with some justice, believed that the army had come of age by defeating a Western power, and the lessons learned on the plains of Manchuria against Imperial Russia became the defining principles of military doctrine. After 1905, Japanese military leaders looked to their victorious past for what they considered the central lesson: "the decisive role of morale or spirit in combat." The Imperial army excelled at inculcating a spirit of sacrifice and loyalty in its young soldiers, and the Russo-Japanese War stood as an outstanding example of what "'sheer tenacity and courage—high morale' could do in fighting a superior enemy."[20] The *hohei soten* (the infantry field manual), published in 1909, rejected the implications of the new, revolutionary technology that the Japanese army had encountered—the machine gun in particular. This new, murderous weapon necessitated fighting in open order,

> rather than in closed order as before. In open order combat each soldier is expected to fight on his own whenever he is separated from his commanding officer or when that officer himself has fallen in battle. Logically, this type of combat requires considerable initiative on the part of the individual soldier, but the military elites resisted this logic because it threatened the social order and the army's position in it.

The solution was to ignore, or at least to downplay, the new battlefield realities, and exhort soldiers to overcome "material forces" with "spiritual forces."[21] The new army literature was replete with phrases such as "the attack spirit" and "sacrifice one's life to the country, absolute obedience to superiors" and the non-negotiable importance of hand-to-hand combat.[22] After its victories against enemies Asian and Caucasian, the army leadership was convinced that the tactics it pursued with success—massed infantry assaults with bayonets fixed—was the *sine qua non* for all future conflicts.

Victory certainly seemed to justify all the Japanese blood spilled on Bataan. I cross the Lamao river and at obelisk #20 approach the town where General Edward King met Colonel

Nakayama, Homma's senior operations officer, to arrange surrender on April 9. I wander a bit helplessly, and can't find the surrender site anywhere, though I ask a half-dozen people. Finally, behind an elementary school, I find the life-sized rendering of the ceremony in statues, taken exactly from a Japanese propaganda photo, showing General Ned King with his legs crossed, and one of his other officers with his head in his hands. Here in work-a-day Lamao this tableaux seems overdone, as if trying too hard. The plaque tells me, "King showed great courage by his decision to end the bloodbath." As I stand and look, a pigeon lands on the table, finds nothing to eat, and flies away. A little boy wearing a Los Angeles Dodger baseball cap walks past with his mother. I turn away and walk north.

At this intersection, such insistence was not as irrational as one might expect. During the American Civil War, most observers, North and South, agreed that only about half of the men in combat units actually remained in the firing line. The slang of the era defined them as "beats or deadbeats, skulkers, sneaks, stragglers, or coffee-coolers," men who disappeared during battle.[23] If the remaining half fired their weapons at a Yankee or Rebel, more participated than did their descendants in World War II. Data obtained by Colonel SLA Marshall from interviews of over four hundred infantry companies clearly indicated that, between 1943 and 1945, in both the European and Pacific theaters, on average no more than 15 percent of U.S. trained infantrymen fired their weapons at the enemy in battle. Clearly, men not under close supervision or in the close company of their fellows chose not to participate in the ultimate purpose of battle—to kill the enemy. Yet the crew-served weapons were all fired—when under the scrutiny of his fellows, all did their jobs.[24]

The advent of modern firepower forced dispersion on bodies of soldiers, so that those visible would be only ten or so men. Gwen Dyer's *War* suggests that for the soldier, by World War II "the battlefield ha[d] become a desperately lonely place, deceptively empty but bristling with menace, where he can expect neither direct supervision by his officer or NCO in combat, nor the comforting presence of a group of other men beside him."[25] The new reality highlighted a central fact of the modern battlefield—most men, out of sight of their comrades, do not like to kill each other and it is difficult to compel them to do so, even on a battlefield after training designed to remove their reluctance.

The American response to this dilemma can be seen in a 1943 training film, an installment of the "Fighting Men" series entitled *Kill or Be Killed*. The film's purpose was to instruct recruits how to use the right weapon in the right way at the right time. Here the young men were told to discard their cultural predilections about fair play, that war was "the law of the jungle" that required them to "go after your enemy all out ... to hurt, to cripple, to kill." Then comes a series of shots demonstrating the use of the bludgeon, brass knuckles, blackjack, trench knife, the sawed-off shotgun and other, standard infantry weapons. One scene shows a GI in hand-to-hand combat with a German, at the end of which he gouges the enemy's eye with his thumb. "No army ever won a battle," the narrator intones, "without getting its hands dirty ... and bloody." Yet such efforts were hardly effective, considering the minimal fire discipline of Americans in combat.

This refusal by a large majority of men to fire at their enemies, if assumed to be a human, rather than simply an American or Allied proclivity, sheds considerable light on Japanese battle tactics. Dave Grossman, in his book *On Killing*, suggests that "the simple and demonstrable fact that there is within most men an intense resistance to killing their fellow man. A resistance so strong that ... soldiers on the battlefield will die before they can overcome it."[26] In a culture where the group so often takes precedence over the individual, Japanese infantry tactics recognized the salient fact that gave men the liberty to refuse—the loneliness of the modern battlefield:

> The battlefield is cold. It is the lonesomest place which men may share together.... The harshest thing about the field is that it is empty. No people stir about. There are little or no signs of action.... It is the emptiness which chills a man's blood and makes the apple harden in his throat. It is the emptiness which grips him as with paralysis.

In training, soldiers grew accustomed to the close, constant company of their fellows. They take the confidence they derive from such company into the field, and think of "battle as the shock impact of large and seeable forces, a kind of head-on collision between visible lines of men and machines extending as far as the eye can see." Under fire on the battlefield, however, units break up, and seeking cover, lose sight of each other. As hostile fire intensifies, men spread out further, a few firing their weapons.

> Some fail to act mainly because they are puzzled what to do and their leaders will not tell them; other are wholly unnerved and can neither think nor move in sensible relation to the situation. Such response as the men make to enemy fire tends mainly to produce greater separation ... thereby intensifying the feeling of isolation and insecurity in its individuals.[27]

The Japanese surely sensed that the modern battlefield was not conducive to individual soldiers' effective use of their weapons. On the assumption that a preponderance of Japanese soldiers might have shared in this refusal, the insistence on massed infantry tactics begins to make sense. The army, aware that a man advancing in the close company of his comrades could be controlled more easily and was much more likely to use his weapon, simply carried the logic of orchestrated, collective action to at least one of its reasonable conclusions. This was, perhaps, not as much a rejection of the realities of modern combat as much as recognition of that reality, and an attempt to overcome it.

* * * * *

One thoughtful observer has suggested, "Britain is a tradition. Russia is a mood. America is a way of life. Japan is a spirit, insular and protesting. It is a spirit that hurls itself in the face of physical facts—a troublesome spirit, unsure of its place, but jealous of its station."[28] The insight is telling, and suggests a pronounced irony. Just as the Japanese spirit—in the form of massed infantry attacks with bayonets fixed—had overcome the Russian behemoth, the society in whose defense the blood was shed began to turn away, unappreciative, from its protector and spiritual example. After 1905, the army found itself increasingly unsure of its place and jealous of its station, ready to lash out at foes domestic as well as foreign.

General Nogi Maresuke, who had led Japanese forces during the Russo-Japanese War, decided in 1912 to follow the emperor Meiji into death. He knelt in front of a portrait of his sovereign and committed ritual *seppuku*, leaving behind a testament calling for a renaissance of the Japanese spirit and bemoaning what he considered the growing spiritual decay of the era.[29] Indeed, the army looked with great suspicion on developments outside of Japan—currents of thought and behavior that it believed undermined the essence of what it considered to be the heart of the nation. The army, an entity that once considered itself the chief agent of modernization and progress, began increasingly to regard itself as the custodian of older values, ones it considered essential to the Japanese soul. Thirty years earlier, it stamped out opposition to the consolidation of central power; now it looked with growing suspicion at elements within Japan that began to question the fruits of that consolidation.

Japan faced wrenching change in the space of about forty years, and the simultaneous shock to the nation's sensibilities at the levels of politics, culture, and social organization is incalculable. Lacking roots in the classical Greek experience, the Enlightenment and the luxury of leisurely experimentation that defined the development of democratic thought and institutions in the U.S., Japan had grafted a patina of Western structures over a traditional culture that remained wary of the outside world and its potentially "contaminating" influences.

Fin de siècle Japan faced new and unexpected challenges. The war had stimulated industrial output and the accompanying shift toward a more materialistic, capitalistic society. Between 1905 and the outbreak of the First World War, Japanese youth, especially those in the urban centers, experienced a "new consciousness of the individual." The previous thirty-five years had seen strenuous efforts to catch up with the West crowned with success. But now, new terms such as *seiko* (success) and *risshin shusse* (getting ahead in the world) entered the vocabulary of the young. The ideas of influential writers such as Nietzsche and Ibsen affected educated city youth, and issues such as women's status, romantic love, and material wealth challenged older, traditional ethics. A kind of malaise set in. Now that the goal of attaining first-rank status was achieved, and so much effort and blood had been expended to that end, the nation's youth wondered what it had all been for.

The ethic of sacrifice for the nation seemed to be eroding, and one anxious observer was forced to "admit to signs of intoxication with idleness, profligacy, and indifference toward national affairs [and] indications that the Japanese people will ... lose their high aspirations and adopt a posture of indifference toward government." Older Japanese, upon whose labors and loyalty the nation had risen, scoffed at what they considered the hedonistic, dissolute behavior of the young, ridiculing them as effeminate "stars and violets."[30] The new century brought Japanese citizens into contact with the new, potentially disruptive ideas of democracy, individualism, and material culture. In response, top officials such as Tanaka Giichi and Ugaki Kazushige saw the army as the custodian of traditional values—seeking to shield the country from the change that any kind of diversity—ideological, political, social—would bring.[31]

Sinister movements were afoot. Just as the Nye Commission in the U.S. accused a nascent military-industrial complex of amassing grossly inappropriate profits from World War I, so did Japan's military resent the accumulated wartime wealth of a class of *niwaka narikin* (suddenly rich) whose conspicuous consumption emanated from a Thorstein Veblen nightmare. One general told the story of a *narikin* who, driving illegally through a section of Tokyo, found his car mired to the axles in mud. He demanded that the general's soldiers haul his vehicle out. The soldiers obliged, but when they approached the car, they found the man with three geisha. "Outraged, they overturned the car, leaving the *narikin* and his companions stranded in a sea of mud." Such episodes rankled Japanese officers, whose pay was minimal, but whose sacrifice, they believed, entitled them to the special respect of society.[32]

Extravagance, money worship and materialism were expressions of modern culture, especially for urban youth who had increasingly begun to identify individual success as their goal. Older Japanese looked with displeasure and anxiety at a rising generation that seemed to be discarding older values and older modes of behavior. One observer summed up their fears well: "Never since the dawn of world history has the growth of the individual been so respected and material happiness so sought after as in present day Japan."[33]

Hedonism was another threat. Younger Japanese were frequently accused of abandoning filial piety and pursuing pleasure for pleasure's sake. Many held the entertainments of the city responsible for "spreading ideas of romantic love, free love, and female sexuality and focused their criticism on young women as well as young men." Female independence, overt sexual posturing in cafes, all encouraged by new magazines such as *Josei*, challenged traditional male roles and produced unsurprising and sometimes vehement criticism—such unlicensed behavior needed to be "kept in check for the good of society."[34] A generation gap yawned.

In truth, Japan's rapid modernization in the late nineteenth century left the nation ill at ease with its cultural consequences. Flowing back and forth between embracing and rejecting the Western values that came with economic and technological progress, the Japanese found themselves on a cultural tightrope. The ideology of socialism, taking hold among the working classes created by Japan's rapid industrialization, threatened the bedrock foundations of loyalty to the emperor, as some laborers turned to Lenin for inspiration. Confrontations with organized labor in 1919 and again in 1921, with the production of military arms and equipment at issue, highlighted the divisions in Japanese society the military lamented. No longer a family with the emperor at its head, society seemed to be splitting apart under heavy blows from a bewildering variety of contemporary sources.

Those in the countryside felt left behind, unappreciated. Young men who knew little else praised farming as the "great foundation of the country" and found a lesson in the disaster (the great earthquake that killed 150,000) that befell Tokyo in 1923. Seeking to separate himself from city-dwellers, one farmer from Ibaraki Prefecture decried their "elegant clothes and their gold teeth, gold rings and watch chains" and their "trips to the seashore or the mountains to escape the heat" and two months after the earthquake, a young man from Nagano prefecture wrote that

> all the features of modern civilization that youths had long admired flourished in the cities, but what had that civilization wrought but fleeting wealth and power? Did it not depend on the exploitation of others, especially farmers? It made no sense to import urban civilization to the countryside or to yearn for what was basically "deformed and unsound."[35]

The poet Hagiwara Sakutaro called for a "return to Japan," and his poem "The New Koide Road" captures the uncertainty that accompanied change in the 1920s:

> A new path is being routed here,
> A direct access to town.
> At the crossing I stand,
> But failed to master the deserted horizons of all four directions,
> And gloom ruled the day,
> For as the sun dipped below the eaves,
> The coppice had been felled to sparsity.
> This mustn't be, This mustn't be! I churn my mind.
> This road, I shall revolt and refuse to take,
> Where the fresh new trees are all being felled.

Junichiro Tanizaki's famous essay "In Praise of Shadows" struck a similar note, lamenting the appearance of modern household items over the more traditional Japanese. Yet Tanizaki's wife later recalled that he himself preferred not to live in the house his essay so elegantly described.[36] Here we can glimpse the deep ambiguity toward modern culture—an ambiguity that the army, when it took control of Japan in the 1930s, would finally resolve in favor of its definition of "traditional."

Tanizaki's ambivalence about the nature of modernity, and even its definition, was reflected in the *Kindai no chokoku* (Overcoming Modernity) symposium, held in Kyoto just weeks after the conclusion of the Death March. The various participants, from the fields of music, literature, science and history, failed to produce any consensus. Even a working definition of the term "modernity" did not emerge, and those in attendance also disagreed about the role of the West vis-à-vis Japan's ills.[37] Much of the discussion in the "Overcoming Modernity" debate, indeed the name of the meeting itself, was about groping toward the Japanese spirit—something essentially Japanese that these men were trying to identify and recover. By 1942, the year of the meeting, the Japanese army had long since found the answer that eluded more thoughtful men: Japanese *seishin* was a fundamental expression of that essence, applied on the battlefield in defense of Japanese "purity."

One of the customs in the drinking culture in "snacks" (small, usually expensive drinking establishments) is that of the "bottle keep"—the practice of buying an expensive bottle, usually of whiskey, to keep there, labeled with one's name, to encourage customers to return to the uchi. *Just after a payday while out drinking with some Japanese acquaintances, I bought a bottle of Suntory at a snack in Namba, an entertainment area in Osaka, to keep the evening's alcohol flowing. We all drank "mizuwari"—the booze cut with just water. Some weeks later I returned with an English friend, and I asked the master what else he had to mix with the whiskey. As he frowned in disgust, I realized that the Japanese discomfort with adulteration extended to my evening's libation.*

* * * * *

Deeply concerned about the changes wrought by rapid modernization and the attendant social transformation, the army sought to preserve its definition of the moral fiber of the society at large. Among the disturbing bellwethers of change was the level of new recruits' education. Draftees after 1905 came to the ranks with increasingly high (though still modest) levels of education:

> The army was no longer receiving stolid, malleable yeoman of rural Japan with only one or two years of formal education. Postwar draftees had six or more years of school, and increasing numbers of young men came from the morally suspect urban areas. For an army that relied on the *seishin* of its soldiers for victory, it was essential that the content of the soldiers' education foster and support the army's spiritual ideal.[38]

The new army ministry, dominated by men whose experience was shaped by the Russo-Japanese War, set about re-writing the *Guntai Naimusho*, the handbook that regulated the details of army life in camp and barracks. The new volume, issued in 1908, sought to create and foster a "family system" infused with Confucian values. Henceforth, the army saw itself "as a great family of soldiers who suffer and rejoice together and live or die as one." Pulling ever more deeply into its shell and, siege mentality hardening, the army came to regard itself as the sole custodian of the nation's essence.

It promulgated the idea that its mission was to shape the character of the entire nation, articulated later in the phrase, "The army is the school of the people." Now, as both the repository and guardian of the nation's "proper values," the army went about isolating itself from the contaminants coursing through society at large. An army song spoke clearly to the sensibilities of those who felt at the same time uniquely qualified to redeem society, yet thoroughly unappreciated for their ability to do so: "In the muddy stream that is the world ... it rises steeply to the heights of Ichigaya (the location of the military academy in Tokyo). The world is a muddy stream, and only we are pure."[39]

The main battle with modernity would be fought in the countryside. The world of the peasant was the hamlet, the basic agricultural unit, and here the army sought to inculcate the values that would serve it best. Here fields surrounded a grouping of houses where all worked in close cooperation to manage irrigation, roads, and the back-breaking requirements of rice growing and harvest. Families depended on each other in ways that made conformity essential and nonparticipation in the hamlet's basic economic functions unacceptable—sometimes resulting in the worst of all punishments: *mura-hachibu* (ostracism).

Faced with new challenges, the army refined its notion of *soto*—now drawing in on itself as a new, well-defined *uchi*, ranged against emerging dangers within Japan, as well as without. To extend its reach in the face of internal threats and to insulate itself against them, it created several kinds of organizations. One of the most important was the *Teikoku zaigo gunjinkai* (Imperial Military Reserve Association), established in 1910. By the mid-1930s it had "14,000 branches and enrolled three million volunteers between the ages of 20 and 40." Other organizations extended the army's reach and influence into the countryside. The *Dainihon seinendan* (Greater Japan Youth Association) and the *Dai nippon kokubo fujunkai* (National Defense Women's Association), brought more than nine million more into the army's sphere of direct influence. By the outbreak of war with the U.S., these "organizations were so totally integrated into the nation's hamlets and villages that loyalty to the army and loyalty to the hamlet and village had become synonymous."[40]

Conformity had often been enforced from above in Japanese history, and in the police state of the late 1930s the Japanese army was able to extract the maximum number of men from its existing demographic pool. Young men received the *Aka gami* (Red Letter) that came from national conscription center through local ward or village office, and few escaped the draft; nationwide campaigns encouraging the public to report those who failed to register kept numbers of draft dodgers low. War ministry records indicated that "the number of draft dodgers increased proportionate to the higher degree of formal education and was always higher in the cities than in the farming villages."[41] It was possible to beat the system by drinking soy sauce to indicate heart problems, or by fasting to ensure being categorized as underweight, but the risk of detection and its consequences was high.

The enthusiasm for war and its impending death seemed hollow sometimes. When their men were called up, the families started making *sennin bari* (thousand stitch belts for the soldiers to wear, in the belief that the belts protected them from bullets), and village mayors assured the men that if they fell, they would be enshrined at Yasukuni, to be honored forever as guardians of the nation. Cheers of *Banzai!* echoed in their ears as they departed, but Denbu added laconically, "You had to say it." One official even sent his own younger brother, even though the boy was only fifteen years old. His rather cold description is heart-rending nonetheless:

> My brother was in his third year at Takaoka Commercial school.... He cried and said, "I don't want to go." But I told him he must. I brought out ... a razor and made him cut his finger and write a petition on the finest paper to volunteer in his own blood. His blood dropped into a sake cup. He had to squeeze more out from his finger to finish writing it, since the paper soaked up the blood. We submitted the paper to the prefectural governor.... My parents were silent, It had to be done because I was the military affairs clerk. I had to send men to the front. Even just one more man.[42]

On the ground, at the village level, the line between enthusiastic and coerced recruit tended to blur.

Speaking with the few Japanese prisoners taken on Bataan, Carlos Romulo called them "typical front-line fodder." He "listened to their stories and wondered how Japan had been able to present herself as a formidable power out of such paucity of physical and intellectual material."[43] Wartime authorities in Japan had no such doubts, and spoke to the mythic family of Japan, "the peculiar psychology of the Nipponese people, who are not only willing, but deem it the highest honor, to serve" in the armed forces. All twenty-year-old young men were required to report for physical exams, and in peacetime only the most robust physical specimens qualified for conscription. In 1937, the last year of peace, the army only took in approximately 23 percent of those it examined.

This percentage is significant—"for the peasant lad, conscription was a mark of status. It placed the recruit, particularly the peasant, in a hierarchical relationship to his peers.... He was acknowledged as one of the best physically, and the Japanese peasantry in the 1930s demanded physical ability to endure the backbreaking labor attendant to wet rice agriculture."[44] Acceptable physical dimensions were: taller than four feet ten and a half inches, a chest measuring more than half his height, at least 103 pounds in weight. Flat feet or complete baldness (though even a small tuft of hair negated this exemption), were grounds for rejection.[45]

During the annual inspection, reservists showed their hook *bukuro* (service bag) to the inspecting officers, a receptacle that hung in the *tokonoma* of every home. Therein resided, among other precious items, "his orders, his soldier's notebook, which contained his service records, all his awards and medals, his will, his photograph, his personal daily needs ... a lock of hair and fingernail clippings to be used for burial if he died in combat." Inspectors ensured that all prescribed items were included, and when one reservist was asked where he kept his bag, he answered, *kokoro ni kakete arimasu* (hanging in my heart), a response that pleased the inspector.[46]

In Toyama prefecture, Denbu Shigenobu was one of more than 10,000 military affairs clerks in Japan responsible for filling the ranks of the army. He stated proudly that the Japanese system "could raise large-scale units in less than twenty-four hours.... No one had a more thorough and efficient system for mobilizing soldiers to the colors than Japan." The system Denbu described was reminiscent of the controls on Tokugawa peasants centuries before:

> With a single red paper all unit organization could be accomplished. Each man's physical condition, work situation, classification according to his military status—all these things had to be memorized by the military-affairs clerk.... You had to know conditions in their families, too.... I often walked around in the village to learn what the villagers were up to. Even those walks belonged to the realm of military secrets. I couldn't say, "I came to check on you," so I'd just ask, "Your son who's working in Osaka as a barber—how's he doing?" In that way I would find out.

Denbu's reports included "the soldier's family background, whether it included a criminal or not, the size of the family's rice fields, the value of their properties, but the individual had no idea what [had] been sent to the unit." It even included what Denbu called the recruit's "thoughts." The thoughts of these young men, what one American prisoner described as "kids, seventeen or eighteen-year-old peasants fresh from the misty rice paddies and terraced valleys of Nippon," centered on their primary definition of *uchi*—the village. Since each Japanese unit was associated with a specific locality, many young peasant boys entered the service with the simple motivations of avoiding disgrace to family and village by delinquent service, and moving from second class private, to first class, and ultimately to superior private rank.[47]

The mystical connection to the furusato *(hometown) remains strong in Japan. In Japanese* Enka *music, dozens of song titles suggest this, especially to those whose companies have relocated them. One of my students was a young salaryman, employed by Sumitomo Electric in Osaka, who hailed from a small island in the inland sea called Naoshima. Late one night in a small Osaka bar, I watched him offer a tearful rendition of a song called* Mujō no Umi:

>Shima wa miete mo watarenai
>Kokoro hiki-saku mujō no umi yo
>Aitai yo aitai yo
>Umi no mukō ni furusato ga aru
>Aitai yo aitai yo

He could see the island, but could not get to it, the cruel sea rent his heart, he longed to see it, his hometown across the sea, longed to see it. I poured him another of the tiny beers that cost ¥ 500, missed the last train and had to take a taxi home.

When a soldier was drafted, he remained connected to his community and all its potential sanctions in ways that suggested he never actually left—in many ways his concept of *uchi* changed little. Rituals that surrounded his departure reminded him of the obligations he carried with him as his family accompanied him to the local shrine and offered prayers for his safe return, then an *omi-okuri* (send-off) at the railroad station with more final farewells. While in the barracks, village officials visited the draftees and encouraged them with the delivery of *imon bukuro* (comfort bags) filled with sundries such as candy and tobacco; upon their return they sponsored letter-writing campaigns to keep the connection to the hamlet strong. Many soldiers went off to active duty wearing the time-honored *sennin bari*, a stitch at a time added by community members at the request of female relatives.[48] Though the belts warded off no bullets, they bore the touch of his community's women in a tangible way.

Formal education reached the vast majority of Japanese, and reinforced the sense of duty and the state's power to enforce it. The seventh lesson in the 1904 *Elementary School Reader #8* was "Takeo Joins the Service," wherein students learned this conversation:

>TAKEO: Father, the idea of "joining the service of my country" makes me so proud and happy. I'll be trained and when the war comes, I will not be afraid to die. I'll give everything I have to show what a good Japanese fighting man is made of.
>FATHER: That's the spirit! You must be that determined. Don't be afraid to die. Don't worry about us here. And you must always be faithful to the Imperial Precepts to Soldiers and Sailors.[49]

These young men were trained to aspire to more than promotion. In the mid–1920s, a school reader contained a story called "A Sailor's Mother":

A sailor receives a letter from his mother: "You wrote that you did not participate in the battle of Toshima Island. You were in the August attack on Weihaiwei but you didn't distinguish yourself with an individual exploit. To me this is deplorable. Why have you gone to war? Your life is to be offered up to requite your obligations to your benevolent Emperor." An officer, seeing him reading the letter and crying, comforted the sailor: "Son, there'll surely be another glorious war before long. Let's accomplish great feats of bravery then and bring honor to our ship.... Explain that to your mother and put her mind at ease."

Lesson twenty-four of the standard elementary school ethics book for second graders, published the year before the Russo-Japanese War, reminded students:

> Kiguchi Kohei was not the least bit afraid before the enemy. He bravely sounded the call to advance on his bugle three times. Inspired by his brave example, our troops attacked and defeated the enemy, but Kiguchi was hit by a bullet and fell to the ground mortally wounded. Later they found his body with the bugle still to his lips.[50]

Expanding its role as the custodian of the national essence, the army began to reach into the public school system as early as 1925. The indoctrination was powerful, with schoolchildren taught that dying in the service of the emperor was not only acceptable, but desirable. Six-year-olds memorized a children's song: "Shoulder to shoulder with my elder brother, I can go to school today. Thanks to the soldiers, thanks to the soldiers, who fought for our country, for our country." The first lesson in school readers intoned:

> March on, march on,
> Soldiers march on.
> The sun is red,
> The rising sun is red.
> The flag of the sun!
> *Banzai! Banzai!*[51]

As part of the reforms of the period, more than 2,000 active duty officers were assigned to secondary school and colleges as military instructors. By the early 1930s, the system became an accepted feature of public education, along with its clearly articulated purpose: "to temper the bodies and minds of the students, to foster collective belief and by this means to improve the quality and character of those who are the mainstay of our people, and concurrently to advance our national defense capability." Ultimately these instructors were successful in beginning the process of "inculcating the army worldview in young people." The program was soon extended to four years of military training for those sixteen and older who did not continue in school.[52]

A roundtable discussion with fifth and sixth grade students in 1932 suggests the army's presence in education:

> INTERVIEWER: Do you think there will be a war between Japan and America?
> FUKUZAWA: Yes, I think so. Americans are so arrogant. I'd like to show them a thing or two.
> KATO: They act so big all the time, they need a good beating. I'd annihilate them.
> FUKUTOMI: Oh, I'd like to try that too.
> INTERVIEWER: If Japan becomes more and more isolated, what would you do?
> STUDENTS: We'll keep trying, we'll keep going, we'll stick at it until we die.

These students would be in their early twenties in the spring of 1942. At the end of his schooling, the "average public school graduate was so full of approved 'facts,' myths, and patriotism as to be immune to fresh or radical ideas." After 1933, when Japan withdrew from the League of Nations, the government decreed that fashioning students' moral character was to take precedence over the acquisition of any particular body of knowledge. Teachers were held accountable to emphasize Japan's unique culture, and the nature of *kokutai*, the national essence. Under such conditions, "ideological suppression of teachers was severe."[53]

The high command had a low opinion of regiments recruited in big cities, arguing that the best regiments came from the southern island of Kyushu, where older feudal military traditions were more clearly observed. Other factors, not specific to any one region, were more important. Peasants—the army's raw material—were all the more receptive to its message because of extraordinary economic hardship in the countryside. Rapid economic progress during the late nineteenth century led to the creation of a dual economy—a burgeoning urban, industrial sector, and an agricultural sector that bore the enormous cost of modernization with the taxes it paid to the government. In fact, 70 percent of the Japanese army came from households in economic difficulty, especially the "debt-ridden peasantry."[54]

A familiar pattern of demagoguery emerged—the army blamed rural suffering on corrupt politicians and business leaders, and offered the peasants the simple solution of expansion abroad, selling its program on the basis of creating a safety valve for excess population. The army told peasants that emigration, greater participation in world trade markets, and expansion of territory were the only ways to achieve economic recovery. The West's racism and high tariffs blocked the first two, leaving military expansion the only option.[55]

Conscription to provide the required manpower hit large farming families particularly hard. In 1932, the Japanese novelist Shimomura Chiaki wrote a report of his tour of villages in the northeast, where one old man told the writer,

> This year has been one of the worst famines. This means next year the poor farmers will dry up and starve to death; they will die in the fields. Some will end up hanging themselves. Damn it all! One of my sons is in Manchuria as a soldier. I sent him a letter the other day telling him to fight bravely for our country and die on the battlefield like a man. Then, you know, we'll get some money from the government, and our family will be able to survive the winter. Families with daughters can sell them, but we have only boys. So this is the only way I can sell my son.

Poverty was a grinding presence. One soldier, serving in Manchuria received a letter from his father, warning him that under no circumstances was he to come home alive, since his death would mean a payment of 150 yen to the family.[56]

When the Great Depression arrived in 1930, farmers in the countryside were especially hard hit. Some who faced starvation emigrated to Brazil or Argentina, but the vast majority who remained faced the harshness brought on by tumbling farm prices. The price of silk declined by nearly half in a year, and those of rice, fruits and vegetables fell sharply as well. *Tomo no kai* formed in the countryside to help peasants adapt to new conditions, but these associations improved little for those who had nothing; conditions were severe enough to force thousands of families to sell their daughters.[57]

Out of a population of some seventy million, ten million young Japanese men were called to serve their empire as soldiers or sailors. The young males who left the farms and factories were, as so often in human history, biologically the most disposable members of the society, what their officers called *issen, gorin* (one *sen*, five *rin*, less than a penny, the cost of sending out a draft notice). Life in the countryside in Japan in the 1930s was a hardscrabble affair, defined by dawn to dark toil and for sons who could expect to inherit no land, the army offered both security as well as status. Many entered willingly, as marginal existence as a poor farmer, or as a fisherman or streetcar conductor was often insecure and inferior to life in the army. Taking the sons of peasants rather than city dwellers gave the army less trouble ideologically; the ignorant are always more malleable. They were a stout and strong lot—conscription figures for 1936 show that only 578 of 630,802 examined by medical examiners were unfit for service of any kind.[58]

In 1974, Onoda Hiroo was the last of Japan's World War II soldiers to emerge after surrender. After twenty-nine years in the jungles of the Philippines he was greeted as a hero but, gravely disillusioned by the changes in his homeland, he left to become a rancher in Brazil. Ten years later, claiming that "concrete and cleanliness makes for weak children," he returned home to infuse the old *seishin* into Japan by setting up a survival training camp for young people, grown soft as *Yowamushi* (weak worms) in the material glow of Japan's economic success.[59] Onoda remembered well his experience four decades earlier.

Basic training in the Imperial Japanese Army lasted eight months, twice as long as that of the U.S. army. The first four months saw winter *taikan kogun* (cold endurance marches) and *tainatsu kogun* (heat endurance marches), offering recruits equal opportunity suffering at the extremes of temperature. The *tainatsu* lasted as long as three days, and recruits were often forced to run under full pack loads for miles in Japan's August heat, building up "phenomenal endurance.... Ordering their troops to double time when near complete exhaustion is a familiar method of Japanese officers to prove that even exhausted men can always march one more mile to take an enemy position."[60]

An American officer, attached to a Japanese unit in the 1930s, described the brutal training that was an expression of the need to instill *seishin* in lieu of equipment that Japan could neither financially nor culturally afford. Setting out from camp, he marched thirty-seven miles, twice without sleep for three days and two nights—"The last four day period was the most strenuous. *We started out at five in the morning and marched almost continuously until ten the next morning. In that time we covered fifty-six miles*" (italics in original). Afterwards, the men were sent on routine patrols and outpost duty, whereupon the American asked why they were not allowed to sleep. "That is not necessary," came the answer. "They already know how to sleep. They need training in how to stay awake."[61] Natural remedies for exhaustion were not lacking; some recommended *Mamushi*, a poisonous snake, "especially efficacious in renewing manly vigor after great physical exertion." With or without the snake, men of such sensibilities rejoiced in the popular army saying—"the samurai displays a toothpick even when he hasn't eaten."[62]

Whatever the faults of Japanese training, lack of clarity of purpose was not among them. The nearly complete reliance on *seishin* in battle tactics assured recruits that their training would omit any encouragement of initiative or individual decision-making. Trained in immediate obedience to attack in close order using the bayonet, Japanese soldiers were prepared to replicate the feats of 1905, and only those feats. The offensive spirit was paramount—a relentless emphasis on the attack would overcome the materially superior foe. The tactical imperatives brought about by new battlefield technologies stimulated new methods of training in the West, but by 1942, the Japanese army had long since made its decision to reject those imperatives, and therefore continued to train its recruits for wars past.

The army's officers took no courses in subjects such as international relations or law, comparative government or economics, and formal instruction showed a marked "contempt for a knowledge of broader fields." Naturally, its products were narrow-minded in the extreme:

> Limited by the narrow confines of his education, indifferent to diplomatic viewpoints in London, Washington or Geneva, antagonistic to great concentrations of wealth, unconvinced that army budgets cannot defy the laws of economics, but moved by dreams of Japan's mastery of the world, the typical officer thinks amazingly like the peasant he commands.[63]

Trained by such men, the Japanese *hohei* emerged with no preparation for the independent action, since such action would threaten the very basis of the army's meaning to the broader society—hierarchy, tradition, and the cluster of associated values. When recruits said that life in training camp was *ri ni kanawanai* (unreasonable) they were in one sense wrong: the training they received was born of culture, defined narrowly, but culture nonetheless. As it dispensed its cultural vision, the Japanese army would summon the basest instincts from the darkest places in some of its soldiers.

Like all armies, this one insisted upon a new vocabulary that set its members apart from the contamination of *soto*. If U.S. Marines were punished for referring to "pogey bait" as candy, or to a "head" as a toilet, so were Japanese recruits required to substitute *guni* (military clothing) for *uwagi* (jacket) and *jyoka* (upper leather) for the Anglo-sounding *surippa* (slipper). This fear of non-conformity, one presumes, also led Japanese recruits to arrange their penises on the left side during inspections.[64] Most recruits came as poor peasants, and their extremely low salary insured restriction to the world of the barracks. In the first four months, recruit pay was two *yen*, seventy-five *sen* per month, the equivalent of sixty-five cents in the U.S. in 1936. The lowest paid soldier in the U.S. army at the time received $65 per month. The low pay reflected the emphasis on service to the emperor—mercenaries these soldiers were not.[65]

Low pay barred the Japanese recruit from more than one kind of recreation. He could buy a prophylactic for just one *sen* (1/100 of a yen), but using it was far more costly—all night at an "average" house of prostitution would cost him as much as seven yen; second class for a few hours four yen; a quick and perhaps embarrassing visit to a third class establishment just one yen. As a defender of the realm, he might expect a slight reduction from the occasionally patriotic courtesan. Before 1937, about ten per thousand were guilty of venereal disease; doubtless a modest figure by later standards.[66]

Concern with purity was not the exclusive province of the military. Diversion from poverty and matters imperial came in the second half of 1936. In May, Abe Sada, a prostitute with a checkered and difficult past, had begun an affair with Ishida Kichizo, a restaurant owner she had met. The couple embarked on a sexually adventurous path, employing asphyxiation techniques to heighten pleasure. During one encounter, on the morning of May 18, Abe strangled her lover to death and cut off his penis and testicles, carrying them off and keeping them until she was apprehended four days later.

When interrogated, she claimed that a pure form of love and an overwhelming desire to keep Ishida for herself had motivated the killing. Even before Abe was apprehended, the Yomiuri newspaper wrote that "most people seemed to support the jealousy theory"—that she had simply wished to "control—literally to monopolize—the object of [her] love." After her crime, Sada's plan for suicide and her request for the death penalty both failed, and she was sentenced to six years in prison. The murder provided grist for a variety of interpretations of Abe's motivations, but until her death in the 1970s, she steadfastly maintained that she had killed Ishida out of pure love, not because of any sexual perversion. Her trial and sentencing captured the public's imagination and provided welcome relief from the pressing military and political problems.[67]

Relief was only temporary, however. Beginning with its seizure of Manchuria in 1931, the army began to tighten its grip on the nation. Of the three great Western revolutions—scientific, industrial, political—Japan embraced the first two but not the last. Once in control of the apparatuses of power, ultranationalists "embarked on a massive campaign to purge the nation of the basic features and values of the European Enlightenment: faith in reason and rational thought, intellectual freedom and curiosity, and the secularization of society."[68] The army expanded its role as custodian of what it considered the nation's core values, and soon it produced a propaganda film, *Japan in the National Emergency*, shown in theaters just after the country withdrew from the League of Nations. In the film, a young man smoking a pipe and playing a mandolin, and a young woman who smokes and dances, embody the decadent values of the West. One scene shows an older Japanese stepping on the woman's toe, and her demanding an apology, whereupon the young man shows him how to do it Western-style, bending to clean her shoe with his scarf. The older man—clearly the repository of *kokutai*, brushes the youth aside and states, "Listen to me! This is *Japan*!"[69]

In 1937 the Thought Bureau of the Ministry of Education published *Kokutai no Hongi* (*Cardinal Principles of the National Polity*), whose text asserted Japanese that they were "intrinsically quite different from the so-called citizens of Occidental countries" due to a special "original condition." By March of 1943 the volume had sold nearly two million copies, part of the increasingly complete government, i.e., military, censorship. The thought control apparatus employed by the government in the 1930s—including *1984*-like thought police—produced excellent results, with large percentages of those arrested accepting conversion (*tenko*).

In this, the government found support even among educated elites, who were reluctant to oppose the state policies—especially the slogans glorifying the emperor on which those policies rested. No dissent was tolerated, and few offered resistance. Frank Gibney puts it cogently: "With the military in total charge, all the classic Japanese social virtues—the group loyalties, the solidarity, the patience, the willingness to accept hardships in the hope of future gain—were in a sense turned inside out." If surveillance by *tonari-gumi* (neighborhood associations) was insufficient, the looming threat of the dreaded *kempeitai*, the secret police, stifled any opposition completely. Communists who threatened the social order were particular targets. The journalist John Morris found his house ransacked by police on the eve of Pearl Harbor, with any of his books with red binding, the color associated with the Bolsheviks, removed.[70]

* * * * *

The army had previous opportunities to impose its vision of order and rectitude on a society buffeted by change and unrest. One teaching opportunity came during the *kome sodo* (rice riots) of 1918. World War I had buoyed the Japanese economy to unprecedented heights, but with prosperity came high commodity prices. Great Britain and France, focused on monopolizing their colonies' exports at a time of crisis, prohibited the export of rice to Japan, and this sparked considerable domestic unrest which started in July that year.

The riots spread through two thirds of Japan's prefectures, more than thirty cities and about two hundred towns and villages. Perhaps as many as 700,000 "vented their frustration and wrath on rice dealers, rice brokers, employers, government officials, and peace officers in an unexpected burst of spontaneous popular discontent." Prefectural governors, overwhelmed by the scope of the riots, turned to the military for help in more than fifty instances, including assistance in a half dozen major cities. The army responded with enthusiasm. "Unfortunately, bayonets and live ammunition were used in some cases, and perhaps a score of people died of stab and gunshot wounds."[71]

The catastrophic earthquake that struck Tokyo on September 1, 1923, offered the army a chance to expand its dark pedagogy. Before that event, the Japanese had had considerable experience with Koreans. Although the two peoples were ethnically similar, the Japanese nevertheless managed to contrive a definition of their neighbor that rivaled any racist expression in the West. In this task they faced an interesting dilemma. Unlike Western colonizers who encountered, in Africa and Asia, peoples of different skin color and with vastly different cultural traditions, the Japanese were compelled to contrive their superiority by different means.

In this Americans provided, more than a half-century earlier, an interesting precedent. In the decade before Fort Sumter and the unpleasant interlude of the next four years, Northern Republicans like Frederick Law Olmsted and others travelled throughout the South and described the people they found as indolent, torpid, the antithesis of the Northern "progressive" mentality. To Republicans, "the South appeared as an alien and threatening society, whose values and interests were in fundamental conflict with those of the North." William Seward, who vied for the 1860 Republican nomination and served as Lincoln's Secretary of State, recalled three visits he made below the Mason-Dixon line, where he described the region as afflicted with "exhausted soil, old and decaying towns, wretchedly neglected roads, and, in every respect, an absence of enterprise and improvement."[72] In a series of letters that became three published volumes Olmsted, later to win fame as the designer of New York City's Central Park, echoed this chorus of disdain.

These Northern visitors succeeded in creating a stereotype of a Southern yeomanry that formed part of the basis of the Republican Party's appeal in the 1856 and 1860 elections and defined the North as progressive, dynamic, expanding, while their Southern brethren were mired in backward stasis. Yet at the same time, Lincoln, the most eloquent spokesman for national union, declared that the sections were united by the "mystic chords of memory" waiting, after a misguided interlude, to once again "swell the chorus of the union." And after the war, as much of Republican Reconstruction policy intended, the North would drag its laggard cousins into the future, whether they wanted to come or not. Hence Northerners tried to have it both ways, before and after the war—defining the South as aberrant, but also as a necessary part of the greater concept of nationhood.

A half-century later and a hemisphere away, the Japanese undertook a similar task, with a similar internal contradiction. They succeeded, or failed, at least as well. Like antebellum Northern Americans, Japanese were unable to distinguish "the other" from themselves by means of racial difference, so they turned to other means. With considerable focus, they "constructed images of Koreans that denied them parity with the Japanese through asymmetrical comparisons measuring Korean backwardness against Japanese modernity." With regard to race, and in cultural terms, the Japanese managed to define Korea as part of *uchi*—the two peoples looked alike and existed in a "natural" cultural embrace. Such rhetoric was convenient as Japan sought to justify its political and economic domination of Korea after 1905, and outright annexation in 1910. At such times, the Japanese spoke of Koreans "in the language of amalgamation, merger, and assimilation" with the intent of promulgating an Asian community—always, of course, in Japan's imperial interest.[73]

As an English teacher in the Japanese junior high school system, I was eager to help break down cultural barriers by exposing students to language and ideas beyond their shores. I co-taught with a Japanese instructor, and in one of the classes to which I was assigned, a Korean student named Myung sat in the last row. One of the lessons dealt with a Japanese boy who took pictures and brought them home to his parents. The teacher was a rather unpleasant man whose distaste for sharing his classroom with a foreigner had resulted in an undercurrent of tension throughout the term. During the lesson, he wondered aloud if the pictures would have been as good if the boy had used a baka-chon—*a "camera for stupid Koreans." As the boy collapsed in humiliation, the class roared its approval. I left the classroom that day, certain that the teacher's racism had, in reality, been directed at me, and wondering if the budget for the program that sponsored me should be dumped onto* gomi-no-shima, *the island of trash in Tokyo Bay. I understood better why, during the exodus of Vietnamese boat people, the Japanese government offered asylum to only 3,000.*

Yet Koreans were also part of an outside world—*soto*—that provided a counterpoint to the Japanese self-definition as "modern" and "civilized" while simultaneously reminding Japanese of the proximity of the foreign, contemptible—and impure. The alien features that drew most comment were Koreans' "strangeness," and their "cultural backwardness" (*mindo*). Guidebooks and travel accounts read and produced by newspapermen, government officials and academicians proclaimed Korea an alien culture. One extreme example was Okita Kinjo's travel account, *Rimen no Kankoku (Korea Behind the Mask)*, which listed the country's main products: "shit, tobacco, lice, *kaesang* [courtesans], tigers, pigs and flies." Examining the producers, he found them "smelly, dirty, pitiful, weak, disorderly, asocial, poverty-stricken, barbarous, immature, lazy, dissipated, suspicious, withdrawn" and given to "swindling, larceny, gambling, bribery, adultery, viciousness and intrigue," a list that surely would have pleased Seward or Olmsted.[74] Here was a catalogue worthy of the heart of *soto*'s meaning.

Just before noon on September 1, 1923, the great Kanto earthquake struck Tokyo, toppling cooking fires and causing a conflagration that killed as many as 150,000. Human agency intensified the natural calamity in unexpected and tragic ways, with the army playing an active role. Local police and fire departments were unable to cope with the scale of the disaster, and the army, the "one intact instrument of government control," did its best to assist the dazed survivors. As fear of looting took hold of the inhabitants, neighborhoods formed *jikeidan* (vigilante committees) to protect themselves and their property:

> Armed with the simplest of weapons—old swords, spears, knives and the like—and often led by members of the Reservists Association, men with military experience, they attempted to maintain order, but in doing so in certain districts they perpetrated terrible crimes. There is incontrovertible evidence that the army abetted this criminal behavior to some degree in two

instances—in the slaughter of Koreans (and some Chinese) and in the murder of political radicals.[75]

Observers recalled that martial law was declared on September 2. The army manned checkpoints that sought to identify Koreans, and gathered them in concentration camps. In some cases it remained unclear if soldiers handed Koreans over to vigilante groups, including a farmers group, where they were killed.[76]

Japanese drew on their long-standing racist ideas about Koreans, who were ready targets because they were foreign, lived in a compact mass in squalid slums, and were perceived as a threat by the working-class Japanese who lived near them in only slightly better economic circumstances. Rumors of Korean depredations spread faster than the flames, and the *jikeidan* responded by butchering as many as 6,000 in the streets. Local army units, not just reservists, actively took part: "These local units sallied forth armed with live ammunition, fixed bayonets, and machine guns. The extant unit orders, reports, and citations prove beyond a doubt that they considered action against 'outlaw Koreans,' reportedly looting and setting fires, to be a military action."[77]

Elements of the Japanese army not directly involved with killings either worked in tandem with vigilante groups or "rounded up thousands of Koreans and herded them into police stations and heavily guarded military camps, where most survived, albeit in terrible conditions" and some "military units were packed with fanatical hard-liners who had served on the Korean peninsula and had helped put down the march 1919 rebellion. Some army commanders may have viewed the Great Kanto Earthquake as an opportunity to purge the country of troublemakers."[78] Here, well before its encounter with the West in the 1940s, were shades of an inward-looking, racist, reactionary force, deeply concerned with purging the nation of "impurity."

Late one night in my favorite local robatayaki, *I found myself in a spirited conversation about* sumo *and the effect of the influx of foreign wrestlers on the sport. Two older Japanese men, both of whom I knew from previous evenings, complained that the sport was somehow less pure for its foreign component. They made clear their distaste for foreigners in the sport, and expressed the hope that its upper ranks would remain safe from such contamination. When one of them said,* "Gaikokujin sumo-do zenzen wakaranai"*(Foreigners don't understand "the way of sumo" at all), his mate nodded vigorously. Then an English acquaintance wandered in, and he firmly refuted their position, suggesting that the sport should, like Japan, open its doors more widely to the world. The two Japanese frowned, drained their* saké *cups and took their leave. As their* sayonaras *faded, the Englishman shook his head, and reminded me that Jesse Kuhaulua, the Hawaiian-born wrestler who fought under the name Takamiyama, won the Nagoya tournament in 1972, causing the same saber-rattling we had just heard. Too bad, he lamented, that this kind of xenophobia lingered. He was stunned when I told him I agreed with the salarymen. Frowning, I too drained the last of my* saké *and fled into the night.*

* * * * *

Just after Pearl Harbor, the U.S. physician Alvin Poweleit instructed his men. "It was not unusual for anyone to manifest fear," he said, but they were to carry on, "being as careful as possible of their own lives." John Coleman, among the last U.S. prisoners to leave Mariveles, spoke to an English-speaking Japanese guard as the artillery dual with U.S. batteries on Corregidor began. As shells began to fall, he screamed to his captor, "We had better hit the dirt, hadn't we?" The Japanese responded, "Hell no! If you didn't want to die, why did you join the army?"[79]

Coleman and Poweleit's sensibilities were alien to their captors. The essential difference seemed clear enough—in a Japanese propaganda film dealing with the American surrender at Bataan, the narrator intoned, "In Mariveles there were American soldiers crouching like locusts in a ditch ... why don't they commit suicide to meet their end as they encountered defeat?" Japanese soldiers were told that "duty is weightier than a mountain, while death is lighter than a feather" and their socialization was aimed at the glorification of death, the natural culmination of their service to the emperor, while Americans took a "rational" approach—risking death was expected, soliciting it was not.

Yet for Japanese, solicitation of death sometimes was expected. One American claimed to have heard the story of a Japanese major who received a letter from his home, expressing concern that no one in the family had yet been killed. Their recommendation was that their scion proceed to some combat area south to rectify the situation and restore the clan's "face." When in October 1943 Ebashi Shinshiro spoke on behalf of 25,000 university students leaving for the front, he stated gravely, *Seira motoyori seikan o gosezu* (We do not expect to return alive).[80]

One officer, an easy-going ukulele-playing youth, was drafted early in the Pacific War, after graduating from Keio University. On a family visit, he assured his uncle, "The only thing left for a young man my age is to offer his life for his country. The thing promised to us ... is an opportunity to die for our country." Another well-educated soldier, Nakamura Tokuro, stated, "As one enters military service in readiness for the sacrifice of his own life on behalf of the Emperor, he once again has to stare death straight in the face.... I shall feel death's stern figure standing right beside me. In this way ... I shall come closer to the real meaning of life and death, even as I tighten further the stiff cord of my determination."[81] A song sung by Nakamura and so many of his fellows, expressed his determination:

> ***Umi Yukaba*** **(Across the Sea)**
> Corpses drifting swollen in the sea-depths,
> Corpses rotting in the mountain grass—
> We shall die, by the side of our lord we shall die.
> We shall not look back.[82]

When possible, their bodies were not actually left to rot; some comfort came in the form of knowing one would be returned to the village. Shortly after the surrender conversation at Balanga, an American officer noticed a mortuary with many shelves containing boxes measuring three inches and six inches. A sentry with some English explained that the larger was for "the earth where a Jap soldier falls, the small one for his ashes. The set in each case is shipped home." The practice was taken quite seriously. In October 1942, Izumi Toru, then stationed in Matsuyama, was ordered to receive remains of war dead. The boxes for the men who had died closest to the front were empty, and Izumi decided to take some of the remains from other boxes, "our hands trembling" as he and his comrades did this. He reasoned that since the soldiers had died together, the bereaved families could pray over their remains.[83]

Little suggested such care with the living, as few Japanese commanders during the Pacific War ranked economy with their soldiers' lives an important priority. In their profligate and sanguinary endeavors they had the full cooperation of the soldiers themselves, who believed their own actions "would be publicized only briefly while [they were] alive. Lavish praise and great honors came after death."[84] As modern day Islamic zealots believe they will die heroes and live with virgins in paradise, Japanese were trained to believe in their deification at Yasukuni shrine. The soldier's manual that each recruit read upon entering the barracks defined two states of being with complete clarity: "Living to be overwhelmed with the innumerable and immeasurable blessings of Imperial Goodness; dead, to become one of the guarding Deities of the country and as such to receive unique honors in the temple."[85] Peasants with only rudimentary, state-sponsored education rarely questioned their duty to die, and their letters suggest that "no peasant soldier raised any doubt about why he had to die for the emperor, any more than he questioned why he had to work to support his parents, wife, and children. Both duties were simply taken for granted.... There was also continuity between the ideological socialization of primary school and that of the army."[86]

Leading an assault on Belleau Wood in World War I Dan Daly exhorted his men, "C'mon, you sonsabitches, do you want to live forever?" Such disdain of death may have been exceptional for an American; for his new enemy of 1942 it seemed a commonplace. At the height of the initial battle in January, the hard-bitten Filipino soldiers of the Scout Division marched into battle shouting "*Petay si la*," "They shall die."[87] The Japanese who opposed them, steeped in the ethos of *seishin*, seemed happy to oblige. Indeed, it seemed that the Imperial Japanese Army sought to create a subspecies of *Homo sapiens*—that of *Homo furens*—for whom death was a welcome expression of duty.

On the eve of island invasions, U.S. Marines were informed that the Japanese they faced had a duty to die for the emperor. "Your duty," they were told, was to "assist him in accomplishing his duty in any way possible." On Bataan, such assistance was not difficult to find, and outdated Japanese military doctrine played no small part in the sanguinary drama. The Imperial Japanese Army still regarded the Soviet Union as its primary enemy and must have still recalled its triumphs thirty-five years before on the plains of Manchuria; just weeks before the invasion of the Philippines, the army carried out the large-scale "Fuji Experimental Maneuvers" as practice for operations against the Soviet army in Manchuria. The historian Edward Drea puts the matter cogently: "[F]or the Japanese army the war in the South Pacific was one against an unknown enemy in an unstudied climate and unfamiliar terrain."[88]

Unfamiliar terrain mattered little to an army that believed *seishin*, employed in the crude tactics of frontal attack, would overcome the enemy. At one point in January, twenty-four artillery pieces opened on an advancing Japanese column. "Under similar circumstances," an astonished observer wrote, "American troops would have disbursed immediately. But the disciplined enemy advanced blindly for another fifteen casualty-filled minutes." Repulsed, the Japanese came on again, into a line of Philippine Scouts, who fired their "weapons until the barrels became too hot to touch, they held the attackers for twelve long hours.... Though the enemy attacked almost continuously for three days and nights, he was unable to break the line. His dead and wounded lay five deep around the Scout positions."[89]

After losing a hard-fought squash game, I was having a beer with my partner in a nearby izakaya. *The Olympics were underway at that moment, and conversation turned to Japan's performance when Tokyo hosted the games in 1964. My partner's mother had been a classmate of one of the members of the women's volleyball team when it overcame the Russians in a dramatic final to win the gold medal. Their victory, he explained to me with considerable condescension, was due to the perfect "fighting spirit" they had exhibited. Feeling contrary that day, I pointed out that in the same Olympics Kaminaga Akio, who was widely expected to win the gold medal in judo, went down to ignominious defeat at the hands of the Dutchman Anton Geesink.*

Irritated, my partner sharply pointed out that Kaminaga had been injured, his loss an aberration. Taking up the challenge, I mentioned that fighting spirit was supposed to have driven the Tokyo Giants and the Japanese all-stars to victory when the Baltimore Orioles came to Japan just six years later, after the 1971 season. Japan's combined best in baseball, widely expected to overcome size with seishin, *were humiliated, managing to win just two of the twenty-two games they played. He went silent. I had struck a blow as a Baltimore native—and as a foreigner happy to subvert, just for a moment, the special Japanese claim on spirit's muscle.*

Joseph Grew, the U.S. ambassador to Japan from 1932 to 1941, called the emphasis on the offensive spirit the key factor in the initial victories the Japanese won. "This spirit ... the most vital intangible factor in achieving victory, has been nourished and perpetuated since the foundation of the modern Japanese army." Grew was correct, but the victories came at extraordinary cost. After another encounter near Mount Natib, a Japanese column was caught in the open by artillery fire—"The road on the hillside, and the ... grass meadow ... were littered with hundreds of dead Jap soldiers.... They had started their bayonet charge about 300 meters too soon and exposed themselves to the destructive fire from the muzzles of all the weapons we had." An American lieutenant commanding a Filipino unit watched with fascination as a Japanese unit rushed his line of defense: "Our machine guns and rifles opened up. There must have been 30 well-trained Nips in that patrol and they were determined to silence that machine gun ... they charged the gun, walking doggedly into its lethal fire. As one after another of them was dropped, another took his place." Such horror explained why one American claimed that "officers and enlisted men would carry out orders faithfully after they had become obviously inapplicable, even absurd."[90]

The U.S. propaganda film *Know Your Enemy: Japan* described the Japanese soldier's mentality: "In combat, his single aim is to close with the enemy in hand to hand fighting. He believes that in the attack itself there is some mystic virtue by which greater numbers bearing superior weapons can be vanquished." The assertion was as correct in 1942 as it had been on the plains of Manchuria. While a prisoner, J.D. Merritt recalled seeing Japanese recruits at bayonet practice, two lines facing each other. "With their excitement gaining a fever pitch," he recalled, "the two lines finally met and blood would flow from chests and arms of those who didn't stop in time. Amazingly, most of the recruits ignored their wounds.... We stayed clear of those psyched-up crazies whenever they practiced their daffy drill."[91] Such was the practice; on the battlefield the demonstration of *seishin* left another observer wondering:

> A great shout of Banzai! came from the front and the Japs started an old Civil War charge.... It was slaughter. All of our guns had been sighted for mutual support and the Japs were caught by terrific fire, both frontal and flanking. Even now I can't understand why the Japs launched an attack of this kind against modern weapons.... The attack was smashed before it got under way.... Our casualties were only five wounded.

James Gautier remembered, "We knew they were tough and brave, and yet their suicidal bayonet charges against our machine guns just seemed dumb."[92]

The most striking image of the Pacific War is that of Marines attacking coral islands, while the fanatical Japanese defenders made them pay for every yard of ground with blood before dying to the last man. The first hundred days of the Pacific War, however, present an entirely different picture. The soldiers of 1942 had been thoroughly indoctrinated with the offensive spirit, on the assumption that closing quickly for a decisive encounter was the best hope for victory. That this played conveniently to Japanese notions of racial superiority was a welcome bonus; the Japanese army employed the "weapons of the underdog."[93]

The bayonet is an intimate way to kill a man whose eyes one can see, whose breath one can feel. Americans, more mechanistically inclined, preferred to let longer-range machines do their killing work, and were less inclined during training to take the bayonet very seriously. One officer remembered that "bayonet drill sometimes left them weak with laughter."[94] Their enemies would have been appalled at such disregard. The bayonet Japanese soldiers kept fixed to their 38-M Arisaka was fifteen and a half inches long and weighed about a quarter of a pound. The rifle was some thirty years old at the outbreak of the Pacific War and was too big for the short Japanese soldier, "who had difficulty holding the weapon to his shoulder while operating the bolt."

Even so, no weapon was more suited to the lunging attack than the bayonet. In hand-to-hand fighting it expressed Japanese *seishin* best, and had "the power to frighten Western enemies out of all proportion to the damage the weapons actually caused." To one observer, "they seemed to exult in struggle body to body." Bemused and perhaps horrified, he went on: "They produced gestures of defiance and glee and also of fear which, by most other soldiers, were regarded as childish. A skirmish was accompanied by grunts, gasps and blood-curdling yells.... It made him a surprising and alarming adversary."[95]

> For the Japanese enlisted man, the bayonet was the poor man's counterpart to the samurai sword carried by officers; and for the Freudian analyst, the wanton frenzy with which these conscripts plunged this weapon into Allied prisoners ... must be of more than passing interest.... But for many Japanese (including popular graphic artists, who turned it into the Japanese common man's sword of righteousness), the bayonet possessed a peculiar fascination.[96]

There was indeed a "disproportionate emphasis on cold steel. Japanese infantrymen were taught that their primary weapon was the bayonet.... The fixing of bayonets is more than a fixing of steel to the rifle since it puts iron into the soul of the soldier doing the fixing."[97] Some souls received less iron than others. Nagata Kazuo reflected on the bayonet training he underwent:

> This extremely harsh bayonet training goes on day after day. I am totally exhausted from morning to night, and even while I am asleep. As soon as we are awakened by a bugle in the morning, the full day of bayonet training begins immediately.... All the joints in my body hurt.... In addition to all this, I am not getting any more skillful with the bayonet. My awareness of this fact, that my capability does not improve regardless of how hard I train, seems to double the exhaustion.[98]

Lack of skill was irrelevant, however, when the soldier could not get close enough to use it.

In the Japanese feature film *Mud and Soldiers*, when the "platoon attack" order is given, every soldier responds by springing forward, heedless of danger. On Bataan life, and death, imitated art with great precision. The term *issen gorin* was given specific meaning when soldiers of the 65th Independent Brigade were hurled into battle against American artillery—

The face of *seishin* (courtesy Christopher Leet).

"Whenever the barrage slackened, the troops dutifully reformed into their columns and renewed their trudge toward death and destruction, for what the defenders could only describe as a 'turkey shoot.'"[99]

Early in the battle, Colonel Richard Mallonee described the carnage caused by a unit of field artillery, firing across open fields: "As attack after attack came on, broke and went back" he recorded, "I knew what Cushing's artillerymen must have felt with the muzzles of their guns in the front line as the Confederate wave came on and broke on the high water mark at Gettysburg." The tanker William Kindler recalled the result as the Japanese assaulted his defensive line: "There was a moon and the Japs attacked. Some were wearing white shirts and they came across the field shouting. They were clearly visible and we inflicted a lot of damage." The carnage lasted three hours with the Japanese restricting their effort to frontal assault directly into the "deadly steel curtain."[100]

During the campaign, the Associated Press correspondent Clark Lee called the Japanese army "an ill-uniformed, untrained mass ... equipped with small-caliber guns and driven forward by a desperate determination to die." The carnage that resulted from their determination was incredible; Japanese desperation to close for bayonet fighting seemed to know no bounds. Again and again, they advanced against the Allied line, human waves breaking in bloody masses, those in front hurling themselves onto barbed wire obstacles, "forming human bridges over which succeeding waves could pass." In the aftermath of such attacks, some remembered the lingering reminders: "The stench of dead Japanese in the surrounding jungle hung everywhere."[101] Yet retreat was impossible, as an infantry song with specific reference to a victory of forty years before made clear:

Hohei no Henryō (Infantry song)
If born as a Japanese,
Fall as a blossom on the line...
What we did at the battle of Mukden
is the essence of Japanese infantry.
We do not know the tactics of retreat
Onward, ever onward!
Close until we are the human bullets.

In late January, an American captain in a Filipino unit watched "Japanese attack and die in such numbers that their bodies stacked up along the final protective line of the machine guns. K Company killed thirty Japanese ... and counted ninety-seven dead along a front of 150 yards, a score of whom died within ten yards of the Filipinos." Even after the sanguinary experience of the first six weeks of battle and the horrendous casualties, the Japanese "stepped up their training for open warfare, for bayonet charges against artillery at close quarters." Such tactics had contributed directly to initial Japanese failure, since many of the best officers fell in the opening phase of the campaign.[102]

The fruitless bloodletting continued until mid–February, when Homma drew his battered army back to lick its wounds. Thwarted in their frontal attacks, he turned to infiltration and amphibious assaults designed to bring his soldiers behind the Allied lines. These encounters, known as the "Battle of the Points," poorly coordinated and inadequately supported, failed miserably to achieve their objective. In the battle at Longoskawayan Point, the Japanese suffered nearly three hundred dead, at a cost to the Allies of twenty-two killed and sixty-six wounded. Even so, Japanese attacking contingents, contained immediately after they landed, fought fiercely. Some, "pushed to the edge of a precipice ... threw away their weapons and then hurled themselves from the cliffs into the water where they either drowned or fell victim to marksmen."[103] At the end of the battle at Quinauan Point, Americans were astonished to see scores of Japanese jumping from the caves in which they had been trapped, down cliffs and into the water. Others grimly fought on until dynamite collapsed their caves; the episode cost the Japanese 900 dead. Their corpses filled the landscape declivities and some, having looted American dead while alive, were wearing four wristwatches.[104]

"Sports Day" in Japanese junior high schools is an opportunity for teams of students, not individuals, to compete in various activities. Though no classes were taught, I was expected to be present, along with many parents, as part of the day's festivities. I was asked to stand at the finish line of a relay race between different classes of seventh graders, and could not help but notice that, regardless of whether the student crossing the line was first or last, boy or girl, all hurled themselves on the ground at the end of the race. Nonplussed, I asked the school's English teacher, why the unnecessary skinned knees? His response spoke volumes. "We know," he said in his awkward English, "they try so hard." Later that week I watched as the male students in the school kendo club practiced to the guttural exhortations of their instructor. At the end of the session the gruff sensei told the smallest fellow in the class, who was smarting from the taunts of

his opponents and near tears from several consecutive defeats, that his size was quite irrelevant, he simply lacked sufficient kon-jo, *or fighting spirit.*

Battlefield *seishin* was not without its strange moments. During one encounter, two Japanese *heitai* (foot soldiers), frustrated by their inability to stop an American tank assault, "took off their shoes and hurled them at a tank." Ignoring invitations to surrender, the Japanese continued to resist until the tanks crushed them to death." When resistance ceased, Americans found hundreds of Japanese dead who had elected to make a last defense "piled up on top of each other like sardines." The power of *seishin* was occasionally exaggerated—some were admonished: "If your arms are broken kick the enemy; if your legs are injured, bite him; if your teeth break glare him to death."[105] Perhaps the seventeenth century poet Bashō, then making his own dangerous journey, spoke to what was left:

Natsugusa ya	The summer grasses—
Tsuwamono domo ga	Of brave soldiers' dreams
Yume no ato	The aftermath

* * * * *

Unlike the American soldier who saw his service in the military as a temporary detour away from his civilian life, the Japanese made no such distinction, and he brought with him all the attitudes he had absorbed since infancy—attitudes that, after the militarists took control of Japan in the 1930s, had been overwhelmingly defined by the army's agenda. He was born and raised in a context that provided little alternative to the conformity that life in the *mura* required, and he brought to Bataan his fear of *soto*, the quest for purity, xenophobia, his pride, his racism and a belief that Western ideas were destructive and antithetical to his way of life.

The famous war correspondent Ernie Pyle, shortly after his transfer to the Pacific after years reporting in North Africa and Europe, wrote after one battle that Japanese prisoners "give me the creeps, and I wanted a mental bath after looking at them."[106] Pyle articulated a response far more common among his enemies. In Japan, foreigners were, and to some degree remain, essentially "impure, foul, polluted" since they did not "share in the grace" of the divine Japan. The Japanese wartime reporter Hino Ashihei's book on Bataan, *Bātan Hantō Kōjōki*, offers a view of the outside that summons up the most fearful dimensions of this notion. Watching the procession of American captives, he wrote, "I feel like I am watching filthy water running from the sewage of a nation which derives from impure origins and has lost its pride of race." Such a mindset led to "perception of the foe as literally something that could not be tolerated.... Since the enemy was regarded, ideologically speaking, as quite alien—in essence as a hostile and contemptible 'other.'" American prisoners were considered "part of the unfinished business of the battlefield."[107]

During the campaign, Japanese soldiers suffered nearly as much from disease as did their enemies. Even so, officers and enlisted men alike refused to eat rice cut with barley, even though they were told it reduced incidence of beriberi. Such "adulterated" rice, they claimed, was fed to men in prison.[108] Discomfort with impurity had other, more symbolic expression as well. Just weeks after the last of the American prisoners straggled into Camp O'Donnell, the May issue of the officially sponsored Japanese publication *Manga* contained an image of a woman on her knees, combing scruff from her hair. The individual flakes are

The start of the Death March, a propaganda shot for the benefit of the Japanese home front. Both POWs and guards are looking at the camera, and prisoners were instructed to raise their hands (Mansell/The LIFE Picture Collection/Getty Images).

labeled "extravagance, selfishness, hedonism, liberalism, money worship, individualism, Anglo-American ideas" and they reveal much about the way the Japanese government understood the threat of modernity.[109]

Certain that their enemies were creatures of the outside, at some fundamental level unworthy, and convinced of the moral superiority of the individual Japanese soldier, army leaders disregarded reports of American industrial capacity, and "made light of America's spiritual fiber. The majority believed that the United States would find it difficult to instill a martial spirit throughout the nation as a whole ... [it was] remarkable for its tendency to overestimate Germany and underestimate other countries."[110]

* * * * *

Writing during the war, the anthropologist Ruth Benedict wondered about the "peculiarities of Japanese behavior which obtruded themselves upon us," ones that "raised questions about the whole way of life to which [Japanese] were conditioned, the ways their institutions functioned and the habits of thought and action they had learned."[111] Well-concealed from wartime observers lay fundamental aspects of that way of life, and the comprehensive degree to which Japanese soldiers had been conditioned.

The army that fought Americans and Filipinos on the Bataan peninsula was far more than a military organization. It was an entity conceived to stave off change—essentially to reject the consequences of entering a more modern age with the inevitable disruption of what the army deemed to be traditional values and modes of behavior. Its purpose was to maintain unity around a profoundly ethnocentric ideal of Japaneseness, from which all others were excluded. When on Bataan the Japanese army came to grips with yet another aspect of the external, contaminating, threatening world, it responded as it had since its inception. Some soldiers, now victorious, in an army that had been decimated by its enemies, understood they had a license to wield their bayonets freely against those others.

3

An Army Apart

These are they which came out of great tribulation.—Revelation 7:14

In the Philippines, the Imperial Japanese Army struck an instrument that was raw and unprepared. Who were these Americans, and what kind of soldiers, here at war's dawn for the U.S., did they make? What were the fault lines in the Allied, Filipino-American force that faced the Japanese Fourteenth Army? How did the fourteen-week campaign unfold and, most important, what was the condition of the American soldier, physically and in terms of his training, attitudes toward authority, morale and unit cohesion, at the moment of surrender?

In the wartime film *Bataan*, Sergeant Dane, the central character, says that the Americans in his squad "never served together before" and that "three months ago they were all jerking sodas or selling shoes or punching adding machines." The film proceeds to show that such inexperienced citizen-soldiers could pull together as a coherent military force. The place the men defend—both geographic and metaphorical—is orderly in a special *e pluribus unum* kind of way, and set the pattern for many a "melting pot" war film to follow, including *Saving Private Ryan* and many others. *Bataan*'s hodge-podge unit comprises an African American, two Filipinos (including Desi Arnaz in his pre–Lucy career), the obligatory Irishman, an Eastern European, a Hispanic and a Jew. The two officers are West Point men, suggesting that class divisions are overcome by the need to unite in the face of the savage enemy. Order is sustained by Dane's brisk commands and by the presence of religion—one soldier makes a cross for a fallen officer, the black soldier is studying to be preacher, and another dies of fever while reciting Latin.

In many ways, the essence of the film resides in the character of Leonard Purckett, a stranded sailor whose innocence resonates widely as the "kid next door." The film follows his transformation from innocence to experience as he witnesses a Japanese atrocity and, over his machine gun, articulates his desire to kill lots of Japanese "monkeys." Later, in hand-to-hand combat, Purckett strangles a Japanese who had offered to surrender, then tried to kill him; he shakes his enemy's body in righteous anger. The film's central purpose was to educate the American viewing public about the necessity to unite in opposition to a savage enemy, but the actual Allied army lacked the mythic coherence so clear in the film.[1] Rather than that army exceeding the sum of its parts, something of the reverse was, in fact, true.

* * * * *

GIs left messages stating that "Kilroy" had been to all the places Americans soldiers conquered in the European and Pacific theaters. He left his name on village walls, on tanks, in latrines, and sometimes even appeared in soldiers' letters home. If the origins of the term "Kilroy" are unclear, its metaphorical meaning was not. This purely American everyman "was a character fulfilling everyone's army fantasies of success, indeed, victory, without effort or strain or fear. He is ubiquitous and agile, cleverly overcoming all limitations of time and space ... he is immortal, impervious to shot and shell, terror and humiliation."[2] Contrived this way, he would be the instrument of Axis defeat Winston Churchill imagined as he rejoiced at the American declaration of war against Germany. "As for the Japanese," he intoned, "they would be ground to a powder. All the rest was merely the proper application of overwhelming force." Tin Pan Alley agreed, its crude lyrics expressing early-war bravado:

> We're gonna have to slap the dirty little Jap
> And Uncle Sam's the guy who can do it
> We'll skin the streak of yellow from this sneaky little fellow
> And he'll think a cyclone hit him when he's thru it
> We'll take the double crosser to the old woodshed
> We'll start on his bottom and go to his head
> When we get thru with him he'll wish that he was dead
> We gotta slap the dirty little Jap

Other early wartime ditties with unfortunate titles included "Goodbye Mama, I'm Off to Yokohama," "The Jap's Haven't Got a Chinaman's Chance," "They're Going to Be Playing Taps on the Japs," "Slap the Jap Right off the Map" and "When Those Little Yellow Bellies Meet the Cohens and the Kellys." One Bataan veteran described his officer's attitude, assuring the enlisted men that "those poor little buggers have shot their wad in China already" and "The Japs aren't ready to fight real soldiers like us superior Americans."[3]

To be sure, the pre-war U.S. was not without its often virulent racism; such stereotyping and fear-mongering reflected the general belief in white superiority. Books such as Madison Grant's *The Passing of the Great Race*, James F. Abbott's *Japanese Expansion and American Policies* and Carl Crow's *Japan and America*, all published in 1916, stoked the nativist fears of those for whom miscegenation was an abomination.[4] Homer Lea had already published a best-seller in 1909 entitled *The Valor of Ignorance*, a book about a future war with Japan, including detailed projections about Japanese landings on the West Coast. Popular works more likely familiar to the American rank-and-file in the Philippines included that of Wallace Irwin, who wrote for *Collier's* magazine and created the comic figure of Hashimura Togo, a "garrulous, arrogant, buck-toothed student," whose "Letters from a Japanese Schoolboy" fed the pre-war stereotype.

More specific anti–Japanese sentiment was expressed in a ten-part film, *Patria*, released in 1917. Here Japan was shown in collusion with Mexico, internal spies and a Japanese nobleman in charge of the Japanese secret service in the U.S. Viewers were treated to footage of a Japanese invasion and requisite atrocities, including "violation" of the film star Irene Castle. More generally, the "Fu Manchu" stereotype was probably more of an influence on soldiers in the Philippines, the conflation of Asian stereotypes as a looming "oriental menace."[5]

The Japanese returned the stereotypical criticism with interest. For a start, their enemy's army ranked twentieth in size in 1940, smaller than that of Greece and Switzerland. It was not simply a matter of size, however—"a widespread feeling pervaded Imperial army circles that the United States was an isolationist, business-as-usual, unmotivated, flabby country, whose soldiers would flee at the first whiff of grapeshot." General Sato Kojiro spoke for many when he asserted that "the Americans are the worst of all nationalities: U.S. officers' method of command was infantile compared to the Japanese army." In times of war, America's ethnic diversity would surely cripple its ability to wage war, as its individual ethnic components were thought to be weak, with some seen "embracing girlfriends in public in train stations

A bestial-looking Japanese is shown earning the wages of defeat in this wartime sketch. Wishful thinking and poetic justice aside, it would be MacArthur, not Wainwright, for whom the glory of re-conquest was reserved (Library of Congress).

and weeping." Sato Kenryo, posted in the U.S. in the early 1930s, was surprised that the army did not work on Sunday, and had picnics even during maneuvers. "With respect to training in particular," he added, "I felt like teaching them a thing or two."[6]

* * * * *

Some Americans heartily agreed with their enemy's critique. One officer named Hayes railed against recruiters advertising the luxuries available in the modern U.S. army—"libraries, baths, all modern conveniences." Instead, he wanted the army to tout "how far Johnny can march, on such a darn little, how Johnny can put out and accomplish real physical tasks when denied the niceties and luxuries of our soft existence. When these ... are denied Johnny in war time, he doesn't do well." One enlisted man, D.E. Smith, reflecting on his enemy, suggested that a natural war-like spirit was to be found in "have-not peoples." He stated, "Altho blind (as it should be) their discipline is probably better than that of a conglomerate USAFFE (U.S. Armed Forces, Far East) force of mutually suspicious people reared in ease, luxury and complete freedom of thought, expression and sympathy."[7]

In December 1941, Geoffrey Ames tried to describe the ethos he saw in the Philippine force in a letter to his wife Kaye. "Our soldiers out here," he wrote, "are just an average lot of American young men ... mostly from the families which earn just about enough to keep a family and home together ... most are downright poor. They don't actually like to work hard. They'd honestly like to take it easy, just talking of women and liquor or otherwise entertaining themselves." A.K Whitehead was more critical, stating that the "average private is undisciplined, discourteous, and ignorant ... his sole interests to sleep, eat and chase a woman down periodically and it is difficult to get him to do anything else."[8]

Only 50,000 men remained in the service after the doughboys came home at World War I's conclusion. As a result, army leaders were eager to build up the ranks. Inducements to keep veterans accounted for some retention, but more men were needed, and "both physical and mental standards were lowered. Illiterates, foreigners who had not yet learned English, and men whose intelligence tests showed that they were at the eight year old level were now accepted." Only half of those seeking induction were rejected, compared to 83 percent between 1909 and 1915. army administration was not happy with the new specimens. One post surgeon called his new wards "morons," and others complained of the generally poor physical condition of the men. Army officials hoped that new educational programs would bring the substandard up to par. Some, no doubt, benefitted from the courses offered, but the training was in some sense counter-productive. Between 1890 and 1940, after a year of service, soldiers could buy a discharge, a policy that tended to drain the army of its better recruits. Some 30,000 men left between 1934 and 1938, especially those who, seeking higher paying jobs in civilian life, had completed technical training of one kind or another.[9]

Douglas MacArthur once said, "The Japanese are the greatest exploiters of inefficient and incompetent troops the world has ever seen."[10] Though the first part of his assertion is questionable, the latter describes the Allied army in 1942 with some accuracy. In the early months of 1942, true American might existed only as potential. At the time of Pearl Harbor, the country was barely past the searing debates between those who favored an isolationist stance and those who saw intervention abroad as either necessary or inevitable.

War Department records show that in 1940, about 4,500 U.S. soldiers were stationed in the islands. By 1941, after the expansion of the military authorized by Congress, the figure had risen to 10,569.[11] This sudden growth accounts for a basic division between two groups of American soldiers—on the one hand the career army men, on the other recent draftees who entered the ranks after the draft law was passed in the fall of 1940, and National Guardsmen whose units had recently been federalized as the War Department reached for the first available troops. Some of the men had arrived in the Philippines only weeks before the Japanese invasion of December 1941. About 13,500 Americans found themselves on Bataan, some 10,000 of whom had been in country less than eight months. Few in the first group had any experience of combat; none did in the second.[12] On the eve of hostilities, MacArthur commanded 31,000 Americans, 12,000 Filipino Scouts, and 100,000 conscripts of the Philippine army.

The initial core of the American contingent of the USAFFE was a small cadre soldiers from the peacetime "old army." Protected historically by broad oceans and weak neighbors and ever mistrustful of a standing army, Americans had invested only minimally in their peacetime military. The historian Ronald Spector described the force as "an army of polo ponies and long golf games, of cheap domestic help, and shopping trips to Shanghai and Hong Kong" where sports were as important as any other function. It was a "tight-knit, hard-drinking, hard-bitten, long-service army: an army of inspections and close-order drill, and of long evenings over drinks at the officers' club."[13]

Many recalled pre-war life on the islands as a soldier's paradise—a highly sought-after assignment. In the summer and autumn of 1941, old-timers and recruits alike found their post idyllic, in spite of the heat. Fort Stotsenberg and its environs boasted facilities for golf, tennis, softball and other athletic endeavors. During peace time in the Philippines, "the military was on duty only in the morning from eight o'clock to eleven o'clock" since many believed that "a white person could not survive in the tropical sun after eleven o'clock." Enlisted men wore "their new life like the latest fashion" and the modest pay of enlisted men went far indeed. Initial pay was $21 per month; rising to $30 after four months; with sixty pesos ($30), life was easier.

One soldier wrote that "each company had its own Chinese tailor" who cut each uniform to fit perfectly. For most, the day consisted of "reveille, followed by breakfast served by Filipino waiters, followed by unit drill or other military training" which ended at 11:30 a.m. Then came a large lunch, followed by a three hour siesta to escape the midday heat. Those opting not to sleep were free to wander into town, play cards, or shoot pool. For old timers the Philippines was "the best damn duty in the whole damn army.... The living was opulent and inexpensive."[14] Edwin Ramsey recalled that his life on base

> was that of the old colonial army. We had servants who lived in the back of the house and acted as our cooks and cleaners, and each officer was assigned an orderly who attended to his horse. Our commanding general enforced the imperial image strictly. We were required to wear the old-fashioned, high-collared white mess jacket in the evenings, and we had to shower and change uniforms twice a day.[15]

Officers worked until noon, after which servants saw to their needs. Lieutenant Charlie Ivins came back to his quarters and left his clothes for washing by the *lavendera*, the duration of his afternoon nap determined by his plans to golf or not. If he did not manage a course outing, he changed, showered, and came to dinner and cocktails in his formal white uniform.

Those playing golf at the Zamboanga Golf and Country Club encountered interesting hazards. Crocodiles haunted a water hazard, various domestic animals wandered the fairways, and monkeys "harassed players at the fourth tee." At one point on the course Ivins killed a cobra, but whether he beat it to death with his seven iron went unrecorded.[16]

Charles Willeford, an enlisted man, quickly bored of his duties as a truck driver, but found that guard duty at least allowed him to steal gas and sell it to soldiers who owned cars. A fellow soldier assured him that in the army, "everything is always done as it was done before" but he still felt like anything but a soldier. Relieved of the need to spend time on any domestic tasks, he found time to visit the Fort Stotsenburg library and read several books a week. James Bollich remembered that there were "Filipinos all over our camp site looking for something to do to make a little money. They would make up your cot, straighten up your tent, wash your clothes, shine your shoes, run errands for you, etc. You did not have to lift a finger around camp if you took on one of these guys. They even did all the KP work for the outfit." Not everyone was fully satisfied—one disgruntled private, sniffing his starched and folded laundry, complained that "they smelled like carabao, because they washed in creeks, and we got that same smell, just like the Filipinos." Officers lived even better. One officer's monthly mess bill exceeded $7 and "included every fancy dessert you could name, and scotch and soda noon and night."[17]

The services of "Bunkboys" were essential and, at five pesos a month ($2.50), well within the reach of the lowest paid GI. These helpers washed clothes, kept uniforms in top trim, and looked after army gear, even cleaning the GI's rifle. Other benefits included language help and advice on the location of crap and poker games on base. He was his GI's "Father Confessor, letter-writer, and occasional pimp, and was expected to lie convincingly to any officer inquiring after his patron's location or condition.[18]

Compelling testimony suggests that this force was anything but battle-ready. One contemporary described the old soldiers as "career army and Navy men, and they were going to take the easiest and sweetest road out, [they] weren't over there to soldier. They were over there to have a helluva good time. The Philippines was the softest duty station in the world, and that's the reason they stayed there."[19] Such men were neither well-educated nor stimulated toward behavior beyond routine. Among the enlisted men, "high school graduates were rare; outright illiterates were common. Of regular enlisted men in the army prior to Pearl Harbor, over 75 percent had failed to complete high school and 41 percent had never been to high school at all." Military life "bred mental stagnation, reverence for routine, parochialism—and indifference."[20]

Enlisted men for most of the interwar period were long term recruits, often referred to as "thirty-year men" some of whom "could not make a living in the civilian world." Ed Thomas recalled one such man, his company's first sergeant, a man nicknamed "Hambone," whom he called a *dhobie*—an American who had gone native. Thomas recalled that Hambone could not read or write. Another illiterate was a master sergeant and maintenance chief who had been in the service since World War I. He had an assistant who read directives to him, his inability to read well-concealed from the officers.[21]

The summer of 1941 was as somnolent as the ones preceding. American officers apprehended no threat from Japan, noted occasional references to China, worked till noon, then took a siesta, played golf, went to the Army-Navy Club. Lieutenant Allison Ind arrived in Manila in May 1941 and later recalled "the effect struck me with impact, that Headquarters of the Philippines Department ... the pivot round which this vast drum of war would spin ... was soft. Utterly soft! Call it what you will, the tropics, Manila heat, American indifference.... There was a flaccidity, a torpidity, and an all-pervading lack of movement or resolution, not in one department, not in just a few individuals, but fearfully widespread." In fact, posting to the Philippines

> had long been looked upon by the War Department and officers of long rank and short distances to retirement, as an ideal place to polish off a career in the army. Or, again, it was a good tropic Siberia for the relegation of those whose overambitions worried their superiors and thereby indicated the need for a little isolation treatment. On the Philippine station you could take it easy, and take it rightfully so.[22]

For many officers, the Philippines was a kind if retirement zone for the unwanted. Disgusted with their poor leadership, Geoffrey Ames wrote, "In any other area, incompetents, blunderers, pettifoggers and people just too old to get about have been weeded out. Out here they couldn't be disposed of. We have plenty of them."[23]

Some of the enlisted men did virtually nothing, spending excessive portions of their days asleep, what soldiers called the "blanket drill." One critic recorded, "These were the old guys, the professional privates, men who had been in the Army since the Great War. These men had never been promoted, had always been privates, and had never developed skills of any kind. In the States they could be assigned to clean latrines or to sweep porches, but in the Philippines, where all the menial tasks were performed by Filipino houseboys, there was nothing at all for them to do."[24]

In tones dripping with sarcasm, Lieutenant Ind described the routine at HQ—work beginning at eight, slowly opening official mail, applying "heavy thoughts to the contents," waiting for "a little black-eyed Tagalog in blue denim" to spray offices for mosquitoes, overcoming the antiquated switchboard to make a phone call, breaking for a half hour for a cool drink and a chat, followed by "the hard work of the day"—some dictation, then launching a "buck sheet" on its "pompous round of officialdom." Perhaps a conference, then one o'clock and sleep till four, after which one did not return to the office.[25]

The numbers were small and the society close, but size and proximity did not translate to reliable unit cohesion. Standard procedure called for both officers and men to rotate into overseas regiments every three years, and this practice clearly affected the units' discipline and efficiency. The result was that for "its entire existence, the Pacific Army was composed of units in constant flux of new recruits, men halfway through their enlistment, and shorttimers." The inevitable result of this system was the sacrifice of regimental spirit. On a complicated rotation system, these officers were assigned two year duty overseas duty, with the possibility of a one year extension before leaving the islands.[26]

A few irritations specific to the P.I. (Philippine Islands) required the exercise of caution. James Bollich remembered a soldier cutting down a tree and being showered with a huge nest of "large ferocious ants," and another soldier was bitten by hundreds of ants, causing excruciating pain, vomiting and swelling. The heat and exotic environment sometimes left men enervated, and some buckled. Psychological problems were not uncommon; veterans called the malaise "Philippinitis," an affliction wherein the victim experienced "apathy, inertia, fatigue, and depression." An officer stationed on Corregidor remembered, "I can see in the faces of most of the officers the expression of tropical lassitude and indifference that gets hold of one here." One officer was known to have "gone Asiatic" after eight years in Philippines—he loved flowers and sometimes talked to them and to insects. Others were called "Sunshiners," old army men "who had missed too many ships to the States" who sometimes sang a popular song, "The monkeys have no tails in Zamboanga"—the monkeys obviously meaning the native Filipinos.[27]

* * * * *

Pacific veteran and military historian Robert Leckie described Marines as divided into "two distinct camps—the Old Salts and the Boots—who are forever warring: the Old Salt defending his past and his traditions against the furious assault of the Boot who is striving to exalt the Present at the expense of the Past, seeking to deflate the aplomb of the Old Salt by collapsing this puffed-up Past upon which it reposes."[28] Such a division, equally pronounced, defined the Fil-American force as well.

A man drafted in 1940 "had to stand at least five feet tall and weigh 105 pounds, possess twelve or more of his natural thirty-two teeth; and be free of flat feet, venereal disease, and hernias."[29] Into the insular world of the Old Army poured such new recruits, a trickle in the fall of 1940, a deluge by the spring of 1941. Raymond Knight's experience was not atypical. After acclimating to the heat, he and his company spent "few miserable weeks learning how to be infantrymen" after which he enjoyed the cheap food and drink and the relaxed regimen of work. Knight had entered a world that was "languorous, torpid, flaccid. The steamy days, unhurried pace and 'sluggish officialdom' wore down even the most ambitious and active men. Older officers nearing retirement came here to pass their final days in honorable quiet, a two-year vacation.... Even in line units, there was little urgency in preparing the men for war." One recruit remembered his training as "going to the field in the mornings for a couple of hours and sitting under palm trees." David Brenzel, who arrived in November 1940, recalled that "every day is Sunday in the army."[30]

For the new men who heard the announcement of the attack on Pearl Harbor, "Their first feeling of outrage gave way to the awful fear that they would be sent away, green and untrained and helpless." These were recently inducted citizen-soldiers, "taken from all walks of life" and "only partially hardened to the rigors of life in the field. Once in the Islands they found themselves with the additional challenge of trying to acclimitize themselves to the heat and discomforts of the tropics." The men who met these less than rigorous specifications comprised a hodgepodge of units and specialties—officers in the newly organized Filipino units, officers in the Philippine Scouts, the American 31st Infantry regiment, grounded airmen recycled as infantry, and various specialized units, such as small tank force and two antiaircraft battalions of the New Mexico National Guard. These disconnected groups of soldiers were quite distinct from the later force, far better trained, that swept across the Pacific toward Japan from 1943 to 1945.[31]

Charles Willeford lied about his age and enlisted at age sixteen in the National Guard in the Depression-ridden year of 1935, enticed by the dollar-a-day bounty paid during training. A third of the members of his unit were under eighteen, either drop-outs or high school students. Living with his grandmother, unable to find work and so desperate for money that he could no longer ask her for the ten cent streetcar fare downtown, Willeford enlisted in the Air Corps. There he complained that most of the jobs required no special training and, with considerable bitterness, he pointed out "the waste of manpower, the sheer incompetence of the setup, and the feeling of worthlessness it engendered in those of us who were assigned to these meaningless jobs." As National Guardsmen whose units had been federalized, these were the first men the government could reach. Deprived of the close intimacy of twelve weeks of basic training, men in the Guard units underwent none of the rigorous training that would have served as the basis for initial bonding—and pride in unit—that any military organization seeks to create.[32]

The novelist James Jones once observed that there was "a lot more bitterness in World War II than historians allow." Much of it existed between different groups in the American army, and these newly arrived were not warmly welcomed. Sometimes newcomers endured the mild hazing of being sent to find the "cannon report," the "biscuit gun," the "flagpole key" or the "rubber flag" flown during inclement weather. More often they encountered serious difficulty. When a New Mexican National Guard unit was made part of the regular army, its members felt the chasm between old and new: "From the first, the 'regulars' looked down their hierarchical noses at the Guard units." The chasm did not disappear when the unit arrived in the Philippines. At the NCO club in Manila, the New Mexicans "drew glassy glances. The Hispanics and Indians felt it doubly. The felony of being Guardsmen, compounded by race, drew snide insinuation or outright rudeness." The ensuing brawls forced a declaration of "off limits" to the newcomers.[33]

The hard bitten (if rather soft-living) old soldiers soon found themselves situated between two new groups. As non-coms and corporals they commanded the newly recruited, inexperienced privates, and in turn were commanded by newly commissioned, equally inexperienced officers, further defining fault lines in this hybrid force. Different levels of education among these soldiers were one divisive issue. "The Regular army enlisted man was a youth of less than average education, to whom the security of pay, low as it was, and the routines of army life appealed more than the competitive struggle of civilian life.... This was the kind of soldier to whom the old army was adapted and who on the eve of World War II would, as a non-com, be the immediate boss and teacher of the new selectee."[34] By June 1941, the new draftees comprised up to 50 percent of those in the regular divisions.

The clash of cultures was pronounced. The first survey conducted showed that 32 percent of draftees had finished high school; 16 percent had finished college, while regulars' percentages were 20 and 3 respectively, while one third of sergeants had not entered high school. Between the world wars, public education exploded in the U.S. The year 1916 saw some 1.7 million students attending high school, with 400,000 in college. By the eve of hostilities with Japan, there were 7.1 million in high school, and 1.4 million in college, and these better-educated men were preparing for white collar jobs in an increasingly sophisticated society. As they flooded into the army, they clashed with soldiers whose military culture and level of education they either failed to understand or resented if they did understand it.[35]

The "basic orientation" of these men was "still civilian rather than military. They looked over their shoulders at the civilian life they had temporarily left behind them and were already making plans about what they would do after the war." Their attitudes were reflected in their preference for dress while on leave—62 percent of regulars preferred to wear their uniforms, compared to only 30 percent of draftees.[36] The gap in experience and education could "hardly fail to be productive of tensions"; better-educated draftees complained accordingly:

> The non-commissioned officers are not efficient enough to operate in war. There are so many who have received stripes and don't know what the score is. Anybody can be an NCO. Under the present army, no tests are given, you are just told that you have been made corporal, sergeant, or what have you, and that is all.

Another dissatisfied draftee wrote,

> This new era in the army brought about by the Selective Service Act should be dealt with accordingly. My First Sergeant knows that the NCOs are not too intelligent—he admits this. He also admits that the SS [selective service] men are, by far, more intelligent than the army's regular NCO's. But he says there is nothing can be done about this. My advice is to run an IQ test and let the men who have the most knowledge be the bosses.

The old regulars responded as might be expected of men whose smaller club was being overrun by civilians in uniform: "I think discipline was relaxed on Selective Service men, from what it was formerly on Regular army men. Selectees have been allowed to wise off too much. Many of them are too smart for their own good." Another, in less than elegant prose, continued,

> The army is nothing like it use to be say five years ago. The men are too use to doing their on way. So it is hard to change. Sense the number men [selectees] has too be here the regulars men get put on K.P. over the week-end so the number boys can go home. I don't like that cause I was one of the boys that got put on K.P during Easter. I think I am as good as any man. Number men and regulars should be treated the same way. I mean what is good for the goose is good for the ganger.[37]

Addie Martin expressed the irritation of many new recruits who found themselves inferior in rank to those who had preceded them into the army and chose to distinguish between goose and "ganger." In August 1941 he wrote, "It's a goddamn shame to see some of the punks they've got in good positions. Some of them can't pronounce anything over a two-syllable word…. So, if anyone ever asks … about progress in the army, tell them there isn't a hell of a lot of chance."[38]

With respect to the interplay between officers and their men, again the wartime film *Bataan* offers an interesting perspective and reference point. Early in the film, Captain Henry Lassiter has his initial conversation with Sergeant Bill Dane, during which he admits his inexperience immediately, telling Dane that he graduated West Point in 1940. Dane responds by telling Lassiter of his two enlistments, during which he earned "no serious demerits." Lassiter instinctively recognizes Dane's competence and signals his intent to rely on it—he states, "We'll get along" to end their initial conversation.

Later, after seeing Dane's obvious competence and command presence, Lassiter cogently defines the ideal American leader. First, he explains the overall strategic situation to Dane, on the assumption that his democratically-oriented and can-do sergeant requires more than simple orders from above to function well. He then tells Dane to use his own initiative—without reference to making Lassiter "look good," and even encourages him to correct any improper orders. Here is the ideal officer—NCO—enlisted man relationship: a competent, experienced and respected officer who nonetheless allows the archetypical well-springs of American culture to flow—individual initiative unimpeded by unnecessary hierarchy, applied to maximum efficiency.

The reality, of course, was quite different. Most of the officers under which these men fought on Bataan were fresh from state-side ROTC training.[39] Resentment against what soldiers considered Mickey Mouse or Chicken Shit was ubiquitous, and more pronounced when dispensed from such inexperienced leaders. Segregated facilities and officers' privileges in general rankled lower ranks—better food, access to cheaper liquor, even better latrines. Many soldiers assumed that those awarded commission were "immediately corrupted" and thereafter tended to refer to the superiors in "caste and class terms."[40]

The new draftees, many of whom had aspirations to become officers themselves, had mixed feelings about their officers, but many were openly critical of what they called the army's "caste system." One draftee stated, "I thought the caste system was restricted to India. Those officers think they are tin gods." Another wrote:

> The sanctity attached to rank is such that man-to-man relationship down the chain of communication is discouraged. The efficiency of the army should be valued more highly than the sanctity of a commission, or somebody's pride, or the feelings of some inefficient man of long service. That kind of thing may be alright in peacetime, but when everything is at stake, as it is now, it is no longer harmless. The men are smart and they can see how they suffer by the insufficiency of the officers and the system, and it is bad for morale when they are kept in the army to train their officers to carry it on.[41]

One of the factors that limited tension between enlisted men and officers was "the inclination of some combat soldiers to think of their own officers in ways at odds with their view of the officer corps." Doubtless this factors were present to some extent during the battles on Bataan. Japanese snipers (amply represented in the film *Bataan*) discouraged the wearing of officers insignia, and distinctions of rank must have faded. Four months of intermittent combat no doubt cemented the bond between some officers and some men, but there were many fault lines to overcome. In the lull after repelling the first Japanese offensive, "As far as possible, inefficient leaders were replaced," and "those that had made good were promoted."[42]

* * * * *

Whether old-timer or newly arrived, the soldiers had ample opportunity to spend their copious free time on amusements common to single men. The American Thirty-First Regiment was known in Manila as the "Thirsty-First" for its hard drinking ways. The unit had been organized in Manila during World War I and had long since settled into garrison life there. It fought briefly in Siberia in 1919 and served in Shanghai in 1932. As a unit it had never been to the U.S. Its members haunted favorite places in the capital, one of which was an establishment called La Playa, "a bar and restaurant run by a syndicate of American gamblers from Shanghai," where Americans and Filipinos hovered over roulette tables and mixed while playing craps and blackjack.

Sometimes the encounters turned violent. Lieutenant Edward Ramsey recalled an incident after a long night of playing craps when his squadron commander saw a Filipino break a glass in his commander's face. Filipinos and Americans squared off in a general melee until one Filipino wearing a white suit produced a revolver. Before Ramsey passed out from his own wounds, he heard his commander had been taken to the hospital. Others took a more peaceful approach. One young officer from a wealthy New York family owned a "brand new red Buick convertible," a useful accessory while cruising the bars of Manila.[43]

The search for Filipino women—the young girls were called *dalagas* in Tagalog—was, of course, most soldiers' chief off-duty concern. Abel Ortega, a bi-lingual Mexican-American, found himself besieged by fellow soldiers when he arrived in the islands in November 1941. Many of his buddies thought his facility with language could "get some local women for them," but when they discovered that Ortega could not speak Tagalog, his popularity declined considerably. Ortega, who had trained as a radio operator, remembered, "Since I didn't drink, curse, play cards, or chase women, I didn't fit in very well with the other soldiers."[44]

No doubt in this he was exceptional; for most men other attractions offset both the hot climate and, for newcomers, the cold reception from old-timers. Sex was cheap and readily available in Manila's brothels and elsewhere from local women, and the rates of venereal disease indicate substantial indulgence. After his arrival in September 1941, recruit Addie Martin remembered "one guy in the barracks who used to go down to 'Sloppy Bottom' [a barrio near his fort] looking for women to screw." At one dollar per visit, opportunities were plentiful. Martin sometimes reminded him "that he had better leave a trust fund for the education of all the children he was fathering." When returning after a night with prostitutes, the men reported to "Ward Six" to undergo "prophylaxis," and were required to sign in to prove their compliance.[45]

Although army medics provided prophylactics and regularly checked the women for

Thirty-year men at play (courtesy Christopher Leet).

STD, one outfit in Manila unofficially reported an infection incidence of 200 percent—two cases per man per year. J.D. Merritt recalled one such genital inquisition, when the doctor "rudely jerked and squeezed each passing penis and its cowering attendants" while a group of Filipino civilians watched. Others, perhaps less modest, were happy to show their wares. Once, while some GIs were showering in an area visible to a gathered host of young Filipino women, the water inexplicably stopped. Some of the women, horrified at what they saw, began screaming *Simula ang tubig* (Turn the water on), but the soldiers, not understanding Tagalog, understood only "too big" and "began wildly waving their penises like batons" to either the delight or, possibly, the continuing horror of those assembled. Physicians who examined organs shy and less shy were called by various names—"pecker checker," "prick smith" and "penis machinist." Soldiers with other conditions were warned by a sign on a latrine: "Bucks with short horns stand close."[46]

With such enticements, a private's $30 per month only went so far. The experience of William R. Dunn, who enlisted at seventeen in 1934, was typical. His salary was eroded by deductions of $5 for post-exchange coupons, $2 for theater tickets, $3 for laundry, and 25 cents for the soldiers' home, leaving him less than $8 for amusement. Some entrepreneurs saw opportunity and took it. One young corporal served the essential purpose of banker for those whose appetites outran their purses. Such men, desperate for further entertainment, came to the corporal, who was widely known as a "ten percenter," lending money to his fellow soldiers at 10 percent interest until next payday. John Bumgarner, one of the base physicians, was incensed by this practice, but was told that such men were "very important to the army's scheme of things."[47] These men would soon learn that such behavior was equally important in the Japanese prison camps, though not all were to benefit.

Old-timers had been enjoying sex with local women for years and, after the new recruits arrived, all who were interested in reaching beyond local prostitutes could enjoy the "fringe benefits" of easy sexual liaisons with Filipinas. Young soldiers, perhaps fresh from the face-slappings that followed clumsy advances in stateside movie theaters, found a different world, one where sex was easy—perhaps even difficult to avoid. Charles Willeford, who had been in the islands since 1935, memorized one phrase in Tagalog: *Ahko mall-ah-guy-ah eenie gee-tah* (I am happy because I love you). He reported that the phrase was usually effective, eliciting claps of glee, and claimed that he was "positive that some of the pieces of ass [he] got in P.I. were directly attributable to that lone sentence." Willeford found this vocabulary, along with *Lalaki* and *Babai* (man and woman), adequate for his needs.[48]

Longer-term liaisons were of mutual benefit. A number of "shack rats" paid to keep women in their own separate houses, and many of these women tried to get pregnant as quickly as possible, hoping that the father would acknowledge paternity with the army's finance department. This ensured common-law wife status for the woman, which in turn produced a monthly payment to the family. When terms of enlistment expired, departing soldiers, many of whom had no families of their own, sometimes "transferred" these families to new arrivals. "Now the kids still belonged to the first guy, but if the woman could get passed on for two or three hitches and have five or six kids, the per diem for these kids got to the point where she could live in the high society part of town." The morality of such business arrangements apparently disturbed few. "Hell," stated one observer, "every Filipino woman had a cunt. She was lucky to have one she could sell.... The women were in competition to snag a soldier if they could." The crude appeal of the system to pragmatic American youth was clear to Forrest Knox, who remembered at home "a soldier ha[d] to hassle around for quite a while to find one that w[ould] even put out. Over there you had to beat them off you." A letter one soldier received from a Filipina suggested something of the relationship between economy and emotion: "I love you Joe. No shit. Send me ten pesos."[49]

Richard Gordon recalled seeing Filipinas crying as their erstwhile lovers departed for the U.S., but the girls would soon be attached to a new soldier. Many stayed with one woman out of fear of STD; not all Filipinas thus impregnated managed the transition. Shades of Madame Butterfly, when ships bearing new soldiers arrived, "hundreds of melancholy Filipinos met the ship at the dock, many of them women looking for soldiers who had promised them" they would return. Some of the women held up *mestizo* babies as evidence of their liaisons. Love was "indeed grand" in the Philippines.[50]

Those receiving a "Dear John" letter (a "green banana," so named because it caused stomach pain) from girls left in the U.S. did not have far to look for comfort. Those not favoring longer-term liaisons indulged in "sex on the arm" whereby bar owners, seeking to attract trade, would allow the men to have sex and then settle accounts on payday. This was commonly referred to as "jawboning," a term that originated during the Indian wars, when a man without cash recorded the amount of his debts at the trading post on the jawbone of a buffalo. This led to occasionally awkward situations. When Filipino pimps came to collect, their "sex tabs" sometimes contained names such as "Tyrone Power" or "Spencer Tracy."[51] One can only imagine such scenes, complicated by the language barrier.

Perhaps understanding something essential about their enemy's proclivities, Japanese propaganda during the campaign attempted to capitalize. Americans were showered with one series of leaflets showing a progressive striptease—first the face of a beautiful woman, then the woman in a shawl from waist up, then a third, full length, with the shawl over her whole body. The fourth revealed her naked and the fifth the sex act itself.[52] Some may have looked at the images fondly before using the paper in the latrine.

* * * * *

James Jones has written that the last stage of the combat soldier's attitude was "final, full acceptance of the fact that his name is already written down in the rolls of the already dead. Every combat soldier, if he follows far enough along the path that began with his induction, must ... lead to that awareness. He must make a compact with himself or with Fate that he is lost. Only then can he function as he ought to function.... He knows and accepts beforehand that he's dead, although he may be still walking around for a while."[53] In Jones' novel *The Thin Red Line*, a soldier named Fife dreams a horrible dream, and wakes in a

> cold sweat of fear and panic the essential essence of which was a feeling of complete entrapment. Trapped in every direction no matter where he turned, trapped by patriotic doctors, trapped by longfaced crewcut infantry Colonels who demanded the willingness to die, trapped by Japanese colonial ambitions ... trapped by his own government and its faceless nameless administrators.[54]

Lieutenant Speirs, a character in the HBO series *Band of Brothers*, makes the same assertion, explaining the simple reality to a dazed trooper:

> The only hope you have is to accept the fact that you're already dead, and the sooner you accept that, the sooner you'll be able to function as a soldier is supposed to function ... without mercy, without compassion, without remorse. All war depends upon it.

The recruits entering the army on the eve of hostilities brought such essentially civilian sensibilities with them and were perhaps slower to adapt to the terror of Pacific combat one veteran described:

> There was a crackling in the jungle like herds of elephants trampling all the gathered twigs in the world—and then suddenly there they were in the clearing: lumps of ghostly dancing figures who swelled monstrously without advancing, changed aspect in an agony of trance to flapping birds, to goats, to antlike crabs with helmets glinting; came on in bands, in spidery striations, and everywhere was the wild ghostly scream: *aaaaaiiiii*..."[55]

The novelist and the filmmaker's lieutenant capture the soldier's horror and reluctance to accept this reality.

Such recognition and acceptance came more slowly to Americans than to Japanese. In his novel *The Naked and the Dead*, Norman Mailer has General Cummings offer a telling critique of his men: "We have the highest standard of living in the world ... and the worst individual fighting soldiers of any big power ... as Americans they share most of them the peculiar manifestation of our democracy. They have an exaggerated idea of the rights due themselves as individuals." Assessing the U.S. military before Pearl Harbor, a British liaison officer to U.S. War Department stated, "This country is soft and highly organized for peace. Their armed forces are more unready for war than is possible to imagine.... The whole military organization belongs to the days of George Washington."[56]

Indeed, unlike those of their Japanese counterparts, these men's uniforms only partially covered a persistent civilian orientation. The 1942 wartime publication, *See Here, Private Hargrove*, poked fun at such attitudes with considerable accuracy. There Hargrove's fictional Top Sergeant called his likeable but ne'er-do-well recruit "the boy who makes a top kick's life exciting! Hargrove the hopeless—the sloppy bunk on inspection day, the soap in the soup, the thorn in the side." Another superior says to Hargrove, "You're a born civilian, son. You're too fond of sitting up all night talking; you're too fond of sleeping late and eating at ungodly hours; you'll never be satisfied without a lot of fast action and civilian good times."[57]

The book speaks to a central truth—an army sprung from a democracy gestates slowly. One social scientist suggested that "to make a soldier out of the average free American citizen is not unlike domesticating a very wild species of animal." Coming from a culture that values individualism, American soldiers have traditionally balked at learning the discipline necessary in times of war. By the time the Japanese opened their offensive in April, the Fil-American army was already deficient in the "combat personality" necessary to sustain discipline. Such was "not easily achieved in a cultural group so traditionally individualistic and self-assertive as the Americans."[58]

During the American Civil War, armies both north and south overwhelmingly comprised volunteers sprung from "a political culture that celebrated personal autonomy and democracy." The men of Bataan shared with their grandfathers something of the same attitude toward authority. "Reared in a democratic society, undisciplined citizen soldiers were extremely sensitive to rank and behavior. Officers who took themselves too seriously or lorded it over their prewar friends and neighbors paid a high price for their conduct."[59]

The men who fought in the 1860s "depended on their own labor and judgment for survival, fostering confidence in their own decision-making ability. Accustomed to forming their own opinions about matters, and unaccustomed to regimentation or significant intrusions by government, their sense of independence proved both a boon and the bane of their military existence."⁶⁰ The soldier who fought on Bataan eighty years later was similar to his Civil War forebear in his essential civilian orientation. Like their nineteenth century counterparts, these men "considered themselves products of a fundamentally democratic society forced, against their will, to accommodate themselves to submit to the most undemocratic environment in defense of that society." Some soldiers managed this central contradiction better than others; many considered the term "democratic army" an oxymoron.⁶¹

The transformation necessary to accept the regimentation of military life, never complete, took time—the longer one served, presumably the more inured to the necessary discipline one would become. Most of the American soldiers on Bataan lacked the training of the men who later entered the service as part of a much better organized war effort. During the Civil War, a Union general might have been describing the problem on Bataan: "Discipline" he wrote, "is the basis of armies. Without it, they are but organized mobs. Men drawn suddenly from home, where liberty was the rule and license was its companion, and placed instantly under the stern control of martial authority, could not be expected to yield to restraint, without showing that change was irksome."⁶²

Whereas his Japanese counterpart left home committed to service to his emperor and with at least the tentative expectation of death, "American men had entered the war effortlessly accepting that home, the world they were leaving, was the only world, and that their military service would function solely as an intermission in their stateside lives."⁶³ They approached the war as a task to be performed, one that could be measured in finite terms. Few believed that the country was in any danger of conquest, so the motivation for fighting was to "get the war over with so that normal life could resume." This meant that

> except for the fact that the resumption of prewar life was contingent on successful completion of the war, it had no relation with anything that had gone before or would come after it. From this point of view, the war was simply a vast detour made from the main course of life in order to get back to that main (civilian) course again, and taking this detour could be regarded as an intelligible procedure only insofar as it was unavoidable.

The feeling of "I've done my part, now it's someone else's turn" was strong among those who had experienced any combat, stronger still among those who had experienced heavy fighting.⁶⁴

The War Department was not unaware of the problem. Section IV of the 1941 *Basic Field Manual* dealt with disciplinary exercises, defined as having "no particular value in physical development but are of great importance in instilling in the men that sense of discipline which is necessary for the efficient conduct of the physical training instruction." There was, of course, broad recognition that the individualistic tendencies of the American soldier had to be curbed in order to fight a successful war—especially against enemies that were assumed to be products of authoritarian societies. Indeed, every six months, an officer read and explained the Articles of War to enlisted men, who were then required to sign a paper stating that the contents were understood. One enlisted man recalled that the semiannual event "reinforced ... how few rights we had.... Enlisted men are not allowed by law to have their feelings hurt or their honor impugned."⁶⁵ In spite of such reminders to the rank-and-file, an official U.S. army report described a distinct lack of discipline among American recruits:

> The average enlistee was a youth of less than average education, to whom the security of pay, low as it was, and the routines of army life appealed more than the competitive struggles of civilian

life. Such men were resentful of their officers, the army's "remote upper class," and resisted the rote training, which many thought fit only for "nitwits."[66]

Such resentment, often justified, would bear bitter fruit on the Death March.

The wartime film offering *Bataan* acknowledges the issue of discipline in the American army, but it is camouflaged as a fundamental character flaw of the soldier Barney Todd, played by Lloyd Nolan. The foil to Robert Taylor's heroic Sergeant Dane, Todd is a man with a criminal past, mildly insubordinate and surly toward authority, at one point threatening desertion, at another bemoaning the fact that the command has been abandoned. Offered a chance to redeem himself, Todd refuses—setting up his just deserts. In the film's dénouement, only he and Dane are left alive, and in the final combat, Todd receives the wages of sin—a sword in the back at the hands of a Japanese soldier. Thus the film reconciles Todd's insubordination by showing him unrepentant, but with biblical justice served.

* * * * *

The reality in the Fil-American army was quite different. For most American soldiers, lack of discipline was not a character flaw, but a function of the chronological point in the war at which they found themselves. In August of 1944, in preparation for the invasion of Peleliu, E.B. Sledge recalled the intensification of training:

> We suffered through an increasing number of weapons and equipment inspections, work parties and petty clean-up details around the camp. The step-up in harassment, coupled with the constant discomforts and harsh living conditions of Pavuvu, drove us all into a state of intense exasperation and disgust with our existence before we embarked for Peleliu.

Yet Sledge recognized the value of his training, and later stated, "I doubt seriously whether I could have coped with the psychological and physical shock and stress encountered on Peleliu and Okinawa had it been otherwise.... Our commanders knew ... we must be trained realistically for it whether we liked it or not."[67]

By the summer of 1944 the U.S. had more than nine million men under arms, and American forces in the Pacific were considerably more battle-hardened, their leaders experienced in the demanding school of combat. American soldiers on Bataan had no such opportunity to undergo or appreciate the training and preparation Sledge described. Even as late as 1943, veterans of campaigns against the Japanese complained of the lack of realism in training, especially on attack procedures and countering infiltration tactics.[68] A year and a half earlier, the gap between training and actual combat yawned much larger. Bataan was America's first full scale battle, and its every feature had a distinctly ad-hoc flavor.

Ideally, training "was to be the process by which the soldier would learn, through forced subordination, that the individual was unimportant relative to the organization and would be persuaded, through daily chastening, that indiscipline would bring down on him penalties that ranged from annoying to life-altering." At this early stage of the war, however, soldiers' natural resistance to military discipline was far more difficult to overcome. One survivor, writing about Bilibad prison after the Death March, apprehended this central truth: "Under proper training and policy, good discipline will not break down—even among prisoners of war.... Our lack of discipline has contributed greatly to our being kicked around in the Philippines—before and after the surrender. But we never learn—we aren't a military people."[69]

Any people can be trained to be "military"; it simply takes time and applying the full weight of governmental authority.

One scans the scores of narratives left by Death March survivors for the boot camp bonding that is the staple of so many others. Many of the memoirs follow the pattern of a brief introduction describing family background and the circumstances of induction into the service, then a section on the Bataan campaign, then the bulk of the pages devoted to the experience of being a POW, followed by a brief section on homecoming. This format leaves little room for descriptions of heart-felt friendships formed in boot camp, because many did not go to boot camp, or only experienced desultory training.

Standing units in the Philippines could not expect the recruits that swelled their ranks to have had much, if any, substantial training before arrival in the islands. Oliver Allen's experience was typical of the men who joined the army in 1940 and 1941. He remembered that his nine weeks of basic training consisted mostly of KP duty, cleaning, assembling and disassembling his rifle, and "a lot of marching to base headquarters to take aptitude tests." By war's outbreak the 31st Infantry Regiment comprised two thirds draftees: "With hardly four months in the army, they were simply processed through a reception station in the States and sent to the Philippines to be trained."[70]

Clemens Kathman remembered rising at six for "fifteen minutes of strenuous exercise, then "the remainder of the morning doing close-order drills in the sun and wind and rocks.... Up and down, back and forth we marched over a newly constructed drill field." The afternoons brought relief in the form of listening to various lectures, learning about his weapons, and driving different army vehicles." After, he enjoyed going to the P.X., drinking beer and playing ping-pong during the balance of his thirteen weeks of basic training.[71]

Ninety-nine men from Janesville, Wisconsin, and Maywood, Illinois, constituted a National Guard unit, the 192nd Tank Company. Training while in the Guard consisted of one day a week, with occasional weekends. Lewis Wallisch remembered that the unit had a social club of sorts, an "invitation only" group whose main activities were drinking, playing cards, smoking, and other vices." Most of these men had never fired their tank weapons, but they knew enough to comment on the rivets holding their vehicle together—welded seams would not have blown apart as readily upon impact.[72]

The War Department's *Basic Field Manual* of March 6, 1941, stated, "A man does not become an effective soldier simply by taking an oath and donning a uniform. The transformation from civilian to soldier is accomplished by training, and it is not complete until the man develops those qualities which characterize the trained soldier."[73] The reality of training could not remotely approximate this stated ideal; unlike his Japanese enemy, at this early stage in the war the American soldier was, in relative terms, both poorly trained and poorly equipped.

The historian of the 31st Regiment states that the unit's level of preparedness at the start of the war was "abysmally low." In the decade before the war started, Americans stationed in the islands "performed their duties on [a] ... half-day schedule." Once annually the regiment engaged in "firing practice and field training" and with the same frequency performed a field exercise to practice the defense of Manila in case of attack. "Classes on soldier skills were usually held in the shade of palm and mimosa trees in the park around Manila's walled city to fend off the oppressive heat. Once a month, companies took a 15-mile forced march with full field pack."[74]

Early attempts at training suggest the chaos associated with quickly making an army from a civilian population. For the recruits of 1941, clothes and equipment were in such short supply, some draftees actually reported for duty in civilian clothes and began their military training "in black and white shoes." Men milled about without direction at Barksdale field in Shreveport, Louisiana, where James Bollich remembered the "parade ground was mass confusion. New recruits were coming in every day and did not know where to go. Even those that had been here before could not remember what group they were in or who their drill sergeant was."

In those early months, Bollich refused drilling with near impunity: "When the first sergeant would tell recruits to report to the parade ground for drill, [he] would just sneak off to the PX or wander around." After three weeks he finally got a uniform, and after a month, he finally reported to his sergeant who, in the confusion, was none the wiser. Marching and drilling were the goals of Bollich's first four weeks of training, but he only did either for a week and a half. One veteran remembered a twenty kilometer hike ending in interesting chaos. The soldiers finished on the beach of Manila, plunged in and several were immediately stung by large man-o-war jellyfish. Some thirty were taken sick with the telltale blotches, and two nearly died.[75]

When the battle was joined, an army that was already struggling to establish a coherent identity saw its pre-war organization shattered even further. The initial Japanese attack had almost entirely destroyed the air force on the ground, leaving hundreds of men untrained as infantry with nowhere else to go but the front lines. army Air Corps personnel, without even the rudimentary basic training of the men in ground units, were rapidly converted to infantry, and during the fighting it was not uncommon for AAC people to be confused about basic tasks such as routine cleaning of weapons and jams. Training such men as foot soldiers was an on-the-job affair of the most challenging kind. Preston J. Hubbard recalled:

> Since my Company and the other groups similarly attached to Air Force Headquarters were considered non-combatant, the principle mission of the training was to teach those unassigned men, whose only firearms training had been in the use of the .45 caliber automatic handgun, how to handle .30 caliber rifles and machine guns. The infantry training was highly contrived if not a farce, and the trainees became the butt of jokes.[76]

Each division now contained personnel untrained to fight as riflemen, men from cannibalized administrative and service units. Even those men considered as trained infantry included thousands of civilians whose first military service came on Bataan.

Airmen and technicians, usually thirty- to thirty-five years old, no longer needed for planes destroyed on the ground or had long since stopped flying, were converted to infantry and sent on patrols after a few days' training. Many of these *ersatz* soldiers went into combat raw, and wounds to the buttocks were common until trained to keep their entire bodies low. Sergeant Jack Bradley remembered that some "had never fired a gun. Sometimes when I took twenty men on a night combat patrol, I was more afraid of the probable accidents with our own men than I was of the Japs." J.D. Merritt "caught a couple of guys peering down the business end of the gun's barrel, checking to see if it was loaded." He concluded, "it was plain we had a big job ahead, teaching the knot-heads how to kill Japs rather than themselves or their instructors."[77]

When Japanese planes began bombing, James Bollich and his company ran blindly, half-dressed into the jungle, and plunged headlong off a cliff into briar patch. The next day they were panicked at a report of Japanese paratroops landing, but when they looked up they saw only "large puffs of smoke" left by the discharge of the anti-aircraft guns. Duly chastened, he admitted, "We still had a lot to learn."[78]

* * * * *

By the end of the second year of the war, especially in the Pacific, "there was virtual unanimity about the superiority of American arms. Early in 1944, almost all soldiers polled believed that "American equipment was better than that of the enemy." In large measure due to their confidence in their equipment, members of a "powerful, well-equipped and well-supplied army—and of a nation that had never experienced military defeat—American soldiers rarely if ever entertained serious doubts about ultimate victory."[79]

The bounty of the wartime American economy was staggering. By 1945 the U.S. had fielded an army of twelve million men:

> Hauling enough sugar for every American serviceman to sweeten his or her morning beverage with a teaspoon of sugar would have tied up two thirty-ton boxcars.... Rivers of machines, tools, weapons and other equipment, from silk parachutes to bulldozers, flowed into the camps to outfit America's legions for battle. To cite but two examples, U.S. factories turned out more than a quarter million artillery pieces (exclusive of anti-aircraft guns) and 2.4 million motor trucks of myriad varieties. Every radar set, LST, and machine gun produced was testament to American industrial might."

The historian William Manchester once observed, "There was something disconcerting about a country which could field an army of twelve million men, fight two awesome empires at the same time, build a Navy larger than the combined fleets of its enemies and its allies— and still record a 20 percent increase in civilian spending over 1939."[80] Few would challenge the notion that American industrial strength and organizational prowess, given time, simply overwhelmed its Axis adversaries. Yet the size of the task facing the nation in 1942 was almost beyond comprehension—fighting two dangerously aggressive empires in different hemispheres, across thousands of miles of oceans with undreamed-of logistical challenges. Eventually the effort would involve the participation of some sixteen million American servicemen, the larger portion of which was drafted.

Much later in the war, American soldiers complained bitterly about aspects of domestic production that threatened their survival—including lapses of concentration on the assembly line resulting in matériel defects, and labor strikes that curtailed production. If the occasional artillery charge or grenade failed to perform as labeled in 1944, two years earlier it was quite common.[81] Soldiers training in the fall of 1941 had none of this bounty to hand. Shortages of ammunition and various equipment in the Philippines plagued the army, but "units in the States were worse off, using stove pipes as mortars, trucks made to look like tanks, and ordinary flour used to mark shell or bomb hits on those 'tanks.'"

Ties to the past persisted. In 1941 the army was in the process of shifting from the old 1903 Springfield rifle, a five round, single action weapon, to a new rifle, the Garand, which was semi-automatic and could fire nine rounds. Many old-timers refused the new weapon, so that they actually learned the new one while in combat. Many Filipinos carried the older weapon. Other equipment was often rusted and far out of date. One member of an anti-aircraft unit complained, "If we could have had the right ammunition, there would have been a helluva lot more planes shot down. The ammunition we had was all corroded. After you took the corrosion off, a lot of them had holes in the casings and you couldn't use them." It was inaccurate because it was "so damn old."[82]

Men of the 31st Infantry fired machine guns without ammunition, "using orange crates to simulate firing"—a soldier would sit on the crate, moving a target until the soldier with the unloaded rifle sighted the target and called out," hardly an exercise that inspired marksmanship. Richard Gordon recalled that his first grenade pitch in combat nearly killed him. Other units struggled as mightily to learn the art of war. Drew Bond described a unit that

> fired rocks for ammunition and shouted "bang." Santana Romero's battery had a gun but no ammunition. "I fed .50 caliber ammunition from the First World War to that .73 millimeter gun. Didn't work." Not one man ever fired a 37-mm shell until the day the war began, A garden hose leashed to the .50-calibers, in an attempt to train the gunners to lead aircraft, failed: the crude model slid too rapidly down the guide wire, and the water flow hit consistently behind the target.

One thoroughly exasperated soldier spoke for many: "Equipment and weaponry were pathetic. Soldiers trained with drainpipes for antitank guns, stovepipes for mortar tubes, and brooms for rifles. Money was short, and little guns were cheaper than big ones; no guns were cheapest of all."[83]

During the actual fighting, some Americans corroborated such penury. When mortars were fired in combat, one report claimed that "20 out of 25 shells failed to detonate on impact." Such equipment failures produced lighter moments, at least for some. Another American observed the same, a mortar shell dud rate of 70 percent, which "so amused the Japanese that they yelled with laughter when it was fired at them."[84] Grenades provided additional amusement to the enemy—a private named Garleb claimed to have thrown fourteen at the Japanese, but only seven exploded. Some claimed that the only reliable use for a hand grenade was fishing, "they were too unreliable to risk on an armed enemy." At least one Japanese agreed, recording in his diary that he feared being hit by grenades as projectiles more than their explosions.[85] With some dark humor, Sgt. Earl Walk recalled the failure rate of faulty mortar rounds, and hoped that duds would "hit Japs on the head. I believe one on the head would put anyone out of action."[86]

The Filipinos fighting alongside received the army's detritus. R.W. Volckman remembered the condition of his Filipino soldiers, barefoot, a mishmash of military and civilian clothes, no helmets, and their equipment, to say the least, problematic. More than 500 of the rifles in his command had broken extractors, causing the men to carry pieces of bamboo used to push out expended cartridges after firing." For this innovation, and for its use of bamboo for many other purposes—beds, shelters and implements—the Filipino force became known as the "bamboo army."[87]

During the siege, a Minnesota congressmen introduced a bill to pay Bataan defenders time-and-a-half for overtime, double wages for fighting on Sunday; when the men heard the bitter joke, they calculated that they'd rather have the planes their wages would buy. Surveying Ed Dyess's one remaining P-40 plane, one wag wrote a brief note to FDR: "Dear Mr. President: Please send us another P-40. The one we have is all shot up."[88]

*****

Other fault lines plagued the Allied force on Bataan. Four months before surrender, two American officers, returning from distributing prophylactics to a medic stationed with prostitutes, stopped at a restaurant for a drink. One of the men ordered a beer and began eating what he believed were peanuts. Perhaps summarizing his attitudes towards things Filipino, he remarked that "the place was hot, the beer was terrible and the peanuts stale." The Filipino proprietor responded that he did not serve peanuts; the American had instead consumed fried grasshoppers. He immediately spat out insect and drink and fled. Americans were surprised that sometimes Filipino coffee came "fortified with ants, spiders, and other creatures," and one veteran of a Filipino meal recoiled as he was offered pig's blood, "curdled and turned brown somehow, and full of some stuff that was probably tripe."[89]

More than purely culinary considerations separated Filipinos and Americans. An American in the 34th Pursuit Squadron who had mastered some Tagalog once said to a group of Filipinos helping his mess crew: *Sabis salita sulang su gawa* (There is much fine talk but little work). They withdrew immediately, Gage said, "distrusting my knowledge of their language." Language was indeed a serious issue. The utility of English was clear when dealing with the Philippine Scouts, a hard-hitting, professional combat unit widely respected by U.S. soldiers. These men often spent more than twenty years in uniform, after which they continued to live on U.S. army bases. One admiring American stated, "These men excelled in every combat situation," typical words of praise.[90]

Americans learned quickly that Filipinos responded to hissing. One recalled, "Holler 'Hey' all day long and get no results. Just say Ssssst and 38 people will turn and look at you." After securing their listeners' attention, however, problems began. Fundamental language problems interfered with unit cohesion and general communication. Tagalog had not been designated the national language until 1937, and in any event it mattered little, since it was spoken mostly by inhabitants of central Luzon, with dozens of other dialects represented in the typical unit. English, spoken to some extent by perhaps a quarter of the Filipino soldiers, often was the only alternative.[91] R.W. Volckman, taking command of the 11th Philippine Infantry, encountered severe language difficulties. His regiment comprised men from a mountain tribe (Igorots) and lowlanders (Ilocanos and Cagayanos), among whom no fewer than eleven dialects were spoken. In one machine gun company, an American captain complained that he faced five different dialects. Even native officers fluent in Tagalog struggled to communicate in this linguistic potpourri.[92]

When English would not do, Americans and Filipinos alike faced the daunting task of communication across multiple language barriers. Each of the nine Filipino divisions had forty American officers and twenty non-coms assigned to it. Barking Non-coms sometimes found their orders being translated several times before they were intelligible to all under their command. In one typical infantry regiment, "there were more than 11 dialects spoken"; in one "company of less than 100 men, five different dialects were spoken." Overcoming the language barrier did not guarantee smooth operation—American ROTC officers, often with only a few months in country, were often assigned as instructors in Filipino units, and Filipino officers with more experience and sometimes higher rank often greeted them with resentment.[93]

Communication between Americans and Filipinos who spoke dozens of dialects was difficult, and solved by the linguistic expediency of simplicity, the word *quan* supplying a

> weak vocabulary with a handy word. Joining the famous marine gizmo, the new American quan will aid you immensely when you want to say thingamajig, doomaflagit, or whatchamacallit. And ... like the GI's can make an entire conversation unintelligible to the laymen with: "Whatcha

These resolute faces belie the tension that often existed between U.S. and Filipino allies (Library of Congress).

quanning in that quan, Joe? Smells very quan. Hows about sharing some quan with me?" Translated, this means, "What are you cooking in that tin can, Joe? It smells very delicious. How about sharing some food with me?"[94]

Yet a few shared words did little to hide deeper tensions.

The U.S. established rule of the islands after the Spanish American War of 1898, and the subsequent years saw the promise of home rule, but only its very gradual introduction. In the army, Filipino recruits (Filipino Scouts) were segregated in their own separate contingents, initially commanded by U.S. officers. Tension over differential treatment of American and Filipino soldiers climaxed in 1936, when six hundred Filipinos mutinied over the denial of equal pay and treatment; equality was never granted. Low-level tension continued during the Bataan campaign, when in February a Filipino officer swam from Bataan to Corregidor to warn of the tension between Filipinos and Americans. Quezon received a clear message: "We feel we should have the same rations as the Americans" and "We eat only salmon and sardines. One can per day for thirty men, twice a day."[95]

The Pacific War Memorial on the island of Corregidor is dedicated to Filipino and U.S. war dead. At one end is a sculpture representation of an eternal flame, in the center a dome with an opening in the top that focuses a sunbeam at the exact center at high noon. In front is a twice life-sized statue of a U.S. soldier helping a wounded Filipino comrade whose left hand has been amputated, on whose pedestal is engraved,

> They died for freedom's right and in
> Heaven's sight theirs was a noble cause

Such solidarity was as much a function of imagination as of reality.

Americans often referred to their Filipino allies in less than flattering terms. One American named McVey, describing the rank-and-file of the PA, spoke for many: "They just couldn't take the guff that you had to take when you were fighting a war. I remember we'd issue them shoes and pretty soon they had sold them and were marching along barefoot.... Most of that regular army was undependable." Sometimes when placed in the front lines, Filipinos would simply move to the rear. When asked for an explanation, they claimed to be the "sole survivor" of their unit.[96] Derogatory names abounded, PA standing for "paper army" among the most widely circulated.

The Fil-American army, with the exception of the Philippine Scouts, a well-trained nucleus of excellent infantry, was poorly trained and poorly equipped, spoke a bewildering variety of languages, and comprised a large contingent of illiterate peasants from the provinces. Officers were sometimes as ignorant of contemporary military practice as their men; "An American advisor once asked a Filipino officer to order his men to dig foxholes, and the Filipino, out of earshot, turned to a subordinate and whispered, 'What is a foxhole?'" One American colonel believed that Filipino soldiers were good for two things, saluting officers and demanding three meals a day. Appalled at the lack of training of the average Filipino, he lamented, "They were the people we had to take into battle."[97]

Such untoward disdain for the Filipino soldiers, most of whom had received scant training, was widespread, and was based on a healthy dose of racism, and the pervasive notion that Filipinos were a "peaceful" people, unsuited to warfare. New Mexican Guardsmen found Filipino soldiers to be "willing but untrained field workers. They'd never worn shoes. They knotted the laces and carried them around their necks.... Half didn't know which end of a damned rifle a bullet came out of. We used 'em to relay ammunition. They'd just stop—'But Joe, I'm tired'—and they'd run off and take a nap."

The culture gap could be potentially lethal. Richard Mallonee reported an ugly incident, an American officer slapping a Filipino subordinate over a promotion dispute. Afterward, the American had to be transferred "to save his life from the enraged men in his battalion. A slapping incident was considered a blood insult to be avenged ... there was a real danger that one of them might have shot [him] in the back." An American doctor with access to the morgue in Manila expressed perhaps the most extreme and revolting disrespect for his Filipino allies. At one point he brought home several Filipino bodies and made "a standing ashtray out of the bones of one body, using the foot, the leg and the skull (hollowing out the top for a glass ash-tray insert); and then he had used the skin of a woman's body ... to make wristwatch bands."[98]

As Americans criticized Filipinos for their amateurish attempts at soldiering, so in North Africa eight months later did the British characterize the Americans. One disappointed Brit claimed that "Americans were frivolous about the war—gifted amateurs." By February 1943, British soldiers, frustrated at American combat behavior, "began referring to American soldiers collectively as 'Alice.'" British General Alexander stated the opinion of many: "My main anxiety is the poor fighting value of the Americans. They simply do not know their job as soldiers and this is the case from the highest to the lowest.... Perhaps the weakest link of all is the junior leader, who just does not lead, with the result that their men don't really fight."[99]

These criticisms were not unfounded. One journalist who had spent time with American combat troops assessed them somewhat ingloriously: "The faults were clear enough ... a certain indiscipline of mind; a tendency toward exaggeration.... Men neglected camouflage because it might smack of over anxiety. Men failed to dig slit trenches because the work was hard." During one action in February 1943, some "were not fighting at all. Most were befuddled and frightened" and at the battle of Kasserine Pass, one commander was alarmed at his soldiers leaving the line on "various pretexts," forcing him to empower the "regimental bandleader to form firing squads if necessary to keep the lines intact." At the end of 1942, a war department report concluded that

> the German army makes war better than we are now making it.... The enemy is regarded as the visiting team, and this is not a major game. Even units suffering heavy casualties did not evince hatred for the enemy.... Both officers and men are psychologically unprepared for war.

Another report cited junior officers' failure to lead their men adequately, "evidenced by the comparatively large proportion of casualties among field officers who have to supply the impetus to their juniors to move forward."[100]

As Japanese bombs fell on Pearl Harbor, some American officers were playing polo, the match refereed by Jonathan Wainwright. Though Lieutenant Edward Ramsey's team lost to the Manila Polo Club, he and the other players showered after their chukker and changed into white dress uniforms for a post-match party, "a raucous affair, rife with liquor and the slender Filipino girls who seemed always magically to appear." Ramsey's evening fun included slipping away with another officer and two girls into nearby rice paddies, where they enjoyed a few hours "cool and comfortable with alcohol and the women." Such was the pre-war life of many. Prewar circumstances bred "mental stagnation, reverence for routine, parochialism—and indifference." After the army's rapid expansion, some "proved unequal to the complex, deadly demands of modern war."[101]

Many of the men who guided their ponies in peacetime proved unfit as combat leaders. Doubtless during the battle the vetting process manifested itself in uncomfortable ways, with officers weeded out, others stepping up to command by force of character.

> Some Americans were able men, clearheaded practitioners of the profession of arms, but the officer corps on Bataan was also filled with men who either were not ready for battle or were simply afraid of it. Many of the junior officers and sergeants seemed to know nothing of the basics of fighting.... And some senior majors and colonels weren't much better. Enervated by age or illness, or just plain frozen with fear, several were caught cowering in their command posts.[102]

John Olson, adjutant of Camp O'Donnell, later wrote, "the bulk of the officers and non-commissioned officers were reservists whose field training had been brief and almost devoid of instruction in matter that would have better prepared them to cope with the rigors of combat and the subsequent incarceration."[103]

Perhaps in recognition of such callow officer material, the *Basic Field Manual* had specific instructions for officers. In order to develop the "command voice" it deemed essential for the necessary gravitas, the manual intoned, "this voice would come from the chest, with the relevant muscles relaxed, the mouth fully opened, with "the assistance of the proper use of the tongue, teeth and lips," with sufficient volume to fit the occasion." Practice involved inhaling in preparation to "utter the word 'hong' moderately loud ... for 3 or 4 seconds" after which the same process was used with the word "kong." Then the young officers were encouraged to gradually increase their volume and substitute the "words 'singsong' and 'dingdong,'" so recommended because "they are simple, easily remembered, and because the sounds required in uttering them adapt themselves best in bringing out the intent of the instruction."[104]

Some, not having absorbed such instruction, simply gave up and could not be bothered. At the moment of surrender, Sam Moody recalled an officer telling a group that the Japanese now had what they wanted,

> "and we'll go back home and mind our business like we should. The hell with these Asiatics anyway. We had no goddam right in the Philippines in the first place. I'm sick of this freaken war." A private asked about escape to the hills, and the officer replied, "What the hell for? ... Let somebody else carry it now. We've had our share. I feel like resting the war in a prison camp."

Unimpressed with this style of leadership, one of his listeners responded, "Go blow it out of your ass, Captain." The officer threatened court-martial as the men laughed at him.[105]

Early in the nation's history, the father of West Point concluded, "To make a good army out of the best men will take three years." The majority of young Americans "bound for Africa in October 1942 had been in the army less than three years, some for less than three months.... Indeed they were not an army at all, but a hodgepodge of units cobbled together." Nine months after the surrender on Bataan, during the actions in North Africa in December 1942, little "cohesion obtained among allied formations or even between American units. They had fought not as an army, but as a disjointed confederation. Neither leaders nor the led had yet proven themselves, despite flashes of competence and many acts of valor."[106] American armies on both sides of the world in 1942 had equal difficulty as they groped toward effectiveness.

* * * * *

Richard Mallonee stated, "Much has been written about the Death March. There have been accounts of atrocities, of massacres, and of men buried alive. I will not say they were not true, but, in the main, the horror of the death march resulted from the physical condition of the men forced to make it." Mallonee's observations and others like it shift the focus somewhat from Japanese cruelty to the inevitable results of a wearing campaign of three months, during which the men's physical condition was diminished by exhaustion, malaria, and the approaching starvation that half rations since January had only partially forestalled. One survivor spoke for most when he described the "deplorable state" of the army; General Wainwright, upon assuming command after MacArthur fled, estimated that his army's combat efficiency was no greater than 20 percent.[107]

Though there was a lull in the fighting from mid–February until early April, the Allied army was frequently under aerial attack, and supplies of food and medicine were dwindling rapidly. Under such conditions, "no motivational structure was adequate to sustain the average soldier in stress of combat indefinitely. It became an axiom that 'Every man has his breaking point.' To win a war ... it was sufficient that men hold out long enough and fight well enough to keep organized and effective armies in the field."[108]

Because of MacArthur's ill-conceived defense strategy that forced the abandonment of huge amounts of supplies, soldiers on the front lines began feeling the pinch of hunger soon after the campaign commenced. Carl Ruse recorded that in February, "the last horses and mules of the 26th Cavalry ... were slaughtered for food. One of the last rations drawn for one unit was "nine medium-sized cans of Salmon and forty-five pounds of musty red rice" that had to feed 175 men."[109] A Filipino soldier, asked how many days it had been since he had eaten, replied, "Three days, sir. Yesterday, today and tomorrow."[110] The soldiers were running out of everything edible. "Lot's wife" (salt), "sweetening compound" (sugar), "cat beer" (milk), "dogfat" (butter), "blood" (ketchup), "Georgia ice cream" (hominy grits), and "punk" (bread) were all vanishing, with no re-supply possible.

The army had been on half rations since early January, and caloric intake declined from 2,000 calories that month to 1,500 during February, and 1,000 during March, even though energy output was estimated at 3,500 to 4,000 calories per man per day. Muscle atrophy, beriberi in conjunction with malnutrition landed thousands in the hospital. Many of those sufferers had malaria, and the inadequate supply of quinine could not stem 500 daily malarial admissions; by April, 1,000 cases were being reported. Recovery was painfully slow due to food and drug shortages, and when the force finally surrendered, the Japanese found more than 12,000 patients in the area hospitals.

The last cavalry horse was slaughtered for food in late March, prompting one officer wag to remark, "So you might say we had eaten our cavalry and had it, too." Mules and carabao had gone before, no doubt without the inverted aphorism; one unit received a single mule's head for eighty-seven men. Under such conditions heartbreaking incidents abounded. In one case, 2,000 quarters of frozen carabao spoiled because the barge carrying it from Corregidor docked in harbor overnight due to a Japanese bombing raid. The following morning, the food was "in such bad condition that even the usual practice of cutting off the green putrid part with its clinging maggots and using the remainder was impossible."[111]

In soldiers' parlance, "riding the sickbook" meant feigning illness to escape duty, but few needed to resort to that ploy as the campaign dragged on. By the end of March, men were streaming into Bataan's two hospitals, where they were laid outside, the cots under canvass long since having been occupied with other sufferers. Gums bleeding from dietary deficiency, they asked for food, many having lost as much as thirty pounds. Few would challenge the "Surgeon of Luzon Force Report," a detailed description of the medical condition of the American force on Bataan from January to April 1942. Its salient conclusions were that "the defensive combat efficiency of the Luzon Force had been reduced more that 75 percent during the final weeks ... due to malnutrition, avitaminosis, malaria and intestinal infections and infestations." Those remaining on duty were physically enervated, and malnutrition had become a serious problem. By March the entire force was "deteriorating rapidly" and by April, little combat efficiency remained.[112]

One surgeon's monologue with himself conveys something of the poignancy of the situation as catastrophe and defeat approached:

> What's the use of trying to save that leg? He'll be a cripple all his life.... Take it off. How would you like to be one-legged at twenty? Give him a chance. Put it in traction. Look at these goddamn worms crawling out of the gut. I wish I were fishing in the Chattahoochee ... I'm sick of this. This skull is thick as a gorilla's I wish we had some electric drills. Jesus, my hands are tired. You killed that last guy fumbling around in his chest. He was on his way out before he got to the

table. Why didn't you leave him alone? He was bleeding. Why didn't you stop it? I couldn't find the God damn bleeding vessel. That's what I thought. You killed him! You killed him!¹¹³

Melville Jacoby, covering the Bataan campaign for *Time* and *Life*, reported at one point that surgeons found interesting objects inside their mangled patients. To the apparent shame of those who had opposed trade embargo on Japan, it was said that "pieces of Ford cars and, on one occasion, a Singer sewing machine screw-driver" were extracted from American bodies.¹¹⁴ Two years later in his poem "Plato Told," e. e. cummings noted that "it took a nipponized bit of the old sixth avenue el in the top of his head" for the short-sightedness of selling scrap metal to Japan to sink in.

While actual disease was widespread, patients seeking admission to hospitals, but diagnosed simply as malingerers, rose as high as 25 percent. Keeping a finger, medical or otherwise, in the rapidly leaking dike was increasingly impossible. On the eve of surrender, the medical officer Ralph Hibbs noted a "minor epidemic of self-inflicted wounds." Several sat, he recalled, "starry-eyed GIs in the dirt holding a boot in one hand and a bloody foot in the other. Their eyes were downcast and tearful."¹¹⁵

The mental toll was also substantial. The report noted that by the end of the campaign, Filipino soldiers increasingly appeared in rear areas, having discarded their weapons and equipment, and they could not be induced to return to the front. Even the rear provided limited relief, as it was "impossible to relieve front line troops and send them to quiet areas in the rear for rest periods. There was no quiet area in Bataan, due to incessant enemy bombing and strafing."¹¹⁶ Administrative consensus held that the "average GI could withstand between 200 and 240 days in combat" but infantrymen on the line decried this as a "grotesque exaggeration," claiming that symptoms of dysfunction appeared as early as a fortnight after entering combat. In the European theater, a pair of psychologists discovered that "after the 30th day in combat, the soldier's effectiveness began to decline precipitously, and by the 45th day ... soldiers ... were close to a vegetative state." Fully 25 percent of medical evacuations throughout the war were neuropsychiatric, a figure collaborated on Bataan. Many officers, seeing their men at close range, readily identified "fatigue of troops from being in combat too long" as having the worst effect on combat effectiveness.¹¹⁷ Yet American soldiers on Bataan endured more than 100 days in a combat zone with no hope of relief.

Many accounts of combat emphasize the process of gradual numbing that soldiers facing combat undergo, and circumstances on Bataan drove men to this state even before the ordeal of the march began. Mental breakdown and nervous collapse were not uncommon—"at the onset, inattention: then behavior more and more robotic; then the vacant look.... Without medical intervention, such signs presaged crackups of striking variety: spastic tremors; the inane repetition of words or phrases; amnesia; infantile regression; paroxysms of crying, laughing, shrieking, and so on." The men fighting on Bataan had no such luxury. An older man in the 200th Regiment of the 31st Division found himself talking to a distraught younger recruit: "One boy came in one night scared to death. The older man reassured him, but a half hour later the boy killed himself. Others simply fled, unable to stand the strain. Members of the 200th regiment recalled that an officer and a sergeant "stole food and deserted to the hills to save their own necks."¹¹⁸

In the weeks preceding surrender, the Fil-American army's efficiency was reduced a full 75 percent from disease, malnutrition and fatigue. Rest was impossible due to daily bombing and artillery attacks. One anti-aircraft battery, not unrepresentative of the general plight, could muster only nineteen healthy men from its original contingent of 100. Tired men were unable to perform even routine tasks on time or at all. What discipline remained began to crumble as stomachs ached—poor inspection procedures led to hijacking of supplies, activity that neither MPs or orders from above could curtail. One survivor spoke for most when he described the "deplorable state" of the army.[119] Deplorable it was, but for many reasons. A comparison to the American military experience in North Africa, begun fully eight months after the surrender on Bataan, highlights the significantly greater problems the American force in the Philippines faced.

From November 1942 until May 1943, the American army learned hard lessons in the school of combat. Whether in the sands of North Africa or the jungles of Bataan, soldiers had to be blooded, learn their necessary skills while under enemy fire, and make the transition from civilian attitudes to the discipline and organization required for military success.

Contact with the enemy did its inevitable job of sorting the competent from the less competent, the steady from the cowardly, those who could adapt their sensibilities to the job at hand, and those who failed to apprehend the nature of the challenges they faced. As the campaign in North Africa unfolded, it became increasingly clear that the "engine of an enemy's destruction could be built only by effectively integrating forces that ranged from industrial capacity to national character to educational systems that produced men able to organize global war." This was the site "where the prodigious weight of American industrial might began to tell, where brute strength emerged as the most conspicuous feature of the allied arsenal."[120]

Along the sanguinary path of discovery American soldiers "learned the importance of terrain, of combined arms, of aggressive patrolling, of stealth.... They now knew what it was like to be bombed, shelled, and machine-gunned, and to fight on. They provided Eisenhower with a blooded hundred thousand, 'high grade stock'" with which to fight the war in Sicily, and on the continent of Europe.[121] Progress toward working out each of these key elements took time and 70,000 casualties, but even after seven months of operations, the U.S. army in North Africa was far from the seasoned instrument that eventually overwhelmed its enemies. At the end of the campaign, General Omar Bradley, hardly an inexperienced observer, believed that his soldiers were still "unwilling to close with the enemy." The historian Eric Larrabee went further, noting that North Africa was "a place to be lousy in, somewhere to let the gift for combat and command be discovered."[122] Seven months of trial and error revealed the gift in sufficient quality to continue the struggle against the Axis in Europe. There was time, and the requisite support in the form of the "Europe first" policy to work out each of the essential elements to a substantial degree.

The situation in the Pacific was quite different. American forces there—Wake Island, Guam—fell like dominoes before the tidal wave of Japanese aggression during the hundred days of advance. The Fil-American army that faced the Japanese in 1941 and early 1942 had none of the advantages, if such a term can be used, that obtained in North Africa. By the time "Operation Reservist" landed on the African coast in November 1942, Americans captured on Bataan had been languishing in Japanese prisons for some seven months, and they had been in combat nearly a year before any American soldier on land in the Atlantic theater fired his first shots.

In both locations American soldiers faced an enemy far more experienced and battle-tested, but beyond this the resemblance ceased. The army in North Africa had to learn to coordinate effort with its English-speaking British allies; on Bataan Americans faced a substantial language barrier. In North Africa Americans remained relatively well-supplied throughout the campaign; on Bataan rations were cut in half four months before surrender and were reduced further as time wore on. In North Africa Americans faced a relatively manageable climate; on Bataan rampant disease destroyed whatever fighting qualities the force began with. The U.S. had had another eight months to plan and execute a large-scale operation, but the salient difference, of course, was that Americans, in spite of the shortcomings their effort betrayed in leadership, organization and tactics, were victorious in North Africa and did not have to endure a Death March.

* * * * *

If the American host in North Africa was an army at dawn, the one in the Philippines was born and extinguished in predawn darkness. Cut off and alone, it fought a determined

Appearing just two days after the fall of Bataan, this drawing shows Secretary of War Henry Stimson frankly admitting the nature of the debacle. Though they agreed with his analysis, few survivors felt their sacrifice was appreciated after the war's end (Library of Congress).

Japanese enemy long before industrial might could be marshaled and deployed. It wrestled with problems of integration both internally and with its large Filipino component; its corpus comprised an often unhappy combination of the remnants of an "old army" and the first, often ill-trained draftees of 1941. The nation was just rousing after the attack on Pearl Harbor, and none of the mechanisms that swung clumsily into place in North Africa could be brought to bear in the Philippines.

J.D. Merritt, still nonplussed a half century after the debacle, asked readers of his book, *Adapt or Die*, "In your wildest imagination, can you believe the U.S. army would send raw troops into battle against a superior, veteran force, battle-hardened after years of fighting in China with ... inadequate training and weaponry?"[123] The answer was as simple as it was unfortunate for those caught in this early war maelstrom—the campaign, doomed from the start, was fought with the army on hand—a far flung force, already in parts opposed to each other before the grinding campaign of nearly four months took its inevitable toll.

As he pondered surrender and its consequences, John Sewall turned to his bible in February and found a comforting verse from the book of Psalms: "A thousand shall fall at thy side, and ten thousand at thy right hand, but it shall not come nigh thee."[124] Such verses offered no protection from what was to come. As much as anything, good fortune or bad would determine his experience, and that of his broken army, after the surrender.

4

Chaos Meets *Kata*

No one is so brave that he is not disturbed by something unexpected.—Julius Caesar

 All societies define their tolerance for disorder according to their environmental and cultural imperatives, and each has its way of ordering proper behavior for individuals. In Japan, geography and cultural heritage have combined to favor the importance of *kata*—or form, a fixed way of behaving. For Japanese, vulnerable to nature's violence, inured to the demands of cooperative labor, and subject to a heritage of strict authoritarian rule, *kata* became a centrally defining feature of their island experience. More than other peoples, the Japanese came to believe that form has a reality of its own, sometimes even taking precedence over substance. Individuals in Japan faced, and continue to face, enormous pressure to conform to fixed patterns of behavior, and the resulting *Weltanschauung* has defined their relationships to each other and to the outside world in profoundly important ways.

 Subject to the demands of myriad specific patterns of behavior in their own culture, speaking a language that prizes using correct form according to specific context, the Japanese are often as unable as they are unwilling to deal with foreigners without significant trauma. Four decades after the fall of Bataan, nearly two thirds of the Japanese population expressed unwillingness to have any contact with foreigners. Such discomfort stems in large measure because foreign behavior is, according to Japanese lights, unpredictable. For Japanese, the unexpected is particularly unwelcome.

 The emphasis on *kata* suggests that deviation from a fixed standard is unacceptable, even immoral. As a result, individuals encountering the truly unfamiliar and unexpected are left very much at sea, the rules that guide behavior in Japan with often hair-splitting precision rendered irrelevant. Knowing that their soldiers were heading into the unknown, Imperial army Headquarters, quite literally, armed their common soldiers with a guide, a text with twelve chapters called *Kore dake Yomeba Ware wa Kateru* (*Read This and the War Is Won*). The guide was written in a simple style, so as to be "understood by all ranks," and was "designed to be read quickly, without strain, in the cramped quarters of a transport vessel." Easily carried into battle, it summarized the "military, ideological and economic aspects" of the campaign in South and Southeast Asia.

 The booklet was intended to render the unfamiliar knowable, to prepare the soldier for circumstances and events beyond his Japanese experience. Here he read descriptions of the physical environment he would encounter, its people, climate and resources. He was warned not to die of disease ("To fall in a hail of bullets is to meet a hero's death, but there is no glory in dying of disease or accident through inattention to hygiene or carelessness"). Chapter III "By What Stages Will the War Progress?" laid out what the soldier should expect from debarkation through occupation. The twelve separate points of Chapter IV "What Are You to Do on the Ship?" addressed the details of the voyage—keeping secrets, settling personal affairs before battle and included a detailed, twelve-step plan to avoid seasickness, specific instructions in case of aerial or submarine attack, and a seven-point list of instructions dealing with clothing ("small spoons and such-like should be tucked into your belt at the rear, or hung from the shoulders on a string"). Other sections dealt with assaults, marching and camping in the tropics, sentry duty, and other miscellaneous aspects of the campaign.[1]

Seishin had won the battle. Yet after their victory, as they moved their prisoners northward, they encountered a reality for which no guide, no matter how detailed, could prepare them, one whose unexpected dimensions left them frustrated and prone to unpredictable, lethal behavior. Already far from home, packing such heavy cultural baggage along with their bayonets and canteens, Japanese soldiers encountered two nightmares—one logistical and the other cultural—as they tried to manage the disorderly, foreign, human traffic of Bataan.

* * * * *

American soldiers preparing to join the occupation forces in Japan after the war received a guide as well—a handy, 78-page *Pocket Guide to Japan*, published by the Armed Forces Information and Education Division. Its first sentence warned, "You are on your way to Japan—and an experience unlike anything you've known before." Servicemen found geographical, historical, linguistic and recreational advice and not a few concise tips on the culture they would encounter. Under the heading "How Their Minds Work," soldiers read:

> Japanese culture is very formalized.... Almost everything has some symbolic significance that you will probably find very farfetched. But, beginning with the belief that the Emperor was divine, the Japanese, through their history, have had a special, rigidly fixed place in the scheme of things for everyone and everything.[2]

Such advice touched on a central feature of Japanese sensibilities. The overweening concern with form, hierarchy and order had its roots in the realities of Japanese history.

A long period of intermittent civil strife preceded the establishment of peace and order at the hands of three great unifiers, the last of whom, Tokugawa Ieyasu, founded the dynasty that lasted from 1603 till the mid-nineteenth century. Deeply concerned with sustaining order where so much chaos had prevailed for so long, Japanese elites set about guaranteeing stability and cementing their own authority within that system. Soon after taking power, the Tokugawa shogun instituted the policy of *sakoku*, or closed country, virtually sealing Japan off from the outside world.

In this new, peaceful world, a large *samurai* class, some 7 percent of the population, dominated the society and polity, with peasants, artisans and merchants below. Peasants, more than 80 percent of the population, stayed alive by bending their backs to the cooperative task of wet rice farming, a process prescribed down to last detail. Here the economic well-being of the group depended on absolute cooperation of all—to provide enough to sustain the village and to give some 40 percent of their crop to the parasite *samurai* class. Peasants had already been deprived of the right to carry swords, insuring that successful rebellion was unlikely. Status derived from birth, and the *samurai*, a military class, imposed an essentially military order on society. The obsession with form extended to the manner in which a person dressed and disrobed and even slept.

Sometimes a foreigner is hired to bring a bit of international flavor. Such was the case with a sports club in Nishinomiya, where I worked for a few hours a week with pre-school children while their mothers played tennis or did yoga. One little girl named Mari was just a bit wilder than others. One day during a chat with her mother, she jokingly acknowledged her child's misbehavior and mentioned that she was even sleeping "like the kanji dai." (大) I had no idea what this referred to, so I asked a Japanese friend, who explained that it meant with arms and legs splayed out—that little boys could sleep that way, but a proper Japanese girl slept in a rigidly straight position, arms and legs at their sides.

Now without influence from abroad except as determined acceptable, the ruling dynasty set about regulating virtually every facet of Japanese life. For those who ranked below the level of *samurai*, this meant being subject to a "harsh orthodoxy" and rigorously "enforced conformism." There life was

> prescribed down to the finest detail. Everyone knew their place, and what was expected of them. At a more detailed level, there were prescriptions for type and place of work and residence for particular classes. At a finer level still, there were prescriptions for the type of clothing that a person of a particular class could wear, the type of present they could give to a child of a particular gender and a particular age, the type of food they could eat, and even where they could build their toilet.[3]

This was life in the *mura*, where regulations made clear the date for the change from winter to summer attire announced, irrespective of the actual weather. It was an enclosed village, a tightly controlled society from within—where all was familiar—and where outsiders were rejected and repelled as a means of self-defense.

The group is the center of Japanese sensibilities, and groups are held together by ties of *giri* (interrelated social duty) and *ninjō* (human feeling). *Giri* suggests the binding force of kinship ties between people, and takes on the equivalent of Christian morality in the West. Obligations between individuals are heavy and reciprocity is practiced in earnest; few will voluntarily take on more *sekinin* (responsibility) and all are careful not to add to others' burden.

These imperatives, though somewhat weaker now, remain strong in modern Japanese society. Forty years after the Death March a nationwide survey showed that nearly 70 percent of Japanese valued *giri-ninjō* above personal beliefs. Relationships held together with such binding force defined village life, where intense loyalty to the group found its complement in deep suspicion of outsiders—human feeling and social duty applied primarily, if not indeed exclusively, to those who were known.[4]

Proper behavior between and among these social strata was more than form for form's sake; for the classes below *samurai* proper form was a matter of personal safety. Peasants were at risk for more than simple rudeness. The verb *tsujigiri* (literally, "crossroads cut") described the samurai's occasional habit of picking a random wayfarer on whom to try the edge of his sword. If he was unable to bisect the victim, cutting from the shoulder to the opposite side, either the sword was too dull or he bungled his stroke. Beyond this, *samurai* could cut down commoners for "acting in an other-than-expected-manner"; the aphorism *Deru kugi wa utareru* (The nail that sticks up is hammered down) could take on an actual, physical meaning. The Tokugawa decreed farmers, craftsmen and merchants "may not behave in a rude manner towards *samurai*. In the Tokugawa village, the rude man was an "other than expected man."[5] These peasants' descendants would encounter many such men on Bataan.

Neighborhood associations were held responsible for the misdeed of any individual, with severe punishments for all. One typical document made clear that "if mistakes … are found … we admit the fault and will accept any kind of punishment." At its worst, punishment might include, as in the case of a woman who had committed arson, being boiled alive. Other examples were misbehaving townsmen whose noses and ears were cut off before being banished. One rather stunning measure of the system's success at maintaining order is that only 350 police were required at the mid-point of the nineteenth century to maintain order in the metropolis of Edo (now Tokyo) and its more than one million inhabitants. For the vast majority of Japanese peasants living in the countryside, no police were present or necessary.[6]

The main ideological currents of this Pax Tokugawa supported the status quo. Much thought during the Tokugawa period was based on the idea that perfection—a lost golden age—lay in the past, a central idea borrowed from the Chinese thinker Confucius. Adapting his ideas to the Japanese political reality, the Tokugawa leaders emphasized the cluster of values that helped to sustain stasis—and their hold on power. At the center were loyalty to one's lord and the notion of *taigi-meibun*, or fulfilling one's duty and knowing one's proper place.[7] Those subscribing to the School of National Learning, though departing somewhat from the ideals of Confucianism, held that "order in the present could best be maintained in the absence of innovation." More than a century into the period of Tokugawa peace, the influential scholar Motoori Norinaga wrote, "Even things that are profitable, if they are of a new form, are customarily to be considered troublesome; and for this reason, things that are traditional … for the most part should remain as they are."[8]

Such rigidity, vigorously enforced by an armed ruling class for two and a half centuries, left a permanent mark on Japanese sensibilities. The notion that everything has a "proper form" is a most powerful cultural imperative that has defined Japanese behavior ever since. Indeed, this was more than "a simple visual aesthetic … it has become a type of ideal to strive for in almost every aspect of behavior … a sort of 'functional ideal' that is very much normative."[9]

The coming of the West was the immediate cause of wide-ranging ferment that led to a brief civil war and the establishment of a new government, thoroughly focused on a form of modernization that would protect the nation from encroaching Western imperialism. The oligarchs who took control of Japan and guided it in its remarkable development did so on the backs of a people inured to obedience and an acceptance of the need to adhere to basic forms in all activities. These new statesmen sought out new forms upon which to base the transformation they deemed necessary for national survival. Shortly after the "Meiji Restoration" of 1868 that defined the emperor as the center of the polity, the Iwakura Embassy, sent abroad to divine the secrets of Western power, recommended which patterns were most successful for rapid modernization, with Prussia the best model for constitutional government, the surest way to curtail popular rights.

The emphasis on form lasted well beyond the changes and upheavals of the nineteenth century. Japanese elites responded to the trauma of World War II in the familiar way—by reassuring the population that they lived in a thoroughly known world. Authorities consistently made statements that seem preposterous until one takes into account the historical context and the long-held emphasis on the need for the security that adherence to a prescribed form ensures. When American bombs began falling on Japanese cities, an Aviation Manufacturer's Association official stated:

> Enemy planes have finally come over our very heads. However, we who are engaged in the aircraft production industry and who had always expected this to happen had made complete preparations to cope with this. Therefore, there is nothing to worry about.

The need to render the world predictable is often one in the same with the need to exercise agency—the planes have come because we have drawn them in. Perhaps the most astonishing pronouncement of this type appeared in a radio report as American soldiers entered Manila. The broadcast described General Yamashita remarking with a broad smile that

> now the enemy is in our bosom.... The rapid fall of Manila, shortly after the enemy landings in Lingayen Bay, was only possible as a result of General Yamashita's tactics and in accordance with his plans. General Yamashita's operations are now making continuous progress.[10]

To be dreaded was not the loss of the city, simply that that loss might somehow be unexpected. Nothing succeeds like failure.

The sociologist Chie Nakane finds that distrust of unwanted deviation in Japanese organizations derives from the reality of intense competition and the need to "imitate the pattern of the similar institution which stands right at the top of the hierarchy: rivals and competitors seek for the sources of success of the institution at the top in its operational pattern. Hence, a 'standard pattern' always tends to appear in every field of activity." Nakane calls this the "one set" mentality, and cites the Japanese newspaper industry as an excellent example. "The three major dailies are virtually indistinguishable from each other, yet they refuse to deviate from a pattern that works. The same applies to educational institutions, wherein the top-ranked universities are able to dominate the landscape."[11]

Lafcadio Hearn, a sensitive observer of Japan in the late nineteenth century, considered the Japanese language to be the most profound expression of cultural difference:

> Experience in the acquisition of European languages can help you learn Japanese about as much as would help you acquire the language spoken by the inhabitants of Mars. To be able to use the Japanese language as a Japanese uses it, one would need to be born again, and to have one's mind completely reconstructed, from the foundation upwards.[12]

The reality of *keigo*, or "respect language," bedevils English-speaking learners of Japanese in part because English speakers construct sentences by choosing words to make them say what one wishes them to say; this facility indicates the originality of the speaker, one who uses the language well. In Japanese, the logic is quite different. The good speaker uses the appropriate forms, "and thus shows his keen awareness of the degrees and kinds of relationships involved. Language is not a search for original expression as much as a search for the patterns appropriate to a time and place."[13]

Features of the Japanese environment also help explain the centrality of form and concern with order. Historically, the Japanese have been subject to more than their share of nature's destructive whims in the form of volcanic eruptions, typhoons, floods and earthquakes. The great Kanto earthquake of September 1, 1923, alone killed some 150,000 in Tokyo. Hearn, writing in 1896, observed that Japan was

> a land of impermanence. Rivers shift their courses; coasts their outline, plains their level; volcanic peaks heighten or crumble, valleys are blocked by lava-floods or landslides; lakes appear and disappear.... Only the general outlines of the land, the general aspects of nature, the general lines of the seasons, remain fixed.[14]

Living in an unpredictable physical environment, the Japanese were all the more inclined to try to exercise control, even if only symbolically. One observer correctly suggests that the Japanese "like to tame nature. They like to tame anything potentially disruptive and threatening."[15] The beauty of any Japanese garden, asymmetrical but defined by an extraordinary degree of planning, is an excellent example.

Where I lived in Ashiya I often walked past a hanaya *(flower shop) near the national railway station in whose window was ranged a beautiful selection of* bonsai *trees. One afternoon I noticed the larger arrangements were complete with rocks to suggest mountains; the trunks of the little trees emerged from lichen and stone. These arrangements, I realized, were not homage to nature. Rather, at base they expressed a fear of nature's power and a strong need to exert control over it.*

* * * * *

In his classic text, *The Art of War*, the Chinese sage Sun Tzu stated, "Let your plans be dark and impenetrable as night, and when you move, fall like a thunderbolt." At one level, the Japanese strikes against Pearl Harbor and the Philippines, as well as the sudden strike against the Russian fleet at the start of the Russo-Japanese War in 1904, are perfect expressions of Sun Tzu's dictum. The subsequent Japanese *Blitzkrieg* in Asia in 1942 contained features of flexibility as well—among them the Japanese assault on Malaya, culminating in the conquest of Singapore, and the decision to detach the 48th Division from Homma's army for service in the invasion of Java when it appeared unnecessary for the Philippines' conquest. Yet throughout the campaign, their enemies noticed that Japanese strategy and tactics in the Bataan campaign were deeply informed by an unmistakable inflexibility and predictability.

Douglas MacArthur, for all his other failings, grasped this fundamental feature of Japanese behavior. He instructed his officers, "Never let the Jap attack you. When the Japanese soldier has a coordinated plan of attack he works smoothly." He continued, "When *he* is attacked—when he doesn't know what is coming—it isn't the same.... A hand that closes, never to open again is useless when the fighting turns to catch-as-catch-can wrestling." A perspicacious American officer agreed:

> Some of my friends who have had the opportunity to observe the army at close quarters have told me that Japanese regimental officers are exceedingly efficient so long as they are not called upon to deal with a situation for which no provision has been made in their official text-books. In novel situations they are apparently apt to lose their heads. It would seem that this weakness is known to the higher command, for there is little doubt that the Japanese army does not, as a rule, undertake any offensive operation before having done the most elaborate rehearsing, during which the smallest details are practiced over and over again; nothing is left to chance.[16]

J.D. Merritt, writing with the bitterness that informs many Bataan memoirs, suggested that "the stupidity of the average Jap pilot" eased the delivery of supplies. "Burdened by inbreeding or drinking his mother's milk too long past puberty," the pilots always chose the same stretch of road to strafe the vehicles instead of changing their pattern.[17]

Early in the Bataan campaign, one American observer noted that Japanese planes concentrated on "portions of Manila" while ignoring the thousands of soldiers retreating to the Bataan peninsula. The Germans, he argued, knew the value of strafing retreating columns to disrupt orderly withdrawal. Instead, the Japanese "hewed to the prescribed plans and, as they would demonstrate throughout the war, lacked an inclination to improvise and exploit unexpected opportunities." The primary historian of the campaign agreed: "Time and again, Japanese aircraft crossed appalling traffic jams and tangled roadways, but they droned blindly away to bomb their assigned targets ... Americans on the ground found it inconceivable that the Japanese did not deem the choked roads a suitable target."[18]

One American recalled looking up from a tangled mass of men and munitions laboring along a road to see formations of Japanese bombers overhead. "They were," he recorded, "not interested." Beyond this, Japanese planes usually stayed on the ground for three hours after lunch, allowing drivers to make deliveries during that time.[19] Another described a related, predictable pattern: "They would bomb our airfields, our engineers would repair them, and the Nips, with characteristic punctuality, would then repeat the bombing at the same time the next day.... Though the pilots were not particularly imaginative or adaptable, many of them were veterans of the campaigns of China, where they had become expert at set pieces." Apparently aerial tactics did not change after Bataan—on Guadalcanal, Robert Leckie remembered that the Japanese planes came overhead to bomb "three times a day and every Sunday morning" a pattern he attributed to "the Jap fixity of idea."[20]

Japanese tactics on the ground, described in detail in Chapter 2, were as predictable as those in the air. They reveal a heavy reliance on the bayonet attack to the exclusion of other approaches. Field exercises after World War I continued to reveal deficiencies, but "they always ended with an infantry breakthrough. In other words, exercises relied more on memorization of predictable tactical solutions than on imagination."[21] Other Japanese activity during the campaign is consistent with patterned behavior as well. During the fighting, Japanese snipers tied themselves into trees spaced 200 yards apart, apparently according to a set plan from which they never varied. Sniper hunting parties took full advantage "after deducing the repetitious placement" of the marksmen. An American colonel divined yet another pattern—infiltration of the "north front every night: little parties that work their way around our strong points." When the main Japanese force attacked from the front, the smaller parties made a huge ruckus with drums and firecrackers, hoping to cause panic.[22]

* * * * *

On the morning of April 9, the 77th anniversary of Lee's surrender at Appomattox, General Edward King met in Lamao with Japanese commanding general Homma Masaharu's representative, Colonel Nakayama Motoo, his senior operations officer. When King's aide, Captain A.C. Tisdale, sat down at the table, he casually crossed his legs and lit a cigarette, whereupon a Japanese officer, "affronted at this lèse majesté," knocked his feet down and the smoke from his mouth.[23] This was Tisdale's first encounter with *kata*; I, however, had been in Japan more than two years and should have known better.

At its inception, the foreign teachers who constituted the initial cohort of a cooperative edu-

cational program assembled at the Kobe Department of Education office. There we were to meet an official from Tokyo as part of a typically formal Japanese "kick-off" affair—a meeting with the important visitor, pictures for the newspaper and a small gathering afterward, all choreographed in great detail. My own understanding of the dance we were performing was, however, inadequate. As we were ushered into the conference room, sat and waited for the top man, I pushed back from the table and crossed my legs. Upon seeing this breach of kata, the local official, who was the driving force behind the program, informed me, in front of the entire group, of the need to "sit well" before the Tokyo official entered. I dutifully uncrossed.

Japanese could insist on proper form during the surrender meeting. Enforcing it during the evacuation of American POWs was another matter entirely.

Thinking of the welfare of his men, King proposed to arrange transport on American vehicles to a place designated by the Japanese for those unable to make the march north from Mariveles, where most of the 10,000 American and 65,000 Filipino prisoners assembled upon surrender. This Nakayama rejected because Homma had already approved a plan for the removal of Fil-American forces. "Like any good leader, Homma had arranged for the logistics of prisoner care and transportation long before the actual surrender, and he had assigned senior staff members to work out the task." Sekiguchi Hisashi of the medical corps was to handle medical care, Wada Moriya of supply to provide food and clothing, Takatsu Toshimitsu would administer the operation, with Kawane Yoshikate overall command. During its first modern test in 1894–95, the "most glaring shortcoming" of the army was its logistics system; now, nearly five decades later, Japanese and American alike would discover that little had improved.[24]

More than a week before final offensive on early April, the staff submitted its plan. The first phase was to be handled by Takatsu—he would supervise the men marching the nineteen miles from Mariveles to Balanga, about half way up the peninsula, a distance of about thirty miles. It was assumed that on this leg the prisoners would bring their own rations. Marching distances of twenty-five miles a day was routine in the Japanese army, and the assumption that their prisoners could do the same defined this phase of the Japanese plan for evacuation.

In the second phase, the prisoners were to be transported by truck from Balanga to San Fernando, fifty-seven kilometers farther on, then board freight trains that would cover the forty-nine kilometers to the town of Capas, where they would disembark and walk the last eleven kilometers to the Camp O'Donnell. The plan provided for two medical stations and four food stops along the way.[25] The major stopping points were the towns of Cabcabuan, Limay, Balanga, Lubao and Orani. Such was the basic outline of the evacuation's anticipated form. For phase two under Kawane, 200 transport trucks had been allotted for the movement of 25,000 men from Balanga to San Fernando. Kawane explained that field hospitals would be set up in Balanga and San Fernando.[26]

The problems with this essentially well-conceived plan were several. First, it was based on a grossly inaccurate estimate of the number of prisoners that would surrender to Homma's Fourteenth Army. His staff had assured him that between 25,000 and 35,000 soldiers defended Bataan, and that resistance was likely to continue until the end of April. When surrender came, the Japanese were overwhelmed by the transportation problem that confronted them three weeks earlier than planned. Furthermore, the plan failed to take into account the physical condition of the Allied force, its near starvation, and especially the extent to which malaria, more prevalent in southern Bataan, had weakened its soldiers.[27] Beyond this, Homma sought to deal with these compounding difficulties while under extreme pressure from Tokyo to complete a campaign that was already badly delayed—Corregidor's big guns continued to boom defiantly and would not be silenced until May 6.

For a period of months, I worked at an English language school that was little more than a shoe-string operation, with classes in a rented three-room space on the top floor of a rather decrepit office building in south Osaka. At Yasashii Eikaiwa *(Easy English Conversation), class scheduling and often classes themselves were haphazard affairs, with anywhere from a few to a dozen students showing up at seemingly random intervals. In deep December it was time for what the president, Mr. Enomoto, hoped would be a company party. At this he made a valiant effort, though his staff, including his wife, all the part-time teachers and the students he could round up, totaled no more than about twenty. Nevertheless, when I walked into the room at a local restaurant reserved for the occasion, I and the other guests were greeted by a large poster board on which was written a detailed agenda, in places broken down into five minute intervals:*

6:00:	The greetings
6:05–6:15:	The talking of people freely
6:15:	The toast of sake or beer
6:20:	The comment from the president
6:25:	The meal is serve
7:00:	The giving the plan for next year
7:10:	The next bar, and so forth

The small size of the gathering, indeed of the whole enterprise, did not mock the specificity of the plan. Enomoto, I and two others carried on until the last train that night; that the toast was not given with the desired punctuality was not, apparently, forgotten until well after "so forth."

The question might be posed—why, after his enemy was cornered in the Bataan peninsula, cut off from supplies, did Homma proceed with the campaign? With no means of re-supply, the Allied army faced certain extinction, and by January it was clear to all that it presented no threat to the southward advance toward the oil of the Dutch East Indies, whose flank the conquest of the Philippines was meant to secure. One answer appears in the form of pressure from the Japanese emperor himself. At this time Hirohito "made his first major intervention in an ongoing Pacific front operation." Hirohito contacted army chief of staff Sugiyama on January 13 and again a week later, wondering about reinforcements needed to end the campaign. Still unsatisfied with the campaign's progress, the emperor again pressed Sugiyama twice more in February.[28] Such inquiries were not to be ignored.

During World War II, the Japanese were by no means alone facing the difficulties attending the capture of more prisoners than anticipated. As the North African campaign drew to a close, Americans faced the prospect of dealing with large numbers of Germans and Italians. In early May 1943, Eisenhower expressed certainty that he would capture no more than 150,000 men in Tunisia. His estimate proved grossly inaccurate; "within a week the prison population would grow to 225,000 and beyond, stuffed into camps built to hold 70,000. For reasons ranging from shipping shortfalls to poor delousing facilities on the piers of New

York, the Allied system for transporting prisoners ... had shown signs of strain even before Tunis collapsed. Now things got much worse." Confusion was rampant:

> Carefully calibrated guard-to-prisoner ratios—one for every twenty Italians and three for every twenty Germans—were immediately scrapped.... Prisoners were shoehorned into boxcars without latrines or sufficient water for the tortuous trip across Africa. One GI described Italian troops in trucks "packed together like sardines, urinating and vomiting."

Other Axis prisoners were "crammed onto Algerian coasters, where they were tormented by thieving Senegalese guards and overwatched by French officers who nibbled chocolate on the bridge and tossed morsels to the lunging men below."[29] No plan survives contact with the enemy, and apparently plans after victorious contact—on both the Allied and Axis sides—did not survive either. Friend and foe alike saw the fruits of victory grow rotten.

* * * * *

The night before the Death March began, the earth spoke to the men of both armies. At 9:30 p.m. on the evening on April 8, soldiers felt the earth tremble. Lt. John Gamble "felt as if he were standing on a mammoth monster that was sluggishly moving in its sleep." Indeed, in Japanese folklore, the god of the earth, Kashima, holds a giant catfish motionless with the *kaname-ishi*, the keystone. Whenever he relaxes his grip, the catfish, upon whose back rests the Japanese islands, thrashes about, causing the earthquakes that afflict the island with such regularity. On the evening of April 8, the night before the Death March began, as if to mock Japanese pretensions and presage the confusion to come, the catfish came to life.

It was just 9:30 p.m. when it struck, and "nature joined the orgy of destruction." Those on the peninsula felt trees swaying "as if in a strong tide, men pitched to the ground, and monkeys screamed in terror. Men tried to run but stumbled and fell and made progress only by crawling. Beds in Hospital 2 bounced.... To the exhausted soldiers, it was the last straw; it seemed as if the world was coming to an end." Lt. William Miller, exhausted from the campaign, thought "Everything else, and now this, too?" Some men, urinating after the first impact, wet themselves as a second shock knocked them down.[30] On the other side, no doubt, the saying, *Naki tsura ni hachi* (When crying, bee stings face) occurred to many.

An American colonel, captured at Little Baguio, spoke to his command: "Men, we're in a mess.... If you become a disheveled, slovenly mob, they will treat you as such.... We must impress the Japs that we are a well-disciplined, smart-looking, smooth-functioning outfit. Their god is discipline." Another soldier recalled that "any captive of the Japanese who was undisciplined, uncooperative or rebellious rarely survived to boast about it."[31] These two Americans spoke to the heart of the conflict that was to define the Death March—Japanese held American prisoners responsible for the failure of order on the march, while the Americans themselves were ill-suited by temperament, training and condition to behave as the Japanese expected.

Yet southern Bataan was a scene of snarling, jumbled, disarray. At the end of the campaign, some 80,000 soldiers, American and Filipino, along with more than 25,000 civilians who had fled southward were crammed into an area ten miles square. The last two days of the battle saw "disintegration and final collapse." The standard military history of the campaign summarizes the chaos:

> Lines were formed and abandoned before they could be fully occupied. Communications broke down and often higher headquarters often did not know the situation on the front lines. Orders

This photograph shows an ideal expression of *kata*—prisoners in a neat line under the supervision of a single guard. Perhaps it was taken at the march's beginning near Mariveles, or at its conclusion outside Camp O'Donnell; such order was unlikely anywhere in between (Keystone/Hulton Archive/Getty Images).

were issued and revoked because they were impossible of execution. Stragglers poured into the rear in increasingly large numbers until they clogged all roads and disrupted all movement forward. Units disappeared into the jungle never to be heard from again, In two days an army evaporated into thin air.[32]

Just before surrender, the confusion intensified. General Bluemel, trying to bring order out of the disorganized mass of retreating Filipinos and Americans, tried to separate his own soldiers from others: "He was grabbing men, trying to thrust them back into the line. This thing was hopeless. He tried to stop the officers. One officer all but hit Bluemel trying to move him out of the way."[33] Transportation of basic necessities to the front broke down almost completely, gasoline and drivers sometimes in equally short supply.

As manifest disaster overtook the army, "more and more American officers began drifting from their units. Not all the men who ran were frightened, inexperienced recruits. Some were professionals. Even field grade officers found one excuse or another to leave their duties and head south."[34] The disaster was not without elements of sheer panic. Along the coastal road, the rout swelled to epic proportions, a tangled mass of Americans, Filipinos, tanks, miscellaneous vehicles all competing for space on the road away from the advancing Japanese—"The panic and mindless desire to go south was contagious." One American colonel gave an order to move his command, but before he could intervene, half his men vanished, joining the broken masses passing by. An American colonel named Fry remarked with the eloquence of simplicity, "I hope never to see a broken army again. It was a terrible sight!" William Evans compared the scene to Dante's Inferno.[35]

Conditions in the hospitals were no better. The last six days of the siege saw patient population of Hospital # 2 swell from 2,500 to 6,000. Hospital personnel, reduced to eating rice meant for pigs, tried to deal with a tidal wave of men afflicted with malaria, dysentery, malnutrition and fatigue. By April 8 the overflow of sufferers, now among the 24,000 sick and wounded, were simply laid on bare ground.[36]

When the American garrison on Wake Island surrendered, the Japanese victors found a manageably small group of men to control, nothing like the swarming chaos they faced on Bataan. A corporal on Wake described the Japanese method of controlling their prisoners: "They stripped us down balls and ass naked and hogtied us." Gregory Urwin, the historian of Wake Island's capitulation, suggests that "many Wake Island defenders viewed such conduct as proof of Japanese barbarity, but it was actually an effective way for a limited quantity of captors to neutralize growing numbers of captives."[37] A small number of captives—only some 500 were taken on Wake—could be controlled in such ways. But Melvin Rosen, taken prisoner on April 9, spoke to the reality of Bataan in a burst of insight: "in fairness to the Japanese, I think that they were caught by surprise at so many people being surrendered, they really didn't know what to do with us."[38]

Even so, Kawane's plan—the form the march was to take—made its way from the staff to the officers who would be responsible for its execution, to the Japanese soldiers who would do the actual guarding of the prisoners. Of paramount importance was moving prisoners along to the designated rest and food points on the march with as much dispatch as possible. Yet proposed form and actual result would bear little relationship to each other as the Japanese struggled to implement Kawane's plan. A historian of modern Japan has observed that "Japanese organizations are weak on top-level control, and section or department chiefs have considerable authority. The closer the department is to the detail work, the more authority it has."[39]

Little describes the logistical reality of the Death March more accurately—poorly transmitted, general instructions came to the guards from above who then, at the many confusing points of contact with their prisoners, sought to apply their notions of *kata* whenever and however they could. The guards were even from entirely different areas of the Japanese army. In theory, "Line of Communications" units were to receive POWs from combat units. In practice, some were turned over, but others made their way north guarded by soldiers from infantry units that captured them.[40]

For an individual Japanese guarding American prisoners on the Death March, the details were simple—move a specific number of men to a specific point on the map as quickly as possible. Sato Tokutaro, responsible for movement of prisoners, stated that "each front line unit was responsible for PsW [POWs], within their operation sector," but soon their "boundaries became confused and there was overlapping which caused obscurity in areas of responsibility."[41] Considering the overwhelming volume of human traffic on just two roads, and the enormous tangle when the columns converged at Balanga, it was inevitable that individual guards, unaware of the overall plan and focusing intently on the details of their assignments, would frequently find themselves at cross purposes.

American and Filipino units received word to surrender at different times and made their way to the rendezvous point of Mariveles piecemeal, sometimes singly or in pairs, sometimes in much larger groups, forming into a confused mass to be disarmed and somehow started northward. Confusion began early on and only increased during the march. Abel Ortega, in a telling phrase, described the moment of surrender—"in the area where we were, it was raining confusion. No one knew what to do or where to go. There was no food or water and we were not permitted to try and locate these necessities. We couldn't depend on our officers because they didn't know any more than we did." After the first mile, organization was lost, the procession "more of a mass group than an organized march."[42]

In the extraordinary chaos in the days following surrender, the Japanese, eager to clear the peninsula of impediments, prodded more than 5,000 wounded, mostly Filipinos, out of one of the two hospitals on Bataan. Believing they had leave to go home, these unfortunates, many wounded or gravely ill from a variety of maladies, flowed onto the route of the march and blended in with the POWs. One American estimated that some eight hundred died "from thirst, starvation, disease, and atrocities committed by the Japanese."[43] The battle's historian concurs:

> Struck with mass hysteria, few listened and almost none remained. Amputees, using tree limbs for crutches, joined the pathetic procession. A row of blind patients formed a human chain behind one of the walking wounded and headed for the road. Men holding their hands over fresh stomach wounds, to keep them from breaking open, staggered out—most to become just another one of the hundreds of corpses that, within a few days, would line the roads leading out of Bataan.[44]

How many died of which cause will remain forever unknown, but it is certain that many of the corpses reported by Death March survivors were those of these men.

Beginning on April 9, groups of one hundred, but sometimes smaller, began making their way up the peninsula. Dick Bilyeu remembered, "I hadn't been able to figure out what type of organization the Japanese had for this forced march. There weren't any rosters, no head counts, nothing. They just pointed with their bayonets in the direction they wanted us to go, and we moved in that direction." Sam Moody remembered that by day four of his march, organization had vanished—"We were strung out in any way possible."[45]

Another recalled, "As we tramped along ... we were joined at irregular intervals by small bands of men coming down jungle trails to surrender, and continually impeded by a steady stream of Japanese tanks, trucks and soldiers pouring southward to begin the assault on Corregidor."[46] The lack of officer control was apparent from the beginning, as guards started groups of prisoners in one direction, stopped, reversed direction, and re-traced their steps. Sam Grashio was astonished to note that once "the guards even turned us about in the hottest part of the day and marched us nine miles *back the way we had come*" (italics in original).

Bernard Fitzpatrick walked several miles out from Mariveles, then back the same distance before staying on a northerly route. Robert Levering marched through Cabcaben, then doubled back, then east and north again. Many observers noted what John Olson saw: "There was no pattern to the speed at which the various columns were moved. The officers ... in command of the guards appeared almost as confused as the captives with whom they were charged." Vincent Silva remembered being forced to stand in formation from dawn until about noon, then the Japanese "started us off at double-time, and when the line was stretched out, they would bring us back together and have us stand again in the hot sun."[47]

A score or more of the Bataan narratives mention that the guards on the march were changed frequently, no doubt as part of the overall Japanese evacuation plan. Guards marched their groups of prisoners, sometimes more than 100, to designated points, where new guards took over. This practice, observed throughout the march, had the inevitable effect of further taxing prisoners already exhausted and suffering from the general debilitation of malnutrition. The new guards, rested and well-fed, insisted on following their specific instructions, hurrying the men along to new rendezvous points. Survivors recalled that these men "would tolerate no stopping at any place other than the spots where they had been instructed to halt."[48]

Japanese officers were not in the habit of explaining their orders to subordinates, and doubtless the guards assigned to the long columns were simply told to move as quickly as possible. *Meirei no shikata*, a way of managing, or of giving orders, sheds considerable light:

> It does not consist of giving orders in the Western sense. It is creating a situation in which individual workers know what they are supposed to do, are given the necessary incentive to do it, and are rewarded when they do. The system is designed to avoid singling individuals out, to diffuse responsibility and to give each person the opportunity to do his or her best—always within the confines of the group and its interests.[49]

The interests of the group had been made clear—move the POWs out of Bataan with dispatch. But as each guard attempted to do his best, in the turmoil of the march he frequently found himself in conflict with others attempting to do the same. According to Japanese military doctrine, prisoners—either Japan's or those of any enemy—had no official status. *Kore dake Yomeba Ware wa Kateru* was silent on the issue of guarding prisoners, and individual guards were left to their own devices when groups of prisoners became uncontrollable.

What can be said of the guards who walked with their American wards? Some assigned to escort the American prisoners were "hardened veterans of the 16th Division. Almost all of them had been wounded in the first attacks on Bataan in January and early February. Many of their sergeants had officiated under Prince Asaka and Nakajima Kesago at the rape of Nanking in December-January 1937–38."[50] Some others were Koreans conscripted into the Imperial Japanese Army, perhaps eager to prove their loyalty by enthusiastically carrying out their given tasks, as well as being inclined to behave cruelly to prisoners because of their own treatment at the hands of the Japanese. Perhaps most important was the salient fact that the individual Japanese guard walked alone, next to a throng of foreigners, mostly out of touch with his fellows, and unsupervised by his officers.

Murray Sneddon observed the effects of such solitary work: "From the very first time I sighted a Japanese soldier to the final day of the Death March, I never saw one of them smile.... They were all sullen and mean-looking." Ralph Levering remembered that his group was guarded by Japanese "who were nervous, didn't know what was going on." Virtually no survivor's account refers to more than a few guards in any one place, and many refer to "small escorts" or only one guard.[51] One source claims that occasionally Japanese section chiefs moved up and down the road, and that "any guard who failed to enforce marching discipline was yanked aside and beaten on the spot."[52] This may have occasionally happened; any officer could claim authority over any soldier of lower rank, all *jōshi* (superiors) could play a supervisory role. The on-going confusion of the march suggests such officers were either ineffective or actually added to the disorder.

Each guard had instructions from an immediate superior that he was desperate to carry out, but in the chaos that only increased day by day, each guard conducted what was essentially a separate March, reacting to events as they occurred.

> When two or three guards were given the job of taking a group of 100 prisoners up the road, they probably were told little more than their immediate destination. How far the prisoners had already come, when they had last rested or tasted food and water, and how much farther they had to go beyond the next stopping point was information that a guard would neither expect nor receive.... All the Japanese soldier knew was that he was responsible for moving a large number of prisoners a certain distance ... and that he would be severely punished if any captive escaped.[53]

As the procession unfolded, an obvious reality, one perhaps easy to overlook, was the size differential between captor and captured; the average American POW towered over his Japanese captor. Toyoshige Karashima recalled, "I think we were all rather shocked ... to see the size of them.... We thought, How on earth are we going to look after people of this size?"[54]

Guards were relieved and changed every five kilometers or so, so any chance for continuity of communication was dramatically reduced. One result was that any real possibility of developing a connection with their captives was severely diminished or eliminated. Later, in the prison camps at O'Donnell and Cabanantuan, prisoners named guards: Half Pint, Minus Five, Donald Duck, Big Speedo, Air Raid, Mabel, Charlie Chaplin, Web Foot, Little Speedo. Guards at the camps must not have seemed as remotely monolithic—prisoners noted their guards' personality characteristics and some were kinder than others.[55] Such distinctions were not possible on the Death March, a reality that certainly enabled the crueler guards to impose their will with greater impunity and little concern for any human context.

The focus was on control. Guards frequently insisted on silence during the march; many recalled that talking of any kind brought wrath down upon them. Clear communication with their prisoners was already practically impossible, but the gap widened even further due to the constant changing of guards. Many veterans commented on this, some on the fact that more kindly guards were frequently replaced by new, more demanding and cruel ones.[56] In the confusion of the march, such *Nikumare-yaku* (inflexible martinets) might become especially dangerous.

Once, after I had been teaching for about three months, some students asked me how many Japanese kanji *I knew. If the foreigner responds with a fair number, a rapid exhalation of breath with accompanying sounds from the back of the throat indicate awe at having ascended the linguistic slope even a few steps. A small number confirms that the language is, as hoped, too difficult for non–Japanese to master. On this occasion, I responded that I knew a few. A chorus followed— would I write something in Japanese? On the board I dutifully wrote the two* kanji *for "Nippon," one indicating the sun, the other the meaning "at the origin." Hoots of friendly disapproval followed, and while I stood by nonplussed, the oldest student in the group demonstrated that, while I had produced the* kanji *correctly, I had written the individual strokes comprising each one in the wrong order. Duly chastised, I asked the group if my result, since it was correct, had any value. The room resounded with shaking heads. I watched with greater understanding when, the following week, on a trip down the coast to a town called Himeji, a girl with her food cart bowed to a completely empty car on the* Shinkansen *(Bullet Train) as she made her way forward.*

The Japanese historian Sakaiya Taiichi suggests that a basic cultural characteristic of people working diligently in a resource-poor society is that large amounts of labor are inevitably poured into limited resources and scarce land. To cope with this problem, Japan developed an aesthetic

This photograph of a Japanese soldier searching the pockets of his captives suggests the height differential between victor and vanquished (U.S. Air Force National Museum).

of devoting great labor to details. Concentrating hard work on a limited object proved that a worker was a good person. Attention to detail became intense, even when the results could not be seen.... Japanese specialists so emphasize the details that they tend to ignore the item as a whole.[57]

Even in dire circumstances, concern for detail defined Japanese behavior. Trapped behind Fil-American lines in February, desperate to break out, half his men dead or wounded, a certain Colonel Yoshioka ordered his heavy equipment items buried—"At each spot where equipment was interred, the Japanese set a piece of wood like a small tombstone listing the items left there."[58]

As the prisoners lurched northward, it became increasingly clear that some groups were moving with no guard supervision at all. Alfred Schreiber noted, "with the exception of the railroad cars at San Fernando, I had a pretty straight march. In fact, there was a stretch of several miles when my group had no guards in sight."[59] Other prisoners walked long distances unsupervised, and obviously set their own pace. Filipino observers noted that sometimes there were "thousands of men on the road at the same time. And at other times there were but a few individuals—depending on how busy the Japs had been in rounding up the scattered forces in the jungle. Prisoners moved over the seventy miles of road between Mariveles and San Fernando for a period of seventeen days. It took the Japs that long to find and ferret them out."[60] Unguarded, the prisoners walked at their own pace and paused for water wherever they found it from the numerous artesian wells along the route, all contributing mightily to the traffic jam.

Some who walked under guard described what they called the "sun treatment"—the

A Filipino contingent, possibly somewhere near Limay. Note the single Japanese guard in the distance to the right (indicated by arrow). Large numbers of men made their way north unguarded or with minimal supervision (Library of Congress).

experience of being made to stand without shade for periods lasting from an hour to several hours, sometimes without headgear. One veteran remembered, "they'd close you up again and they might keep you standing another hour in that hot sun.... There are ways you can rest one leg and shift your weight, it's not too noticeable and you can slough off and rest a bit. But, if they caught you at it, it meant a butt stroke with a rifle or a beating over the head."[61]

Several survivors, including Edward Dyess, interpreted such treatment as clear evidence of wanton Japanese cruelty. If this were the case, it suggests that individual Japanese guards were willing to put aside their assigned task of moving the men in the most efficient way possible, in order to punish groups of prisoners for infractions of rules. While some guards' punitive proclivities may account for this, it seems far more likely that requiring groups of prisoners to stand in the sun was a function of the jumbled human traffic on the peninsula. In their attempts to coordinate arrival at designated places for food and rest, guards had no choice but to delay or speed up their groups' movement. As for the absence of shade, the impossibility of coordinating stops to coincide with the availability of shade, for groups of 100 men, in a landscape denuded of foliage by months of combat, seems obvious.

The Japanese sociologist Chie Nakane observed, "A Japanese is rarely satisfied in a job unless he is able to visualize the whole of the operation being undertaken by the group of which he is a member." Kano Tsutomo, a Japanese social scientist, identified "certain long-term psychological and historical attributes" that defined Japanese sensibilities. "A Japanese," he suggested, "tends to be insecure ... unless he can clearly define his relationship with others around him."[62] These insights shed considerable light on the behavior of Japanese guards. He could not, in the confusion of the march, come close to visualizing the entire operation and his relationship to others—physically separated as he was from his fellows and without supervision by his own officers—was tenuous at best.

Whatever minimal order might have defined early stages of the march from Mariveles was gone when POWs coming north converged with those moving east along the only road that bisected the peninsula. Here, at Balanga, the Japanese had planned to set up a field hospital, and some slit trenches for disposal of waste had, in fact, been dug in preparation. The disorganized mobs straggled in, in groups as large as 100 and as small as forty, many guarded by only one Japanese, other groups arriving unguarded. By this half-way point in the march, many who had drunk filthy water along the way had dysentery, and were unable to reach the already inadequate slit trenches dug by the Japanese sanitation units.

With nowhere else to put the sick, the less sick or the well, the Japanese packed their wards into every available building in the town to overflowing. Those who could not fit were herded into barbwire pens outside of town. The sanitation in some places was non-existent; everywhere inadequate. The stench of unwashed bodies, effluvia of every kind, and death were all in the air and on the ground. All by this time were debilitated from the long campaign, tired, hungry and thirsty, and captive and captor alike were covered with the fine, powdery, tan dust that the columns kicked up as they marched.[63] The Japanese were overwhelmed by what had become a seething mass of foreign humanity.

Milling about in the crowds as the Japanese tried to sort American from Filipino POWS from Filipino civilian refugees, it seemed to Bernard Fitzpatrick that "no Japanese seemed to know what to do." Frustration reached the boiling point, tempers flared. Alvin Poweleit remembered guards "running back and forth all night, kicking the men, beating them with their rifles." Charley Ross slept in a compound through which Japanese guards ran throughout the night "with fixed bayonets, screaming and hollering, and we didn't understand Jap. We knew we were supposed to do something, but we didn't know what the hell it was."[64]

One American recalled, after Balanga, that "the brutality began to increase ... they really began to put it on us from here to Orani." A corporal named Koury stated, "We went from Mariveles to Cabcaben to Limay in one day without too much strain. This is where they started trying to get our attention—that we were prisoners of war and they were God's children." At Balanga another recalled, "As usual, the Japs were operating in a sheer state of confusion. There was a great deal of the now familiar high-pitched gibberish and lots of running around."[65] The guards, no doubt, sought direction, which, in the intense confusion of the moment, was simply not forthcoming.

Small numbers of guards for large numbers of prisoners created numerous dilemmas. If a guard believed a prisoner was trying to escape, he was justified in shooting him. When American prisoners could not continue because of exhaustion, however, the guard could not leave the column to which he was assigned. Falk suggests that "faced with a seemingly insoluble dilemma, his normal tendency was to become excited, even hysterical. Hence the frenzied blows and kicks rained on the fallen prisoners and the ultimate bayonet thrust or rifle shot which solved the guard's problem and put everything neatly back in place."[66]

Halfway to San Fernando from Balanga, the prisoners stopped at Lubao, where they were herded into a warehouse formerly used by the National Rice Company. Thousands were crammed into a space only large enough for hundreds. Those with dysentery could not make it to the latrine, and some were forced to stand all night in the stench and humidity. Richard Gordon, who suffered through the night, thought he would "go mad."[67] Irvin Alexander had visited the village of Lubao the year before the Death March, when his son had not heard the name correctly, calling it "loose bowels." Alexander remembered the story with wry humor when he spent the night in a latrine there a year later.[68] From Lubao and beyond the prisoners made their way to San Fernando, where trains awaited them for their trip to Capas.

Alexander's description of the train ride to Capas is brief, stating only that there "was standing room only in the cars, which the sun soon made into sweat boxes." The accounts of most prisoners, however, describe the train ride from San Fernando to Capas, lasting about three hours, as horrific. Japanese guards herded their captives into small railroad cars from the World War I era, 33' × 8' and 7' tall, and the prisoners were packed tightly, often a hundred at a time into one small boxcar. Many found the next excruciating three hours to be among the worst in their lives. There was so little room that men who fainted with no place to fall, and the feces of those with dysentery made the air unbearably fetid.

Robert Gaskill, the chief medical officer at O'Donnell, stated that in his car aboard the train that carried him from San Fernando to Capas, "the strongest men forced their way to the open door and ate everything tossed up to them, refusing to pass anything back to their fellows." Gene Jacobsen remembered that some who died from suffocation simply remained standing. Hubert Gater remembered that as "the car swayed, the urine, the sweat, and the vomit rolled three inches deep back and forth around and in our shoes." Fitzpatrick recalled feeling like a "sardine in a can."[69]

Somewhere past obelisk # 80, the road's name changes to—what else?—MacArthur Highway, and I haul myself into San Fernando, walking the last five kilometers along a busy four-lane road after succumbing to the heat and taking a jeepney from a point north of Lubao. I unsling at what seems an unlikely place, the Sogo Hotel. The map of the city I get from the clerk has the name in katakana; *I suppose this is where Nipponese tourists stay, though I don't see any. I wander out, eat at a* Turu-turò *(point-point restaurant), and find the rail station where the POWs were loaded onto trains for the ride to Capas, from whence they walked the last leg to Camp O'Donnell. The plaque there tells me that the men were "loaded like cattle" onto the boxcars, and "many suffocated or were crushed to death during the trip to Capas." There near the blue obelisk #102 I see the replica of the "40 and 8" (forty men or eight horses) box car into which some men were packed. The model sits on a concrete slab; gray color, wood sides, metal roof, no windows. I remember that hordes of children gathered to watch as the prisoners arrived at the station. Now, a man with his son, a boy of about five, wants to climb into the car. His father laughs and says no, promises the child ice cream.*

The guards doing the herding no doubt recalled several months earlier when they themselves were packed into the holds of the transport ships that brought them to the Philippines. *Kore dake Yomeba Ware wa Kateru* admonished, "Not only will conditions on the ship be exceedingly cramped and uncomfortable, but the heat will be extreme. In these circumstances, troops may easily suffer from seasickness or similar stomach disorders" and referred to "men sleeping side by side on the mess decks, like sardines in a tin." The relevant fish simile, that of the sardine, was used by Americans describing Italian prisoners, Americans describing themselves, and *Kore dake Yomeba Ware wa Kateru* describing Japanese. Transport preparation for the Malayan campaign that resulted in the capture of Singapore was brutal:

> In temperatures of 120 degrees, men and horses would have to be packed like sardines into the ships, travel through heavy seas and disembark on open beaches. How could this be done without heavy loss? To ascertain the limit of the endurance of the men, they were embarked "three to a mat" (an area of about 6 feet by 3 feet), and for about a week given a ration of water which had to be economized to the utmost.

Such conditions were no surprise to Japanese, who lacked what Westerners would broadly define as a sense of privacy—meaning "a private sphere separated from the group" with regard to physical space.[70]

Virtually all Japanese domiciles have a genkan, *the small space where shoes are taken off and slippers are donned before entering the house proper. My first Japanese residence was a* danchi, *one of many a small three room apartment with entrances from a central corridor. Since I owned nothing to steal, I had fallen into the habit of leaving my door unlocked. I had failed to realize that visitors—the frequent door-to-door denizens of Japan that punctuate the day, collecting for utilities, TV service, and the like—consider the* genkan *an essentially public space. Soon after I moved in, a bill collector knocked politely, came in, and stood in my* genkan *to transact her business. Slightly appalled at what I considered the violation of my privacy, I told her in halting Japanese that it was rude to enter someone's home, even after knocking, and I was completely nonplussed at her reaction of horror. I had forgotten Lafcadio Hearn's admonition: "Everybody's house must be open to visitors, to close its gates ... would be regarded as an insult to the community.... And to displease the community ... is a serious matter."*[71]

* * * * *

After he left Luggnagg, Lemuel Gulliver sailed to Japan but stayed only briefly. There he said, "I was so entirely a Stranger to the Language, that I was not qualified to make any

Enquiries." Those on the Death March familiar with Swift would understand all too well. Upon his capture one American, perhaps anticipating the ordeal before him, stated, "I don't know about you guys, but if a Jap soldier tells me to kiss his foot, I'm going to kiss his foot." The soldier's desideratum assumed his captors could make such a request intelligible. The language problem bedeviled captor and captive alike throughout the march, and it is significant that survivors claimed to remember much more linguistic confusion, and therefore greater abuse, after Balanga. One source claims that perhaps 15 percent of Japanese could read and write English to some extent, but the vast majority had virtually no spoken ability outside of a few words, "speedo" perhaps the most commonly used.[72] Since almost no Americans had any Japanese at all, the linguistic chasm was wide indeed.

During this war, Americans and Japanese had faced each other across the language divide once already. When Americans surrendered on Wake island in December, "a serious problem presented itself. None of the Americans spoke Japanese.... Wake's conquerors could hardly be expected to exercise much patience.... When unintelligible shouts failed to produce the reactions the Japanese desired, they resorted to the universal language of the rifle butt and naked bayonet." John Olson noted this inevitable reality on Bataan—"Since few of the captors could speak English and fewer of the captives Japanese, the mediums of command and direction became the grunt, the jab of the bayonet, the blow from the back of a saber, or, at best, gestures."[73]

To be sure, the language barrier exacerbated the fear and apprehension of the Americans. Lester Tenney recalled, "In some situations ... the guards were simply ignorant of the outside world and thought that everyone understood Japanese. They became irritated by our slowness to respond and our inability to understand their commands and vented their frustration on us."[74] Hearing Japanese for the first time, many American survivors commented on the incomprehensibility of the language, referring to it with terms such as "jabbering." Clearly the guttural enunciations of their guards were disconcerting at best, terrifying at worst for the starved, often sickly Americans, none of whom had any idea about their ultimate destination, how long they would be walking, or what kind of treatment to expect. Rumors sped up and down the column of captured soldiers like darting shadows, as men imagined the best and worst results of their circumstances.

Listening to guards repeat orders in Japanese, Tenney thought that these "were not the brightest members of the Japanese army. In fact, [he] concluded, they were probably the poorest educated and could not connect the fact that we did not respond with our inability to understand what they were saying." Tenney was no doubt correct. While many Japanese soldiers were literate to some degree, most were the extremely parochial products of the countryside. When prisoners failed to understand, their captors were always irritated, and sometimes enraged. James Bollich recalled that "a Jap soldier came up to me muttering something and at the same time flapping his hand up and down." Nonplussed, Bollich stared, whereupon "the Jap kept up his puzzling gestures, and I could tell he was getting more furious by the minute." Bollich turned to his fellow captives, one of whom said that the Japanese wanted him to sit. The Japanese immediately hit him in the head with his rifle butt, so Bollich stood, after which "he came and gave me a shove.... He wanted us to start walking."[75]

An officer named Fields listened without understanding on another occasion, when "a saber-rattling Jap officer strode in like a ham actor trying for a grand entrance, and let loose with a bellow and a string of gibberish. He soon worked himself into a foaming rage and ran up and down the line, slapping the Americans." Once, when Lester Tenney failed to respond instantly to a question he did not understand, Japanese soldiers broke his nose and some of his teeth. Bert Bank recalled being summoned to speak with a Japanese in a command car—"He asked me something in Japanese and since I was unable to understand, he hit me over the head several times and pushed me on."[76] Japanese guards often screamed *Kura!* at prisoners, a word usually used when addressing children or animals. During his first night in captivity, William Evans remembered shots and cries, while "the Japs were hollering 'Kora,' but we didn't know what the fuck they were talking about." John Playter commented on the word, saying, "I don't know the precise meaning of the word 'kora,' but we learned early that it meant danger for us."[77]

Irvin Alexander believed that horror on the Death March was "aggravated by the vast differences between the Americans and Japanese in language, temperament, customs, manners, training and discipline, which all combined, created a colossal misunderstanding."[78] From the guards' point of view, the language problem was severe. Marching and often counter-marching their wards in confusion, remaining with their captives for only a short period of time, guards could not, in the vast majority of cases, make themselves understood to their captives except with sign language and their pointing bayonets. Already performing the strange and perhaps relatively ignominious task of guarding prisoners, surrounded by the unfamiliar, these guards were encountering that which any Japanese sought to avoid—the unexpected.

Trained to obey orders instantly themselves, the guards shouted orders at stumbling or fallen prisoners. When the POWs did not respond, they sometimes bayoneted men who had no understanding of the language. At one point Abie Abraham "misinterpreted a command of some kind, and in punishment for his peccadillo received a bayonet tip through the hand." Survivors recalled that the language problem sometimes had fatal consequences. Just north of Lubao, a prisoner stepped off the road to defecate, and a Japanese guard urged him back with a cry of *Kura!* "The guy made some kind of sign with his hands meaning he'd be right there. I don't know what the Jap thought, but he just stepped over and ran the guy through with his bayonet."[79]

Those with serviceable English were almost always of higher rank, had likely been abroad, and were unlikely to be guarding prisoners directly on the route north. Those assigned were rank-and-file privates with limited education, the vast majority of whom had no functional English. One could also prevent criticism from one's fellows by refusing to speak any English one knew. A few Japanese, some of them what Americans called "Frisco Nips," spoke English, some fluently. These men, however, were reluctant to demonstrate such language ability in front of comrades for "fear of being accused of having pro–American sympathies."[80] Here the Japanese phrase *Kao-ni kakawaru* (it will damage my reputation) obtains.

After two years in Japan I had become fairly friendly with Aoki, one of the racquetball partners I knew from the Kobe YMCA. He spoke English fairly well, and we conversed mostly in that language, occasionally drinking beer together or singing karaoke *at a neighborhood bar. Ours was a sports, alcohol and song acquaintance, and each knew little about the rest of the other's life. One day, on my way home from Osaka, I saw him on a train, dressed in the standard uniform of the salaryman—blue pin-striped suit, maroon tie and white socks, standing among a group of like-dressed men. Smiling broadly, I threaded my way through the swaying throng, and greeted him in English. His response stunned me—he frowned, quickly grunted in brief recognition and then simply turned away and said something to his colleagues in rapid colloquial Japanese I could not follow that produced a round of laughter. The next time I saw him on the courts, he acted as if nothing had happened. Another lesson learned.*

* * * * *

Survivors' narratives devote much space to water—the reality of thirst, and the manner in which it was either given or denied by the Japanese. The Death March occurred at the height of the Filipino summer, and rain came only once, near the end of the ordeal. In such an environment, nothing was more important than water, and the manner in which Japanese guards withheld or allowed it to thirsty prisoners is at the center of the Death March drama. As they acted their part, Americans found that the cost of poor discipline and inadequate leadership was high. Circumstances of the march were challenging enough for those with a certain level of discipline; for those without, the probability of death was higher.

One POW recalled that during rests, "every three or four hours, they might let you line up and get some water from a hydrant and fill your canteen. Sometimes they did, and sometimes they didn't." When they did not, what the soldiers called "GI lemonade" was the "paramount issue. It became something to think about, then to yearn for, and finally to dream about.... Some of the men had reached a state of mind closely bordering insanity, from the lack of water."[81]

The body rebels at the lack of water, and the vast majority of men die after seventy to eighty hours without it. Initial discomfort is followed by reddening of the skin, dizziness and a feeling of exhaustion. Maintaining a steady walking pace becomes difficult, and dyspnea and cynosis appear, and an inability to stand alone—impaired coordination and fainting are common. In the latter stages of acute dehydration, the tongue swells, swallowing is impossible, and feeling disappears from the mouth. Later the skin shrinks, eyes become sunken, the vision dims, and hearing becomes impaired. In the stage of "functional derangement" the tongue clings to the teeth, swallowing cannot dislodge a lump in the throat, ears itch and eye discomfort grows. Sufferers feel a "fullness in the face and head" due to a shrinking of the skin, pain travels down the neck into the upper spine and hallucinations begin:

> irascibility arises, and companions quarrel and separate, perhaps to reunite for the very satisfaction of further dispute; the solitary sufferer may soliloquize, largely on impassioned invective— though the voice becomes cracked, husky or hoarse, and given to unexpected breaking into high tenor or dropping into an absurd whisper. The intellections are insensibly distorted more and more as the phase advances; prejudices are intensified, unreasoned revulsions arise against persons and things, while water and wetness are subconsciously exalted as the end of all excellence, the victim may gravely, after deliberate discussion ... discard hat or shoes.

A captain in the U.S. Medical Corps described the "euphoric delirium" of a soldier who "thought he was at his own funeral ... and uttered the usual lamentations ... for more than an hour, he issued orders ... until the moment a veritable epileptic fit seized him. Uttering inarticulate cries, he shook violently, rolling on the ground, the whole thing accompanied by unrestrained movements."[82]

After counter-marching in the sun and confusion, Dick Mallonee described similar effects—loss of balance, falling. "Finally," he wrote, "I became delirious. Someone in the column had a canteen banging against a piece of metal. It sounded exactly like a bellboy coming down a hotel corridor with a pitcher of cracked ice. But he never arrived. My friends told me that I raved at that bellboy for miles.... Finally my eyes wouldn't track. I saw double, my legs gave way, and I fell."[83] Understandably, the men who sat down to write their memoirs understood the denial of water as either manifest cruelty or simply as unpredictable Japanese whim.

In fact, the Japanese soldier had been given instructions that specified how he was to deal with water—its availability and scarcity. This guide was a specific expression of *kata*, one that Japanese guards, in the confusion of the march, remembered and applied. *Kore dake Yomeba Ware wa Kateru* contained a section entitled "Guarding Strategic Areas" in which the soldiers were instructed as follows: "Small bodies of troops will be left to control large areas ... you must seek to tire the enemy without exhausting yourselves.... Together with taking proper measures to ensure your own water supplies, you should contrive ways of denying water to the enemy." Red Allen witnessed the application of this admonition, recalling that Japanese soldiers would sometimes wade into the midst of the prisoners, take their canteens from them, pour out their contents, throw the canteens on the ground and smash them with their rifles, then hand them back, smiling.[84]

It was a raw and rainy November evening, the kind that told me not to face my drafty apartment alone and unfortified, so I gathered a Japanese friend and, three bottles of saké later, we took an angular course home, the gauze of our breath visible in the cold. At about ten, three blocks away, we were stunned to see a man, perhaps mid-twenties, standing just outside the gate of a private residence, bowing to passers-by and holding a large poster board sign which held a not insubstantial amount of Japanese writing. I maneuvered past as slowly as possible, squinting through the cold mist to see if I could recognize any of the key kanji *but, not wanting to stare and appear rude, I could discern nothing. Fascinated and nonplussed in equal measure, I persuaded my Japanese companion to wait a moment for decorum's sake, then walk back past, his duty as translator clear. So we did, affecting nonchalance. Safely out of sight, he told me that the sign stated simply that inside a student was studying for his entrance exams to college with great sincerity* (makoto); *all those passing by should please be quiet out of respect for his effort. A strategic area well-guarded indeed.*

One section of the pamphlet, dealing with the dangers of dehydration in the tropics, warned soldiers to "use [water] economically and to replenish your supplies whenever good water is found. And, no matter how thirsty you are, do not drink in large quantities—it is always better to drink a little at a time." Soldiers were told to expect to consume ten liters of water a day, their horses sixty liters. The watering of horses received as much attention as that of men—*Kore dake Yomeba Ware wa Kateru* reminded soldiers to be aware that horses became exhausted and were warned to "treat them with kindness and sympathy." The instruction to "give the horses fresh water several times a day" was not, apparently, to be ignored with impunity.[85] Tony Bilek remembered well an encounter with a Japanese cavalry troop:

> The trooper stopped our column and gathered up about a dozen canteens, with varying amounts of water, from the parched POWs. He dumped the contents into his leather nosebag, then heaved the empty canteens into the ditch. He turned and held the feedbag so his horse could

drink. The animal took it all and then the trooper mounted up. The rest of his comrades laughed uproariously as they cantered off.

Robert Levering and Cletis Overton remembered nearly identical episodes, and they seemed to each man the height of intentional barbarity.[86] Yet there existed a context for even this seemingly wanton cruelty. During their training,

> new conscripts were humiliated until they felt less worthy than their horses. Some squad leaders publicly announced that horses were more precious than men, since men could easily be recruited whereas horses could not be replaced overnight. Thus horses were treated with meticulous care. On the occasion of a horse inspection, the soldiers assigned to stop galloping horses suddenly were often kicked and injured by the horses, but they preferred to risk this danger rather than be reprimanded by their superiors.

Richard Mallonee recalled seeing horse-drawn artillery whose "animals looked good in flesh, well groomed and well-handled by the drivers."[87]

In this he agreed with what Hino Ashihei, an official correspondent attached to the Japanese army, had observed five years earlier in a letter to his brother. Speaking of horses in the hold of a ship on its way to China, he wrote that they "have the best food and water. Actually, they get better care than the men ... the horses get all the water they need ... the supply of water for the men is limited, barely enough for washing."[88]

Prisoners dealt with thirst in a variety of ways. Some men were able to demonstrate sufficient discipline and suffered less on the march. Native Americans from New Mexico's recently federalized National Guard units, "used to long treks in the southwestern deserts, taught their white brothers to suck a pebble in the daytime and save their water for the night, when it better satisfied." Abel Ortega, a draftee in the army since March 1941, remembered, "I learned very quickly how to manage my water supply."[89] Richard Gordon described water stops as bedlam with no one in charge: "Many times the rush of prisoners to the well would prevent me from completely filling my canteen, but regardless of how much I got, I conserved it until the next well."

> Once I had my water I would put some in my mouth, move it about to quench the dry mouth, swallow a little bit of it, and then spit the remainder back into the canteen. Hardly dining in accord with Emily Post's book on etiquette, but it saved my life. At no time on the march did I ever allow myself to run out of water, despite my urge to take deep swallows as others did.

He thanked the training he had received from his sergeant: "Men such as myself who had soldiered in the Philippines for some time before the war and had some training in water conservation."[90] But not all young soldiers were as disciplined as Ortega or Gordon.

Since unit cohesion of any type had long since vanished, the strong began to prey on the weak. When Sergeant Earl Dodson asked two other prisoners for a swallow of the water they carried in a large container, they flatly refused. Facing such responses, some turned to other means. Dick Bilyeu remembered desperate fellow prisoners, not from his unit, snatching his canteen from his hands as he drank, after which he hid his water as best he could. Dodson later remembered standing in line several hours to get a canteen of water and then going to sleep among strangers and, even though he put the water under his head, it was still gone in the morning. John Playter remembered that "it was advisable to look around" before drinking water, for fear that someone would take it.[91]

Those too weak, considerate or fearful to take from their fellows turned to other means of slaking their thirst. Sometimes the Japanese guards allowed their prisoners to drink from polluted sources, and men desperate enough risked the disease that the water's parasites were almost sure to deliver. Abie Abraham recalled seeing one group of men: "The heat of the day was so intense that they were half crazy from thirst. They arrived at a small stream that was contaminated with filthy water, a bloated corpse filled with maggots, this filthy stream the P.O.W's were allowed to drink from, as the Japanese guards laughed at them."[92]

Even before surrender, many young, inexperienced soldiers, following orders to avoid making fires that would attract aerial attack, had begun to drink un-boiled water. These "thirst-crazed men drank water they knew to be polluted, from carabao wallows and stagnant mountain pools. At least 30 percent of the troops had bacillary dysentery, 10 percent amoebic dysentery, and the rest some variety of worm infestation of the bowel."[93]

Mark Wohlfield remembered the measures the inexperienced and undisciplined took to obtain a drink: "Some of our young guys started asking the Japs whether they could have a drink of water. I looked to my right and saw a buffalo wallow about fifty yards off the road. It looked like green scum. The guards started to laugh and said 'OK, OK.' So all these kids, eighteen- or nineteen-year-old enlisted men, ran for the water and began drowning each other trying to get a drink." Irvin Alexander's recollection was similar:

> Many times I have seen heat-crazed young soldiers, who did not know how to conserve the water in their canteens, throw themselves down by the ditches and drink the filthy water. I never saw an old soldier or an officer make that mistake.... It did you no good to try to stop any man from doing such an absurd thing, for he told you very positively that it was none of your business and did it anyway.[94]

Two Americans, aware of the dangers of drinking the filthy water they passed in carabao wallows, goaded each other—when one was tempted to dash for water, one said, "Go on, you goddamned sonofabitch, drink it—die—go on" and returned the favor when his buddy's resolve weakened.[95] Others exhibited less willpower or judgment.

Concern with water extended beyond the Death March into captivity at O'Donnell. Dick Mallonee recalled,

> A fact impressed on me at O'Donnell was that the heaviest death rate from illness during the Bataan campaign and the POW days occurred among the youngsters, the recruits, and the civilian army, both officers and men. The old-timers had a big difference in our favor—water discipline. We had years of training and experience in getting along on a minimum of water and avoiding contaminated water at all costs. The young men had never learned to deny themselves anything, and bad water killed them by the hundreds.

Some lacked such discipline or a friend. After drinking from a stream befouled by a rotting corpse, another American began to cry—"Look there," he said, "I'll be dead in three days." Others lacked the strength to fend off their fellows. When Chuck Dragich returned to the road with a canteen, he was set upon. "The guys all mugged me," he stated, "they took my canteen.... I didn't get a drop of that water."[96]

* * * * *

While stopped at the village of Lubao, Irvin Alexander encountered a Japanese officer who sat at a table with his sword unsheathed. The officer called on an interpreter to instruct Alexander's men on conduct: "They must be quiet," he said, "the water line must maintain discipline."[97] Such was the communication possible when one Japanese officer spoke to one American officer through an interpreter. On the march, however, such simple clarity was impossible, and utterly unenforceable.

All along the route of the march, artesian water flowed from pipes protruding from the ground into concrete basins, and many accounts describe columns being halted tantalizingly close to them. The proximity was more than many of the undisciplined soldiers could bear. Many accounts speak of the pandemonium that ensued when prisoners, desperate for water, lost control and ran to its source. The scenario is repeated as a perverse liturgy: a thirsty throng sees an artesian near the road, the men break and run for it, screaming Japanese guards respond with bullets and bayonets.

The frequency of what might be termed "unprovoked" cruelty on the Death March was relatively low. Ninety-four percent of Americans who started the Death March arrived at Camp O'Donnell. Of the six percent who were shot, bayoneted, or otherwise expired along the way, most died near the artesian wells found along the road. It was here, at the sites with flowing water, that Americans' lack of discipline collided with Japanese insistence on order—with lethal result. John Playter remembered that during his six-day march, he only ever saw one man bayoneted, "one who dashed to [a] well and was down on his stomach drinking when the guard killed him."[98]

Just beyond obelisk #18, I see an artesian pool, with kids swimming and splashing. They don't see me looming over them, and it's nice to be invisible, even for a few minutes. I make my way through their little settlement, then out again into the countryside, where lush, green rice fields expand to the left, cross a sluggish river (more tantalizing water for the men of 1942) and, with a jolt, see a large sign:

Accident Prone Area

Just beyond, I see another of the many churches along the way, the sign for this one offering Isaiah 41:18: "I will open rivers in high places, and fountains in the midst of valleys." The irony seeps.

Denying water to the enemy went hand-in-hand with maintaining control during the march, and the first response of the Japanese guards in some cases was to shoot or stab. Panic bred the wild responses that some remembered: "They'd shoot indiscriminately into the crowd and some got shot and laid there."[99] Oliver Allen described a typical scene:

> I was trying to fill my empty canteen, but the thirsty men behind me began to push and shove to get to the well, much like thirsty cattle stampeding at the smell of water. Soon I had been shoved to the ground; I was down and I couldn't get up. About the time I worked myself into a position to rise to my feet, someone would step on me, kick me or push me back down. The longer it lasted the worse it got, as more and more men were piling on top of each other. I was getting trampled to death.[100]

No guard, trained to instantly obey orders, was prepared to deal with such disorder.

Japanese guards were aware that their prisoners needed water, and often gave permission. They soon discovered, though, the liabilities of such largesse. When they allowed prisoners to approach the artesians, Cletis Overton recalled, "we'd storm it like a stampede." Dick Bilyeu remembered that some of his "group had been granted permission to leave the column for water, but other guards reasoned they might be trying to escape and opened fire on them with their rifles." William Evans conjured the same image: "In almost every little barrio we

At artesian wells and other water sites, chaos born of prisoners' lack of discipline was responsible for many deaths (courtesy Christopher Leet).

passed through, there was an artesian well with crystal clear water flowing into a concrete holding tank. Several bodies of Americans and Filipinos would be lying around these wells as evidence that they had not controlled themselves, had broken ranks to get a drink of water, and had been summarily shot."[101]

The artesian wells in the barrios, which for centuries had been the peaceful, free water source for Filipino peasants, now saw blood flow as freely as their crystal clear waters. No standing Japanese guards were on permanent duty at the water sites, and one can easily imagine the surging throng as word spread in the columns that water was near.

Japanese guards, frustrated, without guidance from their officers, alone and responsible for maintaining order, unable to make themselves understood to their wards, began to deal with the unexpected in the only way available to them.

Lester Tenney's account is one of dozens similar. He and a friend ran for an artesian well, drank, and filled their canteens, after which ten or fifteen others followed. Five of those drank their fill, then suddenly the Japanese guard appeared and bayoneted the sixth. Red Allen grimly observed that the worse the chaos, the more lethal; the ground he saw was "littered with the bodies of dead Americans, especially around the water wells, where the guards, infuriated with the mass of pushing humanity, bayoneted anyone within reach. Those in the rear said it soon became impossible to get to the wells without stepping over dead men."[102]

Just after obelisk #4 comes a downpour—the sky opens up and sharp bends in the zig-zag road now guide small rivers down over my shoes. I put on the slicker and think of nature's way of ignoring human needs—how the soldiers of 1942 would have thanked their gods for even a few drops of the torrent that assails me. While listening to the squish of my shoes, I remember that it rained only once on the Death March.

Richard Gordon remembered men running for the artesian wells along the roadway, many shot or bayoneted while doing this. Others remembered that when the prisoners broke and ran for the water, guards would "shoot indiscriminately into the crowd." Guards remained with POWs long enough to offer deterrents; presumably to prevent such disorder among their prisoners, they may have sometimes selected some unlucky American for execution. Among such incidents was that of a young soldier accused of crashing the water line at Orion, taken away and summarily shot.[103]

Yet from an unlikely source comes insight regarding this gruesome reality. Corporal Koury went to the heart of the matter:

> [I]f a guy had been walking for four or five hours, he gets thirsty and sees an artesian well, and he thinks, "My God, I'll get a drink of water!" Well, they would shoot him because they told him not to do this. Who is to say they were wrong? I can't criticize the Japs too severely for it. I think they should have let us have that water, but, on the other hand, they told me not to drink that water, so I wasn't going to drink it. I never saw anybody shot, beaten or stabbed unless they did something against what we had already been told not to do.[104]

Earlier in the war, a smaller group of Americans, tempted by the same urges, found their officers unwilling to allow the descent into chaos.

On Wake Island American POWs had faced a similar hydraulic situation. As parched men waited to be given water after their surrender, a Japanese truck approached bearing a 55 gallon drum. "The prospect of getting a drink ... filled them with almost frantic energy. With no officers or foremen exerting control, the least disciplined prisoners refused to wait their turn and rushed the truck." One observer compared their behavior to wolves, and the Japanese, "panicked at the sight of this unruly crowd" deposited the drum and fled. American officers found this scene more horrifying than did the Japanese:

> Few things can frighten a professional soldier more than the sight of his men degenerating into a mob. The lawless scene triggered by the water truck's arrival finally galvanized the Marine officers on the airfield into taking command of the situation. They could see that their survival and that of every other American depended on reinstating discipline and order. Unless the current state of anarchy was curbed.... The next delivery would set off yet another mad scramble, with the strong and selfish trampling the weak. And if the men continued to run amuck, the Japanese might mistake such behavior for an uprising and start shooting.

Major George Potter took control of the situation, and separated the soldiers from the civilian contractors. This division, and Potter's moral authority, helped restore order, and the next delivery of water and food was met by POWs waiting their turn to be served.[105] At the artesian springs along Bataan's roads, there were too many prisoners, with too little discipline, supervised by too few guards or American or Japanese officers, to curb the anarchy in which so many were killed.

* * * * *

Many survivors' accounts explain the killing at the water sites as pure, vindictive cruelty. Samuel Grashio, who survived the Death March and later escaped, reflected later, "there is no reason other than sheer malice why they could not have let us stop periodically to drink from steams that ran along the road ... the pace of the march was not rapid.... There was no rationale ... save the sadistic desire to make us suffer."[106] Some more dispassionate observers thought differently. In his 1942 offering, *How the Japanese Army Fights*, the military observer Paul Thompson suggested that the Japanese soldier killed innocents simply because he "had little discipline once he is in the field" due to the "feminine and emotional quality of the race, which makes the Japanese lose control of their nerves."[107]

But some survivors recognized the actual logic, however cruelly applied, of the Japanese management of water sites. One such was an American corporal named Read, who thought more deeply about the subject: "I don't know why they wouldn't allow the prisoners to get water." Then he answered his own question with considerable insight:

> I think it was just a matter of organization. They were afraid they would lose control if they let us all dive out into these streams and wallows that we passed. If they had done it in an organized manner, it would have taken all day for a couple of thousand people to go and fill their canteens. I am sure they felt like they would lose control with the number of guards they had and so forth.[108]

Read was certainly correct. Just as there were not enough trucks to transport the prisoners, there were also not enough guards to guard them. Richard Gordon criticized his fellows for their inability to ration their own water supply:

> All during the march I would wait until I saw a well near a village when we stopped. Many times the rush of prisoners to the well would prohibit me from completely filling my canteen, but regardless of how much I got I conserved it until the next well. Obtaining water at "authorized" stops was permitted. Unfortunately no one took charge of such efforts and bedlam usually ensued. This could have been avoided if we were still a disciplined force. We were not.[109]

The two observations neatly summarize the reality of this most unfortunate cultural encounter—American indiscipline meeting Japanese *kata*. Many individual Japanese soldiers, confronted by a situation in the field for which their training in no way prepared them, responded in the way their socialization and army training demanded. Sam Grashio observed that although Japanese "military tactics were often predictable, when it came to personal conduct one never knew what they might do."[110] While individual Japanese might exhibit inconsistent behavior that baffled their American prisoners, their captors' response to the chaos of the water sites was quite predictable.

* * * * *

After a siege that lasted from March 13 to May 8, 1954, the French garrison at Dien Bien Phu in northwest Vietnam surrendered to Vietnamese forces. The numbers of the

French garrison, about 7,000, were similar to those of the Americans who surrendered on Bataan. Like the Americans, the defeated French were "in a state of severe physical breakdown after their long combat ordeal." However, the French prisoners' Death March was considerably longer—from the site of their defeat the French were forced to march between one and two months at a pace of twenty kilometers per day for the duration of a 500 mile trek to distant prison camps. The rations along the way were meager—fourteen ounces of rice and occasional peanuts, with inadequate water. Bernard Fall described behavior along the route of "this incredible Calvary":

> Small groups of men were fighting off death as best they could. The Foreign Legionnaires, with their fair skins, were least equipped to withstand the murderous climate, and their highly individualistic attitude led them to let each man fend for himself.... The mainland Frenchmen were hardly better equipped for such a march but displayed a psychological quality for which they had already been known in Nazi prison camps during World War II: a great amount of group cohesion and devotion to their wounded and sick comrades.

Cohesion was especially strong among the paratroopers, "who would grimly carry their wounded or sick comrades as long as they were physically able," even including their dead.[111]

The documentary *In the Hands of the Enemy: American Heroes of the Bataan Death March* imagines the American experience to have been like that of the mainland French. It features the deep and convincing narration of Brian Dennehy, interspersed with scenes cut from the wartime production *Know Your Enemy: Japan*. Here the past is well distilled. The film describes the special sense of small town community in Janesville, Wisconsin, and the ninety-nine men it gave to the 192nd Tank Battalion, and it concludes with one of the survivors summarizing their experience: "They were a team. They had faith in each other, and trusted each other and they'd fight for each other ... and that makes a good unit." Time passes and gauzy, rose-colored visions of fellowship and battlefield cohesion come to replace nasty reality. American behavior more closely resembled that of the French Legionnaires.

As for the Japanese guards, they encountered a world of the unfamiliar for which they were unprepared by virtue of language and culture. Form renders the world knowable, and the Japanese, in the confused and confusing circumstances of their own victory, found themselves without any reference points for proper behavior. Indeed, their sense of vulnerability and insistence on order, combined with prisoners' poor discipline and lack of unit cohesion, all complicated by the language barrier, explains a great deal about the chaos and death at the water sites along the route of the march.

5

The Lens of Memory

There is nothing either good or bad, but thinking makes it so.—Shakespeare, *Hamlet*

In 1967, Ralph Hibbs returned to Bataan to retrieve a camera he had hidden away, just before surrender, in a hollow tree. He looked, but could not orient himself in a local landscape denuded of trees. There he "wandered around, hopelessly lost," his treasure forever gone.[1] Hibbs' photographic record was lost, but he was among the many survivors whose constructed memory was, in its own way, as seemingly unchallengeable as a series of photographs. Certain they occupied a kind of moral high ground, these men offered their accounts as victims—of malign fate, of the Japanese, of each other in the camps, and of a largely unsympathetic and ungrateful society upon their return.

Ironically, though the greater society denied these men the recognition they craved, the veracity of their individual accounts goes unchallenged. Our understanding of those two weeks in April, for better or worse, has depended solely upon the scores of reminiscences, diaries and transcripts of oral interviews left by the survivors. For this reason, the student of the Death March faces a difficult and fascinating problem with sources. Any claim of Japanese cruelty can only be corroborated by other authors whose agenda was the same—to highlight that cruelty and their own suffering.

The records upon which understanding of the Death March rests are a series of *reflections*, almost always written long after 1942. As such they are not truly primary sources at all, but rather "what an individual thinks spontaneously about the past, the values and affective impressions with which he characterizes the past and makes it relevant to his own present situation." The historian William Moss goes further, stating that reflections

> must not be confused with the past on which they focus. A reflection is a contemporary event of contemplating and evaluating the past, but it is not the past which is the subject of the evaluation. The historian must use reflections with the same caution that he uses recollections, as clues to the significance and meaning that past events have for people in the present. Reflections are hardly to be classed as evidence about the past at all, and thus they must be separated from recollections as a level of historical evidence.[2]

Working with this material, then, is to confront a central, unavoidable reality: what these narratives describe cannot be verified in the absence of an external source. The problem is thrown into even sharper relief upon reading the secondary works dealing with the Death March. These authors accept without modification the accounts that were filtered through the distorting lenses of time and the unreliability of memory.

This chapter, then, is about words and their troublesome claims on meaning, about what caused these men to blur the line between dream and memory, or to substitute imagination for either. It questions the often gruesome images the narratives have offered with such compelling power, and why subsequent authors and other readers have found them so pruriently attractive. It seeks to pierce the hard interpretive shell that has formed around the Death March. To read their words with creative doubt is both challenging and liberating. Between the highly implausible and the oft corroborated lies an unexplored terrain of memory.

* * * * *

In Hesiod's *Theogony*, a seventh century BCE work dealing with the genealogies of the Greek gods, poets receive their powers of authoritative speech from their possession of Mnemosyne, the personification of memory in Greek mythology. Such was the authority, born of the power of their suffering, assumed by the men who wrote of the Death March. One scholar speaks to this reality, dividing "autobiographers into two unequal camps: the overwhelming majority, who place their trust in the concept of an invariant memory that preserves the past intact ... and a small group of dissenters, who argue against such a possibility."[3] Among those who wrote of their experience on the Death March I have found no such dissent. Taken as a whole, the records left by these men illustrate what the historian Gavin Daws has called "moral truth according to the POW." They reflect what the historian and literary critic Hayden White defines as the need for "moral meaning, a demand that sequences of real events be assessed as to their significance as elements in a moral drama." White is certain that all historical narratives are "informed not only by moral awareness but specifically by the moral authority of the narrator."[4]

For Bataan survivors, that authority derived in substantial measure from membership in a very exclusive club. Some sixteen million American men served in the armed forces during the war; by 1945 eleven million remained. Of these, two million were in combat divisions, of those, 700,000 were in the infantry. The stark reality was that infantry units made up only 14 percent of U.S. strength overseas, but suffered nearly three quarters of the casualties. In many theaters of operation, the actual fighting was done by about 10 percent of the total manpower, the rest in support of those who actually toted rifles and threw grenades.[5] Between those who actually fought and anyone else, the chasm between experience and innocence grows wider still. The World War I poet Siegfried Sassoon spoke to this gulf in his poem "Suicide in the Trenches":

> You smug-faced crowds with kindling eye
> Who cheer when soldier lads march by,
> Sneak home and pray you'll never know
> The hell where youth and laughter go.

Many since have echoed the fundamental distinction between those who have known combat and those who have not. A scene in Nunnally Johnson's 1956 film *The Man in the Gray Flannel Suit* speaks to the wide divide between peace and war, the mundane and the soldier's terror. We see Tom Rath riding the train to work with an acquaintance who is looking at the newspaper, saying that he cannot get used to the idea of the Brooklyn Dodgers as world champions. Then a flashback, Rath in Italy, killing a German soldier for his coat, to keep from freezing to death.

Many veterans maintain that those outside the relatively small group fraternity of combat veterans can never understand the experience, "even if they possess very wide-ranging imaginations and warm sympathies.... In general, the principle is, the farther from the scene of horror, the easier the talk."[6] The monumental study of U.S. combat soldiers undertaken by Samuel Stouffer, *The American Soldier: Combat and Its Aftermath*, illustrates the special fraternity of fighting men:

> Any individual's action which had conceivable bearing on the safety of others in the group became a matter of proper concern for the group as a whole. Mutual dependence, however, was more than a matter of mere survival. Isolated as he was from contact with the rest of the world, the combat man was thrown back on his outfit to meet the various affectional needs for response, recognition, approval, and in general for appreciation as a significant person rather than a means—needs which he would normally satisfy in his relations with his family and with friends of his own choosing."[7]

Bill Mauldin, the author of popular wartime cartoons featuring the infantrymen "Willie and Joe," described the interaction between those who had "seen the elephant" and the green replacement:

> While men in combat outfits kid each other around, they have a sort of family complex about it. No outsiders may join.... If a stranger comes up to a group when they are bulling, they ignore him. If he takes it upon himself to laugh at something funny they have said, they freeze their expressions, turn slowly around, stare at him until his stature has shrunk to about four inches.... Combat people are an exclusive set, and if they want to be that way, it's their privilege.[8]

Experiencing the world of combat, some men derived a "sense of enhanced moral values" that somehow "nourished a widespread conviction that those at the front were better people than they had been before the war or than others were elsewhere."[9] To that world the unblooded, among others, were denied entry.

Some 13,000 Americans were on Bataan at the start of the Japanese invasion, and all of them had a claim on proximity to the terror of the front lines. About 9900 made the Death March, and 9300 arrived at Camp O'Donnell; around four thousand returned to the U.S. after the war ended. Of those we have records left by sixty-one survivors, with twenty-seven mentioned in Knox's oral history volume—fewer than one hundred men are left to speak for the experience of nearly 10,000. This demography leads directly to what one survivor asserted: that such men are "members of the world's most exclusive and impenetrable club."[10]

The club of Bataan survivors even excludes those captured a month later on Corregidor. The men who surrendered on May 6 had the advantage of a greater food supply during the siege, a source of enormous resentment. Later in prison, when they mingled with the Bataan survivors, it was obvious who was who. James Murphy noted that men from Corregidor arrived in Cabanatuan with "suitcases and dufflebags and clothing and food" and Richard Gordon "never failed to recognize a man captured on Corregidor as opposed to one taken on Bataan. Healthier and heavier than their fellow Americans from Bataan, it was usually this group who participated in the camp shows put on periodically. To have the energy to do so was beyond the capability of most Bataan survivors."[11]

General Edward King, who had surrendered his army on Bataan, wrote the foreword to Sam Moody's book, *Reprieve from Hell*:

> Courage is a quality God had given fit to dispense with utmost care. His limits it to His special favorites. He knows they will reward him well, using the power with dignity, strength and distinction. The men of Bataan ... were His chosen favorites. They walked through unbearable Hell and labored on under conditions history had never before recorded.[12]

By January 1945, when a special force of raiders liberated Death March survivors, they "were a special lot, a subset of a subset of bad fortune, an elite of the damned."[13] Moody, speaking with a fellow prisoner while interned in the Philippines, looked to the future to give meaning to his experience: "We ought to get some bunch together after this is over and remember all the guys that were out here and have an organization to keep it holy ... and let's just keep it for the guys in the prison camp here."[14]

Decades later, the internet age provided the means to realize his hope. A website for the group of veterans known as the "Battling Bastards of Bataan" proclaims its motto "In Pursuit of Truth," and in the march 2007 newsletter, Tillman J. Rutledge, the group's commander, stated:

> We still receive inquiries from next of kin, families, and friends that were told their relative was on the Bataan Death March.... Most of the time ... we can verify such claims or disapprove it. We expose such "wannabees" without mercy. Why so many want to claim they were on the Death March is very puzzling to us ... it amounts to stolen valor. It degrades those that were on the Bataan Death March and is an insult to the memory of those we lost on the march and at O'Donnell.

The website custodians guard the integrity of the group assiduously. The application for membership states:

> ALL ACTIVE MEMBERS MUST HAVE SERVED ON BATAAN DURING THE PERIOD 2 JANUARY 1942 AND 9 APRIL 1942. A FALSE APPLICATION WILL RESULT IN DISMISSAL OF MEMBER.

These men—with the most tenacious claim on truth—were the ones most certain to tell only part of the story. Of the thousands who never wrote of their experiences, perhaps many wanted only to forget, and they took whatever memories with them to the grave. Doubtless others had less about which to write.

All the narratives, though their titles often make specific reference to the Death March, devote relatively few pages to it. Many begin with autobiographical details—where the men were born, where they were schooled, and the circumstances of their entrance into military service. Often they continue with descriptions of their training, or lack of it, their trip overseas to the Philippines, the Japanese attack, and whatever combat they may have experienced between December 1941 and April 9, 1942, when the Fil-American army surrendered. The longest descriptions of what survivors called "The Hike" run to no more than twenty pages, followed by their experience in Camp O'Donnell and other prisons in the Philippines, transport away to Manchuria, Taiwan or Japan in "Hell Ships" and the work they did as prisoners before liberation at war's end.

Why did these men put pen to paper—often decades after their return to the U.S.? At some basic level, the impulse to record one's history is, for anyone, an escape from the oblivion of death. Friedrich Nietzsche, in his *Untimely Meditations*, spoke to men's shared hope for posterity: "But one thing will live, the monogram of their most essential being, a work, an act, a piece of rare enlightenment, a creation: it will live because posterity cannot do without it." Paul Fussell, never to be outdone in darkness of perspective, suggested that "life is short and almost always ends messily ... that no one thinks as well of you as you do yourself, and that one or two generations from now you will be forgotten entirely and that the world will go on as if you had never existed."[15]

Death March survivors, however, felt a special anxiety, a heightened need to speak to the future—to deny the possibility that their variety of suffering could be forgotten. Sissela Bok's essay "Autobiography as Moral Battleground" makes the point cogently:

> It is first and foremost against oblivion, against the confusing of their persons with others after death, against the wiping out of all traces of their lives, that many autobiographers write.... Their activities and efforts ... were not for naught. Even their suffering must have had meaning. For the brief duration of their lives, they had a unique perspective on the world that they knew. They saw, felt, heard, loved and hated from their own vantage point. Why should it be, how *could* it be, that in the long run none should care to know?[16]

Decades later, the past under construction (courtesy Christopher Leet).

They wanted to preserve what they saw and heard, whom they loved and hated, that born of an ordeal whose contours defied their powers of description. Some were ambivalent about how to record their ordeal, but not why.

James Bollich thought it was "impossible to describe what we went through. Impossible to tell and impossible to describe by written word. I have since read many good books on the subject and seen film documentaries made, but you had to be there and experience it to know what it was like. I know that my meager attempt will also fail, but I will write about it anyway."[17] Philip Brain wrote three essays dealing with his experience, in 1965, 1983 and 1986. He remembered the first attempt to collect repressed memories was an emotional ordeal, but "the support and understanding of Rotarians helped [him] to open the door to memories and feelings kept hidden for years." His two later attempts allowed him "to express thoughts that [he] was not able to express earlier." Yet he was still frustrated:

> While I am grateful for the opportunity to recall, and attempt to communicate, one soldier's response to such an experience, I am still unable to put into words feelings I most want to convey. This is a reality I have come to accept without fully understanding why, and I must beg forbearance by those who may read my words.[18]

Perhaps such awkwardness is "an eloquence problem—most of those with firsthand experience of the war at its worst were not elaborately educated people. Relatively inarticulate, most have remained silent about what they know." These men were not destined "to become our most effective men of letters or impressive ethical theorists or professors of contemporary history or international law. The testimony of experience has tended to come from rough diamonds."[19]

For these men, memory was a simple matter. One survivor's book, echoing the certitude of my dinner host's proclamation, is simply titled *I Was There, Charley*, and it carries with it the message of many others' recollections of Bataan. The poignancy of such testimony surely outweighs whatever it lacks in eloquence—*The Forgotten of Bataan; The Hard Way Home; Parade of the Dead; Surviving Bataan and Beyond; POW: Tears That Never Dry; With Only the Will to Live; Horror Trek; Journey Through Hell; My Hitch in Hell* and, perhaps most telling, *Horror Trek: A True Story of Bataan*.

Whatever difficulties attended writing, the result was certain. Alvin Poweleit stated that he wrote his memoir "without embellishment or superlatives.... Only factual information ... is included.[20] On the copy I used in writing this book I found the following inscription by the author:

> To Ray Horn—
> The way it really was 1941–45
> Sincerely, Alvin C Poweleit

Major Poweleit wrote those words in 1975, forty years after his release from Japanese prison, but the descriptions in his book, often matter-of-fact, sometimes gruesome, occasionally bitter, always compelling, carry the peculiar moral weight of "one who was there." J.D. Merritt's book, *Adapt or Die*, bears a similar message:

> To Kevin Murphy—
> Truth is the Soul of this book and it is written exactly as I lived it.
> —J D Merritt

In his book about the Holocaust, James Young observed, "Violent events and massive human suffering of the kind exemplified in wars and massacres ... seem always to have stimulated an outpouring of what might be called 'factually insistent' narrative." Such are the records left by Death March survivors. Sam Grashio sought this crucial distinction, making clear in his narrative that "the events described are things that happened to me or that I saw; not just atrocities I heard about or read about afterward." William Evans stated that "the American people should never be permitted to forget" the atrocities of the Japanese, and that his was "a true story without exaggerations, embellishments, or cover-ups." Another survivor, Alfred Weinstein, spoke with passion about why he set pen to paper: "I wrote a story. I had to write it. Every fiber of a brain and body which has survived forty months in Japanese prison camps cried out for it. It had to be written from memory." Weinstein "needed no diary" because his experience was "indelibly seared into [his] brain."[21] Survivors repeat such claims with frequency and occasional shrillness—Theodore Abraham's memoir is titled *"Do You Understand, Huh?" A POW's Lament*.

What survivors wished their readers to understand was a simple and compelling story. One such author, waiting for the Japanese to arrive after surrender on April 9, had a premonition, "a funny feeling about what these people would do and what type of people they were—savage and sadistic by nature." Another stated simply, "I was to learn that what we knew as a western civilization had not yet reached Japan." Oliver Allen, writing sixty years later, stated, "The Japanese may be Westernized to a great extent now, but in 1942 they were as Oriental as Genghis Khan." Richard Gordon stated flatly, "No survivor of Bataan will ever question the fact that the Japanese were to a man 'barbarians.'" Some believed even savagery was inadequate to explain Japanese behavior: "the raw brutality exhibited by Japanese soldiers is incomprehensible and can only be explained by the existence of evil."[22]

For Abie Abraham, as for many others, the story of the Death March was more complete insofar as it recorded and honored their suffering at the hands of the enemy. He groped toward what he considered the essence of the experience:

> The story of Bataan's fall to the Japanese has been told many times.... But for many more years to come, new light will continue to be shed on the gallant, heart-breaking story.... A true story will bring home closer in all their starkness the sufferings endured by Filipino and American troops.... A true story will be told one of these days. A story will be told on what really happened on the Death March.[23]

What Abraham wanted was an elaboration of the POW story, not a challenge to it. For most Bataan survivors, that story—centrally concerned with their suffering—existed in a realm beyond interpretation, and certainly beyond revision.

* * * * *

John Steinbeck noted that during the war, correspondents lived and wrote by a "rule book" among whose components were that "there were no cowards in the American army, and of all the brave men the private in the infantry was the bravest and noblest." Years later, the influence of that rule book, appropriately expanded, has defined the reverent approach taken by the authors of secondary works on the Death March. Typical is John Toland, the author of *The Rising Sun*, who wrote the foreword to Manny Lawton's *Some Survived*, calling Lawton's recollections "of special interest because he is a sensitive, objective man with a remarkable sense of recall."[24]

The influence of the original wartime Death March story, that of William E. Dyess, remains strong. Brian MacArthur's *Surviving the Sword: Prisoners of the Japanese, 1942–45* devotes six pages to describing the march, all of which is taken from Dyess, nearly verbatim. MacArthur prefaced his book with "The Fepow [Far Eastern Prisoner of War] Prayer," suggesting that memory was, however unfortunately, the exclusive province of the men themselves:

> As we that are left grow old with the years
> Remembering the heartaches, the pains and the tears,
> Hoping and praying that never again
> Will man sink to such sorrow and shame,
> The price that was paid—we will always remember
> Every day, every month—not just in November.

MacArthur's 2005 book serves his central purpose of telling the story of a generation soon to pass—"it is time their story was told, especially to a new generation, most of whom remain ignorant of the suffering they endured. It is time we remembered the quality, the sacrifices, the suffering, and the courage of the fepows."[25] In *The Pacific War*, John Costello waxed slightly sympathetic before turning to the tried and true:

> Some Japanese did show sympathy for the plight of their ragged columns of starving captives, to the extent of sharing their own meager rations, but most obeyed the callous dictates of Bushido. Stragglers would be mercilessly clubbed, those dying from disease and malnutrition were left by the wayside, and men who appeared to be succumbing were buried alive by their comrades at gunpoint.[26]

Another example is Hampton Sides' *Ghost Soldiers: The Epic Account of World War II's Greatest Rescue Mission*, which deals with the daring attack on the prison camp at Cabanatuan in January 1945, during which a number of Death March survivors were liberated. One review called it "A compelling story filled with colorful characters." Another credited Sides with giving "texture to the personalities of captives, captors and rescuers alike," and a third opined, "you'd have to have a heart of stone not to be moved—and inspired—by this book." Certainly at one level the praise is well-earned.

Sides chose three characters to represent the experience of the Death March. The first was hard-luck Edward "Tommie" Thomas, whose father deserted the family. Thomas lived a hardscrabble existence in Grand Rapids, left home and lived in a car for his last two years of high school. When his mother could not support him, he joined the army. The second was Abie Abraham, the son of Syrian immigrants in Pennsylvania. Abraham broke a world record for tree-sitting, did odd jobs, and eventually became a boxing champion. The third was Bert Bank, from Alabama, the son of Russian immigrants whose father lost everything in the Depression. Even so, Banks saved enough to go to college, where he enrolled in ROTC.[27] The personal details draw the reader closer to these men; there is indeed no substitute for the connection felt as we read of sturdy immigrant progeny, hardscrabble youth and boxing matches.

Dorothy Cave contributed *Beyond Courage* in 1992, an overly enthusiastic book dealing with New Mexico National Guardsmen on Bataan. She describes a wide variety of incidents, as unlikely as lurid, without proper citation, sometimes without sources of any kind. One example is that of Virgil Sherwood, whom she claims walked the route of the march barefoot, escaped, was caught "and as punishment [was] taken to Mariveles and forced to make [the march] over again—still barefoot." Among dozens of similar examples, she describes the horrifying scene of a Filipina, eight months pregnant, who passed a rice ball to a soldier, whereupon a guard bayoneted her through the stomach, then through heart, after which a second Japanese cut out the fetus and held it up, laughing. With the same cruelty, another guard saw an old woman giving water to prisoners, after which he "dragged her out by her hair," cut off her ears and breasts, then "threw the bloody pulps into the column."[28]

A.J. Barker's study of prisoners of war asserts, "Americans captured by General Homma's forces on the Bataan Peninsula ... were lucky if they reached a prison camp alive.... When they marched through occupied villages, the Japanese troops would line the route and beat the prisoners with sticks as they marched by." Bruce Bliven's *From Pearl to Okinawa* states that "Japanese guards allowed the Americans and Filipinos practically no food or water, and seemed to enjoy torturing their helpless prisoners.... Anyone too sick or exhausted to keep up with the march was shot, and the stronger prisoners were not allowed to help the weak."[29] Dyess' account, published in wartime for the pupose of stimulating the sale of war bonds, contained understandable embellishments, but ones that have defined secondary accounts for a half century and more.

Occasionally secondary sources embellish further what was unlikely to start with. In his book *Give Us This Day*, the survivor Sidney Stewart describes giving a Japanese guard some sleeping pills, an overdose of which would presumably kill him. William Breuer, in *Great Raid on Cabanatuan* changed this into the guard dying in convulsions and agony a few minutes later, with his Japanese comrades puzzled as to the cause of his demise. In addition to twisting the original story, Breuer cited the page numbers incorrectly.[30]

The most recent work on the Death March is Michael and Elizabeth Norman's *Tears in the Darkness: The Story of the Bataan Death March and Its Aftermath*, a fraction of which deals with the Death March. The narrative lynchpin of the book is the appealing biography and drawings of Ben Steele, one of the survivors. The book would be better named *a* story, as it has distinct novelistic features, with long passages of verbatim quotes from conversations survivors constructed in works written decades after the end of the war. Jan Thompson's 2011 short documentary *The Tragedy of Bataan* echoes the simple themes of cruelty and suffering. There Alec Baldwin's sonorous voice tells viewers that this is "one more story of the greatest generation" about "how courage and sacrifice helped save America during the early months of World War II." It is, according to Baldwin, "the ultimate story of patriotism, gallantry and relentless faith." All these works tell the same story, different only in their level of detail, and sustain a simple interpretation. To a great extent, they share the problem William Moss points out, that frequently such records are "used as the basis for a historical thesis simply because it is the only evidence available."[31]

Unfiltered sympathy for the tribulations of the Bataan veterans also appears in the significantly inflated mortality figures. Without doubt, the most reasonable figure is that provided by Stanley Falk in the only scholarly treatment of the event, *Bataan: The March of Death*, published in 1962. His careful research yielded solid data, including reasonable estimates of the number of men on Bataan before the last Japanese offensive in April, those killed in that offensive, those who eluded capture, the number on hand at the beginning the march (about 9900). Falk concludes that of these, perhaps six hundred did not reach Camp O'Donnell.[32]

This means that about one in seventeen Americans died on the march. If we reasonably assume that perhaps a quarter of those died of disease or exposure along the route, this leaves about four hundred killed by their Japanese guards, or about 4 percent. Even so, numerous works published after Falk's volume cite the death toll as 2,300 or more, nearly four times the actual figure. The origin of this figure is obscure, but its traction is undeniable. Of twelve secondary sources citing a figure, three chose several hundred, seven chose between two and three thousand (three at 2300 and two at 2330), and two works opting for 5,000 or more.[33]

One scholar of memory has suggested, "To report on one's memories is not so much a matter of consulting mental images as it is engaging in a sanctioned form of telling."[34] All these works (Falk's excepted) share one additional, fundamental feature: each takes in and reproduces what might be termed the "sanctity" of POWs' narratives at face value, allowing the survivors to impose their perspective—without editorial resistance. In the absence of such creative doubt, much of the nuance and texture of those two weeks in April 1942 is lost. None examine how or why the memories of the survivors would be distorted; each is content to remain within the comfortable interpretive triangle: Japanese impose their cruel will, innocent Americans suffer, Filipinos watch, helpless and sympathetic.

The contents of these men's narratives have gone unchallenged for a variety of reasons. One is the marketplace, understood by publishers to contain a healthy demand for gruesome accounts with appealingly disturbing titles. Publishers know that such works sell for the same reason people go to horror films—because "the deepest satisfaction lies in the sense of personal exemption from the fate of others. We watch them being exposed to powers that overwhelm them, and we enjoy the feelings of superiority of the secure."[35] To be sure, jejune accounts or ones offering some positive perspective on Japanese humanity would serve no cathartic purpose for their authors, and have little appeal to publishers concerned with the sensibilities of a post–World War II reading public eager to sustain the righteous verdict of the good war. Still, the public response to these narratives requires a deeper explanation.

In 1995, Binjamin Wilkomirski published a memoir entitled *Bruchstücke* (*Fragments*) which, translated into nine languages, received a great deal of international attention. The book describes his childhood in Riga, his flight from Nazi persecution, incarceration in two concentration camps, and his eventual residence in Switzerland. Although a few initially expressed mild reservations about the authenticity of the work, most reviewers and critics were elegiac in their praise. Typical was *The Guardian*, calling it "one of the great works about the Holocaust," equal to that of Primo Levi.[36]

The world Wilkomirski had created, both in what he claimed was his memoir and the public response that memoir had generated, collapsed in August 1998. That month saw Daniel Ganzfried, a writer for the Swiss weekly *Die Weltwoche*, publish an explosive two page article, stating that Wilkomirski's real name was in fact Bruno Dössekker, and that *Fragments* was a work of pure fiction, "an internalized collection of images by a man whose imagination has run away with him," and that his knowledge of Auschwitz was that of a tourist only. The following year, the Zurich literary agency that had assigned the publishing rights to *Fragments*, engaged Stefan Mächler, a professional historian, to investigate the entire affair. The resulting work, *The Wilkomirski Affair: A Study in Biographical Truth*, published in 2000, offered a compelling sixteen-point refutation of Wilkomirski's memoir, and concluded that

> the elements of Wilkomirski's story are full of contradictions both in their particulars and in regard to historical reality. Above all, however, they are incompatible with his own biographical reality. There is not the least doubt that ... the story he wrote in *Fragments* and has told elsewhere took place solely within the world of his thoughts and emotions."

Yet even in the face of Mächler's destruction of his memoir's veracity, Wilkomirski stubbornly clung to his version of the past, and made clear that, in principle, he rejected the entire critique.[37]

Clifford Geertz once stated, "Every man has the right to create his own savage for his own purposes. Perhaps every man does."[38] Clearly Wilkomirski did so, but of interest to a student of the Death March is not that he invented his savages, or why he might have done so. The fascinating issue is why anyone believed him. Mächler points out that "Paradoxically, the automatic belief in the authenticity of these narrated memories ... ultimately rest[s] on a collective memory that has established itself in the Western world." Indeed, the "horror that Wilkomirski describes ... still retains its collective and historical, albeit not its biographical, truth." Images of death camps, barking dogs, black-uniformed Nazis are common currency, and supply the context for any story that confirms those images. Readers of *Fragments* wanted, and expected, to believe his story; considering its compelling nature, questions of accuracy were unseemly. This is what the literature professor Peter von Matt has called the "moral pact," a "value system" readers accept, wherein

> all the delights and pleasures offered by the text can be had only if the reader says "yes" to its context of norms. The moral pact is thus an important ingredient in experiencing the text, and is called a "pact" because it consists of equally active input by both the text and the reader.

Fragments demands that its readers accept that its author comes "from a world divided into victims and villains," and any reader choosing incorrectly makes clear sympathy to "the side of the villains who planned to murder" Wilkomirski and others like him. Mächler explains that once readers have "established the pact, they must read *all* of the text on those terms. They have to know who is good and who is evil, know whom they are to fear and condemn and with whom they are to share fear and suffering."[39]

Ganzfried goes further, and suggests that the need to sympathize with the fate of the Holocaust victim "releases one from the onerous task of analyzing what is incomprehensible." Reading of his victimization, we become "lost in mindless sympathy, we find the victim the hero with whom we can fraternize on the side of morality." Indeed, as Mächler points out, "It is lovely to be moved by one's own sense of humanity, to relish one's own sensibilities, to watch oneself responding" to the suffering described. Indeed, the "public's reverent pose is one of the most striking hallmarks of the book's reception.... The almost religious zeal that set Wilkomirski the victim on a pedestal, above all standards of measurement." Others have warned of the problems of an event being "sacralized," since the memoirs of many survivors often contain numerous factual errors and exaggerations.[40]

Readers of the Death March narratives, including the authors of secondary accounts based on them, understand them in a similar context. This is a form of reverence for a special group of men. But belief in the authenticity of these works is also a function of the wartime image of the Japanese. In the aftermath of Pearl Harbor, Americans were certain that Japan was a "lawless nation, not fit for the ordinary diplomacy of law-abiding nations."[41] The sneak attack was merely the most horrible and aggressive expression of a culture fundamentally at odds with the Christian, enlightened West. An editorial from the *Infantry Journal* in January 1942 stated that "this war is a fight against.... Nipponese fighters who know no rules."[42] The reader feels solidarity with the innocent victims of such cruelty and barbarism—the corresponding villains rendered comfortably clear.

Between Pearl Harbor and Japanese surrender in Tokyo Bay, the wartime image of the Japanese as a savage enemy expanded, deepened, and general agreement on the nature of the Japanese character defined specific attitudes toward the Death March.[43] The wartime propaganda film *Know Your Enemy: Japan* offered a clear interpretation of Japanese behavior during the Hike. "This march of death was a lasting monument to the insane arrogance and brutality of the Japanese soldier. Thousands dropped out and were bayoneted and shot. Those who made it to prison camp were subjected to unspeakable humiliation and torture." Such notions lingered into the postwar period. Just as the public read Wilkomirski and filled in new details of an existing picture of Nazi cruelty, those who read Death March narratives do the same, relying on images of Japanese wartime cruelty sustained in part by films that offered standard images of wartime fanaticism, kamikaze and *banzai* charges on Pacific islands.

* * * * *

Oscar Wilde once observed, "Most people are other people. Their thoughts are someone else's opinions, their lives a mimicry, their passions a quotation." Wilde's assessment contains more than a kernel of truth and sheds light on the nature of Bataan survivors' accounts. Sam Grashio identified a central reality of survivors' memories: "While I did not personally witness Japanese atrocities ... many others did and there was much talk about them." In his memoir, *Some Survived*, Manny Lawton related a verbatim conversation with a colonel named Irwin, who inexplicably chose to carry some heavy personal effects on the Hike. His description of the colonel's demise is both telling and typical. "I learned later," he wrote,

> that ... one of [the guards] pressed a bayonet against his back, drawing blood.... Finally the impatient and merciless guard pushed him to the side of the road, pressed the rifle to his back and pulled the trigger. Colonel Jack Irwin was among the first of hundreds who were to meet such cruel deaths at the hands of brutal guards who were totally lacking in human kindness and compassion.

Lawton continued, "More frequently now, men fell behind and were shot."[44] Like many, his description begins with a specific incident—the conversation with Irwin—then moves on to an account of Irwin's death as related by another, then to a generalization about the guards' lack of humanity.

The vast majority of other survivors' narratives have another, crucially important feature in common. Reading the narratives, one is struck over and over by the sense that these men are describing events as would an observer who had experienced the march in its entirety, seen it from a universal perspective. At one level, this seems reasonable; there is a kind of safety in folding one's experience into a collective account. Harkening back to the Wilkomirski affair, one critic pointed out that how the author might have drawn on his collective, secondary knowledge of the Shoah: "If you take each of the events he describes, they seem to be the sum of the experience of all survivors."[45]

In many accounts there is a relative paucity of passages that make specific reference to an act of cruelty the narrator *himself* saw or experienced. In this way, survivors assume a common identity, and the cruelty inflicted on one American became that inflicted on all; survivors wanted to describe the unique barbarity of their enemy and the special suffering they experienced, saw or imagined in the most comprehensive terms imaginable. It was detail and structure by consensus. Among many similar accounts is that of Paul Ashton, who stated that numerous "emasculations, disembowelings, decapitations, amputations, hundreds of bayonetings, shootings and just plain bludgeonings to death of defenseless, starved, and wounded soldiers were common on the march, in full view of their helpless comrades."[46]

Lester Tenney remembered that "almost all of us were beaten and tortured beyond the body's normal endurance on the march" and another survivor remembered his guards as "openly sadistic, achieving satisfaction and delight in inflicting torture on us—their victims." Prisoners' frustration and hatred burst forth: "Occasionally, a prisoner gone berserk from the horror of it all jumped up and yelled curses at the Japanese, calling them a race of inhumane, low-down bastards." Such was the natural response to "unreasoning, unchristian brutality, deliberate cruelty and sadistic inclinations" of a barbarous enemy.[47]

Sergeant Vincent Silva devotes two pages to the Death March and mentions seeing one man bayoneted to death when running to drink from a water source, but far more typical are lines such as "Those that couldn't go on died where they fell, or were shot by the guards, or stabbed with bayonets and left to die" and "It is also true that some of our soldiers were buried while still alive" and "If a guard discovered a citizen leaving food or water for the POWs, that Filipino citizen would be shot or beheaded." Murray Sneddon joined the chorus of those describing a general perception of cruelty as opposed to its specific manifestations: "Any man who could not keep up the pace, and as a result fell behind the column, was finished. One of the guards who brought up the rear of the column simply placed the muzzle of his rifle against the skull of the faltering POW and pulled the trigger." Again, "the Japanese threatened to bayonet anyone who attempted to collect water.... The execution of marchers was increasing, drastically." And again, "Anyone who tried to drink water who was not allowed to, was shot. When the men were allowed to rest, they were forced down on burning hot pavement, and those who fell behind even a few yards were bayoneted and shot."[48]

Jesse Knowles expressed the rage of many in his verse, with requisite emphasis on the plural pronoun, now applied to the Japanese:

> It's they that took us that fatal day,
> It's they that made us pay and pay,
> It's they that counted us morn and night,
> It's they that again we wanted to fight,
> It's they that made us as we are...[49]

One American captain referred to the Death March as "Homma's sadistic scheme of savagery." The indictment was as broad as it was deep, yet another survivor describing his captors as an intrinsically evil: "Ever since Pearl Harbor, the Anglo-Saxons have known that Japanese courtesy was merely a mask to hide ulterior motives.... That the white races were duped has been revealed all too tragically ... the inherent character of the Japanese—a cruel, dominating treachery—is a matter of history."[50] Murray Sneddon offered an analysis that many shared:

> The ordinary Jap soldier became a wanton killer during the Death March. He killed simply because it felt good for him to kill, and it gave him the chance to use each one of the weapons he carried, in a variety of ways. Like sharks in the ocean who become stimulated when bait is plentiful and become so excited they enter into a feeding frenzy, the Nip soldier who was stimulated by the great number of ill captives became so excited by the prospect of annihilating his helpless,

unarmed enemies that he entered into a killing frenzy.... Perhaps you can understand now why I question the name Death March. To say that thousands of American and Filipino soldiers died during the Death March gives quite a different impression when stated: Kill-crazed Japanese soldiers brutally murdered thousands of American and Filipino captives during the forced march out of Bataan."[51]

To American soldiers fighting on Bataan, the Japanese were an alien race. Negative images of the Japanese as such stretched back at least a century, and as an enemy they were seen as far more pernicious than the Germans, with whom so many Americans shared a common heritage.

One source that provides some understanding of this is the extensive series of interviews conducted by the Research Branch of the U.S. army's Information and Education division. Its conclusion was telling:

> In spite of the wide currency of atrocity stories about the Japanese ... the proportion of front-line infantrymen who said they had personally witnessed enemy atrocities was the same in three divisions which fought in the Pacific as in the single available division which fought against the Germans, 13 percent. And although a considerably larger proportion in the Pacific said they had heard from others about true cases of atrocities, the majority of front-line infantrymen even there had not. If ... the reason for the greater hatred of the Japanese lay outside of and prior to personal battle experience, the larger proportion in the Pacific who said they had heard true stories of an enemy atrocity can be partially ascribed to the persisting ... predisposition to believe evil of the initially more hated enemy.

In a survey of 4,064 American infantrymen conducted in the spring of 1944, 13 percent claimed first-hand knowledge of Japanese atrocity, stating that they personally saw "cases of Japanese using methods of fighting or treating prisoners" they would call "dirty or inhuman." American predisposition toward Japanese is clear in the response to the next question: "How about the stories you have heard from others? Did you hear any true cases of Japanese using methods of fighting or treating prisoners which you would call dirty or inhuman?" To this, 45 percent responded in the affirmative.[52]

Clearly, more than three times the number who actually saw atrocities were willing to accept stories of Japanese atrocities *from others* as true. Were Japanese guards on the Death March more likely to commit atrocities than Japanese soldiers on the front lines of combat? Perhaps. Were Americans on the Death March more vulnerable to such acts and therefore invited their greater frequency? Perhaps. Satisfactory answers to either question are elusive, yet it seems clear that accounts of the Death March reflect the acceptance and the repetition of hearsay accounts of Japanese cruelty. Such accounts would naturally emphasize information that cast their captors in the worst possible light, a light refracted through a variety of distorting lenses.

* * * * *

In 1981, while many Bataan veterans were still alive, Donald Knox published an oral history, *Death March: The Survivors of Bataan*, containing the words of sixty-eight men. "Only in the memories of the survivors," Knox writes in his preface, "does that story remain alive." He does not question his subjects' sensibilities, suggesting that "little is forgotten, yet much is not spoken of.... Attending a reunion of the Defenders of Bataan and Corregidor is like walking into the village found at the conclusion of Ray Bradbury's *Fahrenheit 451*, where the escapees keep alive in their memories complete books that have been destroyed."[53] Two years earlier, John Neuenschwander published an article in *Oral History Review* that defined Knox's approach with considerable accuracy:

> The theory of long-term memory that coats standard interview guidelines goes something like this: Human memory is a vast storehouse of life experiences. What and how much people will remember will vary due to individual differences in such things as life style, personality and state of health. Whether an interviewee can or will share the contents of this storehouse is heavily dependent upon the interpersonal skill of the oral history interviewer. Ninety-nine percent of what the interviewee does share should be accepted as an honest if not a wholly accurate account of what transpired.[54]

Yet, as Neuenschwander points out, such testimony is questionable, and the assumptions of many practitioners of oral history are deeply flawed. He correctly observes, "Whereas most oral historians tend to be genuinely sanguine about the trustworthiness of the material they extract ... most psychologists are deeply skeptical.... The study of long-term memory has fallen beyond the reach of the psychologist and beneath the grasp of the oral historian." Much has fallen beneath such grasp, and neither survivors' oral testimony nor their written memoirs offer a definitive version of the Death March, they offer *one* version. As one scholar has stated, "most autobiographers proceed to tell their stories with only the most perfunctory and conventional acknowledgement of the memory problems they inevitably encounter."[55]

In *Remembrance of Things Past*, Marcel Proust describes an encounter that has become famous, the "episode of the madeleine":

> No sooner had the warm liquid mixed with the crumbs touched my palate than a shudder ran through me and I stopped, intent upon the extraordinary thing that was happening to me.... The taste was that of the little piece of madeleine which on Sunday mornings at Combray ... when I went to say good morning to her in her bedroom, my aunt Léonie used to give me, dipping it first in her own cup of tea or tisane. The sight of the little madeleine had recalled nothing to my mind before I tasted it. And all from my cup of tea.

Here is the vividness, what seems the unchallengeable accuracy and evocative quality of memory. Such an understanding stands in stark contrast to that offered by Akira Kurosawa's *Rashomon*, the fascinating film recounting a rape and murder of a samurai, told from the points of view of a bandit, the samurai's wife, a woodcutter and the samurai himself. More than anything, the film calls into question the relationship between self-interest and memories that are constructed.

The two ways of understanding memory—its accurate, evocative power for Proust, its unconscious distortions for Kurosawa—reflect the development of the study of memory in the field of cognitive psychology. Broadly speaking, one approach conceives of memories as "stored slides"—wherein the brain maintains snapshot pictures of events which are later retrieved in their original, identical form. A second, where the weight of virtually all of the current scholarship lies, holds that the "subjective experience of remembering does not correspond in any simple way to the reawakening or reactivation of a dormant picture in the mind."[56] Memory's creation, and its substance, are problematic.

There exists considerable tension between the survivors' claims of accurate memory and the admission, in the same works, that the cumulative rigors of the campaign and the march left them in a state of mental confusion. Americans had been intermittently under fire since December, and by April most were malnourished, discouraged, defeated. Many admitted freely that they completely lost their sense of time during the march and that the sequence of events, as well as the events themselves, became blurred. Alf Larson later wrote,

> Once the march started, everything just sort of froze in my mind. I was pretty numb the whole time. I didn't think and I didn't feel. I was like a robot and just kept moving. Other than daylight or dark, I lost all track of time. I had to blank everything out and focus straight ahead. I lived from day to day, in fact, hour by hour.[57]

For many, the overwhelming reality was such numbness.

John Olson stated, "It is significant that many of the survivors frankly confessed that they could remember little, if anything, of those traumatic days," since they arrived at Camp O'Donnell "in a state of mental and physical exhaustion" such that even the strongest were "virtually oblivious to much that went on." Time, he asserted, "stood still." The narratives yield a chorus of similar admissions. James Bollich wrote, "Things were confused in our minds then, and after nearly sixty years it's difficult to be certain about things." John Playter wrote, "exact recollections are hazy to me.... I feel uneasy giving details, but if what I write is not true, it is strictly unintentional." And Calvin G. Jackson's four days on the march caused him to state that after April 11, *"Don't remember days from then on."*[58]

A number of the memoirs refer to the dream-like state brought on by their generally debilitated state on the march. Murray Sneddon recalled, "At times I began to hallucinate.... I knew I had drifted beyond consciousness and I had no way of telling for how long." He continued, "If we started the march, I knew there was at least one day left to go; other than that I was in a mental fog." James Gautier also knew the consequences of fatigue:

> The mind has a way of shutting itself off from suffering.... The body goes on a kind of automatic pilot. We were so exhausted that many men dreamed while they walked, while others hallucinated, delirious from thirst or fever. Trudging through the heat and dust, thinking only of water, put me in a trance-like state, so many details of what happened are fuzzy.[59]

A third of the way to San Fernando, John Hubbard became "thoroughly confused," his memory afterward unclear, able only to recall a high-ranking officer at the end of the Hike who "muttered senselessly as he stumbled down the road in a state of serious mental derangement." Calvin Graef admitted, "It is impossible to try to remember everything that happened."[60]

Another distorting lens was the simple passage of time. In the winter of 2012 Ping Fu, the Chinese expatriate CEO of an American tech firm, published a moving work entitled *Bend, Not Break: A Life in Two Worlds*. There she recounted a horrifying incident while a young girl during the 1960s Cultural Revolution—the quartering of a teacher by four horsemen on a soccer field. When some critical readers pointed out that there was no evidence that the Red Guards ever administered any such punishment, Fu backtracked, stating, "In my mind I always thought I saw it.... Now I'm not sure.... Who can get fifty years of memory right?" Speaking of that time in her life, she admitted, "My dreams felt like memories and my memories faded into dreams—senses fractured, real people and places shaded themselves apart."[61]

Any inquiry into events described by participants years later must engage the issue of time's passage and its distorting effect on memory. The first accounts of events on the Death March did not appear until Homma's trial more than three months after the Japanese surrender. In the closing arguments there, defense counsel George Ott suggested that a variety of testimony against his client was exaggerated or false. He described the testimony on the fourteen instances of alleged atrocity on the march as

> highly incredible and even upon consideration of the evidence adduced by the Prosecution there remains great doubt in the mind of an average man that such things could have occurred. This doubt is based in many instances on the credibility of the witnesses and their obvious antagonism against the Accused.

He pointed in particular to Jimmy Baldassarre who, Ott maintained, did not "willfully state an untruth," but nevertheless had "difficulty in determining a fact from what is not a fact. Certainly his powers of observation and judgment are not of the best. He is the man who said he saw hundreds and hundreds of bodies along the road ... and things of that sort." Ott further pointed out that Baldassarre had misremembered or falsely reported conditions at Lubao.[62]

A few Americans escaped from Japanese prisons and one, William Dyess, was allowed to tell his tale two years later in 1944, at least in part to stimulate the sale of war bonds, but this was exceptional. No one kept a diary on the actual March, and few survivors kept any record of their experience in the prison camps. One who did illustrated the potential for distortion. A POW named P.H. Meier wrote that a soldier named Morgan told a sergeant, who in turn told him that a guard saw another POW in Camp O'Donnell throwing away a small amount of rice. The story went that the man was beaten, forced to stand in the sun for hours, then taken to the Japanese captain, who gave him a sword with which to commit suicide. At this, the captain cut the man's finger and made him sign a paper in his own blood, "contents of paper unknown."[63]

The men who walked the route from Mariveles to Capas and beyond (and those who rode in trucks) had to wait nearly four years before their circumstances began to allow reflection on their experience. Memories of the march lay dormant for years, more often decades. It is a commonplace that the acuity of memory, already blurred by the fatigue and confusion of the march, decreases over time, "reliability ... always inversely proportional to time-lapse between event and recollection, the closer the document is to the event it narrates, the better it is likely to be for historical purposes."[64]

Murray Sneddon began his book in 1985, John Bumgarner, reluctant to talk or write for nearly half a century, wrote his story at the prodding of family and friends. Clem Kathman, also urged by relatives, set pen to paper at almost the same age, hoping to open "the portals of [his] 88 year-old mind."[65] Sometimes the process had several layers. Fifty-five years after the march, Rick Peterson, then working in a zoo, interviewed Alf Larson. Afterward, Kristin Gilpatrick, a local newspaper reporter and editor for a credit union society, "transformed Peterson's transcripts into a book." Gilpatrick is owed thanks for recording a version of Peterson's version of Larson's version of the Death March, but the process could hardly be without distortion. Philip Brain waited four decades and only wrote at the urging of friends; Robert Haney began writing at age sixty-six, and even then it was difficult: "It took four years of trepidation and hurt to produce a manuscript." Yet, as for Holocaust victims, the "events become more and more distorted in their silent retention.... The longer the story remains untold, the more distorted it becomes in the survivor's conception of it."[66]

One study of thirty-five ex–POWs concluded that "mental changes occurred either subjectively or objectively in nearly all the survivors studied. Only 4 of the 35 said that there had been no alteration in their thinking.... The predominant involvement of memory, retention, and recently learned skills" suggested the severity of prison's effect on recollection.[67] Another suggested that usual symptoms among prisoners incarcerated for long periods was the daily complaint of "brain fag" and the

> inability to concentrate for any length of time.... Every prisoner finds that his memory fails him in some way. He cannot remember dates, names, streets, addresses, or his own phone number in his home. The past seems to fade out and there is only the present. Often as a matter of banter one prisoner asks another if he knows his first or middle name this morning. The usual reply is, "Well, as long as I know my first name, I'll get by another day."[68]

For many, such effects lingered well beyond the period of their captivity, the quality of their stories affected by "memory's penchant for trickery." One veteran spoke to the heart of the issue: "We cannot expect the recollections of septuagenarians and octogenarians across half a century to be precise, comprehensive and accurate in every respect.... Some people and incidents will be merged, corrupted or completely forgotten. And, inevitably, there will be factual errors."[69]

Beginning in the late 1980s and accelerating with the 50th anniversary of the end of World War II, a number of studies stimulated interest in the public construction of memory—how societies construct a "usable past" that is consistent with what they believe of themselves. Some causes of such distortion are social and cultural, some result from nationalistic impulses, still others from domestic political tensions. Among the most notable examples is Lincoln's imaginary notion of a "perpetual union" upon which, in part, he denied the Southern Confederacy the right to secede. Another is the collective recasting, starting in the 1880s, of the meaning of the American Civil War away from anything to do with black civil rights.[70]

The memory of individuals is every bit as protean. In his study of German prisoners during World War II, Erich Maschke identified a central problem—those remembering are constantly fitting their memories to current needs, a reality that is painful for the historian approaching sources critically.[71] Scholars who study brain mechanisms and the neuroscience of memory generally agree that "autobiographical memory is a constructive process ... people revise their personal histories. Long-term recollections are often constructions that reflect the impact of people's beliefs, knowledge, and goals at the time of retrieval." The historian Peter Fritzsche agrees. "Narratives," he writes, "whether or not they are written down, are constructed; they require repeated readjustments over time, and thus they incorporate the ... knowledge of the partial, unstable, and tendentious nature of the narrative."[72] For Death March survivors, victims of terribly bad luck, the past was "an artifice, and one susceptible to the most varied and sometimes most culpable manipulations."[73]

For Bataan veterans who had suffered through years in Japanese prisons, had returned to a less than enthusiastic welcome, and continued to suffer from a variety of physical, mental and social problems, the need to create and tell a coherent story was paramount. Understandably enough, survivors' stories found coherence in victimhood. At the Tokyo War Crimes Trial, Donald Ingle described the atrocities he saw, and at the end of the cross-examination, one of the defense attorneys for the Japanese, William Logan, asked Ingle, "You sound rather bitter about this, Mr. Ingle. Are you?" The answer came back after a pause: "Well, there are several thousand buddies that aren't here today that would be here if it weren't for that. Use your own judgment."[74] Ingle's bitterness is reflected in most survivors' accounts.

Acting on their urge to educate, some Holocaust survivors visited schools to tell their stories. As it happened "in the case of one man ... [it was] discovered, accidentally, that he did not actually remember some of the stories he was telling but learned them from his fellow survivors." One can easily imagine the similar evolution of the consensual memories of the Death March, at O'Donnell, with fellow survivors in various camps, and later at the reunions. Ralph Hibbs remembered, "Telling stories was a great pastime ... in captivity.... It seemed to me everyone was sticking to the truth the first year, began to lie the second year, and by the third year it was impossible to distinguish between truth and fiction." Such is suggestibility, one of what Daniel Schacter calls the "seven sins" of memory—"an individual's tendency to incorporate misleading information from external sources—other people, written materials or pictures ... into personal recollections."[75]

Ronald Reagan's oft-repeated story of a belly gunner on a damaged World War II bomber is a good example. While running for president in 1980, he related this incident—of a young belly gunner so seriously wounded he could not bail out of the plane, whereupon the pilot, in an act of selfless loyalty, says, "Never mind. We'll ride it down together." Reagan's campaign easily survived the revelation that the story almost exactly replicated a scene in a 1944 film *A Wing and a Prayer*. Such confusion is more common among the elderly, who are more likely to "forget the source of the misinformation; they cannot remember whether it was part of the original event or something they learned about."[76]

Napoleon Bonaparte once said, "Above all, be distrustful of eyewitnesses ... the only thing my grenadiers saw of Russia was the pack of the man in front." No doubt the vision of some Americans on the Death March was as limited; for others it expanded in the years after the march was over. At Camp Cabanatuan, at least six weeks after the conclusion of the Hike, Manny Lawton wrote that he debriefed with Major Karl Bauer, reviewing the Hike. "Karl," he recorded asking, "did you see many of the atrocities everyone is telling about?" Bauer answered yes—"I saw men shot for trying to get water or for not being able to keep up." They were joined by a sergeant who said he saw two airmen clubbed to death, then by a corporal, who "saw some terrible things. The worst was seeing my good buddy ... get beaten to death with a rifle butt. That Jap kept hitting him after he was down and out. It was horrible." Lawton relates that Peace continued, telling of two Americans "who had been buried alive up to their necks ... only their heads and hands were above ground." Lawton continues with certainty:

> Those eyewitness stories, put together with similar ones from other prisoners, painted a hideous picture of savage and inhumane brutality unbelievable in modern times. But they were true; unreal and unbelievable, yes, but definitely true—and unpardonable.[77]

Any student of the Death March is left with a choice—accept what the major, sergeant and corporal relate, or wonder further about the nature of eyewitness testimony, how it is recorded, by whom and when. Noted authorities on memory Robert Belli and Elizabeth Loftus state what is obvious enough: "As is well known, eyewitnesses are not secluded after witnessing an event." They suggest that "the misinformation effect more dramatically points to occasions in which people may remember an event as real, when in fact, it never occurred."[78]

The psychologist Dan McAdams writes, "The unfolding drama of life is revealed more by the telling than by the actual events told.... Stories are less about facts and more about meanings. In the subjective and embellished telling of the past, the past is constructed—history is made." In this process, changes in memory are especially enabled by frequent oral accounts of them, since the most recent telling is always fresher than the original memory.[79] Tony Bilek, for example, wrote his memoir fifty years after the war ended, but he was confident of its veracity because he had told it so many times. He believed it was most important to "show that we were survivors" and to honor the memory of those who did not make it back. Writing in 2003, he admitted that his recollection of "daily chronology was far from exact," yet his sixteen-page account of the march includes verbatim conversations, and specific, precise observations.[80]

It can be disturbing indeed to come face to face with incontrovertible evidence that memories, however precise and accurate they seem, are, in fact, simply wrong. Oliver Sacks' memoir of his boyhood during the London Blitz contains a vivid description of a bomb that fell into his backyard, and of his father and brothers pouring water on it as it hissed and threw off molten metal. Upon reading the book after it was published, Sacks' older brother told him the memory could not possibly have been his; rather it came from a letter about the incident his brother had written him.

> I was staggered by Michael's words. How could he dispute a memory I would not hesitate to swear on in a court of law, and had never doubted as real? "What do you mean?" I objected. "I can see the bomb in my mind's eye now, Pa with his pump, and Marcus and David with their buckets of water. How could I see it so clearly if I wasn't there? ... Clearly, I had not only been enthralled, but must have constructed the scene in my mind, from David's words, and then appropriated it, and taken it for a memory of my own.

Sacks was describing the "transference" of experiences—being unsure sure whether an event had actually happened or was only something we knew of second hand, or about which we read, or even dreamed. Chastened, he continues,

> It is startling to realize that some of our most cherished memories may never have happened—or may have happened to someone else. I suspect that many of my enthusiasms and impulses, which seem entirely my own, have arisen from others' suggestions, which have powerfully influenced me, consciously or unconsciously, and then been forgotten. I accepted that I must have forgotten or lost a great deal, but assumed that the memories I did have—especially those that were very vivid, concrete, and circumstantial—were essentially valid and reliable; and it was a shock to me when I found that some of them were not.[81]

The memories of Bataan veterans, some of them as vivid and concrete, are subject to the inaccuracy that Sacks describes.

Of central concern to this study is the relationship between intense emotion and memory. If a soldier witnessed a traumatic event, would his memory be poorer or clearer? One literate veteran of the Great War suggested that "fear ... first soften[s] the tablets of memory, so that the impressions ... are clearly and deeply cut, and when time cools them off the impressions are fixed like grooves of a gramophone record, and remain with you as long as your faculties. I have been surprised how accurate my memory has proved about times and places where I was frightened."[82]

Such certainty notwithstanding, the jury is out on the question—the way emotion and memory interact is a very complex matter. A considerable amount of scholarship suggests that "there is no simple relationship between emotion and memory such that emotion or stress impairs memory, or the opposite, that emotion leads to generally detailed, accurate and persistent memory." Christianson and Safer conclude that "memory for information associated with unpleasant emotional events, that is, information preceding and succeeding such events ... seem to be less accurately retained."[83]

Daniel Schacter agrees and states that "even traumatic memories are subject to distortion." His research with children and adults who have experienced traumatic events—kidnapping, a sniper attack, and violent assault revealed considerable inconsistency and inaccuracy in their recollection. Significantly, "people whose symptoms of post-traumatic stress had worsened ... tended to amplify the personal threat they had felt at the time of the shooting.... People appeared to be remembering the event through the filter of their later emotional states."[84] Other research confirms traumatic memory's unreliable dimensions—one pair of scholars posed the question "Is it really possible for vivid recollections to be completely fabricated?" They answer yes, citing experiments where, for example, memories of being lost in a shopping mall are implanted, after which normal adults fully elaborate the incidents, adding precise detail, though in fact no such event occurred.[85]

The word trauma derives from the Greek, meaning "wound." According to Cathy Caruth, the term trauma is understood as a "wound not inflicted upon the body but upon the mind"; it remains with the sufferer in the form of flashbacks. Death March survivor William Evans admitted to this haziness of even traumatic memory:

> I don't believe I ever actually saw a beheading. You might ask, "What do you mean you don't believe you ever saw a beheading? If you saw a guy get his head cut off, you'd remember it." Not necessarily. I sometimes get very dim flashbacks of seeing an American soldier thrashing around on the road with blood spurting out of his neck, but, if I saw this atrocity happen, I have chosen to erase it from my mind.[86]

Such memories "sometimes contain elements of both real and feared or imagined events." John MacCurdy's study of World War I veterans' flashbacks "often involved veterans 'worst fears' rather than actual combat episodes." Another researcher, the psychiatrist Fred Frankel, notes the need to take the veracity of "flashback" episodes with a grain of salt, "unless they are accompanied by corroborating evidence."[87] Yet for any event during the Death March, there is only survivor testimony, men for whom "the brain is an enchanted loom where millions of flashing shuttles weave a dissolving pattern. Since the mind recreates reality from abstractions of sense impressions, it can equally well simulate reality by recall and fantasy. The brain invents stories and runs imagined and remembered events back and forth through time."[88]

* * * * *

At this intersection it becomes necessary to confront the likelihood that many survivors borrowed, exaggerated or simply invented stories of Japanese cruelty. In *The Great War in Modern Memory*, Paul Fussell observed that "the memoir is a kind of fiction, differing from the 'first novel' ... only by continuous implicit attestations of veracity or appeals to documented historical fact.... The further personal written materials move from the form of daily diary, the closer they approach to the figurative and the fictional." Belli and Loftus make clear that false or imagined accounts are

> not confined to situations in which people are witness to an external event, as there is evidence that people can at times remember ... actions that in actuality never took place. In other words,

people may misattribute the source of a memory of their own behavior to reality, when in actuality the source lay elsewhere, perhaps in imagination or suggestion.[89]

Applying these insights to Death March narratives undercuts veterans' claim of *We were there*, and forces a reframing as *They are here*, where "the act of writing memoir allows us to continue participating in what we've witnessed ... we combine what happened with how the exploration of what happened continues to affect us."[90] John Olsen, Adjutant for Camp O'Donnell from April to June, understood this reality, and the historian's central problem. He wrote that

> the ability to judge with certainty the statements of others is extremely difficult. But from the point of view of history it is essential.... Certain verbatim quotes will be made that are exaggerated or specious ... many of these reflect either the ignorance of the originator about the subject or the dismal, pessimistic and distraught mental outlook of most of the hapless captives.

"Man's memory," he continued, "no matter how effective, is at best fragmentary.... If we can sift the factual circumstances from the often emotionally exaggerated tales of those who lived to recount what they saw and endured, we may come to know what was the real story." Abie Abraham apprehended the difficulty as well, suggesting that "many historians have been confused on the Death March.... Many books have been written, but they do not tell the real story.... Some made the Death March greater than it really was. Many told fantastic stories." After the war, he sat in an office reading the testimony against Homma's trial. There he concluded that "most of the stories were fabrications of over-active minds."[91]

In his sensitive treatment of concentration camp survivors, Terrence Des Pres addresses this issue. For the survivor, he writes, "suffering transcends relativity, and when one survivor's account of an event or circumstance is repeated in exactly the same way by dozens of other survivors ... from different nations and cultures, then one comes to trust the validity of such reports." Des Pres' task was "to provide a medium through which these scattered voices might issue one statement. He explains that "the world survivors speak of has been so rigidly shaped by necessity, and so completely shared—almost all survivors say "we" rather than "I"—that from one report to the next the degree of consistency is unusually high. The facts lie in a fixed configuration."[92] Yet I suggest that Death March survivors' narratives differed in a fundamental way—they assume the authority of the collective, but without the supporting substance.

While Japanese cruelty on the Death March is undeniable, it is also unquantifiable. It is possible, however, to eliminate some doubt when many accounts describe the same incident in the same way. Numerous Americans remembered seeing the body of a comrade crushed by Japanese tanks on the steep roadway outside Mariveles, repeatedly run over until it was flat on the road. Many of these descriptions are factual, and graphic enough. Kermit Lay stated that the Japanese "had run over this thing so many times that it looked like one of those small squashed animals you see on the freeway."[93]

Descriptions of Japanese cruelty fall into categories of ascending intensity—psychological, beating with various degrees of severity, bayoneting, beheading, and burial alive. In light of memory's vagaries, perhaps descriptions in each are subject to question. However, an examination of several versions of the most horrifying—burial alive—raises interesting questions. Ed Dyess, who escaped from the Philippines and whose account appeared in 1944, placed his incident in Orani. There he described a Japanese sergeant ordering a detail to bury three comatose men, one of whom regained consciousness as he was being thrown into an open hole. As the man (whose nationality is unclear) struggled to his feet, the guard emitted an order, whereupon one of the gravediggers "brought his shovel down upon [his] head" and he succumbed to his interment. Kermit Lay also remembered an incident where a Filipino, clawing way out of a grave, was beaten on head the head with a shovel.[94] Alf Larson remembered:

> When the [slit] trenches were almost full, the Japanese would take a detail of prisoners to fill them up with dirt. On one occasion I saw a soldier who had diarrhea really bad and went to the bathroom. After he finished, he could barely get up. He slipped and fell backwards into the trench. The Japanese ordered the prisoner detail to cover him up right there, which they did. They had no choice![95]

Lester Tenney's account was that of a delirious prisoner who could not stand, and a Japanese guard ordering two prisoners to dig a grave. One refused and was killed by the guard, after which his replacement helped bury a prisoner alive. Gene Jacobsen described a live burial at Balanga, where

> we watched, horrified, as the Japanese guards forced four Americans soldiers to dig their own common grave. The soldiers were then ... shot as they stood in the grave. One American soldier, only wounded by the volley of shots, struggled to claw his way out of the grave. He was beaten senseless by a shovel-wielding Japanese guard. Atrocities like this became more common as the march continued.

Anthony Czerwien recalled that U.S. soldiers were forced at gunpoint to bury their comrades alive, those with amoebic dysentery and cerebral malaria.[96]

Putting aside the possibility that these accounts recorded this aspect of Japanese cruelty with perfect accuracy, one is struck by the possibility that *one* such event occurred, perhaps something like what Dyess described, and that the other accounts borrowed from an original version, then changed the details. Of particular note are the comments by Jacobsen and Czerwien, both of which generalize Japanese behavior. Were the men who wrote of the Death March after Dyess guided by his account? Did one such story take root in the fertile ground of Camp O'Donnell as men exchanged stories, and grow into several versions?

Other examples of Japanese behavior are offered with hardly any corroboration from other accounts. The inside flap to the Popular Library edition of Sidney Stewart's 1956 narrative, *Give Us This Day*, carries the New York *Herald Tribune's* statement: "If he were never to write another line Sidney Stewart would know the satisfaction of having set down a narrative that belongs in the history of the literature of the war—a narrative that has about it the tragic reality and spiritual grandeur attained only by great novels." Indeed, Stewart's memoir, subtitled *The Powerful Narrative of the Bataan Death March* contains undeniably novelistic features.

The fourteen pages Stewart devoted to the Death March contain verbatim dialog related to a variety of subjects—including quoted lines from Goldsmith's "Deserted Village," and "thousands" of bodies along the road. At the end is a description of four Japanese guards walking among his column near Lubao with severed American heads impaled on their bayonets. James Gautier also remembered a similar grisly sight one night in his enclosure in Balanga, where he claimed he saw "a Jap was coming through the entrance with a GI's head impaled on the end of his rifle. The bayonet went right up through the throat and into the head"; two more Japanese wielding prisoners' heads followed.[97]

5. *The Lens of Memory* 149

These descriptions give pause. Stewart and Gautier are the only Bataan veterans to mention American heads on bayonets. Did these few Japanese engage in such terrorism? Perhaps one account corroborates the other—this indeed happened, with either different perpetrators or the same ones, though Lubao and Balanga are more than twenty miles apart. This is possible. As likely, it did not happen. One wonders about the absence of any other mention of such behavior in the scores of other survivors' accounts, ones whose point was to draw attention to Japanese barbarity. Then there is the reluctance of soldiers in any army to voluntarily carry more weight than absolutely required. Stewart himself suggests the possibility of having invented the story. "Sometimes," he wrote, "I think we all died on that march. Sometimes I feel sure that all the things that came later were just a fevered dream."[98]

Two other stories further highlight the problem. Abel Ortega recalled that Japanese guards tied prisoners to fences in order to "slice them open until their intestines came out and then leave them there to die." Edward Dyess also mentions a similar incident near the town of Lubao: "All eyes were directed toward an object hanging on a barbed wire fence," a Filipino soldier whose "abdomen was open. The bowels had been wrenched loose and were hanging like great grayish purple ropes along the strands or wire that supported the mutilated body."[99] Again, the choice. The events happened as described, or the fact that no other account corroborates them calls their veracity into question. If, as Dyess claimed, "all eyes" fell upon the horror, it seems unclear why only one other account would mention it.

Mark Twain once said, "I am an old man and have known a great many troubles, but most of them never happened"—surely an exaggeration, but in such places these narratives go beyond accuracy, into the realms of meaning, subjectivity, imagination, and emotion. Such realms gave rise to other descriptions. In Ken Burns' epic *The War*, Glenn Frazier told an audience of millions, "I marched six days and seven nights, never stopped. I did not have but one sip of water and no food. Now they say that you can't do this but I did." In the documentary *The Tragedy of Bataan*, Gene Bleil claimed that he "walked five days and four nights with no food and no water." In the midsummer heat of the Philippines, neither feat was possible.

Other accounts of unlikely events are obviously hearsay. One surgeon remembered a friend telling him of a "soldier crazed with thirst grab the arm of another GI with a freshly bleeding bayonet wound. He lapped up the blood like a cat cleaning its milk dish." Bert Bank, also relying on others' testimony, went further—"One person told me that he, along with other Americans, had been required to eat pieces of human flesh during the march. Another American told me that he had seen several men who had their penis cut off and stuck in their mouths." These are the descriptions that give requisite color to the secondary sources.[100]

Other descriptions with the ring of untruth or gross exaggeration crept into many accounts. Sam Moody mentioned dead children, claiming that the "American Highway to Manila was a holocaust of death.... Bodies of children, strewn along the side with their bony remains, cracked under tramping feet." Alf Larson claimed that Japanese guards amused themselves by pushing prisoners "over cliffs," and another veteran stated that "young girls were pulled out of ranks and raped repeatedly. Frightened mothers would rub human dung on their daughters' faces to make them unattractive to guards." James Bollich claimed that he and his fellows "endured constant beatings, beatings, beatings every time we ran into a new group down the road. They hit us with rifles, sabers, sticks and anything else they could get their hands on" and the next day "beatings and more beatings." Murray Sneddon described a pair of Americans who were forced to kneel with hands tied behind their backs, and "every Japanese soldier or Filipino coming down the road was required to beat them vigorously on their way by." Another remembered, "I saw the body of one American officer. He had been suspended from a tree limb and bayoneted repeatedly in the back and buttocks. Then his arms and legs had been hacked off."[101]

* * * * *

Hayden White asks, "What wish is enacted, what desire is gratified, by the fantasy that real events are properly represented when they can be shown to display the formal coherency of a story?" Part of the answer resides in a vignette from Kenneth Grahame's *Wind in the Willows*. There one of the main characters, Toad, describes an adventure he had to his friend Mole: "The mole was a good listener, and Toad, with no one to check his statements, or to criticize in an unfriendly spirit, rather let himself go." Bataan survivors took a degree of license because they could, because no competing narrative contradicted them and, presumably, because they truly came to believe their stories. Another part of the answer lies in the way their stories have been received—neither readers of survivors' narratives nor authors of secondary works were interested in any sort of critical response. Few have considered how much truth resides in the defense's concluding statement at Homma Masaharu's trial: "Take one or two facts supported by affidavits which admittedly are wrongs, allege but don't prove other and much more horrible facts, mix well, and there you have a real atrocity."[102]

Death March survivors described their experience as they wished and as was possible as their ordeal faded further into the past—"What one remembers is, at least in part, what could have happened or should have happened in one's life."[103] The border between dream and reality blurred, and accuracy diminished, as was inevitable. The lane down which they whispered, and sometimes shouted, was long and difficult. It was also laden with experiences that put a finer point on their self-definition as victims. The poet Anna Akhmatova apprehended something of this sensibility:

> As if I were a river
> The harsh age changed my course,
> Replaced one life with another,
> Flowing in a different channel
> And I do not recognize my shores.

6

Remembering and Forgetting

We have floated upwards from history, from memory, from Time. —Salman Rushdie, *Shame*

Survivors' narratives and the secondary works that grew from them have, almost exclusively, focused on the simple theme of cruelty and suffering. This approach leaves unexplored many aspects of the Death March. The home front responded to the American soldiers' travail on Bataan in particular ways, and put their defeat to peculiar use during the balance of the war. After the guns fell silent, returning survivors found little to suggest that the U.S. at peace had much, if any, interest in addressing their needs or in recognizing their sacrifice. Repatriated, embittered survivors were set adrift in an indifferent and sometimes even hostile peacetime world.

One Death March survivor spoke for many when he asserted, "Time does not heal all wounds; it buries them in very shallow graves."[1] Many wounds, physical and otherwise, never healed completely, and bitterness and anger lingered for decades. Addressing such issues leads to some of the darker terrain of World War II and its aftermath. The survivor of the Death March was caught in a difficult quandary. Resentful that his role in the war had been ignored, he wanted recognition, to be remembered for the sacrifice he had made. Yet this very action would have highlighted his participation, however unwilling, in a defeat his country wanted to forget.

* * * * *

The start of World War II saw memories of the Great War still roaming the American consciousness. A popular interwar tale appeared in a best-selling book by two journalists, Thomas Johnson and Fletcher Pratt. *The Lost Battalion*, published in the late 1930s, was the story of Major Charles W. Wittlesey, described as an erstwhile shy and self-effacing Boston attorney, who led an attack that penetrated German lines during the American offensive in the fall of 1918. His command was surrounded and trapped behind German lines for five days, and of the original 550, only 194 returned. To correspondents eager for drama, the harrowing story made good press. News flashes printed in the New York *Evening Post*, the New York *Sun*, and the *New York Times* spread the story nationwide. One example from the *Times* shouted:

BATTALION SPURNED OFFER OF SAFETY

"Go to Hell!" Shouted Whittlesey When Germans Sent Note Pleading for Surrender

Cheers Heard by Enemy

Beleaguered Force Fell into Trap Through Eagerness, and Were Ready to Fight to the Last

Expanded to book length, the story continued to fascinate Americans between the wars. A poignant vignette even made it into school readers—though missing an eye and leg, a carrier pigeon named Cher Ami, dispatched by the hero to call off the friendly fire that was killing his men, made it through. Johnson and Pratt called their extended kudos to Wittlesey "the supreme American hero-story of the World War."[2]

Another hero caught the country's attention in September 1941. Howard Hawks' vehicle for Gary Cooper, *Sergeant York*, was the highest-grossing film of the year and, since it was in theaters when the Japanese attacked Pearl Harbor, it was credited with stimulating enlistment. Alvin York participated in the same offensive as had the "lost battalion," but his cinematic redemption took a different form. The film portrays York as an undisciplined youth, given to violence, until he is struck by lightning and vows to mend his ways. He objects to U.S. participation in World War I but is drafted into service. There the audience sees him wrestle with the morality of war until finally, inspired by an appropriate bible verse, he leaves the reconciliation of his beliefs to the almighty. In France, he excels in combat, killing Germans and capturing more than 100 prisoners. He is rewarded with the Medal of Honor, comes home to a tickertape parade and, like Cincinnatus, returns to farming—on land grateful residents bought him in his native Tennessee.

Both book and film struck resonant chords. In *The Lost Battalion*, those who died left the field with honor, and the few who were rescued, after eschewing any possibility of surrender, had the courtesy not to have been captured. Heroism, after great suffering, is redeemed. The good sergeant, on the other hand, is redeemed by the hand of his god, his spiritual confusion ameliorated, his marksmanship given the appropriate battlefield target. The message in both works is clear: Americans are peace-loving, fight only when provoked, but do so then with great courage and skill—and they are not captured, they do the capturing.

Yet 1942 was not 1918. The Japanese tidal wave had overrun the U.S. garrisons on Wake Island and Guam. Bataan, though holding out for the agonizing three month siege, finally succumbed on the anniversary of Lee's capitulation to Grant in 1865. Such catastrophic humiliations directly contradicted the nation's concept of itself. Unaccustomed to defeat, Americans desperately needed to somehow to force the events of the first six months of the year into a less disconcerting form. This was a tall order, as the meanings offered in *The Lost Battalion* and *Sergeant York* were clear enough to Americans of that generation. This process was intimately bound up with guilt, wartime prosperity, the need to fund the war effort, and the creation, against much evidence to the contrary, of a phony hero.

* * * * *

America is historically unkind to the unsuccessful. Bataan's uncomfortable tale rather directly contradicts salient American notions of progress, moral certainty and material success. It is a story of abandonment, leaving the forlorn to their fate. Neither does the story comport well with the central images of the Pacific War—heroic Marines and GIs wading ashore at Guadalcanal, Tarawa, Saipan, the flag-raising on Iwo Jima and the final chapter of Okinawa on the bloody and inexorable path to the heart of the Japanese empire. Three months of starving combat after the disaster of Pearl Harbor, then ignominious surrender followed by three years' imprisonment, is a sidebar easily swallowed up by the later sweep across the Pacific to righteous victory.

During the agonizing fourteen weeks of the siege, the men stayed connected to the home front via a reliable short wave radio connection. Throughout their Gethsemane, they were able to hear two hours of broadcasts from San Francisco every day from five to seven p.m. The government made an effort to entertain, in one show offering Bing Crosby the opportunity to sing "When Those Caissons Go Rolling Along" to the artillerymen, after which he added, "those 155s keep dishing it out." The British actress Madeleine Carroll, whom the men no doubt recalled from her 1936 role in *The General Died at Dawn*, announced that all her dates were for service men. Soon enough many on Bataan would wish that cinematic fate on their commander.

Perhaps unaware or unconcerned that MacArthur had already cut the defenders' rations in half, the broadcast included a sample commercial from Kraft—"These are days when good nutrition takes on new importance. It's downright patriotic to know your vitamin alphabet and to see that your three meals ... are well balanced. America must be strong—Americans must be strong!" One message "urged listeners to hurry to their friendly neighborhood grocery and bring home a generous supply of mouth-watering cheese."[3] Jack Benny, Bob Hope, Eddie Cantor, Rudy Vallée and Cavalcade of America all found air time. In late March, as they pondered their impending *Götterdämmerung*, the men were treated to a work by Zoltán Kodály, written to celebrate the 250th anniversary of Budapest's emancipation from Turkey.[4] It remains unclear the degree to which such ironic tones soured in their ears.

On the home front, published articles included the expected apocrypha about the men's heroism—one sergeant, shot in the neck, simply "put a bandaid over the holes on either side ... and, incredibly, went on fighting." The reporting did not omit the *E pluribus unum* character of the American army. One piece described the exploits of Roland Sauiner, Edward Archie MacIntosh, Charles Steel, and the Native Americans Peter Flame and Joe Longknife, from a Montana reservation.[5] The end drew nearer and, in compensation for the impending disaster, the media painted MacArthur in ever more glowing terms. Earlier, readers were told that their hero was dreadfully outnumbered—at least 150,000 to his 20,000, although these figures exaggerated the Japanese force by 300 percent and omitted entirely the Filipino contingent of U.S. force. On March 2, *Time* magazine imagined that his men adored him as much as its correspondent:

> The men on Bataan kept watching for him.... Everything about him—the angle of his heavily braided cap, the swing of his brown, curve-handled cane, the uptilt of his long black cigaret holder, the shine of his four stars and brown shoes—everything was always jaunty ... day after dreary day, Douglas MacArthur cheered his tired men. He himself must have been sustained by the growing realization that he was a national hero.

An insurance man in Topeka, Kansas, confused about rank but sure of his symbol's meaning, stated simply, "MacArthur is the greatest general since Sergeant York."[6]

When the general arrived in Australia, *Time* trumpeted, "The U.S. and all the United

Headlines on April 10, 1942, blare the disaster. The front page of the *Examiner* still had room for an article on women's wartime clothing styles (Library of Congress).

Nations breathed a sigh of relief and hope: By God, they got him out!" MacArthur apparently believed that they, and others before them, were but agents of a larger force—once, speaking of his presence in the Philippines he announced, "By God, it was destiny that brought me here!" The correspondent generously described those left behind as "cheering men and officers who said farewell in the Philippines."[7]

Lt. Col. John Sewall wrote to his wife and children on February 18, "One of the most painful things of this whole war is our complete lack of communication. If I could only get a letter to you, or hear from you, everything would be alright." Sewall and others doing the fighting, now cut off from the home front except by radio, did not entirely share the home front's confidence, or at least that of the correspondents and editors who wrote and vetted the stories. A serious blow to hope came on Washington's birthday, February 22, as FDR gave his fireside chat on the war's progress. Listeners examined maps of the world as he explained the vast distances and the global, monumental task facing the Allies. Those concerned with the much more local geography of Bataan noted with bitterness that the president's message omitted any mention of their dire situation. One American listener, now sure of his fate, concluded that the president had "wiped us off the page and closed the book."[8]

Colonel Allison Ind, responding to a transcript of another FDR broadcast two days later, waxed sarcastic. The president stated, "we mustn't be impatient. The Pacific is a big body of water. Months required for a round trip. Right. Dare one arise to remark that the observation lacks originality?" Ind continued, "Two things do make us mad: (1) flamboyant talks about how much money has been appropriated and how much we'll have in 1943 (when none of us will be around to hear about it) and what men and equipment we're sending to every country under the sun—except this one; (2) a roaring imbecile of a congressman telling the world we should bomb Tokyo off the map."[9]

During Bataan's dark hours, some on the peninsula were appalled at a U.S. station broadcasting pugnacious challenges to Homma's army. "It was almost," recalled one bemused soldier, "as if Americans ... were issuing a challenge to the Japanese and stepping on Japanese pride at the same time.... It was kind of like a loudmouth bystander on the sidelines" egging a bully on to hit "a kid half his size."[10] Still, the disheartening battlefield reality of the war's first five months could not be helped. The bully had won the fight—or at least the first and second rounds very convincingly—and now the kid was left, at the far reach of the airwaves, to deal with that reality.

* * * * *

John Steinbeck, reminding himself of the rules that defined his work as a war correspondent, recalled that one "convention was that we had no cruel or ambitious or ignorant commanders. If the disorganized insanity we were a part of came a cropper, it was not only foreseen but a part of a grander strategy out of which victory would emerge." He also mentioned ruefully that the correspondents knew "that a certain very famous general officer constantly changed press agents because he felt he didn't get enough headlines."[11] In fact, throughout the war, MacArthur sported a swollen publicity organization that emitted a constant stream of information that made clear the general's hunger for attention as well as his infallibility.

Death March survivors overwhelmingly rejected MacArthur's self-assessment, as well as that of those who, ignoring his failures on Bataan, regarded him as a hero. In part, this was understandable scapegoating. Many survivors' narratives omit or downplay the fact that FDR ordered MacArthur to flee from the islands to Australia, there to take command of Allied forces and a portion of the Pacific counterattack. Yet even decades later, many recalled the man with unmistakable bitterness. His haughty manner that alienated many in rank and file, his poor generalship, the fact that he fled, leaving them to starve and suffer, and the accolades showered upon him in spite of the mismanaged defense of the Philippines, all rankled the men for decades afterward. For the men he abandoned, the irony of the MacArthur story was rich indeed.

Even before his mistakes during the campaign, MacArthur did little to endear himself to the common soldier. Except for the core of regulars, the Americans under his command had recently come from civilian life, and the general cultivated a sense of the imperious that rubbed many the wrong way. He spoke in grandiloquent language more suited to the nineteenth century. Before the Japanese invasion, he resided in a luxury apartment in Manila with his second wife, where he maintained a wardrobe consisting of twenty-three suits and uniforms, all "custom-made by a Chinese tailor." In the heat of Manila, it was the general's habit to wear three a day to maintain his appearance of freshness as others wilted.[12]

It was his military leadership, however, that caused Bataan veterans' bile to rise. War Plan ORANGE, the official and long-standing War Department blueprint for the defense of the Philippines, assumed that U.S. forces would engage the Japanese enemy only in central Luzon, their central mission to hold the entrance to Manila Bay. This plan mandated that supplies were to be immediately moved to Bataan upon war's outbreak, until depots there were sufficiently full to supply a garrison of 43,000 men for six months. There the Allied army would hold out and await rescue.

MacArthur regarded this plan as defeatist. In its place, he conceived an aggressive plan "whose object would be the defeat of any enemy that attempted the conquest of the Philippines." Soon his prestige with the War Department bore the desired fruit; by the fall of 1941 he had convinced the highest officials there that he could successfully repel a Japanese attack at the beaches, and in October Chief of Staff George Marshall granted MacArthur the revision he sought. The scope of his new plan, enlarged to take the entire archipelago into account, relied on the assumption that the available air force could disrupt Japanese traffic in the South China Sea, that he could complete the training of the Filipino contingent of the army and, most importantly, that the Japanese would courteously allow him the time required. In fact, he was wrong on all three counts.

MacArthur's ill-conceived substitute—to contest enemy landings at the beaches—meant that "supplies earmarked for Bataan under ORANGE therefore went to advance depots and railheads behind the beaches." As a result, supplies desperately needed on Bataan were scattered in other locations, with neither the time nor the planning necessary to bring them to Bataan. Even worse, "instead of the 43,000 men provided for in ORANGE, the force withdrawing to Bataan would be closer to 80,000." Louis Morton, the author of the most balanced and detailed history of the campaign, stated that such a "change in plans was destined to have a greater effect on the ability of the defenders to hold Bataan than any other phase of the operation."[13]

Unlike War Plan ORANGE, which assumed the necessity of withdrawing all forces and supplies to Bataan, the only defensible area, MacArthur's plan insisted that beaches were to be held at all costs. In the event, they could not. Major R.W. Volckman, recalled a visit from MacArthur and his chief of staff in November 1941:

> Sitting on the edge of my desk, he calmly forecast that the Japs could not possibly land in the Philippines for at least four months. As to our mobilization mission, he stated that we were sitting on it—defend five miles of beach along Lingayen Gulf. He went on to explain that he had no details worked out on paper, but that within a month ... all the details would be developed. Since war came only three weeks later, I have often reflected on the General's statements.[14]

The consequences of lack of preparation were dire. The Japanese achieved complete tactical surprise on December 8, and destroyed the bulk of MacArthur's air force on the ground. When Homma's army landed on Lingayen Gulf on December 22, MacArthur, outflanked and out-generalled, was forced to declare Manila an open city. Within days, watching the disorganized Filipino units fleeing southward, he was forced to concede that his overly ambitious plan had been wholly unrealistic—he declared War Plan ORANGE to be in effect after all, but only when it was too late to implement its central feature—the movement of supplies from Manila and elsewhere into Bataan.

Defending the beaches was impossible with the manpower and supplies available. Volckman described the difficulty of fulfilling his mission with untrained troops and inadequate supplies, at one point observing that "at dawn eleven Jap ships, destroyers and cruisers, had a parade about a thousand yards off our beach and we had nothing larger than a .50 caliber machine gun to fire at them." Owen Sandmore of the 192nd National Guard Tank Battalion recalled, "We had tanks spaced out almost a mile apart and I had a mile of beach to 'so-called protect' with almost a peashooter, a little 37 millimeter cannon and machine guns, which wasn't much good."[15]

Another survivor was nonplussed. "There were," he wrote, "immense quantities of food stored in Rizal stadium in Manila when the war began, but it never seems to have occurred to anyone to move it post haste to Bataan even though all the pre-war military plans called for a last stand to be made on the peninsula." Indeed, after the fall of Corregidor, one American officer bitterly recalled loading American supplies on trucks—for use by the Japanese. Immense quantities of rice and canned goods were abandoned at Tarlac and Cabanatuan. Another, making his way north on the march, recalled seeing "stacks of captured American rations."[16]

Confusion and bureaucratic incompetence reigned as the army retreated into the sanctuary of Bataan—an old order from MacArthur's headquarters even forbade the removal of more than two thousand cases of canned foods because they were owned by Japan, and millions of pounds of rice were abandoned in compliance with a law restricting transport from one province to another. One warehouse alone held rice that could have fed the soldiers and civilians on Bataan for five months.[17] One observer bitterly recalled that "Manila had warehouses filled with food and supplies but MacArthur had expressly forbidden his Quartermaster Corp to requisition these supplies while there still had been time to move them to the Bataan peninsula.... Before he left the Bataan troops were starving, exhausted and dying of disease, even before they surrendered."[18] The bulk of the food supplies on the island were lost.

Even more horrifying, the men on Bataan learned that some soldiers, transferred from Corregidor to Bataan early in the campaign, were being fed from their own mess on the island. Several times a week, supplies were delivered across the strait by boat then to the units by truck. On March 18, near the end of the starving campaign, MPs at a checkpoint discovered cases of ham, bacon, cans of vegetables, potatoes, peaches, and fifty cartons of cigarettes. Salt in the wounds of the starving came with the additional realization that the contingents from Corregidor had also been drawing Bataan rations.[19]

Instead of holding enough food for 43,000 men for six months, Bataan's storehouses could only supply 80,000 for one month. This necessitated all soldiers on Bataan going on half rations in early January (2,000 calories a day), reduced in February to 1,500, and in March to 1,000, when at least 3,500 were needed to perform regular duties. Men who began the campaign at 175 pounds were down to 135. Alf Larson, in his otherwise gently worded reminiscence, declared that the men "were starving to death.... General MacArthur's inept planning wasted all the food, so we received half rations or less on Bataan from day one because there was nothing to eat."[20]

Herein lies much of the explanation for Death March survivors' bitterness toward MacArthur. Many of the men who died or were killed on the march north from Mariveles were so physically debilitated that they simply could not keep up. Falling out, they incurred the wrath of their Japanese guards. Richard Mallonee stated the complaint: "Much has been written about the Death March. There have been accounts of atrocities, of massacres, and of men buried alive. I will not say they were not true, but, in the main, the horror of the death march resulted from the physical condition of the men forced to make it." Wachi Takeji, the Fourteenth Army's chief of staff during the march, agreed. When asked during Homma's trial if he had received any reports of POW deaths, he replied in the affirmative, that "the cause of death was that their bodies were so weak and they were so exhausted, and in some cases malnutrition, and they were unable to keep on the march."[21]

If, as seems more than reasonable, much American mortality on the Death March was due to the weakened condition of the men, the blame for the absence of adequate supplies must attach to MacArthur. One embittered veteran stated the heart of the matter: "First of all he should have known that an army lives on its stomach."[22] The Fil-American garrison would have been overwhelmed by Homma's reinforced army in April, even had it been better fed during the campaign. A healthier force would then have been able to withstand the rigors of the march better, and mortality would have been considerably less.

In his autobiography, the general related his anguish as the soldiers wasted away from hunger and exhaustion as the campaign wore on. "They cursed the enemy and in the same breath cursed and reviled the United States," he wrote. "They spat when they jeered the Navy. But their eyes would light up and they would cheer when they saw my battered ... 'scrambled egg' cap. They would gather round and pat me on the back and 'Mabuhay Macarsar' me."[23] MacArthur's self-portrait did nothing to change the reality in 1942—that these men detested him.

One veteran remembered retaining "a profound faith in [MacArthur's] ultimate ability despite the early catastrophes that had forced the great retreat." If some shared this opinion in January, by March few did. MacArthur offered early assurances that help was coming. An official communiqué, issued on January 15 (and widely, if bitterly, quoted in the survivors' narratives), read: "Help is on the way from the U.S. Thousands of troops and hundreds of planes are being dispatched. The exact time of arrival is unknown, as they will have to fight their way through Japanese attempts against them. It is imperative that our troops hold until these reinforcements arrive."[24]

Days dragged into weeks and it dawned on the men that help of any kind was not, in fact, coming, and morale sagged. As the campaign wore on, MacArthur was hardly an inspirational presence. His headquarters were in the Malinta tunnel on Corregidor and, while his men on Bataan suffered and starved, he made only one visit across the narrow strait during his seventy-seven days in command, on January 10. This in spite of the short journey, easily managed in five minutes by torpedo boat. His behavior contrasted sharply with that of Jonathan Wainwright, who was to inherit MacArthur's command. Wainwright understood the situation and repeatedly exposed himself to enemy fire in full view of his soldiers. When asked why he did so, he responded that since he was unable to offer his soldiers food, ammu-

MacArthur, with Jonathan "Skinny" Wainwright, before the commander fled to Australia. MacArthur would later try to prevent Wainwright, who languished in Japanese prison until liberated in 1945, from participating in the Japanese surrender ceremony on the battleship *Missouri* (Library of Congress).

nition, supplies, equipment or medicine, he could at least give them a boost in morale. "That's why I go to the front every day."[25]

James Murphy, a radio operator turned machine gunner, recalled that senior officers promoted rumors that the promised aid would arrive at any moment. In lieu of material help, rumors sufficed for a time. One held that Chiang Kai-shek was sending soldiers to

Bataan; some claimed to have seen them. Incredibly, another asserted that "Negroes on white horses had landed ... across the bay, American Negro Cavalry divisions, and the long-expected reinforcements from the States were offshore, ready to land and catch the Nips from the rear." Officers' optimism began to wane, but many still hoped against hope that the TNT ("Terrible 'n Terrific") force would arrive to save them.[26] Another rumor held that the 1930s isolationist U.S. had betrayed the men even before the war began—"It's true," stated one officer, "repeatedly we have identified among exploded fragments scrap automobile parts which our country so consistently sold to Japan on a policy indignantly defended ... long after it was known that we would some day, soon, meet Japan in war. Also included in bombs: razor blades, bottle caps, cement."[27]

Disillusionment came creeping nevertheless, with none of the promised reinforcements in sight. Morale sank lower and lower as it became obvious the army had been abandoned. Dark humor crept in as men listened to Manila radio playing "Waiting for Ships That Never Come In" every night and began to tell each other that the "V" they had inscribed on their helmets was for "victim," not "victory."[28] An anonymous composer wrote a parody of the tune of "Ramblin' Wreck":

> I'm a hungry man from old Bataan
> And there's nothing on the pot,
> I guess that I'm the buckaroo
> The nation has forgot.
>
> Now Franklin says, "I love you"
> Now boys, you know I do—
> I'll have to risk the Navy's neck,
> There's nothing I can do.

Sergeant David Johns lamented, "The Voice of Freedom kept telling us, 'Hold out for two more days. Help is on the way.' We could have taken the truth. But they lied to us."[29]

Bitter humor crackled out—"Sure, they'll send reinforcements! Haven't you heard how they are coming? Over a bridge from San Francisco. And, say—they've got a quarter of a mile of it done already!" Men passing through one HQ saw, nailed to a tree, a calendar sporting the image of a sailing ship, under which some wag had written, "We told you so, help is on the way." Sarcasm increased with the realization of their desperate situation—some started a mock campaign: "Better buy one bomber than be buried on Bataan." When a Japanese sub off California coast lobbed shells onto the mainland, the story spread that MacArthur cabled San Francisco: "Will send relief if you can hold out for a month." One soldier wrote some verse entitled "MacArthur's Promise in Every Mind":

> The time is secret but I can say
> That swift relief ships are on the way
> Thousand of men and hundreds of planes—
> Back in Manila before it rains!
> With decorations and honors, too.
> MacArthur said it, it must be true.[30]

Common soldiers, justly feeling abandoned, named him "Dougout Doug" and sang the derisive lyrics to the "Battle Hymn of the Republic":

> Dugout Doug MacArthur lies ashaking on the Rock
> Safe from all the bombers and from any sudden shock

6. Remembering and Forgetting

> Dugout Doug is eating of the best food on Bataan
> And his troops go starving on.
> Dugout Doug's not timid, he's just cautious, not afraid
> He's protecting carefully the stars that Franklin made
> Four-star generals are rare as good food on Bataan
> And his troops go starving on.
> Dugout Doug is ready in his Kris Craft for the flee
> Over bounding billows and the wildly raging sea
> For the Japs are pounding on the gates of Old Bataan
> And his troops go starving on...

Other lyrics soon made the rounds:

> Dugout Doug come out of hiding,
> Dugout Doug come out of hiding,
> We have fought this war the hard way since they said the war was on,
> all the way from Lingayen to the hills of old Bataan
> and we'll continue fighting till old Dugout Doug is gone—
> and still go starving on!

As the campaign progressed, it became clear that the "Europe first" policy left no possibility for the relief and reinforcement of the soldiers on Bataan. As early as January, Eisenhower's War Plans Division killed any possibility of sending relief to the Philippines, and Secretary of War Henry Stimson bluntly stated the rather stark reality: "There are times when men have to die."[31]

MacArthur maintained his headquarters deep inside the Malinta on Corregidor. Now, guides lead groups up the island's highest point, where from a Spanish lighthouse one can see all the way across the bay to Bataan. I opt not to climb its many steps, wanting instead a moment of repose inside the "MacArthur Café and Souvenir Shop." As I sit having an orange juice, among much litter on the ground I see an empty packet of Japanese Seven Stars cigarettes, the kind I used to smoke when I lived there. Somehow I think MacArthur might feel demeaned by having his name on this place. Inside, however, there are small, badly made busts of the general for sale. Turning one over, I am astonished to see "Made in Japan."

Those doomed on Bataan did not, however, include the commander. Roosevelt, on the advice of the Joint Chiefs, decided to order MacArthur to escape the noose rapidly closing on the Philippines in order to take command of the Allied forces in the southwest Pacific. With characteristic ego, MacArthur pleaded with the president to determine the timing of his departure himself—"the right moment for so delicate an operation" lest his command suffer a "sudden collapse." The day selected was March 11, his departure seared into the bitter memory of those he left behind.

One scholar of trauma and aging has suggested that "the challenge in the acceptance of one's old age [is] to acquiesce and embrace what had happened" as *"justified by its causes."* For those who, like Holocaust victims, who have suffered trauma, this is difficult:

> For the survivors of the Holocaust to accept that what has happened to them was justified by its causes implies an acceptance of Hitler and Nazism ... and such an acceptance is too closely reminiscent of the submission to persecution. The process of making peace with one's self becomes impossible when it is experienced as bringing back the helplessness and the shame of the past.[32]

Likewise, survivors of the Death March would have to accept that their surrender was justified by its cause. Whether accurate or not, in the minds of many, the cause was MacArthur.

When German soldiers, huddled in a dugout in Stalingrad, heard Hermann Goering broadcasting news of their surrender from Berlin, one embittered *Soldat* responded, "That fat swine has sold us." So it was for Bataan's defenders when they received the news their commander was gone. Richard Gordon claimed that "most defenders of Bataan ... will go or have already gone to their graves with the firm conviction that they were truly 'sold down the river' and for better or worse they place most of the blame for their fate on MacArthur." Jude North, whose book *Lost in the Wilderness* is based on information from the group "Battling Bastards of Bataan" agreed: "If anyone was cavalier about the abandonment of his soldiers it was certainly Douglas MacArthur." Speaking of the BBB, "the men left here are consumed by bitterness for General MacArthur for abandoning them."[33]

On April 1, just eight days before the surrender, Captain Albert Brown spoke for many as he wrote in his diary, "We certainly are the biggest fools of this war, fighting for the biggest and strongest nation in the world ... every day is April Fool's day." Seventy years later, Glenn Frazier, as bitter as ever, still wondered about MacArthur's motives—"Why did he ... when we were down to nothing ... order us to fight to the last man? He didn't want some of the things told when we came back." Frazier spoke for many when he said, "He didn't like the GIs."[34] The Japanese were not asleep to the men's sensibilities. One of the surrender leaflets dropped on Bataan in March read:

> The Imperial Japanese
> troops never kill those who
> surrender to them. Stop this
> futile fighting and surrender.
> General MacArthur
> has deserted you.

Even as the soldiers used the papers in the latrine, the message rankled.

General Brougher, one of the divisional commanders on Bataan, spoke for many: "A foul trick of deception has been played on a large group of Americans by a commander in chief and small staff who are now eating steak and eggs in Australia. God damn them!"[35] After MacArthur fled the islands, uncomplimentary stories abounded. One dealt with the abandonment of seriously ill nurses so that the furniture from the general's Manila hotel, including a piano, in some versions, could be loaded onto the PT boats. Another source of resentment was the general's Cantonese nurse, Ah Cheu, for whom room was made on the boat. MacArthur's defense, recorded in piquant prose in his autobiography, was that "few people outside the Orient know how completely a member of the family an *amah* can become" and that the nurse had been with him since his son's birth.[36] But bitterness continued to crackle in others verses:

Ang Puno Nanawala (The Lost Leader)
Our leader has vanished like last summer's rose.
"Gone to get help" he would have us suppose.
May his medallion grow tarnished with tears,
Now that his honor is built on our fears.
May the ghosts glimmering in nebulous mist,
Ghouls of thirty thousand tombs haunt him....[37]

MacArthur's departure was depressing indeed. Many were unaware that FDR had ordered the general out and simply called him a coward. Rumors that he had escaped with smuggled gold, that he had taken "a staff of servants, and all his household possessions" swirled among the embittered, whose jokes testified to their attitude: "I shall return" some said as they went off to eat or urinate. The general's departure "left no one in doubt that the fate of Bataan ... was sealed." Comparing his survival to their lives' uncertain future, some may have been old enough to recall that in 1932 MacArthur has been picketed by college students in Pittsburgh who carried signs that read, "Generals Die in Bed."[38]

The general arrived safely in Australia, whereupon he announced with customary egotism, "I came through, and I shall return." Safely in Melbourne, wearing his pink silk dressing gown decorated with a dragon, he remarked, in his typically purple prose,

> Our flag lies crumpled, its proud pinions spat upon in the gutter; the wrecks of our faithful Filipino wards ... gasp in the slavery of a conquering soldiery devoid of those ideals of chivalry which have dignified many armies ... from the bottom of a seared and stricken heart, I pray that a merciful God may not delay too long their redemption, that the day of salvation may not be so far removed that they perish, that it not be again too late.

Shortly afterwards, he had dinner at the House of Parliament, made a short speech, then listened to an orchestra playing "For He's a Jolly Good Fellow."[39]

MacArthur then radioed Wainwright in the last agonizing days of the siege, stating that he could entertain no thought of surrender, and ordered him to attack the enemy when food supplies ran out. He reiterated his message to Washington, D.C., on April 1: "I am utterly opposed, under any circumstances or conditions, to the ultimate capitulation of this command. If it is to be destroyed, it should be on the actual field of battle taking full toll from the enemy." Then, in an overt slap at Wainwright, he told Washington, "It is of course possible that with my departure the rigor of application of conservation may have relaxed." Further, he did not trust Wainwright to oversee the apocalypse he envisioned. In these waning days of the siege, he proposed a plan of attack whose "language ... was astonishing and totally unrealistic when compared to the plight of the men expected to execute it." MacArthur's fantasy expected Wainwright to somehow break out from southern Bataan and begin operating in central Luzon, where his starving men could find food.[40]

At the same time, he knew what awaited the soldiers. Just two weeks before the surrender, commanders on Bataan received a memorandum whose contents was "'The Soldier' as defined by MacArthur, "to be reproduced and distributed to all units of your command." For the obtuseness of its contents, the prose is worth quoting in its entirety:

> The SOLDIER, above all other men, is required to perform the highest act of religious teaching, SACRIFICE. In battle and in the face of death, he discloses those divine attributes which his MAKER gave when HE created MAN of HIS own image.... However horrible the incidents of war may be, the SOLDIER who is called upon to offer and give his LIFE for his COUNTRY is the NOBLEST DEVELOPMENT OF MANKIND. I do not know the dignity of his birth but <u>I do know the glory of his death</u>. He dies unquestioning, uncomplaining, with faith in his heart ... he passes beyond that mist that blinds us here to form a part of that beautiful thing which we call the Spirit of the Unknown Soldier. In the chambered temple of Silence, the spirit of his dauntless valor sleeps, waiting, waiting, in the chancery of heaven the final reckoning of Judgment Day. <u>ONLY THOSE ARE FIT TO LIVE WHO ARE NOT AFRAID TO DIE.</u>
>
> (Sgd) MacArthur[41]

Hungry and hopeless men, knowing that their commander was safe in Australia, found the memorandum, tacked to barracks walls and buildings, at a minimum, inappropriate. Bataan veteran Father Robert Phillips had considerable trouble with the last sentence, written by a commander who was leaving. Years later, from behind his Roman collar, he recalled with massive understatement, "I didn't think that was too sensitive." Years later, Owen Sandmire stated, "He thought we should fight to the death ... stand right up there on the front lines, throw your chest out and let a Jap bayonet you or shoot you down. He was kind of a showman."[42] By way of compensation afterward, MacArthur named his plane "Bataan" and often choked up whenever the fate of the army he had abandoned was mentioned.

Any casual examination of the attention paid to MacArthur after he fled the Philippines suggests his public relations machine enjoyed considerable success. On the home front, Americans' insistence on elevating MacArthur to demigod status existed in apparent proportion to their discomfort with the embarrassing failure to defend the Philippines. One veteran of the Death March sought to explain the explosion of MacArthur worship:

This drawing appeared a little more than a week after the fall of Bataan. It shows Wainwright, in command of the remaining Allied force on Corregidor, responding to MacArthur's "I shall return" pledge with obvious disdain. Wainwright would surrender three weeks later (Library of Congress).

As societies we human being are fortunate in that we tend gradually to forget defeat, disaster, pain, injury, unhappiness.... Americans seem to have a special cast of mind which enables them to eventually convince themselves that some unmitigated disaster was really a glorious chapter in the nation's history. Thus Bataan came to be regarded as a symbol of indomitable American courage, the soil from which a generation of national heroes sprang."[43]

Survivors would suggest that a phony hero sprang from such soil; the genuine were buried or captured.

After the debacle of Bataan, the D. Appleton-Century publishing house rushed a book into print, Helen Nicolay's *MacArthur of Bataan*, even before Corregidor fell in May. The combined motivations of guaranteed readership, quick profit and the need to buck up morale on the home front produced the hero-worshipping tome. Readers in Peoria were treated to a MacArthur who was part visionary, part military genius, a paragon of virtue, efficiency, obedience and innovation. In 1931 before a Congressional committee, Nicolay quotes her subject's ruminations on the question of morale: "Only morale will carry a soldier into the dangers and hardships of modern war, and only morale will build up an organization capable of sustaining the shock of present-day battle. Morale, gentlemen, is born of just treatment, efficient leadership, thorough training, and pride in self and in country." For Bataan defenders, the irony was radiant. In the penultimate chapter, "The Miracle Worker of Bataan," Nicolay describes "brilliant generalship," omits completely the mistake of wanting to defend the beaches, the loss of his air force on the ground, and the fact that he made only one visit to Bataan from his HQ on Corregidor.[44]

Five months after MacArthur fled the Philippines, another American general, Joseph Stilwell, endured the collapse of the Allied defense of Burma, walked out, and stated with characteristic honesty, "I claim we got a hell of a beating. We got run out of Burma and it is humiliating as hell." MacArthur's censor, however, refused to allow his escape to be termed anything but a "breakout." Congress agreed, allowing a motion naming June 13 "Douglas MacArthur Day," the Library of Congress published a bibliography comprising 253 references to MacArthur, and men in and out of government in the U.S. and Australia were more than effusive in their praise of his generalship. He was awarded the Congressional Medal of Honor, diners named sandwiches for him, proud parents named their babies after him, bridges and dams were named for him, the Blackfoot Indians of South Dakota made him a member of their tribe, calling him Mo-Kahki-Peta (Chief Wise Eagle). One man on the street in Texas spoke for many when he said simply, "All the people I know think God comes first and then MacArthur."[45]

Indeed, there sprang up nothing less than a "MacArthur industry" that spring and summer of 1942. Buttons and pennants sprouted on lapels. More books appeared, including *MacArthur the Magnificent*; another biographer, Francis T. Miller, enjoyed exquisite timing when his work, *General Douglas MacArthur: Fighter for Freedom*, had its first printing on March 12, the day after the general left the Philippines. Its twenty-one chapters drip with admiration, and the last, "MacArthur's Gallant Stand Thrills the World," made clear that the Fil-American army on Bataan was vastly outnumbered, though in fact the Allied force always outnumbered the Japanese. At home, MacArthur's reputation rose in proportion to patriotic fervor. Boys Clubs, Post Offices and boulevards were re-named in his honor, his home in Little Rock, Arkansas, was made into a museum, and one patriot proposed that the "graveyard shift" in the shipyards of Oakland be re-named the "MacArthur shift" to sustain productivity. For those who endured the Death March, again the irony shone brightly.

One wonders what the survivors of the Death March knew of MacArthur's small-minded, ungenerous behavior after the war. He refused to recommend the Medal of Honor for Jonathan Wainwright and resisted Wainwright's appearance on the battleship *Missouri* at the surrender ceremony in Tokyo Bay. Most cruelly, when MacArthur spoke to Congress in 1951 after being fired by Truman, Ned King, who had endured the humiliation of surrender in MacArthur's place, approached the general to speak to him, but MacArthur affected not knowing him. MacArthur's memoirs hardly mention King and omit any praise of him whatever. Perhaps the Death March survivors would have taken comfort knowing that King spent his retirement volunteering for the Red Cross and other causes.[46]

* * * * *

Between Pearl Harbor and Hiroshima, there were resources to divert, morale to sustain, a war to be won, and the U.S. could scarcely afford to leave any propaganda potential, however painful, unexplored. Hollywood's reaction was slow in coming. Three months had passed when, with the epic on Bataan reaching its dénouement in March, filmmakers saw fit to refer to the debacle at Pearl Harbor. A Warner Brothers official stated the matter cogently—"we felt it wise to leave Pearl Harbor out of it, for all this can do is remind us of defeat." American radio was similarly cautious, the National Association of Broadcasters code of 1941 banning radio programs "which might unduly affect the listener's peace of mind."[47]

Early in the war, the government's office of censorship forbade "films which paint Americans as supermen winning battles single-handedly or assuming a general air of nationalistic superiority."[48] At this stage of the war, such restrictions might more logically have come from the victorious Japanese but, by the autumn of 1942, Hollywood avoided these twin dangers by finding its voice in a spate of "Last Stand" films. *Wake Island*, like all others of this genre, centered on an identifiable hero, in this case William Bendix. The fall of the Philippines, not surprisingly, was shown as a strategic victory—delaying the Japanese advance long enough to allow America to rearm, a theme pounded home in Clark Gable's *Somewhere I'll Find You* and *So Proudly We Hail*, the story of army nurses on Bataan. The most finely wrought of the "last stand" films was, appropriately enough, *Bataan*. Released in 1943, the film begins with a dedication that gives meaning to the largest surrender of American forces in history: "To those immortal dead, who heroically stayed the wave of barbaric conquest, this picture is reverently dedicated."

Viewers were treated to standard *E pluribus unum* stuff—each member of the besieged squad represented an ethnic "type" of American, with Japanese back-stabbing perfidy amply displayed. Its last scene shows the star Robert Taylor, after his entire squad has been killed, savagely pouring machinegun fire, against overwhelming odds, into the advancing Japanese in a violent climax that denies the dark reality of defeat. The film ends with a stirring coda: "So fought the heroes of Bataan. Their sacrifice made possible our victories in the Coral and Bismarck seas, at Midway, on New Guinea and Guadalcanal. Their spirit will lead us back to Bataan."

The other genuflection at Bataan's altar in 1943 was *Salute to the Marines*, starring a rather inappropriately corpulent Wallace Beery as Marine drill sergeant Bill Bailey at the end of a thirty year career. The film begins with an endless sea of perfectly disciplined soldiers marching in cadence, not so subtly pounding home the theme of power and readiness, a clear and intended contrast to the military's condition two years earlier. During Bailey's last assignment, training Filipinos, the Japanese horde, speaking a form of gibberish meant to pass for their language, invade, saving him the humiliation of completing his career *sans* combat experience. During the final battle he even co-opts Japanese battle tactics, telling his men, "A bayonet charge pushed home at the right minute will win for you when nothing else will." His wife, previously opposed to his continued service, joins him on the battlefield, where they are both killed by enemy bombs. The film ends with the ceremony at which his daughter, now a Marine herself, receives his posthumously-awarded Congressional Medal of Honor. As the credits roll, a sea of Marines marches directly into the camera.

Such efforts sought to give the Bataan debacle a usable meaning. During the war, the Bureau of Motion Pictures asked all filmmakers the following question: "Does the picture tell the truth or will the young people of today scorn it a few years hence, when they are running the world, and say they were misled by propaganda?" Americans safe in movie theaters might not be concerned with the difference, but those who returned from Bataan were likely to notice. In the short term, had they known the immediate effect of their failure to defend the Philippines on the film industry, no doubt the soldiers would have smiled sardonically—the breakaway chairs that crashed routinely over the heads of Hollywood villains were no longer available, since the balsa used to make them came from the forests, and the trade, they had failed to keep from Japanese hands.[49]

One radio script put a finer point on the domestic consideration: "They're going to die in the jungles for the shape of a Virginia field and the crossroads store back home—they're going to die in the cold, for the clear air of Montana and the smell of a New York Street." Did Americans want, or need, to see the deaths, even if heroic, of the doomed all-American squad in Bataan and the all-American drill sergeant? Perhaps the historian Alan Nevins divined some of the essence of the national mood in 1943—that somehow the U.S. had reneged on its international responsibility after World War I, and now had a second chance, and this was "the American conscience speaking to itself." This was war as atonement; a picture like *Bataan* "functioned as a kind of catharsis for its audiences by providing a bit of masochistic scourging of their complacent souls." Yet even the production of such films, with their attendant morality, abated after peaking in 1943. More than a third of all films made that year dealt with the war in some way, but the falloff afterward was due to a sated marketplace.[50]

By 1943 some were criticizing the Office of War Information's tendency to promote a "war that refreshes—in six delicious flavors." Tempted by the nation's emergence from the Depression, commercials exploited the war in their ads—"Lucky Strike Green has gone to war!" Advertising reached a kind of nadir when a cemetery firm in New York offered, between flashes of casualty figures, its wares: "You never know when to expect bad news, so be prepared. Buy a lot." Whether ads were in good or exceedingly bad taste, revenues skyrocketed during the war, up by some 85 percent.[51]

As the survivors of the Death March were, after their time in O'Donnell, making the transition to more permanent camps, the government initiated the "V for Victory" campaign. Vegetable gardens, taxicab companies, movie theaters, and even teenage girls enamored of soldiers, all took on the appellation. Advertisers found in the term a kind of bonanza. Four months after the soldiers, no doubt happy that they could no longer hear American radio, straggled to the end of the march, the Pabst beer company asked its patrons to "Drink a

Blue Ribbon Toast to Victory," while lipstick, red in color, was designated V-for-Victory, and shop merchandise, whenever possible, was arranged in the shape of the letter, as were the wings of the eagle on a newly minted postage stamp. A hemisphere away, as it became clear that the promised reinforcements were not coming, the beleaguered on Bataan told each other that the "V" they had inscribed on their helmets stood for "victim."[52]

In his radio broadcast, Bing Crosby expressed requisite gratitude at being able to communicate to the men on Bataan "the general feeling of what's going on in the United States." In truth, for some, a kind of victory was arriving at home more rapidly than on the battlefront. Eric Sevareid, who later attained fame as a newscaster, remembered his "indignation at the luxury" of the home front as he saw it, that men's faces were white, their "clean jowls folded over white collars ... somehow a repulsive sight." Talk of manicures, taxes, profits were disturbing, but magazine ads made him furious:

> They always showed a clean-cut American youth.... Then followed a few crocodile tears in chic type about "our boys," a few gratuitous remarks about how we must all do our bit. And finally, the coy little "plug" for whatever gadget it was.... A nice, clean streamlined, plastic superheterodyne world struggle ... directed by smartly-dressed men ... who manipulated the forces of democracy by tapping with sharp pencils on neat graphs hung around the walls of tastefully furnished, indirectly lighted offices.[53]

Whatever the profit to the Wall Street elite, the war was a relief to so many on the home front in so many ways. During its nearly four years, wages rose nearly 70 percent, the cost of goods and services only 23. Some seven million unemployed found work, and another seven million entered the labor force. The administrative expansion to support all this was staggering—by 1943 each night of the week, "a thirteen car train left Washington railroad yards loaded with wastepaper."[54]

Prosperity on the home front sometimes led to dead ends. During the Bataan survivors' first autumn of captivity, Buck Jones, a famous star of cowboy films, was touring the country to sell war bonds. On the last Saturday of November, although he was ill, movie agents persuaded him to have dinner at Cocoanut Grove, a popular club near Park Square in Boston. That evening, along with a thousand other patrons, he was caught in a horrible fire, ignited when a busboy lit a match to locate an empty light bulb socket on an artificial palm tree. Jones lingered for two days and died, his duties in the war bond campaign, no doubt, taken up by others. The fire that raged through the establishment took less than an hour to kill 490 revelers, only 100 fewer than had died on the Death March over two weeks in April, eight months earlier.[55]

Notwithstanding tragedies such as Cocoanut Grove, it was proving difficult to be prosperous and sympathetic at the same time. As early as the summer of 1942, support for the war on the home front was already waning. Henry Fonda, an established star, was recruited to narrate a moving documentary called *It's Everybody's War*, about the fictional town of Jefferson and the boys it sent off to the Philippines as a National Guard unit. At one point, a bereaved mother says that her son would still be fighting if he only had the matériel. Duly chastened, the town resolves to do everything possible to aid the war effort. The Office of War Information's official manual advocated the "casual insertion" of scenes in all media—showing Americans making modest sacrifices such as giving up seats to servicemen, accepting rationing cheerfully, carrying their own parcels when shopping, and showing "well-dressed persons, obviously car owners, riding in crowded buses and streetcars."[56]

Clearly the public needed guidance, and powerful reminders came in 1943 and early 1944. In April, word came that the Japanese had condemned to death the Doolittle flyers who had been captured after their bombing raid on Japan in April 1942, just days after the Death March concluded. In October came the story of a Japanese soldier's diary detailing the beheading of an American captured on New Guinea. Three months later, the government released more gruesome information—the story of Colonel William E. Dyess, who had been captured on Bataan and made the march north to San Fernando, then later escaped. Putnam's Sons published his account, *The Dyess Story: The Eye-Witness Account of the Death March from Bataan and the Narrative Experiences in Japanese Prison Camps and of Eventual Escape* in 1944, and the public got its first taste of the news from an article published in *Time* magazine on February 7 of that year.

The article included outraged comments from elected representatives. Andrew May, chairman of the House Military Affairs Committee, perhaps without consulting a map of the Pacific campaign in progress, called on the "entire fleet to steam into Tokyo harbor and blow the city to bits." Sol Bloom of the House Foreign Affairs Committee screamed, "We'll hold the rats responsible—from the Emperor down to the lowest ditchdigger—for a million years." Sales of war bonds "zoomed, even doubled several days after publication" as the nation thirsted for revenge and a reckoning.[57] Re-conquest of the Philippines, however, would have to wait another nine months.

Wartime prosperity, fading memories of defeat (courtesy Christopher Leet).

A wartime poster making the direct appeal—to guilt and responsibility (National Archives).

The Dyess Story devoted twenty-nine pages to the Death March. Its *leitmotif* was deliberate Japanese cruelty, an expression of an alien, inhuman sensibility. Dyess related how he and his companions were shaken down for valuables shortly after surrender, and the first execution he witnessed—of an American in possession of some Japanese currency, summarily beheaded. He described various kinds of Japanese horror, ranging from minor harassment to wanton murder. "We were succumbing," he said, "to the oriental tortures that subdue men, break their spirits and reduce them below the level of animals." He detailed a litany of Japanese barbarity, culminating in the horrifying sight of a Filipino soldier, eviscerated, hanging on a barbed wire fence. His response was both visceral and understandable: "Now, as never before," he related, "I wanted to kill Japs for the pleasure of it."[58] His account touched off a torrent of atrocity stories in the U.S. and the U.K. that painted the Japanese as barbarians, beyond the pale of civilized behavior.

Speculating on the two year interval before the government released the information, the *Time* magazine piece suggested that, since the government had abandoned hope of aiding the prisoners by 1944, the story would do them no additional harm. Moreover, if the government told the story of "Japanese bestiality" truthfully, the enemy might treat American captives better. A third explanation, however, rankled some. V. H. Spensley, a dentist whose son had perished in a Japanese prison camp, stated, "I can't understand why such information should be brought out now ... except to sell bonds. For that purpose it's absolutely rotten. If the morality of America has sunk so low it required this kind of propaganda to sell bonds, we wonder what the boys are fighting for." Spensley's outrage notwithstanding, bond sales skyrocketed.[59]

To pay for an expensive war, the government was happy to stoke hatred of the Japanese for exactly the reason Spensley specified. For eighteen months after his escape from the Philippines in 1943, Sam Grashio spoke in half the states of the union, crisscrossing the country to appear at dozens of clubs and associations, and "endlessly at rallies to sell war bonds.... On one memorable (and exhausting) occasion [he] gave fifteen speeches in a single day in Jersey City." During his journeys, he enjoyed fabulous treatment accorded a hero. He sat for photos, artists and sculptors, met celebrities, ate expensive meals, and once signed a 4000 pound bomb addressed to Tojo, "In appreciation of your hospitality." All this made him feel, he later wrote, "like visiting royalty permanently on tour."

When the government decided that Dyess and other POWs who had escaped could tell their stories, publishers began circling. Grashio wrote that these "people chattered endlessly about rights, slices, cut-ins, percentages, residuals, and agents fees." Dyess concluded a deal with the *Chicago Tribune*, and an editor there converted his story into a book. A representative of that paper also approached Grashio, but his account was published by *Life* magazine, for which he received "a sizeable sum of money." Though initially told that the money he received was not taxable, was later required to pay both tax and penalty. He learned, he later wrote, that "fame is evanescent and gratitude is fleeting."[60]

If the Dyess story and those of others stoked anger, later that year came a guilt-inducing offering. *A Letter from Bataan* reinforced the idea that the defense of the Philippines had value to the war effort. The film centers on the apparition of a dead soldier, eerily sitting in the front yard of his erstwhile home, reading a letter he wrote to his family while alive and serving in the field. A young Susan Hayward, who plays the soldier's girlfriend, and other family members sit on their porch and listen to his central message—that the defenders of Bataan were unprepared, both as soldiers and in terms of the equipment they lacked.

The soldier's stark testimony hammers home the theme of conservation, that those on the home front, shown in their various wasteful leisure activities, must learn to "do without," so that the steel, rubber, kitchen fat and other resources can be directed toward the war effort. The stark contrast between the luxury of the civilian world and the hardships of the front-line soldier is clear. At the end of the letter, the ghostly presence walks up onto the porch and kisses his girlfriend, a poignant act of affection she seems to sense as he walks into the yard and disappears, putting on his helmet as he fades away. The film ends with the arrival of the telegram dreaded by all—John Lewis was killed on Bataan.

If such was the government's favored message, there was information it did not wish disseminated. In the autumn of 1944, a ship was sunk on which Calvin Graef, a Bataan survivor, was being transported. Graef miraculously escaped and, upon his return, the army asked him to tour the U.S. to "conduct meetings with the relatives of the POWs who were still imprisoned at the time" and to speak to the kin of those killed "in order to give them as much information" as possible, although he was forbidden to inform the families of those he knew to be dead of their fate at the hands of the Japanese. At those meetings, "One after another," he recalled, "approached me with hope in their eyes. They implored me to tell them how their relatives were faring."[61] His response to their entreaties is lost to history.

As the war reached its gruesome dénouement with the delivery of the atomic bombs, Death March survivors appeared in the context of revenge. President Truman, announcing the dropping of the bombs, stated that the Japanese "have been paid back many times" for their treachery. George Marshall, then head of the Joint Chiefs of Staff, told Leslie Groves, the director of the Manhattan Project, to restrain his joy over the bombs because of the horrific loss of life. Groves answered that he was not thinking of Japanese dead, but rather "the men of the Bataan March." General Hap Arnold, the architect of the bombing campaign against Japan, agreed with Groves, and added, "I'm glad you said that—that's just the way I feel."[62] That the civilians of Hiroshima and Nagasaki had nothing to do with the actions of Homma's army in 1942 seemed irrelevant. A ubiquitous wartime poster showed a gaunt American soldier, helmet in hand, saying,

>Remember Me? I was at Bataan

Underneath was the exhortation,

>BUY WAR BONDS

As the posters began to fade in 1945, the ill-fated defenders were presented once more to the public in the film *Back to Bataan*. During production, American commandos staged a successful raid on Cabanatuan prison on January 30, freeing some 500 POWs, many of whom had survived the Death March. The film opens with John Wayne (who else?) leading the raid along with Anthony Quinn as his Filipino subordinate. The action then shifts to a welcoming parade at home. As the freed soldiers march to the strains of "California Here I Come," the voiceover proudly declares, "The men you are about to see are actual survivors of three terrible years in the Jap prison camp at Cabanatuan" and the four men selected, Emmett Manson, Earl Baumgardner, Dennis Rainwater and Eugene Commander, file past. The camera, reverently positioned below to suggest their hero status, records each of their smiles.

The choice of music may have related to the geography of disaster. The Bataan debacle was particularly wrenching for certain communities that had given large numbers of men to National Guard units later federalized and sent to the Philippines. Salinas, California, the site of Steinbeck's novels, had a population of 11,586 and lost nearly 150 men on Bataan, while tiny Harrodsburg, Kentucky, population 4,673, lost seventy-six.[63] Indeed, in the context of the all-pervading war effort, the American government strained to remember, honor and exploit those who fought on Bataan, the living and the dead. Afterwards, they had largely served their purpose. The postwar experience of the survivors would demonstrate that few remembered or cared.

* * * * *

During the war, films as well as other government-sponsored productions dealing with Bataan all assigned meaning to its victims—American valor in contrast to the barbarism of the Japanese horde, a heroic Thermopylae contributing to eventual victory. This was palatable while the fighting raged. After the champagne of VJ day was drunk, some ten million soldiers returned, "nervous out of the service." If they had fought for anything, it was for the status quo antebellum, and now they once again sought their places in peacetime society. The war had altered the U.S., both internationally and domestically, but Americans in 1945 did not understand its impact in such terms. Most looked forward to a restoration of routine and "normalcy" after the Axis powers were defeated, a time when the dislocation and disruption would end. Many saw the changes of the war years as temporary aberrations.

In the flush of satisfied victory, the veterans of Bataan—the war's largest, most visible reminder of defeat and victimhood—were an awkward, even unwanted story. Janoff-Bulman's book, *Shattered Assumptions*, suggests, "Victims are threatening to non-victims, for they are manifestations of a malevolent universe rather than a benevolent one.... Victims are stigmatized because they violate the expectations established by people's illusions." Victims' presence causes people to question their "most fundamental assumptions, core beliefs that enable us to feel safe, secure and confident."[64] The nation turned away, to stories that once again confirmed what it wished most devoutly to believe of itself.

In 1951, at the height of the Korean War, the American TV viewing audience was treated to a twenty-six part series entitled "Crusade in the Pacific," part five of which was entitled "The U.S. and the Philippines." The thirty minute narrative mentioned Bataan only in passing, and omitted any discussion of the Death March, this lacking relevance to a crusade. After 1945, Hollywood dealt with the Philippines in wartime, but gave Bataan a wide berth. *American Guerrilla in the Philippines* (1950) and *Cry of Battle* (1963) both told of heroic guerrilla and partisan warfare against the Japanese. *I Was an American Spy* (1951) chronicled the wartime activities of Claire Phillips, who transmitted information to the Filipino underground during the Japanese occupation, while *Back Door to Hell* (1964) and *Ambush Bay* (1966) told the story of American military heroism preceding MacArthur's re-conquest of the islands. *Battle at Bloody Beach* (1961) dealt with the romantic and professional life of a U.S. Navy contractor supplying Filipino guerrillas.

Films about the broader sweep of the war in the Pacific typically ignored the 1942 Bataan campaign in favor of memorializing the triumphant sweep across the Pacific. At one level or another, *Sands of Iwo Jima* (1949), *Battlecry* (1955), *Tarawa Beachhead* (1958), *The Gallant Hours* (1960), *Merrill's Marauders* (1962) and *The Thin Red Line* (1964) all advanced on simple ideological terrain—fanatic Japanese defenders resist stalwart American attackers, until the Japanese retreat or, more commonly, are wiped out. This was more comfortable than remembering that the Japanese did the attacking and the Americans the surrendering in 1942.

If these films, omitting mention of Bataan and defeat, accurately measured the nature of American interest in their Pacific war, the upheaval of the 1960s was bound up in the rejection of the 1945 victory itself. A serious challenge to the war's meaning came from a generation of college students, blacks and women who rejected the uses of enormous American international power and the consumer culture the war had helped produce. This critique of free-market capitalism and its commitment to "containing" the antithetical Soviet Communist system also left little room for recognition of the POW plight.[65] If the war's meaning derived from its role in bringing forth U.S. power on the international stage, the critique rejected whatever heroism—and indeed suffering—that attended its birth. Many of those who came of age during the pointless slaughter of Vietnamese and Americans beginning in 1965 had little enough use for war in general, and the POWs who languished on the Death March and in Japanese prisons could hardly be expected to register with them.

Later films about Vietnam offered Americans ample opportunity for masochistic self-examination. Films such as *The Deer Hunter*, *Apocalypse Now* and *Coming Home* dealt with the excruciating emotional trauma of defeat as the nation tried coming to terms with that war's meaning. World War II required no such emotional reckoning, containing as it did so few examples of defeat. Local aberrations like Bataan were relegated to the province of the small documentary. The 1980s saw the publication of Studs Terkel's *"The Good War"* and John Dower's *War Without Mercy*, both in their own way questioning the American motivation and behavior, but left little room for specific rumination on Bataan.

By the time the 1990s arrived, it was virtually too late for the recognition POWs desired, even if the broader society or its government had been willing to offer it. During that decade, the formal delivery of history in college-level textbooks did little to advance any awareness of World War II's significance. The historian Warren F. Kimball observed that for most textbook authors, World War II disappears "under the icy onslaught of the Cold War." Surveying the books available to U.S. college students, he noted that a typical text devoted an entire chapter to the coming of the war, but the war itself and wartime diplomacy rated only twelve of the book's 518 pages. Americans were still being treated to versions of their war on TV and movie screens, but few dealt with POWs' wartime travail. At the century's turn, World War II veterans were dying at a rate of 1100 per day, and one can only imagine Death March survivors' response as they watched Tom Brokaw's *The Greatest Generation* rise to the best seller list, or Major Dick Winters soar to the status of icon in *Band of Brothers*.[66]

Films such as *The Thin Red Line* (1998) arrived for an audience prepared to take note of the war without glorifying either war or its participants. More recent films such as *Windtalkers* (2002) and *Flags of Our Fathers* (2006), though offering some sense of moral ambiguity, also deal with later, ultimately victorious combat; the futility of battle and defeat is left to the Japanese in *Letters from Iwo Jima* (2006). In 2003 Walter Cronkite hosted the documentary series "The War in the Pacific," the second volume of which spends just eight minutes on the Bataan and Corregidor battles, and shows scenes of capture at the start of the Death March. Later segments, "Freedom for the Philippines" and "Promises Made and Kept," emphasize—what else?—MacArthur returning in triumph. The public was more interested in books such as Patrick K. O'Donnell's *Into the Rising Sun, In Their Own Words, World War II's Pacific Veterans Reveal the Heart of Combat* (2002), whose subjects, active in nearly every campaign of the war, "individually and collectively, have an amazing story to tell." The one missing campaign was Bataan.[67]

Finally, in 2007, Ken Burns' *The War* offered the POWs some wider recognition. The

The poster for the 1945 film, the last gasp of publicity for survivors as the war neared its end (Library of Congress).

first episode opened with an interview of Glenn Frazier, a moving piece lasting seven minutes in which Frazier, before an audience of millions, told a story about his experience on the Death March and in Camp O'Donnell. Yet the 2010 miniseries *The Pacific*, focusing on the lives of three Marines, mentions the Philippines only as prelude to the rest of the campaigns in the Pacific Theater. Episode one begins with Guadalcanal, the first American victory in that theater; Bataan is not mentioned at all. And the video games that absorb the attention of contemporary youth, "Call of Duty," "Medal of Honor," and "Battlefield," deal overwhelmingly with the European Theater.

* * * * *

William Wyler's 1946 film *The Best Years of Our Lives* touches on the sense of dislocation and anomie experienced by so many returning veterans. The re-connection was difficult—Air Force captain Fred Derry finds himself married to a shallow harpy, and without skills to cope in the civilian world, Sergeant Al Stephenson seems to be slipping into alcoholism, and the sailor Homer Parrish's physical disability mirrors his inability to emotionally connect with the woman who loves him. By the end of Wyler's sensitive film, all three characters seem to be finding their way into meaningful civilian life, but the reality for the returning veteran was often substantially different—the dislocation and suffering of the Bataan survivors did not end upon repatriation in 1945.

Men undergoing the tribulations of prison camp, largely cut off from outside information, imagined a world that would recognize their suffering and honor their contribution to ultimate victory, and their imaginations while in prison reflected this need. At various times, rumors flew that, upon their return, survivors would receive an automobile from Henry Ford, a kangaroo from Australians who appreciated the Americans' role in saving their country, free homestead land, Lincoln Zephyrs (only for medics), and $2.50 per day for time in captivity from all but three states—Arizona, New Mexico and Oklahoma offering land instead.[68] These hopes and more were to be disappointed—what had once been the home front was now a society with little interest in the specifics of soldiers' service or captivity. H.J. Fleeger, waiting to rejoin his wife, wrote to her in anguish, hoping she could love him, even though she

> could never understand that the animal returned to you will be mentally at least 60 percent ossified from exposure to tropical sun and several years of prison; physically intact perhaps but with all reserves exhausted by starvation, quite unaccustomed to writing anything except to sign his name once or twice a year, bewildered by electric lights, traffic, trains and autos, overcome by the vision of swaying hips and breasts (white) ... terrified by conversation—especially feminine, vitamin insane, love intoxicated, work alurgic [*sic*], and to top it all off, subject to horrifying nightmares."[69]

Speaking to survivors of the Holocaust in his book *One Generation After*, Elie Wiesel asked, "And you, how did you manage to survive? Had you known the art of survival from before? And how were you able to keep your sanity? And today: how can you sleep, work, go to restaurants and movies, how can you mingle with people and share their meals?" His words apply equally to Americans returning after their four year ordeal of combat, surrender and incarceration. The degrading experience of prison left some in despair. After months in prison, one stated flatly, "I'm depressed as hell today. As far as my life is concerned, for the first time I'm beginning to have doubts whether I'll ever get back to America. If I do return, there will be no pieces to pick up. Everything will be new and I'll have to go it alone.... The futility of love, service, loyalty, sentiment—even life, coldly reveals itself like an icy blast from the dark poles."[70] Thomas Hayes spoke to the sense of dislocation upon his return:

> To go for days and never have shoes on your feet—to gather around a rice bucket and dip your ration out with a wooden stick ... to squat around a fire with a half dozen practically naked comrades and heat mongo beans.... You can't do these things day in and day out ... and then snap back into a world that can never comprehend what it's like—or even believe it could happen.

Hayes described prisoners' minds being "distorted—our concepts out of step with the world back home. It makes one wonder if we are missing all that much—if we really want to go back to neckties, lambchops and scotch and soda."[71]

The 1956 film *The Man in the Gray Flannel Suit*, based on the novel of the previous year by Sloan Wilson, also probes the plight of the veteran. In the title role, Gregory Peck is pressured by a wife who tells him that the war has sapped him of his competitive spirit as he struggles with a career change to make more money. In flashbacks, it becomes apparent that he is also wrestling with the ethical dilemma wrought by the child his Italian mistress bore him during the war. Ultimately, Peck's Tom Rath finds meaning by uniting the two severed halves of his life—he tells his wife about the liaison and takes responsibility for his child. Bataan veterans, however, were unable to reconcile their wartime and peacetime experiences as neatly as could the art of a novelist or filmmaker.

Many Death March survivors were plagued by years of poor health. Physical exams upon return to the U.S. revealed that they had already lost between 20 and 110 pounds; even this underestimated their weight, since most had lost between thirty and fifty pounds during the campaign preceding surrender. In addition to weight loss, the physical deprivation most prisoners had suffered left many with lingering effects of malnutrition, recurrent bouts of malaria, traces of dysentery, beri-beri and diminished eyesight. Thomas Hewlett, a physician who spent time in Japanese camp #17 in Fukuoka, listed the physical problems as various gastrointestinal diseases, including diarrhea (Hirohito's Curse), acute enteritis (Benjo Boogie), acute colitis, various respiratory diseases, tuberculosis, Dengue fever and, of course, malaria, which most of the men had already contracted on Bataan.[72]

Many required years to recover most of their pre-war health, if they ever did at all. One sample of 1,830 men taken in 1951 showed an exceptionally high incidence of TB and accidental death (read: suicide), the latter more than twice rate of general population. In 1950, the psychiatrist Thomas Holman wrote a report entitled "Status of 30 Survivors of the Bataan March of Death" that stated, "I believe when an ex–POW of Japan visits ... any physician in fulltime employ of the government, subconscious mechanisms promptly come into play.... The doctor becomes symbolic of the government that ... he felt abandoned him." This circumstance made it impossible for the ex–POW to disclose his entire medical history, thereby preventing adequate treatment, even if available.[73]

Less obvious but even more insidious were psychological problems. Most of the repatriated POWs who had been on the Death March suffered from some symptoms of post-traumatic stress disorder. One sample of forty-seven POWs captured in the Pacific revealed that more than half of those surveyed remained "seriously troubled" for decades after the war.[74]

Another study of forty-one survivors of Japanese prisons agreed—most continued to have symptoms such as flashbacks, problems sleeping and nightmares four decades later. Another sample showed other effects, including survivor guilt, hyperalertness, and discomfort in the presence of Asians. The study concluded that "at least a form of the disorder is characterized more by internalized anxiety than by the more well-known acting out characteristics of some forms of post-traumatic stress disorder."[75]

Some could not work their pre-war professions, and many ex-prisoners complained of inability to concentrate, an antipathy toward strangers, and a powerful need for solitude. After six months in prison, one American officer stated, "Much better to die in captivity than to go home so deteriorated ... mentally, morally ... that my own loved ones would regard me with a combination of pity and loathing.... I fear there are to be casualties from the captivity not reckoned in terms of dead and missing." The casualties were indeed reckoned beyond that measure. Glenn Frazier was haunted by nightmares and hatred of the Japanese for three decades until he found peace—his book, *Hell's Guest*, was doubtless a form of therapy. Joe Merritt, now in his eighties, recently completed a book that explains his "personal metamorphosis" from a "callow, carefree youth into a calculating executioner" that helped banish his nightmares. Frazier and Merritt were among the fortunate who were able to reconcile their experiences with their lives as civilians to some extent.[76]

Many others reported terrible dreams that persisted for decades after the end of the war. Preston Hubbard described a typical episode:

> My dream would begin as a rather pleasant episode, but after a while the setting and thematic structure would break up, producing strange and often grotesque images. Suddenly, I was again in a Japanese prisoner of war camp. My prison-related dreams were nearly always filled with horrible images: executions, beatings, bloated or emaciated dead bodies, and human feces—always human feces. The feces seemed to take the place of blood.

Hubbard wrote his book "because of the pressure produced by a great irony.... The sense of internal conflict between the horror of war and the love of country is common among soldiers, especially POWs, who have seen and experienced the indescribable agonies that live on in unending nightmares."[77] Difficulties extended into waking hours as well. Robert Haney reported trouble concentrating in school: "Sometimes I would sit for hours, with my mind darting off to the other side of the world and a war that was supposed to be over, before completing a few pages." Joseph Petak wrote that his manuscript was "the result of psychiatric counseling and treatment. The doctors insisted that I write my experiences to help me overcome the problems I was having with nightmares and other bad memories."[78]

Guy Kelnhofer, a Bataan veteran and author of *Life After Liberation: Understanding the Former Prisoner of War*, complained bitterly about the absence of special recognition of POW problems; theirs were lumped in with those of all returning vets. Problems included psychic numbing, depression, fatigue, neuropathy, disturbed sleep patterns and nightmares, sexual dysfunction and financial loss. Such afflictions, and the anger and stress they generated, took an enormous toll on marriages. John Wipple spoke for many, writing after his wife divorced him in 1982 that

> the stress I feel now—perhaps more insidious because I have denied it in the past and feel almost ashamed to admit it now ... causes me a great deal of emotional pain. I am filled with guilt, self-doubts, distrust, anger, frustration, fear, loneliness, and powerlessness. I have been subjected to such great stress as a POW to just stay alive, and such degradation and abuse by the enemy and

by unthinking Americans after the war, and by such loneliness because I cannot establish deep, lasting relationships with other people or allow myself to feel any deep emotion (either joy or sorrow) because of my experiences as a POW, and I feel guilty because I feel that way.[79]

Such disconnection from one's fellows was not uncommon.

The 2005 film *The Great Raid* chronicles the daring commando rescue on January 30, 1945, of 511 American POWs from the prison at Cabanatuan. Many of the men rescued had endured the Death March, and the film concludes with several minutes of period footage of the smiling GIs. As the credits roll, ships bearing the ex–POWs approach the West Coast, and the film concludes with scenes of waving crowds lining the dock to welcome their long-lost warriors. The heart-warming scene was indeed real, but short-lived. Others shared such experience. Greg "Pappy" Boyington, the leading Marine ace of the Pacific, was shot down in January 1944 and spent twenty months in Japanese prisons. Upon his homecoming, after his receipt of the Medal of Honor, he was feted with a tickertape parade in the backseat of a Cadillac convertible. At one point, a man broke through the line of police and, before officers could stop him, grabbed Boyington by the arm and said, "Enjoy it today, my boy, because they won't give you a job cleaning up the streets tomorrow."[80] Bataan's survivors were sometimes denied even the welcome.

Many easily confirmed the ephemeral nature of their welcome's sincerity. Whatever degree of physical or psychic pain survivors endured, virtually all observed that they were denied public recognition of their service and sacrifice; some were not even welcomed as heroes. When their ships anchored, some POWs were forced to wait for nightfall to disembark, and loaded onto a bus with darkened windows to take them to the hospital. Many were told not to discuss their POW experiences in the newspaper or radio without express clearance from the military; some were ordered to comply with such restrictions in writing. One hometown newspaper sent a reporter to speak with James Brennan in San Francisco, but an army intelligence officer terminated the interview.[81]

After the brief moment of elation subsided, survivors looked in vain for the recognition they craved. Like Boyington, some would drift into alcoholism and from job to job after the war, searching for their place in society. As the years slipped by, they sometimes encountered complete ignorance of their history. In 1985, while visiting the site of Camp O'Donnell, Richard Gordon met an American Marine guarding a nearby tower used to transmit intelligence data. While waiting for permission to enter, he spoke with the sentry and discovered to his horror that the soldier knew nothing of the camp, or the memorial cross Gordon had come to visit. "Here was an American soldier," Gordon wrote, "stationed where thousands of prisoners of war had died ... totally ignorant of the site's history. I was aghast."[82]

Seventeen years later, Red Allen, then nearing eighty, stated, "It gets harder and harder to give satisfactory interviews. The interviewers get younger and younger as time goes by, and many appear to know nothing of the history of our time. Some will say, 'Just answer my questions' and don't know what to ask. One young lady even asked me, 'What does "POW" mean?'" It often meant something inglorious, the kind of experience "about which most nations have felt more comfortable ... suppressing and keeping out of sight, much like leprosy, plague, social decay.... The prisoner of war has had rather few spokesmen over the years." Abie Abraham, after months locating bodies of dead on Bataan after the war, arrived home in Butler, Pennsylvania. On his way home a cab driver asked him, "Were you in the war, Sergeant?" Abraham could not reply, and he later wrote, "I was powerless to move or speak and stood staring at him, suffering pangs of homesickness for the Philippines where people did not ask such a question."[83] Being politely asked about the war reminded Abraham and many others of the merely perfunctory interest, or none at all, that civilian America evinced in soldiers' overseas service. Eugene Sledge spoke for many when he wrote,

> I was totally unprepared for how rapidly most Americans who did not experience combat would forget about the war, the evils we faced, and how incredibly tough it had been for us to defeat the Japanese and the Nazis.... [I] felt like some sort of alien, and I realized that this sort of thing would confront me the rest of my days.[84]

One survivor, who later became a psychiatrist, suggested the range and depth of returning prisoners' problems. The returning ex–POW faced a world where civilians compared rationing and cramped housing to the nightmare of his imprisonment, as well as

> estranged wives, his own children who didn't know him and even worse did not like him; a changed economy, work situation or service; the distinct material handicap of loss of pay, promotion and professional competence in comparison with his non-captured service contemporaries; physical disabilities; troublesome feelings of guilt, chronic depression; headaches; chronic fatigue and a confused self-picture of being part hero, part coward, part oddity and part junior version of Rip Van Winkle.

Upon his return, George Faulkner, a native San Franciscan, promised his friends a tour of the pulchritude in his black book. The voice on the other end of his first phone calls reminded him of time's passage: "Sara? Sara who? Nobody by that name lives here; Jean got married three years ago." Halfway through his book of names, he realized that "girls of marriageable age just don't sit around for four years waiting" for soldiers to return.[85]

The majority of men captured by the Germans, unless captured in North Africa, could only have remained in prison for about twelve months. The men captured on Bataan, after surviving the Death March, faced years in prison. Life went on in their absence. Siblings grew up. Old girlfriends married. The society they left had changed into one bursting with material wealth. Disappointment increased with time away: "No place, no person, can reproduce his fantasies. The returning soldier envies the prosperity of the civilian world, feeling cut off and resentful. Re-establishment of normal life is hard, sexually, socially, in terms of dress and manner."[86] Sometimes disinterest or neutrality bled over into discomfort or even fear:

> In many cases, American society saw the soldier as a monster who would fall into a life of crime and debauchery. Newspapers and experts argued that it was impossible for a soldier to turn off the killer instincts rewarded during times of war. Rumors circulated through the papers that an island had been set aside ... where the most brutal Marine Corps units would be quarantined for the remainder of their lives.... Anytime a veteran reacted violently to a situation ... newspaper headlines barked about psychotic soldiers.[87]

In fact, the survivor occupied an odd place in post-war America. Often he was ignored because few wished to hear his tales of horror, upsetting to peacetime sensibilities and unwanted in a country the war had not touched at home.

Robert Haney, waiting for repatriation in Japan in 1945, believed that "all of us were orphaned from the beginning and still are orphans. We feel stigmatized for not fighting to the death.... We need a gesture that says the country cares....We need the country to reach out to us, but it didn't.... We have no poets to voice our feelings." William Manchester, a

Marine who saw excruciating combat on Okinawa, sought to calm his demons in his book, *Goodbye Darkness*. "Those of us who fought in the Pacific," he wrote, "believed we would be remembered, that schoolchildren would be taught the names of our greatest battles. But we didn't anticipate the velocity of postwar history ... swamping the past in an endless flood of sensationalism."[88]

For many Bataan veterans, the darkness persisted. Soldiers who had experienced combat wore the Combat Infantryman's Badge, an honor much prized by their wearers, as it carried with it considerable prestige as well as an additional ten dollars in monthly pay.[89] Needless to say, the men who surrendered on Bataan had no one from whom the award could come, though many had experienced the terror of combat. Instead, after the war, ex–POWs were asked to content themselves with receipt of a "POW Medal," sent in the mail following President Reagan's proclamation of National POW Remembrance Day on April 9, 1987. The award, coming more than forty years after their release, rankled the survivors. Former prisoner Guy Kelnhofer considered it

> inadequate recognition ... the only official acknowledgement we have ever been accorded for the suffering we endured for our country. The manner of its presentation left a great deal to be desired. How much significance can be given to a decoration that is sent ... in the mail without the minimum courtesy of an accompanying letter of explanation or gratitude? Where is the honor in that?[90]

Equally sad it was to have been recognized twenty years earlier by a foreign government—Abie Abraham was presented the "Altar of Courage" award by Ferdinand Marcos on April 9, 1967. Forty-six years later, recognition trickled to Phillip Coon, a member of the Creek Nation. At age ninety-four he was finally awarded the Prisoner of War Medal, Bronze Star and Combat Infantryman Badge in Tulsa, "having been overlooked by the military after the war ended."[91]

As the men of Bataan began their second decade since imprisonment, the country took note of the passing of other soldiers from another war. In 1956, Albert Woolson, the last surviving veteran of the Civil War's Union army, passed into history. He had been a drummer boy in the Tennessee campaigns at the end of the war, and his death was marked by lowered flags in his native Minnesota and throughout the country. More than two thousand attended his funeral, and his passing even warranted a statement from President Eisenhower.[92] Perhaps some of 1942's survivors joined the many well-wishers as the era ended, as Woolson was, in fact, the last who wore the uniform of either side. What followed in the next three years, no doubt, tried patience already stretched thin.

Three men purporting to be surviving Confederate soldiers—all of them complete frauds—claimed the country's attention. Although census records proved he was born in 1860, William A. Lundy managed to convince the Florida legislature that he deserved a veteran's pension, and by the time he died in 1957, he was found on the cover of *Progressive Farmer* magazine and both Alabama and Florida claimed him as their own.[93] The second was a rail-thin man named John Stalling, who claimed to have performed the distinctly unglorious task of digging saltpeter for the Confederacy near his Appalachian home. Even so, a country desperate for 1860s nostalgia managed to make him into something of a hero. Stallings delighted in his designated place in the lore, dispensing his version of country humor and wisdom, receiving medals and a gray general's uniform, his old age softened by a $500 soldier's bonus and an honorary military pension of $135 per month. The last, Walter

Williams, died in 1959, claiming to be 117 years old. He had been, he said, a forage master for Hood's Texas Brigade during the war but, like Lundy and Stalling, census records showed him to have been far too young to have served in the war.

On September 3, Bataan veterans might have felt justice served when a newspaper exposé appeared, picked up by national newspapers, making clear on the basis of census records that Williams was only 103, "a mere lad of eight on his father's Mississippi farm when the unit he now believes he fought with was making its final stand in Virginia." What no doubt astonished them was the wave of indignation that followed the article. Though some agreed he was a fake, dozens of outraged readers wrote that their ancestors had served with Williams. The United Daughters of the Confederacy and the Sons of Confederate Veterans supported his claim, as did officials in Texas. The White House also chose to ignore serious doubts about Williams, Eisenhower setting aside a national day for mourning, the U.S. flag lowered to half-mast until Williams' putative Confederate corpse was interred. A dissenting article in *Time* magazine spoke to what had happened. Many had known well enough that Williams' claim was spurious, but "they had showered him with Confederate honors; then, when a too-enterprising reporter proved in the records that Williams could have been only five years old when Hood was marching, they decided to go right on believing just the same."[94]

For Bataan survivors, obituaries were a bleak coda. On August 15, 2011, the New York *Times* reported that Albert Brown, the oldest American survivor of the Death March, died at the age of 105 in Pinckneyville, Illinois. The obituary genuflects appropriately before his suffering, mentioning that Brown was reduced to ninety pounds during captivity and that he knew an eighteen year-old who fell, after which "a guard came along and put a gun to his head, pulled the trigger and walked away." Three years earlier, the paper printed the death notice for Sidney Stewart. It mentioned that Stewart, suffering from PTSD, went to France after the war for his degree in psychoanalysis. The obituary also mentioned a letter Stewart wrote home, explaining why he did not hate the Japanese. In this he was perhaps exceptional.[95]

* * * * *

When Alf Larson went to collect the back pay due him after more than forty months as a POW, some $6,000, he was told that the IRS initially wanted to tax his money. Later, he recorded with satisfaction, "the government finally worked it out so no prisoners of war had to pay any back taxes."[96] Many other Bataan survivors would suggest, some not politely, that Larson's experience with the U.S. government was hardly typical. George Wallace, editor of *The Quan* POW magazine, states that POWs were abandoned three times—in 1942 by MacArthur and the government; again in 1951, when the peace treaty with Japan made no provision for compensation to POWs, and a third time in subsequent years as they tried without success to correct the 1951 problem.[97]

Many Death March survivors, after their imprisonment in the Philippines, were taken to various locations in Japan, where they were forced to work as slave labor. Upon their return, the U.S. government paid them $1 per day for missed meals and $1.50 per day for lost wages—hardly fair compensation considering the conditions of their work. Two books, neither exactly Book-of-the-Month selections, deal with the POWs' tilting at the government windmill in search of additional compensation for their suffering at the hands of the Japanese firms in question. Their titles bespeak frustration and bitterness: *Unjust Enrichment: How*

Japan's Companies Built Postwar Fortunes Using American POWs (2001) and *Soldier Slaves: Abandoned by the White House, Courts and Congress* (2006).

Holmes' *Unjust Enrichment* details the manner in which some Japanese companies exploited the labor and skills of U.S. prisoners. Clearly the postwar Japanese economic miracle was due to a number of factors, but Holmes argues that "for Americans who were forced to work in the war production for at least forty-four Japanese companies, the haunting perception is that their slave labor also fueled the postwar prosperity of those organizations. Too often, the miraculous recovery of Japan's industries began on the backs of our prisoners of war." Most of the companies were still producing goods at the end of the war; some of the shipyards and factories might have had to close down without POW labor. He concludes:

> In its effort to avoid embarrassing the Japanese in postwar years ... the U.S. government ... has instead indulged in "survivor bashing." Beginning with the homecoming orders to ex–POWs not to discuss their captivity and continuing in repeated rebuffs by the State Department to ex–POWs and members of Congress seeking a means of compensation from the Japanese on their behalf, the government has made ex-prisoners of the Japanese feel that their experience was not as worthy of redress as that of German slave-labor victims, or people of Japanese ancestry interned in the United States during the war years. In many ways ... Pacific ex-prisoners of war have been made to feel like the forgotten victims of WWII.[98]

Such a reality explains the bitterness of Bob Aldrich, who while watching ships with the Mitsui logo steam into the harbor from his porch in St. Augustine, Florida, muttered, "Those SOBs. They still owe me money." Aldrich filed a claim against the Japanese firm in 1987 in Florida Circuit court, only to have the judge dismiss it. One survivor put it bluntly: "The Allies rebuilt Japan and Germany and Italy—nobody rebuilt our lives."[99]

The 1951 treaty that formally ended the war with Japan forbade Americans from bringing suit against the Japanese government or the companies that profited from labor extracted from prisoners. Article 14, paragraph Vb states: "the Allied Powers waive all reparations claims of the Allied Powers, other claims of the Allied Powers and their nationals arising out of any actions taken by Japan and its nationals in the course of the prosecution of the war." In an effort to circumvent the restriction, in 1984, Congressman Manuel Lujan brought a bill to a congressional committee, asking that survivors of the Death March be allowed to petition for damages in claims court, leaving it up to "the jurisdiction of the claims court to determine if an apology or reparation should be awarded." The committee heard testimony from Arthur Bressi, Past National Commander, American Defenders of Bataan and Corregidor, and Death March survivor Raymond Pelkey, and was presented with a petition signed by 166 people in support.[100] The bill never became law; no doubt survivors of the Death March watched in tight-lipped frustration and reflected on what was, for them, an extraordinary miscarriage of justice.

If Japanese firms would have compensated them, survivors were looking at a potential bonanza. Lester Tenney, for example, worked at a Mitsui coal mine for about twenty-five months. Using a Japanese pay scale, Tenney was entitled to $1.15 an hour for each of the 8,000 hours he worked. By such calculation, Mitsui owed him $9,000 at war's end. However, fifty-five years of interest compounded at 7 percent came to $550,000. The suit failed. The court concluded that the treaty ending the war with Japan "was intended to bar claims such as those advanced by plaintiffs in this litigation." By one interesting standard, Tenny's calculations were quite reasonable. In an irony that Bataan's survivors found stunning, after the war it was finally made public that Philippine president Quezon paid MacArthur a half million dollars in mid–February 1942 for his "skill" defending Bataan.[101]

In June 2000, the Senate Judiciary Committee held a hearing on POW survivors of the Bataan Death March and their claims against Japanese companies they allege used them as slave laborers. Although attempts to give POWs additional U.S. compensation failed in the 106th Congress, legislation was passed to find, declassify, and release any Japanese records that the United States might have relating to Japanese World War II war crimes, and Congress passed a resolution that asked the administration to facilitate discussions between POWs and Japanese companies over slave labor claims. In the 107th Congress, several pieces of legislation were introduced, including one to give a tax-free gratuity of $20,000 to Armed Forces personnel and civilian employees of the federal government who were forced to perform slave labor by Japan in World War II; none became law. As the number of living POWs and civilian internees dwindles, those that survive continue to press the issue.[102]

Bataan veterans were soundly rebuffed by the courts and governments of both Japan and the U.S. Then, in what they considered the final twisting of the legal bayonet in their wounds, they were forced to watch as their own government helped facilitate compensation for Jewish Holocaust survivors and, most difficult to bear, directly compensate, of all possible groups, Japanese-Americans. Shortly after Pearl Harbor, FDR signed executive order 9033, which required residents of the West Coast of Japanese ancestry to report to relocation centers. Deprived of their property, more than 100,000 spent the war years in camps in the interior. In 1980, Congress directed a commission to study this incident. The report issued in 1983, *Personal Justice Denied*, defined the internment as "unjust and motivated by racism rather than real military necessity" and recommended that $20,000 be paid to those who had suffered as a result of Roosevelt's action. Several years later the Japanese and their heirs began receiving the payments.[103]

Surviving ex–POWs also watched as legal maneuvering that brought millions of dollars to survivors of the Holocaust finally came to fruition starting in the 1990s. Holocaust survivors had to wait decades for compensation for the labor they performed in Nazi camps. Their fate had been a low priority in the aftermath of the war, when rebuilding Europe and fighting the Cold War were the overriding priorities. Yet by the mid–1990s circumstances had changed. The attorney Stuart Eisenstat and U.S. Senator Alfonse D'Amato attacked the Swiss banks that had been the repositories of millions in assets stashed by Germany during the war and obtained a massive settlement, with some victim's families being awarded more than $90,000. Eisenstat's 2003 book *Imperfect Justice: Looted Assets, Slave Labor, and the Unfinished Business of World War II* concluded, "The Holocaust victims, and others injured by the Nazis, many of whom were now U.S. citizens, were particularly deserving of some justice at the end of difficult lives." In some modest recognition of POW rage, the Japanese government later offered all-expense paid trips to Japan for six survivors to visit their place of incarceration. They declined. And when Japanese Ambassador Ichiro Fujisaki offered a formal apology for Japan's wartime behavior at a 2009 American Defenders of Bataan and Corregidor reunion, not all those present accepted it.[104]

* * * * *

As they emerged from their ordeal, survivors of the Death March found that their experience was inconsistent with the basic narrative myths of their civilization. The pattern of male biography was set in antiquity with powerful tales of heroic quest, great myth-narratives such as the *Odyssey*, the *Aeneid*, *Gilgamesh* and *Beowulf*. Such male initiation supplies a continuous flow of competent men to sustain society, very basic indeed as a cultural reference point. It is this "myth of the heroic quest, which is perhaps the most important archetype underlying American cultural mythology. The quest involves the departure of the hero from his common-day world to ... the underworld, the eternal kingdom of death and dreams from which all men emerge." Such a journey was "an initiation into a higher level of existence and power, echoing the movement of the boy from childhood into manhood."[105]

Unlike that of Japan, where the cooperative demands of rice culture and severe limitations on arable land have deeply influenced national character, American history has been fundamentally defined by a surfeit of land and a relative scarcity of labor. Such a relationship formed the basis for development of pronounced form of male individualism. The steady growth of a market economy, technological development, the industrial revolution, the emergence of a middle class and the promise of westward expansion converged to redefine gender roles. The vastness of the West and its opportunities, though only unevenly realized, gave rise to a new male ethos, that of the self-made man. Here was a new era of individualism, where "the old male passion of deference was transformed into the modern virtue of independence. Now, a man was expected to be jealous of his autonomy and free from reliance on external authority. In this world where a man was supposed to prove his superiority, the urge for dominance was seen as a virtue."[106]

Americans have ever sought to situate themselves between the extremes of European stasis and tyranny (too much order) and the chaotic savagery (too little) they saw to their west. This was the world of the American frontier hero, making his way into and over the savage wilderness of the West, the central theme in American history and its most potent symbol. In his book *Tristes Tropiques*, the anthropologist Claude Lévi-Strauss wrote of his experience among the "savages" in the Brazilian rainforest. Its structure follows a familiar pattern of a "civilized" man striking out on a quest into a dark world brimming with tests of physical and moral courage, then returning wizened by experience and now obligated to communicate his adventure to his less wise and less adventurous countrymen.[107]

Closer to prisoners' cultural home are the "captivity narratives" that appear as a recurring theme in American literature and film. As the country expanded, it rubbed abrasively against a frontier inhabited by "savages," and this became a defining aspect of the American experience. The border between white and Indian, between civilization and savagery was a place on the map but, more importantly, it became a place in the mind of Americans who sought to resolve the tension the encounter wrought. This they did by inventing a certain type of hero, one who crossed into the uncivilized wilderness of Indian country and experienced the moral "regression"

> to a more primitive and natural condition of life so that the false values of the "metropolis" can be purged and a new, purified social contract enacted. Although the Indian and the Wilderness are the settler's enemy, they also provide him with the new consciousness through which he will transform the world.... Because the border between savagery and civilization runs through their moral center, the Indian wars are, for these heroes, a spiritual or psychological struggle which they win by learning to discipline or suppress the savage or "dark" side of their own human nature.[108]

For much of the eighteenth century, such narratives were quite popular. Their heroes were women or men captured by Indians who, by virtue of their moral superiority, resist the "physical threats and spiritual temptations of the Indians" to legitimate their own cultural values.[109] Jonathan Dickinson's *God's Protecting Providence,* Ann Eliza Bleecker's *The History of Maria Kittle* and Mary Rowlandson's classic account are all early examples, but the frontier lasted in American geography until officially closed in 1890, and this mythology, in one form or another, persisted as a central American cultural theme. Lest we assume that these archetypes were passé in the 1940s, they have survived well into the twentieth century in various forms of literature and film, notably Martine Scorcese's 1976 offering, *Taxi Driver,* an interesting if disturbing variation on the old theme.

The novels of James Fennimore Cooper offer a different way of reconciling civilization's encounter with the wilderness. At the center of Cooper's series of novels stands Hawkeye. Inspired by the historical Daniel Boone, this character "became the model for future versions of the frontier hero" as a man who stood at a central intersection:

> As "the man who knows Indians" the frontier hero stands between the opposed worlds of savagery and civilization, acting sometimes as mediator or interpreter between races and cultures, but more often as civilization's most effective instrument against savagery—a man who knows how to think and fight like an Indian, to turn their own methods against them. In its most extreme development, the frontier hero takes the form of the "Indian-hater," whose suffering at savage hands has made him correspondingly savage, and avenger determined at all costs to "exterminate the brutes."[110]

Anyone familiar with the character of Ethan Edwards in John Ford's classic *The Searchers* or Clint Eastwood's "Dirty Harry" series of films immediately recognizes the persistent type.

Prisoners of the Japanese had little doubt that their ordeal came at the hands of a savage enemy, one to rival those of any settler encountering the Indians of previous centuries. Americans had no doubt what its guns and swords expressed about Japanese culture. In the aftermath of Pearl Harbor, they were certain that Japan was a "lawless nation, not fit for the ordinary diplomacy of law-abiding nations." The sneak attack was merely the most horrible and aggressive expression of a culture fundamentally at odds with the Christian, enlightened West.[111]

Manny Lawton stated simply, "I was to learn that what we knew as a western civilization had not yet reached Japan." Richard Gordon stated flatly that "no survivor of Bataan will ever question the fact that the Japanese were to a man 'barbarians.'" Indeed, between Pearl Harbor and Japanese surrender in Tokyo Bay, the wartime image of the Japanese as a savage enemy expanded, deepened, and general agreement on the nature of the Japanese character defined specific attitudes toward the Death March.[112]

American soldiers had little difficulty understanding their battle with the Japanese as an encounter with the savage on his own ground. The dark, inhospitable and disease-ridden jungle of Bataan was a perfect stand-in for the wilderness his forebears had faced. The wartime film *Bataan* made a point of showing Americans as an island of civilization, and the savage Japanese now replaced the Indian as his "other," and survivors described their captors in terms that American colonists or frontiersmen of the previous three centuries would not have found unfamiliar. At one level, the American POW experience was consistent with the familiar, if mythic, theme of regeneration through the encounter with a savage wilderness. Most of these men had been civilians not long before their capture, and they carried with them the domestic values of American civilization. The Philippine Islands, especially the jungles of Bataan, answered the description of a wilderness perfectly, and the Japanese—

alien racially, culturally and militarily—were more than adequate to fulfill the role of "savage."

Deeply-rooted stereotypes of Asians already defined American attitudes at the time of Pearl Harbor. Immediately after, President Roosevelt issued executive order 9033, providing for the rounding up of 110,000 ethnic Japanese for internment in the interior. There was, no doubt, legitimate fear of fifth column activity, but a West Coast free of Japanese meant "they were no longer around to contradict, by the trivialities of their daily lives within the community, the image of Japan and the Japanese that propaganda demanded.... A Japanese buying groceries in the local store would have been all too likely to remind" Americans that he was a fellow human being.[113]

Richard Slotkin, a preeminent analyst of the American frontier, defines the man who wanders West in terms that might well describe children of the Depression whose poverty prompted them to join the army or National Guard. Such a man had only

> marginal connections to the Metropolis and its culture. He is a poor and uneducated borderer or an orphan lacking the parental tie to anchor him ... and is generally disinclined to learn from book culture when the book of nature is free to read before him. His going to the wilderness breaks or attenuates the Metropolis tie, but it gives him access to something far more important than anything the Metropolis contains—the wisdom, morality, power and freedom of Nature in its pure wild form.[114]

Survivors did not describe the Bataan wilderness as a purifying force, full of the promise of renewal. Instead, the focus remains on the destructive features of the encounter with the Japanese "savage"—their ordeal was one simply to be endured, their task merely survival. For the survivors, the return to civilization was a physical achievement, nothing more. Survive they did, but the world to which they returned had little use for whatever wisdom their ordeal had given them.

After taming the wilderness, the Indians, or the cattle barons, the Western hero—like Alan Ladd's iconic figure in the film *Shane*—always moves on, further west into the sunset, but with a grateful nod from the community he has made safe for civilization. The community's attitude toward the hero was deeply ambivalent, but it always acknowledged his indispensable role in the on-going march of progress. The returning POW's relationship to his community could not be the same. His community's attitude was equally ambivalent, but with different results. The Bataan campaign ended in ignominy and defeat, and the suffering that followed placed the survivors in a special category. Hero status was denied him; he did not help to overcome the savage, he was overcome *by* the savage. Hence, Death March survivors acted out only a portion of the mythic drama—if heroes were overwhelmed, they at least had the courtesy to die fighting —like Davy Crockett at the Alamo or Custer at the Little Big Horn—and leave a useful symbolic footprint for others to follow.

Another possible source of meaning for the Death March survivor was the idea of Christian suffering. Terence Des Pres, speaking of Holocaust survivors, offers an insightful analysis: "Since the middle of the nineteenth century, suffering has come to be equated with moral stature, with spiritual depth, with refinement of perception and sensibility" with its origins in the

> Christian belief in salvation through pain; Kierkegaard's emphasis on despair and Nietzsche's on the abyss; and not least, the Marxist celebration of the oppressed and down-trodden. The roots

are manifold, but the net result is simple: the more poignant one's suffering ... the more one rises superior to others, the more authentic one becomes.[115]

The image of the hero who perishes in Christianity and in literature is powerful; "we reserve our highest praise for action which culminates in death.... Our serious models draw their sanction and compelling force from death." Figures such as Christ, Lincoln, and Houseman's young athlete "all resolve conflict by dying and through death ensure that the spirit they spoke or fought for" lives on. In death they remain "beyond compromise, beyond the erosion of time, and the truth for which he stood is solemnized ... through the drama of his sacrifice."[116]

However, the meaning of suffering—as part of coming of age, as movement toward spiritual redemption—was losing currency by the 1940s. Survivors naturally made suffering the centerpiece of their stories—little else could sustain their narratives. The consumer culture of the post-war period would have little or none of this, however. The millions of returning servicemen entered an economy in which, between 1939 and 1945, per capita income had doubled and personal saving had jumped from 2.6 billion to nearly 30 billion. At war's end, spending replaced saving, ushering in a period of enormous economic growth. In the film *The Best Years of Our Lives*, one of the central characters, Al Stephenson, speaks to this reality. The morning after he returns home to his wife and family, he says, "I've got to make money. Last year it was kill Japs and this year it's *make money*."

It is difficult indeed to imagine moving the central idea in Lincoln's second inaugural forward seventy-five years. As he groped for the meaning of the war, he seemed to conclude that only the profound sin of slavery explained the nation's immense and proportionate suffering. As the depression and war bore down upon them, Americans of the 1940s believed they had committed no sin, and Death March survivors were left without an altar on which to offer their suffering.

* * * * *

While imprisoned at Camp O'Donnell, American POWs erected a monument to their dead on which they inscribed *Omnia pro Patria*. The post-war world they encountered did not honor them either materially or symbolically, and it seemed to many that though they were "all for their country," it was not, in fact, for them. Solzhenitsyn's Kostoglotov in *The Cancer Ward*, contemplating treatment that will render him impotent, wonders, "Whom shall I seek, with whom share the heavy-hearted joy of my survival?"[117] Americans who wrote about their experiences on the Death March asked the same question, often finding that they had no one to talk to except each other. These men answered to the description Elie Wiesel provided for Holocaust survivors, left as they were with "a sense of both impotence and guilt ... to have badgered a world wishing to take no notice ... people did not look. Worse, many looked and did not see." Ralph Levenburg stated the plaintive refrain of many at an American Defenders of Bataan & Corregidor reunion, where he said, "Our stories are not pretty stories," he said. "They're not exciting stories, but they're stories of life that should be told and over and over again so that people will understand."[118]

The war correspondent Ernie Pyle once concluded his description of a combat action in Europe with the words, "The American soldier could be majestic when he needed to be."[119] Americans noted such majesty only on a selective basis, and only until the guns fell silent.

6. Remembering and Forgetting

Afterward, these men were left to themselves, to make the memories they needed, in what they believed was well-deserved compensation for the broader society's amnesia. For many, the stories were an expression of outrage. One scholar of POW narratives states the matter cogently:

> In lament, captivity narrators evaluate the cost of wasted time, reflect upon their lost material opportunities, and purposefully grieve for their dead comrades. The lament functions too as an ethical forum for former prisoners to express individual and collective outrage against willful, and often illegal acts of inhumanity.[120]

Yet these men were left to solemnize the truth of their suffering on their own, often without the redemption they believed they deserved.

7

The Wages of Defeat

The people made their recollection fit in with their sufferings. —Thucydides, *History of the Peloponnesian War*

Reflecting on the process of composition that produced *Leaves of Grass*, Walt Whitman included these lines in his masterwork: "I often think how little or nothing of my real life, only a few hints, a few diffused faint clews and indirections I seek for my own use to trace out here." For most survivors of the Death March, those useful hints and clues pertained to the image of themselves as victims. In their narratives and at their reunions, survivors vigorously claimed this special status—of malign fate, of Japanese cruelty and their own countrymen's insensitivity. Though Death March narratives contain a significant amount of evidence to the contrary, the secondary works, reluctant to stray beyond the agreed-upon boundaries, focus exclusively on the themes of Japanese cruelty and innocent American suffering. These works omit information that called survivors' status as victims into question or offer a source of cruelty other than the Japanese oppressor.

In light of this, it seems odd indeed that the Japanese experience of the war and its aftermath would in some ways resemble that of American POWs. Defeated, their cities in smoking ruins, the Japanese insisted on victim status as well, and on the omission of any substantial discussion of their depredations throughout Asia. Such silence served the interests of the U.S., as it constructed the appropriate image of a new Japan, a staunch East-Asian ally in the Cold War against Communist China and a nuclear-armed USSR.

While the fighting raged, proper agencies ensured that folks on the home front were spared any evidence of American greed, waste, misbehavior or cowardice; fighting the Good War and displacing evil onto the Japanese left little room for inconvenient contradiction. However, a minority of survivors' accounts explores an uncomfortable terrain, and they blur the antiseptic nature of the existing version of these men's experience. Among war's many nasty environs, one of the most unpleasant to remember is that of the POW camp, where the white light of human behavior refracted ugly hues. There these men were frequently in conflict with each other, indeed many survived at the expense of their fellows.

* * * * *

John Keegan, seeking to capture something of the essence of the horrific battles on the eastern front in World War I, lamented the fact that the campaigns produced such scant literature. Tens of thousands of Russians who fought and died there were illiterate, and no one collected the accounts of those who were not—"without amanuenses, the voice of the Russian peasant soldier could not speak to posterity." Echoes of his observation reverberate in another war. During the campaign Richard Gordon, a sergeant in the 31st Infantry, took a diary off of the body of dead Japanese soldier. Warned against keeping anything with Japanese writing, he buried the tome, which "contained ... a Japanese soldier's impressions of all the action he had witnessed ... until just before he died for his emperor on Mt. Samat in Bataan. Returning to the place where I had buried it some years later, I found out what the tropical climate of Bataan can do to anything placed in the ground.... My treasure was nothing but soil."[1] The fate of such lost material is the historian's lament.

A sometimes shrill insistence on victimhood does much to explain the imbalance of source material on the Death March. The Japanese, defeated and humiliated, were eager to forget the war, and the conquering Americans were happy to support the requisite amnesia. This reality meant that no competing view of the Death March would emerge, nothing to refute or at least refashion what seems upon first blush to require no refashioning at all. William Evans wrote with understandable bitterness about Japanese who were

> probably living in comfortable retirement because of the lenient policies ... applied to the Japanese. One wonders what they say when the little ones ask, "What did you do during the war, grandpa?" You can bet they don't say, "I bayoneted a few American and Filipino prisoners at a place called Bataan" ... And there are precious few of them writing books about their deeds.[2]

Government records are equally unavailable. In the weeks after Japan accepted the Potsdam declaration, "vast amounts of secret materials pertaining to Japanese war crimes and the war responsibility of the nation's highest leaders went up in smoke—in accordance with the August 14 decision of the Suzuki cabinet." Indeed, in Japan since 1945 there has been only limited talk of wartime behavior, and virtually nothing from the men who guarded American POWs in the march. Any discussion has been accompanied by controversy.[3]

Elie Wiesel, seeking to "unravel the mystery" of the Holocaust, believed that "one would have had to question many executioners and many of the dead. The first had long since escaped, the latter were still without graves." Some of those killed on the Death March remain graveless; some survivors speak for them. But their captors have escaped into the silence of post-war Japanese society. With few exceptions, Japanese ex-soldiers existed in what the historian John Dower has called "a milieu of willful forgetting."[4]

A sense of victimhood, sometimes rendered as *higaisha ishiki*, derived from the perception, so prevalent in Japanese thinking, of constant foreign, outside threat. The grand symbol of Japan as victim is, of course, Hiroshima. *Heiwa Koen* (Peace Park) contains many iconic images, but one of the most moving is a statue of Sasaki Sadako, a young girl who died of leukemia after exposure to the atomic radiation. She was trying to fold 1,000 paper cranes to be granted her wish for life, but she died tragically after only folding six hundred forty-four. Now her image stands in the park as a compelling symbol of martyred innocence, bedecked with thousands of cranes every August. In the Peace Memorial Museum, it is possible to find reference to the wider context of Japanese imperial aggression, but one must look hard. The main displays are graphic depictions of immeasurable suffering, and the essential reality of victimhood is assiduously protected. Requests to include histories of Japanese aggression have been summarily turned down, effectively preserving the event as timeless, other-worldly, universal, and disconnected from what came before.[5]

One rainy April day bursting with cherry blossoms, I visited the only museum in Japan dedicated solely to the kamikaze *pilots who died in the war, at Chiran, in southern Kyushu. In front of the museum's entrance stand two statues, to the left a life-size statue of a pilot in flight gear high on a pedestal, standing firmly, his gaze directed beyond to the place where he will die, his face placid. Across from the pilot's statue, and looking at him, is* Yasurakani, *a statue of a mother in a plain wartime kimono, holding her hands clasped in front of her. She projects a powerful image of strong, patient, essentially feminine sacrifice. On the back of her statue the inscription reads, "Mother and son soon will be together forever."*

The inn where I stayed was owned by Torihama Tome, the woman who, on the eve of their flights, substituted for the absent mother of each pilot. Frequently she heard the young men crying themselves to sleep with murmurs of "Okaasan" (mother) and when she changed the covers of the futons *on which they slept, she sometimes found them soaked with tears. Upstairs, preserved with reverence, are the rice bowls, chopsticks and* saké *cups she used to serve the pilots their last meals. On a keychain I bought at the train station is the image of this round-faced, smiling grandmother, the kindly woman who gently shepherded militarism's ultimate victims to their fate.*

Long isolation, cultural insularity and claims of uniqueness have defined Japanese attitudes for centuries, and many still vigorously maintain that their nation remains misunderstood because non–Japanese cannot fathom its subtle complexity. The sensibility of victimhood is not far behind; such Japanese self-perceptions have roots in the physical convulsions of their islands. The famous Hokusai woodblock print, "The Great Wave," gives some indication of the Japanese relationship to nature and its power to destroy. From the perspective of the fishermen huddled in their three *oshiokuri-bune,* the wave and its threatening fingers dwarfs even the majesty of Mount Fuji in the background, and the boats are folded into the churning ocean in ways that suggest submission to nature's overwhelming power.

The great mountain has not erupted since 1707, but terrible disturbances have always been a part of Japan's natural world—the terrifying earthquake of 1923 killed more than 100,000, and 7,000 more died in the Kobe quake of 1995. In 1973 the Japanese reading public was morbidly fascinated by Komatsu Sakyō's apocalyptic novel, *Nihon Chinbotsu* (*The Submerging of Japan*), which chillingly described the nation disappearing into the sea after a giant tsunami. In March 2011, the nightmare became reality, when an earthquake off the coast caused a giant tsunami that took the lives of more than 15,000 and caused billions in property damage. There is something essential in the Japanese sensibility of poverty and vulnerability in the face of nature—"For a thousand years or more perhaps the Japanese had lived like seedy caretakers watching over precious jewels. They tilled the land, expended their lives upon it, and left nothing for themselves."[6]

For Japan, the experience of defeat and victimization was far more compelling than any reality of the cruelty her soldiers had inflicted abroad. Though Norman Mailer's *The Naked and the Dead* (with its appealing descriptions of American battlefield cruelty) achieved bestseller status in 1950, a far more significant publication was *Kike—Wadatsumi no Koe* (*Listen—Voices from the Deep*). The seventy-five entries, carefully selected by a "team of liberal and leftist scholars," all were written by young men who had died in the war, and the "overwhelming tone of the collection was a sense of wasted lives and tragic loss ... their deaths, rather than the deaths of those they might have killed ... commanded attention and were truly tragic." These letters immediately found their way onto the bestseller lists and became the basis of a film.⁷ The Yasukuni war museum in Tokyo, not to be outdone on this theme, offers praise to the *kamikaze* pilots, "incomparable in their tragic bravery," who "struck terror into the hearts of our foes. The entire nation sheds tears of gratitude for their unstinting loyalty and selfless sacrifice."⁸

Victimization took other forms as well. In the first half of the 1950s, more than a dozen edited volumes appeared containing the last words of those who had been executed as war criminals. *Seiki no Isho* (*Testaments of the Century*) was the largest, offering readers nearly seven hundred entries. Certain themes ran through the texts, the men's attachment to their mothers, the reality of becoming *gisei* (sacrifices) for the country or for world peace, and such emphasis made clear the publications were "designed to humanize men who had died in apparent disgrace and to absolve them—at least some of them—of war crimes.... Their gentle words were quoted, while their actual deeds went all but ignored." Such requiems were a salve to a thoroughly defeated nation; the last words of war criminals revealed "that the majority of them made every attempt to glorify their death rather than to become respectful of human lives."⁹

Indeed, the population turned away from its militarist past with as much celerity as the defeated nation could muster. Novels such as Dazai Osamu's *The Setting Sun* articulated a "self-pity that resonated strongly with the deep strain of victim consciousness" in post-war Japan.

> Where the victors asked who was responsible for Japanese aggression and the atrocities committed by the imperial forces, the more pressing question on the Japanese side was: who was responsible *for defeat*? And where the victors focused on Japan's guilt vis-à-vis other countries and peoples, the Japanese were overwhelmed by grief and guilt toward their own dead countrymen. The victors could comfort the souls of their dead, and console themselves, by reporting that the outcome of the war had been great and good.... Triumph gave a measure of closure to grief. Defeat left the meaning of these war deaths ... raw and open.... The millions of deaths inflicted by the emperor's soldiers ... remained difficult to imagine as humans rather than just abstract numbers.¹⁰

Beyond the obsession with her own dead was the issue of responsibility. Japanese dealt with defeat by placing blame on a small coterie of militarist leaders. Many still refer to the summer of 1945 with the neutral term *shusen* (war's end), and another term, *damasareta*, a passive verb meaning "to have been deceived" was a common expression for surrender. In this iteration, "foolhardy leaders" guilty of "collective dementia" were responsible, not the Japanese themselves, either soldier or civilian. "Defeat, victimization, an overwhelming sense of powerlessness in the face of undreamed-of weapons of destruction soon coalesced to become the basis of a new kind of anti-military nationalism." Popular tastes ranged toward the extreme after the U.S. occupation ended in 1952, after which

> movie audiences had a pornographic fascination for the seamy side of American military bases: the crime, the prostitution, the raping of innocent Japanese women ... the scene of an American soldier (usually black) raping a Japanese girl (always young, always innocent), usually in a pristine rice field (innocent, pastoral Japan), is a stock image in postwar movies about the occupation.¹¹

All of this left precious little space in Japan for public speculation about wartime atrocities of any kind, let alone an interested reading public for individual soldiers' purgative narratives.

"Far from achieving a pacifist utopia of popular solidarity," however, Japan became "a country driven by materialism, conservatism, and selective historical amnesia."[12]

For the past twenty years, *Rekishi Kyōiku-Sha Kyōgi-Kai* (Association of History Teachers and Educators) annually asks students aged six to eighteen their views on recent Japanese history. The results indicate that their image of the war is that of "Japan being the victim ... the atomic bomb occupies a large place in their image ... and their victim mentality sharpens in reverse proportion to their awareness of the Nanjing Great Massacre and other atrocities in Asia."[13] The salaryman's devotion to his company displaced any unpleasant recollections; such "economic animals" proliferated during the income-doubling decade of the 1960s.

* * * * *

On the American side, the meaning of their participation in World War II was clear to some. John Steinbeck observed, "in the ranks, billeted with the stinking, cheating, foul-mouthed goldbricks, there were true heroes, kindly men, intelligent men who knew or thought they knew what they were fighting for." Others were grateful for the adventure and to have contributed. One such soldier stated,

> I had the most tremendous experiences of all of life: of fear, of jubilance, of misery, of hope, of comradeship, and of endless excitement. I honestly feel grateful for having been a witness to an event as monumental as anything in history and, in a very small way, a participant.

A soldier on Bataan wrote to his parents, "It looks pretty bad for me right now, if I don't get back don't worry about me, you will know that I went down fighting for Uncle Sam and the good old U.S.A.... When we get through with the Axis powers this time they will never be able to bring war on anybody else." Two years later, Jack Hogan, an infantryman preparing to retake the Philippines in 1944, seemed equally sure of the war's purpose. Reflecting on the death that had visited so many American homes, he wrote, "I realized ... more than ever that there was in reality not one war but two; that unless we fought and won the battle against moral anarchy, against fear and hate in men's hearts our victory over Germany and Japan would be a hollow mockery, and an unforgiveable waste."[14] Such ideological overtones were rare indeed.

The sixteen million men who fought World War II were overwhelmingly civilians, and the 97.5 percent who avoided death were eager to return to civilian pursuits. When asked why they were fighting, many simply said "to go home." In the film *Saving Private Ryan*, Captain Miller justified retrieving his ward simply enough: "If that earns me the right to get back to my wife, well then ... then that's my mission." His comment suggests the war's essential inconvenience, an interruption, with whatever requisite travail, whose victorious conclusion was never in real doubt. This was the "ideological vacuum" within which the war was fought. Most saw it as little more than an interruption of the trajectory of the civilian lives. Glen Gray, author of one of the most insightful reflections on World War II, went a bit further:

> The deepest fear of my war years, one still with me, is that these happenings had no real purpose. Just as chance seemed to rule my course then, so the more ordered paths of peace might well signify nothing or nothing much.... How often I wrote in my war journals that unless that day had some positive significance for my future life, it could not possibly be worth the pain it cost.

Such nihilistic thoughts emanated from a veteran of European battlefields who was, at least, part of a victorious campaign. Gray wondered: "What was I doing here? How did this mad war concern me?" He continued, "So often in the war I felt an utter dissociation from what had gone before in my life; since then I have experienced an absence of continuity between those years and what I have become.[15]

Once upon a time Americans had been moved to battle by abstractions. James McPherson and others have ably testified to the motivations of Civil War soldiers whose competing, yet equally powerful, notions of individual freedom impelled them to the bloody battlefields of Shiloh, Antietam and Cold Harbor. McPherson's examination of Confederate and Union soldiers' letters revealed that they were motivated by forms of patriotism that the World War II GI would find quaint, or even openly mock. Many of the soldiers of the 1860s put on their uniforms to defend liberty as each side understood the concept and with an acute awareness of the Revolutionary generation's legacy. The concepts of democracy, majority rule, and the validity of the constitution were central to their worldview.[16]

North or South, these volunteers were certain of the justice of their cause—"That of the Union or of the South was bound up with one's community, one's home and family, and one's God." These binding ties, argues historian Reid Mitchell, "is why the Civil War volunteer not only submitted to his transformation as a soldier, but took pride in it. Ultimately, the worth of the cause was the worth of the soldier." A fundamental irony accompanied these men as they entered the military: "Only the justice of the cause for which they fought and its meaning for the civil life to which they planned to return could reconcile many volunteers to their new identity as soldiers."[17]

By 1942 such irony had disappeared. As Americans walked through the doorway separating the nineteenth and twentieth centuries, they left much of their ideological baggage behind. The soldier serving on Bataan was fundamentally different in that he, unlike his ancestor, was not a volunteer whose motivation for enlisting bore a direct connection to the war's purpose. The nation had travelled considerable distance, on its way to what historian Christopher Lasch has called the "culture of narcissism" of the 1970s, wherein the meaning of suffering in a just cause had greatly diminished. Urbanization, industrialization, the pragmatism of William James, the sociological jurisprudence of the early 20th century, the disillusionment of the "lost generation" after World War I, the Scopes Trial and the Great Depression all contributed in their way to accelerate the growth of a new, secular, material culture. Abraham Lincoln explained the bloodletting of the Civil War as punishment for the sin of slavery, but eighty years later Americans were at a loss to explain the suffering of the 1930s, or the greater suffering some would endure after Pearl Harbor. The man who would serve on Bataan entered the service because he was an "old army hand," he was in the National Guard and his unit was federalized, or because he was drafted. If the rank-and-file generally fought the war in an ideological vacuum, the men unlucky enough to find themselves on Bataan lived somewhere near its dark center.

Propaganda on the other side spent no time explaining or justifying Japan's war. In films such as *Nishizumi Senshacho-den (The Story of Tank Commander Nishizumi)*, unquestioning acceptance of duty and loyalty to the state were simply assumed.[18] Across the Pacific, however, the Office of War Information understood the weak ideological underpinnings of the war and recruited the director Frank Capra to inform American soldiers why they were fighting. One of his installments was the 1944 offering "War Comes to America" in which the men were reminded just what America was—a place of peace and progress. Nearly an hour long, the film took dead aim at what the OWI assumed was a vast ideological vacuum among the draftees. After a brief history lesson and a succession of images that showed American workers and material progress—accompanied by rhapsodic strains of Gershwin—the soldiers were offered the sinister chronology of totalitarianism's growth.

Here American youth of the 1930s are shown as blissfully ignorant of growing German and Japanese power that crept incrementally, like a cancer, "while most of you were playing ball on a sandlot," "as you graduated from high school," "when you had your first date," and "when you were running around in jalopies." Americans needed jolting out of their teenage isolationist sensibilities, and the OWI had the answer, telling the soldiers exactly why they toted rifles—to defend the idea of freedom, both in the abstract and the practical. If, the film argued, the cancer of totalitarianism was allowed to grow unchecked to the east and west, its material superiority would eventually overwhelm the U.S. The soldiers watched the film, but few were persuaded that their goal amounted to more than what most openly admitted: the simple desire to go home.

* * * * *

If wringing meaning from the coarse fabric of war was difficult for the ordinary American-at-arms, the task was much greater for the defeated, those who failed to avoid the ignominy of capture. Soon after the end of the war in Europe, a German observer spoke to the moral confusion of defeat felt by so many Bataan veterans:

> One can only regard our present situation as the quintessence of irony.... We will never get over this bloody Calvary. We have grown old and weary to death. One sits and searches one's brain for an explanation.... What was the point of it all, what rhyme or reason was there for this desperate, ruinous destruction? Was it just a Satanic game?[19]

Some met defeat with a certain fatalism, tempered with dark humor. One American captain recalled that a "terrible lethargy" fell over the defeated multitude at the end of the campaign: "After the months of being beaten and bettered at every turn in the road, it seemed that being killed in action wasn't so bad. I thought a bayonet job would be a little clumsy. I didn't want to be done in by some ignorant Jap. If he'd had a Ph.D., I'd have felt a little more comfortable about the event."[20] Others were more inclined toward desolation. On the day of surrender, Sidney Stewart built a fire to burn his company's records:

> As its flames danced, it reduced to ashes all records of what we were and who we were. Then the company flag was brought forward and laid on the fire and I turned my face and looked back toward the jungle. I could not stand to see those colors burning. Suddenly I heard Weldon crying beside me, and the sobs shook his body. "The Americans didn't even try to send us help. They deserted us."

When General Ned King finally called his commanders to inform them of surrender, exhaustion gave way to tears. "Many a seasoned soldier wept unashamed. So this was to be the end!" remembered one.[21]

One study of ex–POWs states, "Fighting men speak of 'the fortunes of war.' In combat, luck cannot smile on all participants. Some are bound to lose. The man taken captive is one of the unlucky—a Solider of Misfortune. That can be one definition of a war-prisoner." Few survivors of the Death March would disagree with this assessment. Guy Sajer's verse in his wartime biography *The Forgotten Soldier* articulates this feeling:

> Only victors have stories to tell,
> we the vanquished were then thought of
> as cowards and weaklings whose memories
> and fears should not be remembered.

Such memories and fears were a heavy burden. While in prison, Red Allen spoke to one of his friends, who on the verge of death, told Allen that he was, in surrender, a traitor to his country, and could not face the shame of seeing his family.[22]

Those captured on Bataan, at best, could claim credit for what wartime propaganda called a delaying action, a definition that had expired when peace arrived, hardly the stuff of heroic tales. John Playter spoke to the problem of defeat when he described the end of his trek:

> Thus ended four months of combat and nine days of marching.... There were no brass bands this day with fanfares of trumpets or rolls of drums echoing sounds of glory. Rather, those of us that once marched with chins up and all the pride of parade dress now heard sobs. Many of us felt the lives of buddies had been sacrificed for nothing. If we had done anything of worth, it was that our blood greased the wheels of an out-dated war machine of a blind and neglectful nation. The story of most American veterans ends in victory. Ours ended in bitter defeat. We were to miss the great moments of war.... In our beaten and dazed minds, it felt as if we had come to the end of a civilization.[23]

These were sobering thoughts with which to enter upon long captivity. As Americans languished in Japanese prisons, they had time to reflect on the might-have-beens of their lives as soldiers—the random chance that landed them in the Philippines on the eve of a geo-political conflict they only vaguely understood, the good or bad luck that defined their proximity to starvation during the campaign, and perhaps the missed opportunity to have escaped when the chance presented itself.

In the obvious confusion of their hike north, why didn't more Americans escape? The long siege had taken a toll on soldiers' physical condition, and many, though suffering on the march, must have believed that some kind of relief waited at its conclusion. The ordeal had affected the men's rational faculties as well. Tankers from the 192nd Tank Battalion, thinking of escape, were told by English-speaking Japanese that they would be trucked to Manila and sent to the U.S. in exchange for Japanese in America. Though an incredible proposition, those listening apparently abandoned their escape plans and acquiesced.[24]

A few did not, and instead fled to the jungle interior and joined the guerrilla movement. Ed Thomas claimed that "hundreds of men, both Filipinos and Americans, took off from the Hike," though the vast majority of these were Filipinos, who had the obvious advantage of shedding their uniforms and blending into civilian population. Leon Beck, one of the few Americans to leave, was certain that no glory awaited him in a prison camp, and he decided,

> I'm not going to march in the prison camp. If I have to die, I'm going to die in the attempt or I'll die free. But, I'm not going to go in prison camp. We were taught [that] you had a moral, legal, and ethical responsibility if you were ever captured, that you should make an attempt to escape and if that attempt was successful, you had to continue to resist to your enemy, until such time as you could re-join friendly forces. That's the way it was taught to us, every time they read the Articles of War to us.[25]

In the confusion of the march, with no guards in sight, Beck simply chose a propitious moment and walked away. He remembered, "every time you did anything, the Japanese counted you. They started out with 100, but five or six would drop out, or maybe someone would escape, but it didn't matter how many were in the group, they just counted you over and over like you were precious gold." Beck did not remain among the glitter:

> I just rolled off of the road and got into the edge of the river and there's a lot of palmetto brush and weeds and one thing or another growing and as soon as the group marched on past me, and got a ways down the road, and out of sight and there wasn't anything in sight, coming up the road, I went up, swam and waded across that river and got out into a cut rice field and I could see a shack over there.

Some Filipinos came to his aid and he later joined other American guerrillas.[26] Others' escapes carried only slightly more risk. Between Lubao and San Fernando, Blair Robinett waited until a passing truck convoy kicked up a cloud of thick dust and under its cover "took off, jumped through the hedge, ran 150 feet, and dropped over the edge into a marsh." He lay there for an hour until helped by a young Filipino boy who came back after dark and guided him away.[27] Those who stayed in the dusty, demoralized ranks making their way north would have years in prison and afterward to contemplate the might-have-been of escape.

* * * * *

Surveying the battlefield of Antietam, the novelist James Jones' son asked his father why those men killed each other with such wanton fury in 1862. Jones answered, "because they didn't want to appear unmanly in front of their friends." Jones' cogent response is echoed in an army survey which concluded that the "code of the combat soldier can be summarized by saying that behavior in combat was recognized as a test of being a man." The code did not include defeat and surrender. Manny Lawton felt humiliation shared by many others on Bataan: "I felt shame and remorse for having let our Filipino allies down."[28] The aftermath of defeat lingered, and one imprisoned poet lamented,

> How long, Oh Lord, can men endure the fate
> Of blasted hopes, defeat, and vengeful hate?
> How long can spirit live, can wit survive,
> And keep the flik'ring flame of Faith alive?
> In thralldom dark, depressed with cank'ring cave,
> How long can hope contend with black despair?

In prison, the American captive was overwhelmed with a "feeling of helplessness and defencelessness" and with "feelings of shame, guilt and belittlement. He fears that he will be regarded as a failure, that he showed insufficient courage, and that he should have died fighting."[29]

After the war, the fellowship of other survivors was a salve for such despair. The last reunion of the American Defenders of Bataan & Corregidor occurred in 2009, and footage shot there and at two previous reunions formed the basis for the documentary, *Forsaken Legion: The Bataan Death March and the Defenders of the Philippines in World War II*. During the program, some half dozen surviving veterans held forth about their experiences as prisoners of the Japanese. Their reminiscences echoed that of W.E. Brougher, an officer who believed that Americans in prison were "aggressive, friendly, happy, generous, making friends easily ... democratic, hopeful, defiant, refusing to look at the dark side of even their own most unhappy situation ... singing, laughing and happy even tho hungry." Others shared his rosy view of the experience, one claiming that "nearly every ex–POW will claim that he learned more of human nature in a couple of years of captivity than he could have done in two decades of normal life. There are few who do not speak nostalgically of the comradeship of their days of captivity."[30] Such were the sentiments of optimism:

> When one has touched bottom, become the lowest of the low and unwillingly plumbed the depths of human misery, there comes from it a silent understanding and appreciation of what solidarity, friendship and human kindness to others can mean. Something that is difficult to explain to those unfortunates who are outside of our "club." Who have never experienced what it means to be dirt and yet be privileged to be surrounded by live-saving comradeship.[31]

The reality of incarceration in a Japanese prison was different. In his classic memoir of the Holocaust, Elie Wiesel recalled two examples of advice about survival in the concentration camps. An old prisoner advised newly arrived inmates: "We are all brothers, and we are all suffering the same fate ... help one another. It is the only way to survive." Another inmate offered this: "Here, every man has to fight for himself and not think of anyone else.... Everyone lives and dies for himself alone."[32] To what extent did this latter reality obtain among Americans? What happened in those camps that their pens later glossed over, or in some cases omitted entirely? A different, dark picture emerges when exploring these questions.

One survivor narrative lamented, "In many respects, the legacy of the Bataan Death March is the mystery of how one group of people could be so cruel to another." He referred to his captors' cruelty, but he might have as well described the behavior of many of his fellows.

Richard Gordon directed his bitterness at other Americans, disdaining what he called the "professional prisoner of war" mentality and false claims of solidarity and wartime friendship. "In many ways," he wrote, "I hold my fellow American prisoners more accountable for their loss of manhood and self-respect than I do the Japanese for their brutality." His book, *Horyo: Memoirs of an American POW*, was meant to inform the American people "to what level an American prisoner of war, poorly led and poorly disciplined, can sink" while in captivity.[33]

Gordon, whose father abandoned his alcoholic mother, had grown up in New York's Hell's Kitchen, left home at sixteen, and at eighteen joined the army in August 1940. His main recollections of his time as a prisoner, including that spent on the Death March, were "the heartless actions of my fellow American prisoners." He decried what he called the false camaraderie of Bataan alumni—"In gatherings of former prisoners of war I see men who meet and greet each other as though they had been lifelong friends. This leaves me with an impression of artificial friendliness and shallow insincerity." The epilogue of the book is a scathing indictment of the dog-eat-dog character of American behavior and the lack of leadership by officers.[34]

Notwithstanding a few rosy descriptions of solidarity, prison life hardly showed these Americans at their best. Though surely out of place in the nostalgic glow of an ADBC reunion, discomfiting stories of Americans turning on each other during their imprisonment—officers using their position to monopolize resources, and the strong taking advantage of the weak in the harsh, unforgiving society and economy of the prisons—were a large part of their experience. As it is uncomfortable to explore the behavior of the Jewish *capo* in Nazi concentration camps, so are we reminded that, in the zero-sum game of prison life, some survived, whether directly or indirectly, at the cost of their fellows' lives and well-being.

These men were captured at the war's dawn, and the Death March occupied but two weeks of their three and a half year wait until the war's end and liberation. As a result, most survivors' narratives devote the majority of their space to the time they spent in various Japanese prisons. After about six weeks in Camp O'Donnell, most Death March survivors were transferred to Camp Cabanatuan, northeast of Manila. Most spent at least two months there, after which, at various times and in various contingents, the men were sent off in "Hell Ships" to Bilibid prison in Manila, other locations in the southern Philippines, Taiwan and Manchuria.

As the U.S. forces drew nearer to the Philippines, thousands of Americans were transported to other facilities, several of which were in Japan. American submarines, unable to distinguish these ships from others transporting war matériel, torpedoed and sank several, with great loss of life. These voyages, with the men in cramped and filthy conditions in the holds, sometimes lasted as much as a month. In October 1944 alone, two ships with nearly 3500 prisoners were sunk, with fewer than 700 survivors. Some eleven of these ships left the Philippines between October and December, with some 5000 men never making it to their next destination.[35] Many who survived transportation finished the war in Japan—the Hanawa copper mines of northern Honshu, in the Mitsui Miike mines off the coast of Kyushu, and in Osaka and Kawasaki. Understandably, much of their narrative concerns the deprivation they undoubtedly suffered—starvation, disease without proper medicines, beatings and other punishments, some of which resulted in death.

Shortly after the surrender, William Evans recalled a feeling of optimism: "I figured the Japs would bus us to some nice, comfortable POW camp where we would sit out the war, and that it should take Uncle Sam about six months to kick the shit out of these slant-eyed bastards." Along with some 9,400 other survivors of the Death March, however, Evans arrived at Camp O'Donnell, where the world of incarceration revealed itself. One of the more cogent descriptions of conditions at O'Donnell is that of Alfred Weinstein, a camp physician who confronted a stark reality:

> Amoebic and bacillary dysentery, beriberi and malaria ravaged the starved, exhausted, beaten men who lacked food, shelter, clothing, medicine, and not infrequently the will to live. Heartbroken by their defeat, bodies broken by the Nips on the march, hungry, overwhelmed by their isolation, with no hope of immediate recapture, with nothing to look forward to but more thirst and starvation, it was easy for men to turn their faces to the wall, refuse rice and water ... and pass away.[36]

At O'Donnell the death rate was appalling. Six hundred fifty Americans had died during the two weeks of the march, but nearly three times that number died in the six weeks that followed before the POWs were transferred elsewhere.[37] The procession of men carrying corpses out of the camp for burial seemed endless. Horrifying incidents abounded. Once, on burial detail in the pouring rain, four Americans were carrying a number of corpses swollen with beriberi, when one stepped in a mudhole, and the resulting misstep caused the tipping of the board supporting the bodies. One of the corpses slid off, and when it hit him it burst and its juices flowed over him, while the other three cursed him for a clumsy dolt.[38]

After six weeks in Camp O'Donnell, the survivors of the Death March arrived in Cabanatuan, previously an American agricultural experiment station located 100 miles north of Manila, as so much of the war's detritus. Commander Thomas Hayes noted that their "emaciated carcasses look up with staring eyeballs sunk deep in bony sockets. Their broken bodies, starved and bloated, hover near death ... most of them are past manifesting anything—or even caring." At Cabanatuan, the diary of Steve Mellnik, a general officer, describes a slice of time in what he called "indecent prose":

> 6 June. 1,500 PWs came from O'Donnell ... most in horrible shape from dysentery, malaria and malnutrition.... They collapse in camp streets, die and lie for days ... 7 June.... We dig drainage ditches for dysentery-ridden O'Donnell group. Paths to their latrines lines with feces each morning—men just too weak to make it.... Buried thirty today ... 29 June. Buried fifty-two today. Three majors died this month. Camp is gloomy morgue. Dead men lie on streets until noon..."[39]

Yet death did not visit all types of American prisoners at the same rate.

Younger soldiers' lesser ability to cope with capture, obvious on the Death March, continued to inform their experience in prison; at Camp O'Donnell their lack of discipline often had fatal effects. A slow-moving river, covered with green slime, was the main source of non-potable water there, and younger soldiers, in spite of the supervision of officers, would slip out of line and drink the foul liquid. Colonel John Olson recalled, "The old-timers had a big difference in our favor—water discipline. We had years of experience on getting along on a minimum of water and avoiding contaminated water at all costs. The young men never learned to deny themselves anything and bad water killed them by the hundreds." One analyst described the typical pattern:

> Those who gave up earliest and easiest were the younger men ... in the 18–22 year span, who lacked the maturity, philosophic concepts, fortitude, independence, and the buffering effect of at least several years of military experience needed to sustain themselves.... Emotionally, the plodding, unresponsive, insensitive individuals did well, while more sensitive, previously sheltered, dependent individuals did badly.[40]

Soon enough, the young, sensitive and dependent discovered a world of raw exploitation.

John Steinbeck, in the introduction to his book of war correspondence, noted that the American army comprised "the good, the bad, the beautiful, the ugly, the cruel, the gentle, the brutal, the kindly, the strong and the weak." In such a laboratory the weak would suffer an inordinate share of captivity's abrasions. Japanese prisons were not, in some respects, unlike Nazi concentration camps. One survivor of the Holocaust saw the Nazi camps as loci of "vigorous underworld exchange" with all engaged in a struggle to survive, some with "suspicion and cunning." Even the smallest item worthy of barter became part of a prisoner's capital, traded carefully. Constant hunger and "transformed men into irresponsible beasts. Even those who had formerly passed for honorable men stole from their comrades."[41] A similar reality defined POWs' experience at Camp O'Donnell.

Although survivors arrived in poor condition, conditions improved somewhat in succeeding weeks.[42] However, uniform relief for all was not forthcoming; better conditions provided more opportunities for predators. One prisoner mused: "Here we are settling down. Our death rate is falling. We eat rice three times a day. And the Japs haven't threatened to shoot me in three weeks. But danged if our own people aren't making trouble! I've had reports that ... guys are stealing from weaker PWs and hiding from work details." At Cabanatuan, one American POW remembered that men stole money from weaker companions and then bought extra food from the guards. Another complained that life was "a constant fight against personal selfishness.... A continual battle against individuals who sacrifice their comrades for personal gain." Little was safe. Forrest Knox recalled a friend named Garland telling him to give his bible, with his wedding ring, to his wife. The man died during the night, but

Often labeled incorrectly as part of the Death March, this photograph shows bodies being carried out of Camp O'Donnell sometime after the march ended (National Archives).

the bible and ring had already been stolen. He appealed to those around him, explaining his hope of fulfilling a promise to a dead man, but the book was never returned. Ruefully he remembered that "these New Testaments were stole [*sic*] like crazy."[43]

Typical was one survivor's memory of a fellow prisoner who repeatedly employed a ruse to get water for himself and others—filling a five gallon container and claiming it was for sick patients in the hospital, then sharing it with his cronies. Red Allen recalled that a major, working in a camp kitchen, responsible for distributing gravy, withheld it for himself. More ominously, when he was down with malaria, a friend offered Allen capsules of quinine, but warned him to keep them concealed, for fear that others would kill him for the medicine. Another embittered survivor spared nothing as he laid bare the essentials of prison camp morality:

> Were you the medic who refused me quinine ... but offered to sell it to me? Were you the one who wanted to sell me that diseased piece of sugar cane candy for twenty *pesos* (ten dollars) after you had purchased it for twenty centavos (ten cents)? ... are you the one who stole milk from the sick and dying patients at O'Donnell so that you could use it in your ersatz coffee at an officers' party? Are you the one who deprived me of a drink of water ... by "crashing" the water line under the excuse that you were obtaining water for the sick?[44]

Manny Lawton found himself on the end of such a transaction. In desperate need of protein, he approached an old friend for a loan to buy food, was coldly rebuffed, then went to a "sub dealer" to ask for a line of credit. Though many were starving in the camp, well-fed American bodyguards stood watch over piles of canned goods. The dealer offered the food against

Lawton's credit, but only at higher prices, for a period of a month. Lawton was grateful to write a check for $130, feeling fortunate to have been the victim of only this much usury.[45]

Many narratives mention the tremendous advantage enjoyed by select POWs who drove trucks in and out of camp. These men had access to the marketplace outside camp and, under lax Japanese supervision, were able to acquire and sell goods for profit, sometimes with near impunity. One prisoner drove a bus to and from Manila, and for weeks on end he came and went freely, even taking an apartment where he "entertained" Filipinas, and gained sixty-five pounds.[46]

The strong controlled the economy of the camps, including the distribution of medical supplies—for a price (courtesy Christopher Leet).

Another POW, Corporal L. Arhutik, drove a truck back and forth between San Fernando and O'Donnell. Once, in games of chance with his captors, he won 475 *pesos* and a "15 jewel Hamilton wristwatch." The Japanese with whom he drove often gave him "cakes and fags" (cigarettes), and by mid-May he had earned a Japanese name—"Nickachee." Often he passed a small store where he bought candy, eggs, fags, pancakes and bananas. "I was eating well," he wrote, "and had variety, as well as all the rice and soup I wanted, three times a day." One of his trips into San Fernando reads like a weekend with friends. He drove into town with a Japanese companion, got a haircut, then went to a hotel for dinner, where the Japanese treated him to "a few bottles of beer." The pair then moved on to the market, where Arhutik bought a quart of whiskey for himself, gin for his companion. They then repaired to quarters, where they met a group of ten Japanese, one of whom could speak some English. There he got "drunk as hell and had to be helped to bed." With perhaps a substantial hangover, he remained in town for several days, with plenty to eat and smoke, then back to O'Donnell.[47]

Resentment against such men was proportional. One survivor, bitterly complaining about these "black marketers," stated that they "sold us food and medicines for very high prices, indeed, while their own countrymen died of starvation and diseases only a few yards away." The working parties that accompanied the drivers were an equally privileged lot, and contributed greatly to "deplorable state of the needy." One observer posited a dark equation—"moral integrity could be pretty well judged by inverse ratio to one's state of nutrition."[48]

Some omitted such descriptions. John Wright, who was captured on Corregidor and had not experienced the deprivation of Camp O'Donnell, described Cabanatuan as relatively well managed by a hierarchy of American officers, with a library where POWs studied foreign languages, and work details supervised by officers, with enlisted men generally cooperative and well cared for. In particular, he described negotiations with Filipinos outside camp to bring in money, which was then given to a "camp welfare officer" who distributed it to those in need, enabling them to buy "extra food ... usually beans or eggs for their high protein value."[49] Other accounts offer quite a different version of POW life.

The general lack of discipline that had defined the Death March extended to camp life. It was "an established fact," wrote Richard Gordon, that "discipline was almost nonexistent among American prisoners of the Japanese." The resulting marketplace of greed and exploitation was hardly conducive to fellow feeling or cooperation. One captive wondered, "How low in animal-like behavior can man sink and still revert to manliness?"[50] Another's account of prison life suggested that there "was no escape from continued daily contacts with irritating, incompatible fellow prisoners. In many cases hostile feelings were obviously turned inward and joined with appropriate feelings of frustration to produce serious waves of depression." A surgeon who dealt with more prisoners than most recalled that "we became suspicious and hypercritical of each other.... After years of this life it was difficult to tolerate the presence or conversation of even our best friends.... Bitter arguments over stupid trifles raged constantly." He recalled numerous fistfights over food, and he himself, enraged upon seeing a fellow prisoner use a page of *Reader's Digest* in the toilet, sought to preserve the precious reading material with his fists.[51]

At the prison camp at Las Pinas, fistfights between prisoners were common. As conditions improved, men had more strength to expend on each other, and "these fights could erupt from any conceivable thing—words, unequal quantities of rice being dished out, etc., but mostly because of short tempers" and sometimes, as one remembered, prisoners fought "for the simple reason that we hated each other." Men argued and fought over when lights were turned out, and whose bunk was under a leak "assume[d] monumental proportions in the minds of this bunch of caged human animals."[52] Yet those who profited protected the status quo. Reluctant to leave Cabanatuan, some bribed the American officers in charge of identifying workers bound for Japan. Others, aware of Japanese reluctance to import workers with dysentery, bought stool samples from hospital patients and presented them as their own in order to remain where they could continue their operations.[53]

* * * * *

Where death hovered, survival was precarious, and often purchased with money. Sam Moody learned early the rules governing the harsh economy of his new environment. One afternoon he saw a Filipino on the outside of the barbed wire fence at O'Donnell holding two cans of corned beef, offering them at $10 a can. Moody grabbed them across the wire, then sold them to a fellow inmate for $25 and a box of aspirin. This was his "first lesson in ... the law of supply and demand." Others stated and profited from the laws with more vigor— "There were prisoners that would steal food from each other, or wait for a dying man to breathe his last breath just to get his cot or his water ration. Some would somehow obtain medicines and try to sell them to an ailing man.... These men are not the heroes we've always heard about. They were the scum of the prison camp."[54]

Sanitary facilities in Japanese prison camps were ersatz affairs. At one point in Cabanatuan, a campaign was necessary to bring the population of disease-carrying flies under control. Signed sprouted in camp admonishing POWs to

> Think not of beri-beri,
> Let's wipe out dysentery!
> Kill flies!

And

> Who's going to die,
> you or the fly?
> Kill flies!

For a time each man, armed with a swatter, was required to turn in fifty dead flies per day.[55] The identity of the men assigned to count the corpses, and the manner of verification, is lost to history.

Disposal of waste was another matter. In one location, large declivities were scooped out to form pools into which men urinated; afterwards the men dumped small amounts of lime on the surface and sides of the ever-deepening pools. On one occasion Joseph Petak observed two prisoners urinating and counting out money at the same time, when a sudden gust of wind blew some of the bills into the pool, scattering them across the surface. Without hesitation and without covering his organ, the owner of the cash plunged armpit deep into the pool, chasing stray bills to add to the stack he held above the miasma. As men gathered to laugh at his predicament, he responded, "Go ahead and laugh you lousy bastards ... laugh, you dumb shits. Its money, and money means living. And its mine!" Perhaps those watching had the last laugh—no one would help him out of the pool until he paid fifty *pesos* each to three men who dragged him out with a long bamboo pole. Others profited from the episode as well—he had to pay a man who brought him buckets of water to cleanse himself, and another for a piece of soap. Such was the economy of the camps.[56]

At O'Donnell, one slow-running spigot served the needs of thousands of men, causing them to stand in line for as long as six hours to fill a canteen. Fifty-five years after the fact, Alf Larson's memory of line discipline was roseate. He recalled that the "stronger prisoners helped the weaker" in true democratic style. "Instead of each prisoner standing in line to fill his canteen, the more able men would gather as many canteens as they could possibly carry, and then distribute the water to the owners of the canteens."[57]

Others, less affected by misty visions of pleasant cooperation, disagreed. John Olson remembered that "a deplorable aspect of the water shortage was that it encouraged some avaricious men to exploit their fellow sufferers." Another prisoner concurred: "I remember the long water lines, 3–4 hours to get a canteen. Unfortunately we had some Americans that sold water, sulpha pills and quinine. Water sold for $10–20.00 a canteen. Sulpha and quinine sold for $10–20.00 a pill. Those of us who had no money were out of luck."[58] Richard Gordon posed a salient question:

> How pervasive were prison camp predators? Those surviving today will claim they were few in number. I state the opposite, emphatically. Medication sold by medics—and I include doctors—was a way of life (and a means of sustaining their own lives) at O'Donnell. I know of numerous cases where soapy water was sold as medicine to un-suspecting prisoners in order to turn a profit. Survival at the expense of fellow prisoners became routine ... it cannot and should not be brushed aside with the easy term "relatively few."

He estimated that "perhaps thousands" died as a result of such predation, the exceptions were men "fortunate enough to have money [who] lived that much longer and probably owe[d] their lives to the predators." Sam Grashio recalled, "It was not uncommon for a can of pork and beans, fish or corned beef to sell for as much as $100. If a man was sufficiently parched a canteen of water might command a similar sum." Non-smokers took advantage of smokers' desperation, trading cigarettes for food and medicine. Soldiers gladly paid $20 for a pack of cigarettes. In Cabanatuan, one could "pay $75 for a box of tea, three pineapples and 100 eight oz cans of pilchards." Grashio thought the prisoners at Cabanatuan were "disgraceful ... inexcusably soft, selfish, spiritless, and lacking in heroism." The crude capitalism of the camps allowed some prisoners to accumulate significant wealth—one prisoner reportedly left the Philippines for Japan with some $100,000 in checks and cash he extorted over a period of six months.[59]

Many transactions went on with the full knowledge of the Japanese guards, and their active participation. Corporal Eugene Evers stated that "a lot of fellows would slip out of camp and bring food back.... A lot of the Jap guards knew of this and paid no attention since they knew the men would return to camp."[60] Although Alf Larson recalled that most POWs "shunned the Quisling turncoats that actually collaborated with the Japs, and they got little help from their fellow POWs," many engaged in exactly such cooperation—for money. Testimony at the War Crimes trials of 1948 makes clear that American POWs and Japanese guards worked hand-in-hand. One Bataan veteran stated that in June 1942 "three American prisoners of war had arranged with a Japanese guard to permit them to go to a neighboring barrio and buy food to be brought back to the POW camp and sold. Profits to be split with the guard." These "camp operators" enjoyed access to a circle of supply comprising drivers,

Filipinos in Manila and elsewhere, and some Japanese guards, who were dutifully paid "cuts from the whole operation."[61]

The gulf between officers and men, already wide on the Death March, widened further in the camps. J.D. Merritt, describing the immediate aftermath of the surrender, recorded his impression of the "total chaos at the time with little control from our American officers. The code word of the time was FUJIGM. (Fuck you, Joe, I got mine.)"[62] The hard logic in Merritt's observation accurately defined many officers' behavior after arrival in Camp O'Donnell. They had been unable to exert any significant control during the Death March but now many claimed due deference based on their rank alone. The historian Gregory Unwin states,

> The protracted fight for Bataan and the subsequent Death March morally shattered the American troops who reached Camp O'Donnell.... For months afterward U.S. army officers taken at Bataan ... wallowed in self-pity. They balked at reasserting their authority and restoring order. There was a lot of breakdown in discipline and cussing by enlisted men to officers and blaming them for the predicament we were in.... Denied direction and inspiration, many army survivors from Bataan ... turned on each other. The strong preyed on the weak, stealing rations from anyone unable to stop them.

Colonel J.V. Collier, a senior officer at O'Donnell, concurred. "Food and water details were not supervised," he recalled. "Thirst crazed men were drinking the stream water. Food was not equally distributed to messes, and it looked as tho the main officer's mess was never the loser.... Men were found dead who had apparently died alone and unnoticed until the odor called attention to the decaying body."[63]

Long after the Death March, Thomas Hayes complained bitterly about his fellow officers, a "griping, unmilitary, argumentative group of 'sitter-downers'—who do little or nothing other than look after their own hides. They don't know how to take orders or give them. They haggle and complain and haven't an ounce of military sense. What they need is indoctrination, training and discipline." Yet Hayes' demand was unrealistic considering the state of training that most American soldiers had undergone. When the rapid expansion of the army in 1940 and 1941 "catapulted these officers into positions of great responsibility ... many shook off the lethargy of the interwar years. Some did not ... and proved unequal to the complex, deadly demands of modern war."[64] Among the numerous complaints about officers was their apparent sloth. An enlisted man named Hayes recorded with bitterness,

> So many officers were helpless. They couldn't even find libido or whatever it takes to go get their own drinking water ... everyone has to have someone to do everything for him.... They were mostly "stuffed shirt" officers—not real professional soldiers.... Dog eat Dog was the order of the day. When food came it was every man for himself—get all you can, look out for "me"—to hell with "you."

Strong antipathy against officers stemmed from the belief that they should have protected the men better from Japanese depredations.[65]

Having failed to do so, officers proceeded to protect themselves. In one camp Hayes remembered that officers "would buy fruit, sugar, coffee, tobacco and resell to their own prisoner comrades at outrageous enormous prices. Cigarettes at 100 *pesos* a carton—$5 a pack and food in accordance. Officers who were appointed Camp Commanders frequently curried Jap favor at expense of [their] own countrymen, profiteered, excited personal spite." He recalled that many "were vicious against the Medical Corps chiefly because it lay with [them] to determine those fit to leave hospital areas. Although Hayes believed the Medical Corps generally performed its duties according to the Geneva Treaty, this "was bitterly resented in many quarters" by those wishing to bribe physicians. Through Filipino contacts, officers had easier access to loans to buy the medicines and food that kept them alive.[66]

Reflecting on the leveling effect of Manila's fall, an officer named John Sewall wrote to his wife, "I bought a beautiful wardrobe trunk and stored everything in it except my toilet articles and one change of clothing. All that is lost to me now as it is in Jap hands. I have lost everything but what I stand up in, but so has everyone else." Yet soon enough, officers were using their position for their own advantage. C.D. Quinlenn observed that some ordered that water be used only for essential purposes, but they, "and others of like privilege ... always appeared clean, well-shaved, etc. These Gents of course had not made the march and had their foot lockers and bedding rolls with them when they rode to O'Donnell and let their orderlies bust the line at any time to get a bucket of water for their bath or laundry purposes." Once, a Navy officer asked Thomas Hayes' opinion of lending out $1,000 at interest. Disgusted, Hayes responded, "The son of a bitch! ... this bastard wants to lend them money at interest! An American Navy officer with pawnbroker propensities. If that's the crap we commission as an officer and a gentleman, they can have my suit anytime."[67]

By September 1942, Japanese changed classification of Americans from "captive" to "prisoner" and began paying them according to requirements of Geneva Convention. Privates received fifteen *centavos* per day, NCOs twenty-five *centavos* and officers "sometimes as much as ten *pesos* per day."[68] Yet officers then put out an order restricting enlisted men to the possession of not more than fifteen *pesos*, excess cash to be turned in to a "collecting committee." One embittered corporal bitterly intoned that such officers "disgraced themselves for life for so swindling their helpless fellows, for it was nothing but a racket.... Even men of good character and honesty before the war weakened and became unreliable under such revolting conditions as prevailed at the camp." Officers with stateside checking accounts bought goods to insure their own survival, a practice that was far from exceptional.[69]

Lack of discipline among the enlisted men and the fundamental lack of leadership among the officers encouraged this Hobbsian nightmare. Generals and colonels were sent to different locations, leaving junior officers, many of whom were Reservists or National Guardsmen lacking any military experience, to look after their own survival. Resentment against officers crackled out in ways not unexpected. Once, while standing in line for their morning rice, two POWs saw three officers tied to fenceposts, bleeding profusely from severe beatings. One speculated that the three had tried to escape. "'Yes,' came the answer. 'They're officers, too. Tough.'" Another time, a major named Horton, who had confiscated food from the sick in order to have a special meal for officers to celebrate July 4, 1942, later came down with dysentery and died at Cabanatuan. The Japanese made a practice of having officers buried separately from enlisted men, but the group that buried him took their final revenge, removing dogtags so that he would "spend eternity" among the enlisted men he had mistreated. He was, an embittered enlisted man recalled, "a disgrace to West Point."[70]

Enlisted men relished stories, whether apocryphal or not, that saw officers brought low. One such held that in some theater of operations, the Japanese set aside a house for prostitution and brought in some three hundred "geisha" girls from Japan to staff it. The Americans who saw the women were less than impressed, and thought they looked like "cheap sluts." Though unattractive to the men, their bodily functions went on, and one officer was ordered to dig a latrine for the ladies. He later stated that when his children inquired about his war record, he could say in summary, "I dug a shithouse for a whorehouse." For some after the war, enmity seemed to evaporate, and "very, very few were ever held accountable in all the excitement of victory.... All was forgiven." For others, the bitterness remained. One survivor watched a colonel "who had been a despicable and cowardly major in camp attempting to convince others after the war of his bravery" and choked back bile.[71]

All of this was in stark contrast to British behavior in Japanese prisons. There officers retained almost all their prerogatives, and they controlled camp committees dealing with various aspects of life. "Tempering dire but inescapable circumstances with familiar organization, the British sustained pride, organized large-scale education and recreation programs, and maintained a comradeship ... minimizing conflict with the Japanese and predaciousness among themselves." The greater British comfort with hierarchy "served soldiers well when, in one of the war's sternest ordeals, survival often hinged on the preservation of military cohesiveness. And it was here ... that the cost of American convictions came due." Among American POWs, "Imprisonment weakened further the American soldier's willingness to be bound by formal authority."[72] At the moment they needed it most, the American rank-and-file roundly rejected the discipline officers, had they been more competent, might have provided.

* * * * *

Surely one of the least accessible recesses of the POW experience is sexual behavior. John Steinbeck once observed that one of the conventions of war reporting held that

> five million perfectly normal, young, energetic, and concupiscent men and boys had for the period of the War Effort put aside their habitual preoccupation with girls.... When army Supply ordered millions of rubber contraceptives ... it had to be explained that they were used to keep moisture out of machine-gun barrels.

If men were expected to put their sex drives on hold while corralling Tojo and Hitler, there was no question about its proper object before and after. During World War II, some eighteen million men were examined for military service, and about five million were rejected, some on what was termed "moral" grounds. If a potential recruit stated he did not like girls, he was deemed unfit. Once in the barracks, he was informed that army regulations specifically forbade sleeping with genitals uncovered.[73]

Starvation and the strain of intermittent battle eliminated, or at least diminished, men's sex drives during the campaign. This was certainly the case in the Nazi concentration camps. One survivor of Auschwitz recalled that "even in his dreams the prisoner did not seem to concern himself with sex." The same reality obtained for American prisoners—for a time. In March, as the siege was coming to a close, an officer approached Ed Dyess to initiate a party for his men and the nurses of Hospital #2. At the end of the evening, one participant recalled that the "boy-girl relationships remained on a brother-sister-comrade-in-arms level. Starving men and women lust for food, not for each other."[74]

Alf Larson recalled that, for a time, "everything was devoted to food. Guys would talk about a beautiful woman walking down the street with a basket of bananas on her head and all they could think about" was the fruit. "When you thought of a woman, you thought of her stirring gravy or serving food; you never thought about sex." Such testimony did suggest that combat and imprisonment anesthetized the sexual urge. In the narrow confines of combat's danger, men became physically intimate with each other, sharing food, supplies, foxholes, but Gerald Linderman's *World Within War* contains two pages on the subject and concludes, "A reasonable estimate was that ... sexual desire diminished as a function of time spent in combat, and that explicit sexual expression in comradeship was, in the 1940s, slight."[75] Linderman's analysis did not, however, deal with the reality of prison life.

In the trying conditions of Camp O'Donnell, concern with survival trumped any desire for sex. Sam Grashio recalled that although Japanese guards sometimes went into town and returned to "regale us with tales of their exotic exploits ... prolonged malnutrition so deadens the sex drive that few prisoners talked about women. The only time the subject even came up was after the arrival of Red Cross packages which would fill our bellies and stimulate normal appetites for a few days."[76] Considering the language barrier, images of interesting pantomimes come to mind.

Donald Knox, in the preface to his oral history, *Death March: The Survivors of Bataan*, stated, "I believe there are deeply personal stories that were not told to me, stories that lay behind a wall, guarded by emotions these men do not want to share.... It was as if, once remembered, the survivor decided to seal off from the curious this new part of his memory." Alvin Poweleit explained omissions from the diary he kept in Camp O'Donnell: "Certain incidents involving men of our group were deliberately left out because they might prove offensive to survivors." One American GI suggested possibilities without naming specifics: "The absence of women hits men two ways. Some guys take on nasty habits. I've seen men do things I never believed anybody would do. And those men go from bad to worse and nothing can stop them. It's a terrible thing."[77]

Some of the specific nasty or offensive habits must have referred to sexual activity with other men. Pacific War veteran William Manchester spoke for many when he claimed ignorance of what was then thought to be sexual perversion—"we knew almost nothing about homosexuality ... we were aware that homosexuals existed—they were regarded as degenerates and called 'sex perverts'—most of us had never, to our knowledge, encountered one." Doubtless many were repelled by the suggestion of such activity. Sam Grashio described an incident motivated by "perverted sexuality" when a Japanese guard ordered a sergeant to masturbate. When the man refused, the guard beat him "so mercilessly that he went mad and died two or three days later."[78]

Whatever amount of such sexual behavior informed camp life, few would refer to it openly. The narratives these men wrote were intended to redeem and explain themselves to the general audience; their publishers sought to make a profit from their tales of victimhood—compelling, sad, even gruesome. That any incidents of homosexuality would be omitted is obvious considering the post–World War II audience of the American middle class and its notions of proper manhood and sexual mores. Hayden White has observed:

> It is this need or impulse to rank events with respect to their significance for the culture or group that is writing its own history that makes a narrative representation of real events possible.... Every narrative, however seemingly "full," is constructed on the basis of a set of events that might have been included but were left out.

As Friedrich Nietzsche suggested, "It is possible to live almost without memory ... but it is altogether impossible to live at all without forgetting ... there is a degree of historical sense which is harmful and ultimately fatal to the living thing." Years after the war's conclusion, one Bataan veteran wrote, "It isn't easy to take three and half years and wrap them up in a little ball and say here it is. There are some high points and low points and a lot of things that just can't be included."[79] Indeed,

> the main power that life history narrators have ... is the power to talk or write about their lives, or to remain silent; to reveal truths as they see them, or to distort or lie about them. Their interest ... is to have theirs be the version of history preserved, and told to a well-chosen, relatively influential, or well-connected listener or other selected audience. Of course the temptation or the unconscious tendency will be there to omit painful or embarrassing incidents.[80]

In James Jones' novel of Pacific combat *The Thin Red Line*, widely praised for its gritty realism, two characters, Bead and Fife, have a homosexual encounter. Jones describes Bead's initiation of the tryst inside a two-man tent:

> Apparently it made no difference to him and did not worry him that he was suggesting something homosexual. And, perhaps, being eighteen and just out of school, he didn't see it that way. But it could not be entirely true ... because as he started to crawl over to Fife's side of the little tent, he stopped and said, "I just don't want you to think I'm no queer, or nothing like that." "Well, don't you get the idea I am, either," Fife had answered.[81]

A soldier reluctant to risk the wages of contact with women, "was not a homosexual by choice. The very same soldier who would consider such a relationship normal in Manila would most likely have nothing but disgust for the 'queer' soliciting him on the streets of San Francisco." Military life in the Philippines was not without such evidence. To the dismay of some newly arriving recruits, old soldiers "openly bragged about their 'binny boys'" yet it was generally understood never to refer to these men as "queer." The binny-boys could be found in drag at dance halls.[82]

After the deprivation of O'Donnell, new possibilities arose when conditions improved at Cabanatuan. Alfred Weinstein, concerned about the ragged appearance of men there, approached a soldier he called "Queenie" and asked him about sewing. This young soldier, whom Weinstein described as having "exhibited homosexual tendencies since adolescence," had been posted at Shanghai, where he assumed "it was easier for him to express his abnormal sex drive without excessive comment. As a prisoner ... he had to endure the taunts of his fellow prisoners because of his peculiarities." One POW recalled, "While the military had its share of homosexuals before the war, they were of the 'closet' variety. The upswing in the men's condition did much to encourage and create homosexuality."[83]

"Queenie" may have been taunted in public, but some testimony suggests that private matters were different. A medical officer imprisoned at Cabanatuan observed that between February and October 1943, "sexual rejuvenescence was apparent." During that period,

> sexual interest was reflected by an increased incidence of nocturnal emissions, by masturbation, and by homosexual practices—overt in a small susceptible group, covert in a much larger number of men.... Homosexual practices became a subject of group knowledge and discussion and almost reached a level where internal official measures were needed to be applied.[84]

Some, tempted toward the abyss, may have referred to the "Prayer for a Pure Heart" contained in the 3" × 4½" bible they had been issued, but another American recalled that homosexuality was indeed a problem:

> The Japs relieved the situation in the only way possible. They segregated the homosexuals from the rest of the camp. Putting them all together made the situation desperate for them but saved

the rest of us from contamination. When a man, starved for months without a woman, began to show certain signs, he was chided by his friends to stay straight and not become a member of the "Queenie Brigade." It seemed that once the Japs segregated the known queers from the rest of the camp, the problem ceased.[85]

Yet the memory of the problem's management by a third American—a doctor in the same camp—was quite different. He recalled that Cabanatuan contained "about a dozen" homosexuals, and that after conditions and the food supply improved, these men "found themselves in a pervert's seventh heaven. They had no competition from female chippies. They had no fear of punishment." Though officers requested they be quarantined, the Japanese refused, and the men "drifted loose in the camp—notorious prostitutes." Perhaps it was these men, a "few known overt homosexuals [who] were observed to be in unusually high spirits during periods when they were able to practice their arts."[86]

One study of thirty-five ex–POWs suggested that when food was available, "overt homosexuality and masturbation were common" which "gave rise to considerable guilt feelings." Richard Gordon stated that homosexuality was "rampant," though it was generally the "passive" variety—by which one assumes he meant that men did not reject the overtures of the more aggressive homosexuals. The percentage of prisoners who engaged in homosexual activity can, of course, never be known. According to the expectations of male behavior in the 1940s, few would have admitted to such a perceived aberration. But, as Steinbeck observed, "It is in the things not mentioned that the untruth lies." A scholar of memory concludes the obvious—that "memory is selective. Remembering one thing requires forgetting another."[87] Memory, like the way that camp resources were mal-distributed, was a zero-sum game.

* * * * *

At the opening of the documentary film *The War*, the narrator describes a young man, jilted by his girlfriend and angry at being denied service at a restaurant, crashing his motorcycle into the establishment. He then fled, chased by the gun-wielding owner. The next morning, humiliated and fearing arrest, he joined the army and volunteered for the Philippines. There he experienced the barbarism of his Japanese enemy, and the young man, Glenn Frazier of Mobile Alabama, overcame his Christian scruples about killing. Afterward, he said he actually hunted the enemy. "If I didn't kill a Japanese in a day," he said, "I felt I didn't do my job." Frazier described having seen men buried alive, others run over deliberately by trucks, still others beaten to death, and Filipinos and Americans beheaded. Other horrors included seeing POWs' throats cut by bayonet-wielding soldiers in passing trucks, and Filipinas' stomachs cut open.

Frazier's story has all the earmarks of a parable—young man, fleeing youthful hijinks, lands in the wilderness, whereupon he encounters evil. He responds with justified rage, lashing out at a cruel and heartless enemy until captured, whereupon he changes from righteous avenger to helpless victim, one stretched to the limit of suffering. Frazier's account, like scores of others, is an example of the first stages of the form most POW narratives take:

> The American vision of success demands victory in war. Capture initially signals defeat and failure.... Finding a bridge between failure and success requires some analysis of what happened, for the experience itself takes place in sequential stages.... Prisoners explain what went wrong; why they were forced to surrender, and how their world collapsed in front of their eyes. In the second

8

Facing Filipinos

A friend cannot be known in prosperity and an enemy cannot be hidden in adversity.—Ecclesiasticus 12:8

The Death March was a drama that played out in front of thousands of spectators, the Filipinos who lined the road and *barrios* through which the prisoners passed. In survivors' narratives, this population is described in three distinct categories. The first is that of sympathetic observer, often confirming with tears the suffering of the POWs. The second is that of the active helper, offering Americans food, water or shelter, sometimes at considerable risk to their safety. The third involves the results of that risk—actual suffering at the hands of the Japanese.

Here American victimhood joins with that of Filipinos—*both* suffered during the Death March, Americans because they were defeated, Filipinos because they mourned that defeat. Using the sword and bayonet against a defeated enemy denoted one level of barbarity, but the torture and murder of innocent civilians, especially women and children, defined the enemy as beyond the pale. As with descriptions of Japanese brutality against prisoners, the absence of any competing narrative renders claims of cruelty to Filipinos questionable, the relationship to truth unclear. The narratives constructed a perfect foil to the Japanese—cruelty balanced by equal measures of kindness. Sam Grashio spoke for many of his fellows when he stated, "I never knew an American who went through any part of the war ... who did not come away impressed by the humanity and generosity of the great majority of the Filipino people," and many others spoke of Filipinos' brutal treatment at the hands of the Japanese.[1]

No doubt *some* Japanese treated *some* Filipinos brutally, but the power and prurient appeal of the primary focus on Japanese cruelty has crowded out other interpretive possibilities. Veterans' accounts reveal bespeak unexpected dimensions of the relationship between Americans and Filipinos. A closer examination of Death March stories suggests that, even if Filipinos were not necessarily the victims the narratives claim, they were far more than simply passive observers.

* * * * *

Americans and Filipinos had ample reason to make common cause against the Japanese oppressor. Soon after Japanese forces waded ashore on the island of Luzon in December 1941, the new Japanese government articulated the defining principles of a "new order" to replace American governance. The U.S. had scheduled Philippine independence in 1934, effective in 1946, but the Japanese occupying authorities sought "to make the people understand the position of the Philippines as a member of the East Asia Prosperity Sphere, the true meaning of the establishment of a New Order in the Sphere, and the share which the Philippines should take for the realization of the New Order."[2]

In the early twentieth century, the Japanese initiative involved "sending emigrants to the Philippines to integrate with the Filipino people and fight side-by-side with them" against Spanish imperialism. The implied cooperation against Western imperialists was articulated in the last line of a poem written by Suganuma Tadakaze as he left for Manila in 1889: *Manira no asa motte Nippon no hata o tsunagu ni tariru* (It is Manila hemp that will tether the Flag of the Rising Sun). A generation later, some Japanese policymakers and theorists saw the Co-Prosperity Sphere as a cooperative venture with "southern peoples." In 1939 the Navy National Policy Research Committee offered a "Summary Draft of a Policy for the South" that clearly emphasized cooperation and conciliation over exploitation and oppression.[3]

Early in 1942, Prime Minister Tojo Hideki established the Greater East Asian Ministry, a vehicle intended to sustain enthusiasm for Asia's common war against Western imperialists one and all. The following spring, Leocadia De Asis and thirty other young Filipino elites came to Japan for study of language and customs. By the fall of that year, however, De Asis was struck by a seeming anomaly: "The enormous difference between the Japanese at home, friendly, kindly and generous, and the Japanese in the Philippines—overbearing, heartless and arrogant." Any notion of cooperation rapidly disappeared. Streets were renamed in Japanese, and new posters appeared:

> Watch the Philippines Grow
> Wherever the Japanese army is, There is Peace
> United in Happiness

Such did little to persuade the population of benevolent intentions; as the Japanese settled into the capital, the Manila *Tribune* announced that anyone inflicting an injury on any Japanese, soldier or not, would be shot.[4]

At obelisk #28 in Limay I walk off the main road toward the bay for relief, buy an orange drink, and plop down in Judy's Park, named for I-don't-know-who. After a short rest in the mild bay breeze, I wander toward an old warehouse, on whose wall is an old, shredded notice of a public meeting, circa 1985. On my third try asking passers-by, a grizzled man of about fifty tells me in very broken English that it was to protest the "big fisher boats" that have, he says, ruined the once decent living he and his two sons earned from the bay. In 1973, the Philippines signed a Treaty of Amity, Commerce and Navigation, an agreement that gave large Japanese vessels the right to fish where small-scale fishers had worked without such competition. The awkward relationship to Japan continues.

Unlike Indonesia, where the Japanese were to a large extent welcomed as liberators, the Philippines had already been promised independence, and the majority of Filipinos opposed the occupation—as Homma's victorious army entered Manila, it was "greeted with silence by lines of sullen Filipinos."[5] In practice, this "New Order" meant that democracy and self-government, the delayed goal of the U.S. occupation, was now replaced by the "gospel of Co-Prosperity." Teachers were expected to cooperate in expunging U.S. influence—stories in textbooks such as "The First Thanksgiving," "Henry Wadsworth Longfellow" and "Abraham Lincoln" were eliminated and replaced with Japanese history and heroes. Songs promoting wrong virtues (democracy and individualism) were replaced by Japanese songs such as *Hi no maru* and *Asa no uta* which extolled the virtues of loyalty to Japan. To facilitate understanding, the curricula of schools was (at least in theory) modified to allow language instruction, with *Hanasi Kotoba* (a Japanese reader) occupying a central position. Government employees were required to learn Japanese, and a normal institute and special teachers' institutes were established to impart the language.[6]

Unlike many Japanese officials, Homma advocated a lenient occupation policy. Speaking of the Americans Japan replaced, he told General Terauchi Hisaichi, commander of the southern army, "They administered a very benevolent supervision over the Philippines. Japan should establish an even better and more enlightened supervision." Homma had already suppressed an anti–American propaganda pamphlet, and such actions marked him as excessively liberal. In response, the influential clique led by Colonel Tsuji Masanobu and others set about reversing his policies. Just as the Fil-American army on Bataan was surrendering, Japanese soldiers captured Chief Justice Jose Abad Santos on Negros Island and, though Santos made clear his willingness to work with the Japanese conquerors, he died before a firing squad two weeks later. Though Homma was "dumbfounded" at Santos' execution, the pattern of the occupation's heavy hand was set. That occupation imposed martial law, required residents to wear "rising sun" armbands and made bowing to imperial soldiers compulsory. The year 1942 was changed to 2062 to mark the anniversary of the first emperor's ascension, the *Kempeitai* (Japan's secret police) began its search for seditious elements, and Chinese residents came in for especially harsh treatment.[7]

In response to such policies, a young Filipino sarcastically stated that the Japanese were "reconstructing" his homeland—"They give us many lectures about Japan and Japan's Co-Prosperity Sphere. They show us many movies of Japanese victories. They give us Japanese military training. They tell us we are their brothers. Then they beat us." One Japanese writer, trying to explain the habit of face-slapping, wrote to a Philippine newspaper soon after the conquest of Luzon: "Could it be," he asked,

> the failure of some people to appreciate the very rigid and strict discipline of the Japanese army.... Take the matter of slapping, for instance. In the Japanese way, the *binta*, as the soldiers call slapping, is the slightest disciplinary measure administered in the case of violation of military rules. People who understand this take slapping in this spirit.

A young Filipina was among those who regarded the Japanese with disdain. On one occasion, an American POW who drove a supply truck stopped for sex at a brothel in Manila frequented by Japanese soldiers. There he approached Rosita, a woman he had been with before. She refused, telling the Texan that she had "the clap." The American asked her why she did not stop working and take a cure, whereupon she responded, "I must make many Japs sick. They killed my two brothers in O'Donnell prison."[8]

Maria Martinez, a resident of Manila, spoke of a Japanese "reign of terror," including torture of men, women and children for not bowing to Japanese. "Our conquerors," she wrote, "were worse than beasts. They wanted to win the sympathy of Filipinos with barbaric bloody and murderous tactics. For all true blue Filipinos there was nothing in their hearts but murder for the yellow monkey-faced rats."[9]

Filipinos working overseas are important to the home country. Those OFWs (Overseas Fil-

ipino Workers) who do well in places like Qatar or Canada come home as heroes, relatively wealthy balikbayan *(repatriating citizens), who build houses to take care of their families. Not all are well rewarded for their efforts abroad. One night in a cabaret in Umeda, Osaka, I sat with a young hostess who had taken the Japanese name Yuki—her business card was emblazoned with the address of the club and the outline, she said, of her lips. Like so many young Filipinas, she was sending money home to her family somewhere on the islands. I asked her how much of her earnings she was able to keep, and she said she did not know and did not ask questions. Such women are all over the entertainment districts of Japan, sending back billions that support the home economy. Sometimes lured by absurd promises of wealth, these women have no legal status, and work as hostesses, dancers, and singers at considerable risk to themselves.*[10]

As time went on, the Japanese gave the Filipinos little reason to warm to their definition of "co-prosperity." Sugar fields were ordered converted to cotton, more essential to the war effort, and the standard of living quickly slipped in the disrupted economy. One Japanese historian states that the Japanese were guilty of "an overweening victor's mentality—strutting and ordering the natives about ... the Filipinos watched with bitter resentment."[11]

* * * * *

Just after the surrender on April 9, a Filipino prisoner named Jose Bautista of Paranaque Rizal sat in dazed silence, weeping, on a rock, "with a rosary in his hand as he read his prayer book." He was shaken from his meditation "when a small bag dropped on his lap. He looked behind him and paled in terror, for it was a Japanese officer with a samurai sword. The man's smile, however, reassured him. The Japanese left as silently as when he came. Jose found the bag contained rice."[12] Such kindness was apparently rare. Upon arrival the Japanese assessed Filipinos as inferior. One official intoned, "The natives here are dissolute and lazy.... We must not flatter the natives, and we must exhibit our dignity and strength with a solemn military presence so that they will cast aside their admiration of the United States and cooperate with us with all their hearts."[13] Part of the expected cooperation involved response to any Japanese yelling "*Kora! Kora!*" The Filipino was

> expected to stop on his tracks and, facing the Japanese who uttered it, bow from the waist three times to show submission and deep reverence for a representative of the Land of the Rising Sun. It was, of course, a crude form of humiliating and breaking down the spirit of the Filipinos by their conquerors. As expected, the imposition generated hatred more than anything else.[14]

Japanese behavior was especially loathsome to a people who prized smooth relations between superior and inferior. Such basic similarity in Japanese and Filipino culture rendered the misunderstandings all the more unfortunate and ironic. One authority describes an important aspect of the Tagalog word *pakikisama* as "the stating of an unpleasant truth, opinion, or request as pleasantly as possible. It is an art that has long been prized in Philippine society.... Harsh and insulting speech is correspondingly devalued." A traditional saying summed up this central value:

Ang marahang pangungsap	A gentle manner of
Sa puso'y makalulunas.	speaking soothes the heart.
Ang salitang matatamis	Sweet words win
Sa puso'y nakaalit,	the heart and
Nagpapalubog ng galit.	dispel anger.

The Tagalog proverb *Hindi baling huwag mo akong mahalin; huwag mo lang akong hiyain* (It doesn't matter if you don't love me; just don't shame me) highlights the clash of cultures, and goes some way toward explaining Filipino resentment of Japanese behavior. The unarmed civilian population struck back as it was able. Eleven-year-old Jose Maria Lacambra saw a detail of Japanese soldiers in the streets of Manila, stripped naked and waiting in line to cleanse themselves in an *ersatz ofuro*. He and a friend ignited a firecracker, causing the naked soldiers to run for cover. While they were hiding, Lacambra deposited a dead "mangled toad" in their bath.[15]

The Bataan campaign lasted from late December 1941 until early April 1942, a grueling three and a half months of disease, suffering and bloodshed during which, to some extent, Filipinos and Americans alike defined their attitudes toward the Japanese enemy. As the battle on the peninsula raged, the Japanese showered the Allied lines with leaflets, one of which read:

> Dear Filipino soldiers! There are still one way left for you. That is to give up all your weapons at once and surrender to the Japanese force before it is too late, then we shall fully protect you. We repeat for the last! Surrender at once and build your new Philippines for and by Filipinos.

Others contained "restaurant menus, lascivious pictures, fictitious letters from happy Filipinos who had escaped, and tickets to be given to the Japanese, showing they had authorized surrender." After three months of bitter combat, the appeals became more desperate, inviting Filipinos to kill their American allies and cooperate.[16]

Such possibilities existed mainly in the Japanese imagination. During the chaotic retreat south on the day before the final surrender, a Filipino driving an old, charcoal-burning truck stopped to offer an exhausted American private named Eagle a lift. As the truck proceeded south, the Filipino occupants surrendered their seats. Eagle remembered: "I chocked [sic] up when the Filipinos got off and started walking so that more Americans could come aboard. They left us with a friendly smile and a hand salute, and a "Give 'em hell, Joe!"[17]

Bataan means the place of Bata, the place of children, or little men, named for the original Negritos who occupied the land, and some of its meaning comes home to me as I walk north from Limay. Early in the morning, wanting to cover some ground before the blazing sun extracts its measure of liquid, outside a little barrio near obelisk #31 I find myself suddenly in the midst of a half dozen well-scrubbed urchins on their way to school. They are fascinated by the sudden appearance of a bearded foreigner, their chatter friendly and incessant. One little boy, no more than seven, points to himself and says Pinoy *then, pointing to me, exclaims,* American! *He stays walking with me, holding onto my knapsack for ten meters beyond the turn for school. When his classmates call him he is torn between walking further with his discovery and turning back. He lets go reluctantly, pauses at the top of the lane to school, smiles, waves and screams,* Bye, Joe!

The Fil-American army, some 75,000 men, 12,000 of whom were American, fought and suffered together, and attitudes against the common enemy were forged in the hard crucible of combat. Such solidarity is still reflected in the image on the obelisks that mark every kilometer of the Death March route from Mariveles to San Fernando. Each of the 111 obelisks shows a silhouette of an American soldier bending down to help a Filipino compatriot.

Misunderstanding sometimes led to death, as it did at Hospital # 2, near the tip of the peninsula. The morning after the surrender, the victorious Japanese ordered all Filipino doctors, dentists and some Filipino soldiers to depart Bataan. For reasons that remain somewhat unclear, a rumor spread among the more than 5,000 Filipino sick and wounded that the Japanese were allowing all Filipinos to return to their homes. Against the entreaties of a few American doctors, thousands of patients suffering from dysentery, malaria and wounds struggled north, mingling with the prisoners captured the day before. Weak and dying, they stumbled along, and some were bayoneted by Japanese guards or simply expired in pitiful heaps on the side of the road.[18]

Those Filipinos who survived the march and a month in Camp O'Donnell were finally released. Each was given a paper on which a pledge of allegiance to Japan and the East Asia Co-Prosperity Sphere was printed. The text extolled the benevolence of the Japanese Emperor and his imperial forces. Those inclined toward dark humor amended the lines to read, "*Watakushi domowa, nakayuko na, binayuneta pa!* (Already stooping on bended knees, still bayoneted mercilessly!)[19]

* * * * *

A lovely little antiquarian publication called *Bataan, Land of Valor, People of Peace* contains a story about "Usury and Slavery." In it, a good Christian named Pablo, observing the tension between rich and poor, creditor and debtor, powerful and weak, decides to "restore to their proper owners all ill-gotten goods which he had." Shamed or inspired by Pablo's good heart and generosity, many follow his example and "restore money taken through usury" or free their slaves "without any compulsion." The story ends with moral symmetry, with everyone "just to his neighbor, paying what should be paid and sometimes more than what was just. Hence, conflicts were avoided and there was peace."[20]

The story speaks to the mythic virtues of the Filipino, duly inspired by a Christian priest, and is quite consistent with the manner in which many Americans described the inhabitants of Bataan. Often the feeling was mutual. After the Japanese conquered Manila, General Homma ordered a victory parade, with a local band playing music. The population greeted the tunes with minimal enthusiasm until the band struck up "Stars and Stripes Forever." Homma, unaware of the song's meaning, smiled as the onlookers applauded.[21] Many American survivor narratives describe the Filipino civilian population as a sympathetic backdrop to the suffering of the American soldiers as they ascended their Calvary.

Such sympathy did inform Filipino American relations. Ed Thomas, responsible for paying the Filipino workers employed at his base, was surprised to learn that the hourly workers paid him *coomshaw* or commission, of 10 percent. Unwilling to accept money that other "bosses" of these men had taken, Thomas called the men together and told them that the payment would no longer be necessary. His translator told him, "The men say you are very good to them. They like you. We work very hard for you. We do something for you." The reward for Thomas' generosity was a box of Alhambra cigars every payday. As a further expression of gratitude, Thomas was invited to a *barrio* celebration, where he was royally feted and fed.[22]

The Tagalog word suggesting the need to "just go along with it" is *pakikisama,* and the phrase *bahala na* "leave it to God, come what may" both denote a kind of deference, even passivity as a defining cultural trait. Yet passivity did not denote emotional disconnection from others' suffering—it was shameful to be *walang-habang,* someone "without pity."[23] These terms shed considerable light on the first category of description American survivors applied to the Filipino civilian population—that of passive, sympathetic onlooker. William Dyess described the Filipino civilians who watched the agonies of the captured in tones that are reflected in almost all of the subsequent narratives. Dozens of survivors' stories contain warm descriptions of Filipino onlookers, some of whose number shared the agony of the Death March with a relative—some 60,000 Filipino fellow prisoners walked the route as well.

Typical descriptions suggest a surfeit of pity, if not of agency. Some onlookers ascribed a religious tone to the miserable procession before them:

> As devout Spanish Catholics intimately familiar with Passion plays and the pilgrimage traditions of the *Penitentes*, many of the Filipinos saw in the death march the quality of a tragic passage reminiscent of Christ's progress to Calvary through the Stations of the Cross. In doorways and half shuttered windows, women could be seen openly weeping. Peasants lined the sides of the roads ... offering bottles of water or cool moist rags. Little boys would toss dried mango or sugarcane candy at the staggering prisoners. A woman might emerge from the thickets with her arms full of ripe papayas or a whole cooked chicken.

As Dick Bilyeu came through the small barrios, he took heart when he saw "tears streaming down their faces. This display of affection was overwhelming." Lester Tenney also remembered sympathetic onlookers "with tears in their eyes" and Manny Lawton recalled that "sad-faced Filipino civilians watched from their front yards. Each blow received by a prisoner brought a look of pain to the onlookers' eyes."[24]

On this stretch I am thinking of the Filipino practice of senakulo, *the reenactments of Christ's crucifixion, sometimes complete with real nails. Near noon, just past obelisk #14, on a flat stretch near Cabcaben, sweating profusely, I stop for more water and some bread at Willy's roadside stand. While standing at the makeshift counter, drinking his orange juice, I chat with him while his six kids shyly peek around the corner of the room where a broken refrigerator has given up our two drinks. Willy's English is good; he apologizes for the warm drink, takes thirty pesos from me, and asks where I am going. Between swallows I tell him I am walking the route of the Death March. He says nothing for a moment and disappears, then comes around the counter and takes both of my hands in his and says, "We thought everyone forgot." He tells me that* Araw ng Kagitingan *(Bataan Day) now passes without notice. Improbably, the swing era song* In the Mood *is playing on their radio as I walk away. Such a nice moment.*

* * * * *

Another category of description shows some Filipinos offering succor to the weary American columns, risking their safety in the process—generosity rewarded at the edge of a *samurai* sword or bayonet. In the small park that marks the starting point of the Death March, a metal plaque printed in Tagalog and English describes the relationship between Filipino civilians and the captured soldiers with elegant brevity:

> Already suffering from battle fatigue, the Filipino and American troops were strained to utter exhaustion by this long march on foot. Many were ill, most were feverish, but none might rest, for the enemy was brutal with those who lagged behind. Thousands fell along the way. Townspeople on the roadside risked their lives by slipping food and drink to the Death Marchers as they stumbled by.

As William Dyess passed through the town of Lubao, he remembered, "from the upper windows of a large house a shower of food fell among us. It was followed quickly by other gifts, tossed surreptitiously by sympathetic Filipinos who stood on the sidewalks. There were bits of bread, rice cookies, lumps of sugar and pieces of chocolate. There were cigarettes." By the time the long columns of prisoners reached San Fernando, Filipinos showed more open support, and gave the "V" for victory sign.[25]

On the walk from Capas to Camp O'Donnell, one American remembered young Filipino girls throwing kisses, though the Japanese kicked over the buckets of water that they left for the long columns. One veteran stated, "As they straggled onwards in the unrelenting heat, they passed through small Filipino villages. The compassionate Filipinos tried to throw them bits of chicken, rice cakes and sugarcane. This enraged the Japanese soldiers, and they took particular delight in punishing those who would dare to aid the prisoners."[26]

Americans on the Death March might have understood such help in light of the contributions the U.S. army had made to the islands since its posting there after the Spanish-American War. Historian Brian M. Linn summarized the army's ameliorative effects:

> The army built roads, dams, well, schools, and marketplaces. In dozens of very practical ways, the army improved the lives of Filipinos ... it established health clinics and trade fairs, treated the sick, taught children and adults to read and write, improved agricultural production through planting new crops, quarantines and crop dusting ... and stamped out brigandage and sect violence ... the army was a proud symbol of their connection to the United States.

In this context, Filipinos responded to American travail with *pakikipagkapwa-tao*, what the sociologist Antonio Isidro called the "spirit of neighborliness ... ever present in the Filipino family whether in sickness or happiness, in adversity or prosperity." A death in the neighborhood was an occasion for "all [to] pitch in, helping with small tasks, including financial aid."[27] A monument in Hermosa dedicated to the defenders of Bataan and Corregidor corroborates this comfortable image of generosity:

> The braves of the land who walked the death march from BATAAN to CAMP O'DONNELL-CAPAS, in April 1942 and grateful to the good citizens of HERMOSA, BATAAN who offered food shelter and assistance to the sick, wounded and dying. The FREE WORLD will little note what the unknown-anonymous townfolks did to inspire the defenders but it could never forget what the Death March stood for.

Such generosity was rooted in more elastic notions of private property than those of Americans: "When a Pinoy [Filipino] borrows ... he always thinks the thing he borrows will be lent to him ... Pinoys are open-handed. They lend their happiness and life."

This form of exchange defined activities outside one's own group, and it "compels the recipient to show his gratitude properly by returning the favor *with interest* to be sure that he does not remain in the other's debt.... The type of debt created in the recipient is called *utang no loob* (literally, a debt inside oneself) or sense of gratitude" (italics in original). One scholar has called this "an ancient Filipino operating principle." Failure to repay a kindness freely given produces *hiya*, or shame, and "every service received, solicited or not, demands a return—the nature and proportion of the return determined by the relative statuses of the parties involved, and the kind of exchange at issue."[28]

> In times of crisis or difficulties, expect the Pinoy to help, simply because the person in trouble has lent him an umbrella one drizzling afternoon or a pair of rubber shoes in a basketball game. With his guts and debt of gratitude as weapons, the Pinoy helps put up bail for a friend, saves his friend's kid sister from a speeding truck, and offers his humble hut to a farmer's

family.... For him, trust and harmony come out alive in a relationship where he can borrow and lend.

Filipinos actively expressed these attitudes at sometimes considerable risk. Often guards became enraged at Filipino gifts of food, and they "struck out left and right against the Good Samaritans, slugging, beating and jabbing bayonets indiscriminately. Japs tried to stamp on all the food that hadn't been picked up."[29]

Between obelisks #3 and #4 outside Mariveles the road rises precipitously, zig-zagging to ascend 500 feet every two tenths of a mile. I am well rested after a night in my air-conditioned hotel on Corregidor, but start huffing and puffing as the incline takes its toll. Up ahead I see an improbable crowd gathered at the side of the road—a flatbed Isuzu truck laden with bags of pig feed has run off the road and lies on its side in a ditch. A rescue vehicle is positioned to tow it out, but everything comes to standstill as I pass, rescued and rescuers alike gaping at this be-knapsacked foreigner laboring along. I look up and two nice guys in a small truck offer me a ride. I say no. Smiling and bemused, they drive on, and images of Filipinos offering help to Americans on The Hike come vividly to mind. The road finally flattens, the sun comes out as I reach the site of Hospital #1, a place where so many Filipinos and their allies suffered.

Whatever the motivation, food and sustenance kept coming. One soldier remembered, "The barrio people gave unstintingly from their poverty." In the town of Lubao, natives threw food wrapped in banana leaves, though the Japanese tried to stop them, and again in defiance of the guards they threw food to the starving prisoners in the town of Gaugua. In Balanga, Lester Tenney saw Filipinos standing on the sides of the road throwing rice cakes, pieces of fried chicken and pieces of sugar cane, "gestures [that] lifted our sunken spirits to a new high" as the men shared the food. Richard Gordon remembered that Filipinos "constantly tried to feed us all along the way, often risking their lives." Bernard Fitzpatrick recalled a young Filipino boy darting into his column with a watermelon.[30]

Watching the procession before them, some Pinoys recalled Jesus asking for water on the cross, and their kindness extended through the end of the march. Some sympathetic Filipinos gave a private named Miller and part of his column as much water as they could drink during an unsupervised period on the march. Many of the trains to Capas from San Fernando were driven by Filipino engineers, "and they slowed their engines as they passed through the stations so the locals could toss their gifts into the open doors or run alongside the platform holding up cans of water."[31] Another soldier remembered that on the journey from San Fernando to Capas, Filipinos threw food onto the train, and on the eleven kilometer walk from Capas to Camp O'Donnell, they left five gallon containers of water along pathway, some of which the Japanese kicked over.[32]

Sometimes the help given was poignant indeed. Murray Sneddon recalled feeling fear as he marched past Filipino civilians. "Among the people," he recalled,

> stood a young woman with her shy son who was partly hiding behind her, clinging to her skirt. She leaned over occasionally to confer with the youngster. Then he looked up at her questioningly, she nodded yes, and handed him something she had in the pocket of her skirt. At that moment he left his mother and ran to me. I was terrified! If any guard saw him helping me he would beat him for sure.... Fortunately the guards did not see him as he slipped a sugar cake into my hand. When he returned to his mother I waited a moment, the when all seemed safe I

mouthed the words: *Salamat ... maraming salamat* (thank you very much). Both he and his mother understood and they smiled radiantly and nodded their heads.

An anonymous Filipino kept a diary as he watched the tattered, defeated army pass his home in San Fernando: "To others who have not seen what I saw, I congratulate them because they have been spared of the agony and sleepless nights. To me, my wife and children, we who seen the faces and the way, the way they asked, are something that we could not forget."[33]

* * * * *

The third category of descriptions is that of Filipinos actively suffering at the hands of the Japanese. Some accounts deal with unfortunate Filipino soldiers captured and tortured; one American recalled encountering two terrified Filipinos, whose companion had been captured by a Japanese patrol. The sounds of torture filled the air, "like some animal noise that started low in the throat and rose to a pitch that would bust eardrums. I'd never imagined anything could be so terrible." The sound went on for hours, though those listening never knew what horrors were being inflicted.[34] In February, Philippine Scouts discovered the body of Private Hilario Bernades hanging from a tree; the Japanese used him as a bayonet dummy. During a particularly brutal action, one Filipino prisoner, bleeding from nine bayonet wounds, escaped and reported that his captors had bayoneted and tortured others in his unit.[35]

A much greater number of accounts deal with depredations inflicted on civilians throughout the march. Near Abucay, a nine-year-old boy named Armando Pabustan waited with his mother in the pre-dawn hours for his father, a captured soldier, to pass by. Finally he saw his father and ran and clung to him. As his father told him of thirst and starvation, a Japanese guard kicked the boy in the back and another roughly tossed him to the road.[36]

All along the route, passersby in cars or on motorbikes routinely feel the need to scream something to get my attention, unilateral communication and the Doppler effect. Obelisks #51 and 52 pass in a sweaty blur, and somewhere thereabouts two kids fall in alongside me, selling corn on a stick for five pesos. They giggle and caper, chattering away in Tagalog, and I realize, in the company of the wrong guard, they might have been in some danger in 1942. The pair walk along after I say no many times, their smiles with me for about a kilometer. They ask over and over, "What's your name?" but call me Joe anyway.

One survivor wrote that "if you tried to get food which was thrown by the civilians ... that not only endangered you, but the one who was giving the food or throwing the food to you ... well, those that they could catch, they'd just shoot them there." At Lubao, sympathetic Filipinos showered the prisoners from two-story windows and rooftops, small children darted into the sweating column and gave handfuls of food. When they could, Japanese guards beat back the interlopers with their weapons. William Dyess related how Filipinos threw food over the heads of Japanese guards, only to be chastised and beaten for their efforts. One Filipino merchant wanted to open his store to the prisoners, but was forbidden, others left buckets of water that were kicked over by Japanese guards; Filipino "cries of compassion" greeted this show of Japanese cruelty.[37]

Alf Larson remembered that when Filipinos tried to give him food, the Japanese shot some of them, and he also saw a "Filipino man had been beheaded. His body lay on the ground with blood everywhere. His head was a short distance away. Near Balanga, Alvin Poweleit noticed three Filipinos giving prisoners rice wrapped in banana leaves. Guards apprehended the three and took them behind a grass shack. Poweleit watched in horror as the swords flashed downwards: "The bodies jumped around like chickens with the heads cut off. Blood squirted from the necks all over me and the guards. The hands, arms, legs twitched, contracted, until finally only a feeble jerk remained."[38]

The opening scenes of the wartime film *Bataan* show an American soldier carrying a Filipina child, wearing the cap he gave her. After Japanese bombs fall, the camera cuts briefly to a shot of the child's hand protruding from dirt. Other descriptions corroborate such cinematic license. Ralph Hibbs described a Filipino man and wife tied together to a stake, soaked in gasoline, and burned to death for giving food to passing GIs. Another recalled additional horror as he marched past a farm:

> There is nothing like the screams of a human being tortured, and it's something I'll never forget. I can still hear the cries of a group of about five or six Filipinos, who had been tied to a haystack.... I don't know what they did but the Japanese had tied them to the stack and then set it on fire.[39]

Brutality was not limited to men, and reports of Japanese atrocities exceeded other boundaries as well. The Filipino aphorism "When a corpse is stiff, another family member will soon follow" seemed horrifyingly true.

Many survivors' accounts highlight Japanese treatment of helpless Filipino women, and this emphasis throws their captors' barbarity into sharpest relief. John Bumgarner, a physician at Bataan's General Hospital #2, remembered that a Filipina, pregnant and near term, came in just before the surrender. She gave birth after April 9, and though Bumgarner and his staff tried to conceal her from the Japanese who wandered freely through the hospital (some with cameras), they discovered her and raped her "repeatedly at gunpoint." Dick Bilyeu remembered a Japanese column purposely marching over a pregnant Filipina, the fetus trampled out of her by their marching feet, and Cletis Overton saw a Japanese soldier knock a Filipina down and summarily bayonet her. Alf Larson's memory continued to haunt him after the war:

> I remember seeing the bodies of decomposing American soldiers and Filipino women who had been mutilated and obviously raped. I'm sure the dogs in the area got fat! Also, there was a dead Filipino woman with her legs spread apart and her dress pulled up over her. She obviously had been raped and there was a bamboo stake in her private area. These are instances I would like to forget.[40]

Russell Grokett added that "young girls were pulled out of ranks and raped repeatedly. Anyone who resisted was shot. Frightened mothers would rub human dung on their daughters' faces to make them unattractive to the guards."[41]

Clarence Bramley remembered hundreds of Filipino civilians watching as the Japanese sorted Americans from Filipinos: "While the prisoners stood in line with Japanese rifles trained on them, a group of the guards seized some of the nearby Filipino women and dragged them into the brush ... [he] heard the women scream and cry and he knew they were being raped and beaten. Such depredations quickly found their way into island lore. Corban Alabado described a "morale-boosting story" that was commonly known as "Remember Erlinda." This woman was a village maiden of a remote barrio of Bataan, aged eighteen, a beautiful virgin. She was gang-raped by seven Japanese soldiers in a most bestial manner as she was washing clothes by the river. She was buried alive, naked, her head above the ground. It achieved the desired effect, as we began to say, she could be our mother, our wife, sister, girlfriend. She was violated by our enemies, committing a crime not only against Erlinda, but also against the entire Filipino nation. "Erlinda must be avenged!" became our battlecry.[42]

One soldier remembered Japanese guards taking a young pregnant woman who was giving the Americans cassava cakes behind a tree, where her live fetus was gouged out by a bayonet. Refugee Rosalina Almario Cruz, six months pregnant, took the risk anyway. She was walking north alongside line of prisoners, pitying their suffering, and she offered water to the thirsty horde, even as she saw men who fell out stabbed. Though she "knew they might stab her too," she continued to pass water anyway to the suffering horde.

Fidel Ongpauco's account suggests a sense of dazed helplessness as he watched his countrymen's anguish. Near Lamao, he remembered seeing "a woman dragging herself with her hands. Her legs were broken, her hair was disheveled, and her dress was torn. We just looked at her as we shuffled on in silence. We came across two parents weeping over a young daughter who had blood on her dress. We looked and went on our way." Though they were pleading "*Mga kasama! Huag ninyo kaming iwan!* (Comrades! Please don't leave us!) we could not possibly help them. We even doubted if we could help ourselves."[43]

J.D. Merritt described horror at Balanga behind a rice warehouse, where a Filipina, holding an infant, was caught tossing food over the enclosure to prisoners. One of the guards ripped the child from her arms and tossed it in the air, trying to catch it on his bayonet. As the mother stared in horror, he threw the child up again and missed. On the third try, he succeeded. Abel Ortega described a similar scene: "The Japanese would even kill [Filipinas'] babies with their bayonets and hold them up in the air to prove something."[44]

More horror appeared in the most gruesome description of Japanese barbarity—the tale of the massacre on Bataan's Pantingan River. By April 14, five days after the surrender, the Filipino Ninety-first Division made its way along an east-west trail south of the Pilar-Bagac Road. There it was halted, its officers separated from enlisted men. The privates were sent on their way, but between 350 and 400 officers and non-coms found their wrists securely bound, each man tied to the one behind him. Lined up along the length of a ravine, a Japanese civilian interpreter addressed them in Tagalog: "My friends, don't take it so hard. You must be patient. Had you surrendered earlier, you would not have met this tragedy. We are doing this because many of our soldiers died fighting against you. If you have any request before we kill you, ask now."

The following two hours were filled with the screams of the victims, officers using their swords for the butchery, enlisted men their bayonets. Major Pedro Felix lay hidden under a pile of corpses and bleeding from four bayonet wounds and while he waited for the Japanese executioners to leave, he heard one of his comrades, writhing in agony, scream, "*P—ninyong mga Hapon! Magbalik kayo ditto! Patayin ninyo kami ng husto!*" (You S—Japanese! Come back here and kill us thoroughly!) A guard returned and obliged by dispatching him with three shots. Felix then painfully gnawed through his bonds, and found succor with farmers who hid and nursed him.[45]

This was the ultimate expression of Japanese cruelty. Felix's story is truly extraordinary, enough so to question its veracity. Here is the problem of sources and their relationship to truth—the issue is whether or not this massacre took place. The sources are two Filipinos who testified against Homma, with obvious unfriendly intent, and Fidel Ongpauco's *They Refused to Die: True Stories About World War II Heroes in the Philippines, 1941–1945*, whose title hardly suggests objectivity.

Against this there is defense counsel John Skeen's closing arguments at Homma's trial, who called Felix's testimony into question, citing "obvious antagonism against the accused." He stated,

> The story itself is beyond the comprehension of an average person. When it is recalled that it was told by two witnesses who had fought against the troops of the Accused and were without question prejudiced it becomes less credible, particularly when it is noted that there was absolutely no scrap of evidence as to the existence of 400 bodies when both the witnesses testified as to the exact location of the alleged massacre. The Prosecution must have investigated. If they had found any trace of the bodies they would have brought in evidence showing what they found. We must assume they found nothing. The story then becomes impossible to believe. Can we believe that 400 bodies, more than two companies of infantry, have disappeared without a trace?[46]

Skeen's observations, the fact that the event was barely mentioned in the Tokyo War Crimes trials, and the absence of corroborating evidence such as is available for the massacre of Chinese in Singapore during the Malay campaign, all suggest a dubious connection to reality.[47]

As with survivors' other descriptions of Japanese cruelty, the line between fact and fiction becomes blurred by time, the condition of fatigue, the vagaries and imprecision of memory, and the need to assign clear roles in the drama. Stories of rape and the lurid tales of the butchery of women and children strain credulity, sometimes to the breaking point. In the process, however, the central goal of emphasizing Japanese cruelty and Filipinos as companions in suffering is well served.

* * * * *

The many accounts that portray Filipinos as allies—either passive, active or themselves suffering—are balanced by a smaller but substantial number of references in the narratives that undercut the stereotype of the sympathetic Filipino. They hint at tensions that shared Fil-American suffering cannot completely disguise.

Crude propaganda leaflets reminding them of atrocities in 1898 and of discrimination against Filipinos in Manila social clubs were not entirely without a basis in fact. Some surely remembered the sordid behavior of American soldiers while putting down the insurrection after the Spanish-American War, well within the memory of older Filipinos. The war Americans had fought against the Filipinos contained elements of terror and torture, and "the paradox was all the greater since we had gone to war with Spain to put an end to such abominations." The U.S. dispatched some 70,000 soldiers to pacify the Philippines, to wage "one of the bloodiest wars of colonization in history" during which Douglas MacArthur's father Arthur directed a campaign that "sought to wipe out guerrilla resistance by annihilating the peasantry which sustained it. Over a quarter of a million Filipinos died."[48] Even thirty years on, Americans on Bataan sometimes faced Ganaps, or Sakdalistas, Filipino sympathizers with the Japanese, those that one observer called "a malignant, anti–American force, a keen-edged, utterly willing tool with the most perfect camouflage in the world. They were everywhere ... of their presence we were to be assured in sinister ways."[49]

Abel Ortega, a Mexican-American who looked Filipino, experienced some of this tension directly. As he stopped just outside Mariveles, he

> noticed that some of the prisoners were looking at me and yelling and cursing obscenities for no reason at all. They were blaming me for their agony and the predicament that they were in. They had thought that I was a Filipino and they were really getting hostile towards me. I felt really sad and deeply hurt that my fellow soldiers were treating me this way.... Not only did I have to deal with hostile Japanese guards but I was also faced with having to deal with hostile American prisoners taking this situation out on me.

Ortega tried to tell them he was Mexican, but their shouting drowned out his words of explanation. Racism was never far from the surface. Twelve years before the Death March, in Watsonville, California, an anti–Filipino riot occurred. In January 1930, a mob of some five hundred white men and boys, angry over the presence of two white girls in a nearby dance hall, attacked the immigrant neighborhood, firing pistols and clubbing residents, driving out nearly fifty "terror-stricken" Filipinos, "beaten, bruised and cowed." One victim of the violence did not survive.[50] Such prejudices made their way across the Pacific.

Other incidents hint at the tension. Once during the Death March, at Balanga, an American soldier took his ease against a wall in an enclosure he shared with hundreds of other prisoners. Suddenly, through a hole in the wall, a Filipino officer began to urinate, splashing the American. Infuriated, the U.S. officer berated his erstwhile ally: "You dumb idiot! Aren't things bad enough without you making them worse? I'd rather be killed by Japs than be urinated on by a stupid Filipino officer. With officers like you, it's no wonder we lost Bataan." The American's logic was wanting, as was perhaps that of another American, who contemplated escape with a fellow prisoner, but hesitated because he was not sure "whether any Filipino we might meet could be trusted."[51]

Privately, Americans disdained Filipino willingness to fight. Some took to calling the Philippine army "the P.A." (paper army). General Wainwright's aide-de-camp, with requisite condescension, noted in his diary, "It is generally accepted that all P.A. units will not fight, but flee to the hills and change to civilian clothes when a fight begins." To some degree, the tension was exacerbated by the enormous cultural distance between some Americans, especially officers, and the Filipino rank and file. Richard Mallonee recalled the frustration of trying to exercise authority over a command comprising Pangasanans, Illocanos, Pampangans, and Bontocs, when English "had to be translated two or three times before it reached the men." He remembered one incident when a Filipino house cook had been charged with having a meal ready by a certain time. When the designated hour came and went, he told Mallonnee he had been unable to work because he had been locked in combat with an evil spirit that "wanted his soul."[52]

At Orani, the road turns inward, away from the bay, and the obelisks blur. It's near 4:00 and I wander into the sizable town of Hermosa and park in the courtyard of the church of Saint Peter of Verona. There an older Filipino named Pepé, with a bright smile and a very large paunch, asks me if I am looking for accommodations for the night and invites me to stay in the extra room in his sprawling place a ten-minute walk away. I am happy to comply, and during a stringy chicken dinner we eat with our hands, he asks me if I've had balut *yet, an egg in which a chicken embryo is just beginning to develop, boiled and eaten in the shell. I have avoided this since arrival but now, rather than violate Pepé's hospitality, I accept. I find it repulsive but choke down part of it while my host lights up a Marlboro cigarette and tells me of Filipino evil spirits.*

The patianic, *he says, is a nasty one that lives in the forests, makes animal sounds, and sometimes invades homes to kill babies and sometimes even eats them. In his own family lore, his grandfather supposedly attended his father's birth by beating the air outside the house with sticks to ward off the evil incursion. Another Marlboro yields his description of the* mangkukulam, *a malevolent spirit that can, he says, "take its body apart" and appear in pieces. People possessed by this spirit lose control of themselves, and can only be cured by exorcism. Between the* balut *and the spirits I do not sleep well, and dream fitfully of a verse I learned in Japan:*

> Nenneko, nennko, nenneko ya!
> Netara o-kaka e tsurete ina!
> Okitara gagama ga totte kama!

Sleep, child! If you sleep I'll fetch your mother! If you stay awake the goblin will catch you!

A central reality was the distinct color line between allies. Virtually all aspects of military and social life were strictly segregated, including separate facilities for white officers. Some attributed the gulf between races to the influence of officers' wives, but proposals such as the one forbidding soldiers from manual labor because it "lowered the status of all whites" clearly indicated more general racist attitudes. One 1924 report suggested that Filipino elites

A wounded Filipino being helped to the rear. This photograph gives some idea of the heavy jungle in which much of the campaign was fought (Library of Congress).

might rebel against American rule in spite of its economic advantages, and five years later a Filipino officer stated that he and some of his fellows had considered resigning due to ill-treatment.[53]

In the late 1930s, tension was in part a function of the disparity in pay—seven dollars a month compared to thirty for U.S. soldiers. Between 1936 and 1940, Filipino draft registrations decreased by nearly half. Although poorly paid by American continental standards, army pay gave U.S. privates a distinct advantage over local Filipino men in the competition for local women. Some were able to secure "shack up" arrangements, and other long-term soldiers married Filipinas. Others frequented the numerous houses of prostitution, and even "hardened regulars" visiting the islands found its depravity shocking—"there seemed to be no limits, no dampers, no matter what the excess." Such behavior inevitably involved fighting, drunkenness and generally rowdy behavior, leading some Filipinos to judge the American presence as "intrusive and perhaps dangerous."[54]

Filipino soldiers were not, however, without utility. One night, Suzuki Murio, a frontline soldier in the Fourteenth Army, remembered being so tired he tried to sleep standing up. When he leaned to his front, he found that it "smelled terrible and was soft, but [he] couldn't see it in the dark. [He] found out it was a breastwork made of corpses. The Americans had piled up native bodies like sandbags. The heads were facing toward us. On the other side there was a firing step.... Our enemy was an allied army of Americans and Filipinos, but the corpses in the wall were all Filipino."[55]

* * * * *

Yet another description appears only piecemeal in the soldiers' narratives, but taken *in toto*, nevertheless forms a distinct category. Here we see Filipinos not as clichéd observers of the Stations of the Cross, but as opportunists whose chief concern was less with American suffering than with the economic opportunity the Death March presented. Though doubtless some evinced the sympathy suggested in so many accounts, it is clear that, to others, the thousands of soldiers passing by looked more like customers than victims.

Perhaps tensions between American and Filipino, either long-standing or a product of the immediate circumstances of April 1942, formed the context for a substantial number of Filipino civilians whose behavior was considerably less than sympathetic. A corporal named Read stated one harsh reality of the Death March baldly: "There were civilians along the way looking at us ... but they pretty much stayed out of sight because I think they were afraid of what might happen to them at that point." Then he stated another. "Beyond Balanga," he wrote,

> there were a lot of civilians along the way, but I found none of them to be helpful. They were trying to sell stuff to the prisoners, but unfortunately most of us had had our money taken away. I never had any Filipino offer me food or anything along the march; they were trying to sell it. Now, later on there were occasions when the Filipinos gave us food, but that was after the march was over, when the cattle-car part of the thing to O'Donnell had started.[56]

Stanley Falk states that "the less altruistic citizens had a lucrative business selling food to those captives who still had any money left ... a few of the Japanese guards allowed the civilians to give or sell to the marchers. Most forbade it." As the men began passing through more populated areas near San Fernando, "Filipinos appeared along the road selling food to men in the column."⁵⁷ During the battle, Filipino soldiers on the front lines had been slipping into nearby barrios, where they paid "exorbitant prices" for food from their countrymen.⁵⁸ The peasants in the barrios saw no reason to spare Americans the same treatment.

As the long columns approached the larger city of San Fernando, John Hubbard noted that "Filipino women lined the road, attempting to provide food and water to POWs, American as well as Filipino. Other groups of Filipinos were "accepting money for their gifts of food and water, and still others were selling goods outright." Richard Gordon noted during one of the shakedowns that a soldier had various types of food and powdered milk, which he may have obtained from "the many civilian Filipinos running alongside us offering such wares for cash."⁵⁹

In San Fernando, while waiting for the train that took them to Capas, many POWs were held in a large warehouse Filipinos used for Sa Bong *(cock fighting), so I ask a man at the central market where I might find one. He jots down a location for me, and that night I grab a tricycle and head out. I arrive, walk to the entrance, offer my 200 pesos and, after the burly Filipino at the door consults with another, am firmly refused entry. I retreat to the parking lot, where a young Filipino introduces himself and offers to take me in. With Benny as my escort, I am allowed in without incident. A man whose cock will fight first is his friend, and as they talk, he holds his bird gently in the crook of his left arm, stroking it from head to tail with his right. An old man shuffles about holding a faded blue wooden case, and I wander over to see that he is renting out razor-sharp* tares *(spurs) according to the heft of the bird in question. Benny enters the glass enclosure, he and his opponent thrust their birds at each other while the horde of bettors scream and gesticulate. Then they remove the green sheaths from their bird's* tares, *they fly at each other, and on the third clash Benny's bird is dead in a heap. He returns, sits next to me, laughs, and tells me that the old man is the only one sure to profit today: "One bird die, two birds die, he still take money." His bird, he tells me, will be dinner tonight.*

James Gautier remembered a Filipino standing on the road near San Fernando "with several canteens of water, trying to sell them to us." One parched prisoner simply grabbed a canteen and blended into the crowd, while the frustrated vendor screamed at him. Enterprising Filipinos even approached Americans on burial details at San Fernando, and often "men on these details returned with purchased food." On the way from San Fernando to Capas, prisoners got food from Filipinos along the track, "freely given or sold at extortionate prices, it did not matter—to a prisoner any price was a good price." Cletis Overton remembered buying a quart of water from a rare Japanese civilian for twenty pesos.⁶⁰

When some exhausted soldiers reached the approximate half-way point of Balanga, they smelled their captors cooking rice and sausage nearby. The meal was not for them, and they were driven "almost frantic," but the Japanese allowed some of the starving men to "buy rice from the Filipino civilians who had returned to Balanga." On the route from Lubao to San Fernando, Richard Mallonee was "able to buy from a roadside stand a couple of mangos and a half dozen duck eggs."⁶¹ Another paid three pesos for bits of rice and fruit. Grateful for the transaction, he said, "It was worth millions to me." Paying for sustenance did not occlude prisoners' flow of gratitude: Alexander Quintard "bought some dirty peanut brittle wrapped in newspaper from a Filipino" and later stated, "I really believe it saved our lives."⁶²

The sales went on after the prisoners arrived at Camp O'Donnell. Corporal Eugenio Lorenzo recalled, "The more fortunate prisoners who belonged to the grass and water details could augment the little food given them with food they secretly bought from vendors outside the camp.... Some Filipinos were unkind for they sold food like dried fish, *bucayo*, meat, etc. at very exorbitant prices to the prisoners." During the three-month siege, Americans had received less than one cigarette per day, and "heavy smokers suffered intensely. They gladly paid five dollars for a five cent pack of cigarettes, and thanked the seller for dealing with them."[63]

One American medical officer recalled that one Filipino prisoner had a pair of pliers for removal and later sale of gold teeth he removed from corpses, a profitable venture since so many of the dead had such dental work. This young entrepreneur expanded business, employing "a couple of his comrades pulling teeth, too." The same officer remarked bitterly on the black market prices prisoners had to pay—"Sardines sold for twenty pesos a can (about $10), dysentery pills ... sold for about sixty-five pesos per one hundred (about $33)" and prices continued to rise as time went on.[64]

How did the American prisoners pay for these goods? When the Americans surrendered

Filipino entrepreneurs often sold food and water to the long line of customers passing their barrios (courtesy Christopher Leet).

and gathered at Mariveles for their trek northward, the Japanese began shaking down the prisoners for personal effects, and a few recalled the executions of those who possessed anything with Japanese writing, items the guards assumed were taken from dead Japanese soldiers. Many who gathered at Mariveles described Japanese rifling through their personal effects and taking whatever of value they could find. Later, at Balanga, guards again relieved prisoners of valuables others might have missed at Mariveles. In between, prisoners were subjected to countless searches. One remembered he was searched five times between Mariveles and Balanga, another remembered twelve—others were searched every time the guards were changed, still others by random Japanese they encountered on the road.[65]

Like everything else after April 9, however, the pilferage of American soldiers' money and personal effects was neither organized nor complete. There were simply too many prisoners: "Despite the searches a number of Americans retained personal items and American and Filipino currency as well. Possession of the latter ... was to make a big difference in their life, or death, as prisoners of war." Russell Grokett managed to sew $1,600 into his jacket and kept it all the way through his stay in the prison camps, where it helped buy medicine and food for him and others.[66]

The Allied army on Bataan surrendered on April 9, but the fortress island of Corregidor held out for another agonizing month, finally succumbing on May 6. For those weeks, the island became a temporary refuge for Americans refusing to surrender, and they desperately sought the means to negotiate the expanse of water separating Bataan from the island. Their desperation was a function of the absence of an evacuation plan as the defense of Bataan collapsed. Although Wainwright, the commander of the garrison on Corregidor, believed that he had room for 12,000 of Bataan's defeated survivors, he authorized no organized transport because of the likelihood that "Corregidor would fall from starvation before the Japanese could capture it by force."[67]

The stranded soldiers of Bataan presented a poignant picture. Jim Collier, an officer on Corregidor, looked out on the sad spectacle and remembered hundreds of men trying desperately to get off of Bataan, and Lt. Commander Morrill, watching from a navy vessel on April 9, recalled, "The most unforgettable sight of all was the groups of men standing on the South Bataan shore in the early half light of the morning, beckoning and signaling with flashlights for help." Nevertheless, about 2,300 soldiers and sailors escaped from Bataan to Corregidor, "most by swimming or by raft, small boat, or bamboo pole."[68]

In some cases the small boats were not operated by Americans, and their failure to sponsor transport was a business opportunity for enterprising young Filipinos. One observer recalled that during the siege, "captains of grimy little boats" asked for fares in gold, half paid in advance, to bring in small amounts of supplies to the besieged and hungry defenders. J.D. Merritt recalled a group of Filipinos asking him for a 500 peso investment to buy black market canned food and cigarettes in Manila and risk running the Japanese blockade in a *banca* (outrigger boat). Paying for supplies on the peninsula made sense only to a point; after hope of rescue evaporated, some sought the means to escape, and they found willing vendors. Filipinos were already engaged in transport; at one coastal barrio near Orion, some civilians had set up a black market food operation, bringing in food from Manila across the bay by *banca*. Poor Filipinos also responded to the bounty of fifty *pesos* placed on Americans who had not surrendered and were suspected of guerrilla activity in the provinces. This, one officer remembered, "made the Filipinos undependable."[69]

On my last day on Corregidor, I mention my plan to walk the Death March route to a waiter named Constantino who, it turns out, lives across the bay in Mariveles. He offers numerous objections to my plan—too far, too dangerous, many "bad guys" with paltiks *(cheap handguns) along the way, the route out of Mariveles is too steeply uphill. But bemused and tolerant, he arranges a* banca *for the following morning that will take me over to Bataan. I have four San Miguel beers with dinner and smile, recalling that Jonathan "Skinny" Wainwright, who ultimately surrendered his army on Corregidor, was put out to pasture here in the Philippines because of a widely recognized drinking problem. Next morning I pay my 1200 pesos, and am on my way, across the same narrow strait Wainwright repeatedly traveled as he tried to sustain his men's morale on Bataan. The current is strong as our little boat makes its way through the floating garbage that defines this stretch of water that saw so much despair in 1942. We plow through ugly flotsam—floating bottles, paper and the foam of pollution. My boat is red with blue outriggers, my captain is stoic and sails today without his usual* nakikisama, *a shareworker who cannot afford his own boat. The water is brown and warm on my fingers. As we approach, the mountain behind Mariveles grows taller.*

Beginning on April 10, Fernando Viray, at fourteen the youngest member of the Fil-American army, used his *banca* to ferry escapees over to the opposite shore, where sympathetic townsfolk at a barrio in Hagonoy welcomed them with open arms, saying, "*Dio mo na dalhin sa amin ang mga kapatid na iyan. Kami ang mag-aalaga sa kanila*" (You give those brothers to us. We will take care of them). Each passenger in his *banca*, however, paid ninety *pesos* "for the death ride." Ricardo Jose also remembered that "*bankeros* in Bataan aided the defenders get away by taking them ... by sea (although some of them charged for it)."[70] Such transactions suggest less than the altruism and solidarity that many Americans recorded. If the common Filipino aphorism "Where there is hardship, there is happiness" denoted a stoic acceptance of poverty, it also suggests a period of entrepreneurial opportunity.

* * * * *

Some Filipinos offered an ominous illustration of tension—as the column of prisoners trudged past Limay, a man shouted, "*Iyan ang mabuti sa inyo! Mga talunan!*" (That's what you deserve! You vanquished soldiers!) While this was an extreme expression of enmity, it is clear that the image of the sympathetic Filipino is, to some degree, misleading. Filipinos took advantage of a captive clientele. Americans' tone of bitterness as they described such Filipino merchant activity is understandable, yet the context was real enough to some who were, quite literally, themselves in dire physical circumstances. As Sam Moody made his way into San Fernando, he recalled,

> I soon became aware that being American was no longer the magic word it had been several weeks before, when we were fighting to defend the Islands. The Filipinos were hurt and embarrassed by our surrender. They had put all their faith and hope in us. We had failed them in their greatest hour of need. As they saw their children murdered, their women raped and their men carted away, they could not understand the necessity for surrender. The Filipinos were a broken and bitter people.[71]

Unrest born of poverty and exploitation at the hands of landlords overlapped with resistance to the Japanese.

The Filipino response to the American occupation had always been ambivalent, though during the war the U.S. image of benevolent guardian was cultivated. In the 1945 film *Back to Bataan*, an American schoolmarm asks her class of Filipino students what the Spanish brought to the islands, and a young girl dutifully responds that they "brought us the holy faith, the blessed virgin and the saints." When asked the same question about the Americans, the students spring from their desks and answer, "Soda pop! Hot dogs! Radios! Movies! Baseball!" The schoolmarm then turns to her first student, who solemnly intones, "America taught us that men are free, or they are nothing." Wartime film scripts promoted such notions, but the reality was far more complex.

The schoolmarm in the film represented the *Thomasites*, so named for the ship *Thomas* on which they came, a large group of American teachers who came to the islands after the U.S. acquisition. Part of McKinley's program of "benevolent assimilation," by 1911, ten years after they arrived, these educators were holding forth in more than 4,000 schools, whose enrollment approached one million by 1920. Even so, the U.S. occupation did little to change the plight of the poor. In 1905, one observer stated that the land the poor Filipino occupied hardly sufficed for his needs. "From time immemorial, the small cultivators have been dependent on the large proprietors for advances of money, or food and seed."[72]

The problems of unequal land and wealth distribution went back to the Spanish colonial period, when the king gave huge land grants to nobles and Catholic friars, a system under which the landless peasants became sharecroppers, giving up half their crop for the privilege of staying on the land. Mark Twain, commenting on these practices, wrote that because of their experience with the friars, Filipinos did not mind "other diseases." Americans inherited the problems of widespread tenancy, and sought to correct it with a kind of Homestead Act, allowing individuals to buy and occupy tracts of cheap land. As with Native Americans thirty years earlier, the program failed, and *caciques* (wealthy landowners) bought most of the land, since impoverished *barangay* (village community) dwellers had neither means nor inclination to move away.

U.S. free trade policy opened new markets for Filipino products, and landowners insisted on growing cash crops to increase their profits, with peasants enjoying few benefits. Newly richer landlords moved away to Manila and hired managers to look after their holdings, men who on behalf of their employers pressed tenants for loan repayment and demanded more labor. Nearly completely under the thumb of the landlords on whom they depended, the poor "could not join organizations of their own choosing" and in any dispute was "defenseless against the landlord ... forced to buy all supplies from the estate stores, which charged exorbitant prices." The pressure on Bataan's poor grew as the province's population doubled, from 46,000 in 1903 to 93,000 in 1948.[73]

On Corregidor, the Filipino Pacific War Memorial is the most interesting, a large bronze statue of a guerrilla fighter, a ploughshare in his left hand, around whose base runs a long series of bas-reliefs—"FM to FM" (Ferdinand Magellan to Ferdinand Marcos), all showing heroic Filipino resistance to tyranny of one kind or another—the simplification of history that nevertheless smacks of truth. The catalog of resistance for Filipinos is long indeed: Chinese pirates in 1225, the Spanish in 1521, British in 1600, Spanish again, then Americans in 1898, Japanese 1942–45, the dictatorship of Marcos and the people's revolution of 1986. Marcos was never one to leave a superstition unexploited. In his 1964 official campaign bio, he claimed to have a talisman embedded in his back, one that allowed him to appear and disappear, as well as to bring the dead back to life. During the Bataan campaign, those who went on patrol with Marcos reportedly rubbed his back for protection. Apparently "several who did not participate in this ceremony did not return." Some Marcos faithful still await his resurrection, when a golden age for the islands will begin.[74]

Perhaps toward that age, two organizations arose in the early 1940s. The first was the *Pambansang Kaisaha ng Mga Magbubukid* (PKM), a socio-economic organization that sought to ameliorate the lot of the masses through socialistic principles. The other, the *Hukbong Bayan Laban sa Hapon* (Hukbalahap), was the military wing of the PKM. The roots of these organizations extended to pre-war times, when in Pampanga and surrounding areas the *Partido Socialista* sought to improve commoners' lives. Landowners in areas under the control of the PKM "were forced to give up proprietary rights to land, and the PKM distributed excess land to the unemployed and needy." The Japanese occupation stimulated membership in the PKM.[75]

A Japanese propaganda film claimed that, in defeat, Filipinos experienced a sense of "emptiness ... after having their delusion shattered and confusion after losing their faith." Perhaps, but the salient fact is that rural communities on the Bataan peninsula along the path of the death march were deeply in debt, with primitive methods of farming and poorly constructed homes. As Luis Taruc, a leader of the Socialist Party in the 1930s, later wrote, "The problems were ages old. The people were land hungry.... The few were fabulously rich; the many were incredibly poor."[76]

Their inhabitants could not look to the national government for support, and families struggled to make ends meet from season to season. Contemporary descriptions bear out the truth of rural conditions. The combat on the peninsula between tens of thousands of Allied and Japanese soldiers left the landscaped denuded and barren. James Bollich remembered that he, along with many others, never contemplated escape on the Death March because if they left, they "would eventually starve to death because there was nothing left to eat on the entire Bataan Peninsula. It looked like a moonscape." Red Allen remembered a "foraging trip to an abandoned barrio" that yielded nothing more than bed sheets. He also recalled finding shelter in an "abandoned hut, one probably used by a whole family, but just right for two GIs trying to get in out of the rain."[77]

Even early in the campaign, American officers in observation posts found whole areas "eerie and depopulated. Filipino civilians had fled their huts and farms, leaving the countryside empty." One officer remembered, "we passed a number of miserable *nipa* houses ... but we found only one living soul, an old man who gave us some fruit." As early as February, more than 25,000 civilian refugees found their way into the rear areas, competing for food and resources. Most occupants of the four refugee camps were destitute, sometimes reduced to boiling bark and leaves for food. A month later the death rate was horrendous.[78]

Doubtless, the military action that had been grinding up the Bataan peninsula since December worsened the peasants' lot. Front-line Japanese soldiers were already grubbing for roots and killing water buffalo in March. Tens of thousands of hungry men on the peninsula for more than three months were tempted to supplement their diets with whatever they could find on the farms they passed through. Farmers with little to spare were also subject to thievery from their own soldiers:

> Hunger made great foragers of Filipino soldiers, who soon learned to secure from Bataan's tiny villages such delicacies as pigs, chickens, sweet potatoes, bananas, mangoes, and tender young

bamboo shoots.... And soldiers on patrol, ostensibly seeking human game, would often gather rice standing unpicked in nearby fields and then laboriously thresh the grain in their individual foxholes.[79]

As the battle wore on, such provisions disappeared. War, often hardest on those with the least, took its toll on Bataan's villages, increasing the already heavy burden of their poverty.

A 1939 survey showed that two million people dependent on the sugar industry needed help, and a case study of 173 families showed that the daily wage of laborers was "too meager to support their families. To supplement the earning of the family head, the wife and children had to work. Women worked in various occupations, such as hat weaving, sewing children's dresses, and fruit selling." Illiteracy ran as high as 85 percent among those whose typical dwelling was a one room bamboo houses without a kitchen. Most income went to food (80 percent) and clothing. "Toothbrushes, tooth paste or powder, bath soap and even shoes and stockings are practically unknown in laborer's homes." Households supplemented their income by the limited means at hand—pottery and hat making, cloth and mat weaving, fishing, furniture making, clothes washing.[80]

Balanga, like the other towns and barrios I pass through, has loads of pawnshops. I count a total of six on the two streets housing the banks, and it occurs to me that there is a significant transfer of wealth here. The clerk at the Ellison Hotel tells me there's a steady stream of the poor coming in from the countryside, hocking valuables to stay afloat. This is standard operating procedure throughout the developing world, but I can't help thinking this is the reverse of what happened in Japan at the end of the war—city folk taking valuables out into the countryside, bartering them for food with peasants who had the only remaining supplies. When I ask the hotel clerk about the pawnshops, he shrugs and says, "Good business, I guess."

A chronic shortage of cash in rural communities meant the inevitable appearance of exploitative loan practices. Borrowing from the landlord, especially before harvest or after a fiesta, became common practice. In one method, the *takalanan*, landlords lent money to peasants and were repaid in crop at the time of harvest. A second was the *pasunod*, in which the loan was imposed by the landlord. The third was the *takipan*, in which rice lent to the tenant was paid back two-fold at harvest time. No written agreements were struck, and minimum interest rates on variations of the three methods never yielded less than 33 percent interest to landlord.[81]

The economic woes of peasants went even deeper. In 1935, Douglas MacArthur, then military advisor to President Quezon, presented a plan, later adopted as the National Defense Act of 1936. Among its basic principles was the obligation of all to serve in the nation's defense, "with all industrial and natural resources made available to the state," the provision for actual military security, not just its appearance, and the need for "current and future economy." Criticism of the plan took the form of Emilio Aguinaldo's claim that true military preparedness was little more than a "useless pretense"—the islands should instead rely directly on U.S. protection. His solution to internal unrest was simple: "Stop hunger."[82]

Another dissenter was Assemblyman Camilo Osias, who called the bill a "saturnalia of extravagance." He argued on the assembly floor, "People are hungry. We say we have no money to give them relief ... we have no rice to feed our people, but we have bullets to give to soldiers that we create." In his view, the military spending would ignore salient problems of disease, educational needs and unemployment. He spoke to the concerns of peasant families, ridiculing the proposal to pay trainees the pittance of five centavos each day, inadequate even for cigarettes—and argued that the extended training period of more than five months would "adversely affect families who depended on the trainees for support, especially agricultural families who would lose much-needed labor during the harvest season."[83]

Many feared that taxes would be raised to support the army, and that the national budget, already stretched thin, could not support the endeavor—actual expenditures on the military eventually accounted for more than 10 percent of the annual budget. MacArthur claimed this was well worth the cost, stating, "Without security, there can eventually be only slavery. With slavery will come national death."[84] In the short run, he was wrong, of course. In light of the inadequacy of the islands' defense against the Japanese, his poor generalship, defeat and ignominious flight from his army, the pledge to return seems a justification for his original defense plan. Filipino peasants must have understood that he was also wrong about the accompanying distribution of resources to places that helped them not at all.

As the campaign progressed, the Fil-American forces were pressed into an ever-narrowing area of the peninsula, and much of the civilian population found refuge in camps, where they shared the life of the besieged. In the early stages, they received rations, but these diminished as the front-line soldiers, naturally, were given priority. Eventually, one can of salmon sufficed for twenty civilians, and a cup of rice for a family. Starvation stalked the camps—children were seen sucking their mothers' dry breasts, and as hunger closed in, civilians approached the battle-lines to beg for food. Many lost all they owned. In one heart-rending case, a Filipino soldier was given leave from his unit to visit his family—his wife and five children—but upon arrival in their refugee camp, he found only his eight-month-old child alive. The others had died of hunger.[85]

* * * * *

As with survivors' accounts of Japanese brutality, ones describing Filipinos as victims of that same brutality are problematic. Americans and Filipinos certainly made common cause against their Japanese enemy in battle and as an oppressive occupying force. However, as in the Fil-American army itself, serious fault lines divided American from Filipino as the drama of the march unfolded. The context of their actions—the physical and economic environment of Bataan—suggests that Filipinos were more than victims; to some degree they were victimizers as well.

9

Kinds of Kindness

Under every grief and pine runs a joy with silken twine. —William Blake, "Auguries of Innocence"

One of the more articulate participants in the Death March was Sam Grashio. Like nearly all other accounts, his spared no hyperbole as it lashed his captors. The Death March was, he wrote, "a macabre litany of heat, dust, starvation, thirst, flies, filth, stench, murder, torture, corpses, and wholesale brutality that numbs the memory. The general impression which overwhelms all others about the Death March is of the savage brutality, the arbitrary cruelty, of our Japanese captors." Contained here are the major themes of all the narratives—some description of the conditions of the march and physical suffering, the mental confusion that resulted, followed by a general statement of what caused both, the cultural characteristics of his captors. All this is standard fare, but then Grashio goes on to say that because "prisoners were strung out for many miles ... the experiences of different individuals and groups varied considerably."[1] In his willingness to offer space for a different understanding, Grashio is exceptional.

About halfway through the march, Red Allen recalled one small incident among thousands during those two weeks in April. Allen watched his friend, Sergeant Ervin, approach the limit of his endurance. A guard was soon hovering over him, his bayonet poised. At that moment, Ervin "raised [his] hand to the tip of the bayonet and he stopped," after which Ervin got up and went on.[2] An interesting moment. Other than the act of face-to-face killing, little in modern warfare is more intensely personal than the relationship between prisoner and his captor, and that nameless Japanese soldier drawing back his bayonet hints at the interpretive possibility Grashio suggested.

Exploring that potential disrupts the uniformity of previous interpretations. Scholars have explained Japanese wartime behavior in a variety of ways—Japanese demonized their enemies, they were the product of militaristic socialization and the emperor system, their society was essentially racist, or that their brutality was simply an amplified form of that common to our species. These explanations complement each other nicely. Each work, from the wartime simplicity of *The Dyess Story* to the subtlety of the best scholarship, fundamentally shares the goal of explaining Japanese *cruelty*. Even allowing for the distortions of memory, the need for survivors' cathartic release, and the fiction that sometimes defines survivor's accounts, the monolithic image of Americans and Filipinos as victims at the complete mercy of "savage" captors is hardly accurate. In the confused swirl of the two weeks it took for nearly 10,000 U.S. soldiers to make their way to Camp O'Donnell, thousands of interactions took place between captor and captive, not all of which fit neatly into simple, well-defined categories.

To explore Japanese comity we must rely on accounts whose purpose, in the main, often assumes its impossibility. Yet examples abound, descriptions of acts of kindness and generosity that reveal the record of the Death March as a complex palimpsest, one whose layers offer fascinating, thematic shading. The sum of those descriptions, distributed among so many survivors' accounts, hint at a much larger body of experience, the memory of which exists in a problematic relationship to its actual frequency. If incidents of cruelty were exaggerated or even invented, perhaps it is reasonable to imagine that incidents denoting comity or kindness were minimized or ignored. Naturally, in no single account is there much recognition of Japanese kindness, generosity, or even humanity. Yet such references accumulate in scores of accounts and yield a version of those two April weeks that blurs the line between virtue and vice, between kindness and cruelty.

Survivors conjured a story whose power and appeal depends on a stark contrast—their own innocence and the cruelty of the Japanese, and those who have written about the March have been content to accept that story. Here now is a different story, with the actors' roles reversed. Theodore Roosevelt once said that "comparison is the thief of joy." If the new comparison robs us of joy, perhaps it is well lost as the old understanding breaks down.

* * * * *

In the aftermath of war, few nations are inclined to acknowledge the sordid behavior of their soldiers. Ignoring one's own depredations is easy. Victory is its own reward. The satisfaction of castigating the enemy is self-evident, and for Americans writing and reading the history of conflict with the Japanese, the task is even easier. American accounts of the battle and its aftermath defined the "savage" Japanese in overarching terms; few contain references to similar American behavior. Yet racism was not the province of the Japanese alone, and the encounter with darker-skinned peoples, both Filipino and Japanese, had ugly dimensions. Just as most Americans omitted their often vicious behavior toward each other in prison, evidence of what must have been brutality toward "lesser" peoples is largely missing from their accounts. Standard campaign histories leave out such information as well—in a fit of honest scholarship, the historian George Feifer states that "ignoring [American] atrocities completely, as virtually every military account does, is too good to war and its phony legends."[3]

If extensive Japanese records of the Bataan campaign were available, no doubt they would contain an indictment of their enemies; this on the valid assumption that no one comes out of a nasty, three-month ordeal with clean hands. Donald Keene, an intelligence officer competent in the Japanese language and later a literary scholar of Japan, wondered at war's end "if these people writing 'inside histories' will include all the dirty stuff that has marked our campaigns." All soldiers in combat for extended periods descend to some level of barbarity—during the Guadalcanal campaign five months after Bataan, American soldiers beheaded Japanese enemies and placed their heads on poles. When their commander accused them of acting "like animals" one of the soldiers responded, "That's right, Colonel, we are animals. We live like animals, we eat and are treated like animals, what the fuck do you expect?"[4]

In his book *The World Within War: America's Combat Experience in World War II* Gerald Linderman devotes fourteen pages to how Americans on Bataan learned the Japanese way of war. Virtually all of his sources are Americans who remembered the battle, and he describes them as naïve, their combat behavior in this, the war's first campaign, defined by an "open, roseate quality."[5] In this view, combat on Bataan was a learning process—Americans only gradually came to understand the need to adapt to the reality of fighting the Japanese. But at this early stage in the war, were Americans as naïve and "open" (read: fair-minded and incapable of brutality) as Linderman, and the vast majority of survivors' narratives, claim? Indeed, survivors offered but few examples of American brutality during the Bataan campaign; such would cast unwelcome shadows on their service and on their status as victims. Yet their conflict was bitter, and one can easily imagine that cruelty was no one's monopoly.

The American combat flyer Greg "Pappy" Boyington, after spending months in Japanese prisons, later wrote that he supposed people expected him to hate his captors. "I know I am expected," he wrote, "to brand them as primitive and brutal and stupid. But we can find right here in the United States, almost in any city ... people who at heart are as primitive and as brutal and as stupid.... All that this type of person needs to assert himself is an opportunity." So it was. As early as the opening months of 1942, reports of American atrocities began to appear; seventy interned Japanese on the island of Mindanao were allegedly murdered. Japanese hospital ships were reported as targets of American attacks, classrooms in Japan sprouted posters telling students to "kill the American devils," and schoolchildren participated in a debate about what to do with thousands of blue-eyed dolls that had found their way into the country as a gesture of goodwill in 1927. Not surprisingly, the dolls were destroyed.[6]

Such claims may well have been wildly exaggerated. Yet some evidence hints at a decidedly ugly side of the American war. Early in the campaign, a small contingent of U.S. soldiers stopped a group of six civilians on their way to a bridge. They found that the men were Japanese, carrying dynamite as saboteurs. Without hesitation, they killed them and left the bodies in a ditch. With respect to the broader campaign, Steve Mellnick remembered it as being one of "no quarter." Allied rear area soldiers "prepared ambushes, booby-trapped approach routes, interrogated infiltrators with oriental practicality" and "stopped taking prisoners. It was a 'no-holds-barred' war in which one killed to survive." Even in the spring of 1942, Americans taking prisoners was an exception—sometime during the offensives that eventually overwhelmed the Fil-American army, two Japanese battalions found themselves cut off and under heavy attack, whereupon one of the Japanese scouts "saw American soldiers killing ... wounded soldiers by rolling over them with a bulldozer."[7]

Alvin Poweleit recalled a story about two tankers who ambushed a contingent of Japanese coming down a road near Zaragoza. After killing them all, they "ran over the Japanese with their tanks." In the aftermath of another engagement, some U.S. tankers "had the disagreeable job of scraping pieces of Japanese out of their tank treads, wheels and sprockets. In desperation, they threw sand against tank hulls to reduce the stench."[8] After one bloody engagement, two sergeants were seen "going around and collecting gold and silver teeth as souvenirs from dead Japs. They had their pockets full." During the same battle, Ed Dyess, spotting a Japanese below his position, instructed a friend, "Go ahead and shoot him. Don't hit that watch; I want it for a souvenir." The U.S. surgeon Alfred Weinstein recalled treating wounded Japanese, one of whom had to be strapped down, "wild-eyed with terror." When he found someone to translate, Weinstein learned that his officers "told him that the Americans torture and kill all prisoners."[9]

Sometimes American officers could not control their Filipino subordinates. In early January, Ed Ramsey's squad captured three wounded Japanese. Though he gave orders to keep them alive for questioning, his Filipino sergeant killed them all. Filipinos responded to reports of abuse of their women by setting booby traps, planning ambushes, and when they captured Japanese, they questioned them using torture. On other occasions, American officers participated more directly. In late February, a Filipino patrol under American officers captured several Japanese prisoners. Delayed making their way back to friendly lines and unwilling to be hampered by their prisoners, the officers ordered the captives killed with knives.[10] One reads scores of survivors' accounts before encountering such rare descriptions; the vast majority are focused on their own victimhood and on Japanese cruelty. To compensate for this paucity, a brief look at American soldiers' behavior elsewhere makes for a more complete picture.

In 1989, the Canadian novelist James Bacque published a sensational book entitled *Other Losses: An Investigation into the Mass Deaths of German Prisoners at the Hands of the French and Americans After World War II*.[11] Bacque's central argument was indeed stunning—that Dwight D. Eisenhower expressed his personal hatred of the Germans by allowing more than one million POWs to starve to death in the months after German surrender in May 1945. In response, a number of professional historians contributed to a volume entitled *Eisenhower and the German POWs: Facts Against Falsehood* in 1992. Those essays show Bacque's research to have been superficial and incomplete, and effectively dismantle his argument.[12]

Even so, *Other Losses* served to highlight some of the disturbing features of the American management of the massive POW problem after the war, many of which the historians accepted. Just as Homma faced nearly insurmountable logistical problems after American surrender on Bataan, Eisenhower confronted a similar situation, though exponentially larger in its scope and complexity. The U.S. army had to deal with some twenty million displaced persons, in addition to suddenly becoming custodian of huge numbers of German soldiers, many of whom had fled westward to avoid capture by the Russians. By the millions, defeated *Wehrmacht* soldiers flooded into holding areas, and the unexpected volume of prisoners was simply too much for either victorious host—Eisenhower expected three million prisoners and received five million; Homma expected 35,000 and received 75,000. The ratios are similar and the comparison is worth noting.

The logistical problem, exacerbated by the refusal of the British to handle half of this vast horde, was monumental. Feeding this unanticipated multitude was a serious problem because of a continent-wide food shortage, the shattered German transportation system, and bad weather that spring. In the face of this nightmare, prisoners' official designation was changed from POW to DEF—"disarmed enemy forces," a change which, according to the Geneva Convention, allowed Allied commanders to feed their prisoners less. The inevitable consequence was that Germans went hungry, and many died, perhaps as many as 56,000 out of about five million captured.[13]

Günter Bischof, co-editor of *Eisenhower and the Germans*, categorically rejects Bacque's estimate of Germans who died in the Allied prison camps, but nevertheless accepts the accuracy of the camp descriptions provided by the six sources in Bacque's book. These accounts describe crowding, acute shortages of water and food, disease and of POWs living in the open without shelter. Georg Weiss remembered that "we couldn't even lie down properly.... But the lack of water was the worst thing of all. For three and a half days, we had no water at all. We would drink our own urine. It tasted terrible, but what could we do? Some men got down on the ground and licked the ground to get some moisture.... The guards sold us water through the wire, and cigarettes.... I saw thousands dying. They took the bodies away on trucks."[14]

In 1956 the West German government established the Maschke Commission for the purpose of writing a comprehensive history of German POWs. Its effort of fifteen years produced twenty-two volumes, including reports from dozens of ex–POWs that indicate "the camps were harsh, even brutal. The commission came to the conclusion that the American policy of punishment was spread to the POWs, that there was cruel indifference" at least in part explained by recent Allied knowledge of the horrors of the concentration camps.[15] Another well-balanced source agrees that conditions in the camps—especially the *Rheinwiesenlager*—were extremely harsh. Germans endured outdoor conditions with no tents, poor hygiene and inadequate water, and were denied Red Cross parcels, even though warehouses were full, and Quakers, YMCA and CARE personnel were forbidden entrance to the camps until February 1946.[16] A German sergeant recalled, "I usually lie on the ground. During the heat I crawl into an earth-hole.... During a thunderstorm one wall of my earth-hole falls in on me. My coat and socks are wet through and through" and later, "Nowhere else would I have been so lost in my thoughts or seen humans in their total nakedness. Nor would I have ever believed the victors to be capable of such cruelties."[17]

A German professor, Karl Brandt, warned a colleague in 1940 that among Americans, "the Puritan character is still alive ... and once America is roused to war you will see it in all its harshness and fury. In such moments they judge men as the children of light or the children of darkness with no half-shades. They will be merciless to Germany." Brandt's opinion was not without a certain accuracy. Just as Japanese guards probably sought revenge against a host that had killed so many of their comrades, American guards were not above seeking revenge, and did not treat their captives with "kid gloves." Administrators tended to assign young, recently arrived recruits without combat experience to positions as guards, and some veterans "remarked that the new men ... were the ones most likely to find some way to show how tough they were. It also happened that when the generals picked officers to run the camps, at times they picked Jewish officers. One of those officers was quoted as saying that the job gave him a chance to get a little revenge."[18]

Even scholars who reject Bacque's conclusions regarding the death count generally agree:

> The Americans treated German POWs harshly. In some cases they did so because of the hatred of particular camp commanders vis-à-vis the Germans.... Others had become callous toward their enemy after many months of fighting the tough resistance of the *Wehrmacht* and the SS divisions, losing their comrades in the process. There was also the vindictiveness of German-Americans who were guards in the prison camps in the United States. "God protect you from storm and wind and from Germans who are in America," noted one adage among German camp prisoners.

Such was the "volatile mix in Germany in May 1945: angry GIs, frustrated recruits, and revenge-seeking Jewish officers, and former slave laborers and German soldiers packed into open camps. The result was unbearable conditions on a massive scale in a few of the large and grossly overpopulated holding camps on the Rhine River."[19]

Earlier in the war American GIs, like soldiers everywhere, found that their uniforms did not alter their cultural assumptions and prejudices. The U.S. army in Britain, awaiting it rendezvous with destiny on D-Day, insisted on pre-war segregation of black and white soldiers. British objections to what they considered unfair practices were loud, and the tension was eventually expressed in race riots, particularly in the city of Bristol. One weekend a fight over which race drank at which pubs erupted, with some four hundred black and white soldiers involved. The melee required more than a hundred truncheon-wielding MPs to restore order, but not before one man was killed and several seriously injured.[20]

Earlier still, in North Africa, Americans expressed racial prejudice in a different way. The historian Stephen Ambrose described the hierarchy of response to foreign peoples—the American soldier "felt the Arabs were despicable, liars, thieves, dirty, awful, without a redeeming feature." Less revolting were, in order, Italians, rural and urban French, British, with the Dutch and Germans believed to be most like himself. Six months after the conclusion of the Death March, American contact with the Arab population in Tunisia had awful consequences. Tension boiled over as Arabs spied on U.S. positions, stole matériel, and sometimes attacked isolated soldiers with stones. Frustrated GIs in North Africa, no doubt tired of seeing dark-skinned Arab women, grateful to Bing Crosby, sang "I'm Dreaming of a White Mistress." But acting on such urges with local women could sometimes be fatal. The *GI Guide* warned Americans about contact with Arab women—"Never stare at her. Never jostle her in a crowd. Never speak to her in public. Never try to remove the veil." Some who ignored the warning were found dead with their testicles sewn into their mouths.[21]

Rick Atkinson's thorough research has revealed one of the darkest sides of the American war effort. One American in North Africa wrote, "We became ruthless with the Arab." If we found them where they were not to be, they were open game, much as rabbits in the States during hunting season." Another recalled, "Here Arabs live all over. Some we shoot on sight, some we search, and some we make a deal with to buy eggs and chickens." Throughout the region, GIs "boasted of using natives for marksmanship practice, daring one another to shoot an Arab coming over a hill like a target in an arcade. Others fired at camels to see the riders bucked off, or shot at the feet of Arab children to 'watch them dance in fear.'"

Simple homicide went unpunished, the perpetrators protected by their uniforms. Edward Boehm, a lieutenant from Montana, remembered seeing some of his comrades "shoot Arabs just to watch them jump and fall.... I could hear them yell and laugh each time and there was nothing I could do about it.... I saw them do it, like you're shooting gophers. I could hear them: 'Wow, I got one!' Those guys were murderers." When Arabs did not respond promptly to demands for a password, men of similar bent made them dig their graves before summarily shooting them.[22]

* * * * *

The second component of our new comparison begins with Japan's ambivalent relationship to the West. The country entered the international community at a time of intense colonial competition among Western powers. Eager to avoid the fate of China at the hands Great Britain, an extraordinary group of statesmen guided the country toward the goal of self-strengthening with a steady, if clearly autocratic, hand. Recognizing their military weakness, the Japanese accepted a series of unequal treaties that deprived the nation of tariff autonomy and the right to try foreign citizens in Japanese courts of law. Desperate to escape such humiliation, the oligarchs introduced various Western-inspired reforms, including an overhaul of their judicial system, the creation of a modern bureaucracy and a thoroughly modernized military.

Under the slogans *fukoku kyohei* (Rich Country, Strong Army) and *bunmei kaika* (Civilization and Enlightenment) the central goal was to enter the circle of "civilized," i.e., powerful nations, to sit at the imperial table rather than be on it. The four decades after 1868, when the Meiji emperor assumed his throne, were a period of enormous and unsettling social and cultural change, as an essentially agricultural economy strained to accommodate the modern imperatives of industrial development. By 1905 Japan had achieved what it sought — the status of "great power."

This process, compressed into only a few decades, brought with it considerable tension, and produced a healthy debate over just what it meant, after all, to be Japanese. In light of the racial hierarchy that Western powers applied to the world, the Japanese identity was deeply bound up with such concepts. After the defeat of the Russian colossus, now fully embracing traditional Western notions of racial hierarchy, Japan expected equal treatment from Western, white nations. Yet just as she was achieving international stature, she discovered that those nations' definition of that color did not extend to what, after her victory against China in 1895, the West termed *die Gelbe Gefahr* (The Yellow Peril).

As the new century wore on, Japan increasingly saw herself as only an "honorary white" nation, yet still entitled to the colonial and economic exploitation of "lesser" peoples and nations — as long as her ambitions did not conflict with those of the West. Excluded from this fellowship by great powers' decision to deprive Japan of her spoils after the Sino-Japanese War, by the refusal of World War I's victorious powers to include a racial equality clause in the Versailles settlement, and by racist U.S. immigration laws, Japan's racial identity became "a contradictory combination of self-identification with the 'superior' white race and latent antagonism toward the white race." To be sure, by "treating white POWs inhumanely in the presence of Asian onlookers during the Philippines campaign, the Japanese hoped to flaunt their superiority and legitimize themselves as the 'substitute whites' in Asia." At a fundamental level, the Japanese were deeply concerned with elevating themselves in the eyes of both Asia and the West.[23]

The ambivalence took other forms as well. While American wartime films emphasized already extant stereotypes of the cunning oriental (Sax Rohmer's Fu Manchu, for example), Japanese films betrayed an ambivalence toward the Western enemy that seemed to contradict the militarists' jingoism. Japanese actors playing the parts of Westerners did not evince the heavy accents of American actors playing Japanese roles. Further evidence appears in newsreels showing conquering Japanese armies. Western music was used as background — the conquest of Burma is accompanied by a choir, that of Sumatra by Haydn, Japanese paratroopers fall from the sky to Wagner's *Ritt der Walküren*, and Tchaikovsky accompanies an Allied airfield's destruction.[24]

While the media was severely censored by the late 1930s, some aspects of an earlier humanism were still discernable. Three films illustrate a pattern. In *Tsuchi to Heitai* (*Mud and Soldiers*), soldiers' simple humanity is the central theme. They wander, their final objective both unclear and seemingly unattainable. The film *Go-nin no Sekkohei* (*Five Scouts*), released in 1939, suggests an unexpectedly humanistic stance on the part of the director, Tasaka Tomotaka. His story is also simple, the five men endure and experience the "terrifying effect of the enemy's fire.... The enemy is like a fire or a flood." The soldiers are shown as eminently human—bored, looking for flowers that remind them of home, searching for substitutes for tatami mats. Donald Richie, the foremost analyst of Japanese film, suggests the film showed something more than the face of war—it showed something that is "common to humanity."[25]

Nishizumi Senshacho-den (*The Story of Tank Commander Nishizumi*), released in 1940, shows its protagonist to be clean and modest, a soldier who dies a quiet death, mourned by his men. As in many other films, the focus remains on the "pure self" of the Japanese at war; the enemy is identified as Chinese, but they are "expressionless and almost robotlike figures." Here there was simply no personalization of the enemy and therefore no hatred of him. If anti-foreign venom frequently characterized Japanese cartoons and popular language, it was conspicuously absent from films and literature. Until the outbreak of widespread warfare in 1937, some Japanese media even handled military themes with irony that sometimes bordered on outright derision of military adventurism on the continent. This period saw military service simply as "a rite of passage, a chance to learn to shoot a rifle and use a bayonet, establish lifelong friendships, collect souvenirs, compile a scrapbook ... and then come home and start a new life with savings and severance pay."[26]

Such aspirations had little to do with the stereotype of the "barbaric" Japanese soldier's disregard of his prisoners' lives. There was, perhaps, a connection between the sensibilities that survived the government's militarist agenda and Japanese behavior on the Death March. The censorship of the late 1930s saw the deletion of a few pages in Pearl Buck's novel, *The Patriot*, wherein an anti-war Japanese kills himself rather than accept conscription. This did not deter two students who died by hurling themselves in front of trains instead of reporting for army duty. Afterwards, their friends explained that the two did not resist military training *per se*, but rather because of their "overwhelming belief that the army's domination of their country was not in Japan's best interests."[27] Young, urban Japanese under the age of twenty-five had gone to primary school during the more liberal 1920s; doubtless many were equipped to resist, even if only privately, the militarists' jingoistic nationalism of the late 1930s.

John Morris, living in Tokyo during the two years before Pearl Harbor, stated with assurance that "military training is the most unpopular feature of Japanese life. Every student I knew loathed it and would seize eagerly upon the slightest opportunity to avoid attendance." In this the young urbanites ran against the grain of the army, whose only interest in education was "to get it over with as quickly as possible in order to swell the flow of recruits." Among university students, Morris found a "fairly widespread dislike of the army ... if it were left to individual choice, only a comparatively small number of them would enlist ... there is always a good deal of passive resistance to the officers in charge of military instruction." As Morris came to know a number of Japanese university students, he was "surprised by their sensitiveness, their sensibility, and the range of their interests, which were often remarkably wide. [He] found in most of them an overwhelming desire to understand Western thought." Students able to read English examined the works of Meredith, James, Carlyle, Emerson, Huxley, Lawrence, Hemingway, Eliot, some of which, by the late 1930s, had been proscribed.[28]

Noma Hiroshi's novel *Shinkū chitai* (*Zone of Emptiness*) describes a soldier's alienation from civilization and from a sense of purpose: "He felt separated from everything he had once loved. What was left of the boy who had studied history and economics with such passion, the high school teacher full of faith in the greatness of his calling? The boy was penned up behind the gates of the post.... At the post, my only image is alive, and that image is blindly obedient."[29] Tasaki's novel *Long the Imperial Way* is centrally concerned with the same theme, the process by which a Japanese farmer was "transformed into a machine of war." For all who endured it, punished and punishers alike, it was a

> system which tried to make powerful destructive machines of them even beyond the endurable limit of inherently constructive mankind. Shells of the warm, constructive individuals they were born to become, the men lived unhappily within a perversion which tried not to recognize the ethics, constructiveness, and fair play their souls constantly hungered for in their relations with their fellow men.

Tasaki's novel views mankind as "inherently constructive," whose instincts toward "fair play" and more broadly defined ethical behavior were destroyed in a wartime context whose ethos was one of narrowly-defined and ultimately destructive nationalism. Its pessimistic conclusion makes clear its quintessentially anti-war message.[30] Both works harkened to a time less bellicose, and less permissive of the emperor's subjects' darker instincts.

* * * * *

Just four years before the Death March, the Japanese author Hino Ashihei began publishing a trio of novels that glorified the empire's soldiers. *Mugi to Heitai* (*Wheat and Soldiers*), *Tsuchi to Heitai* (*Mud and Soldiers*) and *Hana to Heitai* (*Flowers and Soldiers*). Ashihei's work showed the Japanese soldier in the most glowing light. The books reassured the homefolks that those they had sent to the fighting front in China retained his *nasake* (humanity) in the face of war and remained a member of the invincible imperial army and represented the very best of the homeland.[31]

Naturally, during the war Allied propaganda rejected this and often portrayed the Japanese as inherently barbaric and abusive throughout their history. This view ignores the fact that prisoners taken during earlier wars were treated in an exemplary manner. Early in the century, such treatment was an expression of a national policy designed to impress Western powers sufficiently in order to escape the unequal treaties to which the country had been subjected since 1859. One legal scholar, writing in 1929, observed that during the nineteenth century, "there was a system of Laws of War to which governments paid homage ... and these laws were last observed by the Japanese in their war with Russia, in 1904, and with a fidelity surpassing that of any Western government." For example, Article Two of the official Japanese *Army Regulations for Handling Prisoners of War*, dating from to the Russo-Japanese War of 1904–05, stated, "Prisoners of war shall be treated with a spirit of goodwill and shall never be subjected to cruelties or humiliation."[32]

When Japan fought China in 1894–95 and Russia in 1904–05, the nation's primary goal was to achieve "great power" status in the eyes of the dominant Western powers, especially Great Britain and the U.S. Treating prisoners well who were captured in these two wars was an excellent way to advertise Japan's arrival as a "civilized" power, worthy of international respect. During the long and sanguinary struggle with imperial Russia, Japan captured some 80,000 thousand prisoners, many of whom "received the same pay and subsistence allowances as Japanese troops ... and were not required to do any work." During their captivity, "their good treatment was praised at an International Red Cross Conference by the renowned jurist, diplomat, international arbiter and former director of Russia's POW Information Bureau, F.F. Martins, who after the war addressed a letter of thanks to the Japanese government." Good Japanese treatment of prisoners was so well known that surrendering Russians were reported to capitulate, screaming "Matsuyama! Matsuyama!" where they knew they would be held.[33]

The worldwide depression of the 1930s saw Western powers raise tariff barriers in an effort to protect their economies, effectively closing Japan out of the international trade necessary for its economic health. This, along with the exclusionary American Immigration Act of 1924, which the Japanese found to be an overt expression of racism, helped stoke support for the ultranationalists, who blamed Japan's ills, in large measure, on the West. The descent into militarism brought with it a new policy that overtly rejected any need for international recognition. Instead, the new Greater East Asia Co-Prosperity Sphere would impose its own xenophobic ethos. By 1942 General Uemura Mikio, the POW Information Bureau's first director, spoke to the heart of the matter: "In the war with Russia we gave them excellent treatment in order to gain recognition as a civilized country. To-day such need no longer applies."[34]

The absence of abstract notions of right and wrong has long fascinated many observers of Japan, but there do exist moral imperatives in Japanese thinking, certainly no weaker than so-called Christian ones. Once in Komatsu, up on the Sea of Japan, I visited a representation of Buddhist hell. There I entered a large cave through the throat of a giant Buddha rising from the bowels of the earth. Descending, I passed numerous paintings and sculptures—one showed a man entwined by snakes, writhing in eternal agony. I was struck most by a sculpture of a man in a small alcove—his legs outstretched and between them his giant penis, moss-speckled with age. Eternal priapism for what must have been flagrant and repeated sexual transgressions.

The *Senjin kun* (Code of Battlefield Conduct, issued January 1941) stated, "Do not despise your enemy or the inhabitants" and instructed imperial soldiers to "take care to protect the property of the enemy. Requisition, confiscation, destruction of enemy resources, etc. are all governed by regulations." It continued:

> The true military spirit is to receive the noble will of the Emperor, to be strong in righteousness and benevolent in strength ... strength must be austere; benevolence requires breadth ... the true martial spirit is incomplete if one is lacking in the virtue that causes one not to strike down those who submit and to treat tenderly those who obey.... It is the providence of the imperial army to temper justice with mercy, to revere the broad majesty of the Emperor.

The code was issued "in an attempt to counter the widespread collapse of military discipline on the Chinese front, the "violence against superior officers, desertions, rape, arson, pillage." Shirane Takayuki, who was assigned to write the code, had studied philosophy and education at Kyushu's Imperial University, and its intent was to remind Japanese soldiers "of the importance of upholding the honor of Imperial soldiers." It warned, "Don't get drunk, don't get carried away by lust, do treat non-combatants with kindness."[35] On the ground a thousand interactions would approximate this ideal according to circumstances and individual impulses.

During the war, American propaganda emphasized the degraded nature of the enemy—

with the inevitable implication that he was beyond redemption. Japanese behavior on the Death March and elsewhere, according to one typical response, showed "the true nature of the enemy ... an enemy that seems to be a beast which sometimes stands erect."[36] Americans offered images of the Japanese as essentially subhuman, as monkeys or lice, literally in need of extermination. The War Department's 1945 film *Know Your Enemy: Japan* asserted that "treachery, brutality, rape and torture are all justified if used against non–Japanese."

Shortly afterward, however, the Cold War defined a new context, one wherein the old images were of no use in the global struggle with Communism. By 1949, facing the "loss" of China to Mao Zedong's Communists and a nuclear-armed Soviet Union, and in need of a reliable ally in the Far East, the U.S. immediately set about the task of refashioning the wartime image of the Japanese. American policy turned favorable toward a resurgent, economically strong Japan as a bulwark against the Asian Red Menace, and forgetting Japan's wartime past became a shared endeavor for victor and vanquished alike. Japan would evermore be a beacon of peace, its wartime past renounced, even expunged according to a new geo-political imperative.

Instructional materials used for training Americans at California's Civil Affairs Staging Area attempted to reverse the wartime image with soothing words. The Japanese were not "treacherous, brutal, sadistic," neither were all of them "the monkey-man type." Instead, the emphasis fell on different features, ones that apparently had always been there, though submerged during wartime:

> There are other traits of character—reliability, ingenuity, industriousness, thrift, bravery, aggressiveness, honesty. With some exceptions, depending on individual personality, sex, age, social standing, income, profession ... the average Japanese displays these characteristics in about the same manner and measure as other people in other lands.

Taking a page directly from John Locke, the War Department film *Our Job in Japan* instructed Americans in the occupation force that the Japanese brain (graphically shown on screen) simply absorbed what was poured into it. The seventy million Japanese brains were just as *tabula rasa* as any in the West, capable of "good things" (presumably West-inspired) or "bad things" (learned from the militarists who led Japan down the wrong historical path). The message was clear: "Neither blood, culture nor history drove the Japanese to war, but rather socialization and indoctrination of recent vintage."[37]

So, the images are clear in three phases. At the conclusion of the Russo-Japanese War, we see a Japan kind to her prisoners, eager to conform to Western notions of right behavior. Then during the Pacific War, another Japan emerged—xenophobic, inward-looking, militaristic, dismissive of Western standards. Last came a Japan that had, apparently, re-discovered her earlier humanity. Yet the apparent aberration of the middle phase was neither clear nor complete, and attitudes reflected in statements such as *Senjin kun* were not completely ignored.

* * * * *

The chapter "Chaos Meets *Kata*" (Chapter 4) makes clear the rather signal failure of the Japanese plan to evacuate the Bataan peninsula. Surrender had been projected much later, and Japanese staff work underestimated the number of POWs by two thirds. Indeed, there is no doubt that the Japanese were unprepared for this crush of humanity.[38] General

Wachi Takeji, Homma's chief of staff, spoke to this issue during Homma's the post-war trial: "The Bataan Death March," he stated,

> is a phrase coined later for propaganda purposes. There is not a single officer from Homma down who ever intended to perpetrate a "Death March." But conditions at the time were very bad. Many of the 70,000 P.O.W.s were suffering from malaria or malnutrition, due to the long fight in a jungle area. There were no vehicles to transport them. Even Japanese forces which were being transferred from Bataan elsewhere were all made to march on foot.... I hope it will be understood that the Japanese army was operating under the same discomforts as the P.O.W.s.

Wachi further asserted that General Edward King did not turn over a sufficient number of vehicles for transporting the prisoners north after his surrender. With or without American trucks, insufficient transport was the reality. One authority on the Imperial Japanese Army noted that the Japanese military, from the early twentieth century on, was marked by a serious structural flaw—its logistical system.[39]

Such difficulties were the reality on Bataan. Yet in the swirling confusion of the next two weeks, the outlines of the original plan were visible, even if only vaguely. Virtually all the material on the Death March, primary as well as secondary, trumpets the degree to which the Japanese fell short of their intention to quickly, efficiently and humanely remove their horde of prisoners. With full awareness of implementation's shortcomings, here we examine the degree to which that intention was realized. Central to addressing this issue is the question of motorized transport. The original plan called for the POWs to walk from the gathering point at Mariveles to Balanga, from whence they would be put on trucks and taken to the railhead at Capas.

At Homma's trial, James Baldassarre testified that "the Japanese never evacuated any prisoners with the trucks, because I know." The number of Americans who rode in trucks, and the ground they covered, cannot, of course, be known with any precision. It is clear, however, that most survivors who wrote of their experience either walked most or all of the way—or claimed that they did so. Reflecting on the selective nature of prisoners' memory, Richard Gordon wrote, "A number were taken out of Bataan by Japanese trucks.... Yet to this day I have yet to meet anyone from Bataan who admits to riding out of that place.... Everyone claims to have been among the vast majority of those who spent five, six, seven eight and even nine days walking."[40]

By four o'clock on day three of my Hike I am all in, ready to surrender to the summer sun. Coming up a long hill outside Limay, and eager to conserve a bit of energy, I leap onto garishly painted jeepney as it thrashes and groans its way the last few thousand meters into town. My driver is a grizzled, happy man of indeterminate age, who accepts my peso *donation with a nod and motions me to grab a hold onto the rear scaffolding as we lurch ahead. Most jeepney drivers only rent their chariots, paying a "boundry" (a corruption of "bounty," a set price to the owner) no matter how much or little they collect. Jeepneys have names and mine, prominently displayed in English, is "Drunken Monster." Later I find out that their engines, constantly rebuilt, are usually Mitsubishi gas or Isuzu diesels.*

Many Americans stated emphatically that those who fell out of the march from sickness or exhaustion were killed by trailing "buzzard squads" who shot or bayoneted them. James Murphy at first believed that these men were being picked up and transported by truck. As it happened, his first supposition was not entirely wrong. During Homma's trial, his former chief of staff, Wachi Takeji, testified, "As much as possible we tried to accommodate the soldiers who fell on the wayside by moving the load of the trucks and cars and placing them on and sending them down to the nearest prisoner of war camp and hand them over to the doctors." Among those who spent considerably less time on foot were some of the sick and disabled. One American remembered, "A few hours later a Japanese truck convoy, returning from Bataan ... stopped outside our shed. They loaded all the sick, the lame, and the lazy onto those trucks and moved us to San Fernando."[41]

Another survivor recalled, "On the second day, I did see some acts of compassion because some of the guys who fell down were picked up by the Japs and taken to prison camp in trucks." A third remembered, "As the days went by and the march continued.... Trucks came along and picked up the men who appeared to be too sick and too weak to keep going."[42] Some wily prisoners took ready advantage of Japanese disorganization. The holding area at Lubao was a confused mass of about two thousand men where, according to William Hauser, "If you played it smart you could remain there a day or so while you rested. So we stayed there. We noticed that at some of the stops guys who had turned themselves in sick would get a truck ride to the next stopping point." Franklin Lacoste recalled riding with thirty sick or disabled men into Camp O'Donnell.[43]

At his trial, Homma testified that his army's lack of motor transport was so acute that it "purchased about 3,000 Filipino ponies" to supplement the "grossly inadequate" number of trucks. However many trucks existed on Bataan, it is clear that the Imperial Japanese Army used some of them to transport American prisoners. As with so much on the Death March, random chance seemed to determine who benefitted from the plan and who did not. As Oliver Allen sat waiting with his captain in Mariveles, shells began to fall and the two were separated. When he found his captain later, the officer asked, "Why didn't you stay with me? You could have ridden." C.D. Quinlenn recalled being "marched to Lamao where we were allowed to get water at an artesian well. We then were marched to Limay where all officers of captain and above were loaded onto trucks and rode to Balanga." Though the plan called for prisoners to walk to Balanga, some rode from various other locations. At Limay, the "Japanese announced to one group that all prisoners who were captains or higher would ride in trucks." Colonel Albert Ives promptly instructed his artillery officers to share their insignia with those who would have to walk, and "over 200 officers and some of the more fortunate enlisted men boarded trucks and rode in relative comfort to Balanga."[44]

Other survivors remembered the overarching reality of random chance as well: "just being in the right place at the right time.... American prisoners ended up riding all the way to our first prison camp, Camp O'Donnell." John Gamble's anti-aircraft regiment rode from Cabcaben to Orani, where they spent the night, were fed and then trucked to Camp O'Donnell. Others remembered being trucked the entire distance from Mariveles to Camp O'Donnell—Addie Martin and two hundred others arrived at the camp within twenty-four hours of surrender, though he stated that "no list of who rode ever existed." Others were left behind. Gene Jacobsen remembered his group being kept in a barren field near Mariveles for three days without food or water, while the Japanese told them that they were waiting for trucks to transport them out of the combat area.[45]

Colonel John Olson recalled that more than a hundred men from a headquarters group and a number of stragglers "were permitted to load into a few U.S. vehicles." They rode as far as Orani, then were put on different trucks all the way to San Fernando. "Another group of ... about two hundred fifty arrived in fourteen trucks later the same day." Others who fell out during the Death March were often "inexplicably loaded into trucks at various points and driven the remainder of the journey." Private E.B. Miller remembered his good luck, when a bus coming from the direction of Bataan with "quite a number of Americans" on it stopped near him:

> The Americans said they had been picked up in southern Bataan and had been ordered by the Japanese to get into this bus, and told the driver to go to San Fernando. Why the Japs ordered them to ride is more than anyone can understand. It was just one of those innumerable quirks of the Japanese mind. No one could tell what they would do next.

Abie Abraham stated, "I saw other Americans in trucks and busses. It was estimated that thousands of the more fortunate men who traveled in the vehicles suffered relatively little, or not at all."[46]

This reality bore at least some relationship to Japanese intentions. One staff officer, Hirano Kurataro, "gave specific instructions that stragglers were to be assembled at suitable locations and allowed to rest, from which point they were to be transported by appropriate means (letting them ride in empty vehicles, etc.)." Piecing together his memory of the Hike, Oliver Allen stated, "Then a strange thing happened ... five trucks stopped and picked some of us up, as many as could get in, and carried us a few miles, maybe five or six, and then stopped.... I never questioned the value of it, for it put me closer to the front of the line." John Playter remembered a Japanese truck stopping to pick him up along with several others as he was laboring up a hill. He jumped off the truck and rested, unmolested, in a roadside ditch for an entire day. He was awakened the next day by a bayonet-wielding Japanese, who offered him a "large, unopened can of sauerkraut." Playter, perhaps unwilling to credit Japanese goodwill, believed the hand of his god spared him.[47]

Trucks made their haphazard way up and down the route of the march, and some surprised Americans suddenly found themselves inside them. A Filipino observer recalled, "A few units had the extraordinary experience of riding over the death route. The Japs had a handful of trucks which shuttled up and down the road. If a group of prisoners happened to be waiting at the end of the line, the trucks picked them up and hauled them to San Fernando." One of those picked up Mark Wohlfield and he rode most of the way, with men trying to cling to the truck as it went by.[48]

The Hike took many different forms depending on when the prisoners left Mariveles, the nature of the congestion encountered, the proclivities of guards, and other factors. Some remembered grueling marches interrupted only by brief respites. Others, however, recall walking at a measured pace with reasonable intervals of rest. Alf Larson recalled, "It depended on us. If we got below a certain walking speed, they would start hollering. As long as you kept a fairly decent pace, they didn't say or do anything. It wasn't a fast pace, just kind of shuffling along. The last two days we walked in close formation."[49]

Lt. Colonel David Hardee was part of a group of seventy U.S. senior officers that received good treatment. When the English-speaking Japanese sergeant in charge agreed to slow their pace and allow more rest stops, Hardee and others tried to reward him with money and a wristwatch. The guard declined, stating that he was "a professional soldier and 'a gentlemen like yourselves.'" James Bollich noted for his group, "As we walked in no particular order, you could walk as fast as you liked or stall to help conserve energy."[50]

Harold Johnson recalled, "Everyone had a different pace he followed during the march because there were plenty of opportunities to hide out.... Some days I just hid out, rested and the [Philippine] Scouts gave me a hand. There were stops at regular intervals where the Japanese tried to take care of us." Bollich, nearing exhaustion, "decided to get some rest regardless of the consequences" and darted out of line into a copse of trees near the road. There he and another American found a *nipa* hut and remained for an hour of rest before rejoining the column. Late in the Hike, Sam Moody and three fellows decided to escape, and simply rolled off the road into some tall grass and remained there until the nearest Japanese guards moved away. The foursome made their way to a nearby house, where they found sympathetic Filipinos who gave them soup, fruits, candy and eggs. On the second day, a Japanese officer discovered them, but simply turned and left. They remained in the house recuperating for three days and then decided to rejoin the prisoners' journey north.[51]

A private named Guiles described the march from Mariveles to Balanga as fairly easy to manage: "They would march us for a distance, and then they would gather us into a compact group for a rest period, as they called it." Others had equally manageable walks. Gene Jacobsen remembered the pattern. "Beginning in the middle of the night, we would be jammed together on the road and would be marched until the hot Filipino sun was high in the sky. When the day became very hot, the Japanese would move us off the road and into a field." Red Allen maintained that men, passed out off to the side, were left alone, "many of them, after resting for a few hours, would be able to leave with the next group that came through. Some of the men did this more than once. It prolonged their march, but it enabled them to live."[52]

An American corporal named Read spoke directly to a broad misconception about the Death March:

> I would like to clarify a point because many people think that the Death March was a great distance made in a short time. But it was not. I don't know how far it was, but I have always figured it was about seventy miles at the most. I was on the march for the better part of a week, and the actual rigors of actually walking on this march were absolutely nothing—absolutely nothing. The fact is I was on this march for ten or eleven days, but some of this time was spent in holding camps for two or three days at a time. Most of the walking was for short distances. The Japs themselves didn't want to walk in the heat of the day.... They changed guard shifts every few miles, but even so they would march us into a rice paddy or open field.... Then, in the evening, we would move out and march a few miles. And that's why it took so long.

Read was describing the instructions on marching found in *Kore dake Yomeba Ware wa Kateru* (*Read This and the War Is Won*): "it is necessary to have a long two or three hour rest during the hottest period of the day."[53]

Clips of Japanese propaganda films show POWs making their way northward in dense columns, four or more abreast as they left the Mariveles area. As the columns advanced, however, they were strung out, often with no guards at all. Alfred Schreiber noted, "with the exception of the railroad cars at San Fernando, I had a pretty straight march. In fact, there was a stretch of several miles when my group had no guards in sight." General Morioka Susumu, commander of the 16th Division, confirmed this reality, noting that disarmed prisoners were "sent up the coast road without any guards from our unit ... it wasn't thought necessary to control the line of march since there was no place else for them to go but toward Balanga."[54]

Other prisoners walked long distances alone and obviously set their own pace. Filipino observers noted that sometimes there were "thousands of men on the road at the same time. And at other times there were but a few individuals—depending on how busy the Japs had been in rounding up the scattered forces in the jungle. Prisoners moved over the seventy miles of road between Mariveles and San Fernando for a period of seventeen days. It took the Japs that long to find and ferret them out." Many so ferreted received help, however unexpected. Near the end of the march John Coleman, earlier wounded in the leg by shrapnel, fell to his knees, unable to continue. He passed out, came to, and wandered into a *barrio*, where he encountered four Japanese who sprang at him with bayonets. With sign language, he explained his wound, whereupon two of the Japanese accompanied him along the road, "They were very reasonable," he remembered, "letting me set my own pace, which was slow."[55]

Though their own training had been brutal, sometimes guards sympathized with prisoners at the end of their endurance. At the end of the long march, just outside San Fernando, four Americans reached their limit, fell and could not rise to continue. Their companions watched as the sentry ordered Filipinos and their *calesa*s (buggies) to carry the exhausted men the remaining two miles to the city. Others recalled similar consideration. When Colonel Ernest Miller explained to his guards that his men were exhausted and ill, "the Japanese proved to be courteous and understanding. They allowed frequent rests and even permitted the captives to forage for food. Another column of prisoners was pleasantly surprised when a Japanese soldier, riding past the men in a truck, tossed them several bottles of soft drinks and a few packs of cigarettes."[56]

Throughout the 1930s Japanese schoolchildren sat through *Dotoku no jikan* (moral hour) during which they were taught right behavior. One lesson in an elementary school reader used after 1911 was *Ikimono o kurushimeruna* (Do not be cruel to living things), another was *Ikimono o awareme* (Be compassionate to living things).[57] Their value was made apparent by some Japanese on the march. A corporal named Koury saw another Japanese "pull an American into the shade and kind of prop him up and wipe his brow off and everything." After getting out of the train at Capas, Manny Lawton remembered that the guards "seemed sympathetic. Prisoners who fell by the roadside were picked up and given rides into camp by truck. To my knowledge, no one was clubbed or shot in that last eight miles of the Death March." On the last leg of the march, from Capas to Camp O'Donnell, Clarence Bramley passed out from an attack of malaria when a Japanese officer "ordered that [he] be placed on a pony-drawn cart with five or six other sick or wounded men." Bill Schuetz, sweating profusely, was stunned when a Japanese guard gave him his fan. The surprised American thanked him and tried to return it, but the Japanese said, "No, you keep."[58]

Some received very personal help. E.R. Fendall, nearing the end of his endurance, fell farther and farther behind, and eventually collapsed under a tree. A Japanese guard saw a *calesa* coming up the road, into which he put a surprised Fendall, then climbed in himself. Together they rode to the head of the column, where the Japanese motioned his prisoner to pay the driver, then got out. Later, again exhausted and unable to walk, other Japanese guards put Fendall on a bull cart, and then on a truck bound for San Fernando. He recalled that on the trip to Capas, the train was not too crowded, with some able to sit in the car, and the guards left the doors open.[59]

Sergeant William Sniezko was just as nonplussed the day before he reached Balanga, utterly at the end of physical endurance. As he lay exhausted, he remembered, a "Japanese officer came up and moved me into the shade of a tree. He told me to rest. Then he had food brought to me ... he let me rest there for two days before he came over again," at which time the officer told him that if he did not move, he would have to kill him. As it happened, the officer was following orders. At Homma's trial, Wachi Takeji described the procedure: "In

9. *Kinds of Kindness*　　　　255

Survivors' postwar bitterness often crowded out memory of such acts of kindness by their conquerors (courtesy Christopher Leet).

cases where ... prisoners were sitting under trees, or who had fallen on the roadside, I had the Japanese soldiers give a hand and carry these prisoners to a place such as beneath the eaves of a building and place them down there."[60]

* * * * *

In one of the two most comprehensive treatments of Japanese wartime cruelty, Gavin Daws makes clear his approach. "For my own part," he wrote, "I have not set out to bash the Japanese with words. I record what POWs say it was like ... with the Japanese physically bashing their prisoners, to the death." Of the Death March, Daws states,

> It was true on the march out of Bataan that every so often along the road a good-hearted Japanese enlisted man, or an honorable sergeant, or even an officer, a warrior of bushido, might behave kindly toward a prisoner, or at least not unkindly—offer a ride on a truck, return loot, show consideration about the pace of the march, come up with a cigarette or a swig of water. But this kind of thing was so unusual that the prisoners took indelible note of it. Receiving a kindness from a Japanese was as rare as winning a prize in a lottery.[61]

Depending on which words one reads, the odds were not as long as Daws supposed.

Twenty years after the war ended, a Marine Corps historian asked one American survivor of Japanese prisons about his experience. Major Paulo Putnam responded, "I would feel better if greater and broader recognition were given to the really surprising number of Japanese who really went far out of their way, and even risked their own safety, to make things a little better for the prisoners."[62] *Osusowake* sharing (literally, "giving away the hem") was deeply ingrained in traditional, group-oriented Japanese society.

The soldiers of the Imperial Japanese Army hailed from villages in the countryside where life was defined by complex webs of obligation. In the world outside the village, those obligations ceased to apply. Along with the brutality of his own training, this sheds considerable light on the nature of the Japanese soldier's occasional cruelty to his captives. The phrase *Tabi no haji o kakizute* (a man away from home feels no shame) speaks volumes about the sense of release Japanese feel when abroad, freed from the often crushing web of mutual obligations at home. Indeed some Japanese guards on the Death March, encountering foreigners outside any frame of reference that was meaningful to them (*soto*), sometimes took full advantage of interactions without consequences and behaved with considerable barbarity.

For Japanese, obligations exist at many levels—to parents and siblings, to the community, to the larger concentric circles in which the individual finds himself and, in 1942, to the emperor. *Sekinin* (responsibility, obligation) is at the center of life, and Japanese are careful indeed about adding additional relationships defined by favor and counter-favor, entanglements from which there is no easy escape. Fulfilling one's obligations is the essence of *ninjo*—humaneness, sympathy, or understanding all bound up in the word's meaning.[63]

Outside of that web of obligation, just as they were free to be cruel, Japanese were equally free to offer kindness, even to an enemy whose defeat represented "purification" of Asia. Indeed the virtue of *nasake* (sympathy, pity) was alive and well among the guards on the march. In this new environment kindness could be offered without complication, to men literally passing through their lives. From the Japanese point of view, these men had no understanding of the complexity of human relations. They were disconnected from all that gave humanity its meaning in Japan, an indigent mob, a palette on which figures of both cruelty *and* kindness could be drawn and erased.

On a long flight one will sometimes speak freely and reveal intimate details to the person sitting in the next seat because it is cathartic and without consequence; goodbye upon debarkation is final. Foreigners in Japan exist in this kind of nether world, one that brings with it certain advantages. Late one night, after a long day on a ski trip in the Japan Alps, I found myself listening with grim fascination to a long diatribe by a man named Tsuruta I had just met that day. His English was excellent, and as we faced each other in our futons, *he held forth in that language about his job at Matsushita Electric, how much he disliked his manager and one particularly disagreeable colleague, how he hated the interminable meetings he had to attend and how, at those meetings, he was forbidden to express his opinion. Such complaints back home in Nagoya were unthinkable.*

One observer stated that "Japan can feed twelve soldiers on the daily food cost of one American private.... Give a soldier a few pounds of rice, a little tea, and he is self-sustaining for days ... independent of canteens and food kitchens."[64] Inured to hardships as a recruit, having suffered through the privations and hardships of a three month campaign, the guards who made their way north with American prisoners might have been expected to view American hunger with disdain. Even so, the occasional distribution of food began at the surrender, when Colonel Takasaki gave General Edward King heated evaporated milk, warm San Miguel beer and cigarettes. Shortly after surrender, Ed Betts recalled, "our captors were not too bad to us. The Japanese tank commander ... asked for our C.O. and then asked Lieutenant Markham how long it had been since we had anything to eat. The lieutenant told him three days. A Japanese warrant officer had 12 cases of our field rations. He lined us up and we each received six cans of meat and beans."[65]

Tom Motosko made the unlikely claim that he went nine days without food. Perhaps, but numerous other Americans received victuals throughout the Hike. Bernard Fitzpatrick's guard shared jarred pickles with him, gave him water from his canteen, showed him "a blister on his right heel," then "pulled some papers out of his pocket and carefully showed [him] worn photos of his wife and their two small children." At a *barrio* in Cabcaben, a Japanese guard offered Lester Tenney a can of fish and Captain John Spainhower, prostrate with sunstroke, was carried into medical shack at Orani where "There was a Jap, I don't know who he was, brought me a sort of broth, it was kind of green and seaweedy." Robert Levering received biscuits from one of his guards. Corban Alabado remembered that on his march, Japanese supplied the prisoners with "barrels of boiled *camotes* (sweet potatoes), which they dumped on the road for us to pick up and eat."[66]

One witness at Homma's trial noted that Japanese guards helped themselves to the food in Filipino houses, and unguarded POWs perhaps had at least some of the same opportunities. Food sometimes appeared on the march in unexpected places, and sometimes Japanese guards did not prevent their prisoners from taking it. One group of soldiers crowded into small field near Balanga, found turnips, and everyone dug for them while the Japanese watched, leaving them unmolested. Mel Madero remembered prisoners from his column breaking and running into sugar cane field, "a vast army of locusts descending on a field to devour it" while his guards looked on without interfering. Pinky Martin's experience was similar. Tired and willing to risk bolting into nearby sugar cane fields, Martin ran for the food, and as he fell back into column, "one of the Japanese guards grabbed his arm and helped him catch up." Holding his stalk of sugar cane, he distributed pieces to others in need. Later, as Martin and another soldier helped a severely wounded chaplain, they noticed that a Japanese guard purposely ignored them as they fell farther and farther behind.[67]

Colonel Sato Tokutaro, one officer responsible for the disposition of POWs, stated, "I heard that the soldier escorts gave stalks of sugar cane to POWs suffering from thirst and let them suck the juice and that they took various other pains and I rejoiced in the fact that they were true soldiers of the Japanese army."[68] James Murphy might have agreed. He wandered off the route of the march, found a cache of guava fruits, was lugging them back to his mates, and encountered a Japanese who allowed him to distribute the fruit as the men started north again. James Gautier remembered that his guards herded his group into a field, and allowed the men to dig up vegetables: "After eating as many as we could find, we actually felt refreshed." Sam Moody's friend O.C. Jones had drunk contaminated water, and Moody was helping him along when a Japanese soldier approached. Moody patted his stomach, whereupon the Japanese "looked around to see if anyone was watching. He took a little package from his sack. It contained five cookies. He gave one cookie to each of us, smiled and turned away."[69]

Another example was that of Harold Feiner, whose young Japanese guard at first screamed and refused to allow an American doctor to remove the shrapnel in his leg. After checking to see if any other guards were watching, he allowed the doctor to proceed. Then, Feiner remembered, "The Jap guard came up to me during the night and gave me a cup of sweetened chocolate, tasted like milk." In fractured English, the guard spoke to him, "'Someday me go to Hollywood, me going to be a movie star' ... All through the night he gave me something, because he knew I needed strength."[70]

In the heat of the Filipino summer, nothing was more important than water, and its apparent absence forms a *leitmotif* of many veterans' narratives—it is clear that many Americans died in the frenzied melees at water sites throughout the Death March. John H. Poncio was one who well remembered the lack of water, one of dozens of survivors who described the heat and humidity, their thirst as they passed the artesians along the road, the Japanese refusal to allow a drink, and the horrible substitute of the polluted water for men desperate with thirst.[71]

Yet other accounts bespeak a far different reality. Those survivors like Bert Bank, who claimed that "for the entire five days the Japanese gave us no water at all" must have gotten water somewhere, else they would have died. Lack of supervision meant access to plentiful water from the numerous artesian wells that so many of the men described on the route. Eddy Laursen remembered simply walking off the road. His buddy was sick and needed a rest, so he saw a Filipino hut on top of a hill, where they found six Japanese soldiers with the same idea. They allowed Laursen and his friend to rest in the shade and get "all the water we wanted." Mel Madero stated, "Occasionally on 'the march' when we were crossing a stream and the guards were not near, I managed to get some water in my canteen."[72]

Many soldiers recorded being allowed access to water in ways that suggest a protean relationship between guard, prisoner and life-sustaining water. Some remembered "kind guards who gathered canteens of the prisoners and filled them with water." Others allowed groups of POWs access to water where it was found. Near Limay, William Garleb remembered "a string of guys ... came off the regular road and went down past me to the stream to get water. The guards allowed them to do that." When prisoners cooperated, guards were more generous with permission. Gene Boyt recalled "kind guards who allowed prisoners to sit down when the column was stopped or to draw water from community wells in the various barrios. These surprising acts of compassion spared American lives. They also kept me from viewing every guard as evil."[73] Not all Americans were forced to march past the bubbling artesian wells along the road. A private named Burns commented on the differences among guards:

> [M]y group was pretty fortunate because this guard told us we could break ranks whenever we came to one of those artesian wells ... and get some water. So the word was passed back. He said that we could not fill our canteens because the holes were too small and it would take too long to fill them, but we could take our canteen cup and get water. The other guards didn't bother our guard.... I do remember this Jap guard pulling a couple of guys out by the shirt because they didn't go and get water.[74]

Some guards showed flexibility even after POWs demonstrated lack of discipline. Colonel Irvin Alexander remembered that near Orion, prisoners saw a spigot, rushed toward it, but were driven away by a Japanese. "After a few moments, " however, "the sentry relented so that we all were able to fill our canteens before we resumed the march." During rests, "every three of four hours, they might let you line up and get some water from a hydrant and fill your canteen. Sometimes they did, and sometimes they didn't."[75]

While some guards intermittently denied their prisoners water, others cooperated in ways that can only reflect recognition of prisoners' basic needs. When he got off the train at Capas for the last trek to Camp O'Donnell, Oliver Allen stated, "One thing stands out in my memory: I saw a Japanese guard send a Filipino man to fill a bucket of water for us."

In other circumstances, Japanese made water readily available. When he arrived at San Fernando, Alvin Poweleit recalled that he was fed a "large quantity of rice (brown) sugar and salt, and drank as much water as possible." In the cramped quarters at Lubao, Japanese guards allowed many to drink from two artesians, and afterward some Americans lay "in runoff ditch, letting the cool water soothe their aching bodies."[76]

Once, I sat with a Japanese friend over coffee and swapped folktales we had heard as kids. I managed to describe Paul Bunyan and John Henry with relative accuracy, and I answered many probing questions about St. Nick's attitude toward good versus bad little boys and girls. The reason for his focus on Christmas became clear as he told me of his fear of "liar's hell." He remembered his father telling him of such Buddhist beliefs—of children who did not eat condemned to eternal hunger, of others screaming in eternal torment. He learned that this special hell, ruled by a king called En-ma-san, *awaited liars, where he kept assiduous count of all lifetime's lies, showed the scroll of record, and brought the mendacious forward to have their tongues cut out.* "Kowai, tottemo kowai dattayo" (It was really scary), *he said, shuddering.*

Even in the chaos wrought by Japanese disorganization, logistical arrangements were occasionally adequate, obviating tension between guard and prisoner. Lest any student of the Death March believe that the Japanese deliberately withheld water, Dick Bilyeu's experience is instructive. He remembered a visit from a Japanese water truck on the first night of his march—"The water tanker was capable of holding several hundred gallons of water and the Japs were allowing us to drink as much as we wanted and fill our canteens if we had them ... the truck remained for what seemed like hours and those with canteens filled them for later." The next day Bilyeu recalled a second Japanese water truck, the day after that, a third, the next morning, a fourth, and a fifth and final visit that night. Another telling incident comes from Clemens Kathman, who after arriving in an open field, was

> directed to sit down in a sort of circle while [the Japanese] took up station just outside the circle. After a while, four carts, pulled by carabao, carrying large drums, approached the area. The guards situated them in four different areas around the circle and directed five or six of us at a time, to come to a cart. The barrels were filled with water. We did not question the quality, but as fast as we could, filled our canteens and moved on so others could do the same. After everyone had made his trip to the cart, the guards motioned that there was still water and come and get it. I think most of us were able to fill our canteens before the guards had the cart driver to move on.

Often those who could not fully slake their thirst during the day did so at night. Alf Larson related, "We were able to get water at night by collecting canteens. You didn't dare get too many or they would rattle. We would handle them very carefully and quietly sneak off to an artesian well. You held a canteen under water and filled two or three of them. Then we came back and passed them around."[77]

* * * * *

Further echoes of a pre-militarist Japan appear elsewhere. Even *Kore dake Yomeba Ware wa Kateru*, though laden with simplistic, racist and imperialistic propaganda, stated that "pillaging, molesting women, and the heedless slaughter or maiming of people who offer no resistance, or any action which may sully the reputation of Japan as a country of moral rectitude, should be condemned by all in the strongest possible terms." The imperial soldier was admonished to "refrain from well-meant expressions of [his] own opinions, to respect the native traditions and customs, and to avoid unnecessary friction." He was reminded that good behavior reflected well on his family, and that as a returning a miscreant he would be shamed.[78]

During the campaign, there was at least some evidence of mutual recognition of humanity between enemies. In the town of Pilar, Alf Larson's unit had an informal arrangement with the Japanese—each side stopped and filled their canteens with molasses at a designated location with the tacit approval of the other. Even after surrender, such material exchange continued. While many prisoners remembered losing their personal effects during the numerous shakedowns throughout the march, the transfer of property sometimes took the form of unexpected barter with captors who, at least in theory, had the power of life and death over them. Abie Abraham saw men exchanging their watches with the guards for water while another passed out cigarettes. At Balanga, an entrepreneurial guard was doing a brisk business: "For a ring or a watch or some other item he would take a man's canteen, fill it with water, and return it to him. Then he would quickly look around for the next bidder for his service. Many of the prisoners got water that way, and the Japanese guard ended up with enough merchandise to open a small jewelry store."[79]

Occasionally the transactions favored the POWs. Calvin Graef had been stationed in El Paso before shipping out to the islands, from whence he and his friends visited Juarez. There they bought "Pancho Villa" money, then completely worthless, but printed in huge denominations. When a Japanese guard found one of Graef's friends carrying a one thousand dollar note, his "eyes bugged out." He took it, and then returned "two or three hundred dollars in Philippine *pesos*." Later, another bill's exchange with a different guard brought the same result; Graef thought this "the epitome of the American dream." Tom Gage enjoyed a brief moment of levity when a "bowlegged little fellow" took his field bag. For the next several miles he smiled, thinking that the only prize the Japanese got was his copy of Hemingway's *For Whom the Bell Tolls*.[80] In light of its main themes, no doubt Gage considered the novel well lost.

Sometimes the equation involved labor or skill. Lieutenant Hadley Watson carried a Japanese guard's pack, and in return got "a piece of cracker and some of that long-haired tea.... Later, we got down to a creek and this Jap guard let me go down and get some water. He gave me all kinds of privileges for toting his pack." Edward Thomas was a signal corps engineer, and his first encounter with the Japanese was anything but expected. Just after the surrender, he took up with an English-speaking Japanese lieutenant who needed a driver. Thomas agreed not to try to escape, and his captor rewarded him with food and cigarettes. Later, he led Thomas to an *ersatz* sumo ring where several well-muscled Japanese were fighting. Invited to wrestle himself, he disrobed to his underwear and imitated the ritual (foot stamping) whereby the wrestlers drove away evil spirits, and commenced. Though the bout ended with Thomas thrown handily to the ground and the referee declared him the loser, his Japanese onlookers applauded his effort enthusiastically. His host said, "They like you."[81]

On his way to Orani at the head of a column of U.S. prisoners, General Albert M. Jones was approached by a Japanese two-star private, who pointed to Jones' two stars, indicating the same rank. The two men "joked back and forth in sign language." The Japanese noticed Jones' watch, and began to take it, whereupon Jones noticed the private's watch. He grasped his captor's wrist and suggested a trade, the Japanese nodded and the men completed the transaction. Some Japanese were interested in specifically trading for American goods. Robert

Haney recalled that Japanese "showed great interest in things American—cars, clothes, leather, glasses, false teeth, Deanna Durbin, Shirley Temple, Western songs—anything American. When they stole the pictures of our mothers, sisters, girlfriends, their interest seemed to be more in the background than in the women. The Japanese soldier's hatred of Americans did not extend to *things* American."[82]

One American airman, holding out hope during the campaign, concluded a letter to his wife with a bible quote, "A thousand shall fall at thy side ... but it shall not come nigh thee."[83] Come nigh to some it did, but bibles had a more practical use. Soldiers were issued a pocket-sized, condensed version, whose editors generously included a selection of patriotic hymns (including "America the Beautiful" and other favorites) and psalms thought to be of special use to those at the front. Men plagued by inappropriate fantasies could read the "Prayer for a Pure Heart"; those facing a crisis, discouraged, lonely and fearful, weary, or fearing death were directed to other appropriate verses. Timothy chapter three was suggested to those facing irretrievably bad situations—"This know also, that in the last days perilous times shall come," bringing men without "natural affection, trucebreakers, false accusers ... fierce, despisers of those that are good." After deriving whatever comfort they could from the verses, soldiers found that the 3" × 4 ½" rice paper pages were just right for rolling cigarettes. They also discovered that not all their captors answered to the biblical description of their enemies.

Americans who kept their bibles found them useful talismans on the Death March. The first time he was ordered to empty his pockets after capture, Red Allen produced his, and offered it to his captor, who declined to take it. "Instead he put his hands together and bowed his head in reverence." Thereafter, he always offered the book, and found the result the same. Pinky Martin remembered the Japanese allowing him to keep his New Testament, thinking "Maybe they were superstitious about touching the holy book." Others recalled that Japanese "seemed ... to fear anything supernatural, so the men with religious medals often saved both them and their attached dog tags. Many also kept their rosaries, and the Indians in the New Mexico National Guard salvaged some of their jewelry by convincing their captors that turquoise was sacred." Sometimes during the shakedowns that punctuated the march, Americans persuaded guards to return stolen goods. Colonel Ray O'Day recalled a Japanese soldier who, after taking, then returning a personal item, looked at him and said, "So sorry. So sorry!"[84]

* * * * *

So many moments of sanity and comity punctuated the two weeks of the Hike. One occurred on the day of surrender, when Claude Fraleigh saw a smiling Japanese leap from a tank and run toward him. Fearing the worst, he was relieved to find that the soldier had been a bellhop at the Tokyo hotel Fraleigh and his wife visited before the war; the Japanese remembered the hefty tip the couple had given him. Another occurred somewhere near Lubao, where a guard smiled at Sam Moody and said in English, "You have wife." Moody agreed, and the Japanese said, "Me have wifey. You look" and produced a picture from his wallet. Moody pronounced the woman "beautiful" and though the guard did not know the word, he "seemed pleased."[85]

Margaret Atwood once observed, "War is what happens when language fails," but the use of language, however minimal, is not without potential benefit between enemies. During the militaristic 1930s, Japanese students studied English for about five hours a week. Even so, John Morris, living in Japan during the two years before Pearl Harbor, remembered that after years of instruction, many were "quite unable to frame the simplest sentence correctly" and that it was "by no means uncommon for a Japanese teacher of English never to have heard the language spoken by a native." Until the outbreak of war with the U.S., interested Japanese could listen to English lessons on the radio at 6:30 a.m. The yield was slim. Morris once recalled seeing a young man on a train, working through cards with English words on them, memorizing vocabulary as so many students were expected to do. Morris was stunned to see the word *floccinaucinihilipification* which, the young man assured him contemptuously, was known to every Japanese schoolboy.[86]

Some were drawn, however awkwardly, to the study of English, but even among Japanese, clear communication is sometimes difficult. At some level in Japanese culture, there is mistrust of the excessively articulate; some will assert, *Me wa kuchi hodo ni mono o ii* (The eyes say as much as the mouth). Those who have wrestled with the Japanese language find it hard to express such phrases as *sasshi ga yoi* (good at guessing another's feeling), *omoiyari ga aru* (considerate of others' feelings), *shinsetsu no oshiuri* (forcing kindness on others), *arigata-meiwaku* (annoyance caused by someone's unwelcome kindness). Japanese themselves sometimes call this *sasshi no bunka* (guessing culture).

Whereas "Western culture is based on the distinction between the observer and the observed, on the opposition of the self versus the other, Japanese culture and sentiment show a strong tendency to overcome this distinction by having the self immerse in the other." Guessing the feelings of the other is challenging enough even when sharing a common language. Engaging foreigners in oral intercourse amplifies the problem. Writing in the early 1970s, Suzuki Takao described a survey on the streets of Tokyo which asked people to respond to simple English sentences: "Such behavior as sneaking away, becoming defiant, and grinning are signals of these peoples' attempts to escape a state of mental insecurity brought on by unexpected contact with the unfamiliar and unplaceable."[87]

It seems that some Japanese guards on the Death March may have spoken English to some degree but were reluctant to show this in front of comrades for "fear of being accused of having pro–American sympathies." It is entirely possible that that some POWs encountered Japanese guards, educated in the U.S., who spoke English, but who were "regarded with suspicion ... because they were considered too unreliable for other purposes." During one rest period on the march, one Japanese non-com announced to a group of prisoners in perfect English that he had gone to school in Chicago and asked if the group "would like to know what the Japanese thought of the United States," whereupon he began beating one of the assembly.[88]

Just weeks after moving to Japan, clutching my minuscule vocabulary with grammatical desperation, I found myself on a national railways train from Himeji back to Ashiya. Across from me was a young family—father, mother, and two children. Neither of the parents could speak a word of English beyond hello and goodbye, so we made do with goodwill and my fractured pronunciation. We were delighted with each other, sharing dried squid, "pocky" chocolate, crackers wrapped in seaweed, Asashi beer and smiles. I showed the kids American coins, we drew maps and pictures on napkins as we jolted along. They got off at Suma, and I rode home, still glowing. Japan was so new and, even if just for a few hours, I felt at home in another hemisphere.

9. *Kinds of Kindness* 263

Whether Japanese knew some English and refused to use it, or knew none, the result was the same. If Japanese knew only a few words of English, Americans knew even fewer of Japanese, especially at this early stage of the war when the two sides were just coming into contact. Irvin Alexander stated that the difficulties of the march "were aggravated by the vast differences between the Americans and Japanese in language, temperament, customs, manners, training and discipline, which all combined, created a colossal misunderstanding." Abel Ortega recalled, "On this march it was really hard for us to understand what they wanted us to do. We wanted to learn their language, but under these circumstances it was hard. There were many a skull cracked by the butt of the Japanese rifle if you didn't do what they wanted. Some of the guys would just stand there and try to figure out what they wanted us to do."[89]

Yet even a single well-placed word could be useful. On the third day of his march, Anthony Czerwien saw a Japanese officer riding in a Buick driven by a childhood friend, who stopped to greet him. At that moment, the Japanese pulled his sidearm and threatened to shoot Czerwien, whereupon his friend screamed, *tomodachi!* (friend), an exclamation that saved his life. Alvin Poweleit was another with at least some Japanese language ability. A doctor with a tank battalion from Kentucky, he had acquired some rudimentary Japanese on the ship on the way to the Philippines and continued his study with help of the few prisoners taken by the army—he referred to working with a Japanese tutor on the interesting date of December 6, 1941. His "vocabulary increased to the point where [he] could understand short, simple sentences" which he employed throughout the march. Stanley Falk, the author of the only previous scholarly study of the Death March, claimed that "this ability obviously not only preserved his own life but also the lives of many others with whom he served on Bataan."[90]

Poweleit used his Japanese right away when he was lined up at Mariveles to be shaken down. As the march began, he had some chipped beef and cans of sardines in his pocket, and when the Japanese reached for the items, the American told him he was *Isya* (doctor). The Japanese asked, *Kusuri Isya?* (medicine doctor?) He answered *Hai*, and the soldier allowed him to keep his food. Later, another guard sought to relive Poweleit of his diary, whereupon he told his captor it was *kami benzyo* (paper for the toilet), and was allowed to keep it. Food and water came easier to Poweleit as well. Near Limay, he asked for water (*mizu kudasai*) and persuaded his guards to allow his men access to an artesian well in small groups, getting as much as needed.

Later he asked for rice in Japanese and a guard brought him and his cohort six tubs. The grateful men "lined up in an orderly manner and everyone had about a half pint of cooked rice." He then thanked the guard, *Arigato, Nipponzin Heitai Taihen Yoi* (Thank you, Japanese soldier very good) after which the guard left him with a pack of cigarettes.[91] Once inside the boxcar from San Fernando, he said *"waruii kuuki"* (terrible air) to a guard, who then opened the door six inches to allow fresh air in. There was even room for a bit of black humor—at Lubao Poweleit pointed to the enclosure into which prisoners were being herded and said to the guard *ookii bensyo* (big toilet). The guard laughed and said, *ookii jodan* (big joke).[92]

At the start of the Death March in Mariveles, John Dempsey, who had studied Japanese at the University of the Philippines, found his language ability useful as well. As Americans stood in line and Japanese rifled through their belongings, one guard saw a pair of Japanese shoestrings. With Dempsey translating, the guard asked where he had obtained them, and the man answered "I got them from a dead Jap." Aware of the danger of this admission, Dempsey changed it, telling the guard in Japanese that item came from a trade with a Japanese for some canned goods. At first the guard refused to believe the story and prepared to bayonet him, but when Dempsey insisted, the guard relaxed.[93]

John Bumgarner observed that "the most obnoxious trait of our captors was their habit, whenever nature called, of squatting in their tracks and relieving themselves." Others on the march claimed that Americans were not afforded that opportunity, their Japanese guards refusing to allow stops to attend to the calls of nature. The frequency of this is subject to the same doubt as other assertions, but Alf Larson and Lloyd Mills, among a few others, claimed this to be the case, with both offering the "global perspective" described earlier. "If anyone had to," he recalled, "they went right in their drawers as they walked. If you stopped or got off to the side, you would have been bayoneted or shot." Mills recalled, "you would just release wherever you were. Generally right on yourself, or somebody else if they happened to be in the way."[94]

In at least some cases, Alvin Poweleit interceded for those walking with him, telling them to ask guards to "let them use the *benzyo* when they wanted to go to the toilet. This worked well with most of the guards. Sometimes they would say, *daiben* or *shoben*."[95] Later, while giving out sulfapyridine tablets, a Japanese guard leveled his rifle at him, whereupon he pointed to himself and said "*Isya-kusuri heitai-taihen byoki—Sikiri* (medicine doctor, very sick soldiers with dysentery). The Japanese put up his rifle and walked away. On another occasion, he prevented a guard from taking one of his possessions by covering it with mud. When the Japanese reached for it, Poweleit told him, "*taihen byoki-takusan daiben shoben* (very sick, much feces and urine)" whereupon the guard "raised his hands and backed away."[96]

While some accounts maintain that all were treated alike on the march, evidence makes clear that guards did distinguish between POWs to some extent. On the road near Balanga, a Filipino captain and physician named Jesus Mendoza bent to tend an American with an infected wound. An observer later recalled, "The Japanese let him alone. They seemed to have great respect for doctors." Calvin Jackson, a physician who had fallen in with the horde of prisoners by mistake, arrived at Balanga exhausted. There he met a Japanese officer, to whom he showed his Red Cross armband and explained that he was a doctor and needed to go back to his hospital near Cabcaban. The officer put him in a car, told him to lie on the floor, and drove him several hours back down the coast to Hospital #2 at Cabcaban, whereupon he let Jackson out with the parting admonition, "You go, do not tell." In the confusion of the final weeks, Japanese bombers hit Hospital #1, killing or wounding more than 100. Wainwright was outraged, but the Japanese apologized immediately over Manila radio, stating that the raid was unintentional.[97]

John Bumgarner was a physician at the same hospital and he watched anxiously as the Japanese came in and established rules for U.S. staff and the 7,000 Filipino patients: No pilfering of supplies, no straying off hospital grounds, with an ominous sign that read, "Anyone caught violating this rule will be shooted." One night Bumgarner went with a staff member to a quartermaster depot in search of food and shoes. On his way back he encountered three Japanese soldiers, but instead of the bullets they expected, they received playful jibes as the Japanese mocked the size of their feet and sent them on their way.[98]

For Americans, there was a far more shocking form of protection. All who saw such behavior were stunned to see Japanese officers punish their own men who committed transgressions against POWs. Ralph Levenberg recalled a guard trying to take his glasses when a Japanese officer interceded, telling him in good English to keep his glasses safe, as he would "need them for a very long time." As Levenberg moved on he watched the officer call the guard to attention and beat him with his sword. Ray Hunt remembered that a guard had taken and crushed the glasses of a sergeant, whereupon a Japanese officer "grabbed the guard and knocked him down with a blow from his fist, one of the commonest modes of enforcing discipline in the Japanese army."[99]

On another occasion, two Americans were standing in line in Mariveles just after the surrender, when a Japanese private took a ring from soldier named Tonelli. A Japanese officer saw this, became enraged and "smashed the enlisted man in the face with his fist and politely handed the ring back." Tonelli's friend had lost an amethyst ring to a different private, and the officer found the offending private, struck him several times, and returned it. He then offered a friendly warning to the pair of surprised Americans: "If you have anything of personal value, hide it."[100] A particularly astonishing incident occurred on Dick Bilyeu's trek:

> Some ten or fifteen yards in front of where I was walking, an American soldier was reeling from side to side.... He was making the maximum effort to remain upright.... There was a guard near him, and he glared at the unfortunate man. Once again he fell ... the guard calmly ran him through with his bayonet. The guard stepped back out of the line of the march, took a cloth from his back pocket, and wiped the blood from the blade. At that moment a military command car pulled alongside. The guard stopped cleaning as an officer jumped from the car. He had witnessed this atrocity. The officer stepped in front of the soldier, stood him at stiff attention, stared directly into his eyes, then removed his sidearm and placed the barrel directly between his eyes and pulled the trigger.[101]

Even in their confusion, the Americans who saw such behavior might have been grateful.

* * * * *

On day three of Gene Boyt's march northward, he recorded what to him was a fascinating incident:

> We were stopped along the road while the guards completed a shift change. As one of the young Japanese walked away, he paused beside a very sick man on the verge of collapse a couple of rows ahead of me. Without making eye contact, the guard whispered, "I'm sorry." Then he walked away.... I thought about it for a moment and arrived at the only logical explanation for what I had heard. The young Japanese soldier must have spent considerable time in America.... I assumed that, much like me, he was a captive.

At another point on the Hike, Franklin Lacoste pleaded for water, holding out his cup to passing Japanese soldier. When the Japanese filled it, his companion said, "I bet that Jap was American-educated.... Or maybe he's a Jap soldier who just committed an act of treason by having some pity."[102]

Lacoste and Boyt wrongly assumed that any Japanese kindness emanated from Western civilization. Some Japanese were, nevertheless, prisoners. The guard who apologized was one Plato might have described as a wise man caught in terrible times, one who "when he sees the others filled with lawlessness," refuses to commit the crimes of his fellows, who takes refuge behind a wall until times change. Those who treated POWs with consideration, even kindness, answered not to "Western" standards of behavior. Instead they were human standards. Scores, hundreds, thousands of Americans made it from Mariveles to Camp O'Donnell unbloodied. Many experienced mercy and kindness from men who offered their captives a different face.

One of the classic memoirs of the Holocaust is Primo Levi's *Survival in Auschwitz*. Four decades later, Levi was moved to tap a different pool of memories, ones that evoked "the few, the different, the ones in whom (if only for a moment) [he] had recognized the will and capacity to react, and hence a rudiment of virtue." *Moments of Reprieve* is a list of incidents of camp life—a Spanish gypsy asking Levi to transcribe a letter to his lover, Levi and a friend attempting to hide a package of chocolates, the mockery of a German prisoner for attempting to conceal a bad case of lice, and other stories about refugees outside the camp. Levi concluded, "In telling this story after forty years, I'm not trying to make excuses for Nazi Germany. One human German does not whitewash the innumerable inhuman or indifferent ones, but it does have the merit of breaking a stereotype."[103]

Such stereotypes need breaking. The number of humane Japanese guards and the catalog of their acts cannot be known with any more precision than that of those who were brutal. But clearly, references to that kindness—in survivors' accounts whose central purpose was to highlight cruelty—suggests a new dimension of the Death March. In spite of the closing of Japan's educational system in the 1930s, the socialization explicit in the Imperial Japanese Army's brutal training, in spite of the racism based on notions of the army's mission to "purify," the simple-minded jingoism and the resulting attitudes toward prisoners and surrender, in spite of the urge for revenge against a stubborn enemy who had inflicted severe casualties on their host, some Japanese answered to a different standard of behavior. Indeed, in the obligation-free vacuum of the Death March could be found the virtues of tolerance, comity and even kindness.

Conclusion

Our obedience to the king wipes the crime out of it for us. —Shakespeare, *Henry V*

Now, at this distance, what might we reasonably conclude about what has come to be called the Death March? The Fil-American army, though undisciplined and poorly led, was able to hold out for three months in large measure because its Japanese enemy rejected the implications of modernity and remained committed to primitive battle tactics. Without question, the Death March after surrender was not deadly to most of its participants. Of the 94 percent of Americans who survived, some arrived in Camp O'Donnell after riding all or part of the way after as little as thirty-six hours. Others walked, with many variations in their experience. MacArthur's strategic miscalculations, the resulting lack of supplies and the debilitated condition of the men by April contributed to many deaths. Others died in the chaotic clash of Japanese and American culture at the watering sites.

Beyond this, the often exaggerated accounts of the men who wrote decades later tell us as much about the men themselves, their circumstances and their bitterness, as they do about the experience itself. At Homma's trial George Ott, one of the defense counsels, stated in his closing arguments,

> Undoubtedly there was mistreatment of the prisoners along this route; I don't think there can be any question about it. I don't think it could be anything near like the picture what the Prosecution presented. I think they presented a very extreme picture, and that if the facts are eventually known, it would not be that picture.[1]

The verdict of time and a deeper analysis of the sources confirm Ott's conclusions.

Even so, questions remain. Men died on the Death March, some of them killed by bayonets, wielded by an alien Japanese enemy. To Winston Churchill, addressing the U.S. Congress in December 1941, the Japanese seemed infinitely mysterious. It was, he stated, "difficult to reconcile Japanese action with prudence or even sanity." A half century earlier, Lafcadio Hearn was equally baffled:

> The whole of the Japanese mental superstructure evolves into forms having nothing in common with Western psychological development.... The ideas of this people are not our ideas; their sentiments are not our sentiments; their ethical life represents for us regions of thought and emotion as yet unexplored, or perhaps long forgotten.[2]

The regions of the Japanese soldier's thought and behavior were defined by a world where cruelty was normal. He came to maturity in an environment where the individual existed in a fundamentally different relationship to those around him, and he had little or no understanding of any values higher than those of the state, expressed in the person of the emperor. Beyond even this reality, imperial soldiers were brutalized by their military training and, in turn, sometimes brutalized their prisoners. Moreover, Japanese sensibilities were, and remain, defined by a flexible, pragmatic morality in which individual responsibility for action is minimal.

* * * * *

Few systems of oppression survive without being rooted in some form of justification. In Japan in the 1930s, this took the form of casting military service in terms the recruit understood above all else—the hierarchical family and his obligations to its members, both above and below. General Iwane Matsui, the commander of a Japanese force in Shanghai, expressed his duty in China using this vocabulary:

> The struggle between Japan and China was always a fight between brothers in the "Asian family." ... We do not do this because we hate them, but on the contrary because we love them too much. It is just the same as in a family when an elder brother has taken all that he can stand from his ill-behaved younger brother and has to chastise him in order to make him behave properly.[3]

Such logic found rigorous application in the barracks. There recruits were told that they were part of a great family that lived and fought together, with the emperor at its head.

In the 1930s the army produced a series of postcards, illustrated and designed to promote a comforting message, showing recruits being sent off by their kin, enjoying barracks life, and doing favors for the more senior members of camp.[4] Just before induction, the War Office sent a "letter of instruction" to the home of the soldier-to-be. Its congratulatory contents read in part:

> When your son and brother enters the barracks the officers of the company will take your place looking after his welfare. We will be to him as a stern father and a loving mother.... We want to be able to teach him in such a way that he ... realize the highest hope of a member of our race.

The letter asked those at home to fill out a detailed form containing questions about the recruit's "personal history and character and the environment of his home." The father was further assured of the regiment's concern that his son

> become a good and faithful soldier ... and put his whole heart into fulfilling the mission of the Imperial Army. On the day your son enters the barracks, we trust that you will accompany him in order that we may meet you and have an intimate talk with you.

Respectfully Yours,
(Commanding Officer)
Imperial Japanese Army

The first drill in new uniforms was then held before family and friends. Since each unit was taken from one area of Japan, recruits were surrounded by those they knew; pressure not to disgrace one's village was immense.[5] According to the *Guntai naimusho* (army handbook for squad administration) the barracks was the soldier's new family hearth, a place where "together soldiers share hardships and joys, life and death ... the company is one household in the one village of the regiment." Second year soldiers were older brothers, and in such an environment, superiors naturally treated their subordinates "as if the latter are of the same flesh and blood."[6]

In *The Origins of Totalitarianism*, Hannah Arendt suggested that a dictatorship can only be built on a popular basis of support. Her observation certainly applied to the visionary statesmen who built Japan into a world power in the late nineteenth century. These men took great care to shape the imperial institution into a mechanism for insuring cooperation for their self-strengthening project, and the militarists in the 1930s easily exploited the population's loyalty to this symbol of the state, indeed the national essence, *kokutai*. The emperor's utility for manipulating commoners is difficult to exaggerate. To the population at large, "the emperor was not merely the supreme symbol of the state, the Japanese equivalent of the American flag; he was also the semi-divine father-figure of a cohesive Japanese *völkisch* community that excluded outsiders." On the emperor coalesced a type of nationalism that bore race at its core: "One might best describe the attitude of Japanese to the figure who unified their nationalism as similar to that of a loyal, filial, nationalistic, and religiously devout Britisher to his employer, father, king, *and* God."[7]

Hirohito was the ultimate *pater familias*, and the army made clear its recruits' direct connection to him, a way of fully exploiting the cultural appeal of harmony within the family, so powerful in Japanese culture. As symbolic head of that family, he was also its commander, accountable to neither the government nor the people. All were now equal, and equally liable to service to the emperor, the touchstone of loyalty among all Japanese. Recruits rarely questioned their duty; their letters home suggest that "no peasant soldier raised any doubt about why he had to die for the emperor, any more than he questioned why he had to work to support his parents, wife, and children. Both duties were simply taken for granted."[8]

A symbol invested with this kind of meaning was not to be taken lightly. John Morris, a resident of Tokyo before Pearl Harbor, noted that when the emperor came down the street, people were expected to avert their gaze and all windows above his level were shuttered to prevent anyone looking down on him. The guards who walked with American POWs attended schools where the portrait of the emperor was an object of religious veneration. The physical location of the portrait—on the eastern side, facing the rising sun—was considered sacred, and all those entering classrooms bowed in this direction. Placement was so important that it defined schools' evacuation procedures in the event of fire; one of the emperor's subjects actually committed suicide to atone for his failure to save a portrait from flames.[9]

In the barracks the emperor was even more of a presence. "It was the absolutely inflexible custom in the army that one should come to attention when the Emperor or anything pertaining to him was mentioned." Each morning all recruits bowed in the direction of the imperial palace before beginning their day's training, and they were told over and over that all equipment, especially their weapons, were gifts from the emperor; the imperial crest on the breech of their rifle reminded all of his generosity. Soldiers were routinely and severely beaten for tiny infractions: "a spot of oil on a rifle, a blemish on a bayonet, a button askew, or dirt on white socks" all meted out in the emperor's name.[10]

* * * * *

An ancient Egyptian, circa 1500 BCE, described a recruit as being "shut up in the barracks. During his training he is always being knocked about. If he makes the least mistake he is beaten, a burning blow on his body, another on his eye, perhaps his head is laid open with a wound. He is battered and bruised with a flogging. On the march ... they hang heavy loads round his neck like that of an ass."[11] Such a description would not be inaccurate in Japan 3500 years later. To be a soldier in the Imperial Japanese Army in 1942 was to stand at the end of a long process by which brutal training and thorough spiritual indoctrination were considered the proper solutions to the nation's defense problems.

In some ways, life in the army did not constitute a severe break with the recruit's previous experience. Beatings and rough physical training were hardly alien to him. In public schools and junior high schools corporal punishment, sometimes severe, was routinely justified as "the rod of love." Such treatment included

> slapping a person across both cheeks, hitting students with a fist, hitting them with bamboo or wooden swords, making them stand whilst holding a heavy object, forcing them to sit erect on their knees, or to run around the playground until they could hardly stand. Sanctions in schools included forcing children to stand barefoot in the snow or be slapped by classmates.

One student, when tested positive for tuberculosis, was compelled to run naked around the school playground and admonished to "use his willpower to drive the [disease] from his body." Collective responsibility for individual transgressions was much in evidence—one young girl brushed hair from her eyes while bowing during an imperial worship ceremony, and each student in the class was hit in the face as punishment.[12]

For a young Japanese, life in the imperial army was a continuation and intensification of what he already knew. Inside the barracks, he encountered a grinding wall of unrelenting brutality that made clear his value as *issen gorin*. He was assigned to a senior private, a *sen yu* (big brother, or fighting companion), and was expected to slavishly perform menial tasks for his "sibling," including cleaning his rifle, polishing his boots, even massaging his back. In this intimate relationship, torture and violence were justified as expressions of "benevolent feelings." Suzuki Murio recalled that he and his fellows "were treated as nothing more than consumable goods." Recruits were told *Soko ni shikkari tatte! Megane o tore!* (Stand firm there! Take your glasses off!) and were beaten until their teeth came out, or their eyes swelled shut. Such benevolence left some nearly deaf or blind, many were knocked unconscious.[13]

If Japanese authorities had not banned it, new recruits might have read Ikeda Kyokugai's semi-documentary work, *Ku? Raku? Shimpei no Seikatsu* (*Agony or Pleasure? A Recruit's Life*) that described grim conditions inside military barracks. Without doubt, *the* salient feature of recruits' life in the barracks was physical punishment, and the capacity to administer physical pain seemed limitless. Beatings, from relatively symbolic slapping to brutal attacks that left scars and even broken bones, were the order of the day, and many accounts of recruits' life in training dwell on this aspect in considerable detail.[14]

A scene from Tasaki's *Long the Imperial Way* illustrates the whimsical omnipotence of the second and third year privates. A drunken senior private, unable to administer his slappings with their intended force, ordered two lines of recruits to slap each other:

> They knew this game well enough and braced themselves for it. "Slap each other! First, start from the front row! ... Each First-year Soldier began slapping his comrade before him ... he heard Yamanaka's drunken voice shouting "Won't you put more strength into it, you fool?" ... Yamanaka kept screaming like a maniac behind Takeo, "Slap faster! Slap faster!"

The punishment continued "until all the faces of the First-year-Soldiers were red and swollen, and the noses of some began to bleed." This would have gone on longer but an officer finally ended the recruits' self-imposed misery.[15]

Kikuyama Hiroo recorded that he and his comrades were beaten with *joka* (leather slippers) and with leather belts. "There were some," he wrote, "who were made to stand for up to two hours and then brutally beaten and kicked senseless because, our seniors said, the serving of rice was too slow." From the moment he arose "there was nothing in the barracks that could not be used as an excuse for being reprimanded."[16]

Beyond the constant beatings, recruits were subjected to a variety of other punishments. One was called "The Crying Cicada," wherein the soldier was forced to hold onto a pillar on which rifles were stacked and make the noise of the insect; unsatisfactory volume meant sure beatings. Another was "Nightingale," where the recruit cried like the bird while repeatedly crawling under the barracks bunks. An apparent variation was "the bush warbler crossing the valley," with its requisite song—*Ho-ho-ke-kyo*. A third, mentioned by several veterans, was "Miss Prostitute." Here the unfortunate was forced to prop his face between rifles arranged vertically, and cry in a high falsetto, "Say mister, come on." If his voice was insufficiently feminine or too quiet, more beatings ensued.

Shikata Masao recalled bunking next to a mentally handicapped recruit named Sumida, who was tormented to the point of wetting the bed. Subjected repeatedly to brutal treatment, Shikada had thoughts of hitting back, but knew that his father, who was his village's chief, would be disgraced. He demurred, once enduring scalding soup poured down his throat, and was subjected to other punishments, such as being forced to lick shoes clean that did not meet the standards of any superior. The only customary recourse was, when working in the kitchen, to scratch one's head vigorously so that dandruff flakes seasoned the *miso* soup and rice served to the tormenters.[17]

One Japanese historian called the Japanese empire "a Kafkaesque state dedicated to the abuse of human rights." Unlike Josef K. in *Der Prozeß*, however, Japanese recruits did not question the purpose of what was happening to them. What appeared to be arbitrary punishment was in fact unrelated to any particular transgression. It was "not based on any system of abstract rules, but only on the whim of their superiors. More often than not, when new recruits were hit or humiliated by their superiors, there were no reasons for the acts other than the need to drive home the necessity of unquestioning obedience." As a result, "anger and contempt were maximized in the socializing agents, while distress, fear and humiliation were maximized in the person socialized."[18]

The beatings were, at least in theory, an expression of love. Officers and non-coms justified their brutality by saying: "I do not beat you because I hate you. I beat you because I care for you. Do you think I perform these acts with hands swollen and bloody in a state of madness?" A senior private asserted that any such beating was "an act of kindness." One recruit recorded that he had, whether from sources sane or kind, received 264 blows during his military service.[19] Kindness of the type specified flowed downward only, from *Joto Hei* (superior private) to *Itto Hei* (first class private) to *Nito Hei* (second class private). Those at the pyramid's bottom "were nonpersons" for whom "the daily routine of barracks life was an unending stream of humiliation and rough treatment."[20]

Lights out carried a stern message: "Oh, you poor recruits!—You will be going to bed in tears again." Without interference from officers, senior privates oversaw "the time of devils," when informal tribunals handed down punishments ranging from mild slappings to the severe and even warped. *Chobatsu* (punishment) was administered by the squad during the hour before lights out, especially dreaded by the new recruits. "in the light of the full moon, the second year soldiers turn into demons." Some recruits, unable to bear the torment, committed suicide.[21]

Ichii Juji entered barracks life a month before the Death March, and his notes contain verses of songs that tell of his desire to escape the punishment simply by surviving long enough to become a second-year soldier:

> Immediately following roll call
>   iron-fisted punishment comes down like rain and hail.
> I crawl into bed, crying miserably,
>   and dream of my mother's face back home.
> Inspection for the first term, second term, third term—
>   The fall exercise has already ended;
> And when, soon, those hateful second-year privates
>   Will leave the company
> Then we will become god-like figures.[22]

For Ichii, the only escape from the brutality was to survive and become a "god-like figure" himself.

I experienced transference during an incident that ended in the only violent physical encounter I ever had in Japan. At a taxi stand late one night in Nishinomiya, I found a very sloppy drunk at the front of the line, in a loud argument with the cabbie. The drunk wanted in; the cabbie would have none of it, and shortly I and the other onlookers learned why—the inebriate vomited copiously over the cab's hood, whereupon the driver bellowed and kicked the man away with vicious blows. The drunk backed away, recovered something like an erect posture, saw me, and started screaming about a foreigner in line, what is a gaijin, ketō *(hairy foreigner) doing in Japan. He came at me full tilt, his assault physical as well as verbal. He left me no choice. I stepped to his left and hit him a hard right, high on his left cheekbone. He went down, gurgling and moaning. No one had interfered. In another minute I was in my cab. Flexing sore knuckles and feeling the need to debrief, I said to my driver,* "Aitsu ga yopparai aho dayo." *After a moment of silence, he replied,* "Shimpai suru koto ja nai yo." *Telling me not to worry about a drunken fool did little to repair my very damaged foreigner's ego.*

Even those on the bottom rung could rely on the passing of a year—the new second-year soldiers inflicted the same punishments on their successors. The psychology was inexorable:

> Where absolute obedience is required on the part of inferiors to their superiors ... those in the relatively inferior positions tend to build up a sense of being suppressed. When this feeling of suppression mounts to a certain point, it tends to produce a displacement.... In strict hierarchical systems, the suppressed affect of a soldier tends to be projected onto his inferior, whose suppressed affect is in turn directed toward his inferior, and so on until the chain reaction reaches the very bottom.[23]

A simple equation, brutality drifting downward. Those "whose own dignity and manhood had been so cruelly violated would hardly refrain from doing the same to defenseless persons under their control. After all, they were just applying what they had learned in basic training."[24] One Bataan veteran understood the logic, even as he decried its results. Ralph Hibbs called the conquering Japanese "ornery yellow bastards, yelling and muttering, with bayonets fixed.... They were sated with the belief of invincibility predestined by a military system resulting in uncontrolled belligerency. Cruelty and bravery were synonymous in the mind of the Japanese soldier."[25]

When the Japanese columns rolled into Mariveles, Bernard Fitzpatrick remembered an exhausted private stumbling and falling, whereupon an officer ordered him to get up. When the soldier remained on the ground, "the officer seized his sword in his scabbard and repeatedly hit the soldier in the head with the ornamental hilt of his sword. Eventually, he strained to his feet, with blood running in furrows down through the sweat and dust on his face." Fitzpatrick knew that "it was a lesson ... to the captured enemy that we will treat him as we treat our own. We can, in honor, do no less." Among POWs' satisfactions was watching such treatment. Sam Moody recalled his amusement while working on the docks of Manila, where he observed what he called the "caste system." There he

> spotted a Jap officer strike another officer in the mouth. The ritual was on. A lower officer was called to the second officer. He was chewed out, then cracked in the face. He turned around and called the name of the nearest sergeant. The sergeant responded ... and was yelled out. Then came the inevitable slap.... The sergeant slapped his nearest corporal. The corporal in turn grabbed the nearest private.

A new prisoner, unfamiliar with the routine, was slapped in turn and then all returned to work.[26]

* * * * *

The scholar and linguist Nakamura Hajime has stated that "Japanese always locate the individual in experience, not in the abstract." Hence, a "person is invariably ... acting in some kind of human relationship, never autonomously." This reality is manifest in the Japanese language, where both "self and other can be expressed only in relational terms."[27] Many observers have commented on the absence of abstract notions of right or wrong in Japanese thinking—that truth exists only in a particular context, within the dynamics of human interaction. One example is the legal system, where the central imperative of conciliation defines dispute resolution. The process has little to do with legal rights, which would be based on individual notions of autonomy, but rather aims to "render highly specific justice, as determined subjectively by the parties to a dispute."

Such a concept of law had little to do with universal principles, since the idea of equality of individuals in the state or before god was absent, as was any clear division between religion and state. Concepts of legality were different in Japan, since

> what determined behavior ... was not primarily a sense of legality, but the consciousness of some force that was higher than they were.... The law was not regarded as some general body of regulations that collectively circumscribed the ruler and the ruled, but simply as a concrete weapon of controls in the hierarchy of authority of which the Emperor was the head.

In this system, morality was based neither on abstract notions of justice nor "an internal sense of right and wrong, nor again any sense of serving the public." Rather, it was "the feeling of being close to the concrete entity known as the Emperor."

The emperor system *in toto* was essentially a "system of irresponsibility" wherein all were responsible to the one immediately above, all the way to the emperor, who was only responsible to his "ancestral gods and goddesses." In this structure, "no one had the opportunity to make a decision which he could consciously recognize as his own, and no one had to take responsibility for the consequences of any decision made or any act committed in the name of the collectivity."[28]

One observer of Japan has suggested that the "Japanese are difficult to understand, not because they are complicated or strange, but because they are so simple."[29] Such simplicity might be understood as resource-poor island nation's search for security. In that quest, Japan has swung, sometimes violently, between extremes. After the West arrived in the 1850s, rabid xenophobia gave way to conditional acceptance of things Western as the nation strove with enormous success to catch up with the imperial powers. Then followed a brief experiment with democracy in the 1920s, then the turn to militarism—the disastrous Greater East Asia Co-Prosperity Sphere. That failure produced broad acceptance of military defeat and stimulated the subsequent quest for national regeneration, a time when stunned Americans were welcomed with questions about democracy and human rights. These shifts from xenophobia, to cosmopolitanism, to democracy, to militarism, to pacifism all suggest a concern with utilitarian values—what works, what is believed to provide security, is of paramount importance.

The soldiers of 1942 were swept along in the strongest of currents, active participants in their nation's racist imperial project, a milieu that encouraged the basest instincts of their tribe. It would seem unlikely indeed to find much goodwill toward Westerners during Japan's violent, militarist experiment. The Pacific War was in many ways the culmination of anti–Western thinking, the associated virulent racism, and intolerance of dissent. Aikawa Takaaki, a teacher at a Baptist mission school during the war, understood himself to be caught in stream of events over which he had no control. "Bataan Death March!" he exclaimed, "We heard about it even in those days. But our military leaders did not make only American captives participate in such [a] march. They made our whole civilian population take part in it! We marched day after day, not knowing our destination nor the time of the end." The young soldier Suzuki Murio agreed: "Setting aside any question of motives, in the time of my youth, my physical strength coincided with the strength of my country. There was a strong tide running, and I was swept away in it without any chance to accede or dissent."[30]

Within a society dominated by a militarist clique intent on expansion, there existed this smaller, even more tightly controlled society of the Japanese army. Each soldier understood his place in a pyramid of authority, with the emperor at the top. Each was expected to obey orders as if they came from the emperor; if the emperor was infallible, then by definition, orders from any superior had validity beyond question.[31]

An American chaplain, Francis Scott, questioned a number of POW camp commanders who were convicted of barbaric treatment of prisoners. His composite explanation of their behavior was that they "had a belief that any enemy of the emperor could not be right, so the more brutally they treated their prisoners, the more loyal to their emperor they were being." Each soldier functioned in such a direct relationship to the emperor:

> As members of the Emperor's forces they were linked to the ultimate value and accordingly enjoyed a position of infinite superiority. Given the nature of Japanese society, it is no wonder that the masses, who in ordinary military or civilian life have no object to which they can transfer oppression, should, when they find themselves in this position, be driven by an explosive impulse to free themselves at a stroke from the pressure that has been hanging over them. Their acts of brutality are a sad testimony to the Japanese system of psychological compensation.[32]

The Imperial Japanese Army's ethos was based on "irrational awe, making it a deadly weapon in the hands of those who could mobilize it. The Japanese soldier more than any other was discouraged from thinking about what he was doing. Individual conscience was not, in any case, a Japanese concept, but in the military sphere it was strictly proscribed." The result was the lack, from a Western point of view, of a moral sense—"Japanese war criminals rarely expressed guilt or even regret; sometimes it seemed as though they saw nothing wrong in what they and their comrades had done."[33]

To Western sensibilities, this refusal of responsibility seems problematic, a basis for action without moral consequences. Yet for Japanese, submerging the individual self in the group is itself virtuous. Edwin Reischauer points out that the

> Japanese is not just the bland product of a social conditioning that has worn off all individualistic corners, but is rather the product of firm inner self-control that has made him master of his less rational and more antisocial instincts. He is not a weak-willed yes-man but the possessor of great self-discipline. In contrast to normal Western perceptions, social conformity to the Japanese is no sign of weakness but rather the proud, tempered product of inner strength.[34]

If submission to such demands was virtuous, then submission to the exponentially more brutal demands of the barracks family was an expression of even higher virtue. Former ambassador Joseph Grew articulated a typical Western response—"Such a mentality is a great deal harder to deal with than a mentality which, however brazen, knows that it is in the wrong." More crudely, Douglas MacArthur observed, "The Germans should have known better. They were traitors to western culture." Presumably the Japanese, ignorant of the West's virtues, did not.[35]

* * * * *

All of this tilts toward a kind of determinism. Uneducated peasants, products of an island nation buffeted by change, grown to maturity in the village *uchi* with its hard labor, fed a diet of emperor worship and the racist, jingoistic propaganda of the military, inured to the violence and brutality of the barracks, were programmed to treat POWs as they had been treated. Indeed, Japanese guards acted on a modified version of the Golden Rule. If they did not treat their prisoners as they themselves *wished* to be treated, they treated Americans the way they *had* been treated, and continued to be treated.

In the West, any "Golden Rule" theory was understood differently. It was "no mere coincidence that American troops were treated relatively better than troops of other nations captured by the Germans in World War II, for there were over a third of a million German prisoners in this country who were at the mercy of the United States, liable to treatment similar to any the Germans might impose upon American prisoners."[36] Since Japan's official position denied even the existence of prisoners, no such reciprocal understanding existed. Donald Keene spoke to the problem as well, stating that while

> Japanese can consider it absolutely bad to be taken prisoner, bad without qualification, we do not agree at all. On the other hand, we are infuriated by Japanese treatment of our prisoners, little imagining that it may result more from a Japanese divergence of opinion on treatment of prisoners than from deliberate evil, our absolute judgment.

Fluent in Japanese, Keene argued with prisoners, insisting that they adopt Western morality, if only because the Japanese were "outnumbered in the world." His logic appealed as Japan lay in ruins at war's end, but in 1942 the nation was experiencing the full flush of victory as her tide spread across the Pacific, by the end of the year encompassing nearly one sixth of the earth's surface. At such a moment things Western, including its morality, seemed quite irrelevant. Reluctant to place blame on individual Japanese, Keene concluded that "guilt for the war rests with the entire Japanese nation."[37]

Surely some Japanese, products of 1930s militarist Japan, were content to ascribe ultimate responsibility to their emperor. They felt no guilt when they killed POWs, especially considering their panic when Americans broke and ran for water. Those devotees of a narrowly construed cultural relativism might suggest that these Japanese, the ones who bloodied their bayonets, were simply ignorant, and therefore blameless. Plato's "Allegory of the Cave" from the *Republic* speaks to the issue:

> Imagine human beings living in an underground, cavelike dwelling.... They have been there since childhood, with their necks and legs fettered, so that they are fixed in the same place, able to see only in front of them, because their fetter prevents them from turning their heads around. Light is provided by a fire burning far above and behind them.

A question then follows—"do you think these prisoners have ever seen anything of themselves and one another besides the shadows that the fire casts on the wall of the cave in front of them?"[38] How one acts depends on what one understands—"all evil is ignorance." The Japanese peasant-turned-soldier surely lived in such a cave, and there were no philosopher-kings among the Japanese militarists.

Is it either fair or possible to judge the Japanese soldier by a standard of behavior about whose existence he was unaware? This seems a short route to excusing any atrocity that litters the human record. Among others, Aristotle rejected such logic, instead arguing that sometimes people can and should be held accountable for their actions. Here the idea of "soft determinism" seems relevant—although everything in the material world is part of a chain of hereditary and environmental forces, free will is still possible as long as we are not constrained—physically forced or prevented from doing something. Decisions are causally based, but on the infinite variety and complexity of the individual's experience, feelings, wishes, state of mind.[39]

Many Bataan veterans were certain that Japanese cruelty was *intentional*. Indeed, intentionality denotes choice, the essential stuff of free will. If some intended to act with cruelty, others intended otherwise, choosing to express goodwill toward their prisoners. Clearly some Japanese acted in ways beyond what their socialization suggested was likely, or even possible. One Japanese veteran stated, "When you think about it, the ones who fight wars are the people. Each soldier fought the war."[40] In spite of all that seemed to predetermine Japanese behavior on Bataan in 1942, some defied what seemed the prescribed pattern. Since the guards' voices are silent, others must speak for them.

As the Pacific War with the U.S. began and Japan rejoiced at its early military triumphs, the teacher of a second grade class asked her students what they would do if they were walking toward an American flag on the ground. Fifteen hundred voices at that morning assembly shouted, "Trample on it as we pass by." One little girl, Arita Suzuko, answered, "Bow deeply as I pass by." She was denounced by her classmates and school authorities called her mother.[41] Such dissent appeared in the sensibilities of soldiers as well. As the Death March was getting underway, Sasaki Hachiro was entering the University of Tokyo's school of economics. His writings contain ideas entirely alien to the purpose of Japanese training, and barracks life barely dented his humanistic attitude:

> If we insist on being only Japanese and on maintaining only Japanese positions, then we shall really have to hate our enemies, Great Britain and America. My own attitude, however, is much more humanistic.... This way of looking at things does not require me to hate people whom I do

not have to hate.... In all honesty, those slogans that our military leaders spread around ... are basically empty.

Another soldier quoted Descartes: "In order to be able to view my conduct with clarity, and to walk surely in this life, I have always maintained the strongest desire to distinguish the truth from the untruth." Hasegawa Shin lamented, "I feel a kind of despair about human beings, and especially about the humanity of our contemporary Japanese. I believe that never in history has there been a time when human beings were as far removed from the gods as they are now."[42]

Of course, the common Japanese soldier did not read Greek philosophy or Descartes when lamenting the oppressive nature of the Japanese state. Yet, alone in a sea of what his government told him was a contaminating mass of foreigners, individual Japanese expressed goodwill and kindness that gave expression to universal, humanistic impulses. To some degree they were free to do so outside the web of obligations that defined their relationships in Japan. And perhaps as well, their goodwill emanated from a common wellspring of humanity.

* * * * *

In the autumn of 1945, just after surrender, Donald Keene stood on a train platform, watching the "grief-stricken parting of an American soldier and a Japanese woman." He wondered about the rapid changes in a people's emotions, and concluded, "perhaps friendship is the normal feeling between peoples, and war is only an aberration." And now, as I write the last words of this book, Aristotle's words come to mind: "One may also observe in one's travels to distant countries the feelings of recognition and affiliation that link every human being to every other human being."[43]

Just before New Year, on the last day of an introductory English class, as the students and I stood milling around saying goodbye, an old man named Yamada, who was just starting to learn English and had made almost no progress at all in twelve weeks, called us all back to our seats. I had just pulled on the genuine World War II U.S. Navy pea coat my father had given me when Yamada, with everyone watching respectfully, came forward and in horribly awkward English (which he had obviously practiced for the occasion) explained that he had seen many such pea coats, and was "so very proud and happy" to be taught by the son of an American sailor.

During the war he had been an officer at a holding station for captured soldiers and sailors on Guam. As he spoke, tears ran down his cheeks and when he took my hand he whispered "ureshii" in my ear. I was happy, too, and concealed my own with the business of turning up the collar of my father's coat. I remember pausing on the walk home to stand for some time on the bridge over the Hankyu tracks eating takoyaki, just thinking, wondering about such encounters so pregnant with meaning, and marveling, once again, at the power of the past to reach into the present.

Years later, during one of my many return trips to Japan, I watched the *O-bon* festival in August, where Japanese speak with their ancestors at their graves and place floating lanterns in rivers and lakes to guide the spirits back to the world of the dead. I watched them, each representing a soul, slowly spreading out on the Inland Sea, and I remembered again my encounter with Yamada. I wanted him to be among the flickering lights. The image is clear and bright as the moon that evening, glistening in the prism of my memory.

Chapter Notes

Introduction

1. Hayashi, *Kogun*, 30.
2. Morton, *The Fall of the Philippines*, 57.
3. Whitman, *Bataan: Our Last Ditch*, 15–16.
4. Harries, *Soldiers of the Sun*, 314.
5. Falk, *Bataan: The March of Death*, 56–63; Kerr, *Surrender and Survival*, 53. Japanese medical services were barely adequate for their own soldiers coming south for assault on Corregidor. Ibid. Lack of material and facilities was obvious even before the Death March began. To Stanley Smith, a naval officer, "it was obvious the Japanese were totally unprepared, and perhaps understandably so, to establish prisoner-of-war facilities when they arrived in Manila." Smith, *Prisoner of the Emperor*, 33.
6. Wagner, *World War II: 365 Days*, Introduction.
7. Atkinson, *An Army at Dawn*, 465–66.
8. Terkel, *"The Good War"*; Brokaw, *The Greatest Generation*.
9. Other works deal more generally with Japanese wartime behavior and reach into culture—psychology, ideology and socialization—to explain Japanese soldiers' wartime behavior. John Dower's much-lauded *War Without Mercy* emphasizes the creation of a stereotypical "other" during the conflict, which resulted in virulent racial stereotyping and the routinization of killing and cruelty. Kazuko Tsurumi focuses on Japan in the 1930s and 1940s, and delves deeply into the process of soldiers' socialization with special attention to the emperor system and attitudes toward death as understood and taught by the army. Philip Towle has suggested that German influence and the experience of war with China in the 1930s as salient factors. Gavin Dawes sees Japanese brutality essentially as a function of virulent racism. The purpose of Saburo Iegana's two contributions was to "prevent collective amnesia" and remind the Japanese generation coming of age in the 1970s that "its peace and prosperity have roots in the fascism and aggression of the 1930s." See Dower, *War Without Mercy*; Tsurumi, *Social Change and the Individual*, chapters 2 and 3; Towle, "The Japanese Army and Prisoners of War"; Daws, *Prisoners of the Japanese*, 17–29; Ienaga, *Japan's Last War* and *The Pacific War: A Critical Perspective on Japan's Role in WWII*. Yuki Tanaka offers a related explanation, casting wartime Japanese brutality in the much larger context of soldiers' wartime behavior across time, culture and geography. Arguing that Japanese behavior is neither exceptional nor particularly excusable, Tanaka lays the blame on the emperor system, soldiers' brutalization by officers and their need to "transfer" violence to others. Tanaka, *Hidden Horrors*.
10. Irokawa, *The Age of Hirohito*, 3.
11. Brokaw, *Greatest Generation*, vi, xxx.
12. Des Pres, *The Survivor*, 208.
13. See Linenthal, *History Wars: The Enola Gay and Other Battles for the American Past*.
14. King, *The Alamo of the Pacific*, 137.
15. Gordon, *Horyo*, xviii.
16. Garner, "Revisiting Wartime: 66 Miles of Cruelty," *New York Times*, June 17, 2009.
17. Cowley, *No End Save Victory*, xi.
18. Knox, *Death March*, 139.
19. Evans, *Kora!*, 145.
20. Bradbury, *Dandelion Wine*, xii.
21. Ellison, *Imelda: Steel Butterfly of the Philippines*, 73.

Chapter 1

1. NARA, RG 407, Philippines Archive Collection, Box 125; Kerr, *Surrender and Survival*, 60–61; Quinn, *Love Letters to Mike*, 6. At fifty years old, Tsuneyoshi was only a captain; most of his classmates from military academy were colonels. He had been a reserve officer recalled to active duty in 1937.
2. Friday, "Bushido or Bull?" 6.
3. Ibid., 340.
4. Yamamoto, *Hagakure*, 23.
5. Tanaka, *Hidden Horrors*, 206–7. At the annual inspection of Japanese soldiers in reserve units, when asked to recite the five ideals of the Rescript of January 1882, the reservist did well to respond: "A soldier must strive to be loyal, a soldier must be decorous, a soldier must revere bravery, a soldier must honor fidelity, a soldier must aim at simplicity." Smethurst, *Social Basis for Prewar Japanese Militarism*, 161.
6. Harries, *Soldiers of the Sun*, 24.
7. Howes, *Nitobe*, 41–3, chapter V, passim. Begin-

ning in 1878, in rapid succession came *Gunjin Kunkai* (Admonition to Soldiers), *Gunjin Chokuyu* (Imperial Precepts to Soldiers and Sailors), *Hohei Soten* (Infantry Drill Book) and *Guntai Naimusho* (Rules of Domestic Affairs in the Army) to regulate soldiers' private lives. Servicemen were required to memorize all or at least parts of these texts, and "samurai behavior" was presented as a great honor to all Japanese men Tsurumi, *Social Change and the Individual*, 85–6.

8. In the introduction to the 1905 edition, William Eliot Griffis, himself an interpreter of Japan, bore witness to "the essential truth of Dr. Nitobe's descriptions" and to the "faithfulness of his analysis." Griffis noted that Nitobe "has limed with masterly art and reproduced the colouring of the picture which a thousand years of Japanese literature reflects so gloriously. The Knightly Code grew up during a millennium of evolution, and our author lovingly notes the blooms that have starred the path trodden by millions of noble souls, his countrymen." Not satisfied with this praise, Griffis claims Nitobe's book as a "notable contribution to the solution of this century's grandest problem—the reconciliation and unity of the East and the West." Howes, *Nitobe*, xviii-ix; xxi.

9. We have not outgrown the urge to gaze wistfully to the East for values we believe lost in our own culture, as $400 million in receipts and Academy Award nominations for 2003's abominably clichéd Tom Cruise vehicle, *The Last Samurai*, suggests.

10. Kerr, *Surrender and Survival*, 43.

11. Daws, *Prisoners of the Japanese*, 66, 70; Martin, *Brothers from Bataan*, 68.

12. Fuller, *Shokan*, 103; Bergamini, *Japan's Imperial Conspiracy*, 558.

13. Harries, *Soldiers of the Sun*, 340; Taylor, *A Trial of Generals*, 151; *USA v. Homma*, 3033–35, 3276, 3280.

14. Toland, *Rising Sun*, 313–14; Sides, "Trial of General Homma," 41.

15. Harries, *Soldiers of the Sun*, 340; Bergamini, *Japan's Imperial Conspiracy*, 1117, note 6. Major Fujiwara Iwaichi, active in helping organize the first Indian National Army to fight for Indian independence, expressed the same idealism when suggested the importance of seeing that "no heartless conduct occurs toward the inhabitants or toward POWs such as has been criticized in China." Lebra, *Japan's Greater East Asia Co-Prosperity Sphere*, 123–4.

16. Murakami, *Japan: The Years of Trial, 1919–52*, 111; Toland, *Rising Sun*, 258. When Filipino Chief Justice Jose Abad Santos was executed, Homma knew nothing of the event. Staff officers "under the sway of Tsuji" had issued the order. Murakami, *Japan: The Years of Trial, 1919–52*, 111; *USA v. Homma*, 3104. Further evidence of the general's sensibilities is his removal of Captain Yoshio Tsuneyoshi, the commander of Camp O'Donnell, when Homma learned of the conditions and abuses there. Olson, *O'Donnell: Andersonville of the Pacific*, 171.

17. Taylor, *A Trial of Generals*, 72–3; Swinson, *Four Samurai*, 73.

18. At his trial, referring to the Malayan and Dutch East Indies campaigns, Homma stated, "those campaigns came to an end while my campaign was delayed, and I knew that Tokyo was displeased." *USA v. Homma*, 3150.

19. Swinson, *Four Samurai*, 235.

20. The Tokyo Trial of Japanese war criminals went on for thirty-one months, and the tribunal concluded that seven former Japanese leaders would go to the gallows, sixteen were sentenced to life in prison, one to twenty years, one to seven years. Five died in prison; none served their full terms. See Minear, *Victors' Justice: Tokyo War Crimes*.

21. *USA v. Homma*, 876–79.

22. Olson, *O'Donnell: Andersonville of the Pacific*, 167.

23. Wachi Takeji testimony, *USA v. Homma*, 2464. See also Falk, *Bataan: The March of Death*, 225; Edgerton, *Warriors of the Rising Sun*, 270, 340; Toland, *Rising Sun*, 313–14; Taylor, *A Trial of Generals*, 72.

24. Quoted in Atkinson, *An Army at Dawn*, 170.

25. The formal charge read that Homma "did unlawfully disregard and fail to discharge his duties as commander to control the operations of members of his command, permitting them to commit brutal atrocities and other high crimes." The portion of the changes relating to the Death March contained eleven separate charges that specified individual acts." *USA v. Homma*, 23, 30.

26. Manchester, *American Caesar*, 485; Hoyt, *Japan's War*, 275; Sides, "Trial of General Homma," 41. In his comprehensive treatment of the Death March, Stanley Falk concluded that Homma's claim of ignorance "may well have been true." Falk, *Bataan: The March of Death*, 225.

27. The defense was allowed only three weeks to prepare, and the prosecution never established any connection between Homma and any atrocities. Considering MacArthur's humiliation at Homma's hands, his ignominious flight from his army in the field, and his enormous ego, vindictiveness as a motivating factor cannot be ruled out.

28. http://caselaw.lp.findlaw.com/scripts/getcase.pl?court=US&vol=327&invol=759.

29. Manchester, *American Caesar*, 488.

30. Bergamini, *Japan's Imperial Conspiracy*, 1116–7.

31. Manchester, *American Caesar*, 484.

32. *USA v. Homma*, 3144; Taylor, *A Trial of Generals*, 149; Swinson, *Four Samurai*, 235, 243.

33. Dower, *Embracing Defeat*, 516.

34. Tsurumi, *Social Change and the Individual*, 85–6.

35. Daws, *Prisoners of the Japanese*, 83.

36. Hall, *Kokutai no Hongi*, 10, 39, 79, 129.

37. Tsuji, *Japan's Greatest Victory*, 242, 238–39, 257.

38. Quoted in Toland, *Rising Sun*, 376.

39. Ward, *Killer They Called a God*, 50; Hayashi, "The Battle of Singapore," 238.

40. Harries, *Soldiers of the Sun*, 343.

41. Ward, *Killer They Called a God*, 89.

42. Hayashi, "The Battle of Singapore"; Ward, *Killer They Called a God*, 63–4. For detailed descriptions of the massacres, see Ward, *Killer They Called a God*, 54–79 and Russell, *Knights of Bushido*, 243–51.

43. Hayashi, "The Battle of Singapore," 6; Ward, *Killer They Called a God*, 83–4.

44. Ward, *Killer They Called a God*, 245.
45. Hoyt, *Japan's War*, 269; *USA v. Homma*, 2480.
46. Ward, *Killer They Called a God*, 247; Toland, *Rising Sun*, 368.
47. Ward, *Killer They Called a God*, 248; Toland, *Rising Sun*, 375; Dower, *Embracing Defeat*, 511.
48. Ward, *Killer They Called a God*, 259–60. The Americans rushed to put Yamashita on trial, and they got to him before the British could follow up on crimes in Singapore. Had Yamashita been tried by the British, instead of by Americans at MacArthur's insistence, the real responsibility for the massacres at Singapore would have been discovered. As it was, Yamashita went to his death shouldering blame for which he was not responsible. Ibid., 131–32.
49. Ward, *Killer They Called a God*, 264–66; Hayashi, "The Battle of Singapore," 238; Dower, *Embracing Defeat*, 511.
50. For a discussion of Unit 731's extraordinary activities, see Tanaka, *Hidden Horrors*, 135–65.
51. Ward, *Killer They Called a God*, 272, 297.
52. Dower, *Embracing Defeat*, 511–13.
53. Harries, *Soldiers of the Sun*, 342; Ward, *Killer They Called a God*, 305, 312, 330. For the full Tsuji treatment, see Brailey, *Masanobu Tsuji's "Underground Escape."*
54. Harries, *Soldiers of the Sun*, 343.
55. Gray, *The Warriors*, xi, 14–15.

Chapter 2

1. Dower, *Japan in War and Peace*, 102. For some of the foolishness, see Roy Miller's *Japan's Modern Myth*, a book that debunks linguists trying to prove the unique superiority of the Japanese language.
2. Hata, "From Consideration to Contempt," 269; quoted in MacKenzie, "Treatment of Prisoners of War in World War II," 516. See also Fedorowich, "Understanding the Enemy," 65–7.
3. Tasker, *The Japanese: Portrait of a Nation*, 16.
4. Henshall, *Dimensions of Japanese Society*, 179.
5. Dower, *Ways of Forgetting*, 53. Scholarship dealing with conflict in modern Japanese history includes Minichiello, *Japan's Competing Modernities*; Najita and Koschmann, *Conflict in Modern Japanese History*; Moore, *The Other Japan: Conflict, Compromise and Resistance Since 1945*.
6. Reischauer, *The Japanese Today*, 128; Masatsugu, *Samurai Society*, 87.
7. Henshall, *Dimensions of Japanese Society*, 48–107.
8. Dyer, *War*, 106.
9. Drea, *Japan's Imperial Army*, 85–6.
10. Hayashi, *Kogun*, 3.
11. SLA Marshall, *World War I*, 45–6. The French army did not instruct its soldiers on how to use entrenching tools: "To dig one's self in diminishes the intensity of one's fire and depresses the offensive spirit." It was "an article of faith" that the French common soldier could carry all before him in attack. Ibid., 59–60.
12. Keegan, *World War I*, 175–176.
13. Ibid., 218, 316–17.
14. Leckie, *Wars of America*, 2: 161.
15. By 1941, the U.S. army clearly recognized that "no one arm wins battles. The combined actions of all arms and services is essential to success." American tactical doctrine called for close coordination between infantry and artillery. After World War I, the U.S. army had created a number of motorized artillery batteries and developed sophisticated fire direction centers capable of directing and coordinating artillery fire with lethal effect. While the U.S. army learned from its experience in World War I and adapted new technology, the Japanese army, facing budget cuts in the 1920s, "opted for large-scale reduction of artillery firepower" hoping to compensate with the fighting spirit of its infantry units. Drea, *In the Service of the Emperor*, 61–3. See also Coffman, *The Regulars*, 415–16.
16. Millet, *Military Effectiveness*, 19.
17. Tsurumi, *Social Change and the Individual*, 99.
18. Millet, *Military Effectiveness*, 39; Drea, *In the Service of the Emperor*, 13.
19. Gibney, *Senso*, 24. As late as 1940, Japan's oil production ranked twenty-second in the world, a mere one tenth of one percent of the global total, or 1/700 of U.S. production, where Japan still received 80 percent of her oil. To a significant extent, it was this shortage of raw materials and "feeble productive capacity" that helped defined military doctrine. Millet, *Military Effectiveness*, 19.
20. Humphreys, *Way of the Heavenly Sword*, 100. In further defiance of the advancing technological imperatives of the new century, the army undertook the complicated overhaul of its field manuals. The *hohei soten* defined the army's approach to combat for the next thirty-six years. The influence of the Russo-Japanese War was clearly in evidence, as the manual placed the entire burden of victory on the infantry.
21. Tsurumi, *Social Change and the Individual*, 87.
22. Ienaga, *Pacific War*, 48–9. After the Russo-Japanese War, a military commission ignored evidence that very few bayonet charges had succeeded and none had overwhelmed a fortified enemy position, and nevertheless "endorsed the merits of a bayonet charge and further recommended that infantrymen had to advance regardless of artillery support." Drea, *Japan's Imperial Army*, 132.
23. McPherson, *What They Fought For*, 17.
24. The sample of engagements made clear that some 80 percent of these men could have fired at the enemy, but chose not to do so. Terrain, the length of the engagement, individual soldiers' pre-battle behavior patterns, even the relative combat experience of the soldiers had virtually no effect on the number of men willing to draw a bead on an enemy and pull the trigger. Marshall, *Men Against Fire*, 54–7.
25. Dyer, *War*, 106.
26. Grossman, *On Killing*, 4.
27. Marshall, *Men Against Fire*, 44–45, 46–8.
28. Gibney, *Five Gentlemen*, 3.
29. Boyle, *Modern Japan*, 152.
30. Oka, "Generational Conflict After the Russo-Japanese War," 198, 199, 209.
31. Smethurst, *Social Basis for Prewar Japanese Militarism*, Introduction.

32. Humphreys, *Way of the Heavenly Sword*, 50.
33. Quoted in Tipton, "Intellectual Life, Culture, and the Challenge of Modernity," 191.
34. Tipton, "Intellectual Life, Culture, and the Challenge of Modernity," 194–95.
35. Waswo, "The Transformation of Rural Society, 1900–1950," 593.
36. Tipton, "Intellectual Life, Culture, and the Challenge of Modernity," 192.
37. Quoted in ibid., 202. Regarding the "Debate on Modernity," one scholar has suggested, "For most, 'modern' was invariably associated closely with rational 'science'" and such a rejection led toward the irrational, or at least toward the mythological. Hayashi Fusao stated that in the West, men were always in conflict with their gods, but in Japan, "gods and men did not contend with each other, as conflict occurred among the gods alone. This reference to mythology was aimed at showing that Western science was fundamentally inappropriate to the spirit of the Japanese people." Harutoonian, "Japanese Revolt Against the West," 760.
38. Humphreys, *Way of the Heavenly Sword*, 14.
39. Ibid., 14–5, 51.
40. Smethurst, *Social Basis for Prewar Japanese Militarism*, xiv-vi.
41. Drea, *In the Service of the Emperor*, 79.
42. Cooke, *Japan at War*, 125, 126.
43. Romulo, *I Saw the Fall of the Philippines*, 203.
44. Drea, *In the Service of the Emperor*, 78–9. "Civil village officials mobilized all of the Army's organizations —that is, virtually the whole community—to ensure that the conscription examination worked smoothly.... The reservist branch chief, several of his top officials, the mayor and some of his subordinates ... and a few local school principals spent the day at the examination center ... to encourage the youths, that is to guarantee their obedience." Smethurst, *Social Basis for Prewar Japanese Militarism*, 159.
45. Millet, *Military Effectiveness*, 8. Army reports concerning Japanese captured during the Philippine campaign say that the average weight of a prisoner was 125.8 pounds, average age 23–29 years, the youngest was 19, oldest 31. The average length of service was one and a half years. Sixty-five percent were from the infantry, 70 percent had elementary school education, 15 percent had completed high school. Becoming a proud soldier of the Emperor constituted the high point in a man's life. To be rejected for military service was a disgrace. Coox, *Unfought War*, 31.
46. Smethurst, *Social Basis for Prewar Japanese Militarism*, 161–62. The connection to home is clear from what Americans routinely found on captured Japanese. "Every prisoner carried a wad of photographs—of his parents, of his wife and children, and so on. He had on him also a national flag, signed by his relatives, and containing heartening messages—usually a *sennin bari* ... many had diaries and notebooks. Hata, "From Consideration to Contempt," 275, note 47.
47. Cook, *Japan at War*, 123–4; Sides, *Ghost Soldiers*, 82; Thompson, *How the Japanese Army Fights*, 132; Drea, *In Service to the Emperor*, 80.
48. Smethurst, *Social Basis for Prewar Japanese Militarism*, 153.

49. Ienaga, *Pacific War*, 25. Perhaps 2 percent were university educated, 2 percent had the equivalent of junior college, 11 percent middle school, 85 percent sixth grade. Lory, *Japan's Military Masters*, 23.
50. Ienaga, *Pacific War*, 26, 24.
51. Gibney, *Five Gentlemen*, 138–39.
52. Humphreys, *Way of the Heavenly Sword*, 92.
53. Ienaga, *Pacific War*, 29–31; Khan, *Japanese Moral Education*, 93.
54. Morris, *Traveller from Tokyo*, 135; Lory, *Japan's Military Masters*, 17.
55. Japan's increasing population outpaced her rice-growing capability by a significant margin. The squeeze in the countryside was severe, since the traditional safety valve of emigration was closed off by both the U.S. and Australia, each fearful of the "yellow peril." Western tariff barriers, designed to protect industry during the depressed 1930s, caused Japan to feel all the more constricted. Johnson, *Modern Times*, 188–9. The U.S. Immigration Act of 1924 singled out the Japanese for total exclusion. One Tokyo newspaper asserted that the law "stamps Japanese as of an inferior race." The Cincinnati *Enquirer* did not disagree: "The crux of this matter is that the United States, like Canada and Australia, must be kept a white man's country." Boyle, *Modern Japan: The American Nexus*, 152. News of the exclusion act came in the near aftermath of the great Kanto earthquake of September 1, 1923, in which more than 100,000 Japanese had died. One Japanese observer wrote, "In the midst of our afflictions, the nation that had literally shaken open our gates—waved aside a long standing agreement with us and slammed its own gates in our face." O'Connor, *Pacific Destiny*, 438.
56. Earhart, *Certain Victory*, 80–1; Drea, "In the Army Barracks," 340. Conscription in Japan dated from 1872, and was designed to create a national instrument capable of suppressing dissent at home and defending the nation from threats abroad. The system was born at a time in Japanese history when peasants were asked to bear the cost of modernizing the country, and the draft law, regarded by many as a "blood tax," was not popular. The central problem facing the Meiji leadership was how to create a "body of willing fighters" to support an essentially authoritarian regime. "Their problem was how to promote among unrevolutionary troops and in support of their own exploitative regime a zeal comparable to the spirit which infuses soldiers battling on behalf of a revolutionary regime." Tsurumi, *Social Change and the Individual*, 84.
57. Between 1932 and 1934, the number jumped from 12,180 to 58,173; in the six northernmost provinces between 931 and 1937, more than 2,000 geisha, and some 4,400 brothel inmates, 6,000 sake servers and 3,200 waitresses were sold, the latter two categories essentially forced into forms of prostitution. Irokawa, *Age of Hirohito*, 7–9.
58. Tsurumi, *Social Change and the Individual*, 127–8; Thompson, *How the Japanese Army Fights*, 11, 20. In 1936 the average Japanese soldier was 5' 3½" tall and weighed 117 lbs. One quarter had six years or less of formal schooling, slightly more than one half had completed high school. Thompson, *How the Japa-*

nese Army Fights, 20–1; Lory, Japan's Military Masters, 23.

59. The Week, 1-31-14, 35.
60. Lory, Japan's Military Masters, 77.
61. Thompson, How the Japanese Army Fights, 54–5. John Morris saw men returning from long marches, "obviously on the verge of collapse. Some were being dragged along by their comrades with ropes." Morris, Traveler from Tokyo, 132. Later, a Japanese officer named Moto forced his prisoners to "rise in the middle of the night to do push-ups for half an hour or make a cross-country hike." Wolf, "Reactions Among Allied Prisoners of War," 183. In September 1943 a Japanese general inspected a prison camp and remarked on the number of sick who could not stand for roll call. An American officer explained by pointing to the typical meal of rice and soup. The Japanese rejected the explanation out of hand and snapped, "The prisoners are sick because they need more exercise." Weinstein, Barbed-Wire Surgeon, 150.
62. Thompson, How the Japanese Army Fights, 59; Falk, Bataan: The March of Death, 63.
63. Lory, Japan's Military Masters, 99.
64. Drea, "In the Army Barracks," 337; Toland, Rising Sun, 375; Daws, Prisoners of the Japanese, 102.
65. Drea, "In the Service of the Emperor," 85; Lory, Japan's Military Masters, 48–9.
66. Lory, Japan's Military Masters, 69–70.
67. Irokawa, Age of Hirohito 19; Johnston, Geisha, Harlot, Stranger, 111, 156–62.
68. Syka, Japan's Holy War, 263.
69. Rees, Horror in the East, 24.
70. Mitchell, Thought Control in Prewar Japan, 149; Gibney, Five Gentlemen, 169–70; Morris, Traveller from Tokyo, 107.
71. Humphreys, Way of the Heavenly Sword, 42–3.
72. Foner, Free Soil, 40, 41.
73. Duus, Abacus and the Sword, 399.
74. Ibid., 401–03.
75. Humphreys, Way of the Heavenly Sword, 54.
76. Hidden Scars: The Massacre of Koreans from the Arakawa River Bank to Shitamachi in Tokyo, 1923.
77. Humphreys, Way of the Heavenly Sword, 57.
78. Hammer, Yokohama Burning, 161, 156.
79. Poweleit, USAFFE, 16; Coleman, Bataan and Beyond, 72.
80. Feuer, Bilibid Diary, 27; Sato, "Gyokusai," 7.
81. Kato, The Lost War, 194; Yamanouchi, Listen to the Voices, 142.
82. Tsuji, Japan's Greatest Victory, 247. An alternate translation: "If I go away to seas I shall return a corpse awash. If duty calls me to the mountain, a verdant sward will be my pall. Thus for the sake of the emperor, I will not die peacefully at home." Tragedy of Bataan.
83. Chunn, Of Rice and Men, 13; Gibney, Senso, 35.
84. Waterford, Prisoners of the Japanese, 21.
85. Lory, Way of the Heavenly Sword, 46. According to Tsurumi, the glorification of death involved four elements: Imperial Precepts promulgated during popular rights movement of late 19th century, designed to insulate soldiers from agitators considered dangerous to the state; the emperor as head, soldiers limbs, soldiers identifying with father/emperor, and orders issued in his name toward death; soldiers as the emperor's favorite sons, obliged to die for him; positive incentive of prestige, folk belief that any dead member of a family becomes a spirit to protect the surviving members of the family. Dead soldiers were worshipped at Yasukuni shrine and enjoyed the special honor of protecting the whole nation. The achievement of fame for the family name was the "ultimate expression of filial piety" and a strong incentive. Tsurumi, Social Change and the Individual, 123–5.
86. Tsurumi, Social Change and the Individual, 133.
87. Leckie, Wars of America, 2: 124; Whitman, Bataan: Our Last Ditch, 353.
88. Drea, Japan's Imperial Army, 64–5.
89. Mellnik, Philippine Diary, 75.
90. Quoted in Morris, Traveller from Tokyo; 146; Hibbs, Tell MacArthur to Wait, 67–8; Whitman, Bataan: Our Last Ditch, 403; Grashio, Return to Freedom, 91.
91. Merritt, Adapt or Die, 245.
92. Astor, Crisis in the Pacific, 112; Gautier, I Came Back from Bataan, 69.
93. Harries, Soldiers of the Sun, 327.
94. Fussell, Boy's Crusade, 164.
95. Harries, Soldiers of the Sun, 350–51.
96. Dower, War Without Mercy, 43–4.
97. Harries, Soldiers of the Sun, 350.
98. Yamanouchi, Listen to the Voices, 190.
99. Astor, Crisis in the Pacific, 111.
100. Quoted in Morton, Fall of the Philippines, 220; Whitman, Bataan: Our Last Ditch, 66.
101. Morton, Fall of the Philippines, 270; Whitman, Bataan: Our Last Ditch, 389; Cave, Beyond Courage, 119. Carolos Romulo recalled that, in attack, the Japanese shock troops hurled themselves onto mines, exploding them with their bodies, and onto electrified barbed wire, whereupon those following "walked over the bodies spitted on the entanglements." Romulo, I Saw the Fall of the Philippines, 151.
102. Whitman, Bataan: Our Last Ditch, 339–40; 426, 429. Casualties among the Japanese were appalling. The 65th brigade entered combat on January 9 with 6651 men; two weeks later, 1472 were killed or wounded. Its commander, General Nara, concluded that his brigade had "reached the extreme stages of exhaustion." Quoted in Morton, Fall of the Philippines, 295.
103. Whitman, Bataan: Our Last Ditch, 267; Astor, Crisis in the Pacific, 163.
104. Whitman, Bataan: Our Last Ditch, 291–2. By the first week in February, the limits of seishin were apparent, and Homma ordered his battered army to withdraw to defensive positions. Though rumors of Homma's suicide flew through the American lines, Homma's shame was limited to the need to request more troops from Tokyo, where his enemy and superior, Hideki Tojo, brooded over Homma's lack of success. Homma's Fourteenth Army had sustained 2,725 killed, 4,049 wounded, 250 missing, as well as more than

10,000 sick with various diseases. His combat units had been "ground to impotence" and the army as a whole had "ceased to exist as a fighting force." Ibid., 75–77. See also Gailey, *War in the Pacific*, 105–6.
105. Whitman, *Bataan: Our Last Ditch*, 290, 368; Daws, *Prisoners of the Japanese*, 275.
106. Dower, *Japan in War and Peace*, 258.
107. Dower, *Ways of Forgetting*, 51–2; MacKenzie, "Treatment of Prisoners of War in World War II," 519.
108. Drea, *Japan's Imperial Army*, 74.
109. Dower, *War Without Mercy*, 191.
110. Hayashi, *Kogun*, 23.
111. Benedict, *Chrysanthemum and Sword*, 42.

Chapter 3

1. For an interesting discussion of the film as an expression of myth, see Slotkin, *Gunfighter Nation*, 322–25.
2. Fussell, *Wartime*, 261.
3. Lingeman, *Don't You Know There's a War On?*, 219–20, 237; Merritt, *Adapt or Die*, 61.
4. O'Connor, *Pacific Destiny*, 430.
5. Boyle, *Modern Japan*, 149–50. In California, long since the target of Japanese emigration, racial prejudice was more precisely expressed and followed a predictably ugly pattern against patient and hard-working vegetable farmers. "California, it should be noted, exhibited only the more virulent aspects of anti–Japanese prejudice in the United States which ... was probably more deeply felt than anti–Semitism or anti–Negro sentiments." O'Connor, *Pacific Destiny*, 428.
6. Coox, *Unfought War*, 29.
7. Diary of S. Hayes, RG 407 Philippines Archive Collection, Box 130; Diary of D.E. Smith, RG 407 Philippines Archive Collection, Box 143A.
8. NARA, Philippines Archives collection, RG 407, Box 125 Geoffrey Ames, Letter to his wife Kaye, December 10, 1941; Ibid., Diary of A.K. Whitehead Box.
9. Coffman, *The Regulars*, 292–93; 312.
10. Manchester, *American Caesar*, 280.
11. Linn, *Guardians of Empire*, 254. In September 1939, in response to the European crisis, FDR proclaimed a limited national emergency, authorized an increase of 17,000 regulars in the army, and raised the National Guard by 35,000 to its authorized strength of 200,000. One year later, Congress passed Selective Service Act, intending to create an army of 1,400,000. At the start of the war in the Pacific, U.S. forces in the Philippines numbered some 120,000 men. The great majority of these were, however, Filipino soldiers who had never fired a weapon, and had barely any military training at all. About 23,000 American soldiers occupied positions on the island fortress of Corregidor or on bases in the vicinity of Manila. The backbone of the force was the Philippine Division, made up of the Philippine Scouts, a well-trained unit of long-term, professional soldiers, and the American 31st Infantry Regiment, which numbered about 3,100. The remainder of Americans, approximately 20,000, were recently drafted, poorly trained and poorly equipped.
12. Doyle, *Voices from Captivity*, 108. Among these were three National Guard units, the 192nd and 194th tank battalions, comprising men from Illinois, Wisconsin, Ohio, Kentucky, Minnesota, Mississippi, California and Washington, and 200 Coast artillery from New Mexico, and the Fourth Marines.
13. Spector, *Eagle Against the Sun*, 106.
14. Martin, *Brothers from Bataan*, 53; Gordon, *Horyo*, 28. One burden on pay was the requirement to buy a "tailor-made Class A uniform," along with leggings, a cap and black cravat and special campaign hat, all together more than a month's pay. Linn, *Guardians of Empire*, 73; Gordon, *Horyo*, 29; Merritt, *Adapt or Die*, 61.
15. Ramsey, *Lieutenant Ramsey's War*, 35.
16. Coffman, *The Regulars*, 340–41.
17. Bollich, *Bataan Death March*, 33–4; Coffman, *The Regulars*, 343–44; Cave, *Beyond Courage*, 49.
18. Merritt, *Adapt or Die*, 53.
19. Martin, *Brothers from Bataan*, 51–2. Other stations, depending on one's proclivities, were even softer. The army recruiter who spoke with Charles Willeford described Panama as a place where "you can buy marijuana by the mattress-cover-full.... Last time I was in Panama I was in a bar where I could drink a glass of rum, smoke a cigarette, get a shoeshine and a blow job, all at the same time—and for only four bits." Willeford, *Something About a Soldier*, 19.
20. Spector, *Eagle Against the Sun*, 10–11.
21. Linn, *Guardians of Empire*, 74; Thomas, *As I Remember,* 12; Willeford, *Something About a Soldier*, 43.
22. Ind, *Bataan: The Judgment Seat*, 11, 12.
23. NARA, Philippines Archives collection, RG 407 NARA, Box 125, Geoffrey Ames Diary, Letter of 2-26-41.
24. Willeford, *Something About a Soldier*, 46–7.
25. Ind, *Bataan: The Judgment Seat*, 12.
26. Linn, *Guardians of Empire*, 62–4, 66. Another result was that, under the new reforms, enlisted men who held their rank only within their regiments had the unhappy choice between returning to the U.S. as privates, or remaining in the islands permanently. Ibid., 63. Many of the old soldiers went from one overseas post to the next, Hawaii, Panama, the P.I. These men tended to monopolize promotions, as time in service meant they would get the first available promotions in their new unit. Some had been "overzealous" administering discipline and were granted "saltwater warrants" that protected them from retaliation by those they had abused while on shipboard transit to new assignments. Many were disliked. Gordon, *Horyo*, 34.
27. Bollich, *Bataan Death March*, 59; Willeford, *Something About a Soldier*, 58; Linn, *Guardians of Empire*, 74; Bumgarner, *Parade of the Dead*, 41; Hibbs, *Tell MacArthur to Wait*, 76.
28. Leckie, *Helmet for My Pillow*, 130.
29. Atkinson, *Army at Dawn*, 9.
30. Allen, *Abandoned on Bataan*, 20; Whitman,

Bataan: Our Last Ditch, 25; Coffman, *The Regulars,* 346.

31. Hargrove, *See Here, Private Hargrove,* 203; Olson, *O'Donnell: Andersonville of the Pacific,* 16; Holt, *King of Bataan,* 158.

32. Willeford, *Something About a Soldier,* 13, 15–7, 40–2; Linderman, *World Within War,* 275–77.

33. Quoted in Linderman, *World Within War,* 197; Cave, *Beyond Courage,* 23, 50.

34. Stouffer, *American Soldier: Adjustment During Army Life,* 59–61. Serial numbers beginning with six indicated old soldier; two indicated National Guard; three draftee. Gordon, *Horyo,* 13.

35. Coffman, *The Regulars,* 405–07; Stouffer, *American Soldier: Adjustment During Army Life,* 57.

36. Stouffer, *American Soldier: Adjustment During Army Life,* 59, 65.

37. Ibid., 63, 68–9. The survey was taken at time of Pearl Harbor.

38. Martin, *Brothers from Bataan,* 33.

39. The all-American 31st Regiment had "led a soft, garrison-type existence in the very heart of Manila.... When the war broke out, the regiment not only found itself barely over half strength, but also overloaded with young ROTC officers and 12-month trainees fresh from the States." Young, *Battle of Bataan,* 6–7. Older officers who had commanded companies for years became "instructors" with the Philippine Army or returned to the states, leaving companies of the 31st Infantry suddenly commanded by much younger officers. Lowe, *31st Infantry Regiment in War and Peace,* http://31stinfantry.org/Documents/ Chapter%205.pdf chapter 5, page 4.

40. Linderman, *World Within War,* 190–92, 196, 197.

41. Stouffer, *American Soldier: Adjustment During Army Life,* 74–5.

42. Linderman, *World Within War,* 199–200; Vance, *Doomed Garrison,* 106.

43. Ramsey, *Lieutenant Ramsey's War,* 40.

44. Ortega, *Courage on Bataan,* 23–4, 15.

45. Coffman, *The Regulars,* 344; Martin, *Brothers from Bataan,* 51. Charles Willeford's description of the procedure was inexplicable: "After getting a piece of ass, you had to go into the prophylactic station, fill your penis with ptargyrol, hold it for five minutes, and let it out" after which a medic certified the soldier as safe. Inquiries with physicians of my acquaintance yielded no better understanding of Willeford's meaning. Willeford, *Something About a Soldier,* 83.

46. Bumgarner, *Parade of the Dead,* 48; Fussell, *Wartime,* 257; Merritt, *Adapt or Die,* 98, 141, 52.

47. Coffman, *The Regulars,* 315; Bumgarner, *Parade of the Dead,* 47.

48. Willeford, *Something About a Soldier,* 57.

49. Ibid., 62; Martin, *Brothers from Bataan,* 52. Charles Willeford claimed to visit the houses occupied by these women with a bottle of "Honeymoon Lotion," purchased for one peso, and adequate to entice them to have sex with him while their boyfriends were away. Willeford, *Something About a Soldier,* 62–4; NARA, Philippines Archives collection, RG 407, Box 125, Geoffrey R. Ames diary.

50. Gordon, *Horyo,* 32. In recognition of a serious problem with venereal disease, the medical department provided medical check-ups to Filipinas selected for "shack-up" arrangements. Willeford, *Something About a Soldier,* 29.

51. Willeford, *Something About a Soldier,* 61.

52. Toland, *But Not in Shame,* 268.

53. James Jones, *World War II,* 43. Linderman suggests that combat soldiers went through three stages: numbing, coarsening, and finally fatalism. Linderman, *World Within War,* 48–89.

54. Jones, *Thin Red Line,* 390–91.

55. Brookhauser, *This Was Your War,* 223.

56. Mailer, *The Naked and the Dead,* 174; quoted in Breuer, *Great Raid on Cabanatuan,* 10.

57. Hargrove, *See Here, Private Hargrove,* 148, 180.

58. Atkinson, *Army at Dawn,* 9; Grinker, *Men Under Stress,* 45.

59. Mitchell, *Civil War Soldiers,* 57; Glatthaar, "Common Soldier of the Civil War," 128.

60. Glatthaar, "Common Soldier of the Civil War," 120. Though some eighty years had passed since Americans had fought each other, the problems of creating an effective fighting force out of an essentially democratic citizenry had remained essentially the same. Civil war soldiers "entered service with an ignorance of army life and an indifference to discipline. The former disappeared out of necessity; the latter remained a constant problem throughout the war." Robertson, *Soldiers Blue and Gray,* 122. One in ten Union and one in seven Confederate soldiers deserted during the war. Ibid., 135.

61. Linderman, *Embattled Courage,* 198.

62. Quoted in Robertson, *Soldiers Blue and Gray,* 123.

63. Linderman, *World Within War,* 349. On a ship returning to the U.S. after the Japanese surrender, Robert Haney recorded his surprise that so few men had "any intention of making the Navy a career. Some are going to join the 52–20 club ($20 unemployment payments for a year) Others are going to school on a government paid program. Still others are going to jobs they left or hope to get. Others just plan to get 'out—way out.'" Haney, *Caged Dragons,* 196.

64. Stouffer, *American Soldier: Adjustment During Army Life,* 448–9. Even after Bataan fell, American soldiers were optimistic about the anticipated length of the war. In the autumn of 1942, when the war looked darkest, some 25 percent of men in training in the U.S. believed that the war would be over "in a year or less." In July 1943, 76 percent of 2,125 respondents underestimated the length of the war. Stouffer, *American Soldier: Adjustment During Army Life,* 448–9. See also chapter 5.

65. *Basic Field Manual,* 22; Willeford, *Something About a Soldier,* 53.

66. Quoted in Norman, *Tears in the Darkness,* 39.

67. Sledge, *With the Old Guard,* 40–1.

68. Stouffer, *American Soldier: Adjustment During Army Life,* 78–9.

69. Linderman, *World Within War,* 186; Feuer, *Bilibid Diary,* 92.

70. Allen, *Abandoned on Bataan,* 10; Whitman, *Bataan: Our Last Ditch,* 24.

71. Kathman, *I Was There*, 5. New recruits were allowed $150 for clothing, "but what a lot of soldiers were doing was holding back on spending the full amount, the reason being that you could still buy out of the service if you did not like it. A private could buy out for $75; a corporal, $50; and a sergeant, $25. Bollich, *Bataan Death March*, 23.
72. *Tragedy of Bataan*.
73. War Department, *Basic Field Manual*, March 6, 1941, 3.
74. Lowe, *31st Infantry Regiment in War and Peace*, chapter 5, pages 1, 4, 5. http://31stinfantry.org/Documents/Chapter%205.pdf.
75. Bollich, *Bataan Death March*, 22–3; Hibbs, *Tell MacArthur to Wait*, 75.
76. Hubbard, *Apocalypse Undone*, 65.
77. Quoted in Whitman, *Bataan: Our Last Ditch*, 455; Merritt, *Adapt or Die*, 124.
78. Bollich, *Bataan Death March*, 38–9.
79. Stouffer, *American Soldier: Combat and Its Aftermath*, 145–47.
80. Parillo, *We Were in the Big One*, 3; Manchester, *Glory and the Dream*, 1: 354. Stoler notes that the U.S. was an unparalleled behemoth of production during the war years, producing about 65 percent of all war matériel as it lifted itself from the depression.... By early 1943 its economy had already outstripped that of all its enemies combined; two years later it had doubled what Japan and Germany produced. By the time it accepted the twin Axis surrenders, it had spent $300 billion to produce an astonishing 86,000 tanks, 193,000 artillery pieces, 14 million shoulder weapons, 2.4 million trucks and jeeps, 1.200 combat vessels, 82,000 landing craft and ships, and 297,000 planes. Stoler, "Second World War in U.S. Memory," note 1.
81. Linderman, *World Within War*, 336.
82. Gordon, *Horyo*, 33, 41–2; Martin, *Brothers from Bataan*, 69.
83. Gordon, *Horyo*, 33; Cave, *Beyond Courage*, 24; Atkinson, *Army at Dawn*, 9.
84. Gordon, *Horyo*, 79; Whitman, *Bataan: Our Last Ditch*, 32.
85. Cave, *Beyond Courage*, 125; Whitman, *Bataan: Our Last Ditch*, 288; Morton, *Fall of the Philippines*, 288–9.
86. Whitman, *Bataan: Our Last Ditch*, 191. While fishing, one American threw three grenades before one exploded. Merritt, *Adapt or Die*, 151. His 33 percent was better than the 80 percent average for that weapon. One platoon fired seventeen rounds from its mortars, but only four exploded. The Japanese derisively left one of the malfunctioning units in no man's land, decorated with flowers. Manchester, *American Caesar*, 236. Alf Larson, destroying a cache of hand grenades so the Japanese would not get them, threw them into a slit trench, but half failed to explode. "That was the quality of the stuff we had. We were fighting World War II with World War I equipment—literally!" Gilpatrick, *Footprints in Courage*, 40.
87. Volckman, *We Remained*, 21.
88. *Time*, 2-23-42; Ruse, *We Volunteered*, 69.
89. Poweleit, *USAFFE*, 19; Whitman, *Bataan: Our Last Ditch*, 35.
90. Astor, *Crisis in the Pacific*, 108; Gordon, *Horyo*, 47.
91. Martin, *Brothers from Bataan*, 72. Edwin Ramsey recalled that officers spent some time studying Tagalog, but he resisted the lessons, the hours of repetition and mouthing syllables that sounded gibberish ... almost unbearable." Ramsey, *Lieutenant Ramsey's War*, 37.
92. Whitman, *Bataan: Our Last Ditch*, 28–9; Volckman, *We Remained*, 6.
93. Young, *Battle of Bataan*, 9.
94. Chunn, *Of Rice and Men*, 22.
95. Bernad, *Tradition and Discontinuity*, 101; Toland, *Rising Sun*, 332.
96. Martin, *Brothers from Bataan*, 72.
97. Norman, *Tears in the Darkness*, 40; Whitman, *Bataan: Our Last Ditch*, 29.
98. Cave, *Beyond Courage*, 107; Mallonee, *Battle for Bataan*, 115; Willeford, *Something About a Soldier*, 146.
99. Atkinson, *Army at Dawn*, 258, 183, 377.
100. Ibid., 234, 346, 354, 261.
101. Ramsey, *Lieutenant Ramsey's War*, 44; Spector, *Eagle Against the Sun*, 12.
102. Whitman, *Bataan: Our Last Ditch*, 115ff, 134.
103. Olson, *O'Donnell: Andersonville of the Pacific*, 3 "Little more than 10 percent of the officers and men who reached Bataan could be classified as combat ready.... Of an estimated 13,500 Americans on Bataan ... in January, probably no more than three thousand had been in the Philippines over eight months." Ibid., 17.
104. *Basic Field Manual*, 14–5.
105. Moody, *Reprieve from Hell*, 70.
106. Atkinson, *Army at Dawn*, 52–3, 235.
107. Mallonee, *Battle for Bataan*, 146. Quinine on the Allied side had run out in March, and admissions to the hospitals for malaria were running 1000 per day toward the end of the campaign. Kerr, *Surrender and Survival*, 50.
108. Stouffer, *American Soldier: Combat and Its Aftermath*, 191.
109. Ruse, *We Volunteered*, 67. From January until mid–February, daily rations were 3.7 ounces rice, 1.8 ounces sugar, 1.2 ounces canned milk, 2.44 ounces canned fish, salmon or sardines, tomatoes when available, 10 men per can. Mallonee, *Battle for Bataan*, 84.
110. Merritt, *Adapt or Die*, 148.
111. Whitman, *Battle of Bataan*, 413; Vance, *Doomed Garrison*, 105. In its effort to feed its host on diminishing resources, the Quartermaster Corps established a fishery near Lamao. Some 12,000 pounds of fish rolled in every night, but American and Filipino alike began plundering the catches and the fishing stopped. Whitman, *Bataan: Our Last Ditch*, 411.
112. Whitman, *Bataan: Our Last Ditch*, 469.
113. Ibid., 491; Weinstein, *Barbed-Wire Surgeon*, 21–2. "Sounds familiar to the operating pavilion vibrated through the air: the zzz-zzz-zzz of a saw as it cut through bone, the rasp of the file as the freshly cut end, dripping red marrow, was ground smooth, the plop of an amputated leg dropping into a bucket, the grind of a rounded burr drill eating its way through a skull; the tap, tap, tap of a mallet on a chisel gouging

out a shell fragment deeply embedded in bone ... the snip of scissors cutting through muscle; the swish of the mop on the floor cleaning up blood, the strangling, gasping, irregular respiration of soldiers with chest wounds." Weinstein, *Barbed-Wire Surgeon*, 20.

114. Norman, *We Band of Angels*, 54, note 12.
115. Hibbs, *Tell MacArthur to Wait*, 92.
116. Filipino quote in Weinstein, *Barbed-Wire Surgeon*, 32. On 29 January 1946, Gen. Edward P. King, Jr., submitted his Luzon Force Operations Report to Washington. Submitted along with his report were two reports: the G-4 report, explaining the food, supply and equipment conditions, on Bataan, and the Surgeon of the Luzon Force Report which describes the physical and medical conditions on Bataan, during the period 6 January 1942 until 9 April 1942. http://home.pacbell.net/fbaldie/G-4_and_Surgeon_Report.html.
117. Linderman, *World Within War*, 356–57. Dyer states that after an initial period of confusion, the men were at their peak after 3 weeks, after which their effectiveness dropped off gradually to the point of near total inertia. Dyer, *War*, 144; Stouffer, *American Soldier: Combat and Its Aftermath*, 73.
118. Linderman, *World Within War*, 355; Cave, *Beyond Courage*, 122–23; 135.
119. Whitman, *Bataan: Our Last Ditch*, 451.
120. Atkinson, *An Army at Dawn*, 413, 3.
121. Ibid., 537.
122. Ibid., 538.
123. Merritt, *Adapt or Die*, 125.
124. Tapert, *Lines of Battle*, 20. The Bible verse was Psalms, 91:7.

Chapter 4

1. Tsuji, *Japan's Greatest Victory*, 237–69.
2. *A Pocket Guide to Japan*, 39.
3. Henshall, *Dimensions of Japanese Society*, 151.
4. Masatsugu, *Samurai Society*, 89–90.
5. Tasker, *The Japanese*, 19.
6. Beasley, *Japanese Experience*, 167; Smith, *Japanese Society*, 39.
7. Hane, *Modern Japan*, 27.
8. Quoted in Smith, *Japanese Society*, 112.
9. Henshall, *Dimensions of Japanese Society*, 152.
10. Benedict, *Chrysanthemum and the Sword*, 27, 28.
11. Nakane, *Japanese Society*, 99, 100.
12. Hearn, *Japan: An Interpretation*, 9–10.
13. Goldstein, *Japan and America*, 141.
14. Hearn, *Kokoro*, 21.
15. Henshall, *Dimensions of Japanese Society*, 153.
16. Quoted in Manchester, *American Caesar*, 281; Morris, *Traveller from Tokyo*, 133.
17. Merritt, *Adapt or Die*, 130.
18. Astor, *Crisis in the Pacific*, 103–4 ; Whitman, *Bataan: Our Last Ditch*, 43.
19. Whitman, *Bataan: Our Last Ditch*, 45, 463.
20. Grashio, *Return to Freedom*, 13; Lecki, *Helmet for My Pillow*, 89.
21. Drea, *Japan's Imperial Army*, 159.
22. Whitman, *Bataan: Our Last Ditch*, 402; Ind, *Bataan: The Judgment Seat*, 298.
23. Chunn, *Of Rice and Men*, 10; *USA v. Homma*, 2313.
24. Drea, *Japan's Imperial Army*, 83.
25. Kerr, *Surrender and Survival*, 52–3; Toland, *But Not in Shame*, 310; Falk, *Bataan: The March of Death*, 46–50, 194, 196.
26. Falk, *Bataan: The March of Death*, 47–51.
27. "Kawane had only 200 trucks for 64,000 Filipinos, 11,500 Americans, 6,000 civilian employees, and as many as 26,000 refugees. Thousands upon thousands of men were sick, hungry and exhausted." Homma thought the condition was "no worse" than the Japanese troops. Hitome Junske, a staff officer, said "there were far more Americans and Filipinos than we estimated" and we weren't prepared for them in any way." Glusman, *Conduct Under Fire*, 162.
28. Bix, *Hirohito and the Making of Modern Japan*, 447.
29. Atkinson, *An Army at Dawn*, 526–27.
30. Kerr, *Surrender and Survival*, 49; Whitman, *Bataan: Our Last Ditch*, 570; Conroy, *Battle of Bataan*, 53.
31. Weinstein, *Barbed-Wire Surgeon*, 54; Grashio, *Return to Freedom*, 38.
32. Morton, *Fall of the Philippines*, 442.
33. Quoted in Whitman, *Bataan: Our Last Ditch*, 532.
34. Whitman, *Bataan: Our Last Ditch*, 536; Cave, *Beyond Courage*, 143–53.
35. Quoted in Whitman, *Bataan: Our Last Ditch*, 561, 568; Evans, *Kora!*, 3. "As the situation worsened, some of the withdrawals became routs, and many of those in them teetered on the verge of hysteria." Olson, *O'Donnell: Andersonville of the Pacific*, 20.
36. Whitman, *Bataan: Our Last Ditch*, 571–72.
37. Urwin, *Victory in Defeat*, 32.
38. http://www.doingoralhistory.org/project_archive/2004/Papers/PDFs/M_Kleinman.pdf.
39. Sakaiya, *What Is Japan?*, 228–29.
40. NARA, RG 331, SCAP Records, Statement (including "Table of Organization") of Lt. Colonel Nakajima Yoshio, attached to Homma's HQ, June 17, 1948; *USA v. Homma*, 144. One staff officer in Homma's headquarters stated, "During the Prisoners' journey guards were attached to them only at the rate of one for every several hundred, and their march was not conducted under any severe control." NARA, RG 331, SCAP, 11-2-45.
41. NARA, RG 331, SCAP Records, Statement of Sato Tokutaro, July 14, 1948.
42. Ortega, *Courage on Bataan*, 38, 46.
43. Bumgarner, *Parade of the Dead*, 79.
44. Young, *Battle of Bataan*, 318.
45. Bilyeu, *Lost in Action*, 83; Moody, *Reprieve from Hell*, 74.
46. Hunt, *Behind Japanese Lines*, 28.
47. Grashio, *Return to Freedom*, 39; Levering, *Horror Trek*, 68; Fitzpatrick, *Hike into the Sun*, 58–9;

Olson, *O'Donnell: Andersonville of the Pacific*, 22; Silva, *Senso Owari*, 20.
48. Astor, *Crisis in the Pacific*, 218; Bilek, *No Uncle Sam*, 59; Knox, *Death March*, 134–5.
49. De Mente, *Kata*, 101–02.
50. Bergamini, *Japan's Imperial Conspiracy*, 957.
51. See, for example, Sneddon, *Zero Ward*, 20, 21, 29. For Levering, see *Tragedy of Bataan*.
52. Norman, *Tears in the Darkness*, 177.
53. Falk, *Bataan: The March of Death*, 234. Two or three guards per one hundred men seems to have been the goal. *USA v. Homma*, 1098.
54. Rees, *Horror in the East*, 74.
55. Abraham, *Ghost of Bataan*, 93.
56. Some of many examples, include Gautier, *I Came Back from Bataan*, 72; Bilek, *No Uncle Sam*, 59; Knox, *Death March*, 134–5.
57. Saikaiya, *What Is Japan?*, 228–29.
58. Whitman, *Bataan: Our Last Ditch*, 367.
59. Knox, *Death March*, 147. See also LaForte, *With Only the Will to Live*, 85.
60. Ancheta, *Triumph in the Philippines*, 102.
61. http://www.pbs.org/wgbh/amex/macarthur/sfeature/bataan_capture.html. See also Bilek, *No Uncle Sam*, 60; Gordon, *Horyo*, 89.
62. Nakane, *Japanese Society*, 82; Kano, *The Silent Power*, 8.
63. Olson, *O'Donnell: Andersonville of the Pacific*, 18.
64. Fitzpatrick, *Hike into the Sun*, 66; Poweleit, *Kentucky's Fighting 192nd*, 90; Cave, *Beyond Courage*, 181.
65. LaForte, *With Only Will to Live*, 88–9; 87; Miller, *Bataan Uncensored*, 226.
66. Falk, *Bataan: The March of Death*, 234–5.
67. Gordon, *Horyo*, 96.
68. Caracillo, *Surviving Bataan and Beyond*, 36.
69. Grashio, *Return to Freedom*, 44; Caraccilo, *Surviving Bataan and Beyond*, 43; Jacobsen, *We Refused to Die*, 92; Hubert Gater, Knox, *Death March*, 151; Fitzpatrick, *Hike into the Sun*, 73–4.
70. Tsuji, *Japan's Greatest Victory*, 247, 8–9; Masatsugu, *Samurai Society*, 69.
71. Quoted in Gibney, *Five Gentlemen of Japan*, 18.
72. Quoted in Whitman, *Bataan: Our Last Ditch*, 59; Lory, *Japan's Military Masters*, 23.
73. Urwin, *Victory in Defeat*, 31–2; Olson, *O'Donnell: Andersonville of the Pacific*, 18.
74. Tenney, *My Hitch in Hell*, 44.
75. Ibid., 47; Bollich, *Bataan Death March*, 70–1; See also Toland, *But Not in Shame*, 329.
76. Cave, *Beyond Courage*, 169; *People* magazine, "Up Front," December 24, 2004; Bank, *Back from the Living Dead*, 25.
77. Braly, *Hard Way Home*, 1; Evans, *Kora!*, 12; Playter, *Survivor*, 63.
78. Caraccilo, *Surviving Bataan and Beyond*, 32.
79. Sides, *Ghost Soldiers*, 83; Evans, *Kora!*, 21.
80. Tenney, *My Hitch in Hell*, 50.
81. LaForte, *With Only the Will to Live*, 82; Miller, *Bataan Uncensored*, 221.
82. Wolf, *Thirst*, 395, 219, 399, 411.
83. Mallonee, *Battle for Bataan*, 152.

84. Tsuji, *Japan's Greatest Victory*, 258; Allen, *Abandoned on Bataan*, 67.
85. Tsuji, *Japan's Greatest Victory*, 254, 249, 266.
86. Bilek, *No Uncle Sam*, 60; Levering, *Horror Trek*, 64; Knox, *Death March*, 130.
87. Tsurumi, *Social Change and the Individual*, 119; Mallonee, *Battle for Bataan*, 149.
88. Quoted in Keene, *Modern Japanese Literature*, 358.
89. Cave, *Beyond Courage*, 180; Ortega, *Courage on Bataan*, 47.
90. Gordon, *Horyo*, 92.
91. Bilyeu, *Lost in Action*, 59, 74, 77; Kerr, *Surrender and Survival*, 57; Knox, *Death March*, 143; Playter, *Survivor*, 58.
92. Abie Abraham, http://ghostofbataan.com/bataan/page3.html.
93. Weinstein, *Barbed-Wire Surgeon*, 40.
94. Knox, *Death March*, 128; Carcillo, *Surviving Bataan and Beyond*, 34.
95. Cave, *Beyond Courage*, 180.
96. Mallonee, *Battle for Bataan*, 155; Cave, *Beyond Courage*, 180; *Tragedy of Bataan*.
97. Caracillo, *Surviving Bataan and Beyond*, 38.
98. Playter, *Survivor*, 58; Knox, *Death March*, 131; During Homma's trial, one veteran testified, "Now, whenever we approach a place where there is an artesian well, many men break the line and rush ... to drink, and we hear shots." *USA v. Homma*, 976.
99. http://www.pbs.org/wgbh/amex/macarthur/sfeature/bataan_capture.html.
100. Allen, *Abandoned on Bataan*, 69, 75.
101. Miller, *Bataan Uncensored*, 221; Knox, *Death March*, 131; North, *Lost in the Wilderness*, 37; Bilyeu, *Lost in Action*, 85; Evans, *Kora!*, 13.
102. Tenney, *My Hitch in Hell*, 51; Allen, *Abandoned on Bataan*, 73. Calvin Jackson remembered that even when guards allowed prisoners to drink, "many drank too fast and were soon thirsty again." Jackson, *Diary of Col. Calvin G. Jackson*, Preface.
103. Gordon *Horyo*, 91; http://www.pbs.org/wgbh/amex/macarthur/sfeature/bataan_capture.html; Caracillo, *Surviving Bataan and Beyond*, 38–9.
104. LaForte, *With Only the Will to Live*, 87.
105. Urwin, *Victory in Defeat*, 55–6.
106. Grashio, *Return to Freedom*, 49. Grashio further believed that the Japanese "thought they would never be held accountable for their deeds.... So most of them gave free rein to all the cruel impulses that flowed from the bushido tradition and from their accumulated hatred and resentment of occidentals." Ibid.
107. Thompson, *How the Japanese Army Fights*, 16.
108. LaForte, *With Only the Will to Live*, 83.
109. Gordon, *Horyo*, 92.
110. Grashio, *Return to Freedom*, 32.
111. Fall, *Hell in a Very Small Place*, 432, 437. Some 37,000 French had been captured by the Viet-Minh between 1946 and 1954; fewer than 11,000 made it home. Ibid., 438.

Chapter 5

1. Hibbs, *Tell MacArthur to Wait*, 119.
2. Moss, "Oral History," 112.
3. Eakin, "Autobiography, Identity and the Fictions of Memory," 292.
4. Daws, *Prisoners of the Japanese*, 19–20; White, *Content of the Form*, 21.
5. Atkinson, *An Army at Dawn*, 536; Linderman, *The World Within War*, 1.
6. Other survivors of combat's crucible agree. William Manchester, the author a compelling personal memoir of war in the Pacific, asserted that everyone "who wore uniforms are called veterans, but more than 90 percent of them are as uninformed about the killing zones as those on the home front." E.B. Sledge, another veteran of Pacific campaigns, put an even finer point on the distinction, stating that "people just behind our rifle companies couldn't understand what we knew." Fussell, *Thank God for the Atomic Bomb*, 6, 16.
7. Stouffer, *The American Soldier: Combat and Its Aftermath* 98–9. The context produced the well-known bonding peculiar to men who have shared the sustained dangers of combat, a special "feeling of fraternity": "Those who had shot at the enemy and had themselves been fired upon in that thin forward zone, had a consciousness of shared experience under great emotional stress which they felt others could never understand. This consciousness became clear mostly after action, when in the rear or in reminiscence." Ibid., 99–100.That fraternity was exclusive indeed. James Jones' vivid novel of Pacific warfare, *The Thin Red Line*, describes the resistance of blooded combat veterans to shaving off their beards, which "symbolized the comparative freedom of the frontline combat infantryman.... Even the thinnest, most straggly nineteen-year-old beard was worn proudly by its grower as the symbol of a combat man." Jones, *Thin Red Line*, 477.
8. Mauldin, *Up Front*, 58.
9. Gerald Linderman, *The World Within War*, 238.
10. MacArthur, *Surviving the Sword*, xxx. J.E. Nardini served as medical officer in prison camps and in Japan after April 1942. He states that 30,000 Americans were taken prisoner in the Far East, and 40 percent, or 12,000 survived the period of imprisonment. Using this rate of survival and Falk's figure of 9,900 that made the Death March, reasonable number of Death March survivors would be 4,000. Nardini, "Survival Factors in American Prisoners," 240.
11. *Forsaken Legion*; Gordon, *Horyo*, 124–25. Upon arriving at the camp in Cabanatuan, John Wright, captured on Corregidor, stated, "As yet we had not experienced genuine hunger." Wright, *Captured on Corregidor*, 49.
12. Moody, *Reprieve from Hell*, Foreword.
13. Sides, *Ghost Soldiers*, 20.
14. Moody, *Reprieve from Hell*, 105.
15. Nietzsche, *Untimely Meditations*, 69; Fussell, *Atomic Bomb*, 81–2.
16. Bok, "Autobiography as Moral Battleground," 310.
17. Bollich, *Bataan Death March*, 72.
18. Brain, *Soldier of Bataan*, 7.
19. Fussell, *Atomic Bomb*, 2–3.
20. Poweleit, *USAFFE*, vi-vii.
21. Young, 15; Grashio, *Return to Freedom*, 37; Evans, *Kora!*, x-xi; Weinstein, *Barbed-Wire Surgeon*, ix.
22. Masterson, *Ride the Waves to Freedom*, 37–8; Lawton, *Some Survived*, 24; Allen, *Abandoned on Bataan*, 66; LaForte, *With Only the Will to Live*, 80; Gordon, *Horyo*, 102. One wrote that "no survivor of Bataan will ever question the fact that the Japanese were to a man 'barbarians.'" Gordon, *Horyo*, 102. Lawton stated that "western civilization had not yet reached Japan." A third described "brutal guards who were totally lacking in human kindness and compassion." Lawton, *Some Survived*, 19, 24.
23. Abraham, *Ghost of Bataan*, foreword.
24. Steinbeck, *Once There Was a War*, xii; Lawton, *Some Survived*, xvii.
25. MacArthur, *Surviving the Sword*, 16–22, xxv.
26. Costello, *Pacific War*, 228.
27. Sides, *Ghost Soldiers*, 49, 86–7, 97–99.
28. Cave, *Beyond Courage*, 179, 186. Cave claims this latter testimony came from a "Colonel Cain" during Homma's trial, but I have found no such record in the transcript. As for forced shoelessness, the only other references I found is James Baldassarre's very questionable testimony at Homma's trial, and that of one other. *USA v. Homma*, 885, 1184.
29. Barker, *Prisoners of War*, 45–6, and Bliven, *From Pearl Harbor to Okinawa*, 50, are two such examples.
30. Stewart's version appears on page 52, Breuer cited it as 72–3.
31. Moss, "Oral History," 110.
32. Falk, *Bataan: The March of Death*, 196–7.
33. Abie Abraham later wrote, "After our surrender many of the prisoners rode in trucks all the way to Camp O'Donnell and could not have seen what happened along the Death March. Many testified that 2,200 died on the route, and even historians have this wrong information." Abraham, *Ghost of Bataan*, 229. Other inaccurate figures are Daws, *Prisoners of the Japanese*, 80: "between 500 and 1000"; Kerr, *Surrender and Survival*, 59–60: "probable death toll in the hundreds"; Garner, *A Study in Valor*, 71: "generally agreed that 1,000 Americans perished on the march"; Yuki Tanaka, *Hidden Horrors*, 15: 2000; Johnson, *Hour of Redemption*, 28: 2275; Murakami, *Japan: Years of Trial*, 111: 2300; Boston Publishing, *Above and Beyond*, 2300; Conroy, *Battle of Bataan*, 65: 2300; Gailey, *The War in the Pacific*, 108: 2330; Toland, *But Not in Shame*, 329: 2330; Bergamini, *Japan's Imperial Conspiracy*, 958: "between 2,000 and 3,000 ... are known to have died"; Carruth, *What Happened When*, 775: "5200 Americans and many more Filipinos lost their lives." Bliven *From Pearl to Okinawa*, 50: "By the time the gruesome march was over, some 5,000 American prisoners had been murdered." The figure cited in the charges against Homma was 1200, *USA v. Homma*, 30.
34. Quoted in Eakin, "Autobiography, Identity and the Fictions of Memory," 295.

35. Gray, *The Warriors*, 34.
36. Some issues pertain to using Wilkomirski's "memoir" to shed light on those written by Death March survivors. Wilkomirski was inventing memories from childhood, whereas the POWs were adults at the time they claimed their level of trauma. Also, Wilkomirski's recovered memories were assisted by therapy, and no estimate of the number of Bataan survivors who chose to undergo therapy is possible.
37. Mächler, *Wilkomirski Affair*, 129, 263–68. In the afterward to his thoroughly researched exposé, Mächler commented on Wilkomirski's "anguish and insecurity" and stated that, in his response, "one could hear the voice of a person who had become very aggressive, who felt willfully misunderstood, offended, and belittled by almost every page of my report." Ibid., 309.
38. Geertz, *Interpretation of Cultures*, 347.
39. Mächler, *Wilkomirski Affair*, 287, 275, 276.
40. Ibid., 130, 288, 115. Among such warnings is Jean-François Forges, *Éduquer contre Auschwitz: Histoire et mémoire* (*Educating Against Auschwitz: History and Memory*).
41. Iriye, *Power and Culture*, 37.
42. Thompson, *How the Japanese Army Fights*, 121.
43. Dower, *War Without Mercy*.
44. Grashio, *Return to Freedom*, 19; Lawton, *Some Survived*, 19, 22.
45. Quoted in Mächler, *Wilkomirski Affair*, 115.
46. Ashton, *And Somebody Gives a Damn*, 159.
47. Tenney, *My Hitch in Hell*, Czerwien, *POW: Tears That Never Dry*, 33; Lawton, *Some Survived*, 21–2; Levering, *Horror Trek*, 63.
48. Silva, *Senso Owari*, 19–20; Sneddon, *Zero Ward*, 17–31; http://www.u-s-history.com/pages/h1737.html On the seventy-first anniversary of the surrender, Lester Tenney, aged ninety-two, appeared on CNN.com and offered his summary of the Death March experience: "If you stopped, you were killed. If you had to defecate, you were killed. If you just couldn't take another step, you were killed. And they just killed you for no reason except for the fact that you did not move." Tenney is shown filling packages for American soldiers in Iraq and Afghanistan, for the purpose of causing them to believe someone cares. www.cnn.com, "Human Factor."
49. Bollich, *Bataan Death March*, 14.
50. Chunn, *Of Rice and Men*, 14, 95.
51. Sneddon, *Zero Ward*, 30–1.
52. Stouffer, *American Soldier: Combat and Its Aftermath*, 161–3.
53. Knox, *Bataan: The March of Death*, xi-xii.
54. Neuenschwander, "Oral Historians and Long-Term Memory," 325–26.
55. Ibid., 328; Eakin, "Autobiography, Identity and the Fictions of Memory," 292.
56. Schacter, *Memory Distortion*, 24.
57. Larson, http://www.bataansurvivor.com/content/the_bataan_death_march/5.php.
58. Olson, *O'Donnell: Andersonville of the Pacific*, 5; Bollich, *Bataan Death March*, 76; Playter, *Survivor*, 55; Jackson, *Diary of Col. Calvin G. Jackson*, 47.

One survivor no doubt spoke for many when he stated, "When I say I don't know how long I was on the Death March, it indicates more than personal loss of memory; it was symptomatic of the whole enterprise. In the most straightforward sense, I endured twelve days ... but I don't remember how many of those days I actually spent marching down the road accompanied by Japanese guards: seven or eight most likely, possibly ten." Hunt, *Behind Japanese Lines*, 28.
59. Sneddon, *Zero Ward*, 22, 26; Gautier, *I Came Back from Bataan*, 74–5.
60. Hubbard, *Apocalypse Undone*, 86, 93; Masterson, *Ride the Waves to Freedom*, 42.
61. Ping Fu, *Bend, Not Break*, 44, 77; *The Week*, March 22, 2013.
62. *USA v. Homma*, 3292, 3339.
63. Meier continued, "My opinion is that they are the most inhuman people on earth. They have driven [men] away from water on the march, and slashed them with bayonets when [their] eyes were bulging out, their mouths swollen and a hysterical look on their faces" and men were lying "in carabao dung." NARA, Philippines Archives collection, RG 407, Diary of P.H. Meier, Box 136, no date.
64. Gottschalk, "The History and the Historical Document," 16; Schacter, *Seven Sins of Memory*, 20.
65. Bumgarner, *Parade of the Dead*, ix; Kathman, *I Was There*, Charley, xi.
66. Gilpatrick, *Footprints in Courage*, 7–10; Haney, *Caged Dragons*, xiv; Laub, "Truth and Testimony: The Process and the Struggle," 64. In his book, *Hell's Guest*, Glenn Frazier states he was haunted by nightmares and hatred of the Japanese for three decades until, expiating his bile in prose, he found peace. Well into his eighties, J.D. Merritt completed his book, *Adapt or Die*, that explains his "personal metamorphosis" from a "callow, carefree youth into a calculating executioner." In the preface to his 1992 book, *Tears That Never Dry*, Anthony Czerwien stated that he had wanted to write since his liberation in 1945, and that his purpose was to "reveal the inhuman tortures inflicted on the valiant soldiers."
67. Wolf, "Reactions Among Allied Prisoners of War," 185, 191.
68. Lunden, "Captivity Psychosis Among Prisoners of War," 731.
69. Parillo, *We Were in the Big One*, xvi.
70. Kammen, "Some Patterns and meanings of Memory Distortion in American History," 329–45.
71. Für einen quellenkritischen Historiker eine schmerzliche Einsicht. Maschke, *Die deutschen Kriegsgefangenen*, 119.
72. Ross, "Constructing and Appraising Past Selves," 233; Fritzsche quoted in Maynes, *Telling Stories*, 78.
73. Fritzsche, "The Case of Modern Memory," 97.
74. Brackman, *The Other Nuremberg*, 247.
75. Krystal, "Trauma and Aging: A Thirty-Year Follow-Up," 92; Hibbs, *Tell MacArthur to Wait*, 151; Schacter, *Seven Sins of Memory*, 113. Once, a television trivia columnist received a letter asking about the details of a show he could not remember from his youth. He wrote, "Was there ever a TV series called

'The Survivors?' I remember it was about some people who'd been stranded on an island in an airplane crash. I also remember Lily Tomlin appearing on it before she was anybody." It turned out that the letter writer had conflated three different shows, all of which appeared on Monday night in 1969. Ceci, "False Beliefs: Some Developmental and Clinical Considerations," 92–3.

76. Schacter, *Searching for Memory*, 287–9.
77. Lawton, *Some Survived*, 33–7.
78. Belli and Loftus, "The Pliability of Autobiographical Memory," 157. Erich Maschke, in his study of German POWs returning from Russian captivity, found that mistaken or contrived memories can take the place of factual occurrence. Maschke, *Die deutschen Kriegsgefangenen*, 117.
79. Quoted in Schacter, *Searching for Memory*, 93. Bei wiederholten Erzählungen des gleichen Ereignisses greift man weniger auf die erste ursprüngliche Erinnerung als vielmehr auf die Erinnerung der jeweils letzten Verbalisierung zurück. Maschke, *Die deutschen Kriegsgefangenen*, 121.
80. Bilek, *No Uncle Sam*, 49–65.
81. Perhaps some of the same thoughts went through George Harrison's mind in 1970, after the legal problems that attended his composition of "My Sweet Lord," a melody eerily similar to Ronald Mack's "He's So Fine," recorded several years earlier. At the trial for artistic plagiarism, Harrison was found guilty, but the judge was not unaware of memory's tricks when he stated, "Did Harrison deliberately use the music of 'He's So Fine?' I do not believe he did so deliberately. Nevertheless ... this is, under the law, infringement of copyright, and is no less so even though subconsciously accomplished." Sacks, "Speak, Memory."
82. Lyttleton, *From Peace to War*, 152.
83. Christianson and Safer, "Emotional Events and Emotions in Autobiographical Memories," 303, 219–20, 238, 218–38, passim.
84. Studies of children who had been kidnapped on a school bus in California, then were buried underground for hours before escaping suggest this reality. Interviewed several years after the traumatic event, about half of the children's testimony revealed "rather striking errors and distortions." Another case, that of a sniper attack on a school in 1984, revealed that some students, just weeks after the incident, reported they were there when they were not. Again, in 1988, a woman assaulted a Chicago school, killing one child and wounding several others. Five and eighteen months later, when school personal were questioned, "two of six who initially said they had been more than 25 miles away later claimed to have been within a mile." Schacter, *Searching for Memory*, 206–07.
85. Neisser, *The Remembering Self*, 5. Schacter, *Searching for Memory*, chapter 9, "Memory Wars" discusses a phenomenon of the 1990s—young women, responding to therapist's suggestions, who claimed to have been sexually abused as children by male relatives. Most accusations proved to be utterly false.
86. Caruth, *Unclaimed Experience*, 3–4. Evans, *Kora!*, 14.

87. Schacter, *Searching for Memory*, 207.
88. Quoted in van der Kolk, "The Intrusive Past," 441. "Prolonged captivity ... produces profound alterations in the victim's identity. All the psychological structures of the self—the image of the body, the internalized image of others, and the values and ideals that lend a person a sense of coherence and purpose—have been invaded and systematically broken down." Herman, *Trauma and Recovery*, 93.
89. Fussell, *Great War in Modern Memory*, 310; Belli and Loftus, "The Pliability of Autobiographical Memory," 158.
90. Larson, *The Memoir and the Memoirist*, 10.
91. Olson, *O'Donnell: Andersonville of the Pacific*, 3; Abraham, *Ghost of Bataan Speaks*, 61–2, 229.
92. Des Pres, *The Survivor*, 29.
93. Knox, *Death March*, 142. Among the many are Abie Abraham, Alf Larson, John Henry Poncio, Richard Gordon and Kermit Lay.
94. Dyess, *Dyess Story*, 85–6; Knox, *Death March*, 144.
95. Alf Larson http://www.bataansurvivor.com/.
96. Tenney, *My Hitch in Hell*, 57–8. Jacobsen, *We Refused to Die*, 88; Czerwien, *POW: Tears That Never Dry*, 34–5.
97. Stewart, *Give Us This Day*, 46–59; Gautier, *I Came Back from Bataan*, 77–8. I have found only one other reference to beheading of this type—at Camp O'Donnell, Sam Grashio claimed that Japanese soldiers returned from a fight with Filipino guerrillas with a Filipino head on a bamboo pole. Grashio, *Return to Freedom*, 55.
98. Stewart, *Give Us This Day*, 59.
99. Ortega, *Courage on Bataan*, 57; Dyess, *Dyess Story*, 90.
100. Hibbs, *Tell MacArthur to Wait*, 112; Bank, *Back from the Living Dead*, 23; Cave, *Beyond Courage*, 184.
101. Moody, *Reprieve from Hell*, 73; bataansurvivor.com/content/the_bataan_death_march/5.php; Bollich, 73–4, 76; Sneddon, *Zero Ward*, 22; Lee, *They Call It Pacific*, 279.
102. White, *Content of the Form*, 4; *USA v. Homma*, 3306.
103. Barclay and Wellman, "Accuracies and Inaccuracies in Autobiographical Memories," 101.

Chapter 6

1. Haney, *Caged Dragons*, 245.
2. Wittlesey finished the war as a lieutenant colonel, winner of a Congressional Medal of Honor, but celebrity weighed heavily on him. On a cruise ship on the way to Cuba, he committed suicide by jumping overboard in 1921. Johnson and Pratt, *The Lost Battalion*, Introduction, passim, 258–60.
3. Breuer, *Great Raid on Cabanatuan*, 19–20.
4. *Time*, March 16, 1942.
5. Ibid., February 9, 1942; March 9, 1942.
6. Ibid., February 23, 1942; March 2, 1942.
7. Ibid., March 23, 1942.

8. Tapert, *Lines of Battle*, 19; Quoted in Morton, *Fall of the Philippines*, 387–88.
9. Ind, *Bataan: The Judgment Seat*, 302.
10. Masterson, *Ride the Waves to Freedom*, 35.
11. Steinbeck, *Once There Was a War*, xiii, xvii.
12. Manchester, *American Caesar*, 165. Breuer believes MacArthur kept thirty-one uniforms. Breuer, *Great Raid on Cabanatuan*, 9.
13. Morton, *Fall of the Philippines*, 166–67. In a press interview in early 1940, MacArthur claimed that 30,000 Filipinos would be trained each year, and by 1946 would include thirty divisions totaling 300,000. By 1966, it would reach MacArthur's goal of ninety divisions and almost one million men. Hayden, *The Philippines*, 739.
14. Volckman, *We Remained*, 7–8.
15. Ibid., 15; *In the Hands of the Enemy*.
16. Grashio, *Return to Freedom*, 13; Gautier, *I Came Back from Bataan*, 189.
17. Conroy, *Battle of Bataan*, 22–3; Gailey, *Liberation of Guam*, 104.
18. North, *Lost in the Wilderness*, Prologue; "MacArthur unwisely ordered that 10 million bushels of food—enough to feed his troops for a year but heavy and difficult to move—be abandoned during the retreat." Greenberger, *Bataan Death March*, 23.
19. Young, *Battle of Bataan*, 207.
20. Gilpatrick, *Footprints in Courage*, 33.
21. Mallonee, *Battle for Bataan*, 146; *USA v. Homma*, 2511.
22. *In the Hands of the Enemy*.
23. MacArthur, *Reminiscences*, 135–6.
24. Hubbard, *Apocalypse Undone*, 63; Thomas, *As I Remember* 111; Morton, *Fall of the Philippines*, 387.
25. Toland, *But Not in Shame*, 177.
26. *Forsaken Legion*; Thomas, *As I Remember*, 118; Weinstein, *Barbed-Wire Surgeon*, 41; Morton, *Fall of the Philippines*, 387.
27. Ind, *Bataan: The Judgment Seat*, 322–23.
28. Feuer, *Bilibid Diary*, 54; Manchester, *Goodbye Darkness*, 237.
29. Doyle, *Voices from Captivity*, 249; Cave, *Beyond Courage*, 104.
30. Marquardt, *Before Bataan and After*, 255; Nicolay, *MacArthur of Bataan*, 160–61; *Time*, 2-9-42; Quoted in Morton, *Fall of the Philippines*, 387.
31. Merritt, *Adapt or Die*, 188; *Tragedy of Bataan*; Quoted in Costello, *The Pacific War*, 186.
32. Young, *Battle of Bataan*, 208; Krystal, "Trauma and Aging," 83.
33. Barker, *Prisoners of War*, 37; Gordon, *Horyo*, 82; North, *Lost in the Wilderness*, Prologue.
34. April 9, 2012. http://www.youtube.com/watch?v=OxKpqQdMsWg; *Tragedy of Bataan*.
35. Martin, *Brothers from Bataan*, 68; Spector, *Eagle Against the Sun*, 119.
36. MacArthur, *Reminiscences*, 141.
37. Chunn, *Of Rice and Men*, 196.
38. Cave, *Beyond Courage*, 132. John Vance recorded that a submarine brought in antiaircraft ammunition "and took out $5,000,000 worth of gold bars plus several tons of silver coins." Vance, *Doomed Garrison*, 111, 117; Marquardt, *Before Bataan and After*, 258.
39. Manchester, *American Caesar*, 309–313, passim; Nicolay, *MacArthur of Bataan*, 181.
40. Whitman, *Bataan: Our Last Ditch*, 487–88.
41. NARA, Philippines Archive Collection, Box 128, Diary of J.A. Guder, RG 407.
42. *Tragedy of Bataan*; *In the Hands of the Enemy*.
43. Grashio, *Return to Freedom*, 32.
44. Nicolay, *MacArthur of Bataan*, 108, 139–65.
45. Manchester, *American Caesar*, 310–11.
46. Holt, "King of Bataan," 171.
47. Lingeman, *Don't You Know There's a War On?*, 175, 235.
48. Ibid., 201.
49. Ibid., 192, 185.
50. Ibid., 210–11, 235–6, 215.
51. Ibid., 241–42.
52. Fussell, *Wartime*, 149; Manchester, *Goodbye Darkness*, 237.
53. Brookhauser, *This Was Your War*, 390.
54. Brinkley, *David Brinkley*, 48.
55. http://www.bostonfirehistory.org/firestory11281942.html.
56. Lingeman, *Don't You Know There's a War On?*, 191.
57. Falk, *Bataan: The March of Death*, 209–10.
58. Dyess, *Dyess Story*, quotes on 91, 85; 68–97, passim.
59. *Time*, February 7, 1944.
60. Grashio, *Return to Freedom*, 147–50.
61. Masterson, *Ride the Waves to Freedom*, 107.
62. Quoted in Grayling, *Among the Dead Cities*, 170–71.
63. Brookhauser, *This Was Your War*, 56.
64. Janoff-Bulman, *Shattered Assumptions*, 148.
65. Stoler, "The Second World War in U.S. Memory," 386.
66. Kimball, "The Incredible Shrinking War," 348–49; Thomas Farragher, "A Thinning of the Ranks," *Boston Globe*, November 11, 1999.
67. O'Donnell, *Into the Rising Sun*, 2.
68. Martin, *Brothers from Bataan*, 112–13.
69. NARA, Philippines Archives Collection, RG 407, Box 130, Diary of H.J. Fleeger.
70. Wiesel, *One Generation After*, 7; Feuer, *Bilibid Diary*, 181.
71. Ibid., 67–8.
72. *Study of Former Prisoners of War*, 57; Sommers, *The Japanese Story*, 75–6.
73. Cohen and Cooper, *A Follow-Up Study of World War II Prisoners of War*, 23; Sommers, *The Japanese Story*, 66.
74. The survey, taken in the 1980s, revealed that 61 percent reported being "seriously troubled" in the first year; 55 percent from 1946 to 1950; 59 percent from 1950 to 1980; 55 percent from 1980 to 1983. One significant variable was rank; officers had a lower incidence of symptoms. Zeiss, "PTSD 40 Years Later," 83, 86.
75. Goldstein, "Survivors of Imprisonment in the Pacific Theater," 1213.
76. Towle, "The Japanese Army and Prisoners of War," xi; Frazier, *Hell's Guest*.

77. Hubbard, *Apocalypse Undone*, 252–53. Red Allen is another of many who reported on-going nightmares. See Allen, *Abandoned on Bataan*, 203.
78. Haney, *Caged Dragons*, 226; Petak completed a hand-written manuscript in 1947, and stored it away until 1989, when he found it while looking through his attic. Petak, *Never Plan Tomorrow*, 431.
79. Kelnhofer, *Life After Liberation*, 11–80, passim, 88.
80. Boyington, *Baa Baa Black Sheep*, 349.
81. Holmes, *Unjust Enrichment*, 145–46.
82. Gordon, *Horyo*, 104.
83. Allen, *Abandoned on Bataan*, 208; Nardini, "William Porter Lecture," 299; Abraham, *Ghost of Bataan Speaks*, 244.
84. Quoted Wagner, *World War I 365 Days*, VE Day section.
85. Nardini, "William Porter Lecture," 306; Lawton, *Some Survived*, 249.
86. Grinker, *Men Under Stress*, 185–7.
87. Landas, *The Fallen: A True Story of American POWs*, 5.
88. Haney, *Caged Dragons*, 167; Manchester, *Goodbye Darkness*, 141.
89. Fussell, *Boy's Crusade*, 101.
90. Kelnhofer, *Life After Liberation*, 1, 57. Kelnhofer lists the physical symptoms shared by ex-POWs as psychic numbing, depression, fatigue, peripheral neuropathy, sleeplessness, and sexual dysfunction, and emphasizes anger as a defining leitmotif of their behavior.
91. *The Week*, November 1, 2013.
92. Serrano, *Last of the Blue and Gray*, 110, 120.
93. Ibid., 31–33.
94. Ibid., 155–65 passim, 174.
95. *The Week*, September 2, 2012; *New York Times*, April 5, 1998.
96. Gilpatrick, *Footprints in Courage*, 119. The treatment of guerrillas was stingy. The War Claims Act of 1948 provided payment to prisoners in the amount of $1 per day, with an additional $1.50 if they could prove they had been treated inhumanely. Leon Beck, who survived the Death March, escaped and spent three years as a guerrilla, then fought the U.S. government for twelve years since it tried to claim $992 paid him was wrongly dispensed since he had only officially been a prisoner for thirteen days. Hunt, *Behind Japanese Lines*, 222.
97. *Forsaken Legion*.
98. Holmes, *Unjust Enrichment*, 144, 147.
99. Ibid., 137–38, 144. Americans were not the only ones who felt betrayed by their government. Filipinos who served on Bataan had been promised equal pay, to rectify a situation that had rankled since the mid–1930s. Even worse, the 1946 Rescission Act "broke the Roosevelt administration's promise of naturalized citizenship and veteran's benefits for all Filipino members of the USAFFE. Only Filipino soldiers wounded or killed ... were to be recognized as U.S. war veterans; all others were ineligible for most benefits under the G.I. Bill of Rights of 1944." Broad, *Plundering Paradise*, 121.
100. H.R. 3188, June 14, 1984.

101. Parkinson, *Soldier Slaves*, 76, 100–01, 117; Gailey, *Liberation of Guam*, 106; Spector, *Eagle Against the Sun*, 115.
102. "U.S. Prisoners of War and Civilian American Citizens Captured and Interned by Japan in World War II: The Issue of Compensation by Japan," Navy Department Library, http://www.history.navy.mil/library/online/usprisoners_japancomp.htm.
103. www.nps.gov/history/history/online_books/personal_justice_denied/intro.htm.
104. Eizenstat, *Imperfect Justice*, 4; *Forsaken Legion*.
105. Slotkin, *Regeneration Through Violence*, 10.
106. Rotundo, *American Manhood*, 4–5.
107. Levi-Strauss, *Tristes Tropiques*.
108. Slotkin, *Gunfighter Nation*, 14.
109. Ibid., 14–5.
110. Ibid., 16.
111. Iriye, *Power and Culture*, 37.
112. Lawton, *Some Survived*, 24; Gordon, *Horyo*, 102; for a general description, see Dower, *War Without Mercy*.
113. Littlewood, *The Idea of Japan*, 42.
114. Slotkin, *Fatal Environment*, 374.
115. Des Pres, *The Survivor*, 42.
116. Ibid., 5, 9–10.
117. Quoted in Ibid., 23.
118. Wiesel, *One Generation After*, 9–10; *Forsaken Legion*.
119. Fussell, *Boy's Crusade*, 49–50.
120. Doyle, *Voices from Captivity*, 231.

Chapter 7

1. Keegan, *World War I*, 174; Gordon, *Horyo*, 90.
2. Evans, *Kora!*, 145–46. For veterans of the Imperial Japanese Army this must in part have resulted from "a simple desire to repress the consequences of one's own actions while dwelling on one's sufferings." One scholar goes so far as to describe the late twentieth century's "usurpation of the narrative of heroism by the narrative of victimhood." Bartov, *Crimes of War*, xxiii.
3. Bix, *Hirohito and the Making of Modern Japan*, 528; Dower, *War Without Mercy*, 262. Examples of addressing Japanese wartime responsibility include the textbooks written by Ienaga Saburo and the pronouncement in 1988 of the Mayor of Nagasaki, Motoshima Hitoshi, that the emperor of Japan bore responsibility for the war. Buruma, *Wages of Guilt*, 189–201; Field, *In the Realm of a Dying Emperor*, 175–266. By the late 70s and early 80s, new kinds of films were being made, ones that rehabilitated the Japanese soldier. *Dai Nippon Teikoku*, for example, contains a scene showing U.S. soldiers playing football with human skulls, and imperial soldiers full of good will toward the local population.
4. Wiesel, *One Generation After*, 7; Dower, *Embracing Defeat*, 513.
5. Buruma, *Wages of Guilt*, 106–07. For further, nuanced discussion of the theme of victimization, see Ellen Schattsschneider, "The Work of Sacrifice in the Age of Mechanical Reproduction: Bride Dolls and

Ritual Appropriation at Yasukuni Shrine" in Tansman, *The Culture of Japanese Fascism*, 296–317. A museum that confronts the issue of Japanese wartime brutality is Peace Osaka.

6. Mailer, *The Naked and the Dead*, 247.
7. Ibid., 198–99.
8. Buruma, *Wages of Guilt*, 223. The museum in Chiran, Kyushu, dedicated specifically to the *kamikaze* pilots, is another example. A few works have dealt directly with wartime atrocity. Tanuma Taijiro's *Shunpu-den* (*Tale of the Prostitutes*, 1947) dealt with comfort women in Korea, and was later made into a film. Gomikawa Junpei wrote a six volume work, *Ningen no jōken* (*Prerequisites for a Human Being*, 1958) that dealt with atrocities in Manchuria, portions of which became a best seller. Morimura Seiichi's *Akuma no bōshoku* (*Satan's Delirious Feast*, 1981), dealing with biological experiments on Chinese and Russian prisoners, also sold well. On the opposite side stands the "Liberal Historic View" typified by Fujioka Nobukatsu, *Kyokasho ga oshienai rekishi* (*Japanese History no textbook teaches*, 1997), a four-volume series that has sold over one million copies. In the same vein are Nishio Kanji's *Kokumin no rekishi* (*The People's History*, 1999) and Ueyama Shunpei, *Dai Tōa-Sensō no imi* (*Significance of the Greater East Asian War*, 1964) and Hayashi Fusao, *Tōa-Sensō kōtai ron* defending Japanese behavior. Koshiro, "Japan's World and World War II," 428, notes 4, 5; 432, note 17.
9. Dower, *Embracing Defeat*, 515–18; Tsurumi, *Social Change and the Individual*, 178.
10. Dower, *Embracing Defeat*, 148, 158.
11. Ibid., 486, 490–93, 52.
12. Ibid., 61. The Armed Forces Information and Education Division's *Pocket Guide to Japan*, issued to servicemen, devoted exactly four short paragraphs to Japanese history, and a mere three sentences to World War II.
13. Koshiro, "Japan's World and World War II," 436, note 28. The Chinese have made a fetish of victimhood, with frequent reference to *bǎinián guóchǐ*, the narrative of their hundred years of humiliation at the hands of Western and Japanese imperialists. In 2011 and 2012, some 177 shows featuring anti–Japan resistance were approved by the Communist government, some 20 percent of the overall total authorized. This is good business for Chinese TV producers. The trailer for one drama, *Smoke Signals Everywhere*, shows the bullets of Chinese soldiers flying in slow motion on the way to hitting their Japanese targets. *The Economist*, 6–1–13, 48.
14. Steinbeck, *Once There Was a War*, xviii; Terkel, "The Good War," 16; Tapert, *Lines of Battle*, 197; Brookhouser, *This Was Your War*, 56.
15. Fussell, *Wartime*, 129–43; Gray, *The Warriors*, 20, 23–4.
16. McPherson, *What They Fought For*.
17. Mitchell, *Civil War Soldiers*, 82, 57. Religion was one means of controlling an undisciplined population of soldiers. The Confederate soldier experienced greater difficulty, had fewer opportunities to visit home, generally suffered greater privation. "Religion promised significant assistance in the thorny problem of governing the frequently intractable Confederate troops." Faust, "Christian Soldiers and the Meaning of Revivalism," 73.
18. Dower, *Ways of Forgetting*, 101.
19. Fussel, *Boy's Crusade*, xv.
20. Quoted in Whitman, *Bataan: Our Last Ditch*, 562.
21. Stewart, *Give Us This Day*, 49; Whitman, *Bataan: Our Last Ditch*, 566.
22. U.S. Government Printing Office, *Study of Former Prisoners of War*, 23; *Death March from Bataan to Manchuria: Raising a Survivor's Voice*.
23. Playter, *Survivor*, 65.
24. Whitman, *Bataan: Our Last Ditch*, 596.
25. Thomas, *As I Remember*, 150; http://www.pbs.org/wgbh/amex/macarthur/sfeature/bataan_capture.html.
26. http://www.pbs.org/wgbh/amex/macarthur/sfeature/bataan_capture.html.
27. Knox, *Death March*, 144, 148. See also Marquez, *War Memoirs of the Alcala Veterans*, 32. Others, like Sgt. Alfred Schreiber, hesitated, fearing that Japanese would be waiting to shoot him if caught. "As long as we were on the road," he recalled, "we figured we'd make it." Others were either too sick or too tired to run. Knox, *Death March*, 147, 149. Some who refused to surrender fled into hills, but later turned themselves in because of starvation and sickness. Bollich, *Bataan Death March*, 69.
28. Quoted in Fussell, *Wartime*, 117; Stouffer, *The American Soldier: Combat and Its Aftermath*, 132; Lawton, *Some Survived*, 22.
29. James, *South to Bataan*, 108; J.B. Nardini, "The William C. Porter Lecture—1961: Psychiatric Concepts of Prisoners of War Confinement," 300.
30. James, *South to Bataan*, 85; Barker, *Prisoners of War*, 193.
31. MacArthur, *Surviving the Sword*, xxx.
32. Wiesel, *One Generation After*, 52, 122.
33. Gilpatrick, *Footprints in Courage*, 134; Gordon, *Horyo*, 229, xxix.
34. Gordon, *Horyo*, 169–70, 227–29.
35. Sommers, *The Japanese Story*, 34.
36. Evans, *Kora!*, 9; Weinstein, *Barbed-Wire Surgeon*, 74.
37. The most reliable figures are found in Falk, *Bataan*. Overall, some 27 percent of prisoners taken by the Imperial Japanese Army died in captivity, compared to 4 percent held by Germany and Italy. Tanaka, *Hidden Horrors*, 70; Kerr, *Surrender and Survival*, 59–60; MacArthur, *Surviving the Sword*, xxvi. American mortality was worse. Of the 33,587 Americans taken, 12,909 died in captivity, a 38.4 percent mortality rate. But the death rate for the 25,580 Americans who surrendered in the Philippines was even higher—more than 10,000 of these men died, more than forty percent. Urwin, *Victory in Defeat*, 335. Of the 34,648 captured in the Pacific, 12,935 died, or 37 percent. The worst period was the internment from May to October, during which 1,500 of 8,000 at O'Donnell died; 2700 out of 6500 at Cabanatuan during first year. U.S. Government Printing Office, *Study of Former Prisoners of War*, 33.

38. Gordon, *Horyo*, 115–16. John Love, who died March 17, 2014, in Philadelphia at age 91, joined other survivors in 2009 to change the caption of one of the most famous photos taken on Bataan, that of bodies slung on poles carried by pairs of men. "The photo, thought to be of the march, actually was an allied burial detail. After a six-month investigation, the AP corrected the caption in 2010." *Philadelphia Inquirer*, March 24, 2014, B6.

39. Feuer, *Bilibid Diary*, 6; Mellnik, *Philippine Diary*, 167–8.

40. Olson, *O'Donnell: Andersonville of the Pacific*, 86; Nardini, "Survival Factors," 244–46.

41. Steinbeck, *Once There Was a War*, xii; Quoted in Des Pres, *The Survivor*, 109, 140.

42. Some were then transferred to Palawan Barracks, located on an island off the west coast of the Philippines. Ultimately, about 1,000 of these men found their way to Bilibid prison in Manila, and another 1,000 were transferred to Camp Hoten in Manchuria. Others went to a camp on Taiwan. Ultimately, some three quarters of Americans captured by the Japanese ended their careers as POWs in Japan. They were split up among locations in Osaka, Fukuoka, Zentsuji and other locations. Turner Publishing Company, *American Ex-Prisoners of War*, 37–43.

43. Mellnik, *Philippine Diary*, 172; Johnson, *Hour of Redemption*, 58; Feuer, *Bilibid Diary*, 137; Knox, *Death March*, 340.

44. Gordon, *Horyo*, 110; *Death March from Bataan to Manchuria: Raising a Survivor's Voice*; Gordon, *Horyo*, 227–28.

45. Lawton, *Some Survived*, 38–43.

46. Wolf, "Reactions Among Allied Prisoners of War," 184.

47. NARA, Diary of L. Arhutik, RG 407, Philippine Archives Collection, Box 125.

48. Abraham, *Ghost of Bataan*, 88; Feuer, *Bilibid Diary*, 9; Wolf, "Reactions Among Allied Prisoners of War," 182.

49. Wright, *Captured on Corregidor*, 66 and 47–80, passim.

50. Gordon, *Horyo*, 228; Weinstein, *Barbed-Wire Surgeon*, x.

51. Nardini, "Survival Factors," 242; Weinstein, *Barbed-Wire Surgeon*, 158–59.

52. Martin, *Brothers from Bataan*, 137; Feuer, *Bilibid Diary*, 76. J.B. Nardini, who made first-hand observations, wrote that "hungry men were often reduced to attitudes and actions incompatible with their own previously accepted levels of behavior and self-respect. Men quibbled over portions of food, were suspicious of those who were in more favored positions than themselves, participated in unethical, barter, took advantage of less clever or enterprising fellow prisoners, stole, rummaged in garbage, and even curried the favor of their detested captors." Nardini, "Survival Factors," 241–42.

53. Gordon, *Horyo*, xiii.

54. Moody, *Reprieve from Hell*, 93. North, *Lost in the Wilderness*, 61. See also *USA v. Homma*, 1365.

55. Wright, *Captured on Corregidor*, 60.

56. Petak, *Never Plan Tomorrow*, 62–3.

57. Gilpatrick, *Footprints in Courage*, 62.

58. Olson, *O'Donnell: Andersonville of the Pacific*, 91.

59. Grashio, *Return to Freedom*, 57, 74, 68–9; Romulo, *I Saw the Fall of the Philippines*, 193; Gordon, *Horyo*, 118. Inflation soared during the siege. Used coffee grounds were so valuable they were "traded like commodities ... their value based on the number of times they'd been brewed" and "those addicted to cigarettes were going nuts." Merritt, *Adapt or Die*, 180.

60. NARA, RG 153, JAG War Crimes Branch Case Files, 1944–49, Box 1108.

61. Gilpatrick, *Footprints in Courage*, 103; RG 153 JAG War Crimes Branch Case Files, 1944–49, Box 1108; Grashio, *Return to Freedom*, 68.

62. Personal email to author, July 9, 2008.

63. Quoted in Urwin, *Victory in Defeat*, 342–3.

64. Feuer, *Bilibid Diary*, 21; Spector, *Eagle Against the Sun*, 12.

65. Wolf, "Reactions Among Allied Prisoners of War," 182.

66. NARA, RG 407, Philippines Archive Collection, Box 145, Diary of S. Hayes; Martin, *Brothers from Bataan*, 157.

67. Tapert, *Lines of Battle*, 19; NARA, RG 407, Philippines Archive Collection, Box 145, Diary of CD Quinlenn; Feuer, *Bilibid Diary*, 96.

68. Johnson, *Hour of Redemption*, 56. At Cabanatuan, Lt. Colonels received 220 *pesos* per month. Lieutenants got 85, and privates only 3. Caraccilo, *Surviving Bataan and Beyond*, 289, note 5.

69. McBride, *Beyond the Death March*, 100; Gordon, *Horyo*, 118.

70. Mellnik, *Philippine Diary*, 173; Gordon, *Horyo*, 116–17.

71. Feuer, *Bilibid Diary*, 31; Gordon, *Horyo*, 94.

72. Linderman, *World Within War*, 222, 225, 219.

73. Steinbeck, *Once There Was a War*, xiii; Willeford, *Something About a Soldier*, 80.

74. Frankl, *From Death Camp to Existentialism*, 31; Young, *Battle of Bataan*, 210.

75. Gilpatrick, *Footprints in Courage*, 64; Linderman, *World Within War*, 278–79.

76. Grashio, *Return to Freedom*, 58.

77. Knox, *Death March*, xii; Poweleit, *USAFFE*, vi-vii; Miller, *Situation Normal*, 147.

78. Manchester, *Goodbye Darkness*, 100; Grashio, *Return to Freedom*, 64.

79. White, *Content of the Form*, 10; Nietzsche, "On the uses and disadvantages of history for life," 62; Brain, *Soldier of Bataan*, 29.

80. Maynes, *Telling Stories*, 119.

81. Jones, *Thin Red Line*, 122.

82. Gordon, *Horyo*, 39. For binny boys see Willeford, *Something About a Soldier*, 99–100.

83. Weinstein, *Barbed-Wire Surgeon*, 128; Gordon, *Horyo*, xii.

84. Nardini, "Survival Factors," 243.

85. Moody, *Reprieve from Hell*, 111. At one point in Cabanatuan, John Wright, in charge of a particular barracks, "received all men discharged from the lock

ward at the hospital. Mental cases, kleptomaniacs, sex perverts, Bolsheviks." Wright, *Captured on Corregidor*, 66.
 86. Weinstein, *Barbed-Wire Surgeon*, 160; Nardini, "Survival Factors," 247.
 87. Wolf, "Reactions Among Allied Prisoners of War," 185; Steinbeck, *Once There Was a War*, xii; Schudson, "Dynamics of Distortion in Collective Memory," 360.
 88. Doyle, *Voices from Captivity*, 5.
 89. See, for example, Alf Larson's "Letter to God," wherein he imagines the saving hand of a larger force in dangerous moments. http://www.bataansurvivor.com/content/epilogue/1.php.
 90. Olson, *O'Donnell: Andersonville of the Pacific*, 179–80.
 91. Grashio, *Return to Freedom*, 28.
 92. Neisser, *The Remembering Self*, 9; Jerome Bruner, "Self Making Narratives," 41.
 93. Biess, "Between Amnesty and Anti-Communism," 138–160, passim.
 94. Grashio, *Return to Freedom*, 69.

Chapter 8

 1. Grashio, *Return to Freedom*, 43.
 2. Isidro, *Philippine Social Life*, 164–5.
 3. Lebra, *Japan's Greater East Asia Co-Prosperity Sphere*, 64–7.
 4. Hoyt, *Japan's War*, 331–2; Feuer, *Bilibid Diary*, 104, 125; *USA v. Homma*, 259.
 5. Toland, *Rising Sun*, 324.
 6. Isidro, *Philippine Social Life*, 164–5.
 7. Toland, *Rising Sun*, 396–7; Costello, *The Pacific War*, 215.
 8. Hartendorp, *Japanese Occupation of the Philippines*, 225; Weinstein, *Barbed-Wire Surgeon*, 108, 161.
 9. NARA, Philippines Archives Collection, RG 407, Box 136, Affidavit of Maria Martinez.
 10. Those working as domestic maids are often sexual prey. One example is that of Maricris Sioson, whose death was officially explained by disease; physical evidence strongly suggested that she may have been beaten, even tortured. See Francia, *Eye of the Fish*, 153.
 11. Ienaga, *Japan's Last War*, 172; For a different attitude toward MacArthur, see Bernad, *Tradition and Discontinuity*, 94–109. Currently, Japanese companies like dealing with peasant workers in developing countries like the Philippines, but give them low marks on work ethic. Woronoff, *Japan's Commercial Empire*, 224.
 12. Ongpauco, *They Refused to Die*, 136.
 13. Goto, *Tensions of Empire*, 89.
 14. Ongpauco, *They Refused to Die*, 88–9. "Today, the story is different. The Japanese are back but, this time, they are welcome guests who respond to their hosts' hospitality with the true grace and charm of the Japanese people.... They are profusely apologetic, like Gomi Toshiharu, who apologized to Abucay Mayor Maxima de la Fuente in these terms: 'So sorry Japan bring destruction Firipings last war. Japan sodjars make-ku mistakeku Firipinos.'" Ibid., 89.

 15. Lynch, *Four Readings*, 10–11, 47; Lacambra, *Rising Sun Blinking*, 78–9.
 16. Astor, *Crisis in the Pacific*, 122; 191.
 17. Quoted in Whitman, *Bataan: Our Last Ditch*, 569.
 18. Falk, *Bataan: The March of Death*, 97–8.
 19. Alabado, *Bataan: Death March*, 88–9.
 20. Paguio, *Bataan: Land of Valor*, 52–3.
 21. Manchester, *Goodbye, Darkness*, 104.
 22. Thomas, *As I Remember*, 33–5.
 23. Norman, *Tears in the Darkness*, 40, note 65.
 24. Sides, *Ghost Soldiers*, 101; Bilyeu, *Lost in Action*, 81; Tenney, *My Hitch in Hell*, 60; Lawton, *Some Survived*, 19.
 25. Dyess, *Dyess Story*, 90; Jacobsen, *We Refused to Die*, 91.
 26. Sides, *Ghost Soldiers*, 105. http://www.american-partisan.com/cols/2002/ww2/qtr2/0429.htm.
 27. Linn, *Guardians of Empire*, 250; Isidro, *Philippine Social Life*, 110.
 28. Lynch, *Four Readings*, 73, 75, 83.
 29. De La Torre, *Patterns of Philippine Life*, 5–6; Dyess, *Dyess Story*, 90.
 30. Bilek, *No Uncle Sam*, 63; Fitzpatrick, *Hike into the Sun*, 68, 71; Tenney, *My Hitch in Hell*, 55, 60; Gordon, *Horyo*, 97.
 31. Miller, *Bataan Uncensored*, 221–2; Norman, *Tears in the Darkness*, 221.
 32. Gordon, *Horyo*, 99, 101; Caraccilo, *Surviving Bataan and Beyond*, 43.
 33. Sneddon, *Zero Ward*, 28–9; Chunn, *Of Rice and Men*, 127.
 34. Allen, *Abandoned on Bataan*, 61.
 35. Whitman, *Bataan: Our Last Ditch*, 314, 363.
 36. Norman, *Tears in the Darkness*, 196–7.
 37. Ibid., 197; Dyess, *Dyess Story*, 95.
 38. http://www.bataansurvivor.com/; Poweleit, *Kentucky's Fighting 192nd*, 88.
 39. Hibbs, *Tell MacArthur to Wait*, 113; Ortega, *Courage on Bataan*, 50–1.
 40. Bumgarner, *Parade of the Dead*, 79; Bilyeu, *Lost in Action*, 89; Knox, *Death March*, 138; http://www.bataansurvivor.com.
 41. http://home.comcast.net/~rgrokett/POW/POW7.htm.
 42. Garner, *A Study in Valor*, 61–2; Alabado, *Bataan, Death March*, 41.
 43. Ongpauco, *They Refused to Die*, 137, 136.
 44. http://www.american-partisan.com/cols/2002/qtr2/0429.htm; Norman, *Tears in the Darkness*, 194–5; Phone conversation with Joe Merritt, June 2008; Merritt, *Adapt or Die*, 225; Ortega, *Courage on Bataan*, 52; Timothy Ruse claimed to remember a similar story. Ruse, *We Volunteered*, 78. Accounts of bayoneting children are not uncommon when seeking to attribute maximum barbarity to one's enemy. For accounts of such German behavior in World War I, see www.spartacus.schoolnet.co.uk/FWWatrocities.htm.
 45. Falk, *Bataan: The March of Death*, 102–12. Falk suggests that Lieutenant General Nara Akira probably ordered the massacre. See also Ongpauco, *They Refused to Die*, 90–102.

46. *USA v. Homma*, 1010–57, 3339.

47. The only other sources are three interviews Michael and Elizabeth Norman claim they had with Japanese members of the 122nd Infantry who asserted they had some knowledge of the massacre. According to the Normans, Nagai Yoshiaki only watched the massacre, Murakami Isamu bayonetted one man under duress, and Shigeta Takesada also only watched, refusing to participate. At the time of the interviews, all the men were at least in their mid-seventies. Several questions obtain—among them the reliability, after fifty-eight years, of these men's memory, their motivation to describe what they claimed to have seen, the unnamed others who did claim to have participated, the problems of conducting interviews with no knowledge of Japanese and relying on a translator, the lack of evidence concerning the men's membership in the relevant unit(s), and no reference in Norman's account to any kind of written or even oral order. See Norman, *Tears in the Darkness*, 203–24, notes 71, 73, 74.

48. Quoted in Leckie, *Wars of America*, 2: 48; Putzel, *A Captive Land*, 51.

49. Ind, *Bataan: The Judgment Seat*, 109. Ongpauco recalled that the Japanese designated some Filipinos as "tobangs" to help direct prisoners on the trek north. Some of these men treated their co-prisoners kindly, whispering *Magtitiis lang tayo, mga kasama* (Let us be patient). Others were less kindly. One Filipino so designated counted his wards by striking their "heads like so many nuts to crack.... We hated this officer." Ongpauco, *They Refused to Die*, 141.

50. Ortega, *Courage on Bataan*, 48–9; Schirmer, *Philippines Reader*, 61.

51. Jacobsen, *We Refused to Die*, 88; Caracillo, *Surviving Bataan and Beyond*, 31.

52. Norman, *Tears in the Darkness*, 61; Mallonee, *Battle for Bataan*, 12.

53. Linn, *Guardians of Empire*, 123–4.

54. Manchester, *American Caesar*, 182; Linn, *Guardians of Empire*, 127, 136.

55. Cook, *Japan at War*, 133.

56. LaForte, *With Only the Will to Live*, 83.

57. Falk, *Bataan: The March of Death* 159; Kerr, *Surrender and Survival*, 58.

58. Morton, *Fall of the Philippines*, 370.

59. Hubbard, *Apocalypse Undone*, 89; Gordon, *Horyo*, 95. See also Fitzpatrick, *Hike into the Sun*, 68.

60. Gautier, *I Came Back from Bataan*, 79; Kerr, *Surrender and Survival*, 59; Daws, *Prisoners of the Japanese*, 79; Knox, *Death March*, 131.

61. Falk, *Bataan: The March of Death*, 150; Taylor, *Unforgettable Story of Bataan*, 143; Mallonee, *Battle for Bataan*, 153.

62. Falk, *Bataan: The March of Death* 159, 178. Some soldiers had "bought food at San Fernando and accepted change in Japanese 'invasion money.'" Cave, *Beyond Courage*, 188.

63. Marquez, *War Memoir*, 33; Falk, *Bataan: The March of Death*, 35; Morton, *Fall of the Philippines*, 373.

64. Poweleit, *USAFFE*, 65–6.

65. Lawton, *Some Survived*, 15; Czerwien, *POW: Tears That Never Dry*, 31; Falk, *Bataan: The March of Death* 144, 127.

66. Kerr, *Surrender and Survival*, 53; In the camps, Grokett loaned some to other men who promised to pay him back, but he never heard from any of them after the war. http://home.comcast.net/~rgrokett/POW/POW7.htm.

67. Whitman, *Bataan: Our Last Ditch*, 581.

68. *Tragedy of Bataan*; Whitman, *Bataan: Our Last Ditch*, 602.

69. Nicolay, *MacArthur of Bataan*, 160; Merritt, *Adapt or Die*, 166–67; Young, *Battle of Bataan*, 205; Wright, *Captured on Corregidor*, 65–6.

70. Ongpauco, *They Refused to Die*, 103–04; http://www.battlingbastardsbataan.com/rico.htm.

71. Ongpauco, *They Refused to Die*, 137; Moody, *Reprieve from Hell*, 82–3.

72. Calata, "Role of Education in Americanizing Filipinos," 91; Le Roy, *Philippine Life*, 72.

73. Schirmer, *Philippines Reader*, 37, 72; Spencer, *Land and People*, 42.

74. Francia, *Eye of the Fish*, 35.

75. Isidro, *Philippine Social Life*, 252–4.

76. *Tragedy of Bataan*; Schirmer, *Philippines Reader*, 63.

77. Bollich, *Bataan Death March*, 82; Allen, *Abandoned on Bataan*, 51–2.

78. Whitman, *Bataan: Our Last Ditch*, 77, 412.

79. Falk, *Bataan: The March of Death*, 33.

80. Isidro, *Philippine Social Life*, 242.

81. Ibid., 248–9.

82. Jose, *Philippine Army*, 43, 45.

83. Ibid., 46–7.

84. Ibid., 71–2.

85. Laya, *Little Democracies*, 12–13.

Chapter 9

1. Grashio, *Return to Freedom*, 37.

2. Allen, *Abandoned on Bataan*, 75.

3. Feifer, *Tennozan*, 496.

4. Cary, *From a Ruined Empire*, 37–8; Bergerud, *Touched with Fire*, 411–12.

5. Linderman, *World Within War*, 154.

6. Boyington, *Baa Baa Black Sheep*, 270–71; Dower, *War Without Mercy*, 248.

7. Whitman, *Bataan: Our Last Ditch*, 2; Mellnik, *Philippine Diary*, 96; Gibney, *Senso*, 175.

8. Poweleit, *USAFFE*, 26; Whitman, *Bataan: Our Last Ditch*, 364.

9. Ruse, *We Volunteered*, 63; Weinstein, *Barbed-Wire Surgeon*, 37.

10. Ramsey, *Lieutenant Ramsey's War*, 68–9; Grashio, *Return to Freedom*, 19; Whitman, *Bataan: Our Last Ditch*, 402.

11. The book generated considerable controversy. See James Bacque, "The Last Dirty Secret of World War II," *Saturday Night*, September 1989, 31–8; *Globe and Mail*, 25 August 1989, C7; "Eine Lange Nacht der Lugen," *Der Spiegel*, 2 October 1989, 129–32; *Time*, 2 October 1989; *Economist*, 25 November 1989, 102–03. See also Stephen Ambrose, "Ike and the Disappear-

ing Atrocities" *New York Times Book Review*, February 24, 1991, 1, 35–7.

12. Bacque suggests that more than a million, or something beyond 20 percent of the Germans captured, died of starvation, yet the most liberal responsible evidence supports no more than 56,000 at the most. This would be a mortality rate of 1 percent. Albert E. Cowdry, "A Question of Numbers," 78–94. Had Bacque's figures been correct, the mortality rate for American prisoners would have approached the overall rate of mortality for Allied prisoners captured by the Japanese—about 27 percent.

13. Bischof, *Eisenhower and the Germans*, 5–9, 19–20, 169.

14. Bacque, *Other Losses*, 222, 37–49, quote on page 40.

15. Maschke, *Die deutschen Kriegsgefangenen*, 50.

16. Frohn, "Das Schicksal Deutscher Kriegsgefangener," 479–480. Die gefangenen Ärzte hatten nichts, keine Medikamente, kein Verbandszeug, kein Instrumentarium, und so gab es anfangs 'in den meisten Fällen' nicht einmal Hilfen für Sterbende. Ibid., 481.

17. Bacque, *Other Losses*, 41–2.

18. Sullivan, *Thresholds of Peace*, 88; Bischof, *Eisenhower and the Germans*, 15–16.

19. Bischof, *Eisenhower and the Germans*, 18.

20. Fussell, *Boy's Crusade*, 21.

21. Ambrose, *Band of Brothers*, 255; Fussell, *Wartime*, 186; Martin, *The GI War*, 40–1.

22. Atkinson, *An Army at Dawn*, 462–63.

23. Furuya, "Japan's Racial Identity in the Second World War," 119–122; Dower, *War Without Mercy*, 205.

24. Manvell, *Films and the Second World War*, 135, 137–38.

25. Richie, *Japanese Cinema*, 127.

26. Dower, *Japan in War and Peace*, 35–40; Earhart, *Certain Victory*, 85.

27. Morris, *Traveler from Tokyo*, 44, 57. Morris stated that the "present generation of university students, whose preliminary education was completed in comparatively enlightened times, possess for the most part a liberal outlook." Ibid., 124.

28. Morris, *Traveler from Tokyo*, 41, 126, 46, 55.

29. Noma, *Zone of Emptiness*, 153.

30. Tasaki was educated in Honolulu and spent a year at Oberlin College, and he wrote his novel in English. *Long the Imperial Way*, by Hanama Tasaki, and *Beyond Defeat*, by Hans Werner Richter, reviewed by Monroe Engel in *Commentary*, September 1950, www.commentarymagazine.com.

31. Rosenfeld, *Unhappy Soldier*.

32. Edmonds, "Laws of War," 322; Falk, *Bataan: The March of Death*, Appendix A.

33. Hata, "From Consideration to Contempt," 256–57, 262. Some 2,000 Japanese prisoners captured by Russia returned home to public adulation. As they made their way by train from Kobe to Tokyo, "large crowds assembled and showered them with presents." None of the returning prisoners was court-martialed. On an individual basis, returning Japanese were sometimes ostracized from their villages. Ibid., 259–60.

34. Ibid., 266.

35. www.ibiblio.org; Sato, *Gyokusai*, 5; Tanaka, *Hidden Horrors*, 208. Some Japanese policymakers and theorists saw the Co-Prosperity Sphere as a cooperative venture with "southern peoples." In 1939 the Navy National Policy Research Committee offered a "Summary Draft of a Policy for the South" that clearly emphasized cooperation and conciliation over exploitation and oppression. Lebra, *Japan's Greater East Asia Co-Prosperity Sphere*, 64–7. Wachi Takeji, the Japanese Army's chief of staff in the Philippines from February 1942 to March 1944, had seen his army's cruelty alienate China's population, and he sought to avoid make the same mistakes in the Philippines. Friend, *Blue-Eyed Enemy*, 66.

36. *Time*, February 7, 1944, 12.

37. Dower, *Embracing Defeat*, 214–15, 217.

38. "Kawane had only 200 trucks for 64,000 Filipinos, 11,500 Americans, 6,000 civilian employees, and as many as 26,000 refugees. Thousands upon thousands of men were sick, hungry and exhausted." One staff officer, Hitome Junske, said that "there were far more Americans and Filipinos than we estimated and we weren't prepared for them in any way." Glusman, *Conduct Under Fire*, 162.

39. Drea, *Japan's Imperial Army*, 83; Kenworthy, *Tiger of Malaya*, 98. Trucks the Americans turned over supplemented a woefully inadequate number in the Japanese Army. The brutal marching that was part of each Japanese recruit's training was for good reason—each infantry division was allocated a limited number of trucks. Some Japanese generals "paid no attention at all to the practicalities of transport and supplies when formulating their plans ... in general, the army suffered from a shortage of motor transport" and the "average division was allocated roughly five hundred motor vehicles for its whole strength." Harries, *Soldiers of the Sun*, 372. One trained observer stated that the "transportation picture is startling. There are in the Japanese division upwards of 3,000 *horses*—and downwards of three hundred motor vehicles." Thompson, *How the Japanese Army Fights*, 28.

40. *USA v. Homma*, 883; Gordon, *Horyo*, 98; Toland, *Rising Sun*, 375.

41. *Forsaken Legion*; *USA v. Homma*, 2484.

42. Knox, *Death March*, 147; LaForte, *With Only the Will to Live*, 88; Brain, *Soldier of Bataan*, 33.

43. Knox, *Death March*, 140; Fraser, *In the Claw of the Tiger*, 199.

44. *USA v. Homma*, 3075; Allen, *Abandoned on Bataan*, 65; NARA, RG 407, Box 145, Diary of C.D. Quinlenn; Falk, *Bataan: The March of Death*, 126.

45. Tenney, *My Hitch in Hell*, 46; Kerr, *Surrender and Survival*, 53; Martin, *Brothers from Bataan*, 76; Jacobsen, *We Refused to Die*, 83. See also affidavits of Devore and Hayes, both of whom rode most of the way to San Fernando. *USA v. Homma*, 1971.

46. Olson, *O'Donnell*, 19; Miller, *Bataan Uncensored*, 226–7; Abraham, *Ghost of Bataan Speaks*, 63. More than army trucks found their way into service. From Mariveles, Irvin Alexander remembered riding the first ten miles of the march in a bus secured by a Japanese soldier for him and his group. Caracillo, *Surviving Bataan and Beyond*, 27.

47. NARA, RG 331, SCAP Records, Statement of Hirano Kudataro, 11-14-47; Allen, *Abandoned on Bataan*, 69; Playter, *Survivor*, 56.
48. Ancheta, *Triumph in the Philippines*, 102; Knox, *Death March*, 132-3.
49. http://www.bataansurvivor.com.
50. Kerr, *Surrender and Survival*, 58-9; Bollich, *Bataan Death March*, 74. There was perhaps a relationship between guards' education and the level of their goodwill. Concerning his own imprisonment, Greg Boyington later observed that some guards who had been to college refused to beat prisoners at all. Boyington, *Baa Baa Black Sheep*, 325.
51. Astor, *Crisis in the Pacific*, 219; Bollich, *Bataan Death March*, 78-9; Moody, *Reprieve from Hell*, 77-82.
52. LaForte, *With Only the Will to Live*, 88; Jacobsen, *We Refused to Die*, 85-6. Allen, *Abandoned on Bataan*, 75.
53. LaForte, *With Only the Will to Live*, 82; Tsuji, *Japan's Greatest Victory*, 255.
54. Knox, *Death March*, 147. See also LaForte, *With Only the Will to Live*, 85; NARA, RG 331, SCAP Records, Statement of Morioka Susumu, Commanding 16th Division of 14th Army, June 3 1948.
55. Ancheta, *Triumph in the Philippines*, 102; Coleman, *Bataan and Beyond*, 78-80.
56. Caracillo, *Surviving Bataan and Beyond*, 42; Falk, *Bataan: The March of Death*, 120.
57. Khan, *Japanese Moral Education*, 157.
58. LaForte, *With Only the Will to Live*, 88; Lawton, *Some Survived*, 24; Garner, *A Study in Valor*, 70; Cave, *Beyond Courage*, 178.
59. NARA, Philippines Archives Collection, RG 407, Box 129, Diary of E.R. Fendall.
60. Knox, *Death March*, 14; *USA v. Homma*, 2484.
61. Daws, *Prisoners of the Japanese*, 22, 82.
62. Urwin, *Victory in Defeat*, 49. In 1995, three survivors of the battle of Wake Island flew to Japan to thank a Japanese officer named Ozeki Shigeyoshi "for his decency and kindness." Ibid., xii. Urwin, like any student of the Pacific War, admits the sometimes "heartless treatment of helpless foes" but his work "revealed that not every Japanese soldier or sailor was an unfeeling brute." Ibid.
63. Smith, *Japanese Society*, 62.
64. Lory, *Japan's Military Masters*, 62.
65. Toland, *But Not in Shame*, 305; Quoted in Whitman, *Bataan: Our Last Ditch*, 601-2.
66. *Forsaken Legion*; Tenney, *My Hitch in Hell*, 48-9; Fitzpatrick, *Hike into the Sun*, 65; Knox, *Death March*, 147; Levering, *Horror Trek*, 65; Alabado, *Bataan: Death March*, 60.
67. *USA v. Homma*, 872; Jacobsen, *We Refused to Die*, 88; Levering, *Horror Trek*, 70-1; Knox, *Death March*, 145; North, *Lost in the Wilderness*, 38-9.
68. NARA, RG 331, SCAP Records, Statement of Sato Tokutaro, 6-14-48.
69. *Forsaken Legion*; Gautier, *I Came Back from Bataan*, 76; Moody, *Reprieve from Hell*, 76.
70. Knox, *Death March*, 137-8.
71. Poncio, *Girocho*, 59-62.

72. Bank, *Back from the Living Dead*, 21; Knox, *Death March*, 132, 129.
73. Ongpauco, *They Refused to Die*, 137; Knox, *Death March*, 126; Boyt, *Bataan: A Survivor's Story*, 133.
74. LaForte, *With Only the Will to Live*, 86.
75. Caracillo, *Surviving Bataan and Beyond* 33; LaForte, *With Only the Will to Live*, 82.
76. Allen, *Abandoned on Bataan*, 78; Poweleit, *Kentucky's Fighting 192nd*, 93; Bilek, *No Uncle Sam*, 62.
77. Bilyeu, *Lost in Action*, 76, 82, 87, 88, 90; Kathman, *I Was There, Charley*, 36; http://www.bataansurvivor.com.
78. Tsuji, *Japan's Greatest Victory*, 241-43.
79. Gilpatrick, *Footprints in Courage*, 34; Abraham, *Ghost of Bataan Speaks*, 64; Falk, *Bataan: The March of Death*, 148-9.
80. Masterson, *Ride the Waves to Freedom*, 41-2; Astor, *Crisis in the Pacific*, 217-8.
81. Knox, *Death March*, 131; Sides, *Ghost Soldiers*, 52-3.
82. Falk, *Bataan: The March of Death*, 91; Haney, *Caged Dragons*, 174.
83. Tapert, *Lines of Battle*, 20.
84. Allen, *Abandoned on Bataan*, 68; North, *Lost in the Wilderness*, 35; Cave, *Beyond Courage*, 179; Allen, *Abandoned on Bataan*, 68.
85. Whitman, *Bataan: Our Last Ditch*, 598; Moody, *Reprieve from Hell*, 75.
86. Morris, *Traveler from Tokyo*, 47-8, 82, 37. Hideki Tojo, speaking in the Japanese Diet, suggested that Japan should increase its attention to the instruction of English: "We shall require large numbers of English speakers to administer our conquered territories. In Australia alone the figure will be enormous." Ibid., 49.
87. Suzuki, *Japanese and the Japanese*, 145-46.
88. Tenney, *My Hitch in Hell*, 50; Towle, *Japanese Prisoners of War*, 12; *USA v. Homma*, 1266.
89. Caraccilo, *Surviving Bataan and Beyond*, 32; Ortega, *Courage on Bataan*, 47. One American prisoner, long after the Death March, learned enough Japanese to ease his way. He said that in captivity, most Americans considered it disloyal to learn the language, but "as a result many died and many more were beaten needlessly because of this idiotic attitude." He remembered that "case after case continued to surface where a prisoner—unable to understand even fundamental Japanese—was severely beaten and often died from his injuries." Gordon, *Horyo*, 170, 172.
90. Czerwien, *POW: Tears That Never Dry*, 32-33; Poweleit, *Kentucky's Fighting 192nd*, 11, 43, v.
91. Ibid., 49, 50-2, 83, 89.
92. Ibid., 91, 95.
93. *USA v. Homma*, 1149-52.
94. Bumgarner, *Parade of the Dead*, 78; http://www.bataansurvivor.com; Boyt, *Death March*, 128; Knox, *Death March*, 133. See also Tenney, *My Hitch in Hell*, 48. Japanese were not unfamiliar with proximity to human waste. After the horrendous earthquake that destroyed much of Tokyo in 1923, the city did not get a modern sanitation system. The surround-

ing rice fields needed human excrement for fertilizer. Morris, *Traveler from Tokyo*, 12.

95. Poweleit, *Kentucky's Fighting 192nd*, 85–6.

96. Poweleit, *USAFFE*, 50.

97. Ongpauco, *They Refused to Die*, 137; Jackson, *Diary of Col. Calvin G. Jackson*, 47; Whitman, *Bataan: Our Last Ditch*, 471.

98. Bumgarner, *Parade of the Dead*, 81–2.

99. *Forsaken Legion*; Hunt, *Behind Japanese Lines*, 31.

100. Toland, *But Not in Shame*, 307.

101. Bilyeu, *Lost in Action*, 78.

102. Boyt, *Death March*, 132–3; Fraser, *In the Claw of the Tiger*, 196.

103. Levi, *Moments of Reprieve*, 10, 91–2.

Conclusion

1. *USA v. Homma*, 3302.

2. Enright, *Wicked Wit of Winston Churchill*, 66; Hearn, *Japan: An Interpretation*, 9–10.

3. Quoted in Maruyama, *Thought and Behavior in Modern Japanese Politics*, 95.

4. Drea, *In the Service of the Emperor*, 77.

5. Lory, *Japan's Military Masters*, 24–6, 65. Sometimes commanding officers threatened to write the recruit's parents if their son was failing in his duty. Rees, *Horror in the East*, 25–6. The warrant officer occupied a special place in the recruit's life—his duty was seeing after a wide variety of personnel issues, and such duties "made him about the most respected and feared superior to the lowly soldier, whose main preoccupation was centered on the kind of record which might be sent home to his village or ward offices." Tasaki, *Long the Imperial Way*, 194.

6. Tsurumi, *Social Change and the Individual*, 87–8.

7. Arendt, *Origins of Totalitarianism*, 306; Smethurst, *Social Basis for Prewar Japanese Militarism*, xvii-iii.

8. Tsurumi, *Social Change and the Individual*, 133.

9. Khan, *Japanese Moral Education*, 73; Morris, *Traveler from Tokyo*, 43–4. Morris was once forced to remove his coat on a bitterly cold day to show proper respect. Ibid.

10. Tasaki, *Long the Imperial Way*, 37; Drea, *In the Service of the Emperor*, 82.

11. Dyer, *War*, 102.

12. Iritani, *Group Psychology of the Japanese in Wartime*, 191–2. Physical violence extended beyond the Japanese school. Social custom allowed bosses to hit their apprentices, and it was not uncommon "even for mothers to lay hands on their children." Coox, *Year of the Tiger*, 79–80.

13. Iritani, *Group Psychology of the Japanese in Wartime*, 189; Rees, *Horror in the East*, 36; Morris, *Traveller from Tokyo*, 133. See also Cook, *Japan at War*, 131; Gibney, *Senso*, 30.

14. In 1938 Major General Matsushiro Ugaki, an infantry expert, noted that "some of the young non-commissioned officers often misunderstood the demands of spiritual discipline, with the result that abuses ensued." This kind of treatment subverted the basic intentions of the *Senjinkun*, whose purpose was "making the Imperial virtues the object of admiration through the exercise of justice tempered with mercy. Coox, *Year of the Tiger*, 79.

15. Tasaki, *Long the Imperial Way*, 196–7.

16. Yamanouchi, *Listen to the Voices from the Sea*, 116–17.

17. *Japanese Devils*; Gibney, *Senso*, 41–2.

18. Ienaga, *Pacific War*, 52; Tsurumi, *Social Change and the Individual*, 116. Osamu Takei, who entered the barracks in February 1942, criticized his superiors: "What a void these so-called superior officers are! A perfect one-word description of their behavior is '*kyotai*' (disgraceful conduct or crazy behavior)—a word that I should like to pass along to them." Yamanouchi, *Listen to the Voices from the Sea*, 102.

19. Iritani, *Group Psychology of the Japanese in Wartime*, 189–90; Gibney, *Senso*, 54. For reference to torture and violence as evidence of superiors' "benevolent feeling" toward inferiors, see also Tsurumi, *Social Change and the Individual*, 98.

20. Yamanouchi, *Listen to the Voices from the Sea*, 118; Gibney, *Senso*, 45; Ienaga, *Japan's Last War*, 51. Very few Japanese ever referred to the Pacific War equivalent of fragging, though Watanabe Katsumi believed he might have taken such revenge on what he believed was the "disturbed" private who beat him "in a crazed way with no sense of when to stop." He claimed that among the draftees it was said that "bullets come from behind on the battlefield." Gibney, *Senso*, 28.

21. Drea, *In the Service of the Emperor*, 83–4; Yamanouchi, *Listen to the Voices from the Sea*, 117; Drea, "In the Army Barracks of Imperial Japan," 338.

22. Yamanouchi, *Listen to the Voices from the Sea*, 90–1.

23. Maruyama, *Thought and Behavior in Modern Japanese Politics*, 18. "As a result every individual is in one capacity the victim of coercion, while in another capacity he metes out coercion to his fellow men. He both suffers and perpetrates oppression; in one direction he yields, in another he boasts.... Today's joy compensates for yesterday's shame, and thus dissatisfaction is evened out ... Peter is robbed to pay Paul." Ibid., 18. oo

24. Ienaga, *Japan's Last War*, 53.

25. Hibbs, *Tell MacArthur to Wait*, 106.

26. Fitzpatrick, *Hike into the Sun*, 56–7; Moody, *Reprieve from Hell*, 134.

27. Smith, *Japanese Society*, 39–40, 49.

28. Maruyama, *Thought and Behavior in Modern Japanese Politics*, 12–13, 128.

29. Singer, *Mirror, Sword and Jewel*, 47.

30. Harries, *Soldiers of the Sun*, 444–45; Cook, *Japan at War*, 134.

31. Tsurumi, *Social Change and the Individual*, 92–3; Thompson, *How the Japanese Army Fights*, 13.

32. Brackman, *The Other Nuremberg*, 251; Maruyama, *Thought and Behavior in Modern Japanese Politics*, 19.

33. Harries, *Soldiers of the Sun*, 185, 478.

34. Reischauer, *The Japanese Today*, 166.
35. Maruyama, *Thought and Behavior in Modern Japanese Politics*, 95–6.
36. Prugh, "Prisoners at War: The POW Battleground," 126–27.
37. Cary, *From a Ruined Empire*, 40–1.
38. Reeve, *Plato Republic*, 208.
39. Aristotle, *Nicomachean Ethics*, Book III; W.T. A modern version of the same ideas appears in W.T. Stace, *Religion and the Modern Mind*.
40. Cook, *Japan at War*, 125.
41. Gibney, *Japan at War*, 189.
42. Yamanouchi, *Listen to the Voices from the Sea*, 127, 147, 176.
43. Keene, *Chronicles of My Life*, 56–7; Aristotle, *Nicomachean Ethics*, 1155a21–22.

Bibliography

Abraham, Abie. *Ghost of Bataan Speaks*. New York: Vantage Press, 1971.

Abraham, Theodore A. *"Do You Understand, Huh?" A POW's Lament, 1941–1945*. Manhattan, KS: Sunflower University Press, 1992.

Alabado, Corban K. *Bataan, Death March, Capas: A Tale of Japanese Cruelty and American Injustice*. San Francisco: Sulu, 1995.

Allen, Oliver "Red." *Abandoned on Bataan: One Man's Story of Survival*. Boerne, TX: Crimson-Horse, 2002.

Allied Geographical Section, Southwest Pacific Area. *Vegetation Study of the Philippine Islands*, 1944.

Ambrose, Stephen E. *Band of Brothers*. New York: Simon & Schuster, 1992.

Ancheta, Celedonia A. *Triumph in the Philippines*. Manila: The National Bookstore, 1977.

Anderson, Joseph I., and Donald Richie. *The Japanese Film: Art and Industry*. Princeton: Princeton University Press, 1982.

Asahi, Shimbun. *28 Years in the Guam Jungle: Sergeant Yokoi Home from World War II*. Tokyo: Japan Publications, 1972.

Ashton, Paul. *And Somebody Gives a Damn*. Santa Barbara: Ashton Publications, 1990.

Astor, Gerald. *Crisis in the Pacific: The Battles for the Philippine Islands by the Men Who Fought Them*. New York: Dell, 1996.

Atkinson, Rick. *An Army at Dawn: The War in North Africa, 1942–1943*. New York: Henry Holt, 2002.

Bacque, James. *Other Losses: An Investigation into the Mass Deaths of German Prisoners at the Hands of the French and Americans After World War II*. Toronto: Stoddart, 1989.

Bank, Bert. *Back from the Living Dead*. Tuscaloosa: self published, 1945.

Barclay, Craig R. "Accuracies and Inaccuracies in Autobiographical Memories." *Journal of Memory and Language* 25 (1986): 93–103.

Barker, A.J. *Prisoners of War*. New York: Universe Books, 1975.

Bartov, Omer, Atina Grossmann, and Mary Nolan, eds. *Crimes of War: Guilt and Denial in the Twentieth Century*. New York: The New Press, 2002.

Baskett, Michael. *The Attractive Empire: Transnational Film Culture in Imperial Japan*. Honolulu: University of Hawai'i Press, 2008.

Beasley, W.G. *The Japanese Experience: A Short History of Japan*. Berkeley: University of California Press, 1999.

Beevor, Anthony. *Stalingrad*. New York: Penguin, 1998.

Belli, Robert F., and Elizabeth F. Loftus. "The Pliability of Autobiographical Memory: Misinformation and the False Memory Problem." In *Remembering Our Past*, edited by David C. Rubin. Cambridge: Cambridge University Press, 1996.

Benedict, Ruth. *The Chrysanthemum and the Sword*. Rutland, VT: Charles Tuttle, 1975.

Berg, A. Scott. *Lindbergh*. New York: Putnam's Sons, 1998.

Bergamini, David. *Japan's Imperial Conspiracy*. New York: Pocket Books, 1972.

Bergerud, Eric M. *Touched with Fire: The Land War in the South Pacific*. New York: Viking, 1996.

Bernad, Miguel A. *Tradition and Discontinuity: Essays on Philippine History and Culture*. Manila: The National Bookstore, 1983.

Biess, Frank. "Between Amnesty and Anti-Communism, The West German *Kameradenschinder* Trials, 1948–1960." In *Crimes of War: Guilt and Denial in the Twentieth Century*, edited by Omer Bartov, Atina Grossmann and Mary Nolan. New York: The New Press, 2002.

Bilek, Tony, with Gene O'Connell. *No Uncle Sam: The Forgotten of Bataan*. Kent, OH: Kent State University Press, 2003.

Bilyeu, Dick. *Lost in Action: A World War II Soldier's Account of Capture on Bataan and Imprisonment by the Japanese*. Jefferson, NC: McFarland, 1991.

Bischof, Gunter, and Stephen Ambrose, eds. *Eisenhower and the German POWs: Facts Against Falsehood*. Baton Rouge: Louisiana State University Press, 1992.

Bix, Herbert P. *Hirohito and the Making of Modern Japan*. New York: Perennial, 2001.

Blacker, Carmen. "Millenarian Aspects of New Religions in Japan." In *Tradition and Modernization in Japanese Culture*, edited by Donald Shivley. Princeton: Princeton University Press, 1971.

Bliven, Bruce. *From Pearl to Okinawa: The War in the Pacific, 1941–1945*. New York: Random House, 1960.

Bok, Sissela. "Autobiography as Moral Battleground." In *Memory, Brain and Belief*, edited by Daniel L. Schacter. Cambridge: Harvard University Press, 2000, 307–324.

Bollich, James. *Bataan Death March: A Soldier's Story*. Gretna, LA: Pelican, 2003.

Boston Publishing Company. *Above and Beyond: A History of the Medal of Honor from the Civil War to Vietnam*. Boston: Boston Publishing, 1985.

Boxer, C.R. *The Christian Century in Japan, 1549–1650*. Berkeley: University of California Press, 1951.

Boyington, Gregory. *Baa Baa Black Sheep*. New York: Bantam, 1977.

Boyle, John Hunter. *Modern Japan: The American Nexus*. Fort Worth: Harcourt Brace, 1993.

Boyt, Gene, with David L. Burch. *Bataan, A Survivor's Story*. Norman: University of Oklahoma Press, 2004.

Brackman, Arnold C. *The Other Nuremberg: The Untold Story of the Tokyo War Crimes Trials*. New York: William Morrow, 1987.

Bradbury, Ray *Dandelion Wine*. New York: Doubleday, 1975.

Brailey, Nigel, ed. *Masanobu Tsuji's "Underground Escape" from Siam After the Japanese Surrender*. Leiden: Globa Oriental, 2012.

Brain, Philip S. *Soldier of Bataan: Retrospective Observations of a Thoughtful Survivor*. Minneapolis: Rotary Club of Minneapolis, 1990.

Braly, William C. *The Hard Way Home*. Washington: Infantry Journal Press, 1947.

Breuer, William B. *The Great Raid on Cabanatuan: Rescuing the Doomed Ghosts of Bataan and Corregidor*. New York: John Wiley and Sons, 1994.

Brinkley, David. *David Brinkley: A Memoir*. New York: Alfred A. Knopf, 1995.

Broad, Robin, with John Cavanagh. *Plundering Paradise: The Struggle for the Environment in the Philippines*. Berkeley: University of California Press, 1993.

Brokaw, Tom. *The Greatest Generation*. New York: Random House, 1998.

Brookhauser, Frank, ed. *This Was Your War: Great Writings from World War II*. New York: Dell, 1960.

Brownmiller, Susan. *Against Our Will: Men, Women and Rape*. New York: Simon & Schuster, 1975.

Bruner, Jerome. "Self-Making Narratives." In *Autobiographical Memory and the Construction of a Narrative Self*, edited by Robyn Fivush and Catherine A. Haden. Mahwah, NJ: Lawrence Erlbaum, 2003.

Bumgarner, John R. *Parade of the Dead: A U.S. Army Physician's Memoir of Imprisonment by the Japanese, 1942–1945*. Jefferson, NC: McFarland, 1995.

Buruma, Ian. *The Wages of Guilt: Memories of War in Germany and Japan*. New York: Meridian, 1994.

Calata, Alexander A. "The Role of Education in Americanizing Filipinos." In *Mixed Blessing: The Impact of the American Colonial Experience on Politics and Society in the Philippines*, edited by Hazel M. McFerson. Westport, CT: Greenwood Press, 2002.

Caraccilo, Dominic J., ed. *Surviving Bataan and Beyond: Colonel Irvin Alexander's Odyssey as a Japanese Prisoner of War*. Mechanicsburg. PA: Stackpole, 1999.

Caruth, Cathy. *Unclaimed Experience: Trauma, Narrative and History*. Baltimore: Johns Hopkins Press, 1996.

_____, ed. *Trauma, Exploration, Memory*. Baltimore: Johns Hopkins Press, 1995.

Caruth, Gorton. *What Happened When: A Chronology of Life and Events in America*. New York: Penguin, 1991.

Cary, Otis, ed. *From a Ruined Empire, Letters— Japan, China, Korea 1945–46*. San Francisco: Kodansha International, 1975.

Cave, Dorothy. *Beyond Courage: One Regiment Against Japan, 1941–1945*. Las Cruces, NM: Yucca Tree Press, 1996.

Ceci, Stephen J. "False Beliefs: Some Developmental and Clinical Considerations." In *Memory Distortion: How Minds, Brains, and Societies Reconstruct the Past*, edited by Daniel L. Schacter. Cambridge: Harvard University Press, 1995.

Christianson, Sven-Ake. "Emotional Stress and Eyewitness Memory: A Critical Review." *Psychological Bulletin* 112 (1992): 284–309.

_____. "Remembering Emotional Events: The Fate of Detailed Information." *Cognition and Emotion* 5 (1991): 81–108.

Christianson, Sven-Åke, and Martin Safer. "Emotional Events and Emotions in Autobiographical Memories." In *Remembering Our Past*, edited by

David C. Rubin. Cambridge: Cambridge University Press, 1996.

Chunn, Calvin Ellsworth, ed. *Of Rice and Men: Americans Under the Rising Sun*. Los Angeles: Veterans Publishing, 1946.

Coffman, Edward M. *The Regulars: The American Army, 1898–1941*. Cambridge: Harvard University Press, 2004.

Cogan, Frances B. *Captured: The Japanese Internment of American Civilians in the Philippines, 1941–1945*. Athens: University Press of Georgia, 2000.

Cohen, Bernard M., and Maurize Z. Cooper. *A Follow-Up Study of World War II Prisoners of War*. Washington, D.C.: Government Printing Office, 1954.

Coleman, John S. Jr. *Bataan and Beyond: Memories of an American POW*. College Station: Texas A & M University Press, 1978.

Conroy, Robert. *The Battle of Bataan: America's Greatest Defeat*. London: Macmillan, 1969.

Conway, Jill Ker. *When Memory Speaks: Reflections on Autobiography*. New York: Alfred A. Knopf, 1998.

Cook, Haruko Taya, and Theodore F. *Japan at War: An Oral History*. New York: The New Press, 1992.

Coox, Alvin D. *The Unfought War: Japan, 1941–1942*. San Diego: San Diego State University Press, 1992.

_____. *Year of the Tiger*. Tokyo, Philadelphia: Orient/West, 1964.

Costello, John. *The Pacific War, 1941–1945*. New York: Quill, 1982.

Czerwien, Anthony. *POW: Tears That Never Dry*. Monroe, NY: Library Research Associates, 1994.

Daws, Gavin. *Prisoners of the Japanese: POWs of World War II in the Pacific*. New York: William Morrow, 1994.

De Asis, Leocadio. *From Bataan to Tokyo: Diary of a Filipino Student in Wartime Japan, 1943–1944*. Center for East Asian Studies, University of Kansas, 1979.

_____. *The Thread of Fate: A Personal Story in Philippine-Japanese Relations*. Manila: Philippine Foundation of Japan Alumni, 1986.

De La Torre, Visitacion R. *Patterns of Philippine Life*. Manila: Regal Printing, 1978.

De Mente, Boye Lafayette. *Kata: The Key to Understanding and Dealing with the Japanese!* Boston: Tuttle, 2003.

Denham, Robert D., ed. *Anatomy of Criticism: Four Essays*. (*Collected Works of Northrup Frye*, vol. 22.) Toronto: University of Toronto Press, 2006.

Des Pres, Terrence. *The Survivor: An Anatomy of Life in the Death Camps*. New York: Oxford University Press. 1976.

Diokno, Maria Serena I. "'Benevolent Assimilation' and Filipino Responses." In *Mixed Blessing: The Impact of the American Colonial Experience on Politics and Society in the Philippines*, edited by Hazel M. McFerson. Westport, CT: Greenwood Press, 2002.

Dore, Ronald P., and Tsutomo Ouchi. "Rural Origins of Japanese Fascism." In *Dilemmas of Growth in Prewar Japan*, edited by James William Morley. Princeton: Princeton University Press, 1971.

Dower, John W. *Embracing Defeat: Japan in the Wake of World War II*. New York: W.W. Norton, 1999.

_____. *Japan in War and Peace: Selected Essays*. New York: The New Press, 1993.

_____. *War Without Mercy: Race and Power in the Pacific War*. New York: Pantheon, 1986.

_____. *Ways of Forgetting, Ways of Remembering*. New York: The New Press, 2012.

Doyle, Robert C. *Voices from Captivity: Interpreting the American POW Narrative*. Lawrence: University of Kansas Press, 1994.

Drea, Edward J. "In the Army Barracks of Imperial Japan." *Armed Forces and Society* 15, no. 3 (Spring 1989): 329–48.

_____. *In the Service of the Emperor: Essays on the Imperial Japanese Army*. Lincoln: University of Nebraska Press, 1998.

_____. *Japan's Imperial Army: Its Rise and Fall, 1853–1945*. Lawrence: University Press of Kansas, 2009.

Dunaway, David K., and Willa K. Baum, eds. *Oral History: An Interdisciplinary Anthology*. Nashville: American Association for State and Local History, 1984.

Duus, Peter. *The Abacus and the Sword: The Japanese Penetration of Korea, 1895–1910*. Berkeley: University of California Press, 1995.

Dyer, Gwynne. *War*. New York: Crown, 1985.

Dyess, William E. *The Dyess Story: The Eye-Witness Account of the Death March from Bataan and the Narrative Experiences in Japanese Prison Camps and of Eventual Escape*. New York: G.P. Putnam's Sons, 1944.

Eakin, John Paul. "Autobiography, Identity and the Fictions of Memory." In *Memory, Brain and Belief*, edited by Daniel L. Schacter. Cambridge: Harvard University Press, 2000.

Earhart, David C. *Certain Victory: Images of World War II in the Japanese Media*. Armonk, NY: M.E. Sharpe, 2008.

Edgerton, Robert B. *Warriors of the Rising Sun*. New York: W.W. Norton, 1997.

Edmonds, Sterling E. "The Laws of War: Their Rise in the Nineteenth Century and Their Collapse in the Twentieth." *Virginia Law Review* 15 (1928–29): 321–49.

Eizenstat, Stuart E. *Imperfect Justice: Looted Assets, Slave Labor, and the Unfinished Business of World War II*. New York: Perseus, 2003.

Ellison, Katherine. *Imelda: Steel Butterfly of the Philippines*. New York: McGraw Hill, 1988.

Enright, Dominique, ed. *The Wicked Wit of Winston Churchill*. London: Michael Omara, 2001.

Evans, William R. *Kora!* Rogue River, OR: Atwood Publishing, 1986.

Fackler, Martin. "Japan Goes from Dynamic to Disheartened." *New York Times*, October 16, 2010.

Falk, Stanley L. *Bataan: The March of Death*. New York: W.W. Norton, 1962.

———. "The General Who Defeated MacArthur." Unpublished paper.

Fall, Bernard B. *Hell in a Very Small Place: The Siege of Dien Bien Phu*. New York: Vintage, 1966.

Fedorowich, Kent. "Understanding the Enemy: Military Intelligence, Political Warfare and Japanese Prisoners of War in Australia, 1942–45." In *Japanese Prisoners of War*, edited by Philip Towle, Margaret Kosugi, and Yoichi Kibata. London: Hambeldon & London, 2000.

Feifer, George. *Tennozan: The Battle of Okinawa and the Atomic Bomb*. New York: Ticknor and Fields, 1992.

Feuer, A.B., ed. *Bilibid Diary: The Secret Notebooks of Commander Thomas Hayes, POW, the Philippines, 1942–45*. Hamden, CT: Archon Books, 1987.

Field, Norma. *In the Realm of a Dying Emperor: Japan at Century's End*. New York: Vintage, 1993.

Fitzpatrick, Bernard T. *The Hike into the Sun: Memoir of an American Soldier Captured on Bataan in 1942 and Imprisoned by the Japanese Until 1945*. Jefferson, NC: McFarland, 1993.

Foner, Eric. *Free Soil, Free Labor, Free Men: The Ideology of the Republican Party Before the Civil War*. New York: Oxford University Press, 1970.

Francia, Luis H. *Eye of the Fish: A Personal Archipelago*. New York: Kaya Press, 2001.

Frankl, Victor. *From Death Camp to Existentialism*. Boston: Beacon, 1959.

Fraser, Thomson G. *In the Claw of the Tiger*. 2007.

Frazier, Glenn D. *Hell's Guest*. Chambersburg, PA: eGen Co, 2012.

Friday, Karl F. "Bushido or Bull? A Medieval Historian's Perspective on the Imperial Army and the Japanese Warrior Tradition. " *The History Teacher* 27 no. 3 (May 1994): 339–349.

Friedlander, Peter. "Theory, Method and Oral History." In *Oral History: An Interdisciplinary Anthology*, edited by David K. Dunaway and Willa K. Brown. Walnut Creek, CA: Altamira Press, 1996.

Friend, Theodore. *The Blue-Eyed Enemy: Japan Against the West in Java and Luzon, 1942–1945*. Princeton: Princeton University Press, 1988.

Fritzsche, Peter. "The Case of Modern Memory." *The Journal of Modern History* 73 (March 2001): 87–117.

Frohn, Axel. "Das Schicksal Deutscher Kriegsgefangener in Amerikanischen Lagern Nach dem Zweiten Weltkrieg." *Historisches Jahrbuch* III (1991): 466–92.

Fu, Ping. *Bend, Not Break: A Life in Two Worlds*. New York: Penguin, 2012.

Fuller, Richard. *Shokan: Hirohito's Samurai*. London: Arms and Armour, 1992.

Furuya, Harumi. "Japan's Racial Identity in the Second World War: The Cultural Context of the Japanese Treatment of POWs." In *Japanese Prisoners of War*, edited by Philip Towle, Margaret Kosugi and Kibata Yoichi. London: Hambeldon & London, 2000.

Fussell, Paul. *The Boys' Crusade: The American Infantry in Northwestern Europe, 1944–1945*. New York: The Modern Library, 2003.

———. *The Great War and Modern Memory*. London: Oxford University Press, 1975.

———. *Thank God for the Atomic Bomb and Other Essays*. New York: Ballantine, 1988.

———. *Wartime: Understanding and Behavior in the Second World War*. New York: Oxford University Press, 1989.

Gailey, Harry. *The Liberation of Guam*. Novato, CA: Presidio Press, 1988.

———. *The War in the Pacific: From Pearl Harbor to Tokyo Bay*. Novato, CA: Presidio Press, 1995.

Ganzfried, Daniel. "Fakten gegen Erinnerung." *Die Weltwoche*, September 3, 1998.

Garner, William T. *A Study in Valor: The Faith of a Bataan Death March Survivor*. Silverton, ID: Mapletree Publishing, 2010.

Gautier, James Donovan. *I Came Back from Bataan*. Greenville, SC: Emerald House Group, 1997.

Geertz, Clifford. *The Interpretation of Cultures*. New York: Basic Books, 1973.

Gibney, Frank. *Five Gentlemen of Japan: The Portrait of a Nation's Character*. Rutland, VT: Charles E. Tuttle, 1973.

———. *Senso: The Japanese Remember the Pacific War*. Armonk, NY: M.E. Sharpe, 1995.

Gilpatrick, Kristin. *Footprints in Courage: A Bataan Death March Survivor's Story*. Oregon, WI: Badger Books, 2002.

Glusman, John A. *Conduct Under Fire: Four American Doctors and Their Fight for Life as Prisoners of the Japanese, 1941–1945*. New York: Viking, 2005.

Goldstein, Bernice Z., and Kyoko Tamura. *Japan and America: A Comparative Study in Language and Culture*. Rutland, VT: Tuttle, 1975.

Goldstein, Gerald, et al. "Survivors of Imprisonment in the Pacific Theater During World War II." *American Journal of Psychiatry* 144 (1987): 1210–13.

Goodman, Grant. "Philippine Bushido." In *Nitobe Inazo: Japan's Bridge Across the Pacific*, edited by John F. Howes. Boulder, CO: Westview Press, 1995.

Gordon, Richard M. *Horyo: Memoirs of an American POW*. St. Paul: Paragon House, 1999.

Goto, Ken'ichi. *Tensions of Empire: Japan and Southeast Asia in the Colonial and Postcolonial World*. Athens: Ohio University Press, 2003.

Gottschalk, Louis. "The History and the Historical Document." In *The Use of Personal Documents in History, Anthropology and Sociology*. New York: Social Sciences Research Council, 1945.

Grashio, Samuel C., and Bernard Norling. *Return to Freedom: The War Memoirs of Col. Samuel C. Grashio USAF (Ret.)*. Tulsa: MCN Press, 1982.

Gray, J. Glenn. *The Warriors: Reflections on Men in Battle*. Lincoln: University of Nebraska Press, 1959.

Grayling, A.C. *Among the Dead Cities: The History and Moral Legacy of the World War II Bombing of Civilians in Germany and Japan*. New York: Walker & Co., 2006.

Greenberger, Robert. *The Bataan Death March*. Minneapolis: Compass Point Books, 2009.

Grinker, R.R. *Men Under Stress*. Philadelphia: Blakiston, 1945.

Groom, Winston. *1942, The Year That Tried Men's Souls*. New York: Grove Press, 2005.

Grossman, Dave. *On Killing: The Psychological Cost of Learning to Kill in War and Society*. New York: Back Bay Books, 2009.

Hall, Robert King, ed. *Kokutai no Hong: Cardinal Principles of the National Entity in Japan*. Newton, MA: Crofton Publishing, 1974.

Hammer, Joshua. *Yokohama Burning*. New York: Free Press, 2006.

Hane, Mikiso. *Modern Japan: A Historical Survey*. Boulder, CO: Westview Press, 1986.

Haney, Robert E. *Caged Dragons: An American P.O.W. in World War II Japan*. Ann Arbor: Sabre Press, 1991.

Hargrove, Marion. *See Here, Private Hargrove*. New York: Henry Holt, 1942.

Harries, Meirion, and Susie. *Soldiers of the Sun: The Rise and Fall of the Imperial Japanese Army*. New York: Random House, 1991.

Hartendorp, A.V.H. *The Japanese Occupation of the Philippines*. Manila: Bookmark, 1967.

Hata, Ikuhiko. "From Consideration to Contempt: The Changing Nature of Japanese Military and Popular Perceptions of Prisoners of War Through the Ages." In *Prisoners of War and Their Captors in World War II*, edited by Bob Moore and Kent Fedorowich. Washington, D.C.: Berg, 1996.

Hayashi, Hirofumi. "The Battle of Singapore, the Massacre of Chinese and Understanding of the Issue in Postwar Japan." *The Asia-Pacific Journal* 28 (July 13, 2009).

Hayashi, Saburo. *Kogun, The Japanese Army in the Pacific War*. Quantico, VA: The Marine Corps Association, 1959.

Hayden, Joseph Ralson. *The Philippines: A Study in National Development*. New York: Macmillan, 1942.

Hearn, Lafcadio. *Japan: An Attempt at Interpretation*. Rutland VT: Charles Tuttle, 1955.

_____. *Das Japanbuch, Eine Auswahl aus den Werken von Lafacdio Hearn*. Frankfurt a. Main: Rütten und Loening, 1923.

___. *A Japanese Miscellany*. Rutland VT: Charles Tuttle, 1954.

_____. *Kokoro: Hints and Echoes of Japanese Inner Life*. Boston: Houghton Mifflin, 1896.

_____. *Writings from Japan*. New York: Viking Penguin, 1984.

Henshall, Kenneth G. *Dimensions of Japanese Society, Gender, Margins and Mainstream*. New York: Palgrave, 1999.

Herman, Judith Lewis. *Trauma and Recovery*. New York: Basic Books, 1992.

Hersey, John. *Men on Bataan*. New York: Alfred A. Knopf, 1942.

Hewes, Lawrence. "Japan—Land and Men." In *Imperial Japan, 1800–1945*, edited by Jon Livingston, et. al. New York: Pantheon, 1973.

Hibbs, Ralph Emerson. *Tell MacArthur to Wait*. Quezon City: Giraffe Books, 1996.

Holmes, Linda Goetz. *Unjust Enrichment: How Japan's Companies Built Postwar Fortunes Using American POWs*. Mechanicsburg, PA: Stackpole, 2001.

Holt, Thaddeus. "King of Bataan." In *No End Save Victory: Perspectives on World War II*, edited by Robert Cowley. New York: G.P. Putnam's Sons 2001.

Howes, John F., ed. *Nitobe Inazo: Japan's Bridge Across the Pacific*. Boulder, CO: Westview Press, 1995.

Hoyt, Edwin. *Japan's War: The Great Pacific Conflict, 1853–1952*. New York: McGraw Hill, 1986.

Hubbard, John Preston. *Apocalypse Undone: My Survival of Japanese Imprisonment During World War II*. Nashville: Vanderbilt University Press, 1990.

Humphreys, Leonard A. *The Way of the Heavenly Sword: The Japanese Army in the 1920s*. Stanford: Stanford University Press, 1995.

Hunt, Ray C., and Bernard Norling, *Behind Japa-*

nese Lines: An American guerrilla in the Philippines. Lexington: University Press of Kentucky, 1986.

Ienaga, Saburo. *Japan's Last War: World War II and the Japanese, 1931–1945*. Oxford: Basil Blackwell, 1979.

_____. *The Pacific War: A Critical Perspective on Japan's Role in World War II*. New York: Pantheon, 1978.

Ind, Allison. *Bataan: The Judgment Seat*. New York: Macmillan, 1944.

Iritani, Toshio. *Group Psychology of the Japanese in Wartime*. London: Kegan Paul International, 1991.

Iriye, Akira. *Power and Culture: The Japanese-American War, 1941–1945*. Cambridge: Harvard University Press, 1981.

Irokawa, Daikichi. *The Age of Hirohito*. Trans. Mikiso Hane and John K. Urda. New York: The Free Press, 1995.

Isidro, Antonio. *Philippine Social Life and Youth*. Manila: Philippine Education Company, 1951.

Ito, Kimio. "The Invention of *Wa* and the Transformation of the Image of Prince Shotoku in Modern Japan." In *Mirror of Modernity: Invented Traditions of Modern Japan*, edited by Vlastos, Stephen. Berkeley: University of California Press, 1998.

Jackson, Calvin G. *Diary of Col. Calvin G. Jackson*. Ada: Ohio Northern University, 1992.

Jacobsen, Gene S. *We Refused to Die: My Time as a Prisoner of War in Bataan and Japan, 1942–1945*. Salt Lake City: University of Utah Press, 2004.

James, D. Clayton, ed. *South to Bataan, North to Mukden: The Prison Diary of Brigadier General W.E. Brougher*. Athens: University of Georgia Press, 1971.

Janoff-Bulman, Ronnie. *Shattered Assumptions: Towards a New Psychology of Trauma*. New York: The Free Press, 1992.

Japan Center for International Exchange, ed. *The Silent Power: Japan's Identity and World Role*. Tokyo: The Simul Press, 1976.

Johnson, Forrest Bryant. *Hour of Redemption: The Heroic World War II Saga of America's Most Daring POW Rescue*. New York: Warner Books, 1978.

Johnson, Paul. *Modern Times: The World From the Twenties to the Nineties*. New York: HarperCollins, 1992.

Johnson, Thomas M., and Pratt, Fletcher. *The Lost Battalion*. Lincoln: University of Nebraska Press, 2000.

Johnston, William. *Geisha, Harlot, Stranger, Star, A Woman: Sex and Morality in Modern Japan*. New York: Columbia University Press, 2005.

Jones, James. *The Thin Red Line*. New York: Signet, 1964.

_____. *World War II: A Chronicle of Soldiering*. New York: Ballantine, 1975.

Jose, Ricardo Trota. *The Philippine Army, 1935–1942*. Manila: Ateneo De Manila University Press, 1992.

Kahara, Nahoko. "From Folktale Hero to Local Symbol: The Transformation of Momotaro (the Peach Boy) in the Creation of a Local Culture." *Waseda Journal of Asian Studies* 25 (2004): 35–61.

Kammen, Michael. "Some Patterns and Meanings of Memory Distortion in American History." In *Memory Distortion: How Minds, Brains and Societies Reconstruct the Past*, edited by Daniel L. Schacter. Cambridge: Harvard University Press, 1995.

Kano, Tsutomu. "Why the Search for Identity?" In *The Silent Power: Japan's Identity and World Role*, edited by Japan Center for International Exchange. Tokyo: The Simul Press, 1976.

Kathman, Clemens A. *I Was There, Charley*. Bloomington: AuthorHouse, 2005.

Kato, Masuo. *The Lost War: A Japanese Reporter's Inside Story*. New York: Knopf, 1946.

Keegan, John. *The First World War*. London: Pimlico, 1999.

_____. *The Second World War*. New York: Penguin, 1989.

Keene, Donald. *Chronicles of My Life: An American in the Heart of Japan*. New York: Columbia University Press, 2008.

_____. *Dawn to the West: Japanese Literature in the Modern Era*. New York: Columbia University Press, 1998.

_____. *Modern Japanese Literature*. New York: Grove Press, 1956.

Kellet, Anthony. *Combat Motivation: The Behavior of Soldiers in Battle*. Boston: Kluwer, 1982.

Kelnhofer, Guy J. *Life After Liberation: Understanding the Former Prisoner of War*. St. Paul, MN: Banfil Street Press, 1992.

Kenworthy, Aubrey Saint. *The Tiger of Malaya: The Story of General Tomoyuki Yamashita and Death March: General Masaharu Homma*. New York: Exposition Press, 1953.

Kerr, E. Bartlett. *Surrender and Survival: The Experience of American POWs in the Pacific, 1941–1945*. New York: William Morrow, 1985.

Khan, Yoshimitsu. *Japanese Moral Education Past and Present*. Madison, NJ: Fairleigh Dickinson Press, 1997.

Kimball, Warren F. "The Incredible Shrinking War: The Second World War, Not (Just) the Origins of the Cold War." *Diplomatic History* 25 no.3 (Summer 2001): 347–65.

King, Otis H. *The Alamo of the Pacific: The Story of the famed "China Marines" on Bataan and Cor-*

regidor and What They Did to the Enemy as POWs. Fort Worth: Branch-Smith, 1999.

Knox, Donald. *Death March: The Survivors of Bataan*. New York: Harcourt, Brace Jovanovich, 1981.

Koshiro, Yukiko. "Japan's World and World War II." *Diplomatic History* 25 no. 3 (Summer 2001): 425–41.

Krystal, Henry. "Trauma and Aging: A Thirty-Year Follow-Up." In *Trauma, Exploration, Memory*, edited by Cathy Caruth. Baltimore: Johns Hopkins Press, 1995.

Lacambra, Jose Maria. *Rising Sun Blinking: A Young Boy's Memoirs of the Japanese Occupation in the Philippines*. Manila: Sinag-Tala Publishers, 1994.

LaForte, Robert S., Ronald E. Marcello, and Ricahrd L. Himmel, eds. *With Only the Will to Live: Accounts of Americans in Japanese Prison Camps, 1941–1945*. Wilmington, DE: Scholarly Resources, 1994.

Landas, Marc. *The Fallen: A True Story of American POWs and Japanese Wartime Atrocities*. Hoboken, NJ: John Wiley and Sons, 2004.

Lardizabal, Amparo S., and Felicitas Tensuan-Leogardo. *Readings on Philippines Culture and Social Life*. Manila: Rex Book Store, 1970.

Larson, Thomas. *The Memoir and the Memoirist: Reading and Writing Personal Narrative*. Athens, OH: Swallow Press, 2007.

Laub, Dori. "Truth and Testimony: The Process and the Struggle." In *Trauma, Exploration, Memory*, edited by Cathy Caruth. Baltimore: Johns Hopkins Press, 1995

Lawton, Manny. *Some Survived*. Chapel Hill: Algonquin Books of Chapel Hill, 1984.

Laya, J.C. *Little Democracies*. Manila: Inang Wika Publishing, 1951.

Lebra, Joyce C., ed. *Japan's Greater East Asia Co-Prosperity Sphere in World War II*. Kuala Lumpur: Oxford University Press, 1975.

Leckie, Robert. *Helmet for My Pillow: From Parris Island to the Pacific*. New York: Bantam, 2010.

———. *The Wars of America*. 2 vols. New York: Harper and Row, 1968.

Lee, Clark. *They Call It Pacific*. New York: Viking, 1943.

Le Roy, James A. *Philippine Life in Town and Country*. New York: G.P Putnam's Sons, 1905.

Levering, Robert W. *Horror Trek: A True Story of Bataan, the Death March and Three and One-half Years in Japanese Prison Camps*. Dayton, OH: Horstman Printing, 1948.

Levi, Primo. *Moments of Reprieve*. New York: Summit Books, 1979.

Lévi-Strauss, Claude. *Tristes Tropiques*. New York: Atheneum, 1964.

Lindbergh, Charles A. *The Wartime Journals of Charles A. Lindbergh*. New York: Harcourt Brace Jovanovich, 1970.

Linderman, Gerald. *Embattled Courage: The Experience of Combat in the American Civil War*. New York: The Free Press, 1987.

———. *The World Within War: America's Combat Experience in World War II*. New York: The Free Press, 1997.

Linenthal, Edward T., and Tom and Englehardt, eds. *History Wars: The Enola Gay and Other Battles for the American Past*. New York: Metropolitan Books, 1996.

Lingeman, Richard R. *Don't You Know There's a War On? The American Home Front, 1941–1945*. New York: G.P. Putnam's Sons, 1970.

Linn, Brian McAllister. *Guardians of Empire: The U.S. Army and the Pacific, 1902–1940*. Chapel Hill: University of North Carolina Press, 1997.

Littlewood, Ian. *The Idea of Japan: Western Images, Western Myths*. Chicago: Ivan R. Dee, 1996.

Livingston, Jon, Joe Moore, and Felicia Oldfather, eds. *The Japan Reader: Imperial Japan, 1800–1945*. New York: Pantheon, 1973.

Lory, Hillis. *Japan's Military Masters: The Army in Japanese Life*. Westport, CT: Greenwood Press, 1943.

Lumbera, Cynthia Nograles, and Teresita Gimenez-Maceda, eds. *Rediscovery: Essays in Philippine Life and Culture*. Quezon City: Interlino Printing, 1977.

Lunden, Walter A. "Captivity Psychosis Among Prisoners of War." *Journal of Criminal Law and Criminology* 39 (1948–49): 721–33.

Lynch, Frank, and Alfonso de Guzman. *Four Readings on Philippine Values*. Quezon City: Institute of Philippine Culture, 1973.

Lyttelton, Oliver. *From Peace to War: A Study in Contrast, 1857–1918*. London: The Bodley Head, 1968.

MacArthur, Brian. *Surviving the Sword: Prisoners of the Japanese, 1942–45*. London: Time Warner Books, 2005.

MacArthur, Douglas. *Reminiscences*. New York: McGraw Hill, 1964.

MacKenzie, S.P. "The Treatment of Prisoners of War in World War II." *The Journal of Modern History* 66 no. 3 (September 1994): 487–520.

Mächler, Stefan. *The Wilkomirski Affair: A Study in Biographical Truth*. New York: Schocken Books, 2001.

Mailer, Norman. *The Naked and the Dead*. New York: Holt, Reinhart, 1948.

Mallonee, Richard C., ed. *Battle for Bataan: An Eyewitness Account*. Novato, CA: Presidio, 1997.

Manchester, William. *American Caesar, Douglas*

MacArthur, 1880–1964. Boston: Little, Brown, 1978.

———. *The Glory and the Dream.* Boston: Little, Brown, 1973.

———. *Goodbye, Darkness: A Memoir of the Pacific War.* Boston: Little, Brown, 1980.

Manvell, Roger. *Films and the Second World War.* New York: A.S. Barnes, 1974.

Mapes, Victor L., with Scott A. Mills. *The Butchers, the Baker: The World War II Memoir of a United States Army Air Corps Soldier Captured by the Japanese in the Philippines.* Jefferson, NC: McFarland, 2000.

Maring, Ester G., and Joel M. *Historical and Cultural Dictionary of the Philippines.* Metuchen, NJ: Scarecrow Press, 1973.

Marquardt, Frederic S. *Before Bataan and After: A Personalized History of Our Philippine Experiment.* Indianapolis: Bobbs-Merrill, 1943.

Marquez, Alberto T. *War Memoirs of the Alcala Veterans.* Quezon City: New Day Publishers, 1992.

Marshall, S.L.A. *Men Against Fire: The Problem of Battle Command.* Norman: University of Oklahoma Press, 2000.

———. *World War I.* Boston: Houghton Mifflin, 2001.

Martin, Adrian R. *Brothers from Bataan: POWs, 1942–1945.* Manhattan, KS: Sunflower University Press, 1992.

Martin, Ralph G. *The GI War, 1941–1945.* Boston: Little, Brown, 1967.

Maruyama, Masao. *Studies in the Intellectual History of Tokugawa Japan.* Trans. Mikiso Hane. Princeton: Princeton University Press, 1974.

———. *Thought and Behavior in Modern Japanese Politics.* Ivan Morris, ed. London: Oxford University Press, 1963.

Maschke, Erich. *Die deutschen Kriegsgefangenen des Zweiten Weltkrieges, Eine Zusammenfassung.* München: Ernst und Werner, 1974.

Masatsugu, Mitsuyuki. *Samurai Society: Duty and Dependence in Contemporary Japan.* New York: Amacom, 1982.

Masterson, Melissa. *Ride the Waves to Freedom: Calvin Graef's Survival Story of the Bataan Death March and His Escape from a Sinking Hellship.* Kearney, NE: Morris Publishing, 1999.

Mauldin, Bill. *Up Front.* New York: Henry Holt, 1945.

Maynes, Mary Jo, Jennifer L. Pierce, and Barbara Laslett, Barbara. *Telling Stories: The Use of Personal Narratives in the Social Sciences and History.* Ithaca: Cornell University Press, 2008.

McAdams, Dan P. "Identity and the Life Story." In *Autobiographical Memory and the Construction of a Narrative Self,* edited by Robyn Fivush and Catherine Haden. Mahwah, NJ: Lawrence Erlbaum, 2003.

McBride, Myrrl W. *Beyond the Death March: Memoir of a Soldier's Journey from Bataan to Nagasaki.* Jefferson, NC: McFarland, 2010.

McFerson, Hazel M., ed. *Mixed Blessing: The Impact of the American Colonial Experience on Politics and Society in the Philippines.* Westport, CT: Greenwood Press, 2002.

McPherson, James M. *What They Fought For, 1861–1865.* New York: Anchor Books, 1995.

Mellnik, Steve. *Philippine Diary, 1939–1945.* New York: Van Nostrand Reinhold, 1969.

Merritt, J.D. *Adapt or Die.* InstaPubisher.com, 2010.

Miller, Arthur. *Situation Normal.* New York: Reynal and Hitchcock, 1944.

Miller, Donald L. *The Story of World War II.* New York: Simon & Schuster, 2001.

Miller, E.B. *Bataan Uncensored.* Long Prairie, MN: Hart Publications, 1949.

Miller, Francis T. *General Douglas MacArthur, Fighter for Freedom.* Philadelphia: J.C. Winston, 1942.

Miller, Ian. "The Afterlife of Elephants: Imperial Collapse and the Cult of Martyrdom in Wartime Japan." Presentation at American Historical Association, January 9, 2010.

Miller, Roy Andrew. "Levels of Speech (*keigo*) and the Japanese Linguistic Response to Modernization." In *Tradition and Modernization in Japanese Culture,* edited by Donald H. Shiveley. Princeton: Princeton University Press, 1971.

Millet, Alan R. & Murray, Williamson. *Military Effectiveness, Vol. III, The Second World War.* Boston: Allen and Unwin, 1988.

Minear, Richard H. *Victor's Justice: The Tokyo War Crimes Trial.* Princeton, New Jersey: Princeton University Press, 1971.

Minichiello, Sharon, ed. *Japan's Competing Modernities: Issues in Culture and Democracy.* Honolulu: University of Hawai'i Press, 1998.

Mitchell, Reid. *Civil War Soldiers.* New York: Penguin, 1988.

Mitchell, Richard H. *Janus-Faced Justice: Political Criminals in Imperial Japan.* Honolulu: University of Hawai'i Press, 1992.

———. *Thought Control in Prewar Japan.* Ithaca: Cornell University Press, 1976.

Moeller, Robert G. "'In a Thousand Years, Every German Will Speak of This Battle': Celluloid Memories of Stalingrad." In *General Douglas MacArthur, Fighter for Freedom,* edited by Omer Bartov, Atina Grossmann and Mary Nolan, eds. *Crimes of War: Guilt and Denial in the Twentieth Century.* New York: The New Press, 2002.

Moody, Samuel B. *Reprieve from Hell.* New York: Pageant Press, 1961.

Moore, Bob and Fedorowich, Kent. *Prisoners of War and Their Captors in World War II.* Washington, D.C.: Berg, 1996.

Morre, Joe, ed. *The Other Japan: Conflict, Compromise and Resistance Since 1945.* Armonk, NY: M.E. Sharpe, 1997.

Morris, John. *Traveler from Tokyo: My Life in Japan, October 1939 to December, 1941.* London: Keegan Paul, 2004.

Morton, Louis. *The Fall of the Philippines.* Washington, D.C.: Center of Military History, 1993.

Moss, William. "Oral History, An Appreciation." In *Oral History: An Interdisciplinary Anthology,* edited by David K. Dunaway and Willa K. Brown. Walnut Creek, CA: Altamira Press, 1996.

Murakami, Hyoe. *Japan: The Years of Trial, 1919–52.* Tokyo: Kodansha, 1983.

Murray, Michael. *A Jacques Barzun Reader: Selections from His Works.* New York: HarperCollins, 2002.

Najita, Tetsuo, and J. Victor Koschmann, eds. *Conflict in Modern Japanese History: The Neglected Tradition.* Princeton: Princeton University Press, 1982.

Nakane, Chie. *Japanese Society.* Berkeley: University of California Press, 1970.

NARA, RG 153, Records of the Judge Advocate General.

NARA, RG 331, Military Agency Records.

NARA, RG 407, Military Agency Records.

Nardini, J.B. "Survival Factors in American Prisoners of War of the Japanese." *American Journal of Psychiatry* 109 (October 1952): 241–48.

———. "The William C. Porter Lecture—1961: Psychiatric Concepts of Prisoners of War Confinement." *Military Medicine* 127: 299–307.

Neisser, Ulric, and Robyn Fivush. *The Remembering Self: Construction and Accuracy in the Self-Narrative.* Cambridge: Cambridge University Press, 1994.

Neuenschwander, John. "Oral Historians and Long-Term Memory." In *Oral History: An Interdisciplinary Anthology,* edited by David K. Dunaway and Willa K. Baum. Nashville: American Association for State and Local History, 1984.

Nicolay, Helen. *MacArthur of Bataan.* New York: D. Appleton-Century, 1942.

Nietzsche, Friedrich. "On the Uses and Disadvantages of History for Life." In *Untimely Meditations,* translated by R.J. Hollingdale. Cambridge: Cambridge University Press, 1983.

Nitobe, Inazo. *Bushido, The Soul of Japan: An Exposition of Japanese Thought.* Rutland, VT: Charles E. Tuttle, 1969.

Noma, Hiroshi. *Zone of Emptiness.* Cleveland: World Publication, 1956.

Norman, Elizabeth. *We Band of Angels: The Untold Story of American Nurses Trapped on Bataan by the Japanese.* New York: Random House, 1999.

Norman, Michael, and Elizabeth M. Norman. *Tears in the Darkness: The Story of the Bataan Death March and Its Aftermath.* New York: Farrar, Straus & Giroux, 2009.

North, Jude. *Lost in the Wilderness: Remembering the Bataan Death March.* BookSurge, 2004.

O'Connell, Robert L. *Of Arms and Men: A History of War, Weapons, and Aggression.* New York: Oxford University Press, 1989.

O'Connor, Richard. *Pacific Destiny: An Informal History of the U.S. in the Far East: 1776–1968.* Boston: Little, Brown, 1969.

O'Donnell, Patrick K. *Into the Rising Sun: In Their Own Words: World War II's Pacific Veterans Reveal the Heart of Combat.* New York: The Free Press, 2002.

Oka, Yoshitake. "Generational Conflict After the Russo-Japanese War." In *Conflict in Modern Japanese History: The Neglected Tradition,* edited by Tetsuo Najita and J. Victor Koschmann. Princeton: Princeton University Press, 1982, 197–225.

Olson, John E. *O'Donnell: Andersonville of the Pacific.* Self-published, 1985.

O'Neill, William L. *American High: The Years of Confidence, 1945–1960.* New York: The Free Press, 1986.

Ongpauco, Fidel. *They Refused to Die: True Stories About World War II Heroes in the Philippines, 1941–1945.* Levesque Publications, 1982.

Ortega, Abel, Jr. *Courage on Bataan and Beyond: Memories of an American POW Who was a Slave of the Japanese during World War II for 3 ½ Years.* Bloomington: AuthorHouse, 2005.

Osawa, Kiyoshi. *The Japanese Community in the Philippines Before, During and After the War.* Manila: Joshu Bunko Library, 1994.

Page, William Frank. *The Health of Former Prisoners of War.* Washington, D.C.: National Academy Press, 1992.

Paguio, Wilfredo C. *Bataan: Land of Valor, People of Peace.* Manila: Jardi Press, 1997.

Parillo, Mark P., ed. *We Were in the Big One: Experiences of the World War II Generation.* Wilmington, DE: SR Books, 2002.

Parkinson, James W., and Lee Benson. *Soldier Slaves: Abandoned by the White House, Courts and Congress.* Annapolis Naval Institute Press, 2006.

Petak, Joseph A. *Never Plan Tomorrow: The Saga of the Bataan Death March and Battle of Corregidor Survivors, 1942–1945.* Valencia, CA: Delta Lithograph Company, 1991.

Playter, John. *Survivor.* Bolivar, MO: Southwest Baptist University, 2000.

Poncio, John Henry, and Marlin Young. *Girocho: A GI's Story of Bataan and Beyond*. Baton Rouge: Louisiana State University Press, 2003.

Potter, John Dean. *The Life and Death of a Japanese General*. New York: Signet, 1962.

Poweleit, Alvin C. *Kentucky's Fighting 192nd Light G.H.Q. Tank Battalion: A Saga of Kentucky's Part in the Defense of the Philippines*. Newport, KY: Quality Lithographing Company, 1981.

_____. *USAFFE, The Loyal Americans and Faithful Filipinos: A Saga of Atrocities Perpetrated During the Fall of the Philippines, the Bataan Death March, and Japanese Imprisonment and Survival*. 1975.

Prowles, Cyril H. "*Bushido*: Its Admirers and Critics." In *Nitobe Inazo: Japan's Bridge Across the Pacific*, edited by John F. Howes. Boulder, CO: Westview Press, 1995.

Prugh, George S. "Prisoners at War: The POW Battleground." *Dickinson Law Review* 60 (October 1956): 123–38.

Putzel, James. *A Captive Land: The Politics of Agrarian Reform in the Philippines*. New York: Monthly Review Press, 1992.

Quinn, Michael A. *Love Letters to Mike: Forty Months as a Japanese Prisoner of War, April 9, 1942 to September 17, 1945*. New York: Vantage Press, 1977.

Ramsey, Edward Price, and Stephen J. Rivele. *Lieutenant Ramsey's War*. New York: Knightsbridge Publishing, 1990.

Rees, Laurence. *Horror in the East: Japan and the Atrocities of World War II*. London: BBC Books, 2001.

Reeve, C.D.C. *Plato Republic*. Indianapolis: Hackett, 2004.

Reischauer, Edwin O. *The Japanese Today*. Cambridge: Harvard University Press, 1988.

Reynolds, Gary K. *U.S. Prisoners of War and Civilian American Citizens Captured and Interned by Japan in World War II: The Issue of Compensation by Japan*. Washington, D.C.: Congressional Research Service, Library of Congress, 2002.

Richie, Donald. *Japanese Cinema: Film Style and National Character*. Garden City: Doubleday, 1971

_____. *Japanese Portraits: Pictures of Different People*. Tokyo: Tuttle Publishing, 2005.

Robertson, James I. *Soldiers Blue and Gray*. Columbia: University of South Carolina Press, 1989.

Rogers, Everett M., and Nancy R. Barlit. *Silent Voices of World War II*. Santa Fe, 2005.

Romulo, Carlos P. *I Saw the Fall of the Philippines*. Garden City, NY: Doubleday, Doran, 1942.

Rosenfeld, David M. *Unhappy Soldier: Hino Ashihei and Japanese World War II Literature*. Lanham, MD: Lexington Books, 2002.

Ross, Michael, and Anne E. Wilson. "Constructing and Appraising Past Selves." In *Memory, Brain and Belief*, edited by Daniel L. Schacter. Cambridge: Harvard University Press, 2000.

Rotundo, E. Anthony. *American Manhood: Transformations in Masculinity from the Revolution to the Modern Era*. New York: Basic Books, 1993.

Ruse, Timothy C. *We Volunteered: A Biography of Carl Robert Ruse, Survivor of the Bataan Death March and Prisoner of the Japanese 1942–1945*. Washington D.C., 2010

Russell, Lord. *The Knights of Bushido: The Shocking History of Japanese War Atrocities*. New York: E.P. Dutton, 1958.

Sacks, Oliver. "Speak, Memory." *New York Review of Books*, February 21, 2013.

Sakaiya, Taichi. *What Is Japan? Contradictions and Transformations*. New York: Kodansha, 1993.

Sassoon, Siegfried. *Collected Poems*. New York: Viking, 1949.

Sato, Hiroaki. "*Gyokusai* or 'Shattering like a Jewel': Reflection on the Pacific War." *Japan Focus*. http://japanfocus.org.

Schacter, Daniel L. *Memory Distortion: How Minds, Brains, and Societies Reconstruct the Past*. Cambridge: Harvard University Press, 1995.

_____. *Memory, the Brain, the Mind, and the Past*. New York: Basic Books, 1996.

_____. *The Seven Sins of Memory: How the Mind Forgets and Remembers*. Boston: Houghton Mifflin, 2001.

___, ed. *Memory, Brain, and Belief*. Cambridge: Harvard University Press, 2000.

Schattsschneider, Ellen. "The Work of Sacrifice in the Age of Mechanical Reproduction: Bride Dolls and Ritual Appropriation at Yasukuni Shrine." In *The Culture of Japanese Fascism*, edited by Alan Tansman. Durham: Duke University Press, 2009.

Schirmer, Daniel B., and Stephen Rosskamm Shalom, eds. *The Philippines Reader: A History of Colonialism, Neocolonialism, Dictatorship and Resistance*. Boston: South End Press, 1987.

Schudson, Michael. "Dynamics of Distortion in Collective Memory." In *Memory Distortion: How Minds, Brains, and Societies Reconstruct the Past*, edited by Daniel L. Schacter. Cambridge: Harvard University Press, 1995.

Serrano, Richard A. *Last of the Blue and Gray: Old Men, Stolen Glory and the Mystery That Outlived the Civil War*. Washington, D.C.: Smithsonian, 2013.

Shinzo, Hayase. "The Japanese Residents of 'Dabao-kuo.'" In *The Philippines Under Japan: Occupation Policy and Reaction*, edited by Setsuko Ikehata and Ricardo Jose Trota. Manila: Ateneo De Manila University Press, 1999.

Sides, Hampton. *Ghost Soldiers: The Epic Account of World War II's Greatest Rescue Mission.* New York: Anchor Books, 2001.

_____. "The Trial of General Homma." *American Heritage* (February-March 2007): 35–47.

Silva, Vincent. *Senso Owari.* Bloomington: AuthorHouse, 2008.

Simmel, George. *The Philosophy of Money,* 3d ed. London: Routledge, 2004.

Singer, Jefferson A., and Peter Salovey. *The Remembered Self: Emotion and Memory in Personality.* New York: Free Press, 1993.

Singer, Kurt. *Mirror, Sword and Jewel: A Study of Japanese Characteristics.* New York: Braziller, 1973.

Sledge, E.B. *With the Old Breed at Peleliu and Okinawa.* Novato, CA: Presidio Press, 1981.

Sloan, Bill. *Undefeated: America's Heroic Fight for Bataan and Corregidor.* New York: Simon & Schuster, 2012.

Slotkin, Richard. *The Fatal Environment: The Myth of the Frontier in the Age of Industrialization, 1800–1890.* Norman: University of Oklahoma Press, 1985.

_____. *Gunfighter Nation: The Myth of the Frontier in Twentieth-Century America.* Norman: University of Oklahoma Press, 1998.

Smethurst, Richard J. *A Social Basis for Prewar Japanese Militarism: The Army and the Rural Community.* Berkeley: University of California Press, 1974.

Smith, Robert J. *Japanese Society: Tradition, Self, and the Social Order.* Cambridge: Cambridge University Press, 1983.

Smith, Stanley. *Prisoner of the Emperor: An American POW in World War II.* Niwot: University Press of Colorado, 1991.

Sneddon, Murray M. *Zero Ward: A Survivor's Nightmare.* San Jose: Writer's Club Press, 2000.

Sommers, Stan. *The Japanese Story, Packet #10.* Marshfield, WI: National Medical Research Commission, 1980.

Spector, Ronald. *Eagle Against the Sun: The American War with Japan.* New York: The Free Press, 1985.

Spencer, J.E. *Land and People in the Philippines: Geographic Problems in Rural Economy.* Berkeley: University of California Press, 1952.

Stamp, Loren E. *Journey Through Hell: Memoir of a World War II American Navy Medic Captured in the Philippines and Imprisoned by the Japanese.* Jefferson, NC: McFarland, 1993.

Steinbeck, John. *Once There Was a War.* New York: Viking, 1958.

Steiner, Kurt. "Wartime Local Government." In *Imperial Japan, 1800–1945,* edited by Jon Livingston, et al. New York: Pantheon, 1973.

Stewart, Sidney. *Give Us This Day.* New York: W.W. Norton, 1956.

Stoler, Mark A. "The Second World War in U.S. Memory." *Diplomatic History* 25 no. 3 (Summer 2001): 383–92.

Stouffer, Samuel A., et al. *The American Soldier: Adjustment During Army Life.* Princeton: Princeton University Press, 1949.

_____. *The American Soldier: Combat and Its Aftermath.* Princeton: Princeton University Press, 1949.

Sullivan, Matthew Barry. *Thresholds of Peace: Four Hundred Thousand German Prisoners and the People of Britain 1944–1948.* London: Hamish Hamilton, 1979.

Suzuki, Takao. *Japanese and the Japanese: Words into Culture.* Trans. Akira Miura. Tokyo: Kodansha, 1973.

Swinson, Arthur. *Four Samurai: A Quartet of Japanese Army Commanders in the Second World War.* London: Hutchinson of London, 1968.

Syka, Walter A. *Japan's Holy War: The Ideology of Radical Shinto Ultranationalism.* Durham: Duke University Press, 2009.

Tanaka, Yuki. *Hidden Horrors: Japanese War Crimes in World War II.* Boulder, CO: Westview Press, 1998.

Tansman, Alan, ed. *The Culture of Japanese Fascism.* Durham: Duke University Press, 2009.

Tapert, Annette, ed. *Lines of Battle: Letters from American Servicemen, 1941–1945.* New York: Times Books, 1987.

Tasaki, Hanama. *Long the Imperial Way.* Westport, CT: Greenwood Press, 1949.

Tasker, Peter. *The Japanese: Portrait of a Nation.* New York: Penguin, 1987.

Taylor, Frank. *The Unforgettable Story of Bataan, Corregidor.* Visitor's Guide, n.d.

Taylor, Lawrence. *A Trial of Generals: Homma, Yamashita, MacArthur.* South Bend, IN: Icarus Press, 1981.

Tenney, Lester I. *My Hitch in Hell: The Bataan Death March.* Washington, D.C.: Brassey's, 1995.

Terkel, Studs. *"The Good War": An Oral History of World War II.* New York: Pantheon, 1984.

Thomas, Ed "Tommie." *As I Remember: The Death March of Bataan.* Sonoita, AZ: Edward E. Thomas, 1990.

Thompson, Paul W., Harold Doud, and John Scofield. *How the Japanese Army Fights.* New York: Penguin, 1942.

Tierney, Robert Thomas. *Tropics of Savagery: The Culture of Japanese Empire in Comparative Frame.* Berkeley: University of California Press, 2010.

Tipton, Elise K. "Intellectual Life, Culture, and the Challenge of Modernity." In *A Companion to*

Japanese History, edited by William A. Tsutsui. Malden, MA: Blackwell, 2007.

Toland, John. *But Not in Shame: The Six Months After Pearl Harbor*. New York: Random House, 1961.

_____. *The Rising Sun: The Decline and Fall of the Japanese Empire, 1936–1945*. New York: Random House, 1970.

Towle, Philip, Margaret Kosugi and Yoichi Kibata, eds. *Japanese Prisoners of War*. London: Hambeldon & London, 2000.

Tsuji, Masanobu. *Japan's Greatest Victory, Britain's Worst Defeat*. New York: Sarpedon, 1993.

Tsunoda, Ryusaku, ed. *Sources of Japanese Tradition*. New York: Columbia University Press, 1958.

Tsurumi, Kazuko. *Social Change and the Individual: Japan Before and After Defeat in World War II*. Princeton: Princeton University Press, 1970.

Turner Publishing Company. *American Ex-Prisoners of War*. Paducah, KY: Turner Publishing, 1988.

United States of America vs. Masaharu Homma.

U.S. Government Printing Office. *Basic Field Manual, Physical Training*. March 6, 1941.

_____. Hearing Before the Subcommittee on Administrative Law and Government Relations of the Committee on the Judiciary House of Representatives, 98th Congress, 2nd session on H.R. 3188 Permitting Bataan Death March Prisoners to Sue in U.S. Court of Claims. June 14, 1984.

_____. *A Pocket Guide to Japan*. Washington, D.C., 1950.

_____. *Study of Former Prisoners of War: A Study Prepared by the Veteran's Administration Submitted to the Committee on Veterans' Affairs, United States Senate*. June 3, 1980.

Urwin, Gregory J.W. *Victory in Defeat: The Wake Island Defenders in Captivity, 1941–1945*. Annapolis: Naval Institute Press, 2010.

Utsumi, Aiko. "Japan's World War II POW Policy: Indifference and Irresponsibility." *Japan Focus* (May 10, 2005).

Vance, John R. *Doomed Garrison—The Philippines (A POW Story)*. Ashland, OR: Cascade House, 1974.

Van der Kolk, B.A. "The Intrusive Past: The Flexibility of Memory and the Engraving of Trauma." *American Imago* 48 no. 4 (1991): 425–54.

Volckman, R.W. *We Remained: Three Years Behind the Enemy Lines in the Philippines*. New York: W.W. Norton, 1954.

Wagner, Margaret. *World War II: 365 Days*. New York: Abrams, 2009.

Waldron, Ben D. *Corregidor: From Paradise to Hell*. Freeman, SD: Pine Hill Press, 1988.

Ward, Ian. *The Killer They Called a God*. Singapore: Media Masters, 1992.

Waswo, Ann. "The Transformation of Rural Society, 1900–1950." In *The Cambridge History of Japan, Volume 6, The Twentieth Century*, edited by Peter Duus. New York: Cambridge University Press, 1988, 541–605.

Watanabe, Shoichi. *The Peasant Soul of Japan*. New York: St. Martin's Press, 1980.

Watanabe, Shoko. *Japanese Buddhism: A Critical Appraisal*. Tokyo: Kokusai Bunka Shinkokai, 1970.

Waterford, Van. *Prisoners of the Japanese in World War II*. Jefferson, NC: McFarland, 1994.

Weinstein, Alfred A. *Barbed-Wire Surgeon*. New York: Macmillan, 1948.

White, Hayden. *The Content of the Form: Narrative Discourse and Historical Representation*. Baltimore: Johns Hopkins University Press, 1987.

_____. *The Fiction of Narrative: Essays on History, Literature, and Theory*. Baltimore: Johns Hopkins Press, 2010.

Whiting, Robert. *The Chrysanthemum and the Bat, The Game the Japanese Play*. Tokyo: The Permanent Press, 1977.

Whitman, John W. *Bataan: Our Last Ditch*. New York: Hippocrene Books, 1990.

Wiesel, Elie. *Night*. Trans. Stella Rodway. New York: Avon, 1969.

_____. *One Generation After*. New York: Random House, 1965.

Willeford, Charles. *Something About a Soldier*. New York: Random House, 1986.

Wodnik, Bob. *Captured Honor: POW Survival in the Philippines and Japan*. Pullman: Washington State University Press, 2003.

Wolf, A.V. *Thirst: Physiology of the Urge to Drink and Problems of Water Lack*. Springfield, IL: Charles C. Thomas, 1958.

Wolf, Stewart, and Herbert Ripley. "Reactions Among Allied Prisoners of War Subjected to Three Years of Imprisonment and Torture by the Japanese." *American Journal of Psychiatry* 104 (September 1947): 180–93.

Woronoff, Jon. *Japan's Commercial Empire*. Armonk, NY: M.E. Sharpe, 1984.

Wright, John M., Jr. *Captured on Corregidor: Diary of an American P.O.W. in World War II*. Jefferson, NC: McFarland, 1988.

Yamamoto Tsunetomo. *Hagakure: The Book of the Samurai*. Trans. William Scott Wilson. Tokyo: Kodansha, 1979.

Yamanouchi, Midori, and Joseph L. Quinn, eds. *Listen to the Voices from the Sea (Shinpan kike Wadatsumi no Koe)*. Tonawanda, NY: University of Toronto Press, 2000.

Yano, Christine R. *Tears of Longing: Nostalgia and the Nation in Japanese Popular Song*. Cambridge: Harvard University Asia Center, 2002.

Yoshida Kenko, *Essays in Idleness*. New York: Cosimo Classics, 2005.
Young, Donald J. *The Battle of Bataan: A Complete History*, 2d ed. Jefferson, NC: McFarland, 2009.
Young, James E. *Writing and Rewriting the Holocaust: Narrative and the Consequences of Interpretation*. Bloomington: Indiana University Press, 1988.
Young, Marilyn B. "An Incident at No Gun Ri." In *Crimes of War, Guilt and Denial in the Twentieth Century*, edited by Omer Bartov, Atina Grossmann, amd Mary Nolan. New York: The New Press, 2002.
Zeiss, Robert A., and Harold R. Dickman. "PTSD 40 Years Later: Incidence and Person-Situation Correlates in Former POWs." *Journal of Clinical Psychology* 45 (January 1989): 80–7.
Zincke, Herbert, with Scott A. Mills. *Mitsui Madhouse: Memoir of a U.S. Army Air Corps POW in World War II*. Jefferson, NC: McFarland, 2003.

Periodicals

Life
Newsweek
Saturday Evening Post
Time

Feature Films

Back to Bataan, 1945
Bataan, 1943
The Great Raid, 2005
Salute to the Marines, 1943

Documentaries

The Bataan Death March. A&E Television Networks, 2000.
Bataan Rescue: The Most Daring Rescue of World War II. Peter Jones, PBS, 2003.
Death March from Bataan to Manchuria: Raising a Survivor's Voice: Oliver 'Red' Allen Interview. Jean K. Bruce, HomeTree Media, 2008.
Death March of Bataan. Rainer Loeser, United Movietone Pictures, 2009.
Forsaken Legion: The Bataan Death March and the Defenders of the Philippines in World War II. Dan Traub, Dreamkeeper Films, 2010.
Hell in the Pacific: The True Stories. Revolver Entertainment, 2010.
Hidden Scars: The Massacre of Koreans from the Arakawa River Bank to Shitamachi in Tokyo, 1923. Choongkong Oh, 1983.
In the Hands of the Enemy: American Heroes of the Bataan Death March. Reel Productions, n.d.
Know Your Enemy: Japan. Frank Capra, Aberle Media, 2005.
The Pacific. 10 part HBO miniseries, 2010.
The Propaganda Wars: Japan and the U.S. and the Battle for Hearts and Minds. A&E, 1994.
"*Riben Guizi*" (*Japanese Devils, Confessions of Imperial Army Soldiers from Japan's War Against China*). Minoru Matsui, Center for Asian American Media, 2000.
The Tragedy of Bataan. Jan Thompson, PBS, 2011.
World War II with Walter Cronkite, 2005.

Index

Abraham, Abie 116, 132
Aguinaldo, Emilio 237
Aka gami 44
Alexander, Irvin 113, 116, 120
Allen, Oliver 120, 132
Allen, Red 118, 239
American Army 39: after axis surrender in North Africa 244; after German surrender in Europe 242–244; attitude toward Filipino soldiers 228; buying from Filipino civilians 232–234; characteristics 67ff, 78–80; confusion after surrender 107–114; equipment of 83–84; leisure pursuits 74–77, 230 (*see also* sexual behavior); motivation, lack of 194–195; National Guard component 71–72; officers 73–74, 88–89, 105; "old army" contingent 68–71; racism in 244; tension within 72ff; training in 71–72, 80ff
American Civil War 5, 39, 52, 59, 78–79, 143, 181, 195, 198
American propaganda 248–249
Arabs, American killing of 244
Aristotle 276, 277
artesian wells, chaos at 121–123; *see also* guards on Death March
Atkinson, Rick 244
atomic bomb 12
atrocities 8, 19, 134, 224–227; American 240–241

Back to Bataan 172, 175, 235
Bacque, James 242–243
Balanga 112, 113, 231, 237
Baldassarre, Jimmy, 24, 142, 250
Ball, John 19–20
Baltimore 57
Band of Brothers 9, 77, 174
Bank, Bert 116
Barker, A.J. 134
Basic Field Manual 81, 88–89
Bataan (film) 64, 73, 80, 166–167, 186, 225
Bataan campaign 7–8, 23; bitterness of soldiers during 155; confusion in aftermath 104; disease during 91; earthquake during 104; rumors of promised relief 158–160, 168
battle of the points 60
Battling Bastards of Bataan 15, 129, 213
Beard, Charles 15
The Best Years of Our Lives 188
bibles, utility of 94, 211, 261
Bilek, Tony 118

Bilyeu, Dick 107, 221
Bliven, Bert 134
Bok, Sissela 130
Bollich, James 82, 115, 131
Boyington, "Pappy" 179, 241
Bradbury, Ray 16
Brain, Philip 131, 142
Brokaw, Tom 9, 11, 13, 174
bushido 20, 22, 26–27, 28, 255
buzzard squads 250

Cabanatuan, Camp 144, 200; improved conditions in 201
Cabcaben 113
Capas 8, 142; train from San Fernando 113–114, 231
captivity narratives 185–186
Cave, Dorothy 133
Chinese 28–29, 30; *see also* massacres
Churchill, Winston 267
cockfight 231
cold war 30
Coleman, John 54
Corregidor 5, 103, 128, 157, 235
Costello, John 133
cruelty, descriptions 147–150; *see also* POW narratives

Daws, Gavin 127, 255
Des Pres, Terence 11, 147
Dien Bien Phu 124–125
dissertation defense 14
documentaries: postwar 134, 149, 198; wartime 33, 168, 171, 195, 249
Dodson, Earl 119
Dower, John 30, 34
Dyess, Edward (William) 112, 132–133, 142, 147, 148, 169–171, 221, 224, 239, 241

education, Japanese recruits 43, 46–48
Eisenhower, Dwight 9, 92, 103, 242
emperor 269, 273
Enka music 46
Enola Gay controversy 12–13
Evans, William 15, 106, 191
exaggeration in narratives 147–150

Falk, Stanley 113, 134, 230
Felix, Pedro 326–327; *see also* massacres

Filipino soldiers: alleged massacre of 226–227; equipment for 84; Filipino Scouts 86, 87; language barrier 85; tension with Americans 86–87; wounded 107
Filipinos 215ff; cultural characteristics 218, 220–222; death along Death March path 107; discrimination against 229–230; entrepreneurship during Death March 230–234; folk tales 228–229; helping Americans 221–223; hospital patients 107; sympathy for Americans 221; treatment by Japanese 215–219, 224–227; women and Japanese brutality 225–226, 242
films, feature: Japanese 58, 245–246, 247; U.S. 166–167, 172–174, 176, 179, 186, 187
Fitzpatrick, Bernard 107, 112
Fonda, Henry 168
Frazier, Glenn 162, 176, 212
Fu, Ping 141
Fussell, Paul 129–130, 146

Gautier, James 231
Geneva Red Cross Convention 21–22, 24
genocide 17
German POWs 143; trials of 214
Gordon, Richard 14–15, 119, 123, 124, 132, 162, 199, 204
Grahame, Kenneth 150
Grashio, Sam 124, 132, 171
Gray, Glen 31, 194
The Great Raid 179
Grossman, Dave 39
guards on Death March 108–114; aid to American POWs 254–259; barter with POWs 260–261; chain of command 106–108; chaos at water sites 120–123; pace of March 252–253; use of bayonet 121, 123; *see also* artesian wells
Gunjin Chokuyu 26
Gunjin Kunkai 26

Hagiwara, Sakutaro 42
Hanshin Tigers 37
Hearn, Lafcadio (and Jeff) 99, 114, 267
hell ships 129
heroism, World War I 151–152
Hibbs, Ralph 126
Hirohito 103
Hiroshima 191, 194
hohei soten 38
Hokusai 192
Holocaust 11, 131, 135–136, 144, 147, 161, 176, 184, 188, 191, 199, 201, 266
home front: advertising 167–168; attitude during campaign 153–154, 167; Cocoanut Grove fire 168; postwar attitudes 174
Homma, Masaharu, 7, 8, 19, 29, 31, 101, 102, 134, 138, 217, 242; characteristics 22–23; trial of 24–26, 150
homosexuality 210–212; *see also* prison camps; sexual behavior
How the Japanese Army Fights 124

Ind, Allison 155
issen gorin 48
It's Everybody's War 168

Jacoby, Melville 91
Japan: conditions in countryside 48–49; conflict in 34–35; cultural characteristics 96–98, 109–110, 112, 114, 256, 273; education in 46–48, 254, 270; *fin de siècle* 41ff; form, concern with 96ff; images of 137–139; language 99; militarism 274; opening of 35, 98; postwar image 249; purity, notions of 32, 34–35, 43ff, 50–51, 61, 256; relationship to West 244–246; resistance to militarism 246–247; utilitarian values 274–275
Japanese Army: bayonet, reliance on 57–58; confusion during Death March 107ff; English language use 262; evacuation plan 102–103, 106–107, 249–252 (*see also* Kawane, Yoshikate; Wachi, Takeji); expectation of death in 55–56; explanations of cruel behavior 239; family ethos 268; images of U.S. 65–67; life in barracks 268–271; POW treatment, Russo-Japanese War 247–248; predictability of 100–101; prohibition of brutality 259–260; punishment of guards 264–265; reactionary behavior of 40ff, 48, 51, 62–63; recruits 44–46; songs of 55, 60; tactics 35–40, 56–61; training 49–50
Johnson, Nick-bird 2
Jones, James 72, 77, 198, 211

kamikaze 192, 193
Kanto earthquake 52–53, 54
kata 95, 99ff, 101, 118, 124
Kawane, Yoshikate 102; *see also* Japanese Army, evacuation plan
Kill or Be Killed 39
Kilroy 65
Keene, Donald 275–276, 277
King, Edward 8, 38–39, 101–102, 128, 166, 250
Know Your Enemy: Japan 57, 125, 137
Knox, Donald 139, 210
Knox, Forrest 77, 128
Kokutai no Hongi 27
Kore dake Yomeba Ware wa Kateru 27–28, 95–96, 108, 114, 118, 253, 259; *see also* Read This and the War Is Won
Koreans 52–54; *see also* massacre
Kurosawa, Akira 140

language barrier 85–86, 115–116, 261–264
Larson, Alf 142
Lawton, Manny 137
Lay, Kermit 15
Levering, Ralph 107, 108
Levi, Primo 266
Limay 113
Lincoln, Abraham 11, 52, 143, 188, 195
Linderman, Gerald 241
logistical difficulties 8–9
The Lost Battalion 152; *see also* World War I
Lubao 113, 120, 142

MacArthur, Brian 133
MacArthur, Douglas 7, 23, 24, 25, 90, 100, 153, 155–166, 275; characteristics 155–156, 166; egotism 158; lionization on home front 165–166; mockery of 160–162; orders to Wainwright 163; poor generalship 156–158; rumors about 162–163
Mächler, Stefan 135–136
Mailer, Norman 78, 192
Mallonee, Richard 59, 87, 89, 118, 119, 120
The Man in the Gray Flannel Suit 127, 177
Mariveles 6, 107, 113

Martin, Addie 73, 75
massacres 29, 30, 52–54, 226
Mauldin, Bill 128
memorials 5–6, 38, 86–87, 213, 221
memory, scholarship on 130, 131–132, 135, 140, 143–146
Merritt, J.D. 94, 100, 131
Momotarō 19
Moody, Sam 107, 128, 149
Morris, John 246, 262, 269
mortality on Death March 134–135
Moss, William 126
motivation of soldiers: Japanese 195; U.S. 194–196
Murphy, Frank 25; *see also* Homma, Masaharu trial
myths, U.S. & Western civilization 184–188

Nakane, Chie 112
Nietzsche, Friedrich 129
Nishi, Amane 21
Nitobe, Inazo 21
Norman, Elizabeth 134
Norman, Michael 134
North Africa campaign 87–88, 92; evacuation of Axis prisoners 103–104

obituaries 182
O'Donnell, Camp 9, 120, 121, 128, 141, 144, 147, 176, 239, 251; conditions 200–201
officers 88; behavior in prison 207–208; leadership on Death March 68–70, 72–73
Olson, John 88, 115, 141, 147, 251
olympics, 1964 56–57
Onoda, Hiroo 49
Orani 113
Ortega, Abel 107, 119, 228
Ott, George 141–142, 267; *see also* Homma, Masaharu trial
Overton, Cletis 121

The Pacific 9, 176
Philippines: economic context for Death March 234–238; effect of war on 236–237; Japanese occupation 236; tension with U.S. 227–228; U.S. aid 222, 235; U.S. subjugation of 227
Plato 276
Playter, John 119
Pocket Guide to Japan 96
poetry 17, 20, 25, 42, 127, 138, 150, 160–162, 197, 198, 272
POW narratives: atrocity stories 170–171; common characteristics 137–139, 239; descriptions of cruelty 147–150; "global" perspective 137–138; passage of time 141–143; reception 136–137; unreliability 11, 141ff
POWs: attitude toward MacArthur 155–163; attitude toward U.S. government 183ff; bitterness during campaign 160–164; escape, difficulty 197–198; experience of defeat 196; failure to receive compensation 182–184; homecoming upon release 179; Japanese language use 263–264 (*see also* Poweleit, Alvin); payment for stories 171; postwar difficulties 177–179; postwar lack of recognition 179–181
Poweleit, Alvin 54, 13, 263–264; *see also* POWs, Japanese language use
prison, rumors 176

prison camps: behavior in prison 199–203, 205ff; British behavior 209; conflict in prison 204–205; economy 205–206ff; Japanese guards 206; officers in 207–209; sexual behavior 209–212; *see also* Cabanatuan, O'Donnell
propaganda, Japanese 51, 219
Proust, Marcel 140

quan 85–86
Quezon, Manuel 237

radio, contact during campaign 153
Read This and the War Is Won 27–28, 95–96, 114, 118; *see also Kore dake Yomeba Ware wa Kateru*
Reagan, Ronald 144
religious references 10, 64, 94, 187, 211, 220–221, 248, 261; *see also* bibles
reunions, veterans 13, 14, 139
rice riots 51–52
Roosevelt, Franklin 154–155, 161, 184
rural organizations 44
Russo-Japanese War 36, 38, 40, 247

Sacks, Oliver 145
Sallust 24
samurai 20, 21, 34, 35, 37, 96–97
San Fernando 113, 231
Sassoon, Siegfried 127
Saving Private Ryan 9, 194
Schacter, Daniel 146
Schreiber, Alfred 111
secondary work 133–134
See Here, Private Hargrove 78
seishin 32, 36–38, 49, 56, 61, 96
Senjin kun 248
Sergeant York 152
sexual behavior 75–77, 230; *see also* American Army, leisure pursuits
Sides, Hampton 133
Silva, Vincent 107, 138
Singapore massacre 19
Skeen, John 24, 25, 227
Sledge, Eugene 180
Slotkin, Richard 187
Sneddon, Murray 108, 138, 142
songs, wartime U.S. 65
sources, lack of 126–127, 191, 238, 240
Spanish imperialism 235
Steinbeck, John 132, 155, 194, 201
stereotypes, racial 65–66, 139, 187
Stewart, Sidney 134, 148
Stilwell, Joseph 165
Stouffer, Samuel 128
sumo 260
sun treatment 111–112
supplies during campaign 156–158; *see also* MacArthur, Douglas

Tagalog 220
Tanizaki, Junichiro 42
Tenney, Lester 115, 116, 122, 138, 148, 223
Thomasites 235; *see also* Philippines, U.S. aid
Tojo, Hideki 29, 216
Toland, John 132
train transport 113–114

transference: memories 145; punishment 271–273
Tsuji, Masanobu 19; characteristics 28; orders to kill POWs 29; postwar career 30–31
Tsuneyoshi, Yoshio 20

uchi-soto 33–34, 44, 46, 53
Umi Yukaba 55

V for Victory campaign 167–168
victim status: American 143, 160, 173, 213–214; Japanese 190–194
Vietnam 10, 11, 53, 124–125; *see also* Dien Bien Phu
Volckman, R.W. 156–157

Wachi Takeji 29, 250, 254
Wainwright, Jonathan 88, 158–159
Wake Island 106; American POWs on 123–124
The War 12, 149, 174
war bonds 169, 171–172
war plan ORANGE 6, 7, 156, 157
water on Death March 117–123, 124, 258–259
Weinstein, Alfred 132
White, Hayden 127, 150, 210
Whitman, Walt 17–18, 190
Wiesel, Elie 199
Wilkomirski, Binjamin 135–136
Williford, Charles 71–72
Wittlesey, Charles 151
Wohlfield, Mark 120
World War I 151–152, 190
World War II 9

www.ingramcontent.com/pod-product-compliance
Lightning Source LLC
Chambersburg PA
CBHW080758300426
44114CB00020B/2755